Look to ORBIT...

- for innovative software features such as statistical analysis online, true crossfile searching, subaccount invoicing and much more;

- for more new databases in engineering, materials, biology, chemistry, patents, trademarks, energy, health and the environment;

- for a staff ready to give you search assistance and customer service now when you need it.

ORBIT SEARCH SERVICE
A Division of Pergamon ORBIT InfoLine

We're the one to watch!

In North America   Pergamon ORBIT InfoLine, Inc. 8000 Westpark Drive, McLean, VA 22102 Tel: (703) 442-0900; (800) 421-7229

In Europe   Pergamon ORBIT InfoLine Ltd. Achilles House, Western Avenue, London W3 0UA, England Tel: (01) 992-3456

In Australia   ORBIT Search Service P.O. Box 544, Potts Point, NSW 2011 Tel: (02) 360-2691

Our online databases
stand alone
in drug information.

ASHP® databases help you to locate a wide scope of drug information, including fultext drug monographs, patient counseling information and abstracts of articles.

Drug Information Fulltext®

The DIF database contains detailed, comprehensive drug information representing over 50,000 marketed drug products.

Consumer Drug Information™

CDIF is a fulltext database with descriptions written for the patient's understanding. More than 3,000 brand name drug products are covered.

International Pharmaceutical Abstracts®

The IPA database is the practical, efficient way of locating information from over 800 pharmaceutical, medical, cosmetic and other health-related journals throughout the world. IPA's abstract/indexing system works to help you easily locate the information.

ASHP databases are available around the world through international online computer systems. For a brochure or more information, contact ASHP's Database Services at 301-657-3000, or write to:

ASHP Database Services
4630 Montgomery Avenue
Bethesda, MD 20814

National ONLINE MEETING

PROCEEDINGS—1988

New York, May 10–12, 1988

Sponsored by
ONLINE REVIEW
The International Journal
of Online Information Systems

Compiled by
Martha E. Williams
Thomas H. Hogan

Learned Information, Inc.
Medford, NJ

In this game strategy is everything

The right strategy means fewer moves, less wasted action. It's no different when you need to perform a thorough literature search.

Social SciSearch® is the right strategy to employ for searching the world's social sciences literature. You'll move directly to a multidisciplinary database indexing every significant item from more than 1,400 journals in the social sciences.

Like any superior strategy, our online database offers you options at every turn: in addition to the conventional retrieval techniques, you can search by *cited references*. And you choose your source—*Social SciSearch* is available through *DIALOG, BRS,* and *DIMDI.*

If you already subscribe to the print *Social Sciences Citation Index®* then you're one move ahead--you're eligible to search at a substantially reduced rate.

The smartest move of all? Call us free at **1-800-523-1857**, and say that you'd like more information on this strategy. We'll show you how *Social SciSearch* gets you to the other side of the board fast.

CHECK !

Institute for Scientific Information
3501 Market Street, Philadelphia, Pennsylvania 19104, Telephone: (215) 386-0100

S-400-5202

PROGRAM CHAIRMAN

Martha E. Williams

MEETING ORGANIZER

Thomas H. Hogan

ORGANIZING/REVIEWING COMMITTEE

Toni Carbo Bearman .... University of Pittsburgh
Joe Bremner .... Database Development
Corilee S. Christou .... Mead Data Central
Donald W. King .... King Research, Inc.
George Minot .... AITRC
Victor Rosenberg .... Personal Bibliographic Software
Jim Seals .... Chemical Abstracts Services, Inc.
Donna Willmann .... VU/TEXT Information Services, Inc.

ISBN: 0-938734-26-1
©1988 by Learned Information, Inc., Medford, New Jersey. All rights reserved.

Price: $50.00
Order from: Learned Information, Inc.
             143 Old Marlton Pike
             Medford, NJ 08055

THE MOST

CONVENIENT,

COMPREHENSIVE,

EASY-TO-USE

RESOURCE FOR

AG DATA

ON THIS:

IS THIS.

You can search the world over and never find a more convenient, time-saving resource for ag data than DIALOG On Disc™ AGRIBUSINESS U.S.A.℠ Database. Not only does it support DIALOG® commands, it also incorporates a built-in bridge to the weekly updates on our online database. For more information, call 800/826-5944 toll-free today!

DIALOG On Disc™ *Products*

AGRIBUSINESS U.S.A. ℠
DATABASE

A service of Pioneer Hi-Bred International, Inc.
11153 Aurora Avenue
Des Moines, IA 50322

© 1988 Pioneer Hi-Bred International, Inc. ℠ Servicemark, registered or applied for, of Pioneer Hi-Bred International, Inc., Des Moines, IA. DIALOG is a registered servicemark of Dialog Information Services, Inc. DIALOG On Disc is a trademark of Dialog Information Services, Inc.

TABLE OF CONTENTS

**Highlights of the Online Database Field:
New Technologies for Online**
Martha E. Williams 1

**Corporate Library as Online Vendor: Perspectives on
Operating an In-house Text Retrieval Structure**
Nancy Audino and Jack Borbely 5

**Molkick: A Universal Graphics Query Program for
Searching Databases with Chemical Structures**
Robert C. Badger, Clemens Jochum and Sigrid Lesch 7

**Metallurgical Searches in the Chemical Abstracts
Database**
Hanns Bechtel 9

**Implementation Hurdles for International Information
Systems**
Jean Newman Bedord 17

**Searching for the Ultimate Set-Up: Online
Communications for the End-User Environment**
Steven J. Bell 21

**House Resolution 145, The Computer Security Act
of 1987: An Asscssmcnt**
Virgil L.P. Blake 27

**The Electronic Branch Library: Using CD-ROM
Technology and Online Services to Support
Off-Campus Instructional Programs**
Robert L. Burr 37

**Implementing an Expert System for Use by
Undergraduates**
Nancy J. Butkovich, Kathryn L. Taylor and Ann S. Moore 43

The Second Time Around: Adventures in the Production of Public and Private CD-ROMs
Matilda Butler 49

Constructing a Thesaurus for Medical Knowledge
Gina D'Ascenzo Carlos, John K. Vries and Peretz Shoval 53

Highways to Hypertext
Joseph M.A. Cavanagh 59

Student Preferences in Online Search Instruction
Dorice Des Chene 63

CAUTION: Downloading May Be Hazardous to Your Computer's Health
Glen Key Dalessandro 67

WILSONDISC: Training the Trainer
Victoria E. Dow and Gail Kriebel 71

Meeting the CD-ROM Marketing and Sales Challenge
Ralph Ferragamo 79

Finding Statistics, Tables, Charts and Pictures Using NEXIS
Nancy F. Hardy 81

Marketing Strategies for Promoting Online Full-text Primary Information
John A. Hearty and Cynthia G. Smith 91

CD-ROM and Apple Macintosh: Market Opportunities
Lyndon S. Holmes 99

An Evaluation of a Gateway System for Automated Online Database Selection
Chengren Hu 107

Availability of Japanese Scientific and Technical Periodicals in Major English Language Databases
Keiko Ikushima and Carol Tenopir 115

Searching for Industry Information
Leslie R. Jacobs 123

Information Retrieval as Hypermedia: An Outline of InterBrowse
Paul Kahn 131

ABI/Inform on CD-ROM: How Does the Disk Stack Up?
Nancy S. Karp 141

Local Area Networks in an Online Information Retrieval Environment
Harry M. Kibirige 149

Optical Media: Converting High-Tech Library Needs into Market Realities
Linda Joyce Kosmin 161

DOD Gateway Information System (DGIS) Common Command Language: A Summary of the First Prototyping & the Decision for Artificial Intelligence
Allan D. Kuhn 169

Insurance Information Goes Online
Lynda S. Kuntz 185

The Retrieval and Display of Patent Images from Optical Storage
Gary M. Kurtenbach 191

End-User Access to Medline: The Role of CD-ROM
Donna Lee 199

Learning Modes and Online Behavior of Novice Searchers
Elisabeth L. Logan 205

Full Text Newspaper Retrieval is Hard to Manage: Fact or Fiction?
Arlene F. Long 213

Promoting Online Services in State Government
Kathleen Low 217

Image Processing: Technology/Overview
Lois F. Lunin 221

Image Retrieval, Display, and Reproduction
Clifford A. Lynch 227

Monitor Online Search Costs: An Evaluation
Katherine M. Markee 233

Designing an Online Medical 'Hypertextbook'
Bruce McClelland 235

Textual Information Management Systems (TIMS): Powerful Full-Text Retrieval
Michael A. McDonald 239

ABI/Inform: A Database of Mini-Databases
Tim McDonald 247

The Georgia Interactive Network for Medical Information (GaIN)
Kimberly A. McInnis 259

Developing an Electronic Information Service
John F. McLane 265

Ensuring End-User Quality Control: An Academic Model
Chris J. Miko 275

Artificial Inputs, Natural Intelligence: The Database as Mental Peripheral
Tim Miller 281

Factors Used in Selecting Online Databases
Judith E. O'Dell 287

Promoting Medical Literature Databases to the Physician End User
Christine A. Olson, Karen Hackleman and Robert E. Kristofco 293

A Prototype Clustering Program
Miranda Lee Pao 301

Picture Perfect
Allen W. Paschal 307

CD-ROM and Optical Technology: The User Interface
Charles Peters 311

Use of a PC to Search in Japanese Online Databases
Wolfgang Pilch 315

F-TAS: A Full-Text Access System
Michael J. Prasse, Martin Dillon, Martha J. Gordon, Bruce Mortland and Anthony Repka 327

Psych/Neuro Core Concept Database: A Quality-Filtered Database
W. Jean Pugh and Gary Moore 333

Business Uses of Scientific and Technical Databases
Carol L. Rich and Edward W. Badger 337

Training the End-User in a CAS Online Academic Environment
Johanna C. Ross 353

Medical Information on CD-ROM
Peter Schipma 359

Removing the Mystery: Training the End User to Search
Maxine Leeds Snow 365

Front-End Software: The Effect of Theory on Reality
Lisa M. Staggenborg 371

Providing Front Ends for Marketing Executives
Ruth E. Stanat 377

The Software Jungle: To Guide or Not to Guide
Sue E. Stigleman 383

Only the News That You Can Use
Stanley Stillman 389

Gateways: The User has Responsibilities and Rights Too
Betty Unruh 397

The Search Performance of End-Users
Geraldene Walker 403

The Design of Online Thesauri
Bella Hass Weinberg and Julie A. Cunningham 411

Justifying Your Information Center's Budget
Daniel U. Wilde and Nan R. Cooper 421

In Search of GNP and 30 Million Other Series DRI's New Dimension in Online Searching
Roger M. Winsby and Samuel H. Solomon 429

Searchers by the Thousands: The Development of a Program and Some Results of the Experience
Lucy Anne Wozny 437

National Agricultural Text Digitizing Project: System Startup and Operation
Judith A. Zidar 443

You could look for days. Weeks. And still not find the information you need.

But with DIALOG® all the facts about millions of products, companies, and markets are right at your fingertips. You'll have instant access to information from Dun & Bradstreet, Standard & Poors, Disclosure, Predicasts, Moody's, Media General, and more.

In fact, of all the online information services, Dialog has the most valuable collection of business databases.

So, if you'd like to get the jump on your competition and still get home in time for dinner, find out about Dialog. Dialog knows everything.

Except where your high school sweetheart lives.

To find out about Dialog now, call 800-3-DIALOG. Or write: Dialog, 3460 Hillview Avenue, Palo Alto, CA 94304.

DIALOG® INFORMATION SERVICES, INC.
A SUBSIDIARY OF LOCKHEED CORP.

The world's largest online knowledgebank.

Getting the information you need without using Dialog is like trying to find out where your high school sweetheart lives by going door to door.

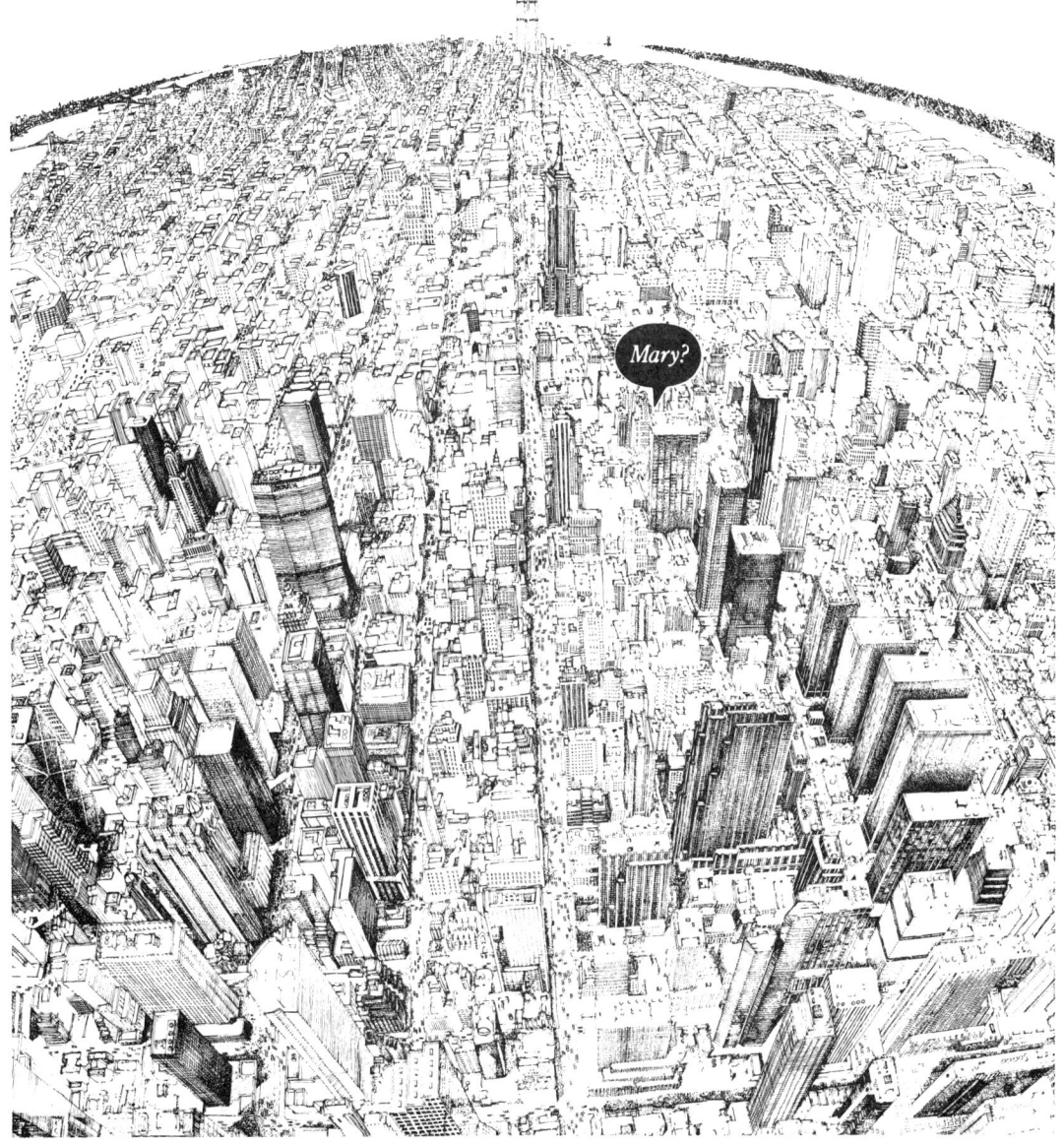

PREFACE

The National Online Meetings, sponsored by Online Review, were initiated in 1980 and have been held annually. The first meeting was entitled National Online Information Meeting and the word "information" was dropped from the name in 1981. There was no Proceedings volume for the 1980 meeting; however, an abstracts volume (National Online Information Meeting: Collected Abstracts, compiled by Carolyn G. Robins) was published by Learned Information, Inc. The National Online Meeting Proceedings volumes were started with the second National Online Meeting, 1981 This is the eighth Proceedings and corresponds to the ninth meeting.

This Proceedings contains 66 of the 76 papers reviewed and selected by the Organizing/Reviewing Committee for presentation at the National Online Meeting, 1988. While the balance of the papers are not included in the Proceedings, their titles, together with authors and author affiliations, are listed in the Proceedings and they have been included in the index. Thus, all technical papers presented at the meeting are cited in this publication. In addition to the papers presented at technical sessions, the meeting included product reviews, exhibits, and a wide variety of satellite events (special seminars and workshops, etc.) which are not represented in this Proceedings.

This volume begins with the introductory presentation of the Program Chairman, "Highlights of the Online Database Field," followed by the balance of the papers which are arranged in alphabetical sequence by the primary author's last name. The computer-generated index includes author names, affiliations, selected title words, and added keywords in the form of an index.

The Proceedings was prepared under the direction of Martha E. Williams and Thomas H. Hogan. Substantial contributions were made by Carol Nixon of Learned Information, Inc., Chengren Hu, and Sheila Carnder of the University of Illinois. Their efforts are gratefully acknowledged.

National ONLINE MEETING

PROCEEDINGS—1988

HIGHLIGHTS OF THE ONLINE DATABASE FIELD: NEW TECHNOLOGIES FOR ONLINE

Martha E. Williams, University of Illinois

1. Introduction.

The database industry in the United States is complex and dynamic. In order to understand it one should see it in terms of past growth, the current status, and trends that are leading us into the 21st century. In this presentation I will trace the worldwide growth of databases, provide detailed data about the use of online databases in the information center/library market in the United States and, discuss the potential for changes in online services as we take advantage of the capabilities that research and technology make available to database producers, online vendors, and entrepreneurs.

2. Database Growth.

Back in the late 1950s and early 1960s nearly all databases were produced by governmental organizations and these were not generally made available to the public. Statistics regarding publicly available databases can be traced back to 1975 (Ref. 1) when there were 301 publicly available databases. By 1985 the number of databases had grown ten-fold to 3010 (Ref. 2) and I estimate the number for 1988 to approach 4000. It is worth noting that in 1975 the number included only word-oriented databases and that the numeric, modelling, image, and transaction type databases had not yet come into the marketplace. The number of databases doubled between 1975 and 1981 and quintupled between 1981 and 1985. Concomitant with the growth in databases was a growth in the number of records contained in those databases and they grew at an even faster rate from 52 million in 1975 to 1.68 billion in 1985 for a 32-fold increase.

Not only did the databases and records within the databases increase, but the use of the databases increased and the increase probably was more than commensurate with the database record growth. There are no worldwide figures on usage of all publicly available databases but recorded use in the United States of the word oriented databases shows a 15-fold increase from 1 million searches in 1975 to 15 million in 1985. Extending the use of the word-oriented databases beyond the United States would probably increase the 1985 number by 50-60%. The use of numeric/transaction databases (stock market, credit checks, etc.) is greater than the use of word-oriented databases, so the total of both is really quite large. The revenue associated with use of numeric/transaction databases is roughly 10 times that of word-oriented databases. It is safe to say that the rate of database use has more than kept pace with the increase in numbers of databases and database records. Database production worldwide shows consistent growth with no evidence of diminution. Although databases die every year, far more new entrants join the ranks than die, thus there is a net increase.

3. The Online Industry.

Next I would like to look in detail at the growth and character of the online database industry in terms of the information center/library market (Ref. 3) and its use of word-oriented databases in the United States that are accessed through the major vendors of word-oriented online databases in the U.S. market. These include Mead, DIALOG, NLM, BRS, STN, ORBIT, Dow Jones, and others.

Over the five years from 1982-1986, use increased in all but four quarters and revenue increased in every quarter. The greatest percentage increase for both use and revenue generally occurs in the first quarter of each year. The increases occur as new budgets come into effect, new semesters start, the holiday period is over, and producer/vendor pricing changes for the new year come into effect. Over the same time period, from the first to last quarter represented, usage increased by a factor of 2.25 and revenue increased by a factor of 2.99. This represents healthy growth for the industry but it does not mean that every database or every database producer enjoyed proportionate increases. One must remember that the number of databases and producers also grew during the same time period. The number of databases grew from 247 to 517 and the number of producers grew from 151 to 270, thus the revenue pie must be split into an increasing number of pieces and the shares differ greatly in size. A small number of producers and databases enjoy large shares and a large number have very small shares.

4. Usage and Revenues.

In order to provide highlights of the market I will provide figures for the distribution of usage and revenues for online vendors, database producers, and databases for one quarter, the fourth quarter of 1986 (Q486). During this quarter 517 databases produced by 270 producers were accessed on 14 vendor services. The amount of usage was 689,000 connect hours and the revenues generated thereby were $85.5 million for an average hourly expenditure of $128.41 where hourly expenditures include all costs (connect time, displays, prints, SDIs, communications, storage, and anything else that is charged to the user and appears on his vendor bill).

The distribution of usage and revenues for the 14 vendors varies from the high end with a small number of vendors enjoying more than 100,000 hours/quarter to the low end where use is less than 1,000 hours/quarter. Similarly, high-end revenues exceed $10,000,000.00 per quarter and low-end revenues are less than $100,000.00 per quarter.

The two highest use vendors were Mead and DIALOG; together they accounted for 72% of the usage market. The next five vendors, BRS, STN, West, NLM, and SDC made up the next 25% of the market leaving seven vendors to share the remaining 3%. The revenue picture is similar. Mead and DIALOG together received 82% of the revenues and the next five, West, STN, BRS, NLM, and SDC together received 15% leaving 3% to the remaining seven vendors.

Distribution of usage and revenues among database producers follows a similar pattern with a small number of producers getting most of the use and revenues, and a large number getting much smaller shares. At the high end, use is classed as more than 100,000 hours of connect time per quarter and the low end is less than 200 hours. High revenues are over $1,000,000.00 per quarter and low end is less than $25,000.00 per quarter. In Q486 one producer had databases that were used > 100,000 hrs, 9 > 10,000 hrs, 94 > 200 hrs, and 166 < 200 hrs in the quarter. In terms of revenue, 11 producers generated > $1 million, 75 > $25,000, and 184 < $25,000 in the quarter.

As would be expected the distribution of usage and revenues at the database level follows the same pattern. The high-end use is classed as more than 100,000 hours per quarter and the low end is less than 200 hours per quarter. In Q486 one database had > 100,000, 7 > 10,000, 151 > 200, and 358 < 200 hours in the quarter. Similarly, one generated revenues > $10,000,000, 10 > $1,000,000, 117 > $25,000, and 389 generated < $25,000 in the quarter.

5. Trends for Online Retrieval.

In light of the background on the growth of databases and the character of the online database industry in the United States information center/library market it is appropriate to look toward the future and discuss changes that are likely to take place with respect to online information retrieval. The goals of retrieval can be said to progress through several stages starting with the retrieval of source information, through the retrieval of information/data, facts, and knowledge with the ultimate goal being the attainment of truth. In order to achieve retrieval, users (searchers) must go through a series of steps, some of which may be iterative in order to satisfy the purpose of the search.

As a part of a National Science Foundation funded research grant (Ref. 4) we analyzed the steps involved in retrieval and broke them down into discretely identifiable functions. We indicated what could be automated and what would be required in terms of user data, system data, query data, and technologies (hardware/equipment, software/firmware, and techniques) to automate each function or portion of a function. Such automated aids we called transparency aids and they fell into four categories, automated converters, automated selectors, automated routers, and automated evaluators/analyzers (for fuller descriptions see Ref. 5).

Beginning in the early 1970s considerable research efforts were carried out by many organizations to develop transparency aids and some of the terms used to describe the resulting prototype products were *front end, intermediary system, post processor, gateway,* and most of them were described with adjectives such as *user friendly* or *user cordial.* All of them had the same general aim of making information retrieval more transparent. A lot of work is currently being carried out by researchers in many countries to help simplify the process of information retrieval through use of AI techniques. AI can be brought to bear on retrieval in four major areas: on the databases through development of knowledge bases, and on preprocessors, processors, and postprocessors. Many transparency aids have been brought to the marketplace advertised as *intelligent* but, I think few really have a legitimate claim. Until systems incorporate intellectual activities such as perceiving, understanding, thinking, learning, intuition, inferring, etc. they cannot truly be called intelligent. AI certainly has a role to play in the development of transparent systems but so also do statistical techniques, associative techniques, dictionary look-ups, and other more traditional approaches.

6. Conclusion and Predictions.

As we look toward the year 2000 and realize that it is only a dozen years away the reluctance to make predictions begins to fade. What is in store for the online world or, more generally, the world of computerized information retrieval? What will the industry look like and what will the technology look like? Answers to both questions can be characterized by the terms *transparency, integration,* and *connectivity.*

The industry will continue to grow so that it will be considerably larger but I suspect that the overall structure will be much the same with a very small number of big players controlling most of the activity and most of the dollars. The trend toward vertical integration will continue because database producers and online vendors realize that market expansion will come through knowing and serving their users and the users they wish to serve include not only their current users but also the end users they are trying to attract. Database producers and service providers must know who the users are, what they want, and what they need. New products will be developed, but more important, they will be integrated with other products and services. Many more database producers and databases will come onto the scene and their products will be narrowly focussed. The very existence of a multiplicity of new databases might seem to provide an even greater burden to those who are having difficulty keeping abreast and making intelligent choices from among the multiplicity of databases, search services, command languages and the like. However, mergers, acquisitions, and cooperative activities between and among database producers and service providers will bring together and integrate many of the new and existing products and services into a smaller number of fuller service offerings.

The information and data needs of professions, industries, and disciplines will be met with integrated information services such as chemical, medical, financial, or banking networks--either through the banding together of information/data producers to provide integrated services, or more likely, through the integration of databases and services in the form of virtual disciplinary, or mission oriented networks.

To a great extent the changes in the industry will be dependent on changes in technology as most new information products are technology driven. Changes in technology that will affect information users will relate to increased transparency of systems, including the integration of sets of transparency aids together with new storage media and devices, as well as new processing and display techniques and devices.

Integration of text, images, and voice will enhance the front ends of retrieval systems, and retrieval will be enhanced and speeded up by the use of techniques and technologies such as associative processing, artificial intelligence (AI), hypertext, and parallel processing. Communications will eventually be improved in terms of simplified protocols and increased bandwidth to facilitate the transmission of images and perhaps even color images from full-text documents. Somewhat later, higher bandwidth lines will permit the transmission of moving images generated by experimental research so that those results can be integrated with other data at remote locations.

The changes I anticipate taking place by the year 2000 will be more dramatic than those that we have seen in the past dozen years. Together with the increased transparency and integration of information and data systems will come an increase in the stature of information scientists and information professionals of all types. Regardless of the increased transparency that will greatly facilitate the use of information resources there will always be a need for human beings who will remain cognizant of what is in the systems in order to know how to interpret the information and to know what is, and what is not, included in search results. However, the increase in stature will occur only if the information professionals stay on top of the situation and remain in the driver's seat to steer the course into the next century.

REFERENCES

1. Williams, Martha E.; Rouse, Sandra K., Eds. *Computer-Readable Bibliographic Databases: A Directory and Data Sourcebook*. Washington, D. C.: American Society for Information Science; 1976.
2. Williams, Martha E.; Lannom, Lawrence; Robins, Carolyn G. *Computer-Readable Databases: A Directory and Data Sourcebook, (2vols.) Vol. 1, Science, Technology, Medicine, Vol. 2, Business, Law, Humanities, Social Science*. Chicago, IL: American Library Association and Amsterdam, The Netherlands: Elsevier Science Publishers (North-Holland); co-publishers. Vol. 1, 705 pp; Vol. 2, 1315 pp; 1985 (available from Gale Research Co., Detroit, MI).
3. Williams, Martha E. *Information Market Indicators: Information Center/Library Market*. (Proprietary Report) Monticello, IL: Information Market Indicators, Inc.; 19; 458 pp.; 1988.
4. Williams, Martha E.; Preece, Scott E. "Elements of a Distributed Transparent Information Retrieval System," In: A. R. Benenfeld; E. J. Kazlauskas, Eds. *Communicating Information: Proceedings of the 43rd American Society for Information Science Annual Meeting*. White Plains, NY: Knowledge Industry Publications, Inc.; 17:401-402; 1980.
5. Williams, Martha E. "Transparent Information Systems Through Gateways, Front Ends, Intermediaries, and Interfaces," *Journal of the American Society for Information Science* 34(4): 204-214, July 1986.

Note: This presentation is based in part on the keynote speech presented 20 January 1988 by the author at Information Online 88: The Key to Our Future; Third Australian Online Information Conference and Exhibition and to be published in the conference proceedings.

CORPORATE LIBRARY AS ONLINE VENDOR—PERSPECTIVES ON OPERATING AN IN-HOUSE TEXT RETRIEVAL SYSTEM

Nancy Audino and Jack Borbeley, Towers Perrin

ABSTRACT:

This paper presents a synopsis of our collective personal experience of the past three years with an in-house text retrieval system known within the Towers Perrin company as IRMS (Information Resource Management System). Starting with a brief overview of the Towers Perrin corporate environment, the paper highlights in particular the business needs which the system addresses and the resources of the firm used in the development of the IRMS application. Next, while the paper focuses somewhat on the experiences during the initial design and development phases of the IRMS project, its principal focus is on the service aspects of the system, i.e., on the insights gained in the operation of IRMS as a full-fledged retrieval service. Particular attention is given to the non-technical policy and procedural issues which development of the system precipitated, as well as to the system support activities such as training, user support, documentation, pricing and marketing which have been implemented in connection with IRMS. Insights pertaining to these non-technical areas are highlighted and discussed in relation to their overall impact on the acceptance and success of the system. The paper also discusses the approaches used to measure and communicate system performance.

MOLKICK: A UNIVERSAL GRAPHICS QUERY PROGRAM FOR SEARCHING DATABASES WITH CHEMICAL STRUCTURES

Robert Badger, Springer-Verlag and Clemens Jochum and Sigrid Lesch, Beilstein Institute, West Germany

This paper presents details about the development of Molkick, a software program now in the final test stage before commercial introduction, that is designed as an easy to use universal graphics query system for searching structures or substructures in chemical oriented databases. The program can be used with any terminal emulation program and it can search multiple hosts.

Description

Molkick is a software program for IBM PC's or compatibles written by the Beilstein Institute in Frankfurt, West Germany and Softron, a computer software company in Munich, West Germany. It is designed as a universal graphics query system for searching structures or substructures on different systems like the CAS Registry File, DARC/Questel and the Beilstein file on STN or Dialog. Molkick supports all common graphic adapters - CGA, EGA, Hercules, AT&T 6300, Toshiba and VAG.

Development and Operational Considerations

The program was developed with several objectives in mind:

- To reduce the costs of conducting structure and substructure searches by allowing the user to frame a structure or substructure search query offline and then have the program upload it to a host for the structure or substructure search.

- To allow the user to develop a single query and then be able to use that query to conduct the same search on different systems. The idea was to develop the capability of translating a single query into the various structure search syntax of the hosts that had chemical structure oriented databases.

- To have the program interact with any terminal emulation program. Thus users could use their own programs and have Molkick memory resident and called on whenever it is needed.

- To incorporate state-of-the-art editor and graphic routines to enable users to build a full range of molecular structures including stereochemistry, nested generic groups and other chemical necessities like varying bond lengths and predefined fragments.

In order to accomplish the various tasks Molkick formulates the user's query into a source graphics file which is then translated, in a key step, into the destination language of the particular system i.e., STN, DARC/Questel that will be queried. In the event that the query is stored before it is uploaded, Molkick translates the query into an ASCII file and it is stored as a ROSDAL string. The ROSDAL string will be the destination language used to search the Beilstein File on Dialog using the Softron Substructure Search System.

Chemical Drawing Capability

The program is easy to use with a mouse to draw freehand or to use with pull down menus. The various menus include a Bond menu, a Stero menu and a predefined fragment menu that includes rings, polycycles and amino acids among other fragments. There are also various help function keys and the program has extended display features like increasing and decreasing molecular size, centering of molecules, tilting plus the capability to delete groups, fragments or whole structures.

Chemical syntax and valence assignments are checked automatically. In addition the program offers the following kinds of chemical drawing capabilities:

- Stereochemistry

- Abnormal charges, radicals, masses and valences

- Varying bond orders

- Nested generic groups

- Exact location of attachment points for generic groups

- 'Free Sites" and a set of special symbols for easy substructure input(i.e., ALK = alkyl groups)

- Predefined and user defined fragments

- Short cuts to help users construct molecules

Using the Program

Molkick is easy to use. After it is installed and loaded into resident memory it can be called from any directory. Thus a structure query can be formulated before or during an online session and then may be modified at any time during the session.

METALLURGICAL SEARCHES IN THE CHEMICAL ABSTRACTS DATABASE

Hanns Bechtel, Metallgesellschaft AG, Fed. Rep. Germany

Keywords: Chemical Abstracts, indexing policy, metal alloys, retrieval strategy

Abstract: Retrieving metal alloys in the Chemical Abstracts database is very difficult. Although individual alloys like any chemical compound are coded by registry numbers, fundamental alloy compositions, which metallurgists characterize by two or three main element names or symbols, are very often not correctly or not at all indexed. The paper shows how the alloy records are structured in the C.A. registry file, and how alloys are indexed in the bibliographic file. Also in the abstract texts alloys are not consistently described by element names or by their symbols, let alone the spelling of percentage figures and their position between element names or symbols.

Some simple rules for indexing and abstracting diction, derived from our daily experience, are proposed to avoid Babylonian confusion, complicated searching and loss of information.

1. Introduction

Metallurgists are accustomed to characterize alloys by the basic element and the first and second alloying element in decreasing weight percentages order. Additional elements may but need not be mentioned. Speaking of a copper-zinc-tin-alloy means that the base element is copper and the additional elements are zinc and tin, regardless of further components. For binary and quarternary alloys the elements should be given likewise in the order of the weight percentage.

The information contents goes far beyond the nomination of the elements, since in most cases the metallurgist associates characteristic alloy properties with the three-element term. The searcher formulating a metallurgical bibliographic search by A(w)B(w)C, where A, B and C are element names or symbols, has unfortunately to consider that the recall of his search is far below 50% with a remarkable amount of false drops. This happens likewise if the fundamental question containing the three elements is first matched to the registry file and then, the resulting registry numbers whether relevant or not, transferred to the bibliographic file. It should be mentioned here, that the number of alloy hits in the registry file, in so many cases, is not much lower than the number of the corresponding records in the bibliographic file.

The example of the following search shows how metallurgical publications are indexed by CAS staff, and how a searcher has to formulate his question in order not to be knocked down by false drops, and yet to retrieve a sufficient number of relevant citations which give him the assurance of not having fallen into an information gap.

2. Searching alloys in the registry file

Tab.1 shows the data structure of a nickel alloy as it typically appears in the registry file. Each alloying element is listed in a synonym line as ALLOY NONBASE, except the base element which is characterized by ALLOY BASE. Each line contains also the symbols of all element components followed by their weight percentages. The percentages, however, can hardly be hit due to their distances from the element symbol they belong to, and due to decimal numbers which shift the distance.

Using the registry file, we have three basic queries to search for alloy types (Tab.2: A, B and C). The queries A and B do not match a three-element formulation: In A as well as in B, chromium and aluminum might be minor constituents of a multinary alloy; in C, the material is limited to three components only. In order to exclude non-nickel base alloys from C, the MF search may be "and"ed with A. Since nickel alloys are widespread in technical application, 206 different nickel alloys out of 228 remain. They show up in only 313 records of the bibliographic file. The third possibility, namely nickel, chromium and aluminum being the main components beside others, can hardly be formulated since the neighboring distances between the symbols on the one hand, and the symbols and their respective percentages on the other hand, cannot be foreseen due to their ranging and to decimal figures. Therefore, the use of neighboring operators cannot be recommended.

In a more specific search (Tab.3) for nickel-chromium-aluminum alloys having an approximate composition of 80, 15 and 5% respectively, we still entered percentage numbers. When doing so, we were, however, aware of the fact that we presumably did not hit several indexed percentage numbers for reasons already discussed. It took a very long time to retrieve such percentage figures and, later on, to transfer lots of registry numbers from the registry file into the bibliographic file.

We compare now the number of nickel base alloys containing more or less chromium and aluminum and other elements, regardless whether they are major or minor constituents, with the number of nickel base alloys which contain nothing else but chromium and aluminum. The first amount is in the order of magnitude of thousands, the second is ten times less. In between lies the amount of multinary alloys which we have found by quasi range searching, applying those sophisticated queries in which element symbols are linked with percentage figures. In order to avoid those time consuming searches and yet to reach our goal, we

```
RN   85747-49-3
IN   Nickel alloy, base, Ni 75-76,Cr 16,Al 4.6-4.8,Y2O3 1.9, ...
SY   Chromium alloy, nonbase,  Ni 75-76,Cr 16,Al 4.6-4.80,Y2O3
SY   Aluminum alloy, nonbase,  Ni 75-76,Cr 16-24,Al 4.6-4.8,Y2O3
SY   Yttrium oxide (Y2O3), alloy, Ni 75-76,Cr 16,Al 4.6-4.8,Y2O3
SY   Tantalum ..........
SY   Cobalt ......
MF   Al.Co.Cr.Fe.Ni.O3Y2.Ta
1 References in File CA (1967 to date)
```

Tab. 1   Data structure of a nickel base alloy in the registry file

```
Search formulations                                    hits
                                       file:    REG      BIB

Multinary alloys
A   NICKEL(w)ALLOY(w)BASE
        and CHROMIUM(w)ALLOY(w)NONBASE
        and ALUMINUM(w)ALLOY(w)NONBASE           2.601    6.380
B   NICKEL(w)ALLOY(w)BASE and CR and AL          3.265    n.d.

Ternary alloys
C   AL.CR.NI/MF                                    229      377
D   AL.CR.NI/MF and NICKEL(w)ALLOY(w)BASE          206      313
```

Tab. 2   General formulations for alloy searching in the registry file (hits as per Dec. 86/Jan. 87)

```
Search formulations (quasi range searching)            hits
                                       file:    REG      BIB

Alloys containing 70 to 89% Ni
NI(w)(7! or 8!)                                  5.354    8.661
NI(w)(7! or 8!) and NICKEL(w)ALLOY(w)BASE
        and CHROMIUM(w)ALLOY(w)NONBASE
        and ALUMINUM(w)ALLOY(w)NONBASE             823    1.080
NI(w)(7! or 8!)
    and CR(w)(10 or 12 or 13 or 15 or 16 or 18 or 20)
    and AL                                         535      600
NI(w)(7! or 8!)
    and CR(w)(10 or 12 or 13 or 15 or 16 or 18 or 20)
    and AL(w)(2 or 3 or 4 or 5 or 6 or 7)          255      264
```

Tab. 3   Narrowed formulations for alloy searching in the registry file (hits as per Jan. 88)

propose (Tab.4)

1. that three-element formulations as previously mentioned should be indexed in a separate synonym field line or

2. that an alternate molecular formula field should contain element symbols in order of the weight percentages, f.e. NI.CR.AL

3. that the synonym lines should be made searchable in the order of decreasing percentages, that means the IN-line should be connected to the first and second SY-line by links or numbered qualifiers.

```
1.  IN    NICKEL ALLOY, BASE ....
    SY    CHROMIUM ALLOY, NONBASE ....
    SY    ALUMINUM ALLOY, NONBASE ....
    SY    ....
    SY    ....
    SY    NICKEL CHROMIUM ALUMINUM

S Nickel Chromium Aluminum/SY

2.  IN    NICKEL ALLOY, BASE ....
    SY    ....
    SY    ....
    AF    NI.CR.AL.

S NI.CR.AL/AF

3.  IN    NICKEL ALLOY, BASE ....
    SY1   CHROMIUM ALLOY, NONBASE ....
    SY2   ALUMINUM ALLOY, NONBASE ....

S Nickel/IN and Chromium/SY1 and Aluminum/SY2
```

Tab. 4 Different ways of improved indexing of three-element compositions and enhanced searching

Alloy descriptions as shown in Tab.5, however, are not matched by three-element searches. According to the C.A.S. system, even alloys with rather stupid compositions have been indexed and given a registry number. If, however, those nonsense compositions are registered at all, there is no reason why binary and ternary short formulas should not be given a registry number, too.

In case of STN's registry file it would also be helpful if all those registry numbers, which appear zero times or only once in the bibliographic file, could be elminated during searching in the registry file.

```
RN  100344-60-3
IN  ALUMINUM ALLOY, BASE, AL 0-100,CR 0-100,NI 0-100
SY  CHROMIUM ALLOY, NONBASE, AL0-100,CR 0-100,NI 0-100
SY  NICKEL ALLOY, NONBASE, AL 0-100,CR 0-100,NI 0-100
MF  AL.CR.NI
AF  UNSPECIFIED
CI  AYS

1 References in file CA (1967 to date)


RN  95079-52-0
IN  CHROMIUM BASE, ALLOY, CR 0-35,NI 0-35, AL 30
SY  NICKEL ALLOY, NONBASE, CR 0-35,NI 0-35,AL 30
SY  ALUMINUM ALLOY, NONBASE, CR 0-35,NI 0-35,AL 30
MF  AL.NI.CR
AF  UNSPECIFIED

1 References in file CA (1967 to date)


RN  101005-46-3
IN  ALUMINUM ALLOY, BASE, AL 80,CR 10,NI 10
SY  CHROMIUM ALLOY, NONBASE, AL 80,CR 10,NI 10
SY  NICKEL ALLOY, NONBASE, AL 80,CR 10,NI 10
MF  AL.CR.NI
AF  UNSPECIFIED
CI  AYS

1 References in file CA (1967 to date)


RN  105568-99-8
IN  INDEX NAME NOT YET ASSIGNED
MF  AL.CR.NI
CI  AYS

0 References in file CA (1967 to date)
```

Tab.5 Alloy compositions as appearing in the registry file

3. Searching in the bibliographic file

Searching for a certain fundamental type of alloy on the basis of its two, three or four main elements in the bibliographic file, without making use of the registry file, is almost impossible. In fact, C.A.S. has sometimes indexed fundamental alloy designations consisting of three element names in the keyword or index term field. But this has not been done consequently enough. Even if the alloying elements are indexed, one never knows how many are mentioned and in which order they appear.

Original spelling as taken from the abstracts

	number of records
Titles	
Nickel-Chromium-Aluminum	32
Nickel-based .... Chromium and Aluminum	2
Nickel-Chromium-Base	1
(Nickel-Cobalt-Iron)-Chromium-Aluminum	1
TD-NiCrAl	1
Ni-Cr-Al-X	1
Nickel-18.6 pct	1
Nickel-15Cr-5Al	1
Nickel-Chromium-6-Aluminum	1
Nickel-15-Chromium-Aluminum	1
Nickel-15 wt % Chromium-Aluminum	1
Aluminum ...... Ni 80-Cr 20	1
Ni-20Cr-4Al	1
Ni-20CR-5Al	1
Appearances in titles	46
Keywords	
Nickel-Chromium-Aluminum	25
Aluminum-Chromium-Nickel	2
Nichrome Aluminum	1
Appearances in keywords	28
Index terms	
Nickel-Chromium-Aluminum	22
Aluminum-Chromium-Nickel	5
Nickel alloys with Chromium and Aluminum	1
Nickel base with Chromium and Aluminum	1
Nichrome Aluminum	1
Nickel-Chromium ..... Aluminum	1
Appearances in indexes (descriptors)	32
Basic index, total	
Nickel-Chromium-Aluminum	47

Tab. 6 Three-element terms in titles, keywords and indexes (desciptors)

Tab. 6 shows the frequency of three-element terms comprising nickel, chromium and aluminium as they appear in a sample of 114 documents. The total frequency in the basic index, however, is only 47. So, if you had searched for NICKEL-CHROMIUM-ALUMINUM in the C.A. file, you would have retrieved only 47 out of 114.

```
Original spelling as taken from abstracts        number of records
Ni-Cr-AL                                                22
NiCrAl                                                   5
Ni alloy(s) ... Cr ... Al                               22
Ni-Cr alloy ... Al                                       6

Hyphenated (continuous) spelling, percentage preceeding element
symbol
   without space
     no decimals              Ni-20Cr-Al
     decimals                 Ni-16.9Cr-3.4Al

   with space or percent sign
     no decimals              Ni-16 Cr-4 Al
     decimals                 Ni-16 Cr-3.5 Al
     ranges                   Ni-(15-29)Cr-1%Al    Ni-10Cr-(2,5)Al

Spaced spelling, percentage preceding element symbol
   no decimals                Ni ... 15-20 Cr ... 2-6wt% Al
   "wrong" order              15-27 Cr ... 2-3% Al ... Ni
   decimals                   Ni .. 19.7-20.45 Cr .. 2.2-4.85 Al

Spaced spelling, element symbol preceding percentage
   no decimals                Ni ... Cr 15 ... Al 4
   decimals                   Ni 72.3 ... Cr 16.72 ... Al 5.07
   ranges                     Ni .. Cr 10.0-16 .. Al 2.5-5.5
   "wrong" order              Cr 15-19 ... Al 1.5-5.7 .. Ni
   two base elements          Ni-Cr .. Cr 14.0-14.8 .. Al 4.5-7.5
```

Tab.7 Irregular spelling of alloy compositions

In the ESA version of the C.A. file, the MF-line has been transferred from the registry to the bibliographic file. Why should it not be possible to transfer to the bibliographic file also a molecular formula, taken from the first three elements of the IN-line or from an MF-line, in which the elements are ranged according to their weight percentages?

4. Searching in the Abstracts

The accomanying abstracts of those 114 records from the C.A. file in which the alloy composition is indexed 47 times describe the alloy type in question as many as 80 times. The effort, however, to retrieve all these different wordings as extracted from the abstracts (Tab.7), is too complicated and would be too costly. The reason is that percentage figures in connection with the element symbols are either whole or decimal numbers standing before or behind the symbol are attached by hyphens or not, consist of character strings or have spaces in between regardless of their function.

15

A few simple rules issued by C.A.S. to their abstracters would turn the abstracts into a very helpful tool for retrieving alloy compositions (Tab.8):

1. The base element should always be expressed as "Ni alloy". If the publication makes alloying elements evident, further element symbols should be inserted in the order of decreasing weight percentage.

2. If percentage values are known, they should be attached to the symbol they belong to. In case of percent ranges, the limiting lower and upper values should be written in the same manner, with a hyphen between both the limiting expressions. Decimal figures may be written because they are not harmful for searching, since the dot is considered by the system as a blank. Base elements need not necessarily be quantified. Percent abbreviations are not only superfluous, but are also interfering with the searchability.

3. In case where several alloy compositions are mentioned in one abstract, false drops can be avoided by the use of neighboring operators. This implies however that the element symbols and their respective percentages are written in a standardized sequence.

```
Without pct:  Ni alloy   NiCr alloy   NiCrAl alloy   NiCrAlTi alloy
With pct:     Ni80 Cr15 Al5   Ni79-Ni82 Cr12-Cr15 Al2-Al6
```

Tab.8 Alloy spelling in the abstracts for enhanced searchability

5. The significance of C.A. for metallurgical searches

Chemical Abstracts Service is offering more than eight million records for the period between 1967 and today. More than 450.000 belong to the sections 55 (ferrous metals) and 56 (non-ferrous metals). The importance of Chemical Abstracts for metallurgical searches lies particularly in the domains of metal chemistry, alloy development and material properties dependent on alloy composition. C.A.S. obviously is unaware of this fact, or has considered it as neglectible.

During the second half of the 70ies the importance of the three-element indexing for metallurgical searches was extensively discussed between members of the German Society for Metallurgy and the Society for Information and Documentation; we came to the conclusion that the three-element indexing would improve the retrieval of metal alloys in the System for Documentation and Information in Metallurgy. In my opinion, metallurgical scientists and engineers as clients of C.A.S. would appreciate an enhanced indexing to increase their information yield. Last not least, it is for the database producer's benefit, too.

IMPLEMENTATION HURDLES FOR INTERNATIONAL INFORMATION SYSTEMS

Jean Newman Bedord, DIALOG Information Services, Inc.

Keywords: International, microcomputer, software, telecommunications, business practices, language, standards

Abstract: Implementing an international network of microcomputers required overcoming a number of hurdles. Acquisition of hardware and software and gaining access to a packet switching network required adapting to the realities of international availability. Compromises were made to resolve issues relating to differences in language, culture and business practices.

1. INTRODUCTION

Crossing international boundaries for information is complex, involving more than just hardware, software and a network. Issues are involved in resolving differences in language, culture and business practices. Solutions actually implemented are compromises which overcome these hurdles to provide a working information system.

2. BACKGROUND

This paper is based on my experiences in implementing an international network of microcomputers for a manufacturer of medical diagnostics. The project originated in the international marketing department to meet needs for more timely and detailed reporting of sales information. The application required transmitting sales data from five international sales offices in the United Kingdom, Sweden, Germany, France and Spain. These were relatively small offices with primarily sales and administrative personnel with limited computer skills. The only technical support available was the local supplier of hardware and software and telephone support from headquarters in the U.S.

An early decision was made to standardize on the hardware and software, though this proved to be more difficult than originally expected. Standardization on the IBM PC hardware was achieved, but the third party add-on cards for additional memory were not readily available at the local equipment suppliers. Availability in Lyon, France, was not the same as in Paris, but as assured by the U.S. supplier, the boards were available in France!

Use of standard software packages was a rational headquarters decision, but met with mixed success. Standardization on the spreadsheet software was achieved with Lotus 1-2-3 and headquarters supplied templates. This worked fairly well since the templates used standard company wide part numbers and numeric input, with no text. In addition, the package was available in all countries, with no strong local competition. However, even this package presented a substantial learning curve since the instructional manual and menus were all in English. The managers in this multinational company spoke English as a requirement of their jobs, but the actual work of data entry fell to their administrative assistants, with a generally lower level of fluency.

Standardization was not achievable for the word-processing software. WORDSTAR was the only package available in all the countries, but we discovered this really meant that the English version was sold in each of these countries. Only the French WORDSTAR had been converted to the French language and keyboard. The Spanish version would not recognize or print the tilde n, thus becoming useless for correspondence. In each country, a local word-processing software was available which was superior.

The IBM Asynchronous Communications software package was used for the communications software, since it was available from the same dealer as the IBM hardware and had instructions on communicating with the IBM host. Of necessity, the network was standardized since the TYMNET ENGINE was installed on the host and access to the TYMNET network was available in all countries. Standardization on modems was impossible due to differences in the telephone systems and government regulations. Generally, modems were available only through the government Postal, Telephone and Telegraph (PT & T) authority, not the local computer vendor; internal modems common in the U.S. were not available in Europe.

Even though the original intent had been standardization, the realities of international availability forced a multi-vendor environment with all the associated support difficulties.

3. LANGUAGE ISSUES

Installation of this PC network involved five countries with five different languages, so these issues surfaced early. Fortunately, the primary vendor, IBM, had recognized the implications of a world-wide market. Even though standardization was a goal for the field offices, hardware and software were purchased locally. The modular design of the IBM PC family meant that language specific keyboards were available, rather than just the U.S. keyboard, an important factor in acceptance of automation by local offices. The French keyboard has a very different key placement, whereas the other countries had additional keys for their special characters.

The international version of MS-DOS had separate drivers for each language, so the machine could be configured for each country. This version was not available in the U.S. so it had to be obtained in the U.K. While having language specific keyboards solved the acceptance problem, there were other problems. For data communication, a control key was likely to be in a different position or labelled differently on each keyboard. A person trouble-shooting from the U.S. telephone using the same software had to have a layout of the caller's keyboard! Even more troubling was the problem encountered in France where the break key needed for communication with the IBM host was not recognized by Transpac until a specific control sequence was entered. Since the day to day operation would be done by the administrative staff, this meant the instruction manuals had to be tailored for each office, more so than originally planned. It also increased the perceived difficulty of the system.

Differences in currency notations were another implication that surfaced. The U.S. dollar sign and British pound sign are single place characters, but the commonly accepted DM for German deutschmarks and FF for French francs require two places; in addition, the period sign is used as a decimal marker for English notation, but the comma is used in Spain. Financial displays had to be modified to incorporate these differences.

The language differences were insurmountable in standardizing on word-processing software. The U.S. software simply didn't have the flexibility to accommodate all the differences in keyboards and displays. Given the smaller European markets and the amount of customization for each language, any future standardization on a world-wide word-processing package is doubtful.

4. CULTURAL DIFFERENCES

A major area of cultural differences emerged in the telecommunications area. Data communications in Europe is based on the CCITT standard and in the U.S. is based on the Bell standard. At the available 300 and 1200 baud speeds, a CCITT modem cannot communicate with a Bell modem. This meant that direct dialup to the host computer in the U.S. was not an option. All data communication required protocol conversion and routing through a packet switching network. To complicate the installation even further, TYMNET was not directly available, but was one of the international record carrier services controlled through each national government. This meant that trouble-shooting had to be routed through the government PT & T, then onto TYMNET, then the host system.

Another area of differences was in the power supplies and plugs that were specific to each country. For this reason, buying hardware locally turned out to be an absolute necessity, in addition to having a local repair service. Interestingly, getting a CCITT modem with a U.S. power supply and plug required a special order and months to obtain, even though the company manufactured the modems for Europe and the U.S. in the same location only a few miles away--international sales were handled by a different group than domestic sales.

5. BUSINESS PRACTICES

International communication turned out to be very time-consuming and led to lengthening the project implementation schedule. Matters that took days to resolve in the U.S. would take weeks in the international environment. Ordinary airmail took too long, but even an air express package sent Thursday or Friday did not arrive until Monday. Routine business communication was done via Telex. Sending a message at the end of the working business day had the advantage of arriving at the beginning of the business day on the other side of the Atlantic. The time window for voice communication was limited due to the obvious differences in time zones, so early A.M. conferences in the U.S. and late P.M. conferences in Europe were common. Differences in European holiday schedules also contributed to limiting communication windows. More subtly, communication of technical requirements took longer since we were dealing with personnel with limited computer experience speaking English as a second language. We also had limited knowledge of the additional constraints in each country and the impact on the schedule.

Modems and user id's were necessary to implement the network, but obtaining them was not a simple matter. Unlike the U.S., where access was controlled by the corporate computing center, internationally, each office had to apply to their government PT & T authority for the new user id and access to TYMNET. In the U.K. and Germany, this procedure took months! Even then, complete technical information was not provided. To establish communication with the headquarters computer required specifying the host address which was not available from the PT & T and not needed in the U.S. Furthermore, each country had a different dialing sequence and logon procedure.

Telecommunications costs were higher and more difficult to control internationally. In the U.S., most field units could reach a TYMNET node by a local call, so no long distance charges were incurred. Packet switching costs were billed to the central computer facility, rather than individual users. Internationally, typically, there were local telephone tolls in addition to the packet switching charges--costs borne by the field unit, rather than headquarters. Reliability was generally lower, due to the number of links. Time of day and weather were important variables; twenty-four hour operation of the host system was crucial.

The issues concerning transborder data flow (TBDF) were handled by not transmitting individual customer information. Only summary numbers were sent to headquarters. This sales information was collected in the local currency, then exchange rates applied as part of the headquarters consolidation procedure. Even exchange rates were not simple. Sales revenue was converted at the average exchange rate for the month, since the assumption was that sales had occurred evenly throughout the month. However, inventories had to be valued at the month end exchange rate. In addition, forecasted sales used the anticipated exchange rate.

As part of the intent to standardize the field units, accounting packages were evaluated. Although all five field offices performed similar functions and reported similarly to the head office, the government reporting requirements were specific to each country. Only two packages were even contenders. There were no plans to add European features to the U.S. package, and the one European package did not have features to satisfy all the countries. The decision was made to allow country specific accounting, sales and inventory software packages since only these could meet the government regulations and local business practices.

6. CONCLUSION

The challenges encountered in this specific implementation were those facing any organization with an international network and information flow. The issues I encountered while implementing a PC network for a multinational manufacturer are the same issues encountered while working for an international online information provider such as Dialog. There are organizational and support reasons for standardizing hardware, software and the network in both environments. However, country specific issues involving language, culture and business practices must be resolved with compromises. The international arena requires more time and effort to implement working systems. The learning curves are numerous and steep!

SEARCHING FOR THE ULTIMATE SET-UP: ONLINE COMMUNICATIONS FOR THE END-USER ENVIRONMENT

Steven J. Bell, University of Pennsylvania

Keywords: End-Users, Communications Software, Software

Abstract: A successful end-user search service using microcomputers as search terminals should make online searching efficient and error-free for the end-user. An ultimate set-up is the result of efforts to "set-up" a communications software package so online communication functions are performed with a high degree of automation. The search to create this set-up will reduce mechanical errors related to online communications.

A properly selected software package is critical in management of the online session. It should have a display screen that clearly shows the online systems available to end-users. The package should be capable of assigning communication functions to specific keys. Logons or downloads can then be performed with a minimum of keystrokes.

There is no one ultimate set-up. Each organization should adapt a communications software package to its end-user service. As communications software becomes more sophisticated a better, more ultimate set-up may be possible. Such a set-up would allow all communication functions to work from function keys with a template to serve as the end-user's guide to searching.

1. INTRODUCTION

User training, fees, availability of end-user databases, and strategies for building end-user clientele are some aspects of end-user search services discussed in the library and online literature. This presentation extends the discussion of end-user searching to the management of the end-user session with microcomputer communications software.

A successful end-user search service should make online searching efficient and trouble-free for the patron. Effective training, reliable documentation and knowledgeable staff contribute to this goal. But online search sessions must also be managed. A database logon must occur, there may be a need to print or download, a patron may need to check the directory of a diskette or staff may need to monitor the elapsed time of searches. Good management of these functions facilitates a service with which end-users will be satisfied.

The goal of searching for the ultimate set-up is to find the communications software package that, when customized to meet the demands of a particular end-user environment, efficiently performs search management tasks. It is characterized by features that make an end-user service easier for staff and users. There is no one single ultimate set-up. Each organization should adapt a communications software package to meet the needs of its end-user service.

2. END-USER SEARCHING AT THE LIPPINCOTT LIBRARY

Since 1984, the Lippincott Library of the Wharton School at the University of Pennsylvania has offered its "Do-It-Yourself" online search program to its students, faculty and staff. This heavily used service provides end-user access to four separate timesharing systems. End-users clocked over 2500 hours of online search time during the 1986-87 academic year. Lippincott was using a popular communications software package with its microcomputers. The software performed adequately and was generally perceived as satisfactory, although staff members indicated there were some features of the software for which they did not care.

There are several reasons why staff may choose to keep using a software package despite apparent deficiencies:

- constraints on staff time for learning new software
- lack of funds to purchase new software
- site licensing agreements may bring in a package and funds may not be approved for other software purchases
- unwillingness to introduce new software to end-users
- staff unwillingness to change from a familiar package
- learning new software may be intimidating

In these situations, the service may adapt itself to the limitations of the communications software. The communications software will determine how certain aspects of the service are managed rather than the individuals operating the service. In developing the ultimate set-up, you find the right communications software package and adapt it to the needs of your staff and end-users.

Lippincott's staff sought to make improvements in its communications software by changing to a package that could be customized. A main concern was ease of use for both staff and end-users. For example, on our existing software the "F4" function key initiated a download. Downloading with the new package was different, which concerned staff. The flexibility of the new package made it possible to program the downloading command to operate from the "F4" key. This is one illustration of adapting your software to meet the needs of your service.

3. SOFTWARE SELECTION

The search for the ultimate set-up begins with the selection of an appropriate software package. The decision to select a communications package is often based on one of the following criteria:

- the software is popular
- the software is already in use at the organization
- the software was recommended by experts

What's popular or right for others may be inappropriate for you. Some factors to consider in selecting software for your ultimate set-up are:

- screen display
- function key programming
- command file editing

The display screen is on the monitor when the package is loaded but not in communications mode. This display may be referred to as the "home" or "status" screen. If end-users log themselves on then they should be able to see what systems are available from the display screen. If staff perform logons, it is still helpful to have available systems clearly indicated. This can reduce unintentional logons to incorrect systems. If different logons are available for the same system, for example a Tymnet and Telenet logon or a 1200 baud and 2400 baud logon, then that distinction should be clearly displayed.

It may not be possible to customize the display screen. It is important to know what the screen appearance is and how it displays available search systems. An illustration of a good display is:

```
--------------------------Available Command Files-------------------------

1)  BRS1200        2)  BRS2400        3)  DIALOG         4)  VUTEXTYM

5)  VUTEXTEL       6)  DOW1200        7)  DOW2400
--------------------------------------------------------------------------
ENTER NUMBER OF FILE TO USE:
```

This display shows the available auto-logons. Choices are BRS at 1200 baud or 2400 baud, DIALOG, VUTEXT on Telenet or Tymnet, and Dow Jones at 1200 baud or 2400 baud. Be concerned if communications software requires you to go through a series of screens or commands to find files available for logon or to initiate a logon sequence.

Single keystroke operations are essential to this set-up. The fewer keys to type, the faster communication functions are performed. Typing errors are reduced. Some packages are designed to operate with single keystrokes. Others allow you to program commands to a specific key or combinations of keys. While it is important to have single keystroke operations, the software shouldn't require sophisticated computer skills to assign functions to the keys.

The ease with which command files are edited is another consideration. A command file is a data file stored on the communications disk. The baud rate used, the logon sequences, phone numbers dialed, names of search systems and other facets of the communications set-up are stored in them. Again, making changes or editing these command files shouldn't require sophisticated computer skills.

A good approach to file editing would use a command that allows any element in a file to be changed. For example:

EDIT(the command) BAUD2400(change baud rate to 2400)

Alternatively, it may be possible to enter the command file and edit specific lines or data items. A command would be used to retrieve the file, and then make changes with editing keys. Communication packages with built-in text editors usually have this type of editing capability.

Finally, in selecting software, consult colleagues and software reviews. If possible, examine the documentation or obtain a demonstration disk from the distributor. To learn more about modifying the package call the vendor's technical assistance hotline. This may also determine the level of help available from the technical assistance staff. In the future, your pursuit of the ultimate set-up may necessitate calls for assistance.

4.   FEATURES FOR THE ULTIMATE SET-UP

Some specific communications functions that can be customized in developing the ultimate set-up are:

- Automated Logons
- Downloading

- Phone Disconnect
- Reloading of Command Files
- System Specific Customizations

Automated system logons are vital to any ultimate set-up. Most communication packages are capable of creating auto-logons although some are far easier than others. Packages that create auto-logons by saving the sequence as it is performed are the easiest to use. Those requiring you to type out the logon commands, including time-out pauses, carriage returns, etc., are more complex.

For those environments where end-users may perform their own logons, fully automated logons are desired. If passwords are included in the customized logons then security is a concern. One security measure used in most online systems is password suppression. The "lock-up" feature found on some communications software is also useful. It allows you to create a password that must be entered before using the software. If the communications disk is copied or stolen, the password would prevent searching. Libraries wanting greater control over system usage need to determine how much, if any, of the logon sequence to automate.

Many end-users want to download their searches. The capture of data to disk is susceptible to error by anyone, especially inexperienced end-user searchers. Common end-user mistakes when downloading that may be reduced by customizing include:

- capturing to the software or hard disk instead of the searcher's disk
- losing the capture file by failing to correctly save it
- failing to correctly initiate the download

Again, single key programming is most effective. The download sequence should begin and end with a single keystroke. At the Lippincott Library, despite instruction sheets for downloading posted at search terminals, end-users still encountered difficulty with downloading. The most frequent error was directing files to incorrect drives.

The software we now use is set-up to deliver a command which begins the download, and also specifies the capture drive. Users only have to type in a file name. The "capture off" command also works from a single key. Communications software offers many approaches to downloading. A simple approach, combined with customizing options, will greatly aid end-users.

Other targets for customization are printer on/off, phone disconnect and command file reload. Each of these functions should be programmed to operate from a single key. Users will find activating the printer easier if the on/off works as a toggle switch. Complicated printers often lead to paper waste.

End-users may finish a search and leave without logging off or disconnecting the phone. To save timesharing costs, the phone should be disconnected immediately after logging off. A single key operation can make this an easy chore for staff or the end-user. Also, as one search ends the software should be reset to show the command files for the next user. Most end-users will leave this to the staff. A single key approach will save time and make this task seem less tiresome.

System specific customizations may also contribute to the ultimate set-up. Repetitious operations may be conducted with a single key. Assume an end-user performs a daily search of the BUSINESS database on Dow Jones NEWS/RETRIEVAL. A key could be programmed to type "//BUSINESS" when needed so the database is quickly accessed. More extensive sets of instructions or commands, referred to as macros, may also be programmed to keys. Additional progamming may be appropriate in some end-user environments but will take more time and effort to develop.

Finally, monitoring search time and checking the disk directory are two useful features in an end-user search service. These are not items you can customize. They must be a feature of the software. A time monitor differs from a time clock. The clock may be set to show the current time or will just run from zero when the software is booted. The monitor keeps time from zero as each search begins. When end-users are limited to a specific amount of search time, the monitor will show the time elapsed since the logon occured. End-users who download often want to check their disk for available space. They may need to erase files to make space. Communications software that handles these requests will save time for staff and patrons.

The ultimate software set-up you create, no matter how carefully developed, will not anticipate the potential abuses it will be subjected to in an online search service. Putting it to use in daily end-user searching will reveal faults. A flexible communications package will adapt to end-user needs that couldn't be anticipated.

5. CONCLUSION

A key advantage of online searching is its ability to enhance research capabilities and increase one's productivity. Database vendors have tried to make their products more inviting to end-users. It would be unfortunate if, in assisting end-users to access these products, information professionals relied on communications software that made online searching a frustrating experience for the end-user.

Part of the challenge in searching for the ultimate set-up is the desire to advance beyond the current set-up. I like to envision a software set-up that would allow all logons and other communication functions to work from function key combinations. There are approximately 40 keys available for programming or macros. These include combinations of the SHIFT, ALT and CONTROL keys with the ten function keys.

A template would be placed over the function keys to guide end-users to the keys needed to effectively manage the search. Function keys would trigger logons, downloading sequences, help screens and possibly some specific commands for individual online systems.

The search software created by Mead Data Central for microcomputer searching of LEXIS/NEXIS illustrates this concept. Many search commands and management functions are executed with function key combinations. A template shows the keys to use for specific functions. For the end-user, particularly infrequent searchers, the template is a quick guide to online searching.

Developing the ultimate set-up for your end-user environment will require time, effort and experimentation. It is a challenge with tangible benefits for your end-user service. I hope others involved in end-user services will be encouraged to customize their communications software, and to share their versions of the ultimate set-up.

H.R. 145, THE COMPUTER SECURITY ACT OF 1987: AN ASSESSMENT

Virgil Blake, Queens College

Keywords: Computer Security, Information Policy, H.R. 145 Telecommunication Security.

ABSTRACT: In 1986 the existence of the "National Policy on Protection of Sensitive but Unclassified Information in Federal Government Telecommunications and Automated Information Systems" was revealed. This policy sought to extend the Federal governments authority to control access to unclassified information in computer and telecommunications system within the Federal government and the private sector. This policy, also known as NTISSP No. 2, was the immediate catalyst for the introduction of the Computer Security Act of 1987, H.R. 145. This bill's objective was to offset the percieved threats to free access to unclassified information helf by government agencies and made available by private operated online information services. Specifically it was viewed as the vehicle to (1) remove the potential authority of military and intelligence agencies to control access to unclassified information; (2) eliminate a new category of information; and (3) restrict the government's authority to secure unclassified information to government computer and telecommunication systems.

Shortly after the introduction of the Computer Security Act of 1987, NTISSP No. 2, promulgated by then National Security Advisor Adminiral Poindexter, was rescinded by his successor, Frank Carlucci. The intense feelings generated by the provisions of the repudiated policy abated as the anticipated legislative solution, proceeded through the Congress.

The major features of H.R. 145, as signed into law, are (1) an augmented role for the National Bureau of Standards in developing the regulations for computer security and telecommunications security of unclassified information; (2) the creation of the Computer Security and Privacy Advisory Board; and (3) the inclusion of a direct role for the President in governing access to unclassified information.

The strengths of the bill include (1) the apparent restoration of civilian control over regulations governing access to unclassified information; (2) restriction of its provisions to Federal Agencies with unclassified information in their computer and telecommunications systems; and (3) an emphasis on protection of the system rather than limiting access to the information the systems contain.

There are areas of apparent weakness as well. A new category of information is given Congressional endorsement. The responsibilities of the individual agency heads are not well defined.

The law as passed is far from an ideal solution to the issues raised by NTISSP No. 2. The operation of H.R. 145 should be closely watched by all information professionals.

"What a Tangled Web We Weave When first we practice to decieve"
                              -Sir Walter Scott,

"Eternal Vigilance is the Price of Liberty"
                              -Wendall Philips, 1852

"A Republic If We Can Keep It"
                              - Benjamin Franklin, 1787

On January 5, 1987 Rep. Jack Brooks (Dem.-Texas) introduced H.R. 145, The Computer Security Act of 1987. The immediate catalyst for its introduction was the disclosure at the Information Industry Association's 1986 convention of a federal directive entitled "National Policy on Protection of Sensitive but Unclassified Information in Federal Government Telecommunications and Automated Information Systems." This policy, also known as NTISSC No. 2, was the product of the National Telecommunications and Information Systems Security Committee (TNISSC), a body created by National Security Decision Directive 145 NSDD 145). The purpose of NSDD 145 was to develop a national policy securing Federal telecommunications and automated information systems. Overseeing the NTISSC was the Systems Security Group. The responsibility for implementing the policy was assigned to the National Manager for Telecommunications who also serves as director of the National Security Agency (NSA).

It is the purpose of this paper to review the grievances raised by NTISSC No. 2, outline the major features of H.R. 145, and assess the strengths and weaknesses of this bill.

1. BACKGROUND

NTISSC No. 2 was severely criticized on several grounds. Objection was raised to the apparent creation of a new category of information-sensitive but unclassified. This was defined as "Information the disclosure, loss, misuse, alteration or destruction of which could adversely affect national security or other Federal interests."[1] Logic argued that information meeting that criteria should not be unclassified in the first place.

The phrase "other government interests" was another cause for concern. It was defined as information "related to the wide range of government or government derived economic, human, financial, industrial, agricultural, technological, and law enforcement information."[2] This was so sweeping in scope that critics pointed out that virtually any type of information, whether in government information systems or in the private sector, could be included.

A third concern was the Federal government's intention to apply the guidelines developed under terms of NTISSC No. 2 to the private sector as well. NSDD 145 stated that "the government shall encourage, advise, and where appropriate, assist the private sector."[3] The government's determination to assist the private sector were made clear by Jack Simpson's report of four visits from Federal authorities to Mead Data General in 1986. The Associate Director of the State University of New York at Buffalo reported the receipt of a subpeona designed to determine the use of online data bases by an Iraqi student.

The dominance of officials from military and intelligence agencies in bodies created by NSDD 145 was also pointed out. On the NTISSC, Jack Simpson noted, "12 of its 22 members are from military or intelligence agencies."[4]. This was regarded as a potentially dangerous extension of their authority to include unclassified as well as classified information.

A final concern was the seeming disparity in the treatment of the on-line databases as opposed to their print cousins. The focus of NSDD 145 was data in its electronic format. This was derived from the so-called mosaic theory by which some Federal officials argued that online databases must be made more secure since it was easier and faster to systematically scan them. These advantages, it followed, made it easier for users of these systems to connect bits of unclassified data found there to deduce classified information. The same could be done with print versions of the same data but it required far greater effort over longer periods of time. This, in the minds of those subscribing to the mosaic theory, made the difference. Counter-arguments were offered that to make these deductions a user would already have a thorough background in the subject to little avail. The larger concern was that this focus on the electronic as opposed to the print format of the information was only a first step toward securing the print versions of the information as well.

The furor over the implications of NTISSP No. 2 intensified until Frank Carlucci, then National Security Advisor, wrote to Rep. Brooks on March 12, 1987 that he had "directed my staff to review immediately NSDD 145..."[5]. "With respect to NTISSP 2," he added, "I have instructed my staff to initiate procedures ... to rescind that document."[6]. Each of the major professional associations directly concerned with the principle of free access to information, the American Library Association, the American Society for Information Science, and the Information Industry Association, proclaimed a victory and turned their attentions toward the passage of H.R. 145.=This bill, regarded as corrective legislation to prevent any future reincarnation of the repudiated NTISSP No. 2, had been proceeding through the legislative process. It was approved by the House on June 22, 1987, by the Senate on December 21, 1987 and signed into law on January 8, 1988.

2. **H.R. 145, THE COMPUTER SECURITY ACT OF 1987**

The objective of H.R. 145 and NSDD 145 were similar. Both sought to prevent unauthorized access to information in Federal computer and telecommunications systems. H.R. 145, however, sought to obtain this end with a policy that would respond to the criticisms NTISSP No. 2 had evoked. H.R. 145 attempted to secure the systems without making the information in those systems inaccessable. It is in that light that the basic features of H.R. 145 should be examined.

Under H.R. 145 the National Bureau of Standards (NBS) regained primacy in the development of "standards, guidelines, and associated techniques for computer systems."[7]. and for "developing technical, management, physical, and administrative standards and guidelines for the cost effective security and privacy of SENSITIVE information."[8]. The NBS authority was limited to unclassified information and the Federal systems in which it was stored. Classified information and the Federal systems in which it was stored were still subject to security regulations approved by the Congress or created by Executive Orders. The specific purpose of the NBS developed standards and guidelines is "to control loss and unauthorized modification or disclosure of sensitive information in such systems."[9]. Once developed the NBS was to submit its standards to the Secretary of Commerce, who was to ensure that they were employed, develop training programs in the use of the newly developed techniques, and evaluate the effectiveness of its programs.

The NBS is also empowered to (1) assist the private sector, UPON REQUEST: (2) provide technical assistance in implementing its standards; and (3) conduct research in computer security. The NBS is directed to co-operate with other government agencies with technical expertise in computer security to "assure, to the maximum extent feasible, that standards developed ... are consistent or comparable..."10. It is specifically directed to consult the NSA but has the option of using their procedures "to the extent that the National Bureau of Standards determines such guidelines are consistant with the requirement of protecting sensitive information."11.

A second feature of H.R. 145 is the creation of a twelve member Computer System and Privacy Advisory Board appointed by the Secretary of Commerce. The board, composed of four members from the private sector associated with the telecommunications or computer industry, four members from the private sector with expertise in computer or telecommunications technology, and four members from the Federal government with experience in computer security. One of the members from the Federal government must be from the NSA. The board is to identify emerging issues related to computer security and advise the NBS.

The Secretary of Commerce is the manager of the NBS policies. He is to make the NBS regulations mandatory for each of the Federal agencies with unclassified information. It is his responsibility to ensure that the NBS recommendations are carried out. The President may disapprove or modify the NBS guidelines but if he does so it must be reported to the House Government Operations Committee and be published in the <u>Federal Register.</u>

The individual agency heads are to use the NBS standards in the agencies under their supervision. Each agency head may, however, introduce standards more stringent than those set down by the Secretary of Commerce. There is also the provision for a waiver of the standards by the Secretary of Commerce if "compliance would adversly affect the accomplishment of the mission of an operator of a Federal computer system, or cause adverse financial impact on the operator."12.

Finally each agency is required to develop a program of training in computer security awareness. Each agency is given six months to identify each Federal computer system containing sensitive information and, within a year, establish a plan for the "security and privacy of each Federal computer system identified."13.

3. H.R. 145--STRENGTHS

The new law has some distinct strengths. The first, and most important, is the restoration of civilian control over unclassified information in civil agencies. NSDD 145 superceded President Carter's directive, PD 24, on governmental information policy. That 1978 directive had assigned the Defense Department the task of securing telecommunications systems containing classified information only. The Commerce Department was given sole responsibility for telecommunications systems containing unclassified information. NSDD 145 gave total responsibility for Federal telecommunications to the Defense Department. Within the Defense Department the responsibility for securing Federal telecommunications was assigned to the NSA. The NSA, in April, 1986, merged its Communications Security and Computer Security units. This new unit, under NSDD 145, announced that it was extending its authority to include all Federal computer and communications systems and the private sector. Shortly thereafter NTISSP No. 2 was promulgated.

H.R. 145 specifically restores to the Commerce Department jurisdiction over all Federal computer and communications systems with unclassified information. The NBS is given primary responsibility for the development of standards and guidelines for such systems. While the NBS is to consult other Federal agencies with technical expertise including the NSA it is relieved of any obligation to employ NSA guidelines in discharging its own unique responsibilities. The self described "shadow role" NBS was forced to play under NTISSP No. 2 was dispelled.

To further ensure civilian control of Federal telecommunications and computer systems with unclassified information H.R. 145 created the Computer

Security and Privacy advisory Board. This body supplanted the NTISSC as the NBS's overseer. Since two-thirds of its membership is to be selected from the private sector, it is unlikely that the military and intelligence agencies could ever exert the degree of control over unclassified information that the composition of the NTISSC might have permitted.

A second major improvement is the limitation of the Federal governments standards to Federal agencies. The NBS, like the NSA under NSDD 145, is authorized to "assist the private sector, UPON REQUEST, in using and applying the results of programs and activities..."[14]. But the key difference is the insertion of the phase "upon request" in H.R. 145. NSDD 145 and NTISSP No. 2 assumed that the Federal government had the authority to extend its regulations to unclassified information in the private sector. Carried to its logical extreme this would have meant government censorship of information not related to national security, a practice alien to the American experience. Inserting the phrase "upon request" will permit the private sector to cooperate with the Federal government when it is convinced that the security measures are warrented. This is more typical of the American experience-- government and private industry working together in the national interest when the Federal government clearly demonstrates the necessity of doing so.

H.R. 145 also tore down the artificial wall that had been created to differentiate the focus on electronic rather than print formats. This dichotomy followed from the mosaic theory. H.R. 145 states that "nothing in this act...shall be construed to authorize any Federal agency to limit, restrict, regulate, or control the collection, maintenance, disclosure, use, transfer, or sale of information (regardless of the medium in which the information may be maintained) that is (A) privately owned information; (B) disclosable...; (C) public domain."[15]. Format is no longer a prime concern. The fear of the power of electronic databases derived from the so called mosaic theory was officially repudiated. The prime concern of H.R. 145 was to prevent unauthorized access to information in any format.

The tone of H.R. 145 is much different. The emphasis in H.R. 145 is clearly the protection of the computer systems themselves, defined as hardware, software, and telecommunications links, and the prevention of unauthorized access to the information contained therein. The very title of NTISSP No. 2, "National Policy on Protection of Sensitive but Unclassified Information in Federal Government Telecommunications and Automated Information Systems," indicates a very different emphasis. Both NSDD 145 and NTISSP No. 2 are rooted in a fear of "technological exploitation as well as other dimensions of the hostile intelligence threat"[16]. and sought to protect information "potential adversaries have targeted."[17]. Making unclassified information inaccessible was the paramount concern of these documents. In H.R. 145 the primary concern is protecting the system. H.R. 145 makes clear that the standards and guidelines developed by the NBS "shall be to control loss and unauthorized modification or disclosure of sensitive information in such systems and to prevent computer related fraud and abuse."[18].

H.R. 145 differs from NSDD 145 and NTISSP No. 2 in one other way. It was concerned with the disclosure of personal and proprietary information. While the definitions of sensitive information in both H.R. 145 and NTISSP No. 2 include this type of information, it was H.R. 145 alone that saw fit to emphasize this concern by including the phrase "Privacy Advisory" in the name of the NBS' supervising board. The preponderant concern of both NSDD 145 and NTISSP No. 2 was information that might be related to national security. The privacy concerns are not mentioned in either document except in the definition of sensitive information dound in NTISSP No. 2.

4. <u>H.R. 145--CONCERNS</u>

Despite the strengths of H.R. 145 outlined above there are some aspects of the bill which might provide the basis for its subversion. The first of these is the inclusion of the charge to the NBS to develop standards and guidelines for the security of SENSITIVE INFORMATION in Federal computer systems. Sensitive information is defined as H.R. 145 as "any information the loss, misuse, or unauthorized access to or modification of could adversely affect the national interest or the conduct of Federal programs."[19]. This is virtually identical to the definition of sensitive information dound in NTISSP No. 2. This apparent legitimization of a new category of information was a central concern during the legislative hearings on H.R. 145. Raymond G. Kammer, Deputy Director of the NBS, testified that the "bill does not provide sufficient guidance or definition of the type of information t hat is to be considered "sensitive but unclassified."[20]. Dr. Howard Rensikoff argued that "it is not possible to draw a sharp distinction between 'sensitive' information and information that is 'not sensitive'."[21]. The Association of Research Libraries urged that "the definition of the term 'sensitive' information should be eliminated or at least more precisely defined."[22]. The ACLU's J. Berman did not believe that either military or civilian Federal agencies should be restricting access to public information they labelled "sensitive." An American Society for Information Science (ASIS) position paper opposed "any proposal to limit access to unclassified information delivered electronically..."[23]. Even Donald Latham, Assistant Secretary of Defense and chairman of the much maligned NTISSC, pointed out that the "bill defines sensitive but unclassified almost identical to what NSA did."[24]. Critical of the fact that both H.R. 145 and NSDD 145 incorporated the concept of unclassified but sensitive information, Rep. Glenn English envisioned "an army of bureaucrats armed with ink pads running around stamping "sensitive" to masses of documents...Any such markings have a way of interfering with public access to documents that belong in the public sector."[25]. Congress has been aware of the problem of overclassification since the early 1970s.[26]. Nevertheless H.R. 145 was approved with a definition of sensitive information that lends a Congressional imprimateur to a new type of information.

The pivotal role of the Secretary of Commerce in H.R. 145 is a second source of concern. The Secretary of Commerce is the official who is to ensure that the NBS standards are followed within those Federal agencies dealing with unclassified information. It is important to note, then, the Commerce Department's thinking on H.R. 145. Then Commerce Secretary Baldridge was one who subscribed to the so called mosaic theory and, in 1985, characterized the National Technical Information Service (NTIS) as a "hemmorage of American technology."[27]. In his testimony before the House Committee on Government Operations, Baldridge made three suggestions to improve H.R. 145--(1) the inclusion of a means of Presidential review to ensure that standards used by the NBS were consistent with National security; (2) that the NBS use the technical standards of the NSA; and (3) that the Computer Security and Privacy Advisory Board be eliminated. Two of these proposals would have emasculated the bill. Mandating the use of NSA standards by the NBS would return the NBS to the subordinate role it held under NSDD 145. The NSA's objective is to ensure the secrecy of information and its standards would reflect that mission. The NBS charge under H.R. 145 is not to secrete unclassified data but only to ensure that it is made available to authorized persons. Elimination of the civilian dominated advisory board would, presumably, have left the NTISSC, dominated by military and intelligence officials, as the sole policy making body for computer security. The combined effect of the two suggestions is to create a situation analgous to that under NSDD 145. These suggestions, it should be recalled, were offered by the official who would have, under H.R. 145, overall responsibility for the program itself. One only has to recall this administration's management of the Environmental Protection Agency to realize the dangers here.

One of the Baldrige suggestions, however, was incorporated into the bill as passed. The Presiden t was given authority to "disapprove or modify such standards if he determines such action to be in the public interest."[28].

But the bill failed to provide a way for the Congress to override a Presidential modification or disapproval. H.R. 145 only required that any such Presidential action by reported to the House Committee on Government Operations and by published in the Federal Register. Should a President modify NBS standards to the point where TNISSP No. 2 is resuscitated, Congress has no rapid means to react.

H.R. 145 permits the heads of individual agencies to develop and employ standards that "are more stringent than the standards promulgated by the Secretary of Commerce."[29]. The bill does not require that these enhanced standards be reported to anyone or published anywhere as is the case with Presidential actions. In his defense of NSDD 145 Donald Latham pointed out that "Federal departmental and agency heads are individually responsible for identifying sensitive but unclassified information and ensuring that telecommunications and automated information systems processing such information are appropriately protected..."[30]. H.R. 145 is not markedly more precise. John Richardson of the Institute of Electrical and Electronic Engineers (IEEE) Washington Office noted that "both H.R. 145 and NTISSP 2 fail to provide workable guidelines for agency heads to identify and designate sensitive but unclassified information."[31]. Failure to include such guidelines or include a requirement that individual agency heads notify a superordinate body or official of their implementation of standards exceeding those required by the Secretary of Commerce is unfortunate on two counts. First, no agency head wishes to be singled out as being lax in securing the information in his agency. This only leads to over use of classification labels that in turn makes access to even unclassified information more difficult. Secondly, the fact that these individual agency heads are not accountable to anyone provided their standards exceed those of the Secretary of Commerce is a loophole that the crafty as well as cautious bureaucrat can easily use to inhibit access to information.

Conclusion

H.R. 145 has been described as a compromise agreed to by the White House. A compromise is usually defined as an agreement in which each side makes some concessions. In H.R. 145 the White House did make some concessions. It did abandon the attempt to extend to the military and intelligence community the power to establish controls for access to unclassified information held by government agencies and in online information systems operated by private firms. Through the NBS and the Computer Security and Privacy Advisory Board civilian control of unclassified information appears to be restored. Private industry is not to be subjected to the NBS standards unless it chooses to be. In addition the false dichotomy between electronic and print formats of unclassified information derived from the mosaic theory is rejected.

But the White House has managed to exact a high price for these concessions. It gained Congressional assent to the creation of an new category of information which is not any better defined than it was in NTISSP No. 2. Key positions in the operating structure created by H.R. 145 are members of the executive branch of government. Presumably the Secretary of Commerce and the individual heads of the Federal agencies first lyalties will be with the execytuve rather than the legislative branch of government. This is magnified in importance when one considers that the authority of both the Secretary of Commerce and individual agency heads are not well defined. The individual agency heads in particular do not seem directly susceptible to Congressional oversight yet they have the option of using standards more stringent than those prescribed by the NBS itself.

H.R. 145, then, has not attained all that many information professionals had hoped. The true measure of it as an individual aspect of the effort to retain access to unclassified information will be the quality of the standards developed by the NBS and their employment by those supervising federal agencies. Information professionals will have to carefully scrutinize the operation of H.R. 145 to ensure that its limited ends are not subverted.

But this is only one of the responsibilities facing information professionals in the near future. NTISSP No. 2 is merely the latest in a series of actions on the part of the Federal government as it seeks to develop a coherent information policy. It is the natural corollary of a number of related actions--the use of the Paperwork Reduction Act of 1979, Executive Order 12356, The Office of Management and Budget's Circular A-130, and the discovery of NASA's "No No List"--which have consistently worked to restrict access to information in general. This administration is not the first to try to develop a national information policy. It is only the most active. Deliberations on the part of the Federal government on the development of a national information policy can be traced back to Nixon's Domestic Council. Until now information professionals have been fortunate . Most Federal efforts in the evolution of a national information policy have been sporadic and uncoordinated. This administration has tried to develop a single coordinated approach to information policy. The development of a national information policy is no longer in question. The real issue facing information professionals is the nature of that policy.

This should be the real lesson of the Experience with H.R. 145 for all information professionals. The essence of these professions is the gathering of information and organizing it for the purpose of making it accessible to users. Any element of an emerging government information policy that restricts access is counter to the core of all information professions. Preserving that essence will require a more active stance on the part of information professionals. Reacting to events that have already been put into effect, as was the case with TNISSP No. 2, may not be good enough any longer. It is time for information professionals to seriously consider what are the essential elements that ought to be incorporated into any future government information policy that serves both the national and our own professional interest. Having done that information professionals can take steps to let Federal policy makers know what must be considered in the development of any national information policy. By taking steps to ensure that the emerging national information policy emphasizes access to information can information professionals best serve their patrons and uphold their professional creed.

1. U.S., Congress, House, Computer Security Act of 1987, Hearings before a Subcommittee of the Committee on Government Operations, House of Representatives, 100th Congress, First Session, 1987, February 25, and March 17, 1987, p. 544.

2. Ibid., p.

3. Ibid.

4. Ibid., p. 530.

5. Ibid., p. 327.

6. Ibid., p. 386.

7. Ibid.

8. U.S., Congress, Senate, The Computer Security Act of 1987, H.R. 145, 100th Congress, 1st Session, 1987, p. 2.

9. Ibid.

10. Ibid.

11. Ibid.

12. Ibid., p. 7.

13. Ibid., p. 13.

14. Ibid., p. 16.

15. Ibid., p. 5.

16. U.S., Congress, House, op. cit., p. 528.

17. Ibid., p. 545.

18. U.S., Congress, Senate, op. cit., p. 4.

19. Ibid., p. 9

20. U.S. Congress, House, Computer Security Act of 1987, Hearings before the Subcommittee on Science, Research, and Technology and the Subcommittee on Transportation, Aviation, and Materials of the Committee on Science, Space, and Technology, 100th Congress, 1st Session, February 26, 1987, p. 82.

21. U.S., Congress, House, Computer Security Act of 1987, Hearings before a Subcommittee of the Committee on Government Operations, House of Representatives, 100th Congress, 1st Session, p. 458.

22. Ibid., p. 503.

23. "Sensitive but Unclassified Update," *Bulletin of the American Society for Information Science*, V. 13, No. 5 (June-July, 1987), p. 11.

24. U.S., Congress, House, *Computer Security Act of 1987, Hearings before a Subcommittee of the Committee on Government Operations, House of Representatives*, 100th Congress, 1st Session, 1987, February 25, 26 and March 17, 1987, p. 305.

25. "Rep. English on Sensitive but Unclassified" Newsletter on Intellectual Freedom, V. 36, 3 May, 1987, p. 108.

26. William G. Phillips, "The Government's Classification System," in *None of Your Business, Government Secrecy in America*, edited by Norman Dorsen and Stephen Gillers (New York: Penguin Books, 1975.)

27. U.S., Congress, House, *Computer Security Act of 1987, Hearings before a Subcommittee of the Committee on Government Operations, House of Representatives*, 100th Congress, 1st Session, 1987, February 25, 26 and March 17, 1987, p. 141.

28. U.S., Congress, Senate, *op. cit.*, p. 12, 13.

29. *Ibid.*, p. 13.

30. U.S., Congress, House, *Computer Security Act of 1987, Hearings before a Subcommittee of the Committee on Government Operations, House of Representatives*, 100th Congress, 1st Session, 1987, February 25, 26 and March 17, 1987, p. 265.

31. U.S., Congress, House, *Computer Security Act of 1987, Hearings before the Subcommittee on Science, Research, and Technology and the Subcommittee on Transportation, Aviation, and Materials of the Committee on Science, Space, and Technology*, 100th Congress, 1st Session, February 26, 1987, p. 190.

THE ELECTRONIC BRANCH LIBRARY: USING CD-ROM AND ONLINE SERVICES TO SUPPORT OFF-CAMPUS INSTRUCTIONAL PROGRAMS

Robert L. Burr, Gonzaga University Libraries

Keywords: CD-ROM, End User Searching, Academic Libraries, Extended Learning Support, Native Americans.

Abstract: This paper reports the experience of the Gonzaga University Library in establishing and operating an on-site electronic information center to support undergraduate level instruction at the Canim Lake Reserve, located in the Cariboo region of British Columbia, Canada, approximately 500 miles distant from the main library in Spokane, Washington. System components include the WLN LaserCat CD-ROM bibliographic data base, end user searching of online data bases, electronic messaging, and FAX document delivery.

1. INTRODUCTION

    In April 1987, Gonzaga University launched an ambitious and innovative program of distance learning with the inauguration of its Bachelor of Education in Native American Leadership program for twenty-eight students at the Canim Lake Reserve in British Columbia, Canada. The Canim Lake Reserve is located in the province's interior Cariboo region, approximately 300 miles northeast of Vancouver and about 500 miles northwest of Spokane.
    Nearly 350 members of the Canim Band live on the reserve. The Canim people are members of the Shuswap Nation, one of the Salish tribes which formerly roamed the interior northwest of the continent from the Rocky Mountains to the Cascades. They are closely related to such American indian tribes as the Flatheads of Montana and the Colvilles and Coeur d'Alenes of Washington and Idaho. While Canadian policy with respect to native peoples in the 19th Century fostered the creation of small scattered reserves for individual bands, rather than the establishment of large consolidated tribal reservations as in the United States, the problems affecting native americans are much the same on both sides of the border: poverty, unemployment, hopelessness, substance abuse, cultural and social fragmentation.
    In 1980 the Canim Lake Band approved a long-range development plan for improving education, community economic development, housing, recreation, and culture on the Reserve (Ref. 1). The plan stressed the importance of securing university-level education for Band members to achieve these goals. The Canim Band recognized that desired improvements in elementary/secondary education would require Band members who were certified teachers; new community business ventures would require Band members trained in management and finance. Thus the development of a cadre of university-trained leaders became a high priority of the Band Council.
    While many Band members had completed high school, the loneliness and dislocation experienced by Canim students enrolled in college or technical courses off the Reserve contributed to an extremely high drop-out rate.

The Band Council felt the establishment of a bachelor's degree program on the Reserve was imperative, and when British Columbia universities declined to consider the possibility, the Band turned to Gonzaga University in Spokane, Washington.

Gonzaga University was founded in 1887 by Jesuit missionaries and is today the leading private university in the Inland Northwest, the 50,000 square mile intermountain region spanning eastern Washington, eastern Oregon, northern Idaho, western Montana, and parts of British Columbia and Alberta. The University presently enrolls approximately 4,000 students in undergraduate and graduate degree programs through the doctoral level. Gonzaga has been engaged in off-campus instructional programs since the early 1970's.. The University's School of Education has been especially active in this regard, offering masters level professional degree programs at a large number of off-campus sites in British Columbia and Alberta. Gonzaga University's demonstrated willingness to bring degree bearing programs to remote locations in Canada, as well as the widely recognized academic quality of its off-campus programs, prompted the Canim Band's inquiry.

Exploratory discussions between the Canim Band and the School of Education began in 1984. Program planning and administrative negotiations involving University officials, the Canim Band Council, British Columbia provincial officials, and the Canadian federal government, extended over the next two years. The formal Agreement establishing the Bachelor of Education in Native American Leadership was signed by University and Band officials in April 1987. Canim students began classes on the University's main campus in Spokane six weeks later.

The program model adopted combines summer residency of the Canim students (and their families) on the Spokane campus with on-site instruction at the Reserve during fall and spring semesters. Over a seven year period, the Canim students will complete an undergraduate curriculum of 128 semester hours including the University's standard liberal arts core of 31 credits, the School of Education's professional core of 19 credits, plus required and elective courses in a subject major totalling 78 credits. Credentialing options include British Columbia teacher certification at the elementary and/or secondary level (Ref. 2).

2. **THE CANIM LAKE LIBRARY CENTER**

The Agreement concluded between the Canim Band and Gonzaga University provided for the establishment of a library resource center on the Reserve to house a basic general reference collection selected by Gonzaga librarians as well as course-specific materials to be selected by Gonzaga staff for each course taught on the Reserve. All library materials placed at the Canim Center are to be retained permanently by the Band. Except during summer sessions, when students are on the main campus, the Center is to be staffed by a half-time library assistant employed by the Band Council. Finally, the Agreement specified the installation of an online information access/retrieval system at the Center for student as well as library administrative use (Ref. 3).

From the outset, online information access, retrieval, and delivery strategies were considered to offer the only practical means to meet the overall library support needs of Canim students. It was clear that on-site print resources of necessity would be limited to a few required and highly recommended texts for each course. Inasmuch as the availability of support from other libraries in the locality was minimal, virtually all materials would have to be supplied from the main library in response to student requests (Ref. 4).

The online information access, retrieval, and delivery system was installed and tested at the Canim Library Center during the period of

August-September 1987, and includes the following components:

> Hardware
> 1   IBM-PC XT Microcomputer, 640K RAM, 20MB Hard Drive, 1 Floppy Drive
> 1   Hayes 1200B Smartmodem
> 2   Hitachi 2500-S CD-ROM Drives
> 1   Ricoh 210 FAX Transceiver
> Software
>   WLN LaserCat Search Software and Database
>   PFS First Choice Integrated Applications Program

3. **ACCESS TO MONOGRAPHS: WLN LASERCAT**

Canim students access the main university library's book and periodical holdings via the Western Library Network's LaserCat CD-ROM database and search software. The database is supplied on three 5-1/4" CD-ROM disks containing approximately 2.5 million monographic and serials cataloging records representing items held by WLN's 300+ member libraries, and is updated quarterly. The search software is supplied on floppy diskette and can be installed on the hard drive. LaserCat's sophisticated retrieval capabilities include keyword searching of author, title, and subject headings fields, Boolean combination of search terms, and the ability to limit search parameters by format, language, date of publication, etc. Utilities for browsing the database and compiling bibliographies are also provided.

The Gonzaga University Library has been a principal member of the Western Library Network since 1977, and the majority of its cataloging records appear in the WLN database. Thus students at the Canim Center have at their fingertips bibliographic access to the book and serial holdings of the main library as well as those of other WLN member libraries. Once students have identified items of interest on LaserCat, requests for delivery are sent to the main library via electronic mail or FAX.

4. **ACCESS TO PERIODICAL LITERATURE: BRS AFTER DARK**

Although the LaserCat database includes extensive serials holding records, it obviously does not provide the indexing and abstracting tools students need to identify relevant periodical literature. Rather than attempting to provide such tools on-site, the Canim Center relies upon online access to these tools through the BRS After Dark information service. The After Dark service was selected because of its database coverage, its accessibility through a nearby Datapac telecommunications node, its reasonable cost, and its menu-based approach which facilitates end user searching.

Canim students search a variety of online databases, though transaction logs to date indicate heaviest use of Magazine Index, Ontario Education Resources Information Database, and ERIC files. The PFS First Choice telecommunications program module used by the students automatically saves the online session as a text file which is later used in several ways. First, the staff library assistant reviews the session offline with the student to evaluate database selection and search strategy, thereby further developing online search skills. Then the search results, i.e., citations, are discussed to determine which documents should be requested from the main library in Spokane. Usually an edited version of the original text file, containing citations and request information, is later uploaded to the electronic mail utility for transmission to the main library.

5. ELECTRONIC MESSAGING: INET 2000

Electronic mail provides the primary communications link between the Canim Center and the main University Library. In addition to transmission of library materials requests, electronic mail is used administratively to report the receipt of course-specific materials ordered from the main library but shipped directly to the Reserve by suppliers. Email is used for routine administrative messages, and in one instance was used to transmit student writing assignments to the main campus for grading by the course instructor in advance of scheduled class sessions on the Reserve. The medium has proven itself to be timely and reliable, both critical concerns given the 50% arrival rate and average 3-4 week period required by the U.S. and Canadian Postal Services to move first class mail between Spokane and Canim Lake.

Electronic messaging is transacted via Telecom Canada's INET 2000 Information Network, marketed in British Columbia by B.C. Tel. The choice of email utilities was influenced by cost considerations, especially the Canim Band's ability to access the INET 2000 system through a toll-free telephone line, but also by the main University Library's interest in securing access to Canadian and European databases available through INET but not presently available from U.S. sources. The resulting enhanced access to current Canadian economic data and business information has been especially useful to the University's School of Business, and to the Spokane business community.

6. DOCUMENT DELIVERY: FAX AND ONLINE

All library materials requests for the Canim Lake Library Center, irrespective of format, are filled by the main library from its own holdings or, when necessary, obtained from other libraries or commercial document sources. Book materials are usually shipped by a commercial parcel delivery service, with an average delivery time of 5-7 days. Occasionally, Gonzaga faculty members travelling to the Canim Reserve to teach classes also transport library materials for student use.

Periodical literature requests which can be filled from the main library collection, or obtained from one of the other libraries in the Spokane area, are sent to the Canim Lake Center by telefacsimile transmission. Periodical articles which cannot be supplied locally are routinely ordered from an online supplier, usually UMI Article Clearinghouse. Online orders are placed and documents received at the main library, then forwarded to Canim by FAX transmission.

7. EVALUATION OF PROGRAM EFFECTIVENESS

A preliminary assessment of the effectiveness of the Canim Lake online information access, retrieval, and delivery system was performed in December 1987, following the completion of first semester classes, by a Program Advisory Board composed of representatives from the Band Council, Gonzaga University, and the Ministry of Indian Affairs. The Canim students expressed a high level of satisfaction with their ability to locate relevant information sources on LaserCat and After Dark, and with the speed of delivery of materials to the Reserve once requested. Active student use of both the CD-ROM system and online services was confirmed by statistical records showing 61 book and 29 periodical article requests filled for Canim students between September 1 and December 15, 1987. The average delivery time for book materials was eleven days, for periodical articles four days.

The most serious deficiency noted in this initial evaluation was in staff and user training. All of the Canim students had participated in a two week short course presented by the Gonzaga reference staff during the on-campus summer session. Lectures, class discussions, demonstrations, and supervised practice sessions were offered to prepare the students to use LaserCat and After Dark effectively. The designated on-site library assistant received a similar, though more intensive, training program. What was overlooked was the equally important need to develop among students, and especially among staff, the more general microcomputing skills needed to successfully operate system hardware and software. While reasonably well prepared to search LaserCat, neither staff nor students were adequately prepared to deal with a hard drive failure which required reinstallation of the search software.

Notwithstanding the obvious problems of training and technical support, Gonzaga University's experience suggests that information technology can be used to provide efficient and effective library support to students enrolled in off-campus academic programs at reasonable cost. CD-ROM technology offers the means to make the library catalog accessible to students at geographically distant locations at minimal cost. Online information services can provide distributed access to the periodical literature. Appropriate use of conventional delivery mechanisms, augmented by telecommunications strategies such as FAX and electronic mail, can enable academic libraries to deliver information to students at remote locations in a timely and cost-effective manner.

8. REFERENCES

1. (Canim Lake Band), Canim Lake Band Planning Policy. 100 Mile House, B.C.: Canim Lake Band, 1980.

2. A Program Proposal for an Off-Campus Program Leading to the Bachelor of Education in Native American Leadership with the People of the Canim Lake Reserve. Spokane, WA: Gonzaga University School of Education, November 1986, p. 17.

3. Letter of Agreement Between Gonzaga University and Canim Lake Band Regarding Bachelor of Education in Native American Leadership, April 23, 1987, p. 2 and Appendix A.

4. The nearest academic collections are at 2-year colleges located in Kamloops, B.C. (approx. 150 miles) and Prince George, B.C. (approx. 175 miles); small public libraries at 100 Mile House and Williams Lake (approx. 35 and 50 miles distant) offer primarily popular reading collections.

IMPLEMENTING AN EXPERT SYSTEM FOR USE BY UNDERGRADUATES

Nancy J. Butkovich, Kathryn L. Taylor, and Ann S. Moore, Texas A&M University

Keywords: Reference Assistance, Expert Systems.

Abstract: This paper will outline the planning and implementation of an expert system for use with technical writing students. Each semester students present the same assignments to reference desk staff. One of these requires students in English classes to compile a list of sources in a particular field which they have chosen for in-depth research. Because this assignment is a recurring one, Evans Library staff devised an expert system to provide the information electronically. Planning for the system began with a few basic decisions. The system would be based on a commercial database manager or "shell" rather than writing a customized program in-house. Criteria for software selection were relatively simple; the purchase price must not exceed $250, and the system should contain natural language capabilities. The software must be easy to use and should allow for the following fields: title, call number, location, format and broad subject areas. Q&A was the only software package which met all the criteria. Student assignments from previous semesters were analyzed to determine the types of sources most frequently used. Class rolls were examined to pinpoint majors most frequently represented. Librarians were assigned broad disciplines in which to collect bibliographic information for the database. Many methods of collecting data were used. Items were selected from standard bibliographies, the subject portion of the card catalog, and the **Index to Indexes,** an in-house bibliography of indices and abstracting services with subject and keyword access. Data entry into the system was relatively simple due to the user-friendly nature of the software package. Statistics on the cost of the microcomputer equipment and software and on the manpower required to construct the database will be provided.

1. INTRODUCTION

Who has not worked at a reference desk where the same reference questions are encountered over and over? Whether it is explaining how to use the **Readers' Guide to Periodical Literature** or finding an address for a company in **Standard and Poor's Register,** there are some tasks which we find ourselves repeating to the point of boredom or, even worse, job burnout. What if we could refer some of those questions to a machine? Many libraries are doing just that by inaugurating various types of expert systems. Expert systems are computer systems which mimic the problem-solving abilities of experts in order to provide a solution to a problem.

Libraries are using expert systems for a variety of tasks. At the National Agricultural Library an expert system has been developed to answer ready reference questions in the field of aquaculture (Ref. 1). An expert system for use at the government documents reference desk has been instituted by the State University of New York at Buffalo (Ref. 2). The University of Waterloo has a very ambitious expert system which uses VAX hardware and performs such functions as interpreting bibliographic references, determining the physical location for an item, and explaining the use of the Library's microfiche serials list (Ref. 3). At the Sterling C. Evans Library, however, we decided to begin with a rather narrowly defined area in which to develop an expert system.

Each semester we assist patrons at the reference desk with an assignment generated by an English 301 class entitled Technical Writing, which is generally required for students in the Colleges of Business, Agriculture, Engineering and Science. For this the students must choose a topic, usually within their major field of study, and write a research paper on that topic. Students are required to locate and use standard reference tools, i.e. dictionaries, handbooks, encyclopedias, indexes, and abstracting services, in that particular field. By completing this assignment, students realize that there are more sources available than just the **Readers' Guide to Periodical Literature** to which most were exposed in high school. Many man-hours were spent at an already busy reference desk assisting these students with the assignment. Since the assignment recurs semester after semester and the clientele is fairly predictable, we decided to develop an expert system to lessen the pressure at the reference desk.

2. CRITERIA

From the outset we had no intention of designing our own software, because we felt that there were sufficient numbers of commercial packages available on the market to give us a reasonable selection without having to invest the time and manpower needed to write new software. Software selection was guided by two general criteria, the first being that of cost. Since this began as an unfunded research project, cost was critical. Although we examined software in a variety of price ranges, practically speaking, we were restricted to the $250.00 maximum allowed by the State of Texas for making spot purchases.

The second criteria was that the software should have a natural language component in order to facilitate use by the students. Because any given student would only have a week in which he or she needed the system, the database needed to be designed to answer questions pertaining to this specific assignment. Natural language ability would alleviate the need to learn a search protocol for only one assignment, and would, therefore, be received more readily by the students.

3. SOFTWARE SELECTION

Several software packages were considered, including NOTEBOOK II, Q&A, PARADOX, 1ST CLASS (ANSWERMAN), and GURU. Since all of these had some difficulty in meeting at least one of the criteria, we decided to read some reviews of these and decide which would be the most likely candidates.

The first examination resulted in two being dropped very quickly. Review excerpts in **Software Review** (Ref. 4) suggested that GURU failed all of our criteria; its list price was over ten times what we could afford, and it did not appear to have a natural language component. Also, several reviews indicated that a significant level of expertise would be required in order to effectively use the system. Since this was not at all what we wanted, we did not consider it further.

1ST CLASS was also eliminated at this time, since it, too, failed to meet either of the two criteria set for this project. Information provided in an article by Samuel Waters of the National Agricultural Library (Ref. 1) indicated that it cost nearly twice as much as we were allowed to spend, and it did not have a natural language component, although it did appear to be able to provide answers to the kinds of questions we were anticipating.

The three remaining candidates also had difficulties in meeting the criteria. However, all were available for demonstration, so we decided to look at each of them in action. PARADOX was quickly eliminated. Cost was a major factor, and the LOTUS 1-2-3 menu style was inappropriate for our purposes. We found it confusing the first time we used it and decided that students who would probably only use the system once would also be confused. Natural language querying ability was not available. The character per field limitation was also too restrictive, since we wanted to index reference materials on the chapter and not the monographic level, and could therefore have fields larger than those allowed. Examination of reviews yielded some other factors which would cause problems, notably with sorting speed and programming (Ref. 5). These factors resulted in its elimination from consideration.

Of the remaining two packages NOTEBOOK II met the cost requirement. From our perspective a major flaw noted in a review in **Social Sciences Microcomputer Review** (Ref.6) was that the stored data cannot be searched on anything less than a field level. Since we did not want to create a separate field for each broad subject heading or format type, we dropped this package from our list of candidates.

Q&A proved to be superior to the other software that we examined. It permitted searching within fields, which we needed for our database, and the addition of natural language to the menu permitted first-time patrons to use the system with minimal help. Database creation could be easily accomplished, and movement from the File mode where the database was created to the Intelligent Assistant mode where the natural language expert system resides could be accomplished simply by changing disks in the floppy drive. The final hurdle to acquiring Q&A was cleared when we found a dealer willing to sell the version 2.0 for a sum within our specifications.

4. DATABASE CREATION

The database was tailored to meet the needs of its audience, students in Technical Writing classes. In order to determine the types of sources which would best answer their questions, we examined copies of assignments from previous semesters and interviewed instructors concerning course content and characteristics of students. The majority of students enrolled in this course are from the Colleges of Agriculture, Engineering, Business, and Science.

We also considered the kinds of questions most frequently asked at the reference desk, the "What do you have...?" and the "Where are they...?" questions, in order to determine what fields would be needed in each record. Broken down into essential elements these questions require the following pieces of information: title, location, subject and format. Because of the way in which our library is organized, we actually have two locations present, call number and actual physical location. Therefore, each individual record in the database contains these five fields: title

of the work, call number, physical location, format of the work, and broad
subject headings.

Each field is searchable, and we permitted format and broad subject
headings to be searched on a sub-field level. This was accomplished by
setting off each searchable portion of a field by semi-colons. Because
Q&A is menu-driven data entry was fairly simple. The operator brought up
the main menu and chose the File function. Data could be entered onto the
screen and saved in two easy steps. The software has a counting mechanism
which automatically counts the number of records entered, thus permitting
the operator to determine the size of the database.

Each author was responsible for collecting bibliographic data in the
broad disciplines selected. Various methods were used to collect the
data. Standard bibliographies such as Eugene P. Sheehy's **Guide to
Reference Works,** tenth edition, and Walford's **Guide to Reference Material,**
fourth edition, were consulted as were special subject bibliographies,
such as **Science and Engineering Literature: A Guide to Reference Sources**
by H. Robert Malinowsky and Jeanne M. Richardson, third edition.
Appropriate subject headings were checked in the subject card catalog.
An in-house bibliography entitled **Index to Indexes** was most useful. This
source is a comprehensive listing of indexing and abstracting services in
the Sterling C. Evans Library with access by subject and keyword.
Librarians also browsed the reference shelves to identify key titles for
the database.

5. <u>EQUIPMENT, SOFTWARE AND MANPOWER COSTS</u>

For testing purposes we ran the system on an IBM PC-AT with 640K
memory, monochrome monitor, and a Hewlett-Packard Think-Jet Printer. This
was, however, a temporary arrangement; the equipment was already committed
to our CD-ROM operations, and we only had the use of the workstation for
one semester. The final configuration will consist of an IBM-XT clone
with a 16-bit (640K bytes) hard disk, monochrome monitor, and printer,
probably a Think-Jet. The cost of this new workstation will be
approximately $1,285, based on the costs given in the state contract
specifications.

Staffing expenses include the time spent in gathering data, inputting
records, and instructing staff. Approximately twenty hours were needed to
gather data for a 440 record database, and 5 hours for inputting data.
Instruction for the rest of the Reference Division staff and faculty
required 6 hours. Data gathering, inputting and instruction were
performed by the three authors for a total estimated salary cost of $350.
An estimate of time spent in patron instruction is not possible, since the
workstation was located in our Wiley Laser Disk Service area, and patron
assistance was provided by the attendants in the area.

6. <u>FUTURE PLANS</u>

Although Q&A met our initial criteria, we decided to apply for a
research grant from the Office of University Research, which we received
in December 1987. A major component of this grant is the funding for the
workstation described above. Another $1000 was provided to purchase a
more sophisticated software package. We will begin the search for that in
Spring 1988 and hope to have a working system for Fall 1988. The work
done on this project has been interesting, and we believe that expert
systems have a definite place in a reference department. By providing

answers to the large quantities of repetitive questions, the expert system can free the librarian to provide in-depth reference service needed by some patrons.

7. REFERENCES

1. Waters, Samuel T. Answerman, the Expert Information Specialist: An Expert System for Retrieval of Information from Library Reference Books. Information Technology and Libraries 47, p. 204-212, September 1986.

2. Smith, Karen F. Robots at the Reference Desk? College and Research Libraries 47, No. 5, p. 486-490, September 1986.

3. Parrott, James R. Expert Systems for Reference Work. Microcomputers for Information Management 3, No. 3, p. 155-171, September 1986.

4. Levy, Abe, ed. GURU. Software Reviews on File 2, No. 10, p. 647-648, October 1986.

5. Thompson, Keith. Paradox: Powerful, Pricey, and Easy. Infoworld 7, No. 43, p. 39, 42, October 25, 1985.

6. Notebook II, Version 2.02. Social Science Microcomputer Review 3, No. 3, p. 284-285, Fall 1985.

THE SECOND TIME AROUND: ADVENTURES IN THE PRODUCTION OF PUBLIC AND PRIVATE CD-ROMS

Matilda Butler, Knowledge Access International

Keywords: Planning, Prototypes, Products, Production, Prospects, Problems, Price, Promotion

Abstract: In 1976, there were about 60 reference databases online and approximately 1,000 reference users. Ten years later, there were in excess of 400 reference databases online and more than 100,000 users. Although 1986 seemed a landmark year for online, it also marked the introduction of a new technology that will change the character of online -- CD-ROM. The first two years in the life of CD-ROM, 1986 and 1987, primarily demonstrated the feasibility of the technology through the use of prototypes. In some cases, these were like trial marriages. In other cases, they were like the marriage of teenagers. Information providers and CD-ROM software developers each had expectations and needs that did not always match. The outcome has been separations, divorces, rocky marriages, and a few happy couples.

In anticipating the "second time around", let's examine the past with its prototypes; the present with initial real products; the prospects for "smart" products; public versus private uses of CD-ROM; the problems -- especially as they relate to price performance; promotion; and people -- the end users.

OVERVIEW

1. PAST

CD-ROM itself was the product until recently. Discs were filled with opportunistic databases of no special value. Their retrieval engines were no better, and sometimes worse, than the online services.

Like many other technologies of the past century, CD-ROM left the laboratory as a solution in search of problems to solve. The early solutions were primarily undertaken as prototypes.

What are some of the adventures in developing prototypes?

What lessons can be drawn to make it better "the second time around"?

2. PRESENT

The present is marked primarily by products that have moved from one storage technology to another -- from print to electronic, from online to ondisc. The functional use of the information remains about the same in the new technology, although there may be a few new bells and whistles.

What are some of the adventures in developing the current "real products"?

What lessons can be drawn to make it better "the second time around"?

3. PROSPECTS

A few products have taken the step beyond retrieval. While their new functions do not go beyond the common microcomputer utilities, the advantages of combining retrieval and information-manipulation utilities in the same program are impressively evident.

Where are these "smart" products heading? It is said that the future, writ small, always exists in the present. CD-ROM "smart" is moving toward CD-ROM "expert". Products under development contain carefully chosen "key resources" for particular professional specialties, containing a variety of information formats. These are not yet expert systems by any stretch of the imagination. Their rules are based on association rather than deduction or inference. However, they are shifting the focus from given databases to given tasks.

What are some of the adventures in developing "smart" products?

What lessons can be drawn to make it better "the second time around"?

4. PUBLIC VERSUS PRIVATE USES

<u>CD-ROM Review</u>, <u>CD Data Report</u>, microcomputer magazines, and even local newspapers are focusing on the <u>public</u>, that is commercial, uses of CD-ROM. An outsider looking at the industry would get a slanted view using these media. The observer would see many products for the library, some products for business, and a few for the professions such as lawyers and doctors. This under-represents the CD-ROM activity level. Many corporations are developing CD-ROM products for mundane applications that can make a difference in the bottom line.

What are the differences and similarities in developing for public versus private users?

5. PROBLEMS

Although there are many problems in planning, producing, and promoting optical products, two are especially interesting to consider -- pricing products and promoting "smart" products.

Pricing CD-ROMs seems to take place even before the disc's contents, functions, promotion, or placement are discussed. Pricing can easily become a problem. If it is priced high and doesn't sell, the publisher always insists that "price is not the problem." If it is priced low and sells well, the publisher says "I should have priced it higher."

If we look at price from the publisher's perspective, it is easy to understand that new functionality in the product merits a higher price than a corresponding print publication, for instance. If we look at this from the customer's perspective, we find that price will usually win in the price versus features trade-off. Assume there are two possible CD-ROM purchases. One has features 1-5 and the other has features 1-10. The first costs less than the second. Because both products are new in the marketplace and represent different information access than was possible before, the one with the lower price will usually be purchased. Selling the value of the extra featuresis a difficult marketing task.

"Smart discs" designed for corpsorate use are well-accepted. Their features have been designed with users' needs clearly in mind. But those designed for vertical markets are still a hard sell, because users have to be trained to make full use of their features. This training has little to do with user-friendliness. For example, the user either does or does not know, from previous trainingh, how to use and interpret the statistical models provided as post-retrieval analysis tools. Power users love the "smart discs". Other users seem to be settling into an attitude of "Can't work with them, can't work without them."

6. PROMOTION

Build a better mousetrap and the world will beat a path to your door. Wrong. CD-ROM products are a hard sell. Smart products are an even harder sell. It is important to not only think about the original marketplace for the information, but also to consider expansion markets. In thinking of expansion markets it helps to play out scenarios such as: What if most users of microcomputers would not hesitate to add a CD-ROM drive for around $500 because of attractive CD-ROM products they want to use? What if business-people and professionals withsout microcomsputers would not hesitate to acquire an entire computer/CD-ROM system for $1500 because of CD-ROM products they can't resist? What if schools and households joined the movement to CD-ROM, with a grwoth curve steeper than that of microcomputers ten years ago? And that,s as a consequence, the price of computer/CD-ROM systems fell by another 50%? What impact would each of these scenarios have on CD-ROM product planning, promotion, pricing, and placement?

There are five major types of expansion markets:

- o additional customers who are similar to original customers, but who have not been reached by previous marketing;

- o additional customers who are similar to original customers, but do not have the same financial resources;

- o additional customers who are similar to original customers, but do not have the same capabilities;

- o additional customers who are attracted by extended features;

- o additional customers who have different needs from the original customers.

How are these new markets reached? What are some of the adventures in reaching these customers?

What lessons can be drawn to make it better "the second time around"?

7. PEOPLE

On the third day of the Microsoft CD-ROM Conference in March, a woman walked into the Knowledge Access booth looking quite confused. She said, "There are so many retrieval systems I don't know how to choose." Instead of slipping into my usual pitch of the advantages of the KAware2 Retrieval System, I found myself saying, "Don't think about the software. First, think about the people who are currently using your information and who you would like to use the information. Think about the problems your information will help them solve. Then think about your information and what kinds of features it will need to have to help people using it to solve those problems. Then, and only then, look for a retrieval system that matches your needs."

In the final analysis, the "second time around" will be better only if the focus is on the needs of people rather than the needs of the technology.

CONSTRUCTING A THESAURUS FOR MEDICAL KNOWLEDGE

Gina D'Ascenzo Carlos, John K. Vries, and Peretz Shoval, University of Pittsburgh

Abstract

This paper discusses LEXX an indexing and retrieval system and a component of the University of Pittsburgh's Medical ARchival System (MARS), a bibliographic retrieval system for biomedical information. The knowledge base for LEXX is a thesaurus of medical terms in which concepts are represented by a large network of interrelated terms. LEXX uses natural language processing tools to allow users to access relevant information through free text expressions thereby eliminating the need for a controlled vocabulary.

1. Introduction

The most common method for storing information in bibliographic databases involves indexing the information using a prospectively established set of controlled vocabulary keywords which form an inverted-index into the database [2-4]. Searching the database involves selecting from those keywords the terms which are appropriate to the users query. The requested information is retrieved by matching a boolean combination of these terms against the keywords in the index vocabulary, which provide pointers to the appropriate information in the database.

This approach, although well accepted, is inadequate for managing many types of information, specifically medical information. The principal limitation of this method is that the user must be familiar with a controlled vocabulary of keywords, a query language, and the procedures used to retrieve data. Those not familiar with the procedures and terminology may find this method cumbersome. Because of these limitations, a complex search requires the assistance of an experienced librarian. With the proliferation of online bibliographic services and the introduction of databases designed for deployment on microcomputers, this type of assistance is not immediately available.

LEXX is an indexing and retrieval system designed to avoid the problems of a traditional inverted index system. It is a component of the University of Pittsburgh's Medical ARchival System (MARS), a bibliographic retrieval system for biomedical information currently under development. Within LEXX, knowledge is represented as a thesaurus of terms arranged in a hierarchical order. For each of the current LEXX topic areas there exists a fully developed knowledge base in which medical concepts are represented as nodes in a network whose structure reflects pragmatic associations among these nodes as viewed from the clinician's perspective. LEXX maps free text user requests into a set of medical terms from the index vocabulary that best capture the contents of the archived information.

Address correspondence to: Gina Carlos, Decision Systems Laboratory and The Office of Biomedical Informatics, University of Pittsburgh, 1360 Scaife Hall, Pittsburgh, Pennsylvania, 15261

2. Shoval's Expert System

The LEXX indexing and retrieval system is based on principles presented by Peretz Shoval in his 1981 dissertation in which he described the design and development of an expert consultation system for a retrieval database [5]. Shoval's system functioned by interfacing between the user and the retrieval-system. It mapped user requests for information into specific vocabulary terms suitable for a database query. The objective was to assist unsophisticated users in selecting the most accurate index terms for a database search without requiring them to be familiar with the controlled vocabulary of the specific index.

The knowledge base for Shoval's expert system was a thesaurus of business terms with *broader-than* and *narrower-than* cross references to other terms. His problem domain took the form of a semantic network, in which nodes represented terms or concepts and links represented relationships among the terms. In addition to the broader-than, and narrower-than terms, each term was also associated with a *synonymous-with* and *general-relatedness-to* category. The structure of the network was a hierarchy which allowed the system to expand each user-entered term in the direction of its links. The main principles of Shoval's system are as follows:

- Users enter a set of terms that express their information needs.
- Terms linked to the user terms by broader-than or synonymous links are also identified in a process called *expansion*.
- At points where expanded terms intersect (*matches*) a relevancy test is performed. A match is considered relevant if its meaning is more specific than the meaning of the originating terms.
- Where relevant terms are identified they replace the originating terms and the process of expansion is restarted from that point.
- This search process terminates when no more terms can be expanded or matched.

Once the search process is terminated, the resulting list of terms is subjected to a process called *selection*. Two factors determine the order in which resultant terms are selected. First, terms are selected on the basis of the number of user terms which are explained by the resultant index term. Index terms which encompass a greater number of the user entry terms are given preference in the selection process. Preference is also given to the remaining terms according to the number of user entry terms explained which were not encompassed by previously selected terms. This is to ensure that the earliest consideration was given to terms which captured the meaning of the greatest number of user terms. This strategy was based on the observation that more specific search information was derived by the smallest number of index terms which explained the greatest number of user terms.

3. The LEXX Retrieval System

The ability of the Shoval system to map concepts expressed in non-specific terms into a set of keywords allowed the development of the LEXX system. The thesaurus for LEXX was structured in a form similar to the system described by Shoval, however, in addition to using broader-than, narrower-than and synonymous links, the LEXX system was also designed to handle morphological descriptors, and links which are not hierarchical. The structure of the data in the LEXX system can be best exemplified with reference to the neuropathology thesaurus.

4. The Neuropathology Thesaurus

The neuropathology thesaurus consists of 7,000 terms with 40,000 links. The terms for the thesaurus were selected from the indicies of five major neuropathology textbooks. The basic entry for a thesaurus term is shown in the following figure using *neoplasm* as the keyword.

Thesaurus Entry of Keyword NEOPLASM

```
KEY....    NEOPLASM
VAR....    NEOPLASMS
SYN....    TUMOR
BT......    NEOPLASTIC-DISEASE
NT......    GLIAL-TUMOR ADAMANTINOMA
           BRAIN-TUMOR VENTRICLE-TUMOR
           MALIGNANT-TUMOR AMELOBLASTOMA
           INTRACRANIAL-TUMOR BENIGN-TUMOR
           ADAMANTOBLASTOMA ADAMANTOMA
AW......
PERSP..    DISEASE
```

The fields in the above entry can be described as follows:

- The *KEY field* (keyword) represents the canonical form of the keyword.
- The *VAR field* (variation) includes the morphological variations of the keyword term.
- The *SYN field* (synonym) represents synonymous relationships. The most important function of this field is to account for the exact meaning understood for certain medical terms.
- The *BT field* (broader-than) lists those terms which are conceptually broader than the keyword term. The accuracy and completeness to which this category is entered determines how extensive the term will be expanded in the semantic network.
- The terms in the *NT field* (narrower-than) are generated automatically for each keyword based on that keyword and the broader-than terms associated with it. The narrower-than links provide the paths for expansion to the most specific applicable terms.
- The *AW field* (associated-with) display terms that are not necessarily hierarchical but, are generally related to the term. This field will be used to develop more complete sets of descriptors by incorporating knowledge acquired from domain experts.
- The *PERSP field* (perspective) represents the domain most commonly associated with the keyword. Examples of perspectives include anatomy, disease, manifestation, substance, physiology. In the present version of LEXX the perspective field is used, to organize the information displayed to the user after a set of terms are expanded in the thesaurus.

Through on-going thesaurus construction certain guidelines have been established to maintain a set of standards and to ensure a coherent relationship among terms in the thesaurus. These guidelines include the following:

- All terms must be entered in their noun form.
- Each term, where applicable, must include any acceptable morphological variation (i.e., plural forms)
- All multiword terms (e.g. *amyotrophic-lateral-sclerosis*), must be reachable in the semantic network by forward and backward tracing of their component parts. Multiword terms and their component terms must be entered as keyword terms in the thesaurus.
- Each term entered that is a disease must backtrack to one or more fundamental disease categories (i.e. congenital, deficiency degenerative, demyelinating, hereditary, immunologic, inflammatory, infectious, neoplastic, psychiatric)

These principles guarantee that each term will inherit a group of classification properties from the associated terms in the network. For example the terms *neoplasm* and *tumor* will automatically inherit the concept of *neoplastic-disease*. The following example shows the terms resulting from an expansion of the terms neoplasm and hereditary-disease in the neuropathology thesaurus.

$$===> \text{Recklinghausen-disease}$$
$$===> \text{Von-Recklinghausen-disease}$$
$$===> \text{Neurofibromatosis}$$

5. Current Applications of the Thesauri

The purpose of the neuropathology thesaurus is to provide an interface to a teaching collection assembled by Dr. John Moossy at the University of Pittsburgh School of Medicine. During his career Dr. Moossy has collected 16,000 images of gross and microscopic neuroanatomy slides which have been pressed into a videodisk. Each image is accompanied by an extensive textual description. These descriptions are expanded by LEXX to yield a set of index terms which point to the appropriate videodisk images. The user terms are, similarly, expanded to generate a rank ordered list of videodisk images that are conceptually related to the input terms.

Based on the success of the neuropatholgy thesaurus a mechanism was developed to enhance the parsing of free text [1]. The purpose of this is to identify multiword combinations for their inclusion in the expansion of the semantic network. Suitable word combinations are determined by selecting potential word pairs using a distance operator to identify the distance between words in the pair as they appear in the query text. Attempts are made to expand these word pairs using LEXX. In order to guarantee that these derived word pairs explain terms in the original query the word-pair terms are backward traced in the network to their root terms. A set difference is performed between the terms on the user list and the union of all terms derived through backtracking. Finally all residual terms from the set difference are combined with the multiword keywords. This module improves the efficiency of the system, and permits the user to interact with the system using free English text. By selecting a threshold for the distance operator the user can vary the sensitivity and alter the specificity of the search strategy.

The ability of the LEXX system to extract relevant descriptors from free text neuropathology statements indicate that the system could automatically index medical reports. Using the parsing module previously mentioned, a neuropathology report was processed using a limited thesaurus, which produced a rank ordered list of terms. The following is an example of the LEXX processing from a report of a patient who die of a cerebral hemorrhage secondary to leukemia.

Neuropathology Report

Microscopic examination of the cns sections reveals the following. The cerebral cortex and basal ganglia demonstrate recent subarachnoid hemorrhage and an extensive meningeal infiltration by leukemic cells. In addition cerebral edema and multiple extensive leukemic infiltrates of the white matter are noted. There is diffuse anoxic and ischemic changes noted. The leukemia cells disclose the same characteristics as in all systemic organs. These cell are immature myeloid. The spinal cord and cerebellum demonstrate minimal to modest subarachnoid hemorrhage associated with meningeal infiltration by similar blast cells. This infiltration is also seen between the folia. There is autolytic change noted in the cerebellum. Edema and mild ischemic changes of anterior horn neurons is seen within the cord. Intracerebral hemorrhage multiple acute secondary to leukemia acute myelogenous. Minimal subarachnoid hemorrhage temporal lobes brainstem spinal cord. Cerebral edema brain weight 1560 grams. The leukemic infiltrate is extensive and is clinically seen in leukemia phases when the white count is greater than 30000. This level of white count leads to disruption of the poorly supported cerebral vessels and subsequent subarachnoid hemorrhage even in the face of an adequate platelet count. No opportunistic infections were noted. Selected coronal sections of the cerebral hemispheres.

The first sixteen terms from the processing the previous text are shown below. The terms appear to be reasonable index terms for a searching an inverted index or the LEXX retrieval system.

Rank Ordered List of Index Terms

1.	NERVOUS-SYSTEM	RANK===> 44
2.	CENTRAL-NERVOUS-SYSTEM	RANK===> 43
3.	CEREBELLUM	RANK===> 7
4.	LEUKEMIA	RANK===> 6
5.	INTRACRANIAL-HEMORRHAGE	RANK===> 6
6.	SPINAL-CORD	RANK===> 6
7.	CEREBRAL-EDEMA	RANK===> 6
8.	ISCHEMIA	RANK===> 5
9.	TELENCEPHALON	RANK===> 5
10.	BRAINSTEM	RANK===> 5
11.	CEREBRAL-HEMISPHERE	RANK===> 5
12.	BASAL-GANGLIA	RANK===> 5
13.	CEREBRAL-CORTEX	RANK===> 5
14.	WHITE-MATTER	RANK===> 5
15.	MENINGES	RANK===> 5
16.	SECONDARY-HEMORRHAGE	RANK===> 5

The success of the neuropathology thesaurus and the capabilities of autoindexing in neuropathology led to the undertaking of a neuroradiology thesaurus. The purpose of the neuroradiology thesaurus is to serve as an interface to a neuroradiology teaching collection which consists of approximately 10,000 patient medical records and their medical images.

An additional thesaurus has been designed to access the Western Psychiatric Institute and Clinic (WPIC) Library collection. The terms for this thesaurus were selected from the WPIC subject heading list, the MeSH (National Library of Medicine medical subject heading list), and the Library of Congress subject heading list. In addition to accessing the WPIC collection the thesaurus has the capabilities of retrieving information from MEDLINE, a National Library of Medicine database.

6. Future Directions

The LEXX system has been proven to be a successful alternative to more traditional archiving and retrieval systems, however, it is clear that there are significant limitations associated with the current implementation which need to be addressed. Research is continuing to improve the structure of the knowledge represented in the database and the procedures applied to this knowledge. Two such areas of research are described, below.

Currently the LEXX system makes no distinction between the procedures applied to the different types of links though two observations seem worthy of implementation as part of the LEXX strategy. It is believed that the closer an intersecting node is to the original term the more likely it is to be relevant. Therefore we plan to consider the distance of any node from the user-supplied term when determining the priority of a search and when the search should be terminated. Also, the number of inherited terms (which is a factor of both the depth and the breadth of the term expansion) should also influence the direction in which to explore expanded nodes.

We are also considering the addition of link weights which would be used to express the relative importance of various links occurring at the same level of an expansion. Such a system may allow us to enhance the expression of the relationship between terms by recognizing that some terms are "more synonymous" than others.

We are also planning to extend the natural language parsing system to recognize whole phrases and their contexts in addition to recognizing multiword and single word terms. This would be accomplished by permitting the parser to identify groups or clusters of terms based on their occurrence in sentences and phrases and then to evaluate the terms within these clusters. For example, while all of the terms returned in the neuropathology report test case are reasonable indicators of the concepts expressed in the chart, additional links are missing because of an incomplete interpretation of the text. The following example is taken from the neuropathology report previously mentioned.

> The leukemia cells disclose the same characteristics in all systemic organs. These cells are immature myeloid. The spinal cord and cerebellum demonstrate minimal to modest subarachnoid hemorrhage associated with meningeal infiltration by similar blast cells. This infiltration is also seen between the folia.

The phrase beginning "These cells" refers to the leukemia cells in the prior sentence. In the subsequent sentence, "similar blast cells", refers to the immature leukemia cells described in the preceding two sentences. "This infiltration", again, refers to the to the infiltration of the [cerebellar] folia by immature leukemic cells. Although the current system identified leukemia and central nervous system as important concepts it was unable to infer a description of "leukemic cell infiltration of the cerebellar folia". The new parser will address the need for improved concept identification and encourage a more powerful information processing system.

7. Summary

It seems clear that the volume of information available to individuals in many different areas will continue to expand at a rate proportional to advances in technology. LEXX is an evolving system developed to help improve strategies for the archiving and retrieval of information by providing some type of intelligence to the user interface.

8. Acknowledgements

We would like to acknowledge the help and cooperation of John Moossy, M. D., Bernadette Marshalek and Theresa Vries in the preparation of the various thesauri and to Bernadette Reddy for her untiring administrative support and assistance. This work was funded through a grant from the Josiah Macy, Jr. Foundation. The resources of the Decision Systems Laboratory were available through NIH Award 5R24-RR01101-10. Equipment was provided through grants from Digital Equipment Corporation and Sun Microsystems, Incorporated.

9. References

J. Allen, in *Natural Language Understanding*, The Benjamin/Cummings Publishing Company, Menlo Park, California, 1987.

J. Egeland and G. Foreman, "Reference Services: searching and search techniques", in *Handbook of Medical Library Practice*, vol. 1 , L. Darling (editor), Medical Library Association, Chicago, Illinois, 1982, 183-235.

S. J. Feinglos, in *Medline: A Basic Guide to Searching*, Medical Library Association, Incorporated, Chicago, Illinois, 1985.

F. W. Roper and J. Borkman, in *Introduction to Reference Sources in the Health Sciences*, 2nd Ed., Medical Library Association, Incorporated, Chicago, Illinois, 1984.

P. Shoval, *An Expert Consultation System for a Retrieval Database with a Semantic Network of Concepts*, Ph.D. Thesis, University of Pittsburgh, 1981.

HIGHWAYS TO HYPERTEXT

Joseph M.A. Cavanagh, State University of New York at Stony Brook

Keywords: Hypertext; Non-Linear Text.

Abstract: This paper describes the nature of Hypertext. A brief overview of the origins of the concept and the development paths towards Hypertext systems is provided.

Synopsis:

The conventional presentation of text is linear. Readers normally start at the beginning and progress to the end; some texts invite readers to skip passages containing information or ideas which may be familiar or too difficult. Some digression in real time is offered by way of footnotes but extensive excursions into related reading usually must be postponed. There is some freedom to capture and pursue ideas generated by what is read but the linear text reflects the author's train of thought, not the reader's. Hypertext breaks this pattern by allowing readers to modify both the sequence and the content of the text as it is being read. Hypertext provides for a highly personalized structuring of knowledge in online shared databases by the creation of multiple pathways to serve different readers at the same time or to serve the same reader at different times. One facet of Hypertext, links between chunks of knowledge, is to be found in conventional encyclopedias where individual articles frequently refer, both explicitly and implicitly, to other articles within the whole and also to other works. Another facet of Hypertext, the ability to reorganize information as needed, is exemplified in the scholar's note cards. The essence of Hypertext is the ability to create, erase, or modify links between chunks of knowledge in a variety of forms and formats, to make the links themselves substantive, and to be able to arrange and rearrange the whole, at will. Jonassen has defined Hypertext as "any text presentation system that permits the user to direct the logical flow of the text presentation" (Ref. 1). Clearly, many of the technologies required to accomplish this are available today: very large databases; very large storage capacities (magnetic and optical); powerful computers; precise retrieval facilities; smart software.

H. G. Wells is usually credited with giving the idea of a "world encyclopedia" or "world brain" its modern interpretation as a dynamic, evolving, compendium of man's knowledge intended to serve social, political and economic purposes (Ref. 2). However, Goodman has stressed that Wells himself acknowledged an intellectual debt to John Amos Comenius, a 17th century Czech scholar (Ref. 3).

The man who gave the world brain concept its machine-based orientation was Vannevar Bush. He emphasised the need to abandon conventional indexing and classification in favor of organization and retrieval by association "in accordance with some intricate web of trails" (Ref. 4). Interestingly, Bush did not suggest a role for computers in mechanizing personal files, to supplement the individual's memory, until more than twenty years after he coined the name "Memex" for such a device (Ref. 5).

Bush's notions about managing information found a responsive chord among researchers. A succession of writers have contributed to the expression and refinement of such ideas in recent years. Douglas Englebart has long been committed to the augmentation of man's intellect through machine aids (Ref. 6). His efforts resulted in an experimental system, NLS, that functioned as a developmental tool; among other things it provided for multi-person distributed conferencing and editing (Ref. 7). Coinciding with Engelbart's early writing, J. C. R Licklider published his _Libraries of the Future_ (Ref. 8). At about the same time Swanson was offering his perceptions of "Dialogues with a Catalog" (Ref. 9). An advanced design to facilitate browsing and navigating in augmented library catalogs has been proposed quite recently by Hjerppe (Ref. 10).

Theodor Nelson, who coined the term Hypertext, has been the most prolific author and, perhaps, the most active researcher in the field. His Project Xanadu, a system for the storage and retrieval and display of linked texts using windowing techniques has a long history (Ref. 11). A more recent description of Xanadu, "a real and currently available product," is offered by Roger Gregory; Xanadu focuses exclusively on textual data (Ref 12). Trigg has furnished the only dissertation identified to date on Hypertext (Ref. 13). His "Textnet" approach to non-linear text was seen as an online system to support the scientific community with authoring, editing, refereeing and retrieval capabilities for information stored in a national distributed depository.

In contrast to these seemingly text-oriented systems, Kay and Goldberg describe the "Dynabook" as being capable of handling text and of manipulating pictures as objects even to the point of animating them (Ref. 14). Weyer discusses the idea of "the dynamic book" in some detail and reports on some tests of a simple version (Ref. 15). The necessity for handling information in a variety of formats has been recognized and pursued most actively, perhaps, at the Institute for Research in Information and Scholarship (IRIS), at Brown University. The IRIS INTERMEDIA system has been discussed by Yankelovich; an illustrated sample session included in this work conveys the richness, power and utility of "hypermedia" (Ref. 16). More detail of "the capabilities necessary for multimedia electronic document systems" is provided by Yankelovich, Meyrowitz and van Dam (Ref. 17). Negroponte seems to go much further in suggesting something more like an experience than a system; a kind of total immersion in information is envisaged (Ref. 18).

One of the most extensive discussions of Hypertext has been offered by Conklin (Ref. 19). He examines the origins and the evolution of non-linear text handling. He also discusses some of the advantages and the disadvantages of Hypertext. In particular he notes that cognitive overhead and disorientation are serious problems in the use of these systems. The cognitive burden in creating, naming and tracking numerous links, especially while trying to assimilate other information, can be overwhelming. Techniques to deal with this problem include: displaying linked items quickly; providing brief explanations of side paths in pop-up windows; giving a graphical depiction of the subnetwork into which a link leads. The tendency to lose one's location and sense of direction in non-linear text can be alleviated with graphical browsers and powerful search mechanisms which can quickly partition large databases. Graphical means of way-finding in very large files seem to be particularly effective; they are featured in several of the developments identified above.

REFERENCES

1. Jonassen, David H. Hypertext Principles for Text and Courseware Design. Educational Psychologist 21, p. 269-292, 1986.

2. Wells, H. G. World Brain. New York, NY: Doubleday, 1938.

3. Goodman, H. J. Abraham. The "World Brain/World Encyclopedia" Concept: Its Historical Roots and the Contributions of H. J. A. Goodman to the Ongoing Evolution and Implementation of the Concept. Proceedings, 50th Annual Meeting of the American Society for Information Science, 1987. p. 91-98.

4. Bush, Vannevar. As We May Think. Atlantic Monthly 176, p. 1-108, July 1945.

5. Bush, Vannevar. Science Is Not Enough. New York, NY: William Morrow, 1967, p.75-101.

6. Engelbart, Douglas C. A Conceptual Framework for the Augmentation of Man's Intellect. in Paul W. Howerton and David C. Weeks (eds.) Vistas in Information Handling, I: The Augmentation of Man's Intellect by Machine. Washington, DC: Spartan Books, 1963, p. 1-29.

7. Engelbart, Douglas C. and W. K. English. A Research Center for Augmenting Human Intellect. AFIPS Proceedings, Fall Joint Computer Conference 33, 1968. p. 395-410.

8. Licklider, J. C. R. Libraries of the Future. Cambridge, MA: MIT Press. 1965.

9. Swanson, Don R. Dialogues with a Catalog. Library Quarterly 34, p. 113-125, 1964.

10. Hjerppe, Roland. Project HYPERCATalog. in B. C. Brookes (ed.) Intelligent Information Systems for the Information Society. Amsterdam: Elsevier, 1986, p. 211-232.

11. Nelson, Theodor H. Replacing the Printed Word: A Complete Literary System. Proceedings of the IFIP Congress, 1980, p. 1013-1023.

12. Gregory, Roger. XANADU: Hypertext from the Future. Dr. Dobb's Journal Number 75, p. 28-35, January 1983.

13 Trigg, Randall Hagner. A Network-Based Approach to Text Handling for the Online Scientific community. Ph.D. Dissertation, University of Maryland, 1983.

14. Kay, Alan and Adele Goldberg. Personal Dynamic Media. Computer 10, p. 31-41, March 1977.

15. Weyer, Stephen A. The Design of a Dynamic Book for Information Search. International Journal of Man-Machine studies 17, p. 87-107, 1982.

16. Yankelovich, Nicole. INTERMEDIA: A System for Linking Multimedia Documents. IRIS Technical Report 86-2. Institute for Research in Information and Scholarship, Brown University, Providence, RI, 1986.

17. Yankelovich, Nicole, Norman Meyrowitz and Andries van Dam. Reading and Writing the Electronic Book. Computer 18, p. 15-30, October 1985.

18. Negroponte, Nicholas. Books Without Pages. IEEE International Conference on Communications, IV. 1979, p. 56.1.1-1.8.

19. Conklin, Jeff. Hypertext: An Introduction and Survey. Computer 20, p. 17-41, September 1987.

STUDENT PREFERENCES IN ONLINE SEARCH INSTRUCTION

Dorice Des Chene, University of Cincinnati

Keywords: Online Searching, Student Instruction, End-User Instruction, CAS ONLINE.

Abstract: CAS ONLINE has been available to graduate students in Chemistry at the University of Cincinnati for about three years. Students have been given individual instruction in the library, or they have taught each other, or faculty members have assisted them. It came to be of interest to learn whether or not more formal instruction would be desirable. Student preferences in instruction in the use of CAS ONLINE were surveyed during fall quarter of 1987. The results are reported.

1. INTRODUCTION

In recent years, end-user searching has been a subject of great interest to librarians, database owners, and vendors of online services. Some libraries have experimented with access to online services for their users. There has been promotion of the use of online databases to end-users through various gateway and front-end services. The vendors or database owners have devised menu-driven, user-friendly versions of the their systems for the benefit of end-users (Ref. 1-4).

How much and what kind of training is appropriate for end-users has been a source of concern to librarians. Some experiments with training have been disappointing, since although the end-users were able to learn how to search, not many of them were willing or eager to perform their own searches afterwards. But vendors have made efforts to improve the user-friendliness of their systems and to provide user aids that are accessible to inexperienced users. So in some cases, online services have been very popular with end users, whether or not there had been very much training. One of the most important factors in end-user searching, after training or without training, is cost, particularly for students (Ref. 5-9).

Chemistry faculty and students and chemists in industry have long had access to intermediary online searching in Chemical Abstracts and in recent years have been encouraged to participate in online searching for themselves. Chemical Abstracts Service has made CAS ONLINE, its own online version of the Abstracts, available at low cost to academic institutions in non-prime time. CAS ONLINE includes a bibliographic file from 1967 to date (CA File), a chemical substance file including substructure search capability (Registry File), and a pre-1967 limited access bibliographic file (CAOLD File), provided now through STN International. using the Messenger command language. There are also two training files: the Learning CA File (LCA) and the Learning Registry File (LREGISTRY).

At the University of Cincinnati, CAS ONLINE has been available to faculty and graduate students in the Department of Chemistry for about three years. An initial workshop was presented by Chemical Abstracts Service staff members to selected faculty members, who in turn instructed their graduate students in the use of the Service, and some of these students taught others. Students have been given individual instruction in the library if they wished. Others have taught themselves from the manuals which they may check out from the library. These are: <u>A Guide to the Commands</u> and <u>Using CAS ONLINE: The CA File</u>.

A majority of the students who search use the CA File, which is the bibliographic file corresponding to the printed <u>Abstracts</u> from 1967 to date. Although there was considerable interest amongst some faculty members in the Registry File at first, few users have pursued it since then. We do not have the graphics capabilities that would make substructure searching easier.

2.   SURVEY RESULTS

Recently, it was decided that it would be of interest to learn whether or not more formal instruction would be desirable, or if other methods of instruction should be pursued. Accordingly, chemistry graduate students' preferences in instruction in the use of CAS ONLINE were surveyed during fall quarter of 1987.

Thirty responses were received, of 130 questionnaires that were distributed, a 23% response. Twenty-two of the students who responded had used CAS ONLINE at least once. Five of them had used it on over eleven occasions. Eight had never used it.

Eleven, or fifty percent of the students who had used CAS ONLINE had learned how to use it from their friends. Another group had taught themselves from the manuals or, as they said, by trial and error. Four had been taught by the librarian. Several had used more than one of these methods. Students who were taught by the librarian were required to study the manuals beforehand.

Seventeen, or 77%, of the students who had used CAS ONLINE, when asked whether or not they would like further instruction, agreed that they would.

A final question gave the students a number of choices of methods of instruction: (1) check out the manuals and learn by myself; (2) ask my friends for help; (3) ask the librarian for individual instruction; (4) ask a faculty member for instruction; (5) use STN Mentor (computerized instruction; (6) attend a workshop; (7) other. Students were to respond to this question whether or not they had ever used CAS ONLINE. They were asked to number their choices in order of preference. Attending a workshop received the most first choice votes (12, or 40%). Asking the librarian for individual instruction was next as a first choice (8, or 27%).

On a point basis, giving first choices six points, second choices five points, and so on, attending a workshop was a clear winner, with 110 points. Asking the librarian for individual instruction was second with 88 points, with teaching oneself by using the manuals nearly the same with 85 points. Asking friends for help received 66 points, and STN Mentor, close with 60 points. Asking faculty members for assistance was less popular, at 42 points.

In the comments, one student suggested that a seminar be conducted to relate the use of CAS ONLINE to finding materials or arranging interlibrary loans in the library, and to the use of equipment in the Department of Chemistry. Another proposed weekly or monthly updates to acquaint students with new developments in CAS ONLINE.

3. PLANS FOR TRAINING

A letter to chemistry graduate students has been prepared, listing the methods of instruction available to them from the library at present: individual instruction by the librarian, the use of the manuals and/or STN Mentor, and printed handouts from Chemical Abstracts Service.

Plans are being made to offer workshops in spring quarter, most likely by the librarian. The students will queried to determine what time of the week or day is most suitable for workshops. We will need to know about how many attendees there might be, so that materials can be assembled.

Training will be limited to graduate students in chemistry, in small groups (5-10). There is limited access to terminals or microcomputers for demonstration or hands-on instruction. Small groups allow more opportunities for questions and discussion for each student. Since most of the students appear to be interested in searching the CA File, that and general instruction in using Boolean logic and the Messenger commands will be the first line of attack. Responses to training efforts up to that time will be reported when this paper is presented.

4. REFERENCES

1. Williams, Martha E. "Electronic Databases." Science 228, No. 4698, p. 445-56, April 26, 1985.

2. Summit, Roger K. and Meadow, Charles T. "Emerging Trends in the Online Industry." Special Libraries 76, p. 88-92, Spring 1985.

3. Neufeld, M. Lynne and Cornog, Martha. "Database History: From Dinosaurs to Compact Discs. Journal of the American Society for Information Science 37, no. 4, p. 183-90, July 1986.

4. O'Leary, Mick. "CompuServe and The Source: Databanks for the End-User." Database 8, No. 2, p. 100-6, June 1985.

5. Buntrock, Robert E. and Valicenti, Aldona K. "End-Users and Chemical Information." Journal of Chemical Information and Computer Sciences 25, No. 2, p. 203-7, May 1985.

6. Buntrock, Robert E. and Valicenti, Aldona K. "End-User Searching: The Amoco Experience." Journal of Chemical Information and Computer Sciences 25, No. 4, p. 415-9, November 1985.

7. Reiter, Martha B. "Can You Teach Me to Do My Own Searching? Or Tailoring Online Training to the Needs of the End-User." Journal of Chemical Information and Computer Sciences 25, No. 4, p. 419-22, November 1985.

8. Palma, Mary Ann S. and Sullivan, Charles. "Meeting the Needs of the End User." Journal of Chemical Information and Computer Sciences 25, No. 4, p. 422-5, November 1985.

9. Warr, Wendy A. "Online Access to Chemical Information: A Review." Database 10, No. 3, p. 122-8, June 1987.

5. TABLE I. RESULTS OF SURVEY

1. Have you used CAS ONLINE?

   yes __22__

   no __8__   If no, skip to Question 5.

2. If so, how many times?

   1 - 5 __14__

   6 - 10 __2__

   11 or more __5__

3. How did you learn to use CAS ONLINE?

   From friends __11__

   Using the manuals __8__

   From the librarian __4__

   Trial and error __2__

   Search done for me __2__

   Short course __1__

4. Would you like to have further instruction?

   yes __17__

   no __4__

   no response __1__

5. Of the following methods of learning to use CAS ONLINE, which do you prefer, either as beginning user or with some experience? Please number in order of preference.

Method	Times Selected as 1st Choice
Check out the manuals	4
Ask my friends	3
Ask the librarian	8
Ask a faculty member	2
Use STN Mentor	1
Attend a workshop	12

CAUTION: DOWNLOADING MAY BE HAZARDOUS TO YOUR COMPUTER'S HEALTH

Glen Key Dalessandro, Continental Insurance

KEYWORDS: Download, Freeware, Pirate, Public Domain, Shareware, Trialware

ABSTRACT: Although information utilities, commercial electronic bulletin boards and public domain bulletin boards constantly monitor and test the contents of public domain, Freeware and user developed software, unlawfully copied or modified programs may exist on these services.

When users download and execute programs, they accept risks ranging from using unauthorized modifications of a program to destroying the information on a hard disk by overwriting the zero track. Pirated, hacked or camouflaged programs pose a threat to business and professional users who download on the same microcomputers used for other applications (spreadsheet, data base and wordprocessing) or are networked to other computers.

Some corporations, aware of the possible loss in information and copyright violation, require designated personnel to download and test programs on non-networked microcomputers containing files that are either expendable or easily reconstructed via backup.

A review of the types of modifications and methods to test and evaluate programs shows that the majority of programs offered to users for other than monetary gain can be useful and projects a comradeship lacking in other professions.

1. OVERVIEW

Most microcomputer users feel confident in downloading different types of software and files from bulletin boards and information utilities. In addition to a microcomputer, modem and a telephone line, a user needs a communication package to 'talk' to a service and access to a bulletin board via subscription or password. While The Source and CompuServe bulletin boards have the highest volume and many services, most of the activity between a program developer and potential users occurs on smaller bulletin boards. The types of programs or utilities available to microcomputer users fall into three categories: Freeware/Public Domain, Shareware and manufacturer's upgrades or Trialware.

Freeware requires no payment and gives no promises on function or performance. Shareware is software that doesn't require payment up front but satisfied users are requested to send in payment covering licensing, registration and documentation fees. Software manufactures supply upgrades and patches for application programs and sometimes sponsor software-specific forums to exchange information and files. Trialware allows a potential software buyer to sample a program with one or more key features disabled or removed. The user tests the software at little or no cost to find out if it will satisfy his or her needs in a particular application. Although users may download a program with computer errors or bugs, the greatest number of errors come from communications failures, not flaws in a program itself. Many users have written off a program when a bad phone line was the actual culprit (Ref. 1).

Software obtained via bulletin boards offer advantages to both the developer and the computer user. The programmer or manufacturer can quickly test the software waters with a new type or kind of software through Shareware, Freeware or Trialware. If the users respond favorably by the 'chat' or interactive electronic mail feature on a bulletin board, the programmer may be encouraged to develop the product for mass distribution. The developers also gain user insight about the software application. The computer user obtains valuable utilities and programs and free upgrades of existing software. There are no guarantees in downloading software, but in most cases, a microcomputer user only loses his or her time and any connect and telephone charges.

This symbiotic environment also has its parasites in the form of a few people who use the bulletin boards to transmit modified copy protected software or destructive programs that may damage files on the hard disk (disk-killer). With the increasing use of computer bulletin boards, killer programs are a threat to personal computer owners. Among bulletin board system operators, or SYSOPS, this has become a big enough problem to warrant circulating lists of disk-killer programs (Ref. 2). One source, THE DIRTY DOZEN, list three types of unlawfully copied or modified programs: Trojan, Hacked and Pirated software.

2. TYPES OF MODIFICATIONS

The Trojan horse is very simple in theory, but also very effective when it works. The program that is written or modified to be a Trojan horse is designed to achieve two major goals: First, it tries to look very innocent and tempting to run, and second, it has within itself a few high-security tasks (Ref. 3). The Trojan horse may also be fused with a "logic bomb," a device that can be timed to go off in a precise number of days or years in the future, or on the occurrence of some specific event (Ref. 4). A Trojan horse program can also be a Worm program. It is a simple program that's installed into the system so that whenever the system is brought up, the worm program is run along with others (Ref. 5). These types of programs have the ability to erase files, lock-up the computer system or overwrite the zero track containing the file index.

Hacked software is an unlawfully modified copy of an otherwise legitimate Freeware or user-supported program. Normally, it is illegal to distribute a modified copy of someone else's work without their permission. If permission has been granted, statements will appear in either the display or the documentation.

Pirated software is an illegal copy of a commercial program product. Examples include, a "cracked" (de-protected) game or application software package, an accidentally or deliberately distributed compiler, editor or utility or a Beta test copy of a program under development (Ref. 6).

A microcomputer user can fall victim to other types of illegal activities or 'thruput' scams in the processing mode, while on-line. Even a neighborly service called Chat, provided on The Source, is not exempt. Chat enables people to strike up an on-line conversation with each other. Recently, some individuals found a way to trick others into revealing their passwords. During a "chat," the perpetrator would mimic commands on the service telling another user that he had been disconnected and to please enter his password to log onto the system again. The user would innocently enter the code, although he was still in the Chat mode, allowing access to the password (Ref. 7).

3.1 PREVENTATIVE MEASURES vs. PRIVACY

Software reliability and product support are governed by the utilities and manufacturer's policies, software user awareness and government concerns about crime and privacy. While SYSOPS monitor communication traffic on their bulletin boards, they may be barred from some 'chat' or private 'talk' areas because of service agreements with computer users. According to Jonathan Wallace, a charter member of Computer Hobbyists Against Raiders and Thieves (CHART), "Legislation will be pushed and passed to address these issues if the various electronic mail companies don't address it themselves first. If they each proclaim it their policy, as CompuServe has, never to invade the privacy of electronic mail, then the government will not see a need to act so quickly" (Ref. 8).

The Source also respects the privacy of electronic mail and makes its policy clear in the subscriber agreement. However, the agreement further states that Source Telecomputing Corporation (STC) "may review any material stored in files or programs to which all subscribers have access... and will remove any material which STC in its sole discretion believes to be unlawful or otherwise objectionable...without notice..." (Ref. 9).

People found modifying or illegally copying software may be subject to criminal penalties. Two laws were passed in October 1986 that offer some protection to computer users. The Computer Fraud and Abuse Act recognizes the contents of a computer as property, while the Electronic Communications Privacy Act makes it a crime for anyone to access electronic mail or other data transmissions without authorization (Ref. 10).

While no on-line utility guarantees downloaded software, the service Exec-PC provides the name of the person who uploaded each program. Any complaints go directly to The Source (Ref. 11).

3.2 METHODS TO TEST SOFTWARE

In addition to eliminating the obvious downloaded programs, such as modified copies of popular games or application software, the computer user can examine and test software prior to implementation. While on the bulletin board, checking the date of the upload (the date software originally arrived on the bulletin board) may show that the software has been around long enough to have been tested by other users. Some bulletin boards also list the number of times a piece of software has been downloaded. A large access number may show that others have confidence in the software.

Some bulletin boards distribute lists of modified programs and a review of the message boards may reveal the names and or version numbers of disk-killer programs. Software vendors offer programs that can be used to test programs that have been downloaded. Digital Dispatch, Inc. of Minneapolis designed detective software called <u>Data Physician</u> that detects and removes a software virus by mathematically sampling a suspect program for dangerous code. A similar program, <u>C4bomb</u> is free on CompuServe (Ref. 12).

In addition to packaged detective software, a knowledgeable user can apply some simple tests to suspect software. In the IBM PC-DOS environment, use the DOS TYPE command to display the contents of a specific file. While most of the information in an object program file (a compiled program) appears unreadable due to the presence of nonalphabetic and non-numeric characters, check for keywords such as "Gotcha," "Boom," or common expletives.

Interpreter BASIC programs can be loaded and then saved as an ASCII file. Use any text editor to check the file for undesirable keywords.

Downloading and executing all software on a non-networked microcomputer with easily reconstructed files, protects both the network and other files and is the best protection from thruput scams.

4. CONCLUSION

Tampering with the contents of bulletin boards affects both personal computer users and business users. The best way to protect this important and in most cases free service is to check the source, if possible, and test the program either by examination or implementation in a nonvolatile environment. For those who have a tendency towards developing disk-killer programs, don't!

REFERENCES

1. Bermant, Charles, "In Search of Utilities Software," Personal Computing (January 1988), p. 126.

2. Gross, Steven, "Computer Virus," Omni (June 1986), p.35.

3. Landreth, Bill, Out of the Inner Circle - A Hacker's Guide to Computer Security. Bellevue, Washington: Microsoft Press, 1985, p. 94.

4. McLellan, Vin, "Of Trojan Horses, Data Diddling and Logic Bombs," Inc. (June 1984), p.106.

5. Landreth, p. 100.

6. Neff, Tom, "The Dirty Dozen - A Program Alert List," Smart Bulletin Board System (June 29, 1986), last screen.

7. Honan, Patrick, "Data Security," Personal Computing (January 1987), p. 102.

8. McClure, Matthew, "At Risk: Your On-Line Freedom," Popular Computing (June 1985), p. 143.

9. Ibid., p. 143.

10. Honan, p. 102.

11. Bermant, p. 131.

12. Gross, p. 35.

WILSONDISC: TRAINING THE TRAINER

Victoria E. Dow and Gail Kriebel, Lehigh University

Keywords: Wilsondisc, training the trainer, college students, training methods, endusers.

Abstract: The Lehigh University Libraries have encouraged end user searching of online databases for several years. In the past we have instructed faculty and students in searching BRS AfterDark and CAS Online. Most end user instruction, however, has been directed toward faculty and graduate students. Our goal in this program was to reach Freshmen and introduce them to online searching concepts. We enlisted the help of the English Composition (Freshmen English) instructors in teaching students the use of several indexes, among them the Readers' Guide to Periodical Literature on WILSONDISC. The instructors were taught about the CD-ROM system and how to construct and execute a search on WILSONDISC. They then taught their students the mechanics of WILSONDISC preparatory to the classes coming to the library for a demonstration of the system by a librarian. This two stage instruction program increased the effectiveness of instruction and reduced staff time in subsequent one-on-one instruction when students came in on their own to use WILSONDISC.

1. INTRODUCTION

Lehigh University is a medium sized university with an enrollment of over 6,500 students. The three university libraries have a combined collection of almost 900,000 volumes. The libraries' online catalog and an integrated voice and data telecommunications network contribute to a "computer literate" environment for students and faculty. The reference staff of the Lehigh University Libraries actively promotes a number of end user database services. A well developed program exists for end user searching of BRS AfterDark. In addition, regular workshops are held to instruct faculty and students in online search techniques and protocol for Dialog, STN, RLIN, and OCLC searching.

In the summer of 1986 Lehigh subscribed to the Infotrac system on a test basis. Infotrac has become a popular index, especially with the undergraduate population. It was, however, not entirely appropriate for the humanities library. In the summer of 1987 the reference staff decided to eliminate the Infotrac search station in the humanities library and install Wilsondisc. The InfoTrac search stations in the science, social science and technology library remain. Initially, only the Wilson database for the Readers Guide was subscribed to.

2. STATEMENT OF THE PROBLEM

It was apparent to the reference staff that the Wilsondisc system required much more training and sophistication on the part of the end user than InfoTrac. Because the system was intended primarily for use by undergraduates, this presented a major training problem for the reference staff. In the past, end users of BRS Afterdark were trained during two hour workshops. Actual searches were carried out under the guidance of a search coach. This approach, which worked well for the 300 users who performed searches during the year, was considered too labor intensive for a system such as Wilsondisc, where it was hoped that usage would be much higher, especially for the undergraduate population.

A long term goal of the reference department has been to involve incoming Freshmen in a structured introduction to the Libraries. Therefore, we decided to introduce Wilsondisc searching to most of the Freshman English sections, with the exception of several sections which were used as a control group. Freshman English is a required course and its sections are taught by graduate students. The professor and graduate students involved agreed to participate in the experiment. Participating sections would be introduced to Wilsondisc as part of a one hour tour of the library, which would include also a brief demonstration of InfoTrac and two paper indexes. This meant that the time alloted for Wilsondisc training would be very brief, about twenty minutes per class. Given the complexity of the system, we thought that students coming in "cold" would not be able to learn to use Wilsondisc in this time period. Therefore, we asked the graduate students to learn Wilsondisc themselves and introduce it to their sections prior to the library tours.

3. GOALS

The experiment began with several clearly defined goals. We wanted to train the seven graduate students who instruct Freshmen English in Wilsondisc searching techniques so that they could introduce their students to the system prior to their library instruction sessions. We wanted to know if this technique of "training the trainer" would be an effective way of reaching a large number of students.

Ultimately we wanted all the Freshmen involved in the program to be able to use Wilsondisc with minimum staff intervention. Given the number of students who would be using Wilsondisc, it was essential that we keep individual instruction to a minimum. A major goal was to instruct students effectively enough in large groups so that when they actually performed their searches they would need little or no assistance.

A further goal was to maximize our investments of time and money by publicizing the availability of the system and thereby encouraging its use. The Wilsondisc search station is in a relatively untrafficked area. It was our hope that by introducing it to a large number of students in a formal way, we would increase its visibility.

Considering the time and expense involved in implementing the Wilson system, a final goal was to evaluate Wilsondisc. We were especially interested in its ease of use, the quality of results, and its popularity with students. Peripherally, we also planned to note hardware or software problems and we felt we were in an ideal situation to compare the system with InfoTrac.

4. **IMPLEMENTATION**:

Implementation of the program had three stages: training the English instructors; preparing the staff members who would take part in the student instruction; and the actual instruction of the Freshman English composition students. The first stage was crucial. If the instructors were not adequately prepared, this program would lose any advantage it might have gained from a two stage instruction format.

We taught only the Browse and Wilsearch modes on Wilsondisc. Because of telecommunications incompatibilities, our station is not configured for online searching and we have not made Wilsonline and Expert mode available to users other than library staff.

Before embarking on this project, we carefully considered the content and level of the course into which we would integrate our program. We felt that for the sake of the library staff it would be easiest to work with the same assignment for all the classes in the program. In our case, this meant that all 500 freshmen composition students whom we trained were reading the same essay and had the same topics - nuclear arms or Darwinism - to write about. What differed for each student was the approach or argument taken in his/her own essay. Each student used two or three articles to support his/her view.

4.1 Instructor training

Preparing the instructors was given careful thought since they would in turn prepare students for their sessions in the library. The instructors needed a clear sense of the goals of the program, namely to train freshmen more effectively in the use of Wilsondisc. It was important the instructors feel confident in their role as intermediaries and not feel that they had relinquished control of their classes.

To start with, it was necessary to review what an index is and to define terms such as subject headings, fields, and Boolean operators. A thorough overview of Wilsondisc, including the print counterpart of the index that the students would be searching, followed. It was also especially important to explain what information is actually in the CD-ROM files: that only bibliographic citations with subject indexing are listed; that the full article is not available on the disc.

Searching concepts, as they apply to Wilsondisc, were covered in some detail. The differences between basic index searches, controlled vocabulary, and specific field searching (authors, organizations, etc.) were stressed. Truncation was covered briefly along with a warning regarding the dangers of creating too short a stem for searching. The instructors also needed lessons in combining terms using Boolean logic as it operates in Wilsondisc. This was easiest to explain with hands on practice after reviewing how "and," "or," and "not" function and finally going over an example using Venn diagrams. This stage of instructor training prepared the way for explanations of how Wilsondisc actually works.

Although teaching Wilsondisc mechanics is best done in a hands-on mode, this was impossible in our situation. Instead, we used visuals taken directly from the screens, describing each step in the search process from those visuals. However, the instructors did have time before their own classes to try what they had seen during the instruction session. We explained Wilsondisc's Browse mode rather quickly. Most users have few problems with Browse since it is not much different than searching through a paper index. However, we covered Wilsearch thoroughly.

A screen-by-screen overview of Wilsearch came first, followed by a detailed discussion of the screen on which the search terms are entered. The difference between subject terms, Wilson subject headings, and title words was explained, as well as what happens when a name is entered on the author/name line or the organization line. We found that subject term searching caused the most problems. Instructors, as well as students, initially had trouble understanding what happens when terms are entered all on one line versus on various lines, and what difference "any" makes in a search. Both groups understood these concepts once they sat down at the Wilsondisc station and tried their searches.

The output from a search, whether in Browse or Wilsearch mode, was quickly explained. Using preliminary results we discussed refining a search. The problem of too small or too large a result set is common with inexperienced searchers. We used a single example throughout the instruction sessions, modifying it as we moved through Browse and Wilsearch. This clearly demonstrated the differences in the search modes.

The final step in the instructor training was perhaps the most difficult. How does one describe how to explain something to a third party? Obviously, the instructors would not retell everything they had just heard to their classes. They had to be selective, providing to their students only the basics necessary for successful instruction in the library. We told the instructors to explain what the students should expect to learn from the instruction session: why they were learning to use an automated index; what its advantages are over other means of gathering information; and finally some basics about the index, what is in it, how that information is organized and accessed.

4.2   Staff preparation/coordination:

The six staff members who would be involved in teaching the students were briefed on the purpose and aims of the program. We gave them an outline of the entire training process, from start to finish, and a full set of teaching materials. All the instructional materials - notes, examples, overheads - were the same for everyone involved to ensure consistency. This reduced overall staff time on the project, which was crucial given the extensive bibliographic instruction program already in place at the Lehigh Libraries. Ms. Dow and Ms. Kriebel coordinated the project and fielded all questions and problems, both from the library and English department staff.

4.3   Student instruction:

Once the first two steps in the Wilsondisc instruction program were completed, the student instruction followed of itself. Most of the initial work in preparing the instructional materials had been done in teaching the instructors. We used the same examples for both groups and then tailored the Wilsondisc segment of the students' tour to fit the 20 minute time span we had allotted for it.

As mentioned above, we followed the outline for instructor training in teaching students. However, these instructions were geared more towards the students' actual needs, i.e. they were to write essays on a particular topic and needed two or three articles to support their views. Before looking at Wilsondisc the students went over two paper indexes to see how they are organized and gain an appreciation of the variety of indexes available.

Of the modes we make available on Wilsondisc, Wilsearch needed more detailed and thorough explanation than the Browse mode. Again, hands on training would have been ideal; that being impracticable we used visuals and allowed for limited practice time after the instruction. Students also needed to know that they could ask for and get help from librarians when they actually came in to do their searches. We pointed out that a one page instructional handout was available next to the search station. This handout was meant to help anyone searching Wilsondisc for the first time. The Wilson documentation, although complete, was not sufficiently succinct to enable users to quickly grasp the essentials of the system. The final step in the student instruction was showing them how to look up the articles for which they found citations on Wilsondisc.

5. MEASUREMENT AND EVALUATION

The "Training the Trainer" project and the student tours which followed it were completed by October 19, 1988. We knew that we could expect heavy usage of the system for the two week period following this, and therefore planned to record data on searches made during this time. A log sheet was maintained for all searches. We recorded information on whether or not the user had been introduced to Wilsondisc; a note on any problems encountered; and an estimation of the individual instruction time required for each search session. A brief questionnaire was designed to measure overall satisfaction with the system. All searchers during the two week period were asked to fill it out. Once the Freshman English composition project was completed we did an informal survey of the graduate student instructors involved in the project. Also, a final written survey was distributed to all of the study participants and to six additional classes which had completed the same Freshman composition assignment without the benefit of instruction in the use of Wilsondisc. This survey gave students who had used both InfoTrac and Wilsondisc an opportunity to comparatively evaluate the systems.

5.2 Instruction Time

The major goal of the project was to effectively train a large number of students to use the Wilsondisc system with minimal staff time spent on individualized instruction. Although the success of this effort was difficult to measure, this goal seems to have been realized. During the two week period of the study, the great majority of users were from the Freshman English classes which had been formally instructed. Only 15% of the searches logged during the two week study were performed by uninstructed students and many of these were assisted by classmates who had received search training. The peer tutoring which was evident throughout the study made it impossible for us to compare the group of trained searchers with a completely uninstructed group. Even so, there were some dramatic differences between the groups.

Many of the difficulties which required staff intervention (37% overall) were due to problems with Wilson software which have since been corrected. Therefore, the instruction time needed to address these problems has been discounted.

Freshman English students who received instruction needed an average of 1.1 minutes of individual instruction time per search when they actually used Wilsondisc. This compares favorably to the 3.64 minutes of instruction time per search required by uninstructed searchers. These figures are more impressive when we take into account the fact that many uninstructed students were receiving additional instruction from classmates. In fact, several of the uninstructed students who searched without a peer tutor needed as much as ten minutes of individualized instruction per search. Another informative measure of the effectiveness of the instruction was the percentage of searchers who were able to operate the system entirely without staff intervention. Of the students in the trained group, over 73% were able to perform their searches without assistance. Uninstructed searchers needed individualized instruction 56% of the time. Had there been no peer tutoring going on, this figure would, no doubt, have been even higher.

A final difference between the two groups of searchers emerged when we looked at the reasons they needed assistance. Most of the untrained searchers asked for help in basic mechanics of the system and in search strategy. The problems encountered by trained searchers were much more varied. A percentage breakdown of problems requiring assistance follows.

Reasons for Individualized Instruction
for Trained Searchers

29%	Assistance in formulating search strategy
18%	Interpreting Wilsearch procedure
12%	Discovering how to begin a new search
12%	Inadvertent use of the f7 automatic connection key
29%	Other

5.3 Instructor Feedback

In addition to objective measurements of instruction time and students search problems, we also performed an informal poll of the graduate student instructors who participated in the experiment.

In general, instructors do not participate in any instruction session before bringing their classes to the library for bibliographic instruction. This is the group to which we loosely compared the instructors in the "training the trainer" program.

The instructors who participated in our program felt more comfortable in explaining to their students the purpose of the instruction sessions than those who were not in the program. The eight instructors in the program knew beforehand what their students would learn and were of the opinion that this helped them better integrate the library instruction session into their classes. They were also better equipped to answer any questions their students had about searching, both in paper indexes and on Wilsondisc, once they were finished with the tours.

However, we did discover some problems in our approach to training the instructors. To make the most of the "training the trainer" method, we found that it was imperative to give the trainers plenty of hands-on time _during_ their instruction session. They needed to practice on Wilsondisc, especially with Wilsearch, in order to gain a thorough understanding of the system. Unfortunately, we did not have as much time for this hands-on practice as we evidently needed. Also, we could not assume, as we had to begin with, that the instructors knew anything more about indexes than how to use a particular one. They were not familiar with some of the terms we used and with the basic structure of an index. Once we had explained these concepts the workings of Wilsondisc became clearer to them.

The single, clearest result of training the instructors was that we could not assume prior knowledge on their part. Also, we had to allow ample time for them to absorb and try out the lessons before they went into their own classes. If their own knowledge of the system was faulty or incomplete, they would not be effective in teaching their students about Wilsondisc.

5.4 Usage

It was clear from the start that we would need publicity in order to attract students to Wilsondisc. The search station is in a somewhat remote area and almost all of the students using the system during the two week study had been introduced to it in class. Of the students who did not receive training in Wilsondisc, only 21% chose to use the system. Most of these indicated that they discovered it through "word of mouth" presumably from students in participating Freshman English classes. Without the initial publicity from the 300 students trained, usage would probably have been appallingly low. We are still concerned about increasing our use of the system, but will probably address this by subscribing to a different database.

5.5 Evaluation

In the two printed surveys we asked searchers to fill out we were primarily concerned with users perceptions about ease of use; their need for additional assistance; and their overall satisfaction with the system. Students who had used both Wilsondisc and InfoTrac were also asked to compare the systems.

Students who received training in Wilsondisc searching were almost unanimous in their satisfaction with the system. Over 80% indicated that they would use the system again. Only 28% thought that the system needed additional instruction. (Keep in mind that they did have a brief guide to the system written in house.) One half of the untrained students thought that the Wilson system needed additional instructions, in spite of the fact that they had access to the same in house guide and often benefited from peer tutoring. However, even without training, this group was still generally satisfied with the system and over half of them indicated that they would use Wilsondisc again.

When it came to comparing Wilsondisc to InfoTrac, our two groups of users were very much in agreement. Both groups found InfoTrac much easier to use, although a sizeable minority (37%) of the group instructed in Wilsondisc thought that Wilson was easier. However, when asked to evaluate the results of their searches, most users preferred Wilsondisc. They were also in agreement on the reasons for their preference. In written comments, both groups indicated that they found documents cited on the Wilson product were easier to locate in the Lehigh Libraries. This is, of course, a reflection of the match between database coverage and the local collection rather than an evaluation of the systems. A striking difference between the two groups is that a large number of instructed searchers found Wilsondisc to be more precise. Of the trained searchers who found Wilsondisc results better than the InfoTrac's, 32% volunteered that it was because searching is more precise on the Wilson product. None of the untrained searchers mentioned this in their evaluations. This is probably because the untrained group did not know about or feel confident enough to use the Wilsearch Mode and were operating entirely in Browse Mode.

When it came to overall preference for one system or another, our users were divided. Searchers who had received no training in Wilsondisc were split. Half of these students preferred Wilson and half preferred InfoTrac. Wilson fared somewhat better with trained users. In this group 61% found their product preferrable while 39% gave InfoTrac a higher rating. Most users indicated that they would use both systems again.

As part of "Training the Trainer" we also saved a representative sample of searches from both trained and untrained groups of searchers. This should produce some interesting information on how end users search. We intend to analyze these searches before the next round of instruction.

6   CONCLUSIONS

In conclusion, we feel that "Training the Trainer" was a success. We learned that we could greatly reduce the amount of individual instruction time required to teach end users to search effectively on Wilsondisc. By combining formal instruction in the library with introductory information imparted by graduate teaching assistants we were able to train a large number of trained searchers to use the system with minimum staff time spent on individual searches. We discovered that although we had somewhat overestimated the sophistication of our graduate student instructors, they were all able to grasp the essentials of the system. The response of our graduate students will be useful in planning the next instruction series. We found that our users were generally satisfied with both automated systems and that the library instruction program enhanced their use of automated indexes.

MEETING THE CD-ROM MARKETING AND SALES CHALLENGE

Ralph Ferragamo, Corporate & Industry Research Reports

Keywords: Decision making, CD ROM, Marketing, Corporate and Industry Research Reports (CIRR).

Abstract: Corporate and Industry Research Reports is a database of over 100,000 analytical research reports. These reports are submitted to JA micro from 68 worldwide securities and investment firms. CIRR offers indexing and abstract with full text in either microfiche or paper. With the advent of the new CD ROM technology, JA decided to offer a CD ROM version of CIRR. Several issues were involved in the decision making process, including file design, production, product enhancements, and marketing. These issues are addressed as experienced by a small database publisher.

Each time a new technology in this case a new publishing media hits the street, the amount of print coverage is extensive and immediate. Almost to the point where the press precedes the technology. New journals appear as well as traditional journals taking new slants. The hype continues for a period and then the lull begins.

Therefore, I don't know that I can tell you anything new that has not already been in the press and this may be repetitious to most of you.

My idea is to discuss the reasons why a publisher decides to venture into new technologies when the traditional publishing media is alive and well.

Not all publications lend themselves to CD ROM technologies but certainly databases have application. Our first CD ROM publication is Indexing and Abstracting to Corporate and Industry Research Reports. CIRR is a collection of 100,000 analytical research reports issued by 68 securities and investment firms. We serve several markets and each is unique. Our academic and public library clients tend to purchase collections in microfiche format with hard bound indexes while our commercial clients search the file on BRS or Dialog and order through our ON DEMAND Service either paper or microfiche.

In determining how to best utilize the new CD ROM, we had to first determine the best fit for our product and markets. Then of course decide on the production, distribution, etc.

Fortunately, we were not the first in the business and we could study the pattern of like products. ERIC and Disclosure seemed like good candidates for study. Both are fiche based products with online and some type of hard copy index. The feedback we received from the market convinced us that CD ROM offered an enhancement to CIRR not easily found in other medium.

PRODUCTION

After making a decision that our product had CD application, the next step was to determine the best way to produce the product. Also, we had to position the CD in such a way that it did not adversely effect our traditional products (print and fiche) or cause confusion in the marketplace.

We examined a variety of opinions:
- a stand alone company produced CD
- as part of another CD product that offered compatibility
- as part of a CD vendor

Our choice was the latter and with SilverPlatter for the following reasons.
- SilverPlatter had similar databases in form and function. Most notably ERIC as an index to the fiche file
- they offered both key word and boolean logic software
- they understood part of our marketplace i.e. academic and public libraries
- they offered certain marketing expertise

As I mentioned before, we wanted to position our CD as an enhancement to our existing products not a replacement, and so designed that the novice user could easily search the file.

This led to a complete restructuring of the on line file that simplified the file structure. As an example, the print product does not allow for look up by product while the CD has a product field. Also the CD contains abstracts and the book does not. In essence, the CD product has convinced us to enter more data per records and at the same time display that data in a user friendly way.

MARKETING THE CD

We are still very much in the learn curve mode for marketing our first CD product. Of course, we have learned a few interesting items in the process.

The major concern is the cost of sale in the CD market. Unless you are an established name, let's say like Wilson, it is almost imperative that you demo your product, even with established customers. This is costly.

We have found that demos at trade shows, etc is an effective way of telling the story but still, extensive followup is necessary.

Other traditional marketing approaches such as direct mail and advertising are helpful but the client still wants to see the product.

In conjunction with SilverPlatter, we have a "try and buy" period of 30 days. In this way, the client can test the product with a variety of applications.

POINT OF USE DISPLAYS

Helping our customers "sell" the end user on the value of our information is an important part of our overall marketing plans and we are developing point of use materials that librarians can display or distribute.

ON DEMAND ON DISK

As our abstracts continue to increase in quality and quantity, we will continue to offer a full text on demand service to those customers who subscribe only to the CD. The instructions for ON DEMAND appear right on the disk and we offer same day (FAX) or next day delivery.

FINDING STATISTICS, TABLES, CHARTS AND PICTURES USING NEXIS™

Nancy F. Hardy, Mead Data Central

Keywords: Statistics, Tables, Charts, NEXIS™, Indexing, Pictures, Photographs, Maps, Cartoons, Full-text

Abstract: Searching for statistics, tables, charts and pictorial material in the online environment can be frustrating and onerous. Understanding how this "nontextual" material is loaded by the database vendor can eliminate user frustration and enhance search effectiveness. Tips for searching this type of material on Mead Data Central's NEXIS service will be discussed. Examples will include searches from Business Week's Financial Figures of the Week, Scoreboard issues, and the "BusinessWeek Index"; statistics from The New York Times; daily and historical currency exchange rates; charts and tables from Newsweek, Time, Fortune and other business publications, and even how to track photo credits for journalists and other pictorial material.

1. INTRODUCTION

The purpose of this paper is to show how nontextual material is loaded by Mead Data Central on its NEXIS service. As many of you know, the same databases or files may appear on the retrieval service of several different vendors. One's "old familiar file" may appear quite differently on another service, because the vendor chooses (or contracts) to load (make available) all or some specific fields -- we call them "segments" at MDC -- which are available in the material provided by the publisher.(1)

It is quite unusual for the producer (publisher) to license different versions of a file to various online vendors. Therefore, the user must divine how given vendor has loaded a file and how best to maneuver a way through the inevitable traps which are encountered. (I might also mention that there may be occasions or circumstances, when a vendor, for one reason or another, may decide to reprocess the publisher's material by rekeying, scanning or some other technique.)

For the purposes of this paper, examples will be drawn from files available on the NEXIS service. The capability to search for graphics in a given file may be limited to the file as it appears on NEXIS. This material may not be searchable in the same file on other services.

2.   YOU CAN'T PLAY WITH MY TOYS

Curiously, even when one is intimately familiar with a publication, records that one might expect to see online, simply are not there. In some cases, a column or a particular story may not be within the copyright of the publication, resting often with the reporter or writer instead. In such cases, the publisher simply cannot offer that material to any vendor unless special arrangements are made with the author. An example is the "My Turn" column of Newsweek, which is only available through 1982. NEXIS simply does not have this column (or certain columns from the Washington Post) available. So much for "full text"!

3.   FAMILIARITY BREEDS SUCCESS

It is very clear that the more familiar one is with a publication in its printed form, the easier it will be to retrieve the desired information online. The best technique is to make the search strategy mimic what you know to be the publication's design or idiosyncracies. For example, if one is looking for caricatures or cartoons representing a political figure -- Gary Hart, let's say -- it is very useful and cost-effective to know that the Christian Science Monitor and the Washington Post are ready sources for these items and that these "graphic" items are indexed in the GRAPHIC field of the online version of the paper. A suitable search strategy would be:

                LIBRARY: NEXIS
                FILE: CSM, WPOST

                GRAPHIC (CARTOON OR CARICATURE AND HART)

                              Figure 1

(Note: NEXIS does not require that the ORs be within parentheses because ORs are always processed first.)

Items retrieved would include:

                    The Christian Science Monitor
                    December 16, 1987, Wednesday

    SECTION: Editorial: Pg. 14

    BYLINE: JEFF DANZIGER - STAFF

    GRAPHIC: Cartoon, Amidst a group of eight spotlighted clowns, Gary Hart emerges from his car, striking a "Here I am!" pose ...

                              Figure 2

While the GRAPHIC segment is generally available for most newspapers in NEXIS the availability and indexing of a particular type of information is a matter of editorial policy at the particular newspaper. (Although cartoons appear in the "Perspectives" section of Newsweek, they are not available on the tape sent to vendors. There are no cartoons of Gary Hart -- or any other political figure -- in the venerable Times!)

4.   BURIED TREASURE

Let's turn our attention to the wonderful tidbits that we can pull out of NEXIS files. The above-mentioned GRAPHIC segment, used by itself or in conjunction with the TYPE or TERMS segment, can provide the searcher with fairly precise retrieval of charts and tables. Should you need to find data on the sales of personal computers, preferably a nice table, try the following:

```
LIBRARY: INFOBK
FILE:    NYT

GRAPHIC (CHART OR TABLE  OR GRAPH AND
        SALES OR REVENUE OR EARNINGS OR INCOME) AND
        PERSONAL COMPUTERS OR MICROCOMPUTERS
```

Figure 3

What the above example specifies is: Look for a chart or table or graph where the legend states "sale(s)" or "earning(s)" or "income(s)" or "revenue(s)" and also that the words "personal computer(s)" or "microcomputer(s)" appear somewhere in the story. Results would include stories featuring PC software companies with their revenues. To insure that the revenues are for personal computers instead of software, use subject indexing by specifying a TERMS segment as well.

```
M; AND TERMS (PERSONAL COMPUTERS)
```

Let's look at the case of the familiar Scoreboard issues of Business Week. To find the R & D expenditures of a particular company, the following (albeit a bit odd) strategy must be used:

```
LIBRARY: NEXIS
FILE:    BUSWK

SECTION(SCOREBOARD AND RESEARCH OR R&D OR R & D)
        AND MEAD
```

Figure 4

I cannot tell you why the Research Scoreboard is not consistently named, but the fact remains that in some issues the word "research" is used and in others the initialism "R&D" or "R & D" is used.

Current and historical financial statistics provide a goldmine of economic information. There are several excellent sources available on NEXIS. Finding the data quickly and cost-effectively however, requires some knowledge of the sources where the data can be found and, more specifically, the nuances of a particular publication's format and design. Although we would _like_ to believe that publications consistently follow a particular format, experience shows that in full text files "It ain't necessarily so."

In 1984, I made what I thought was a sound argument for the inclusion of indexing terms in search strategy.(2) While this practice is most useful for bibliographic files, it is less so for full-text files. Somehow, indexers of full-text documents seem to be less consistent in the application of subject terms -- or alternatively, indexers apply repetitive indexing. To wit: in a newspaper story containing a reporter's byline, <u>New York Times</u> indexers dutifully repeat the name -- inverted, of course -- in the NAME indexing segment. The problem here is that when people use the NAME segment, they expect that the person named is mentioned in the story, <u>not</u> the author of the story.

Meanwhile to cull stories about interest rates, bond rates, etc., from <u>The New York Times</u>, one cannot depend on the indexing. In order to ensure comprehensiveness, the following strategy must be used:

```
LIBRARY: INFOBK
FILE:    NYT

HEADLINE ((CURRENT OR KEY OR CONSUMER W/2 RATES)
         OR CREDIT MARKETS)
```

Figure 5

Because the column name (or headline) is not consistent -- you will note that CURRENT INTEREST RATES, CONSUMER RATES, and KEY RATES appear to be used interchangeably -- the indexing is not consistent, and the type of document identification is also inconsistent, the chance of finding the information one wants is relatively small unless you "know" the publication.

5. <u>CLEAR AS A BELL</u>

Another rich source of financial data is the "Figures of the Week" pages in <u>Business Week</u>. Each page, "Financial Figures of the Week" and "Figures of the Week" provides "current week," "week ago," "month ago," "year ago" and "1977 (or 1967) average," respectively. To retrieve numbers from the NEXIS version of this information, try this:

```
LIBRARY: NEXIS
FILE:    BUSWK
```

SECTION (FIGURES WEEK) AND GOLD

Figure 6

By using the KWIC display, one can zoom directly to the search words and pluck from the page those statistics desired. See Figure 7. The same technique can be used to extract "Financial Figures of the Week."

Two commonly used economic measures are the consumer price index and currency exchange rates. Both of these measures are available in NEXIS in Evans News Service, an Automatic Display File. To retrieve these indicators, the following strategy is used:

```
LIBRARY: GOVNWS
FILE:    ENS
```

(At this point in an ADF, the current day's records are automatically displayed.)

.NS;   (To begin a new search)

CONSUMER PRICE INDEX AND TYPE (FORECAST TABLES)

Figure 8

Other types of documents which might be useful here are ECONOMIC SNAPSHOTS or INSTANT ANALYSIS.

To pull daily historical exchange rates from Evans News Service, try:

.NS; DAILY HISTORICAL EXCHANGE RATES

Another source of information for exchange rates is the World Financial Markets file. Again, one must understand the format of the publication in order to retrieve the appropriate documents. In World Financial Markets, use the following strategy:

```
LIBRARY: NEXIS
FILE:    WLDFIN
```

SECTION (STATISTICAL APPENDIX) AND EXCHANGE RATE

Figure 9

Everyone seems to want that elusive measure "market share." This can often be found in the AMI file in INFOBANK or in Advertising Age (ADAGE) in NEXIS. One of my favorite sources for this information is the COIND file in the COMPNY library.

LEVEL 1 - 1 OF 4 STORIES

Copyright (c) 1987 McGraw-Hill, Inc.;
Business Week

December 28, 1987 / January 4, 1988

SECTION: INDEXES/ FIGURES OF THE WEEK; Business Week Index; Pg. 4

Note: This table may be divided, and additional information on a particular entry may appear on more than one screen.

LENGTH: 2199 words

BODY:

FIGURES OF THE WEEK

Gold/ Wed. final setting, London open mkt., troy oz.   Dec. 16

FIGURES OF THE WEEK

                                                        Latest
                                                        week

Gold/ Wed. final setting, London open mkt., troy oz. $ 486.300

FIGURES OF THE WEEK

                                                        Week
                                                        ago

Gold/ Wed. final setting, London open mkt., troy oz. $ 485.300

FIGURES OF THE WEEK

                                                        Month
                                                        ago

Gold/ Wed. final setting, London open mkt., troy oz. $ 463.700

FIGURES OF THE WEEK

                                                        Year
                                                        ago

Gold/ Wed. final setting, London open mkt., troy oz. $ 392.000

FIGURES OF THE WEEK

                                                        1967
                                                        average

Gold/ Wed. final setting, London open mkt., troy oz. $ 35.000

Figure 7

There is a special, very useful segment in this library called TABLE-INDEX. Here's the scenario:

        LIBRARY: COMPNY
        FILE: COIND

        MARKET W/5 SHARE W/35 TOOTHPASTE

        Figure 10

The above search yields 91 investment/research reports. Since these reports can be quite lengthy, with a wealth of detailed competitive information, we need a fast way to find a nice table displaying market share. Try the following format/display sequence:

        .SE; TABLE-INDEX

This sequence displays the TABLE-INDEX segment which contains a table-of-contents of the tables contained in the report. (See Figure 11). One can then zoom to the table desired by incorporating words or numbers in the table's caption in a subsequent search statement:

        M; AND TABLE 4

and then take advantage of the KWIC display to produce the data shown in Figure 12.

6. A PICTURE'S WORTH A THOUSAND WORDS

Searching for pictorial material, as for bibliographic material, produces an incomplete result. Often the desired information is not exactly in the online record, but the online record will tell us where to get the information. Identifying the source of a picture, map or photograph is fairly simple, but not necessarily straightforward. To find a map of Chile, for example, one might use the following:

        LIBRARY: INFOBK
        FILE: NYT

        GRAPHIC (MAP AND CHILE!)

        Figure 13

Note that the nominative and adjectival forms of the country are both retrieved by truncating the country name. It is also important to include the country name within the parentheses to insure that Chile or Chilean is in the caption of the map.

(c) 1987 Paine Webber Mitchell Hutchins Inc., July 2, 1987

TABLE-INDEX:

... industry Current earnings estimates

Table 2 Personal care industry Advertising by product category

Table 3 Toothpaste   market Advertising expenditures

 Table 4   Toothpaste   market Estimated quarterly market   share trends

Table 5 Feminine hygiene Advertising expenditures

Table 6 Sanitary napkins Estimated quarterly market   share trends

Table 7 Tampons Estimated quarterly market   share trends

Table 8 Shampoo market Advertising expenditures

Table 9 Shampoo market Estimated quarterly market share trends

Figure 11

Note: This table may be divided and additional information on a particular entry may appear on more than one screen.

Table 4
Toothpaste   market
Estimated quarterly market share trends

	1986				1987
	1 QTR	2 QTR	3 QTR	4 QTR	1 QTR
	%	%	%	%	%
PROCTOR & GAMBLE					
Crest	39	37	40	40	38
Gleem	2	2	2	2	2
Total	41	39	42	42	40
COLGATE-PALMOLIVE *					
Colgate	21	23	22	24	26
Ultrabrite	2	2	2	2	2
Total	23	25	24	26	27
UNILEVER					
Aim	5	6	6	6	7
Close-Up	5	5	5	5	6
Pepsodent	1	1	1	1	1
Total	11	12	12	11	13
BEECHAM					
Aquafresh	13	12	10	10	10
S.C. JOHNSON **					
Check-Up	2	2	1	1	1
ALL OTHERS	10	10	11	11	9
GRAND TOTAL	100	100	100	100	100

Figure 12

Use text in the caption to find other maps:

>   LIBRARY: NEXIS
>   FILE: NWEEK
>
>   GRAPHIC (MAP AND MUJAHEDIN)

Figure 14

Retrieval of pictures and photographs follows the same pattern. Need a photo of Texaco's chairman, Alfred DeCrane? Try:

>   LIBRARY: NEXIS
>   FILE: BUSWK
>
>   GRAPHIC (PHOTO! OR PICTURE W/3 DECRANE)

Figure 15

Like a recent photo of "what's-his-name" -- the young guy who's CEO of Microsoft? A snap.

>   LIBRARY: CMPCOM
>   FILE: FULL
>
>   DATE AFT 10/1987 AND
>   GRAPHIC (PHOTO! OR PICTURE AND CEO OR CHAIRMAN
>   AND MICROSOFT)

Figure 16

By using a specialty library (Computers and Communications), the probability is increased that you will find the photo desired.

7. <u>MY PARTING SHOT</u>

Richard Avedon, known primarily as a fashion photographer, has also delved into other areas of photography. To identify a collection of his work, use the following examples:

>   LIBRARY: NEXIS
>   FILE: OMNI
>
>   GRAPHIC (RICHARD AVEDON) OR
>   TERMS (RICHARD AVEDON)
>
>   (to find his photo credits and stories)

also
>   LIBRARY: COMPNY
>   FILE: ALLABS
>
>   RICHARD AVEDON AND NOT JOURNAL-CODE (NYT)
>
>   (because NYT was already found in NEXIS/OMNI)

Figure 17

The above sets will provide 116 photo credits or stories about Richard Avedon.

8. CONCLUSIONS

Successful searching for statistics, chart, tables and pictorial material can be accomplished. For the most part, however, more careful preparation is required in order to achieve the desired results. Rules to follow are:

1. Know which publications are likely to contain the information you need.

2. Determine whether the vendor has loaded graphic information for that publication.

3. Determine the appropriate segments (or fields) which contain the desired information and incorporate them in the search statement.

4. Take advantage of special display formats in a given file in order to format the data appropiately.

5. Ask for help from the vendor or the publisher.

References

1. Hardy, Nancy F. "Maximizing the Effectiveness of Online Searching - A Training and Education Model" Proceedings, 3d International Online Meeting, London, 1979.

2. Hardy, Nancy F. "Vagaries of Full-Text Searching in English" Presented at 8th International Online Meeting, London, 1984. Unpublished.

MARKETING STRATEGIES FOR PROMOTING ONLINE FULL-TEXT PRIMARY INFORMATION

John A. Hearty and Cynthia G. Smith, American Chemical Society

KEYWORD: Full text, integrated systems, primary information, marketing, end user, database.

ABSTRACT: To date, the increased availability of full-text primary journal literature online has not been accompanied by a corresponding growth in file usage and revenues. In light of the fact that research, at least in the hard sciences, can not be effectively pursued without access to primary information, there should be a greater demand reflected by usage for full-text primary journal databases. Use of full-text primary information online can be significantly increased by developing and implementing sound marketing strategies. Database vendors and producers of online full-text journal databases should actively promote the benefits and utility of their files. The concept of full-text by itself does not sell the product. Customers must be made aware of a product's applications. Database vendors and producers can go a long way towards correcting this problem by developing strategies that accent the applications and uses of their products. Before an effective strategy can be implemented by a database supplier, a clear understanding of the relationships between and among the following concepts is necessary: primary and secondary information, end users and search intermediaries, and active and passive customer support. In addition, the vendor and producer of online information must fully comprehend under what conditions their database becomes useful to the customer. Product positioning and user education can only be enhanced by a clear conception of these relationships on the part of the vendor and producer. If these relationships are not completely understood, then developing an effective marketing strategy will be difficult and the user community will suffer as will file usage and bottom-line profitability.

1. TYPOLOGY OF FULL-TEXT INFORMATION

When a database supplier begins to develop a marketing strategy for selling their online full text information, they usually encounter the dilemma of defining and delineating the type of full text database they want to promote. Most often all full text is lumped together and thought of in the aggregate. This is a mistake. Not all full text databases are similar. If increasing usage and bottom line profitability are the primary motivations for mounting a full text file, it is incumbent upon the database supplier to understand how the end user would use the database. In this regard, full text information is not all alike or equally useful.

There are a number of unique ways one can differentiate between types of full text information. Typically, full text online databases are categorized by size (total number of records) or subject area (social sciences, chemistry). In very few cases do database suppliers or vendors market or even discuss their full text products by delineating the way the end user would use them. End users, at least in the sciences, tend to categorize a database by whether its primary, secondary, or tertiary source of information. This definition is generally discipline dependent (i.e. chemistry, law, sociology).

Primary information is generally the first publication of a report, exposure or disclosure of a finding, a journal article or symposia in the hard sciences, a major speech by a political authority in political science, or a legal opinion in law.

Secondary sources of information are abstracts, indexes, or reviews taken from primary sources of information. In general, they are an indexer's or writer's interpretation of the original author's intent; the indexer/writer often does not include secondary or tertiary concepts from the article in the record, abstract, or controlled vocabulary. Certainly very few bibliographic databases or review articles include the author's citations, tables, or graphics, all relevant information to an article's discussion. In addition to bibliographic databases, secondary information can also be the full text of handbooks.

Tertiary sources of information are explanations or inferences drawn from primary information and in some cases secondary sources. Textbooks, technical manuals, or encyclopedias all of which are full text might be viewed as tertiary sources of information.

End users will usually search for and use these different types of information for very specific reasons. If an individual wanted a general feeling for or understanding of a subject area, or a specific numeric piece of noncritical data, one might go to tertiary information. A user not necessarily concerned with timeliness would use secondary information for breath (comprehensive) and depth (in terms of years) of coverage of a specific subject area.

End users will search through and use primary sources of information because it provides detailed, timely data, and/or because it is the record or statement of authority. If they need a critical piece of data, they must go to the primary source. It is generally not enough to know a piece of data or information; one must know how it was generated. In scientific investigation, you need to go back to the primary source; primary full text information is end user information and it is crucial to the research process.

Full text primary, secondary, and tertiary sources of information each has its own unique uses. Users of these sources of information either consciously or subconsciously employ this typology when making decisions on choosing the specific type of information to satisfy their requirements. The marketing professional should be aware of these subtilies in positioning and marketing. For the purposes of this paper, we are discussing marketing strategies for full text primary information. We will also generally be employing our experience from *CHEMICAL JOURNALS ONLINE (CJO)* because of our familiarity with it.

2. PRODUCT INTEGRATION

With the ever increasing number of online files provided by a plethora of vendors and database suppliers, users might feel that they have a large number of choices in fulfilling their information needs. In the sense that most of the information they need is available online, this is true. In most cases, however, one database will not usually provide the complete answer to a research question.

Traditionally, the biggest competitor to the primary full-text database is its corresponding secondary bibliographic database. The latter file has been a major resource for obtaining information on any given subject. The bibliographic database literature coverage is extensive in terms of depth and in terms of content (documents abstracted are usually world-wide). By contrast, the detailed coverage within the full-text files is one of its major benefits. The goal for the marketer is to link these two different types of databases together; to persuade the user to think of secondary and primary information not as competitive but rather as complementary.

There are two available methods for linking similar discipline related primary, secondary, and tertiary databases together. Technically, one can integrate the databases by developing super indexes, allowing simultaneous multi-file searching and displaying, or providing crossover capability between and among different files. All of these technical solutions would allow searchers the capability of taking information obtained in one file and utilizing to search another file or database.

The other method for linking different levels of information together is to market the concept of integrated information systems or holistic information retrieval systems. This method does not require special software development; it only necessitates an understanding on the part of the marketer on how the databases within a specific subject area are related to each other, and why an individual uses them electronically or in hard copy.

It is no longer enough for a marketer only to know his database, he must also be very familiar with other topically related files. Primary information suppliers must work with secondary owners not competitively but congruently. Full text primary database suppliers are the "new guys" on the block. It is thus incumbent upon them to seek the cooperative relationship necessary to ensure the success their files.

3. PRODUCT POSITIONING

There is little question that understanding the differences and relationships between and among primary, secondary, and tertiary sources of information will make a marketer's next task much easier. The relevancy of this typology becomes apparent when one starts to position the product in the market place.

Product positioning is by its very nature the single most important aspect of strategic planning. Before a single brochure can be written, the full text primary database owner must define the database user or segment the market; develop applications and benefits for using the database; and position the database in relationship to other topically similar databases.

Although each particular market has unique characteristics, the position types or job functions within each market are very similar. Due to costs and staff considerations, it is more cost-effective to design promotional strategy around like segments of the markets rather than the markets themselves. In this regard, two unique market segments have been delineated: end users and information specialists.

Full text primary information is primarily an end user database. Although this is by far the largest market, it is also the least advanced in terms of online experience and sophistication. Another important reason is that this group by and large has traditionally had very little online training experience.

The information specialist segment has been, and still remains in 1988, the focal point of most online market strategy. Even though end users are increasingly doing more of their own searching, information specialists are and will continue to be a very important market segment in the foreseeable future. They have assumed the role of teachers of online searching to end users, and they are the repositories of knowledge about online databases (what files contain what kinds of information). In addition, information intermediaries will continue to perform the more difficult searches or the searches for individuals who do not want to go online. For these reasons and for the role information specialists are playing in the budgeting and funding process for online information, database suppliers will have to direct a large percentage of their promotion dollars at this market segment.

The second important aspect to product positioning is defining specific user applications of the primary full text file. One must be aware that the benefits of obtaining the information online might have to be explained. It is still true today that an important competitor of primary online information are the paper editions or microfilm. In addition, the set of unique applications and benefits associated with use of the full-text online database must be end user oriented. It will be the end user (chemist or lab technician in the sciences) who will either be doing the searching or going to the information intermediary to have the searching done.

Some of the full text applications and benefits a database supplier will discover will be generic, such as finding information on secondary or tertiary concepts not indexed in the bibliographic database. Other applications, will by necessity, have to be uncovered. "Focus sessions" with information specialists and end users are an effective means of pinpointing other valuable applications.

A basic premise for developing and promoting a set of unique applications for full-text searches is that often users do not necessarily require a comprehensive retrieval of information; rather some relevant specific information that will help them. If users require a comprehensive search for concepts, they would use the more comprehensive bibliographic database. If they need specific information on unique applications, they would use the full-text database.

Full-text's primary benefit (as defined by our product positioning) is to search for information that is not easily accessable in other databases or in the hard copy. A secondary benefit is to display full-text document records online. The main advantage of displaying full-text records online is to determine whether or not the search has resulted in a relevant retrieval of information. A note of caution, as a document delivery vehicle, the full-text database is not as useful due to high costs.

The third important aspect of product positioning is situating the the database in relationship to other topically similar databases. As stated before, primary full-text information should not be isolated from discipline related secondary or tertiary sources of information. When these different levels information are used together, they form a one stop research supermarket. The capability of searching, browsing and downloading primary information will be an integral part of an integrated database.

In an integrated system, searchers are able to take information obtained in one file and utilize it in context with another file. Single files become more than just single files--they are turned into the building blocks of a total search strategy. The entire file can be used conceptually, rather than just alone.

4. MARKETING STRATEGIES & POSITIONING

The foundation for developing strategy for marketing a database relies on three major factors: the marketer's total understanding of the database and how it fits in the competitive field; the users or target market of the product; and most importantly, why users access the database -- applications. Combining the analysis from all this information and properly integrating it should provide a clear direction on what strategies should be used to properly position the database in each target market.

As previously defined, the major markets for full-text primary journals are information specialists/librarians who tend to be more experienced searchers and, end users, who at this point in time, are mostly novices. It is primarily for this reason that in developing a marketing plan, various strategies and approaches must be considered for each target market. In the case of the more experienced searcher, development of a technical manual, occasional updates on new file applications, availability of a Help Desk and infrequent contact by phone or visit might suffice in getting the product launched to that market. For the more novice end user, obviously more technical training, instructional materials and personal contact is necessary to ensure that the user will be comfortable with the database and thus become a repeat user.

The next logical question is how much marketing effort should be done by a database supplier in conjunction with the host vendor? This can only be answered after thorough analysis of the supplier's internal marketing resources. Is there sufficient marketing staff to handle many of the required functions (ie. sales calls, training, publicity, promotion)? Or is it something best left entirely to the vendor? Or maybe a combination of resources from the vendor and the database supplier? For the purpose of this discussion we will use the following definitions to define the type of marketing participation:

a.	Passive	Total reliance by the database supplier on the vendor for generic marketing of the file;
b.	Moderate	Joint effort between the vendor and the database supplier on defined areas of marketing;
c.	Aggressive	Database supplier is primarily responsible for marketing effort.

5. MARKETING APPROACHES

In developing effective marketing approaches and to what extent the database supplier will participate (passive, moderate, aggressive), three major criteria must be reviewed by the marketer for each defined market: experience level of the searcher; current product awareness; and the vendor's planned marketing activity. It can be assumed that the majority of vendors will provide a range of basic generic marketing services (ie. applicable to all databases) in the following major areas: publicity, promotion, direct sales, customer training and support. These services are usually general in their approach and do not highlight one database over another.

Analyzing what is presently covered by the vendor's plan, combined with the suggested analysis of the database supplier's internal marketing resources, should give the marketer enough direction to integrate the defined approach with the appropriate participatory action in developing a sound marketing plan catered to that particular database.

The following chart illustrates the various levels of marketing participation a database supplier may wish to assume given the choice of participatory action.

DATABASE SUPPLIER MARKETING ACTION PLAN			
MARKETING APPROACHES	(DATABASE SUPPLIER) TYPE OF ACTION		
	PASSIVE	MODERATE	AGGRESSIVE
PUBLICITY			
Press Releases	X	X	X
Exhibits		X	X
Product Presentations/Conferences			X
PROMOTION			
Space Ads	X	X	X
Direct Mail			X
Newsletters/Bulletins		X	X
DIRECT SALES			
Sales Reps			X
Sales Literature		X	X
Demonstration Disks			X
Workshops			X
International Reps			X
CUSTOMER TRAINING/SUPPORT			
Technical Manuals	X	X	X
Training Sessions			X
Learning Modules			X
Help Desks		X	X

Publicity

Publicity's main function is to promote product awareness through press releases and feature articles in targeted media, exhibits at expositions directed at a specific market, and product presentations and papers at related conferences, symposiums, and seminars. Of the three types of publicity, press releases and feature articles are the least expensive and should be part of every database supplier's marketing plan. Both exhibits and product presentations obviously involve more staff and travel, however, provide a unique opportunity to publicize and demonstrate specific applications of a database to the targeted market.

Promotion

Promotion consists of direct communication between the database supplier and targeted market. Development of space ads emphasizing specific database applications to the user is an effective approach in attracting customer interest. Placement of such ads can be in the database supplier's own publications, or if more funds are available, in outside media targeted to the desired audience.

A direct mail program is effective in building a customer prospect list by generating direct requests through specific offers. Example of such offers include free connect time, a special premium such as a poster or learning module, or other database related items. The direct mail package can be a simple self-mailer, a full package with a brochure, or a more expensive three-dimensional type mailing that might include a premium. Size of the potential market and budgetary considerations will dictate what format to use and how large the mailing, bearing in mind that the goal is to generate and develop a defined customer prospect list.

Periodic newsletters or bulletins allow a database supplier to stay in constant contact with both current and prospective customers. It can include: news on the database; latest developments and cost-saving suggestions on full-text searching; announcements on seminars, workshops, and upcoming conferences; specific search examples featuring important applications; question and answer column; information on enhancements. Newsletters can also be an effective tool for generating customer feedback by periodically including mini-surveys.

Direct Sales

Direct sales involves direct, personal contact with current and prospective customers by sales representatives. This is a costly approach but highly effective in building customers and ultimately usage of a database. Sales reps can be assigned by territory or customer type (academic, industrial, government) and are usually compensated by salary plus incentive bonus or commission based on performance goals. Whether a database supplier uses their own sales staff or that of a vendor, sales brochures and leave behind literature should be developed emphasizing the databases' features, benefits, and most importantly, applications.

In addition, sales reps can schedule on-site workshops featuring lectures and hands-on demonstrations for major accounts. For smaller accounts, PC Demo Disks designed to demonstrate the major applications of the database have proved to be cost-effective in maintaining direct contact.

If a database has international appeal, then additional attention should be given to key international areas such as Japan, England, Northern and Central Europe. The international market is best served by establishing international reps in each major targeted region. As in the case with foreign subscription agents who are retained to market printed products, international sales reps specializing in electronic publishing are best suited in locating and handling customers (i.e. workshops, help desks, training manuals in their own language) in their respective regions with support from the database supplier. Compensation for international reps can be in the form of a flat fee or percentage of sales. It is important that the database supplier request detailed action plans from each international rep and establish annual goals as proper measurement of effectiveness.

Customer Training/Support

Customer training/support is the key to developing repeat usage of a database by customers. Bearing in mind that if a database contains information that a customer needs and is easily accessible, then repeat usage will occur. The key to this is providing proper initial search training in an effort to minimize initial customer frustration. Every database should have a technical manual designed uniquely for that database. In addition, other technical materials such as strategy guides, search planners, and specific guides targeted to novice and expert users can be developed to augment the basic manual. Database applications should be emphasized in all technical material.

Technical training sessions developed specifically by the database supplier provide a useful means of dealing directly with customers. They should be designed to not only introduce the customer to the unique applications of the database that may not be covered in a vendor's general training session, but also give enough hands-on instruction to ensure that the customer is comfortable with the database and able to secure desired information. Sessions can be scheduled either onsite for the customer depending on the potential size of an account, or in public sessions in conjunction with the vendor's general training.

Developing and providing interactive (self-taught) learning modules is a relatively new approach of training. It has come about as database suppliers have begun expanding their customer base beyond the traditional information specialists/librarians into the end user market. Learning modules can take shape in many formats: PC Interactive Disks, learning files, and training video tapes. Although initial programming development may be somewhat costly for these modules, the actual production is relatively inexpensive and highly cost effective in reaching a large market. In addition, small fees can be charged for the modules thus recouping initial investment.

Help Desks provided by the vendor should be sufficient in handling typical search strategy questions. However, database suppliers can reinforce customer support by providing additional help desks related to facilitating editorial/database content questions.

6. SUMMARY

- When full text databases are thought of in the aggregate, it often confuses the user and inhibits usage. It would be much clearer to the the user if database suppliers categorized a database by whether its a primary, secondary, or tertiary source of information.

- Full text primary database suppliers need to work with other topically similiar database owners in order to design and develop joint promotions which will conceptually link the different levels of information together.

- Although full text primary information is end user data, information specialists, for the foreseeable future, will be the primary searchers. Promotions to the end user community are still very important.

- Database suppliers should promote the applications and benefits of their information rather than market their databases as an alternative document delivery vehicle.

- Marketing strategy depends on a total understanding of the database's position in the competitive field, the types of users or target market for the database, and the respective applications.

- Based on an internal evaluation of marketing resources, a database supplier must decide the degree of marketing effort they will provide in conjunction with the host vendor -- passive, moderate, or aggressive and apply that to each major marketing approach: Publicity, Promotion, Direct Sales, and Customer Training/Support.

CD-ROM AND APPLE MACINTOSH: MARKET OPPORTUNITIES

Lyndon S. Holmes, Aries Systems Corporation

Keywords: CD-ROM, Apple Macintosh, Information Markets, Database Publishing

Abstract: The growing acceptance of Apple Computer, Inc.'s, Macintosh computer as a serious tool for business and professional applications creates opportunities and challenges for CD-ROM applications. This paper examines the background of CD-ROM application development for the Macintosh, reviews current product offerings, and assesses technological and market challenges associated with such products. It also suggests options, risks and opportunities for database producers and publishers.

1. HISTORICAL BACKGROUND

CD-ROM technology and publications have evolved as peripheral, subordinate components to microcomputer technology. The typical CD-ROM application requires substantial computing power to handle the large amounts of data stored on the optical disc. Accordingly, most CD-ROM applications tend to use the more powerful members of a microcomputer product line.

Microcomputer configurations amenable to CD-ROM integration fall into two principle camps - IBM PC's and clones and derivatives on the one side; and Apple's Macintosh on the other. This categorization does not intend to ignore other vendors or products in the microcomputer arena. However, they tend to occupy more specialized niches, which by their nature and focus diminish their potential as "mass" market opportunities (if one can today talk of CD-ROM and mass markets in the same sentence!).

The vast majority of CD-ROM applications implemented to date have been targeted for the IBM PC/PS family of microcomputers. The reasons for this are several:

- The high market domination and acceptance of IBM PC technology two to three years ago, when today's CD-ROM products were in their formative stages. CD-ROM producers at that time really had only this one, viable microcomputer vehicle through which to deliver their products.
- CD-ROM drive manufacturers facilitated integration of their drives with the PC by developing and offering PC-compatible device controllers.
- Microsoft's CD-ROM High Sierra extension software was perceived by CD-ROM developers to facilitate the software/hardware integration task.

In fact, PC-operable CD titles now number in the hundreds, with a growth rate that is probably logarithmic. And this does not include many privately-published titles, which tend to receive no publicity.

By contrast, and with few exceptions, CD-ROM has yet still to come to the Apple Macintosh. One can look to the reasons that the PC and CD-ROM have married, and see diametric reasons for this not having happened with the Macintosh:

- Until recently, the Macintosh has lacked the professional aura attributed to the PC. It was viewed, variously, as a toy, cute, too small (from a variety of perspectives), etc.
- The Mac uses SCSI to communicate with mass storage peripherals. CD-ROM manufacturers characteristically have not developed SCSI compatibility for their drives until their PC-based products have been proven.
- No facilitating interface software was available to CD-ROM producers, either from Apple or third parties.

2. **THE STATE TODAY**

While the Macintosh is certainly "late out of the gate", we believe that there exist today unique opportunities for Macintosh CD-ROM products. Indeed, any CD-ROM producer not seriously considering Macintosh-based products may be at a serious competitive disadvantage within a couple of years.

2.1 **Acceptance of Macintosh Technology**

The original Macintosh introduced in 1984 was both innovative and underpowered. Its innovativeness, heritage and unusual physical and visual appearance earned it various diminutive characterizations. Its minimal memory of 128KBytes, combined with a scarcity of power applications, made it particularly unattractive to professional users.

Just four years later, the Mac is now a very different machine. With the new 68000 series processors, multiple megabytes of memory, a myriad of large capacity peripherals, powerful software development systems, and an exploding range of application software, it offers serious challenge to the traditional dominance of IBM.

In 1987, Macintosh sales were approximately 500,000 units. However, in typical professional user environments, the Mac now accounts for a small 5%-15% of installations. By contrast, the PC accounts for 60%-70% of installations. One can look at this difference negatively and positively. The pessimist will conclude that the Macintosh base is much too small to merit consideration, and will bypass it. The optimist (and perhaps the opportunist) will see a glowing market opportunity. Since the Macintosh is now experiencing a much higher level of acceptance, the low penetration suggests a large growth potential for the Mac.

Particularly in professional applications, we have seen a trend to favor the Mac over the PC. For users who cannot take a lot of time to learn a new technology, the Mac offers rapid access to powerful computing. The high level of consistency between applications on the Mac means that the time and effort required to learn a new application is considerably less with the Mac than with the PC. Further, the Mac environment seems to encourage the development of more sophisticated applications which appeal to the high expectations of professional users.

All this suggests that the Macintosh today has a high level of appeal to the "upscale" professional market, and may well outpace the PC in associated market segments. In turn, we can expect that high-quality, professional CD-ROM products will experience substantial popularity in these markets.

But perhaps the best characterization of where the Macintosh stands today is given by comments from the leading PC publication, *PC Magazine*. "...when the 'good stuff' hit about a year and a half ago, the [Macintosh] machine finally began to make the metamorphosis from Yuppie totem to business computer." (Ref. 1). And in the same issue (remember, this publication is PC base camp!) "The IBM world has ... *Windows*, which naive users assume is similar to the Mac interface. It's not. The *Windows* Executive is laughable when compared with the Mac operating system and interface." (Ref. 2).

2.2 Current Macintosh CD-ROM Applications

The validity of the CD-ROM market on the Macintosh is to some degree predicated on existing applications. When this paper was written (February, 1988) there existed a small number of commercially available or announced CD-ROM products for Macintosh. Currently available (i.e., deliverable) products include:

- Aries Systems' MEDLINE® Knowledge Finder™ (North Andover, MA).
- Laserscan Systems' RealScan™ Real Estate Market Information System (Miami, FL).
- Multi-Ad's InHouse advertising art (Peoria, IL).

Other products that have been announced include:

- Software Mart's Visual Dictionary (Austin, TX).
- R. R. Bowker's Books-In-Print (New York, NY).
- Point Foundation's Whole Earth Catalog (Sausalito, CA).
- Highlighted Data's Electronic Map Cabinet; Merriam-Webster 9th Collegiate Dictionary (Washington, DC).

Since 1988 is likely to be a pivotal year for CD-ROM product announcements, we can expect to see other product offerings soon, perhaps even before this paper is presented.

2.3 Technology Support for the Macintosh Environment

CD-ROM development and publishing in a particular machine environment requires an infrastructure of supporting tools. Many of these are now available for the Macintosh:

- The SCSI (Small Computer System Interface) protocol for connecting to storage peripherals is fully supported by the Macintosh. Many CD-ROM drives now support SCSI; most or all should in the future. A correctly developed software driver for an SCSI CD-ROM drive has a very high likelihood of working unchanged with other SCSI CD-ROM drives. By contrast, most PC-connected CD-ROM drives each require a different software driver interface, complicating the development and support task.
- The following vendors currently offer packaged CD-ROM development systems:
  - Meridian Data (Capitola, CA)
  - LoDown (Scotts Valley, CA)

These and other packaged development systems run on a Macintosh, provide large capacity magnetic storage for database formatting, offer magnetic tape for data import and export, and may include tools to simulate CD-ROM environment performance. Needless to say, availability of a CD-ROM development system is a prerequisite to developing a CD-ROM product for the Macintosh.

2.4 What the Mac Can Do Today that the PC Can't

The Mac interface and stylistic consistency

Apple's almost religious encouragement to its developers to follow the Macintosh interface standards is not dogmatism - it's a powerful business strategy. Since most successful Mac applications do follow these interface guidelines and standards, a Mac user finds learning a new application simple. Further, intermixed use of multiple applications requires the user to remember considerably fewer sets of disparate commands. As a result, the typical Mac user runs 45% more applications than their PC user counterpart (Ref 3.).

What this says is that the Mac is easier to use than the PC, and that this encourages greater levels of Mac-related purchases.

Inter-machine compatibility

Unlike the PC/PS family, the Macintosh family offers a very high degree of inter-machine compatibility, based on the Motorola 68000-series microprocessor. Many applications written for the Mac Plus have run unmodified on the Mac SE and Mac II, and will most likely run unmodified on future 68000-series processors.

The IBM PC/PS family presently offers a variety of incompatibilities, at both the hardware level (8086/80286/80386 memory management strategies, for example), and at the software level (e.g., DOS versus OS/2; Presentation Manager versus Windows; etc.).

From the perspective of a software developer concerned with strategic evolution of a software product across many generations of hardware, the ability to write the software once, and not have to redevelop it for each new machine family member, is a powerful attraction. This consideration was a primary reason for Aries Systems' choice of the Macintosh as a vehicle for its Knowledge Finder text and bibliographic retrieval system.

Large memory space

All Macintoshes support very large real memory spaces - up to 16MB can be installed (and used!) today on a Mac II. Even the early Mac Plus can support (and use) 4MB of memory. Compared to the DOS PC's 640KB limit, the Mac offers both developer and user substantially greater flexibility and efficiency - more useable memory means that I can do more things in the machine at the same time, and without the need for various convoluted strategies.

Data import and export

Most Macintosh applications are written to allow convenient import and export of data through the cut-and-paste metaphor. For example, a graphic created in MacPaint can be imported into most word processing programs. Bibliographic citations retrieved from Aries Systems' Knowledge Finder can be transferred effortlessly into Personal Bibliographic Software's Pro-Cite™ bibliography management system. Apple's definition of standards for these data transfer functions results in a high level of inter-application compatibility. And this means better, more convenient tools for the user that increase user productivity.

3. **Markets Opportunities for Macintosh CD-ROM Products**

The Macintosh fills an interesting position in the spectrum of microcomputer products. At its low end (the Mac Plus and the Mac SE), it is definitely a "Personal Computer", to be found in the home, schools and colleges, and in a variety of work environments. The high end Mac II is clearly a "Professional Workstation" class machine, appealing to and eligible for demanding processing applications.

Given the current typical costs of CD-ROM drives, production and distribution, the short term opportunities will be found primarily in the professional, academic and work environments. These markets will probably limit individual CD-ROM volumes to hundreds or thousands of a particular publication. Drive and disc prices between $750 and $1,500 (where they are today), will clearly limit volumes.

As the professional markets mature, we can expect growth into personal and consumer markets, with opportunities for tens or hundreds of thousands of copies of a publication. This will occur as a result of growing recognition of CD-ROM as an information dissemination vehicle (both by publishers and consumers), and by prices. We should anticipate CD-ROM drive prices in the $200-$300 range, and disc prices in the range of $30-$50.

3.1 **Existing PC-Based CD-ROM Products**

Many of the more popular PC-based CD-ROM products should be prime candidates for implementation in the Macintosh environment. MEDLINE is already available on the Macintosh through Aries Systems' Knowledge Finder system. ERIC, NTIS and other public domain databases are immediate candidates for implementation on the Macintosh.

As the Mac becomes more accepted within the corporate world (a year ago, 50% of corporations approved Mac's; today over 85% approve), we can expect the producers of business-related CD products to convert them to the Macintosh.

3.2 **Commonly-Mentioned Future Applications**

While delivered applications to date have been few, many have been discussed, and it's perhaps these leading indicators that best foretell the potential for the Macintosh world.

Apple's Hypercard has been billed (amongst other things) as the gateway/frontend to CD-ROM databases. While this may be somewhat wishful and untested (i.e., Hypercard's questionable performance on large databases, and the implications of CD-ROM publishing for the "casual" publisher), there is undoubtedly some level of opportunity through this vehicle.

The Macintosh is ideally suited to the display and manipulation of graphic images. Graphics take up large amounts of storage, typically 40KB to 80KB per image. On any useful scale, floppy disk is logistically impractical for image distribution, high-capacity serial tape is too immature, and hard disk is economically infeasible. This leaves a gaping opportunity for CD-ROM.

Every Macintosh is delivered with flexible audio generation facilities (albeit lacking symphonic capabilities, unless you buy an add-on board!). This means that products incorporating audio are a "natural" for the Macintosh.

Let me suggest a few application areas, where the Mac's unique capabilities (especially graphics) offer exciting opportunities:

- National Real Estate listing services, with pictures, floor layouts, etc.
- Color Clip-Art (the high resolution and wide color range of the Mac II are particularly suited).
- Reference works (encyclopedia and dictionaries) where fine resolution graphics and even audio give significant added value to the product.
- Product catalogs, where a picture is worth a thousand words.
- Chemical structure databases, with three-dimensional representations of structures.

4. POTENTIAL CHALLENGES AND BARRIERS

Despite these potentials, we see a number of hurdles to successful CD-ROM development and marketing in the Macintosh world:

4.1   CD-ROM on the Macintosh?

A common myth that exists today is that CD-ROM does not work on the Macintosh, and only on the PC This clearly is a myth! None the less, this is a perception that exists even amongst many of the more sophisticated buyers in the CD-ROM marketplace. Macintosh CD-ROM vendors will have to spend time, energy and dollars to reverse this perception.

4.2   CD-ROM Player Costs

A typical SCSI-compatible CD-ROM drive today retails for $1200 to $1500. This is up to twice the perceived price in the IBM world, and several times the valued price by end users, who tend not to be able to discriminate between audio CD players at $200-300, and their digital counterpart. The basic reaction is "What a rip-off" (and are they really so far off the mark?). So the CD database buyer's decision is less, today, should I buy the database, as opposed to "Can I afford the player". And when the cost of the player approaches the cost of the computer, the answer is often "No". So, we must find ways to bring the cost of players down. And this can only be accomplished by persuading the manufacturers that there are potentially very large markets. And this in turn requires a healthy number of CD database products. Bring on the entrepreneurs, please!!

As an object lesson, let's just review the decline in CD-ROM mastering costs (which has been driven exclusively by demand from the PC side of the house). Two years ago, typical mastering costs (excluding data preparation) were $10,000 to $15,000, and $20 per disk. Today, we see mastering available for $3,000 to $5,000, and replication as low as $4-5 per disk. Clearly, current and future market opportunity has encouraged the CD-ROM disc manufacturers. Now, we need to apply the same mechanism to the other side of the equation, the database purchasers.

4.3   Complexity of Macintosh Software Development

Good Macintosh software has earned the reputation of being difficult to develop. This is true!

The Mac software environment is intrinsically different than traditional programming environments. Even experienced programmers take many months to master the fundamentals of Macintosh programming. And acquiring the skill to design a good user interface that takes advantage of the Mac's tools can take significantly longer. A common mistake made by PC developers is to assume that the Mac is a PC with graphics, and that PC applications can be easily "ported" to the Macintosh. This strategy invariably fails, since the resulting product does not have the true flavor of a Macintosh application. The programmer must either forget most of what they've learned in the PC environment, or else the Mac development task must be given to an individual who is not prejudiced by the PC applications environment.

Successful Mac software products are also rare because the Mac community demands unusually high quality software, and quickly and vocally rejects substandard offerings. These high expectations place a further burden on the developer, requiring an unwavering commitment to excellence in the software product. However, since high quality almost always sells well, this only suggests market opportunities!

4.4 Will the Mac Last?

The Macintosh has been around for only 3-4 years. So far, its unique properties and characteristics have been emulated but not duplicated. This uniqueness creates the present opportunity. However, there is evidence that a "universal" user interface that possesses many of the Macintosh characteristics may evolve within the next half decade. When (rather than if) this occurs, some portion of the Mac's competitive advantage and appeal will erode. Accordingly, any CD-ROM strategy built around the Macintosh should incorporate an option to migrate to other vendor's technologies within a 3-5 year period. Undoubtedly, any vendor who has adopted Macintosh technology into their product line will have a far easier transition to this universal environment.

5. CONCLUSIONS

The Macintosh is not just a collection of compatible machines. More significantly, Macintosh is a collection of concepts, that says there's a better way for people to use computer and information technology. As with all change, it's taking time to alter the market's perception of what's "right" in computer interface technology.

At the beginning of 1988, many of the "industry experts" are forecasting that CD-ROM will experience explosive growth over the next few years. Simultaneously, we are now experiencing steep increases in the acceptance of the Macintosh technology. And today, there are a mere handful of CD-ROM products for the Macintosh. So, for the venturing publisher, this may be one of the rare occasions to truly "get in on the ground floor".

6. REFERENCES

1. Seymour, Jim. What's Inside. PC Magazine, Vol. 6, No. 20, p. 4, November 24, 1987.
2. Dvorak, John C. Double Standard. PC Magazine, Vol. 6, No. 20, p. 94-101, November 24, 1987.
3. MacWeek, Vol. 1, No. 32, p. 1, December 15, 1987.

AN EVALUATION OF A GATEWAY SYSTEM FOR AUTOMATED ONLINE DATABASE SELECTION

Chengren Hu, University of Illinois

Keywords: Online Systems, Interfaces, Gateways, Database Selection, Artificial Intelligence

Abstract: An evaluation of automated online database selection by an existing gateway system (INFOMASTER, a version of EASYNET) was performed at the University of Illinois at Urbana-Champaign. The results of automated database selection by INFOMASTER were compared with the databases selected manually by four experienced online reference librarians for the same queries. The comparison shows that database selection by INFOMASTER still heavily depends on human judgements, especially the selection by searchers of the subject field in which a query falls. INFOMASTER could select databases as well as human intermediaries when the gateway user properly selected the subject area for a particular query. Some suggestions for improving automated database selection by a gateway system with artificial intelligence techniques are outlined.

1. Introduction

The tremendous growth of computer-readable databases and online systems makes automated database selection very desirable in online services, especially as an aid to inexperienced searchers. Since the 1980s, various kinds of gateway systems (or interfaces, front-ends, and intermediary systems) have converted information among online systems and aided the users in various ways including database selection.[1-2] The research reported in this paper sought to determine the effectiveness, problems, and techniques of gateway systems for automated database selection through an evaluation of an existing gateway system (INFOMASTER of Western Union, which is based on EASYNET of Telebase Systems, Inc.) that includes the capability to select databases in online services.[3]

2. Hypothesis and Methodology

This study was conducted to compare the databases selected by inexperienced online searchers, aided by a particular gateway, with those chosen by experienced searchers performing online searches in response to patron requests in a university library. The topics for which the selections were made were the same for both groups.[4]

The study hypothesized that the inexperienced searchers aided by the gateway would do as well as the experienced professional searchers in selecting databases likely to be most productive in their yield of potentially relevant items. "Likely to be most productive" refers to probabilistic criteria - the more potentially relevant items the database contains, the greater the chance that some at least will be found when the database is searched online. In other words, this comparison was limited to a quantitative measure of search results from the databases selected by both groups.

The study was done at the University of Illinois at Urbana-Champaign from February through March of 1987. Seventy-five students in the Graduate School of Library and Information Science of the University of Illinois at Urbana-Champaign participated in this study. They had just started an online searching course at the end of January 1987 and had no prior online searching experience, so they were considered to be the "inexperienced searchers". Four professional online reference librarians from four departmental libraries (Engineering Library, Education and Social Sciences Library, Agriculture Library, and General Reference Library) participated in the study as the "experienced professional searchers", who had online searching experience of between two and six years. INFOMASTER, as a test gateway system selected for this study, provides access to over 800 databases on seventeen online systems, thus offering a wide subject area for the test of database selection. Fifty search queries were selected from the actual searches which had been conducted by the experienced searchers (librarians) from December 1986 through January 1987 in four departmental libraries. Data about these queries for online searching, such as search topic, type of document needed, the subject field, and the key words for the search topic, as well as a record of the database selected and the search strategy used, were provided by the librarians. Inexperienced searchers were given the information about the queries prior to logging on to INFOMASTER. Each student searched two different topics and each query was searched by three different students, so that there was a total of 150 searches done by seventy-five students searching fifty queries on INFOMASTER.

To effect the comparison of database selections, a Posting Database (PD) for each search query tested was established as the standard. The databases listed in the PD for each query were those that appeared to contain at least one potentially relevant item for the query. These databases were identified on the basis of the occurrence of topical keywords or phrases of the query in database indexes, either through DIALOG's DIALINDEX or through BRS's BRS/CROS, depending on which online system the librarian searched for a particular query because all these fifty queries had been searched by librarians with only BRS or DIALOG system. The search statement for each search topic used for establishing a PD was formulated by the researcher based on information supplied by the librarians (the same information supplied to the students). Only those keywords occurring in the title of the search were used. The number of items for each database in the PD should indicate the relative probability of locating potentially relevant items on the search topic in each database. When performing the comparisons of database selection by librarians and by INFOMASTER operated by students, the standard for numbers of items retrieved from the databases was based on the PD. (See APPENDIX: Example of PD.) In this way, it was possible to avoid the problems caused by the fact that the students and the librarians would be searching at different times and with different search strategies. That is, if a database selected (by INFOMASTER or by the librarian) could be found in the PD for a particular query, the number of items considered to be retrieved from this database for the comparison was the number of items indicated in the PD for this database. If the database selected by INFOMASTER was not already in the PD, the database would be searched with the search strategy used for the PD of the corresponding query to establish the number of postings.

Since three students searched the same query using INFOMASTER, there were three possible cases for the consistency of database selection by INFOMASTER: (1) all three searches selected the same database for a particular query; (2) two searches had the same database selections but another was different; (3) three searches for the same query had all different databases selected. For the inconsistent cases of database selections, there would be three results (for case (2) above, only two results) based on the number of items retrieved from the three databases selected: best result, middle result, and worst result. In this study, only the best and worst gateway results were used to compare with those databases selected by the librarians. That means, it would test whether in the best result of database selection from INFOMASTER, the gateway (INFOMASTER) could (or couldn't) select the database for a particular query as well as the human intermediary; and whether in the worst result, INFOMASTER could (or couldn't) select the databases as well as human intermediaries.

3. Research Results

The 150 searches for fifty queries by seventy-five students (inexperienced searchers) through INFOMASTER used a total of six online systems accessible through INFOMASTER with twenty-four different databases selected for these queries. (For comparison, sixteen databases from two online systems (BRS & DIALOG) were used by librarians for these fifty queries). Among the six online systems involved, ninety-nine of 150 searches were conducted on DIALOG (66 percent of the total number of searches), twenty-eight on BRS (18.7 percent), thirteen on SDC (8.7 percent), five on Data-Star (3.3 percent), three on Pergamon InfoLine (2.0 percent) and two on WilsonLine (1.3 percent). DIALOG and BRS were the major online systems used in the INFOMASTER online network for these searches.

Statistical comparisons of database selections between librarians and INFOMASTER operated by students were conducted to investigate the hypothesis of this research. Two cases were analyzed: gateway best result and gateway worst result (as explained above) with results reported in Table 1. The gateway best result supported the hypothesis, i.e., in the gateway best result INFOMASTER could lead the inexperienced searchers to select databases as good as those selected by the librarians. But the result in the gateway worst case failed to support the hypothesis.

The consistency of database selections between librarians and INFOMASTER operated by students is detailed in Table 2. In the gateway best result, twenty-nine queries (consistency of 0.58) had the same databases selected by librarians and by INFOMASTER. Thirteen queries had the best databases as ranked by PD selected by INFOMASTER (but fourteen queries had the best databases as ranked by PD selected by librarians). Twenty-one queries had inconsistent database selections by librarians and INFOMASTER with the librarian making the better choice in thirteen cases and INFOMASTER making the better choice in eight. In the gateway worst result, twenty-eight queries had the same databases selected by librarians and INFOMASTER (consistency of 0.56). Only five queries had the best databases as ranked by PD selected by INFOMASTER. For the twenty of twenty-two queries, which had different database selections between the two groups, librarians selected the better databases.

The consistency of database selections by INFOMASTER for the same query among three students is shown in Table 3. Thirty-two queries (consistency of 0.64) had consistent database choices. Among those eighteen queries with inconsistent database selection from INFOMASTER, fifteen of them had two different choices and three had with three choices.

In addition, the results of a questionnaire survey to the students who participated in this study are reported in Table 4, which can supplement the evaluation of INFOMASTER for database selection from the viewpoints of searchers. Most of the searchers (92 percent) felt that INFOMASTER was easy to use. Fifty-four of seventy-five searchers (72 percent) thought that INFOMASTER was helpful for database selections. Forty percent of searchers spent less than fifteen minutes for two searches in INFOMASTER (each search was limited to up to ten citations printed out). Fifty-two percent of searchers spent from sixteen to thirty minutes for two searches. Only six searchers spent over thirty minutes but no one spent over one hour.

4. Analysis of Database selection by INFOMASTER

From searching INFOMASTER in this study, one can see that the procedures of automated database selection by INFOMASTER are through narrowing down the subject fields (usually less than six hierarchical subdivisions for a subject category) of a particular query based on the subject selection by a human searcher from a series of menus (including choosing a type of document after the most specific subject field is selected) The subject fields and the types of documents were categorized in a hierarchical structure designed by the INFOMASTER system. All subjects and types of documents selected by searchers must be within the hierarchical subject lists pre-organized by the system.

From the research results, when the subjects and types of documents selected by human searchers of INFOMASTER were the same as those selected by librarians, the databases selected by INFOMASTER could be as good as the librarian's but few could be better than the librarian's choices. When the subjects and types of documents selected by the searchers of INFOMASTER differed from the librarian's, INFOMASTER usually selected different databases, of which some might be better databases (when the subjects selected by INFOMASTER's searchers were better than the librarian's). Therefore, the subject selected by the human searcher is the key factor influencing database selection of INFOMASTER. That is, "automated" database selection by INFOMASTER actually still depends heavily on human judgement.

However, since all subjects selected by the searchers must be limited by the hierarchical lists of subject fields designed by INFOMASTER, the subject selections not only depended on human judgement but are also limited by INFOMASTER's system design for subject categories. Queries in interdisciplinary subjects, of which the subjects might not be covered in the subject lists of INFOMASTER for selections, proved very hard for searchers to select the suitable subjects. It is one of the important reasons leading to the worst results for database selection by INFOMASTER.

As for the consistency of database selections by INFOMASTER for the same query, it was also mainly influenced by the different subjects selected by different searchers of INFOMASTER. Table 3 shows the inconsistency of database selections for the same queries distributed by subject. The queries with low inconsistency of database selection are mostly those queries located in social sciences, education, or agriculture (0 or 18.2 percent).

The queries located in interdisciplinary areas such as materials science and environmental science had the highest inconsistency (87.5 or 100 percent) of database selections for the same query. It might be due to the fact that most searchers of INFOMASTER in this study were graduate students in library school with a social sciences background, and were more familiar with those queries in social sciences than those in the sciences, especially those in interdisciplinary fields of sciences (i.e., materials science). Even when the subjects of queries had been provided by librarians as data about the queries given by the end users, still some students selected different subjects for those queries based on their own judgements or limited by the hierarchical subject lists for categories given by INFOMASTER. These categories were simple and mostly for discrete disciplines, but did not cover all detailed subdivisions, even excluding some categories in high class levels (such as no environmental science in the subject list from INFOMASTER).

But in some cases, the same subject selections from different searchers for the same query still led to inconsistent databases selected by INFOMASTER. This was apparently due to random selection from a group of databases for a particular subject by INFOMASTER. For instance, query 18 (of which the search topic is "Book Theft in European Libraries in the 18th and 19th Centuries") is a topic about library science. All three students selected the same subject (library science) as the librarian's subject selection. But INFOMASTER offered two different databases for three searches (two of these were the same (SOCIAL SCIENCES CITATION INDEX (SSCI)), the other one was a different one (INFORMATION SCIENCE ABSTRACTS (ISA))).

Even with the correct subject selection by the searchers, INFOMASTER's selection of the best database (ranked by PD) for a particular query would also depends on the random selection from a group of databases for a particular category selected by the system. For instance, query 18 mentioned above, had the same and correct subject selection as the librarian's (library science). But neither of the databases selected by INFOMASTER (ISA and SSCI) was as good as the librarian's (LISA) which was ranked as the best database for this query in its PD. There are two possible explanations for this kind of failure by INFOMASTER: (1) The INFOMASTER database selection actually only depends on the subject selection of a query but not the query itself. That is, INFOMASTER can not "think" as the human intermediary to seek information for a particular query in detail: which database is the "best" one to meet this specific query. In this way, INFOMASTER selectes a database randomly among a group of databases only according to the last subject field and type of document selected by the searcher for a query, and does not take the search topic into account. Two tests confirmed this in the study. The last subject category selected for both test searches was Education, with the type of document as "Professional Journals". At the first time the topic input was "Surge Protect/ and Microcomputer", a topic about computer science rather than education. The database selected by INFOMASTER was ERIC. The second time the topic input was a group of "garbage symbols" such as "SALDJFLALE/ AND 88JDKE", but the database selected by INFOMASTER was still ERIC. It seems that the search statements did not influence database selection by INFOMASTER at all. (2) Commercial considerations may be another factor influencing INFOMASTER in selection of databases. For instance, when query 18 (mentioned above, about library science) was searched, the system asked, "This database carries a surcharge. Do you wish to continue?"; it then picked SSCI as the database selected which was not actually the best database for this particular query. If commercial considerations influence database selection, the database chosen may not be the best choice in terms of highest postings.

These two reasons (for influencing the best databases selected by INFOMASTER) also could be considered to be the factors influencing the consistency of databases selected by INFOMASTER for the same query in different searches by INFOMASTER. Random selection from a group of databases can lead to different databases for even te same query as long as the same subject and type of document were selected.

5. Conclusion and Suggestions

Automated database selection by a gateway system among online networks is necessary and possible for online services. The major technique for "automated database selection" by INFOMASTER is through narrowing down the subject selections for a particular query using menu choices by the human searcher, then, selecting a database seemingly at random from among a group of databases for the queries falling in a particular subject field. That is, AI techniques are applied in only a limited way to the database selection by INFOMASTER. Therefore, automated database selection can be termed a "system component" [5] in a "synthetic intelligent system", which is the synthesis of man and machine but not a replacement of man by machine.[6]

There are several problems in database selection by a gateway system found in this study, which could be improved with some AI (artificial intelligence) techniques, as follows:

1. There should be some "Machine Learning" functions for automated database selection by a gateway system. Machine Learning is "to study computational methods for acquiring new knowledge, new skills, and

new ways to organize existing knowledge".[7] In information retrieval, learning functions are to modify the system response during the processing of a particular query in order to retrieve items most likely to meet the needs of the searcher, or, to improve system response over time.[8] When a database selected by the gateway system is not satisfactory (or not available for access in the meantime because of some system problems), the system should be able to change to other suitable databases (or online system) to process searches. But INFOMASTER could not change its selection of database and online system besides the first choice as long as the same subject field and the type of document were selected, unless the searchers returned at a later time when the random selection of databases from INFOMASTER has been changed.

2. As mentioned above, the hierarchical subject structure designed by INFOMASTER should be implemented or use some implemented methods (such as coordinating subject terms) to make the subjects listed for selections have more categories (including some more subdivisions and interdisciplinary fields) or be more flexible to meet queries.

3. More AI techniques (such as heuristics, machine learning, natural language processing) should be applied for automated database selections by a gateway. That means that more decisions should be by machine rather than depending on human searchers, such as increasing machine judgements instead of the subject selections from human searchers' judgements as much as possible.

4. Database selection by the gateway system should focus more on the subject of the search query itself instead of being based on the wide subject field in which the query falls. That means, within the subject field of queries, the details of the query should be taken into account for the BEST database selection.

Many of these suggestions are potentially worthwhile areas for research. But it also can be considered to the trend of gateway for automated database selection in online services in the future.

ACKNOWLEDGEMENTS: The author would like to thank F.W. Lancaster and Linda C. Smith for their advice and assistance throughout her dissertation research and Linda C. Smith help in preparing this conference paper.

REFERENCES

[1] Williams, Martha E., "Transparent Information Systems Through Gateways, Front Ends, Intermediaries, and Interfaces," Journal of the American Society for Information Science 37:4 (July 1986): 205.

[2] Kehoe, Cynthia A., "Interfaces and Expert Systems for Online Retrieval," Onine Review 9:6 (December 1985): 450.

[3] Pemberton, Jeffrey K., "An Interview with Dick Kollin of EasyNet," Online 10:3 (May 1986): 18.

[4] Hu, Chengren, An Evaluation of Online Database Selection by a Gateway System with Artificial Intelligence Techniques, (Ph.D Dissertation) October 1987, the University of Illinois at Urbana-Champaign.

[5] Smith, Linda C., "Artificial Intelligence and Information Retrieval," In: Annual Review of Information Science and Technology, vol. 22, 1987. Ed. Martha E. Williams, New York: Knowledge Industry Publications, Inc., 1987, p. 47.

[6] Bolter, J. David, Turing's Man: Western Culture in the Computer Age, Chapel Hill, North Carolina, The University of North Carolina Press, 1984, p. 238.

[7] Forsyth, Richard and Rada, Roy, Machine Learning: Applications in Expert Systems and Information Retrieval, Chichester, West Sussex, England: Ellis Horwood Limited, 1986. p. 14.

[8] Smith, Linda C., Selected Artificial Intelligence Techniques in Information Retrieval Systems Research, (Ph.D Dissertation) Syracuse University, May 1979. pp. 44, 61, 67.

Table 1. Statistical Results for Comparisons of Database Selection Between Librarians and INFOMASTER Operated by Students
(With Chi-Square Statistical Method)

For the comparison of performances between the two approaches (Librarian vs. INFOMASTER), there were three outcomes: same, librarian better choice of databases, and INFOMASTER better choices of databases, which are listed in the table as **Same**, **Better** (Librarian or INFOMASTER), **Poorer** (Librarian or INFOMASTER).

Hypothesis (H0): The performance of INFOMASTER for database selections is the same as librarians' (at the significance level 0.05).
That is, INFOMASTER can select appropriate databases as well as the librarians.

Cases		Same	Better	Poorer	Critical Value	X^2 Value	df Value	Result
Best Gateway Result	Librarian	29	13	8	5.99	2.38	2	Support H_0
	INFOMASTER	29	8	13				
	Total Number	29	21	21				
Worst Gateway Result	Librarian	28	20	2	5.99	29.45	2	Reject H_0
	INFOMASTER	28	2	20				
	Total Number	28	22	22				

Table 2. Categories of Consistency in Database Selection Between Librarians and INFOMASTER Operated by Students

Notes: Category I : Librarian and INFOMASTER made the same choice, and the choice is the best database ranked in PD;
Category II : Librarian and INFOMASTER made the same choice, but the choice is NOT the best database ranked in PD;
Category III : Librarian made better choice than INFOMASTER did.
Category IV : INFOMASTER made better choice than librarian did.

Cases	Category I	(%)	Category II	(%)	Category III	(%)	Category IV	(%)
Best Gateway Result	8	(16)	21	(42)	13	(26)	8	(16)
Worst Gateway Result	5	(10)	23	(46)	20	(40)	2	(4)

Table 3. Consistency in Database Selection by INFOMASTER
for the Same Query Among Three Students

Query's Subject	Total No. of Queries in This Subject Field	Total No. of Queries with Different Choices (%)		No. of 2 Choices	No. of 3 Choices
Agriculture	11	2	(18.2)	2	0
Environment Science	2	2	(100.0)	2	0
Art & Literature	3	2	(66.7)	1	1
Library Science	1	1	(100.0)	1	0
Education	6	0	(0.0)	0	0
Social Science	7	0	(0.0)	0	0
Computer Science	1	1	(100.0)	1	0
Engineering	8	2	(25.0)	2	0
Materials Science	8	7	(87.5)	5	2
Physical Science	3	1	(33.3)	1	0
Total Queries	50	18	(36.0%)*	15 (30.0%)*	3 (6.0%)*

Total Consistency of Database Selection by INFOMASTER = 64% ((50-18)/50 or 1-0.36)
* The percentages are all based on the total of fifty queries.

Table 4. The Evaluation of INFOMASTER Database Selection by
Students (Inexperienced Searchers of INFOMASTER)
(Questionaire Survey Results)

Items	Contents		Results of Survey		Notes
			Number	(%)	
Evaluation of Use	Easy of	1 (Difficult Use)	1	1.3	
		2	1	1.3	
		3	4	5.3	
		4	12	16.0	
		5 (Easy Use)	57	76.0	
of INFOMASTER	Helpfulness in Database Selection	1 (Not Helpful)	4	5.3	
		2	3	4.0	
		3	13	18.7	
		4	24	32.0	
		5 (Helpful)	30	40.0	
Time Used for Searching INFOMASTER (in minutes)	0 - 15		30	40.0	(Time counted from logon until logoff including two searches.)
	16 - 30		39	52.0	
	31 - 45		4	5.3	
	46 - 60		2	2.7	
	> 60		0	0	

**Appendix. Example of Posting Databases (PD):
Database Selection by Librarians and INFOMASTER Operated by Students
Compared With Posting Databases (PD)**

(Note: DB = Database; Most databases which librarians or INFOMASTER selected will be involved in Posting Databases (PD). If any database was not involved in PD list, it must be the database with 0 item for the corresponding search query.)

No. Search Query	Subject of Search	DBs Selected by Librarian		DBs Selected by INFOMASTER		Posting Databases (PD) List	
		DBs' Name	No. of Items	DBs' Name	No. of Items	DBs' Name	No. of Items
14. Living Realist Sculptors	Art	RILA	85	RILA	85	RILA	85
				RILA	85	ART MODERN	23
				RILA	85	HISTORICAL ABSTRACTS	1
15. Literary Salons in 19th Century France	Literature	MLA	7	MLA	7	HISTORICAL ABSTRACTS	1
				AHCI	4	MLA	7
				MLA	7	AHCI	4
						SOCA	1
						LLBA	1
						AMERICA: HISTORY & LIFE	1
						RELIGION INDEX	1
16. Reviews of Films by Andrei Tarkovskii	Art (Cinema Studies)	MAGILL'S SURVEY OF CINEMA	5	ART INDEX	6	NATIONAL NEWSPAPER INDEX	24
				NATIONAL NEWSPAPER INDEX	24	MAGAZINE INDEX	22
				AHCI	16	AP NEWS	17
						AHCI	16
						UPI NEWS	16
						MLA	15
						CANADIAN BUSINESS	8
						BIOGRAPHY MASTER INDEX	8
						ART INDEX	6
						MAGILL'S SURVEY OF CINEMA	5
						FACTS ON FILE	4
						TRADE AND INDUSTRY INDEX	4
						SSCI	3
						ART MODERN	3
						PSYC	1
						LLBA	1
17. Evaluations of Surge Protectors for Microcomputers	Computer Science	MICROCOMPUTER INDEX	1	COMPUTER DATABASE	18	COMPUTER DATABASE	18
				COMP	0	INSPEC	10
				COMPUTER DATABASE	18	JAPAN TECHNOLOGY	5
						MICROCOMPUTER INDEX	1

AVAILABILITY OF JAPANESE SCIENTIFIC AND TECHNICAL PERIODICALS IN MAJOR ENGLISH LANGUAGE DATABASES

Keiko Ikushima and Carol Tenopir, University of Hawaii at Manoa

Keywords: Databases, Online, Japanese Literature, Japanese Periodicals, Science, Technology.

Abstract: In the last decade the number of Japanese scientific and technical periodicals has increased and the realization of the importance of this information has also increased in the Western world. It is thus expected that the number of Japanese periodicals available in English language databases will have increased significantly. To test this assumption, a random sample of titles from the Directory of Japanese Scientific Periodicals was tested for inclusion in eight major English language databases (AGRICOLA, CA SEARCH, COMPENDEX, BIOSIS, EMBASE, INSPEC, MEDLINE, SCISEARCH). Findings show a significant increase of coverage in most databases when compared to the result a similar study conducted in 1979. Language of the periodicals or summaries is the most important determining factor.

1. INTRODUCTION

Japan has made a concerted national effort to apply science and technology to achieve economic growth since the end of World War II, and now Japan ranks second as a world economic power in the free world. Japan ranks third in research and development spending in the world and has made the advancement of science and technology a central focus of its national policy (Ref. 1). The collection, analysis, translation, and application of scientific and technical information from all over the world by the Japanese have played a major role in making their economy the second largest in the world.

Japan published 8,900 scientific and technical periodicals 9 years ago. Today, about 10,000 scientific and technical scholarly periodicals are published in Japan. Of these periodicals 20% are published fully or partially in Western languages, with 80% published in Japanese (Ref. 2). As of 1979, the most recent year for which this data is available, only 19% of the Japanese scientific and technical periodicals were included in Western indexing and abstracting printed and database sources. Of this 19%, 71% were fully or partially in English or other Western languages, with only 29% printed solely in Japanese (Ref. 3). Users of English language databases were therefore not being made aware of most Japanese literature.

There are several databases devoted to coverage of Japanese technological literature in 1987. JAPIO database (Japanese Patent Information Organization) provides English language abstracts summarizing Japanese patent applications for which no English language summaries were previously available online (Ref. 4). Japan Technology (provided by the Japanese Technical Information Service, University Microfilms International (UMI)), indexes and abstracts approximately 600 technological or business periodicals. NewsNet contains the full text of over a dozen Japanese newsletters which cover Japanese business activities. Japan Economic Newswire Plus contains the complete text of news releases from the Japan Economic Daily (JED) and Kyodo English News Service (KENS) newswires. Japanese researchers have access to scientific and technical information from the west through the Japan Information Center of Science and Technology (JICST). JICST collects information related to science and technology, with a collection including 47% domestic periodicals and 53% from the western countries (Ref. 5) JOIS (JICST Online Information System) is an English language version of a database provided by JICST. Since October 1986 it is available in the U.S.

2. PROBLEM TO BE STUDIED

In 1987 researchers who know they want Japanese materials can search one of the above databases. If the 1979 situation still exists, researchers who use the traditional subject approach to database selection do not have the same access to Japanese scientific and technical information for their research.

Since 1979, the number of Japanese scientific and technical periodicals has been growing, and realization of the importance of this information has been also growing. It is expected that the number of Japanese periodicals available in English language databases will have increased significantly. My study tested this assumption.

A significant comprehensive study was done on the topic by Gibson and Kunkel at the General Motors Research Library in 1979. The findings were: 1) less than 20% of the Japanese scientific and technical periodical literature is covered by the Western indexes and abstracts, 2) about one quarter of Japan's periodical literature is written in Western languages, yet only about one-half of that literature is available to Western researchers through the indexes and abstracts. Of the 75% that is written in Japanese, only 7% is covered by the indexes and abstracts (Ref. 6).

3. RESEARCH DESIGN

To identify the total number of scientific journals currently published in Japan, the Japan National Diet Library's Directory of Japanese Scientific Periodicals was used. It covers 9,569 titles of current serials in science and technology published in Japan as of November, 1984. There are several catalogs and directories of Japanese scientific periodicals, but the Directory of Japanese Scientific Periodicals, 1984 (the most current edition), is the most comprehensive and reliable.

The major English language databases which were surveyed are: 1) AGRICOLA (Bibliography of Agriculture), 2) BIOSIS (Biological Abstracts), 3) CA SEARCH (Chemical Abstracts), 4) COMPENDEX (Engineering Index), 5) EMBASE (Excerpta Medica), 6) MEDLARS (Index Medicus), 7) INSPEC (Computer and Control Abstracts, Electrical and Electronics Abstracts, Physics Abstracts), 8) SCISEARCH (Science Citation Index).

Each database publishes an alphabetic list of periodicals indexed. Each of the randomly selected titles was manually matched against the list for each database.

4. FINDINGS

Table 1 shows that approximately 26% of Japanese scientific and technical periodicals are indexed by the major English language databases. This is an increase of about 7% since Gibson and Kunkel's 1979 study. The percentage of Japanese periodicals included in each database is also shown in Table 1. Coverage in AGRICOLA has decreased about 1% since 1979. The coverage in the other seven databases has increased; the coverage in SCISEARCH has doubled and that of MEDLARS has more than tripled. This growing percentage of coverage in the databases supports the expectation that the number of Japanese periodicals available in the major English language databases has increased since 1979.

The 370 sampling titles were broken down into four broad subjects: agricultural sciences, applied sciences, medical sciences and natural sciences. The percentage of Japanese titles that are covered in the databases in each subject has also increased since 1979.

Table 2 shows for each subject the percentage of the Japanese scientific and technical periodicals that are included in the major English language databases. Twenty-one percent of the agricultural science, 25% of the applied sciences, 24% of the medical sciences and 35% of the natural sciences titles are included.

4.1 STATISTICAL TEST

Since my sampling size was small and I was comparing the increasing rate of indexing in the major English language databases with the General Motors' study of 1979, the Wilcoxon matched-pairs test was applied. The overall increase is significant at the 0.05 level. Each subject title increase is also significant, except agricultural sciences. Applied sciences shows significance at 0.01, and natural sciences at the 0.05 level. Medical sciences is significant at the 0.05 level, although the total percentage of increase is only 0.1%. This test supports the hypothesis that the total number of Japanese scientific and technical periodicals indexed by the major English language databases has significantly increased since 1979. There has been a significant increase since 1979 especially in the applied sciences. This might show the emphasis that Japan has placed on technological research and the realization by Western researchers that they need Japanese technological information.

4.2 ISSUING ORGANIZATION

Societies publish the largest portion (29%) of total periodicals, followed by government (22%), research institutes (21%) and universities (11%). Almost 90% of government published periodicals are written in Japanese, and only 7% of them have an English or Western language summary. Only 9% of government published periodicals are indexed by major English language databases.

Government publishes the largest portion of agricultural sciences periodicals (46%). Even though the percentage of periodical titles indexed by the major English language databases has increased, the increase is not significant in agricultural sciences. This may be because Japanese do not put much emphasis on agricultural research, and most government publications are statistical reports which are written in Japanese and do not have any English or Western language titles. Western researchers would not be interested in these statistics.

4.3 LANGUAGE AS A FACTOR

Figure 1 shows periodicals indexed by major English language databases broken down by languages. Forty-five percent of the periodicals indexed by CA SEARCH are totally written in English or another Western language. Over 50% of Japanese periodicals written totally in English or in another Western language are indexed by the rest of major English language databases. Figure 2 shows periodicals indexed by the databases broken down by language of summary. Over three-fifths of Japanese periodicals indexed by major English databases have English or Western language summaries. 100% of periodicals indexed in EMBASE have English or Western language summaries, followed by BIOSIS (97%), AGRICOLA (93%), MEDLARS (93%), COMPENDEX (83%), SCISEARCH (83%),

INSPEC (71%) and CA SEARCH (62%). This might show that most database services simply take the English or Western language summary to index Japanese periodicals.

Figure 3 shows that 69% of the periodicals indexed in CA SEARCH are in whole or in part in English or another Western language. Eighty-three percent of SCISEARCH is English or Western language, 86% of INSPEC, 92% OF MEDLARS and 100% of AGRICOLA, BIOSIS, COMPENDEX and EMBASE. This shows clearly that major English language databases index more Japanese periodicals that are written in English or other Western languages than those written in Japanese, and that periodicals with English or Western language summaries are more likely to be indexed by the databases.

That the major English language databases favor English language selection is not surprising. Only one database explicitly states this language bias, however, in its selection criteria. The Bibliography of Agriculture (AGRICOLA) states:

> The Bibliography of Agriculture is a monthly index to the literature of agricultural and allied sciences... The National Agricultural Library collects literature related to agriculture from world wide sources. The Bibliography includes citations of journal articles, pamphlets, government documents, special reports, proceedings, ...new serials and, other materials.
>
> Publications are considered for indexing by NAL if a summary, abstract or title is available in a language in which the indexers have expertise...(Ref. 7).

Although language limitations are not stated by the rest of the databases in this study, some selection criteria are used by each indexing and abstracting service. Some criteria may be related to language. As figures 1, 2 and 3 show, three-fourths to 100% of periodicals indexed in the databases are written either completely or partially in English or in Western languages, except CA SEARCH. Chemical Abstracts Service has relationships with many scientific and technical organizations in the world, including the Japan Association for International Chemical Information which provides abstracts of Japanese literature to CAS. This is probably the reason that CA SEARCH indexes more Japanese language periodicals than the other databases.

5. CONCLUSION

The results of this study show that language of the periodicals or summaries seems to be the single most important factor that determines whether Japanese scientific and technical literature is included in the major English language databases. Although some Japanese researchers write articles or summaries in English or in Western languages, still half of the Japanese scientific and technical periodicals are completely written in Japanese. Western researchers are not getting access to a large body of Japanese language technical literature. There are translation services available, but they are often perceived as inconvenient or high cost and many researchers do not use these services. This language bias on the part of English language database producers and, perhaps, of the Western researchers means that a large body of the world's valuable scientific and technical literature is not readily available on the Western world.

6. REFERENCES

1. U.S. Congress. House of Representatives. Committee on Science and Technology. Subcommittee on Science. Research and Technology. The Availability of Japanese Scientific and Technical Information in the United States. Hearings before the Subcommittee on Science, Research and Technology of the Committee on Science and Technology, House of Representatives. 1984.

2. Igarashi, Mitsuo et al. Nihon no Kagakugijutsu zasshi no shoshiteki bunseki (1): Nihon kagakugijutsu kankei chikuji kankobutsu mokuroku 1984 nenban-o-motonishite. Kagakugijutsu bunken sabisu 74, p. 1-12, 1985.

3. Gibson, Robert W. and Barbara K. Kunkel. Japanese Information Network and Bibliographic Control: Scientific and Technical Literature. Special Libraries 71, p. 154-62, March 1980.

4. Simmons. Edlyn S. JAPIO-Japanese Patent Applications Online. Online 10, p. 51-58, July 1986.

5. JICST. The Japan Information Center of Science and Technology. pamphlet. 1987.

6. Gibson, Robert W. and Barbara K. Kunkel. Japanese Scientific and Technical Literature: A Subject Guide. p. 1-64, Westport, Connecticut: Greenwood Press, 1981.

7. Bibliography of Agriculture, v.50-12, p. i-vii, December 1986.

DATABASES	'79 STUDY INDEXING of JAPANESE PERIODICALS %	'87 STUDY INDEXING of JAPANESE PERIODICALS %
Total	17.8	25.7
AGRICOLA (AG)	5.3	4.1
BIOSIS (BI)	4.7	8.6
CA SEARCH (CA)	15.4	23.5
COMPENDEX (CO)	1.2	1.6
EMBASE (EM)	2.5	4.3
INSPEC (IN)	2.0	3.8
MEDLARS (ME)	1.1	3.8
SCISEARCH (SC)	0.9	1.6

Table 1. Comparison between 1979 study and 1987 study

Agricultural Sciences

DATA BASES	'79 18.9%	'87 21.4%
AG	13.1	11.4
BI	4.8	10.0
CA	12.3	18.6
CO	0	0
EM	1.1	0
IN	0	0
ME	0.1	0
SC	0.1	1.4

Applied Sciences

DATA BASES	'79 13.0%	'87 25.4%
AG	1.4	2.2
BI	0.3	1.4
CA	10.9	23.2
CO	1.9	3.6
EM	0.3	2.2
IN	2.8	6.5
ME	0	0.7
SC	0.3	1.4

Medical Sciences

DATA BASES	'79 24.0%	'87 24.1%
AG	1.4	0.9
BI	7.1	13.0
CA	20.4	23.1
CO	0	0
EM	10.5	11.1
IN	0.1	0
ME	2.4	12.0
SC	0.8	0.9

Natural Sciences

DATA BASES	'79 23.1%	'87 35.2%
AG	5.7	5.6
BI	9.1	16.7
CA	17.7	31.5
CO	0.5	1.8
EM	0.7	1.9
IN	3.0	9.3
ME	0.2	0
SC	0.8	3.7

Table 2. Subjects in the database

Note AG: AGRICOLA BI: BIOSIS CA: CA SEARCH CO: COMPENDEX EM: EMBASE
IN: INSPEC ME: MEDLARS SC: SCISEARCH

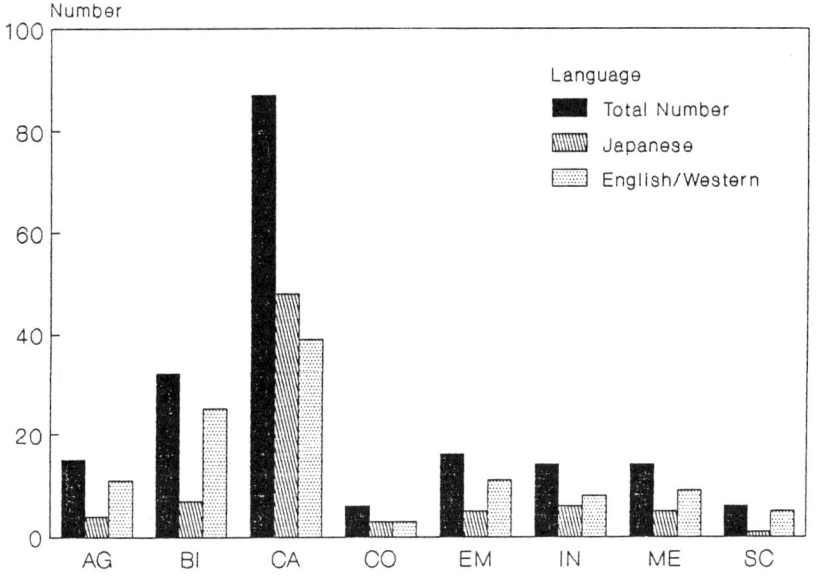

Figure 1. Japanese Periodicals Included in Major English Language Databases by Language (article)

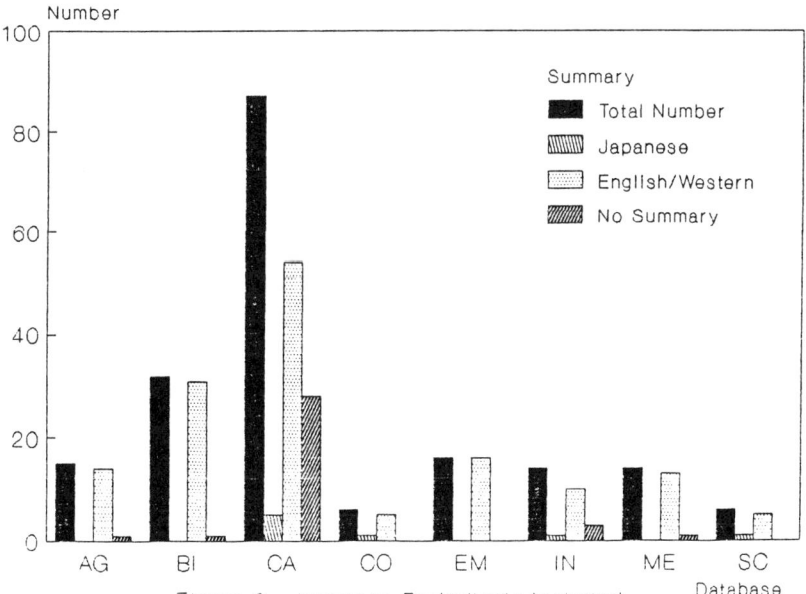

Figure 2. Japanese Periodicals Included in Major English Language Databases by Summary and Language of Summary

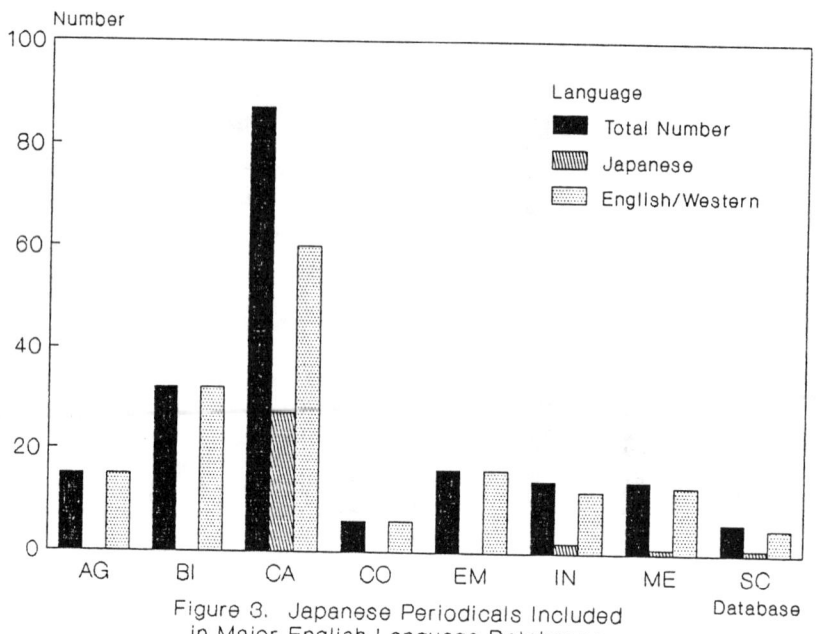

Figure 3. Japanese Periodicals Included in Major English Language Databases by Language (Total: article & summary)

SEARCHING FOR INDUSTRY INFORMATION

Leslie R. Jacobs, DIALOG Information Services, Inc.

Keywords: Industry Information, Standard Industrial Classification Codes, Downloading.

Abstract: Online sources of industry information are plentiful, but can be tricky to locate. Many databases use Standard Industrial Classification (SIC) codes which are often as much of a search hindrance as a search aid. Some of the most valuable industry information can be compiled from company directory databases, but this requires that the database allow for post search manipulation of the retrieved data. If there is a database specific to the industry in question, it can be a goldmine of information, however no single source of information should be considered as 'complete'; it is preferable to triangulate sources. And, of course, the great myth that everything is online must be debunked: if it isn't in the public domain, it isn't online.

This paper focuses on those online vendors which are readily available to the searcher. BRS, DIALOG, Dow Jones, NEXIS, and Pergamon/SDC require little, if any, start up fee, and are essentially on a pay as you use basis. Useful information can also be found on multi-industry databases such as Compustat, or on industry analysts databases such as those from Gartner Group or IDC for the computer industry, but these have fairly steep subscription fees associated with them.

Charts listing Databases for Industry News, Company Directory Databases, Industry-Specific Databases, and Textual Databases for Industry Analysis are included.

SYNOPSIS

There are two methods for retrieving industry information online. One approach is to find records--generally textual records-- about the industry per se. This is the easy method, since once you have found the records, you have what you need. However, this method may not be fine-tuned enough when one is dealing with 'niche' industries, or with competitive analysis. The definition of a given industry within a textual record may be too broad--or may include companies superfluous to the searcher's quest. This is where the second method may be more useful.

The second method requires retrieving several records--usually one record per company from a directory database--and extracting the necessary data from the records. This can be accomplished via user defined formats, or by using a feature, such as DIALOG's Report feature, which allows the data to be aggregated into rows and columns. This method allows the searcher to define the players in the industry.

THE MIXED BLESSING OF THE SIC CODE

Standard Industrial Classification (SIC) codes were created by the

Department of Commerce in 1972 in an attempt to classify all enterprises in the U.S.--manufacturing, retailing, wholesaling, etc.--so that data could be collected and disseminated in some organized fashion. Although SIC's work well most of the time, problems arise in several areas. Some SIC codes are too broad; analysts trying to hone in an industry subset or niche may retrieve a considerable number of irrelevant records. Some companies have more than one appropriate SIC code, and may be indexed under one SIC code in one database, and another SIC code in another database. Still more confusion was added to the SIC cauldron in 1987 when the Department of Commerce updated the codes for the first time in ten years. While many codes have been expanded, or redefined in a highly useful fashion, some codes are still lacking. When searching online, the confusion is amplified since some databases have migrated to the new codes, and many have not.

Some database producers have recognized the problems inherent in SIC codes, and have devised their own indexing to retrieve industry information. Predicasts has addressed the issue with their own coding system which in some cases coincides with SIC codes, and which defines an industry or product to seven digits. (SIC's are rarely used beyond the fouth digit.) Other databases, such as Investext, use controlled nomenclature for industry descriptions.

THE INDUSTRY-SPECIFIC DATABASE

Those databases dedicated to a specific industry are virtual troves of information. Generally, they cover every aspect of the industry--technology as well as market data. The sources indexed in these databases are varied, and cover government and news sources as well as industry dedicated publications. For example, Chemical Industry Notes contains citations to the Asian Wall Street Journal (as well as other editions of the Journal), China Daily, Congressional Record, U.S. Department of Commerce--Current Industrial Report Series, Federal Register, Financial Times, New York Times, as well as just about every journal related to the chemical industry. This paper contains a chart listing those industry-specific databases described to the author by the database vendors.

INDUSTRY DATA FROM COMPANY DATA

The second method of retrieving industry data, mentioned above, requires using a company directory database (see chart). Relevant records can be retrieved from these files by searching on industry codes or descriptors, or by searching on the names of the companies within the industry. If the online system allows the user to arrange the data in tabular format, it can then be down-loaded to a disk and imported to a spread sheet program for further manipulation. This method allows the analyst to incorporate data found from other sources as well.

THE IMPORTANCE OF TRIANGULATION

The role of online searching in industry analysis is one of reconnaissance--the act of gathering information. Most industry information in the public domain is far from complete--there are gaps in the data, there are guesstimates, and currency may be lacking. The best way to validate industry information is to triangulate: to verify the data with a second source, or to interpolate the data from two or more sources.

INDUSTRY SPECIFIC DATABASES

Database	Venders	Features
American Banker	DIALOG NEXIS	full text news for the banking industry.
Agribusiness	DIALOG	abstracts 300+ trade and government publications.
Biobusiness	DIALOG	Abstracts of 110+ technical & business journals, newsletters, proceedings, patents, & books.
Biocommerce Abstracts	DIALOG	Abstracts 100+ publications concerned with business aspects of biotechnology.
Chemical Business Newsbase	DIALOG PERGAMON	Abstracts world-wide chemical news with emphasis on European news.
Chemical Industry News	DIALOG	Indexes regulatory info, market data, resource use, people, products & processes, cost & price info.
Coffeeline	DIALOG	Indexes 5000+ journals, plus books, patents, reports & theses.
DMS Market Intelligence	DIALOG	Full text analysis of aerospace & defense industry. All major defense companies, products & programs.
FINIS: Financial Industry Information Service	BRS DIALOG	Includes items relating to banks, brokers, credit unions, insurance companies, investment houses, real estate firms, thrift institutions & related government agencies.
Foods Adlibra	DIALOG	Provides information on every sector of the food industry. Abstracts over 750 publications.
Materials Business File	DIALOG	Abstracts 1300+ publications for iron & steel, non-ferrous metals, composites, plastics, etc.

INDUSTRY SPECIFIC DATABASES (con't)

Database	Venders	Features
Pharmaceutical News Index	DIALOG	Indexes publications on drugs covering corporation & industry sales, M&A's, legislation & regulations, RFP's, press releases and other news items.
PTS Aerospace/Defense Markets & Technology	DIALOG	Abstracts 1600+ defense & other publications. All major defense contracts awarded by U.S. Dept. of Defense.
Rapra	PERGAMON	Abstracts technology & business publications pertaining to polymors & related compounds.

DATABASES FOR INDUSTRY NEWS

Database	Venders	Features
AP News	DIALOG	Daily updates of Associated Press newswire.
Businesswire	DIALOG NEXIS	Full text of press releases. Updated continuously on DIALOG.
Dow Jones News	Dow Jones	Fifteen minute updating of business news.
Financial Times	DIALOG NEXIS	Full text.
Kyodo Newswire	DIALOG NEXIS	Information on Japanese Industry & companies, and Japanese perspective on world business.
McGraw Hill News	DIALOG	Continuously updated business news and McGraw Hill analysis.
Moody's Corporate News	DIALOG	One database for U.S. news, and one for international.
New York Times	DIALOG NEXIS	Indexed on DIALOG in National Newspapers Index (NNI). Full text on NEXIS.

DATABASES FOR INDUSTRY NEWS (con't)

Database	Venders	Features
Newsearch	DIALOG	Daily updates of National Newspaper Index, Trade & Industry, and others.
PR Newswire	DIALOG NEXIS	Full text of press releases.
Reuters	DIALOG NEXIS	International business news. Updated continuously on DIALOG.
Standard & Poor's News	DIALOG	Daily updates of business news.
UPI News	DIALOG NEXIS	Daily updates of United Press International Newswire.
Wall St. Journal	DIALOG Dow Jones	Full text on Dow Jones. Indexed on DIALOG in National Newspaper Index.
Washington Post	DIALOG Dow Jones NEXIS	Full text.

TEXTUAL FILES FOR INDUSTRY ANALYSIS

Database	Venders	Features
ABI/INFORM	BRS DIALOG NEXIS	Abstracts of 550 primary business publications. Industry info not primary emphasis
Arthur D. Little Online	DIALOG	ADL reports on industries & technologies.
Barrons	Dow Jones	Full text.
BIS Infomat World Business	DIALOG PERGAMON	Abstracts monitoring engineering, financial services, health care, oil/gas/chemicals, biotechnology, electronics/telecommunications, food & drink, packaging/paper/printing/publishing.

TEXTUAL FILES FOR INDUSTRY ANALYSIS (con't)

Database	Venders	Features
Business Dateline	DIALOG Dow Jones	Full text of U.S. regional publications.
Exchange	NEXIS	Full text of investment bankers reports.
Industry Data Sources	DIALOG	Index of directories, journals, articles & other on 65 major industries.
Investext	BRS DIALOG Dow Jones	Full text of investment banker reports. Covers more than 50 industries.
McGraw Hill Publications	DIALOG NEXIS	Full text of 30 publications, many industry-specific.
PTS F&S Indexes	BRS DIALOG	Indexes over 5000 business sources, strong on M&A. No abstracts.
PTS PROMT	BRS DIALOG	Abstracts from thousands of sources covering all industries. Searching with PTS code assures accuracy.
Trade & Industry	DIALOG NEXIS	Full text of 85 journals & abstracts of 1,500 - many industry specific.

COMPANY DIRECTORY DATABASES

Database	Venders	Features
DISCLOSURE	BRS DIALOG Dow Jones NEXIS	10,000 companies full text
D&B-DUN'S FINANCIAL RECORDS	DIALOG Dow Jones	700,000+ public & private companies
D&B-DUN's MARKET IDENTIFIERS	DIALOG	2,000,000+ public & private companies
MEDIA GENERAL DATABANK	DIALOG Dow Jones	4,300+ public companies, 900+ industry records
MOODY'S CORPORATE PROFILES	DIALOG	3600 public companies
STANDARD & POOR'S CORPORATE DESCRIPTIONS	DIALOG Dow Jones	8,000+ public companies

COMPANY DIRECTORY DATABASES (con't)

Database	Venders	Features
TRINET ESTABLISHMENT DATABASE	DIALOG	Market Share and Line of Business Reports

INFORMATION RETRIEVAL AS HYPERMEDIA: AN OUTLINE OF INTERBROWSE

Paul Kahn, Brown University

The need to provide access to electronic information from within the daily environment of a knowledge worker presents many interesting challenges. The current software market contains hundreds of collections of bibliographic and numeric data, reference collections, and collections of digital images, all in discrete and proprietary formats. At the same time, many database management systems are being employed to reorganize and make use of data collected from these discrete sources. A uniform interface to these database resources is needed. To test out our ideas in this area, we are developing an information retrieval application that will run within Intermedia, the hypermedia environment currently under development at Brown's Institute for Research in Information and Scholarship (IRIS). This application, called InterBrowse, will address the issues of information retrieval and management in a hypermedia environment. This paper provides an outline of the requirements for that application

We view this problem as a continuum of need and use. Locating and applying information, i.e. *integrating information*, must be viewed as a continuum of interlocking tasks, beginning with a perceived information need and resulting in that needed information being applied in the user's work environment. We break the solution down into five steps: 1) a high-level browser, 2) a database specific browser and query builder, 3) a set of tools for refining and reapplying queries, 4) a tool for using results to develop queries in other collections, 5) and a personal information management system. The linking structure of our hypermedia environment adds another layer of possible information management: saving links among pieces of information in a way that makes these links easy to navigate and apply.

1 ASSUMPTIONS

Personal computers are being used today to create *personal databases* in which information is gathered, stored, referenced, and manipulated by a single user. When access to large databases via timesharing networks began in the late 1970s, the end-user worked at a terminal, either block mode or teletype in style, connected to a host computer over a telecommunications network. Today, terminal emulation and special purpose front-end software on personal computers is commonplace for searching these same on-line databases. These applications, however, solve only a small part of the problems faced by end users of large databases. They automate a number of repetitive tasks, such as interacting with a telecommunications network (Telenet, Tymnet, etc.), logging on to a timesharing system, and even uploading pre-created queries. But they do not deal well with issues such as: presenting tools to help a user build a reasonable query, resolving queries among different database collections, providing graphical representations of result sets, or downloading information into a personal database.

As 1988 begins the personal computer field is advancing rapidly in three areas:

> *CPU power and memory*: We now have a generation of machines based on a 32-bit CPU architecture (80386, 68020 and 68030, RISC), capable of addressing tens of megabytes RAM and usually configured with 4-10 megabytes of RAM.

> *Size of data storage*: The standard magnetic diskette is now 1-2 megabytes, with most local hard disks in the 80-140 megabyte range. Optical disk options include the 550-600 megabyte CD ROM and WORM cartridges in the 200-800 megabyte ranges.

> *Size and resolution of display*: Display size is increasing on all fronts, with 15-19" monitors, minimum resolutions of 75 dots-per-inch, and 256-1024 colors.

> *Telecommunications*: The 300/1200 baud standards are giving way to higher speeds such as 9600-19,200 baud modems.

The current applications software market lags far behind the potential offered by these advances in computing and storage hardware. The large capacity of an inexpensive optical media such as CD ROM provides the opportunity to deliver very large and complex databases to single users. To take advantage of this new media, however, equally large advances must be made in user interface design.

Since 1983 with the introduction of the Apple Lisa followed by the original 128K Macintosh, windowing systems and pointing devices have clearly demonstrated their ability to increase the potential user base for all applications.

Our experiences with numerous hypermedia projects at Brown have also demonstrated that the use of graphics makes it easier for users to visualize, analyze and manipulate complex information.

2 THE CONTINUUM MODEL

Integrating information must be viewed as a continuum of interlocking tasks, beginning with a perceived information need and resulting in the needed information being placed in the user's work environment. To do this an application must be capable of presenting information about heterogeneous database resources in some open-ended manner. It must be able to deal with the user's needs from beginning to end, an end that is not reached by simply displaying information on a screen. The more complex issues of storing and organizing results in a personal information management must be part of the information retrieval design.

To test our ideas in this area, we are developing an information retrieval application that will run within Intermedia, the hypermedia environment currently under development at Brown's Institute for Research in Information and Scholarship (IRIS) [1]. This application, called InterBrowse, will address the issues of information retrieval and management in a hypermedia environment. For the design of InterBrowse, we are breaking the application into five tasks which are capable of sharing and transferring information in a simple and fluid manner. We identify these as serving the following functions:

1) a high-level browser for viewing collections of available information leading to the selection of a database;

2) a database specific browser and query builder for browsing information in a specific database and developing a query;

3) a set of tools for refining and reapplying queries, for browsing the results of a query to refine and reapply those results to another query, to narrow, broaden, or change the direction of a search, and select from those results the desired information;

4) a tool for using selected results to develop further queries in other database collections available through the high-level browser;

5) a personal information management system to store results locally in a systematic fashion for use in the work environment.

Figure 1 provides a conceptual overview of these interlocking tools. Each of these are described in more detail below.

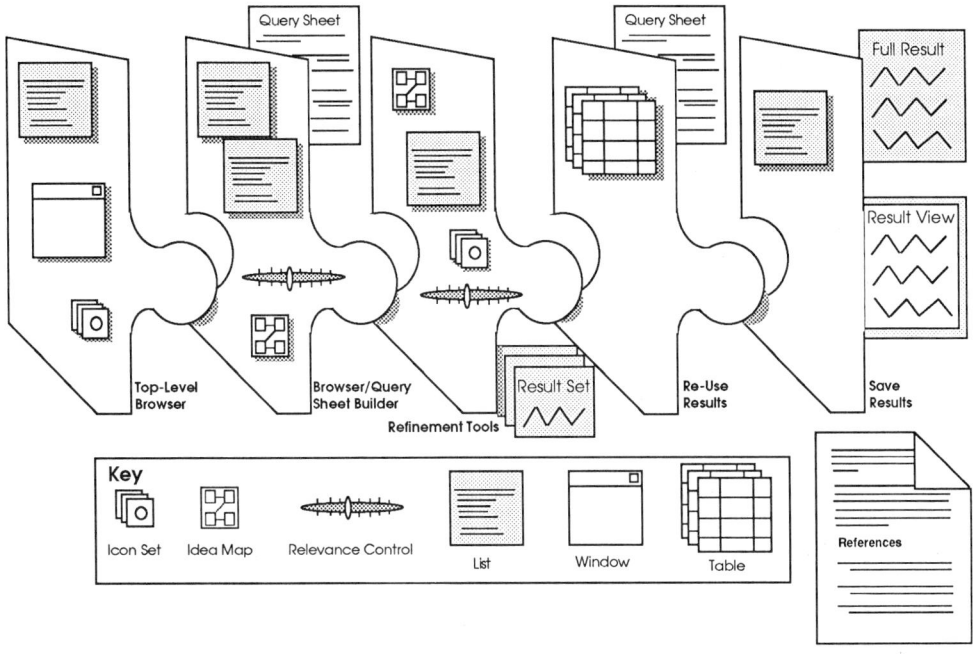

Figure 1: An overview of InterBrowse

2.1 HIGH-LEVEL BROWSER: BROWSING COLLECTIONS OF AVAILABLE INFORMATION LEADING TO THE SELECTION OF A DATABASE

The purpose of this browser is to provide the user with information about the available databases. The browser will present this information in a number of ways, analogous to the way the Macintosh Finder presents file/folder information, i.e. as groups of icons or as sorted lists of names.

An interesting example of this kind of database browser is to be found in Pro-Search, a personal computer application for searching databases on BRS and Dialog.[2] This program provides a high-level interface to the several hundred databases found on these information services. The user walks a tree by selecting one of four general topics (*Art and Social Science*), one of a list of subtopics (*Language*), and is finally presented with a set of "cards" representing the databases that fall under these categories (*Arts & Humanities Search, Language & Language Behavior Abs, MLA Bibliography,* etc.). The same database could be reached from a different subtopic (*Philosophy* also leads to *Arts & Humanities Search*). InterBrowse will provide this functionality using a methodology similar to the "View" function in the Macintosh Finder.

Selecting a database name or icon will allow the user to get information about that database. This will operate in a manner analogous to the "Get Info" function of the Macintosh Finder. Information accessible from any database name or icon will include:

- size, coverage and time-depth of the database, in terms of general subject covered, list of information sources, frequency of update, etc.

- overview of the field structure of the database, showing how records are organized, what is searchable, etc.

- description of the thesaurus, the citation index, or other special features, explaining how subject headings are organized in different structures: flat lists, hierarchical trees, or networks of greater and lesser terms

- a user's or group's history of interaction with this database

The user can then choose to develop a query for one database by following from the information window to the query sheet builder.

2.2 QUERY SHEET BUILDER: BROWSING INFORMATION IN A SPECIFIC DATABASE LEADING TO THE DEVELOPMENT OF A QUERY

The purpose of this tool is to provide the end-user with the means for examining the structure and content of a particular database, and applying that knowledge to developing a query in that collection. The tool provides information about:

- what the database contains

- how the database defines a particular subject

- how the subjects relate to the searcher's ideas

By interacting with the Query Sheet Builder, the user creates a document called a Query Sheet, which can then be used to generate a result set from a database. To do this InterBrowse must know how each database is structured and indexed, and how to request results from the appropriate information retrieval (IR) system.

The process of building a Query Sheet involves two paradigms: *selection* from a sorted list or graphic and *feedback* resulting from that selection in the form of numbers, re-sorted lists of result terms, or graphics.[3]

The Query Sheet Builder will provide graphic *idea maps* showing coverage of subjects, relations among subjects, bibliometric features of the data, and co-citation cluster maps showing central works. Things we would like to model include:

- a view of an entire database or a large subset as a topological *idea map* which presents the coverage of subject areas as surface plots. The tools for calculating the "shape" of these different visualizations will allow the user to select specific areas for further searching.

- the use of co-citation information to calculate directed graphs for locating the "central" authors, subject headings, journals, and citations for a specific search, subject, or combination of subjects.

- graphic representations of bibliometric functions such as author and journal popularity for the entire database.

To find out what the database contains the user will have access to sorted lists of the contents for selected fields such as authors, subject headings, and journal titles. This feature will allow the user to identify, for example, whether the work of a particular author is contained in the database by examining the author list for the author's name. If it is there, the user can then select the correct form of the author's name to build the query. This technique allows the user to build a query by selecting items from the field indices, rather than having to guess the form in which a term exists or whether it exists at all. If the user chooses to supply terms directly from the keyboard, the Query Sheet Builder will parse the input, and match words against indexed terms. There will be a mechanism for notifying the user when input does not match any indexed terms, and this mechanism will allow the user to browse the appropriate list for alternatives.

The way in which a database defines its subjects is best presented in the form of a subject thesaurus. An interesting example of thesaurus access for a single database is found in the Knowledge Finder version of MEDLINE, a Macintosh application which accesses MEDLINE on CD ROM.[4] This application treats the Medical Subject Heading thesaurus (MeSH) as a database to aid the user in locating subject headings appropriate to a query. Usage and history notes for each term, supplied by the National Library of Medicine, are available for display in separate windows. InterBrowse will treat the thesaurus of each database in a similar fashion. Relations among subject headings will be represented in a manner which allows the user to navigate among the connections, so that a user can move among and select networks of related terms.

By supporting multiple windows on a large (19") monitor, InterBrowse will allow the user to maintain visual context among lists of subject headings, information about these headings, list of terms in various fields, while still viewing the current Query Sheet. As terms are selected from these lists a query is built. Once the user is satisfied with the initial query the Query Sheet is *applied* to the database.

2.3 QUERY REFINER: USING THE FEEDBACK FROM A QUERY TO REFINE AND REAPPLY, AND/OR SELECT FROM THOSE RESULTS

The result of applying the Query Sheet will be the creation of a result set. The purpose of the Query Refiner is to provide tools for evaluating the result set and using the information it contains to refine and reapply the Query Sheet.

It is assumed that coarse results (large sets) are just as useful as fine results (small sets) when the purpose is to refine and reapply a query. The Query Refiner will provide tools to browse and represent large or small result sets.

A fundamental aspect of the InterBrowse design which distinguishes it from previous applications is its ability to deal with result sets as sub-databases. For the sake of efficiency, most IR systems produce a result set which consists of a set of pointers to records which satisfy a query. To effectively represent a result set for browsing, InterBrowse requests the IR system to return *all* the information in, not just pointers to, the records which satisfy the query. The Query Refiner tool will receive the entire result set and organize the information as a sub-database for display and refinement purposes.

The Query Refiner will present the following information about the result set:

- sorted lists of the result set's contents for selected fields such as authors, subject headings, journal titles.

- graphic *idea maps* analogous to the pre-calculated maps of the entire database available in the Query Sheet Builder.

- search results as a group of *graphic icons* which visualize features that the user deems important. The graphic attributes of the icon set can be based on applied bibliometrics such as author and journal frequency, numbers of subject headings (generalness or narrowness), etc.[5] The relative weights and graphic presentation of these attributes will be controlled by the user.

- when citation information is included in the result set, the Query Refiner will generate co-citation cluster maps to show central works in a result set.

Each of these displays will provide an easy way for the user to select information to modify, add to, or otherwise refine the current Query Sheet, and to reapply it to create a new result set.

During a session, InterBrowse will keep a version history of the Query Sheet so that the user is free to make and "undo" modifications to the search. Any version of a Query Sheet can be saved as an InterBrowse document.

Two useful *filters* will be provided as options for limiting the view of any result set: Local Holdings and Full-text Online.

The Local Holdings filter will limit the display to only those sources found in the user's library. For journals this can be done by filtering against a list of the serial holdings of the local library. For books it can be done through access to the data in an online union catalog, such as Brown's online catalog, JOSIAH, or a multi-site union catalog such as RLIN. This will help the user evaluate results based on sources that can actually be located.

The Full-text Online will limit a display to those citations which can be used as pointers to the full-text of an article or book in electronic form. This will bring to the user's attention those citations that can be located online for further searching and browsing.

It will be possible, while browsing any of these displays, to select individual records or an entire result set to be used in the Correspondence Builder, and/or saved in the Personal Information System, both of which are described below.

2.4 Correspondence Builder: Make use of results to develop a query in another collection

The InterBrowse design assumes that the information a user needs may be located in any of a number of databases, and that each database may represent similar ideas (subject headings) and identical elements (titles, author names, journal names) in dissimilar ways. The purpose of the Correspondence Builder is to help the user locate information that overlaps with, or is related to, information in saved result sets. It will provide another set of tools that can be applied to the Query Sheet and result sets:

- tools for reapplying a Query Sheet to another database
- tools for showing relations among results from various databases

Tools will be provided for building tables to show the relations between database-supplied subject headings in selected results and user-supplied subject headings assigned to those records in the Personal Information Manager.

For example, a user might be looking for articles about how database software is used to manage bibliographic information. Previous results from a search for information on the concept of *bibliographic data bases* in both ERIC and the MLA Index show that this phrase exists as a subject heading in both databases. In ERIC most of the thirty-three records found also have subject headings such as *online searching* and *databases*. In the MLA the two records with the subject heading *bibliographic data bases* also use the subject heading *research tools*. By browsing the MLA, the user locates three more interesting records with *research tools* and *data base*, and nine others with *data base* and *computer-assisted research* as subject headings. As the user copies each of these records into his Personal Information Manager, the Correspondence Builder will map the user-assigned keywords to the database-supplied subject headings. Based on the results of previous searches, this tool will be able to suggest possible synonyms and related subject headings in these two databases for later searches.

This tool will maintain a table of what sources are indexed in what databases. This will allow the user to look for information that is likely to be found in specific journals. It will also provide the ability to use bibliographic citations from one database as "pointers" to full text versions of an article available in another collection, as described in the Full-text Online filter above.

2.5 Personal Information Manager: Storing results locally in a systematic fashion for use in the work environment

We assume that the user will want to save and use information located in a result set. The Personal Information Manager will be capable of accepting selected "pieces" of information from a result set, and will provide tools to help the user organize the copy of this information.

A result set will be treated as a group of *objects* which the user can directly manipulate. Selecting a result will involve marking or moving a result object into a *save* space.

Transferring (copying) information to the local system will be done in a form that retains the semantic information in each record, and either transfers the complete record or enough information to retrieve more information when necessary.

In citation collections, InterBrowse will bring back full tagged records complete with database-specific subject headings and identifiers for *classification*, along with a selected view of that record for *display*. In full-text, InterBrowse will bring back sentences or paragraphs, as defined by the user, and enough information to return to the complete article if necessary. In numeric collections, InterBrowse will bring back data along with semantic relations to other data in the collection.[6]

Saved results will become part of a local database, built by the Personal Information Manager, which will contain tools for normalizing data in the personal or group work space. These tools will include:

- correlation tables for forms of author names and journal titles
- mapping personal subject classifications to database-specific subject headings

The Personal Information Manager will be capable of integrating information into the text/graphics authoring work environment of other Intermedia applications. It can be used to generate sets of footnotes, bibliographies, or other forms of citation for use with other Intermedia editors.

3 INFORMATION RETRIEVAL AS HYPERMEDIA

Current IR systems do not provide the flexible linking structure characteristic of hypertext/hypermedia systems. Having located an instance of the string "Oliver North" in a newspaper database, there is no way for a user to create a link between that string and the string "William Casey" in another story. At the same time, the current family of hypertext/hypermedia systems do not provide the basic record/field/string retrieval functionality so basic to information retrieval.[7] InterBrowse will provide a bridge between these two domains, providing access to a variety of IR systems from within Intermedia, a sophisticated hypermedia framework.

Using Intermedia, readers can browse through linked information in a non-sequential but orderly manner. Information is entered into Intermedia using one of a variety of applications, which include *InterText*, a text processor; *InterDraw*, a graphics editor; *InterVal*, a timeline editor that for organizing temporal information; *InterPix*, a scanned-image viewer; and *InterSpect*, an application to view three-dimensional models. Figure 2 illustrates an Intermedia session.

Intermedia is both an author's tool and a reader's tool. The system, in fact, makes no distinction between types of users, provided they have appropriate access rights to the material they wish to edit, explore, or create. Creating new materials, such as an InterBrowse Query Sheet, and making and following links are all integrated into a single seamless multi-user environment.

To link information, the user indicates a source selection (a *block*) in a document made with any of these editors and chooses the Start Link command. After performing any number of related or unrelated actions, the user indicates a destination selection (another *block*) in the same or some other document, and chooses the Complete Relation command. The system places a link marker beside each selection. When the operation is finished there is a semantic tie — a navigational link — between the two selections. Whenever the user selects a link marker and issues the Follow command, the document containing the other end of the link is activated and the appropriate information is presented in another window.

Intermedia stores link information is stored in a *web* database, not in the file itself. One implication of this strategy is that any user can create links to otherwise read-only documents, such as an online dictionary or citation database, without in any way corrupting the data itself. Webs present users with a context in which to collect and navigate a set of links. An individual user, a group of users, or even an entire campus can conceivably create a shared web of linked information.

Because InterBrowse is incorporated into Intermedia, users are able to link to and from search results stored as InterBrowse documents. These search results will be stored in two forms:

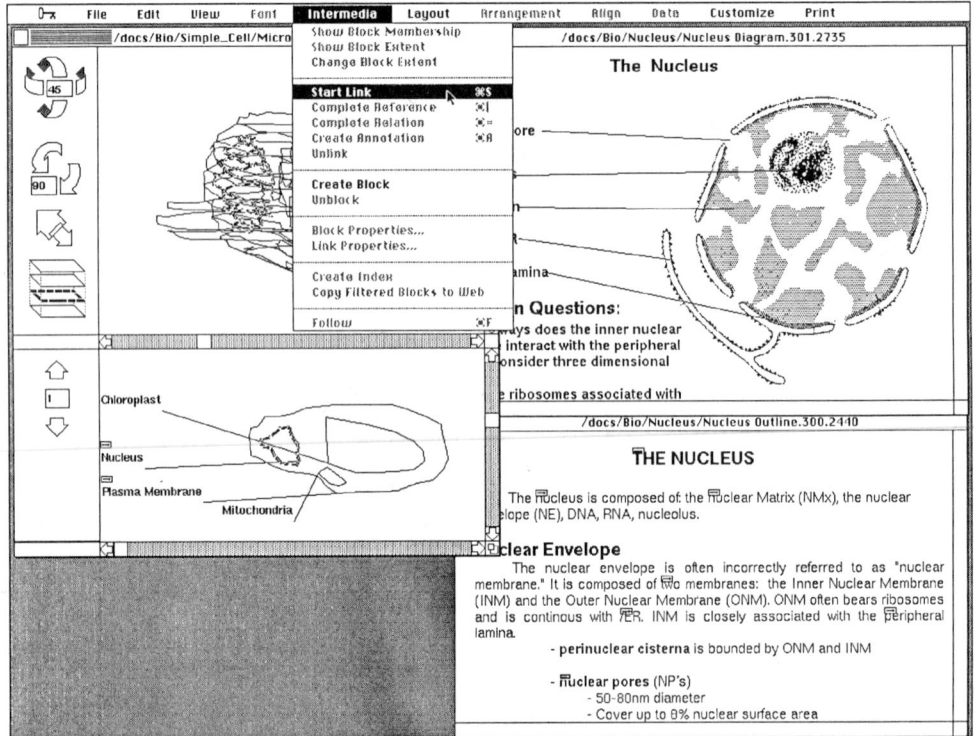

Figure 2: An Intermedia session. Links are created between the two-dimensional bitmap of a cell nucleus on the upper right, the three-dimensional wireframe of the cell on the left, and the text document on the lower right.

- as a Query Sheet containing the algorithm for locating information: the search path to database, and the actual search query

- as a Result sets stored in the Personal Information Manager

The Intermedia linking mechanism is used in InterBrowse to save or create links among pieces of information to make it easy for the user to follow and navigate among related items. InterBrowse will allow for two kinds of links: block to block link and action link. An overview of the linking strucutre is found in Figure 3. Of these, the first is currently implemented in all Intermedia applications. The other is under development.

3.1 BLOCK TO BLOCK LINK

A block to block link is a bidirectional link between two blocks in any Intermedia document. These links are created manually by the user selecting two blocks and making the link. InterBrowse will use block to block links for two purposes:

> Link between a block in any document and a Query Sheet for *viewing* or *editing*:
>
>> Query Sheets can be saved and linked to from any Intermedia document for later reference and modification. Following a link from a text or graphics document to a Query Sheet will start InterBrowse and display the Query Sheet. Similarly, a block in a Query Sheet can be linked to another Query Sheet, or any other Intermedia document.

Link between a block in any document and a view of one or more references stored in the Personal Information Manager:

A link can be made from a any document to a view of a citation. Following this link will open the view of the citation in the Personal Information Manager. Following the link from the citation will bring up another document, or citation.

3.2 ACTION LINK

An action link is a uni-directional link starting from a block and causing some action to take place. The action is specified by information in the document which is the target of the link. InterBrowse supports action links by linking a block in any Intermedia document to a Query Sheet, which is applied with the link is followed. InterBrowse will use action links for two purposes:

Link from a document to a Query Sheet

A link can be made from any block to an existing Query Sheet. Following this link will apply the query, produce a result set and present it to the user in the InterBrowse Query Refiner

Link from the Personal Information Manager to a Query Sheet

A link can be made from a reference stored in the Personal Information Manager to the database from which it came. Following this link goes back to the stored Query Sheet and re-locates the reference in the source database with the InterBrowse Query Refiner. The Refiner tools can then be used to continue browsing this database.

4 CONCLUSION

The design of InterBrowse addresses a large number of issues facing both information retrieval and hypermedia research. The design is based on our speculation, not that these issues need to be addressed, but that they can now be addressed by the methods we have used to create other scholarly tools in Intermedia. Given the advances in personal computer hardware, user interface design, and programming techniques, we feel that the time is right.

The development of InterBrowse will be accomplished in stages over the next few years. It is our hope that this research will prove valuable for other researchers in the field, as well as members of the the Online community at large.

Submitted 21 January 1988. The author wishes to acknowledge the contributions of other members of the InterBrowse design team: Marty Michel, James H. Coombs, and Karen E. Smith.

Notes:

1. The design and functionality of Intermedia are described in a number of articles, the most recent of which is "Intermedia: The Concept and the Construction of a Seamless Information Environment", N. Yankelovich, et al., *IEEE Computer*, January, 1988, pp. 81-96.
2. *Pro-Search* manual, Ann Arbor: Personal Bibliographic Software, 1986.
3. In "Making A Difference: A Review of the User Interface Features in Six CD ROM Database Products" (*Optical InformationSystems Journal* 8:3 May/June 1988) I discuss the selection and feedback aspects of some current CD ROM database applications.
4. *Knowledge Finder* manual, North Andover: Aries Systems Corporation, 1987.
5. The Graphical Icon-driven Search Tool (GIST), a prototype for this kind of graphical representation of bibliographic data, is described in "Graphic Icons for Problem-Oriented Information Retrieval", Page Elmore, Providence: Brown University, IRIS Technical Report 87-1.
6. The initial version of InterBrowse will be limited to handling only bibliographic citation data.
7. See "Hypertext: An Introduction and Survey" J. Conklin, *IEEE Computer*, Sept. 1987 for a useful survey of such systems.

ABI/INFORM ON CD-ROM: HOW DOES THE DISK STACK UP?

Nancy S. Karp, University of Michigan School of Business Administration

Keywords: ABI/Inform Ondisc, CD-ROM

Abstract: This paper reviews and evaluates a new CD-ROM product, ABI/Inform Ondisc, offered by University Microfilms International, through a response to three questions. First, how do the system's retrieval techniques compare to those of the major online systems? The vendor has chosen to use some of the major features from DIALOG, NEXIS, BRS and others. The discussion will review these features, with some attention given to those that might be added or removed. Second, what are the advantages and challenges for librarians? While the librarian's role and image as a provider of information is enhanced, there are collection, staff time and other concerns to be addressed. The cost factor has both negative and positive aspects. Third, how do library users benefit? What are related problems? Users have access to a system that is fast, easy to use, always available and free of per-use charges. It is easy for users to view the computer as a quick source of all available information. They must be educated about the fact that CD-ROMs are to be used in conjunction with online, print and other information sources.

1. INTRODUCTION

    As the CD-ROM revolution continues, librarians who work in various library settings and disciplines are constantly watching for new products to become available in their areas of interest. For business librarians and for others who regularly search the business literature, University Microfilms International is making available in CD-ROM form one of the premier business databases, ABI/Inform. The database itself includes references to business articles in 680 management and business publications. The University of Michigan Kresge Business Administration Library has been a test site for ABI/Inform Ondisc since spring of 1987. We have recently purchased a subscription, as a result of an enthusiastic response from library users and reference librarians. ABI/Inform Ondisc (hereafter referred to as ABI Ondisc) is in general an excellent, easy to use product.

2. LIBRARY SETTING

    The Kresge Business Administration Library serves about 2,500 Business School faculty, students and staff, the majority of whom are masters level students. Most students use computers in their course work or elsewhere, with the result that many are interested in and willing to try out new systems. We have recently purchased an ABI Ondisc subscription, due to an extremely enthusiastic response from students, faculty and library staff. In addition to ABI, our students currently have access to two other optical disk systems. InfoTrac is known to many as a laserdisk subject index to almost 1,000 periodicals, about 600 of which are focused on business. COMPACT DISCLOSURE contains financial and textual information on about 10,000 public U.S. companies. It can be searched via either a menu-driven or command-driven (DIALOG) method. During COMPACT DISCLOSURE training sessions, we have focused on the menu-driven feature. ABI Ondisc offers searchers Boolean logic search capabilities. We are as of this writing (January, 1988) offering users ABI Ondisc workshops, stressing the use of Boolean logic and othermore advanced techniques. We plan to survey workshop attendees in order to assess the value of these sessions.

3. BASIC COMPARISONS: ABI ONDISC AND ONLINE

In the course of this paper, comparisons will be drawn with DIALOG, BRS and NEXIS features and search protocols. In general, the online version covers August, 1971 to the present. In its final form, ABI Ondisc will cover the last five years only, a time period adequate for most student research. As ABI Ondisc achieves the popularity it deserves, the availability of an historical disk may be of interest to university and other researchers.

ABI Ondisc is updated less often than the online databases, but - to UMI's credit - more often than most other databases currently available in CD-ROM form. The time lag for online is approximately four to six weeks, while the ABI Ondisc time lag is expected initially to be about three months.

The ABI Ondisc full record has all the important information that appears in DIALOG, BRS and NEXIS records, including both a Dun's company number and company field. Classification name, language and ISSN number, less important fields, are omitted. The subject terms are listed at the top of the record, making them easy to spot. Terms and phrases searched for are conveniently highlighted in the resulting record.

While the online systems offer many format options, ABI Ondisc currently offers the choice of a title only or a full record, complete with useful abstract. After a search request is processed, searchers first scan a list of titles and then select abstracts they wish to see. It may be useful to offer either a full or a citation format. Searchers would first scan citations, not just titles. Those not interested in reading an abstract can often make quick judgments as to the value of a title if they can immediately see the name of the periodical in which it appears. Many users are not interested in printing out a full abstract just to get a copy of the citation itself. The ability to avoid printing out unwanted abstracts, as valuable as they are to many if not most users, would decrease the amount of time spent at the terminal. This is an important feature in a setting such as ours where ABI Ondisc is an extremely popular service. InfoTrac allows its searchers to print either a single citation or a full page of references. This may be a useful capability for ABI Ondisc searchers a well, to be able to specify which citations or complete records are to be printed.

Records in most online systems are in last-in-first-out (LIFO) order; ABI Ondisc records are now basically retrieved in this order as well. It is possible (and often useful) to be able to limit a search result to specific publication years by specifying a range of dates to be covered. This is currently not possible in the ABI Ondisc version. However, it is possible to "or" the desired years together and combine the result with the concepts being searched. This is a fairly slow process; it takes time for the system to process the request. A date range option would be desirable if processing time could be significantly reduced. If a date range search is not needed because the user is interested in only the current year's articles (e.g. 1988), he or she could (1) "and" the terms with da(1988), (2) scan the LIFO full records, noting the publication dates, or (3) scan one or more screens of citations, as proposed above, if they were available. This last option would require the least processing time.

While it is possible online to sort records by author, periodical, publication year or other factors, no sort capability is currently available on ABI Ondisc. This would be an attractive option. Searchers would find it convenient, for example, to be able to sort records by periodical name in order to be able to locate articles on the library shelves more quickly.

4. SEARCH CAPABILITIES

Quoting from UMI's ABI/Inform Ondisc promotional material, the system is "easy enough for even inexperienced patrons to use, yet powerful enough to perform many of the sophisticated searches online users are accustomed to." It's true - users can find useful results fairly quickly. UMI wisely makes use of many of the best basic and advanced search features from BRS, DIALOG and NEXIS, while adding a few unique features of their own. I like the WORKING sign that flashes on and off while the system is processing, to reassure me that something is happening!

4.1 Basic

Among the many features attractive to the novice and helpful to the more experienced searcher:

Free-Text Searching

The user can enter a free-text phrase without having to include any connectors. The phrase "television advertising campaign" can be entered in just that way, without the BRS "adj" or DIALOG (w). Because of the size of the database, the nature of the search software, the speed of the CD-ROM disc drive, and the uniqueness (or lack of same) of the search terms, the response time is sometimes rather slow, especially with free-text searches, so that an ABI Ondisc search may take longer than an online search. This is understandably frustrating to both the user and to others waiting to use the system.

Usage Information

Information at the bottom of the screen always tells the user what to do next. See Figure 1. On each screen, the user is reminded about two additional sources of help. Pressing the F2 (Commands) key reveals other currently possible steps and lists what keys to press to activate them. Due to space limitations, these commands are often very brief and may require some explanation. Users may press the F1 (Help) key at any time to get further information. The Help key reveals a topics menu or actual information that is geared to the specific search situation at hand. A number of menu-driven system features are skillfully used in a command-driven environment.

Also due to space requirements, not all system features are referred to on the bottom information line. To take full advantage of ABI Ondisc's capabilities, the user needs to read the Help material either on-screen or, as soon promised by UMI, in brief written search guide format. UMI in writing this material has responded to the fact that users want to begin searching right away and spend as little time as possible reading directions! The Help

```
            UMI/DATA COURIER      ABI/INFORM     JAN 1983 -- AUG 1987
─────────────────────────────────────────────────────────────────────
         Search Terms                                  Item Count
─────────────────────────────────────────────────────────────────────
(01):   television - -> TELEVISION                   4358 item(s)
(02):   advertising - -> ADVERTISING               12079 item(s)
(03):   (01) pre/1 (02)                              981 item(s)
(04):   campaign - -> CAMPAIGN                      4597 item(s)
(05):   (03) pre/2 (04)                               28 item(s)

Search results in 28 item(s).
```

To Display List of Titles: Press ⏎.   F1=Help   F2=Commands

Figure 1. Screen displaying search results. Note
           additional information at the bottom of
           the screen.

screens as well as the introductory system screens are very well done. Information is concise; the user is not overwhelmed with detailed directions. A UMI-produced poster kept near the terminal summarizing system commands has proven invaluable.

Stopwords

Common words known to experienced searchers as stopwords are quickly identified as noise words on the processing screen. The searcher need not know what they are and thus does not need to allow for them when structuring the search request.

4.2 Advanced

Many more sophisticated features known to experienced searchers are available and made easy to use:

Truncation

ABI Ondisc allows the searcher to truncate words, using the DIALOG question mark truncation sign. Unlike BRS, DIALOG and NEXIS, it is not possible to specify the maximum number of letters to appear following the sign. To partially compensate for this lack, the plural form of a word is automatically retrieved. It would be useful to the searcher if it <u>were</u> possible to specify the number of letters to follow the truncation sign. Consideration should also be given to eliminating the automatic retrieval capability. These changes would speed up system response time and would also eliminate retrieval of unwanted terms. It is not currently possible to "not out" an unwanted singular or plural. In some cases, an unrelated concept would be retrieved: "communication" would also retrieve "communications." One way to deal with this problem would be to "and" the term with another concept. Both forms of the word would be retrieved, but at least the resulting references would be more relevant.

Field Searching

As noted in Figure 2, searchers can access information via the most frequently searched fields, including controlled vocabulary terms, ABI classification codes and a company field. As DIALOG and BRS searchers know, it is possible to specify single-word or multi-word descriptors. In DIALOG, the use of the /DF suffix after a single word term limits results to that single word only, while the /DE suffix broadens the results by retrieving all descriptors containing the word (or words) given. UMI might want to consider adding this feature to ABI Ondisc. It is clearly important to make searching as efficient as possible; the addition of this capability would decrease the amount of time the user spends at the terminal. At present, if the searcher wanted to search only "te(trade)", he or she would also retrieve "trade secrets", "census of retail trade - US", and a number of additional descriptor terms containing the word. The user can "not out" unwanted terms, but this can sometimes be a time-consuming process.

Field Name	Label
ABSTRACT	ab
AUTHOR	au
CODES	cd
COMPANY	co
DATE	da
DUNS	du
JOURNAL	jo
JRNLCODE	jc
TERMS	te
TITLE	ti

Figure 2. Searching by field. Searcher types a field name or label, then the search term enclosed in parentheses.

Logical (Boolean) Operators

NEXIS calls Boolean and proximity operators connectors; ABI Ondisc uses six of them and follows the NEXIS processing order guidelines. As shown in Figure 3, DIALOG searchers must prioritize only Boolean operators. BRS includes Boolean and proximity operators in its priority order, but they are conveniently processed from the most specific to the most general. The priority order for ABI (following NEXIS) is the most cumbersome to deal with. (Ref. 1) UMI handles this well by advising users to use common sense in grouping related concepts together with parentheses. This is certainly a sound approach for the present. As searchers become experienced with ABI Ondisc and thus more sophisticated, the "rules" may be harder to remember. Thus, it ultimately may be easier for users to deal with either the BRS or DIALOG method.

Modifying a Search Request

ABI Ondisc again borrows from NEXIS and other systems when it encourages users to enter a simple search request and then modify the request later if necessary. With the SuperSELECT command, DIALOG searchers can modify an initially more complex search request by combining and building on set numbers assigned to each element of the request. ABI Ondisc assigns a single set number to the results of a request. If an Ondisc search result

BRS	DIALOG	ABI Ondisc
adj	not	or
with	and	w/# or pre/#
same	or	w/seg
and/not		and
or		and not

Figure 3. Order in which Boolean and proximity operators are processed. DIALOG does not include proximity operators in the processing order.

is to be narrowed or broadened, it is often possible to pair this single set number with a narrowing or broadening term or other concept. When due to the nature of the search request this is not possible, the searcher can use designated keys to edit the previous search request and then re-enter it. This strategy is quite acceptable for the present. Later, when there is more widespread use of Boolean logic among library users, the more sophisticated DIALOG technique may be desired.

Other Techniques

An attractive feature available to ABI Ondisc users is called a "sideways" search. The user can highlight and then search an interesting term or phrase encountered anywhere in a record without having to entirely leave the current search. Then, by pressing a few keys, the searcher can return to the original search at the exact spot of interruption.

5. ADVANTAGES AND CHALLENGES FOR LIBRARIANS

5.1 Advantages

Cost

While the initial cost of an ABI Ondisc subscription is high, the library pays a set annual subscription fee, with none of the connect and communication charges of online systems. Compared to online costs, compact disk technology offers a relatively inexpensive method of teaching users to access automated information retrieval systems. The University of Michigan Business School academic year runs from September through April. Based on a usage rate of 16 half-hour search sessions per day for this eight-month period, the per-session cost is about $1.35. This estimate does not include hardware and supply costs. The system will be used less frequently during May through August. The session cost is even less when this activity is included in the calculations.

Librarian Role

Now that ABI Ondisc is available, Reference Department members have more time to spend dealing with more complex research questions. The user can now do some ready reference searching heretofore done by librarians, such as verifying citations and compiling a brief bibliography on a topic. The library's image as a provider of the new technologies is enhanced. The teacher/consultant role of the librarian is now more visible to users as they learn to access new systems efficiently and effectively.

5.2 Challenges

Cost

The initial cost of ABI Ondisc is high enough so that it is unlikely to be significantly offset by any reduction in purchase of print sources or by doing less online searching. The subscription fee may be too high for smaller public or college libraries.

Librarian Role

Librarians must devote time to teaching users about ABI Ondisc's many special features. A recent UMI survey polled users about their use of advanced search capabilities. Features were reported used, but not extensively. From our observation and based on user questions, a training program would definitely be useful. Students do not want to devote much time to reading documentation, no matter how well it is written. Librarians will need to continually educate users about the fact that many additional information sources exist to supplement and update ABI Ondisc information.

Collection Management

Many issues will surface as CD-ROM products become an increasingly larger part of a library's budget. In our case, ABI Ondisc has been so popular with our users that if we were to decide on a second subscription, we would need to consider how present services would be affected. Will we need to add to our periodical holdings in response to requests from ABI Ondisc users? Should we continue our present subscriptions to printed indexes?

Other

There are other concerns common with many CD-ROM systems. There are security issues related to CD-ROM disks and drives. Librarians must consider arrangement of reference facilities to accommodate CD-ROM products.

6. BENEFITS AND PROBLEMS FOR LIBRARY USERS

6.1 Benefits

General

Library users are able to access a system that is easy to search, available all hours the library is open, and is free of per-use charges. They can browse database references without cost. Results are available immediately. The time-saving ability to access and print full abstracts is very attractive. The scope and size of the database allows users to make significant progress in their research efforts. The self-serve aspect appeals to many. They are able to do research faster and more easily. In one particular instance, students were able to get overviews on hard-to-research industries by reading through relevant ABI Ondisc abstracts.

Library Use Education

ABI Ondisc is providing students with a good introduction to Boolean logic and database searching. Knowledge of these techniques will help them to adapt more easily to using online catalogs, other CD-ROM systems, and online databases.

6.2   Problems

Users have the tendency to view ABI Ondisc and other similar tools as the only sources necessary to do adequate research. This problem relates to the librarian's need to educate users about other available sources. Users also, understandably, expect all indexed periodicals to be easily and immediately available to them.

7.   SUMMARY

Current users of ABI/Inform online now have available to them a high-quality CD-ROM product. Librarians and their clientele who take the time to become familiar with ABI/Inform Ondisc will find it to be a valuable business reference tool.

REFERENCE

1.   Veccia, Susan H. "The Ubiquitous ABI/Inform: DIALOG, NEXIS, DIALCOM et al." Database, p. 38, February 1987.

LOCAL AREA NETWORKS IN AN ONLINE INFORMATION RETRIEVAL ENVIRONMENT

Harry M. Kibirige, Queens College

Keywords: Local Area Networks, LANs, Online Information Retrieval, Information centers, Libraries, Database Searching, Resource Sharing, Office Automation.

Abstract: Information professionals in libraries and information centers are gradually realizing the importance of local area networks in their daily activities. Microcomputers have pervaded all aspects of information work and networking them for optimum effectiveness has become inevitable. The local area network is thus a logical outcome of the micro proliferation to facilitate resource sharing. This paper presents a summary of the findings of a nation-wide research study on local area networks. It was sponsored by the City University of New York (CUNY) Research Foundation and conducted from July 1986 to December 1987. The purpose of the project was to evaluate the relevance of currently available networking systems for use in libraries and information centers. A sample of 600 United States libraries and information centers was randomly selected. In addition, another sample of 200 local area network products manufacturers and vendors was similarly selected. Investigation was done by questionnaires, interviews, and systems demonstrations. Results indicated that data sharing, electronic mail, uploading and downloading, device sharing, and software sharing are the most significant reasons for using local area networks in libraries and information centers.

1. INTRODUCTION

The value of information in society is at a premium. Today individuals and organizations have realized this fact and buy or sell information extensively as a marketable commodity. It is thus not only pertinent but mandatory for information professionals to discuss ways of optimizing it. Although they are relatively new, local area networks have a high potential for helping professionals to attain this goal.
This paper discusses local area networks as catalysts in the society's effort to access online information. It summarizes the results of a nation-wide study of these computer structures in American libraries and information centers. The online revolution which has been around for more than two decades, has pervaded the office, the library, the school, the factory, and the home. Local area networks are adding a very important dimension to it.

2. WHAT IS A LOCAL AREA NETWORK?

Several definitions of the term local area network abound in computer and information science literature. Some are too long or too brief to be adopted as working definitions. For the purposes of this paper a local area network (or LAN) is defined as a privately owned communications facility which links devices in a small area[1]. There are four basic elements in this definition which require further explanation.

First, a LAN must be fully owned and operated privately by the organization which initiated and continue to fund its activities. In other words, the communication links belong to the parent organization as opposed to other networks where links or lines are provided by common carriers like AT&T, Western Union or local telephone companies. Thus this distinction separates LANs from the networks based on large time sharing systems.

Second, it is a communications facility permitting devices to exchange information. It is not a computer network whereby a group of subordinate devices are hard wired or otherwise connected to a central processor or a cluster of processors. Several of the components of a LAN must have independent intelligence and processing power. Some information professionals discuss LANs as if they are limited to data. Although they are currently predominantly data communications facilities, systems are being developed to transmit:
- (a) Data - conventional computer generated messages.
- (b) Video images--like still picture frames, as well as moving images.
- (c) Audio messages--the spoken and machine generated signals.
- (d) Facsimile--replicas of graphic/written representations.

Multi-media LANs are at an advanced experimental stage and will soon be commercially available.

Third, a LAN links devices. A device linked in a local area network must be able to communicate to at least one other device on the network. The wide range of devices may include:
- (a) Central processors (CPU/computers)
- (b) Command and control systems (security, weather, etc.)
- (c) Dumb/intelligent terminals
- (d) Fax systems (Facscimile)
- (e) Interactive video
- (f) Other peripheral devices (disks, tapes, etc.)
- (g) PBXs (telephones/voice)
- (h) Transceivers (message transmitters and receivers)

Devices linked by a LAN may be from the same manufacturer say Apple Computers, AT&T and IBM. From the user's point of view, the more diverse the devices a given LAN can support the higher the utility value. The CUNY study discussed at the end of this paper revealed that most institutions have a variety of microcomputer brands in place. A LAN that permits multi-vendor devices to share data is definitely at higher premium than a single vendor based LAN.

Finally, a LAN is a facility for a small area. This results in ease of management, relative ease of use, and ownership by a single institution, division or department. It does not have to be in one building as suggested by some information professionals, for LANs have been successfully implemented in two or more buildings especially on college campuses or among research laboratories. The extremeties or the furthest nodes should not be more than 2 kilometers (approximately one mile) apart. Beyond that it might be better to use other terms like metropolitan area networks (MANs) or wide area networks (WANs). These limitations in the definition also relate to the main components of LANs, the microcomputer.

3. LAN COMPONENTS

Several pieces are connected together to make a LAN. Any LAN must have at least five elements: the cabling system, workstations, servers, interface units and network software. Depending on the size and configuration of the LAN, the number of the elements may vary. A brief explanation of the elements will indicate their relationships starting with the cabling system. The function of the cabling system is to physically interconnect devices to facilitate the flow of messages among them. There are three generic systems for cabling, coaxial cable, optic fiber and twisted pair wire. When packaged and marketed by different corporations, they may bear proprietary trademarks or brand names. Their characteristics are discussed in a later section.

Workstations form part of the intelligence of the LAN. They are the microcomputers (or personal computers) which are used to access, manipulate data or otherwise aid the end-user to perform his or her activities. They may be used as stand-alone or as LAN access devices. Depending on the user's choice or sometimes dictated by circumstances, they may be from one vendor or multiple vendors. As demonstrated by the CUNY study very few current or potential users of LANs start with a clean slate. The average institution has at least two or more brands of microcomputers before installing a LAN. Consequently, vendors providing protocol conversion, thus permitting use of multiple vendor workstations, would be more attractive to most users.

The third element is composed of servers. These are also microcomputers which facilitate access to shared resources for example a user from workstation X requiring that a file be printed on laser printer D will make the request through printer server W. For each shared device or set of devices, an associated server must be contacted before use. Some systems have independent servers, while others allocate server function to some of the workstations. There may be savings on the hardware in the latter case. However, the efficiency of the server as a workstation may be marred by the additional activity. Decision to have independent servers or use workstations depends on the level of financing available as well as the volume and range of services provided by the LAN.

The last hardware element is composed of interface units. They allow the logical connections to be made between the communicating devices. LAN vendors have various ways of implementing this. Some have circuit boards added to the microcomputer to transform it into a network station. Others have circuits incorporated in a separate box to which one or more micros may be connected.

LAN software is the final element to consider. Like any other computer system a LAN needs software to run and perform all the functions it is designed for. Three types of software are used, the systems software, the network software and the applications software. The systems software manages the hardware and permits other software to operate using the host hardware, examples would be the network versions of the DOS or UNIX. The network software, on the other hand, allows the interconnections between applications and the network. Common systems are Novells Netware and IBMs NETBIOS. The third component, the applications software covers the LAN versions of the ordinary software packages like dBase III, Lotus 1-2-3, Wordperfect and the like.

4. TOPOLOGIES AND TRANSMISSION MEDIA

Local area networks are characterized by three basic topoloogies or configurations namely: The star, the bus/tree and ring (2). These topologies are demonstrated in figure X. A star is a group of connected devices (nodes) served by a central device sometimes referred to as a host (computer). On the other hand, a bus/tree topology has a multiple-access, broadcast medium. Since all devices share a common communication medium, only one device an transmit at a time. As figure X indicates, the bus is the special case of the tree with only one trunk. Finally, the ring consists of a closed loop with each node attached to a repeating element.

Another important feature of networks is the transmission media. Surveying current literature reveals that there are three types of media suitable for networks, the twisted pair wire, coaxial cable and optical fiber. The twisted pair wire is one of the common transmission media. It's main weakness is that it is susceptible to noise. However, with proper shielding this defect can be minimized. Coaxial cable can achieve higher

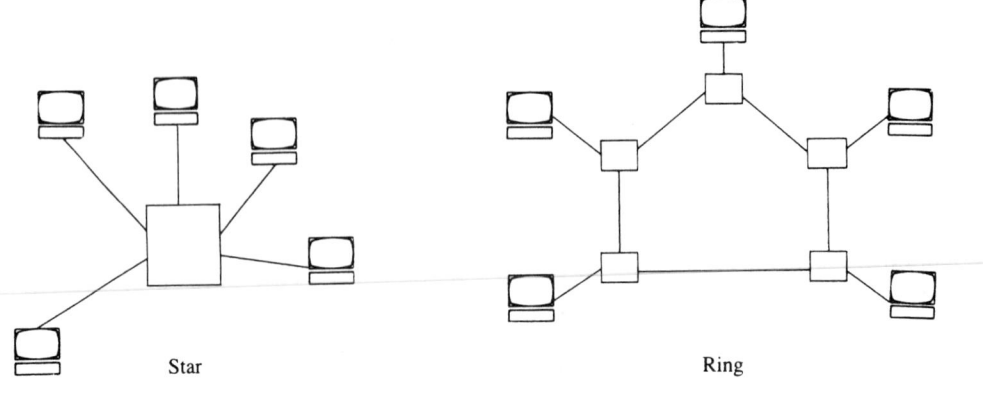

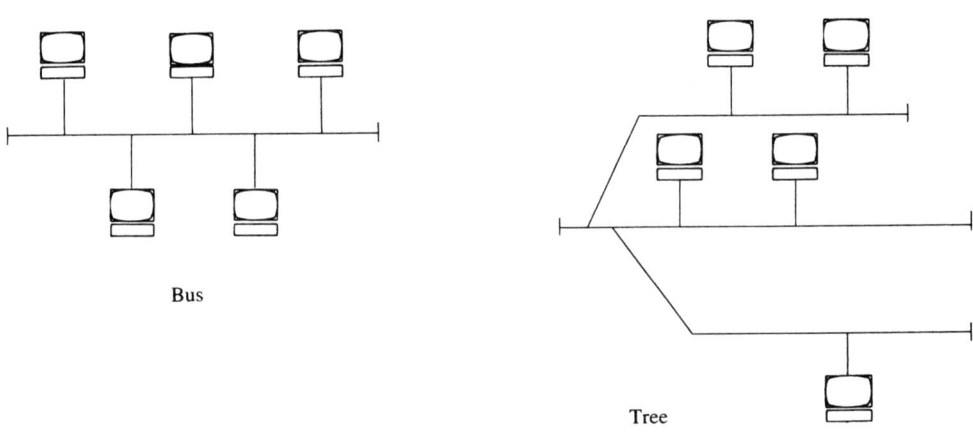

Figure X. Local area network topologies.

performance by providing higher throughput, supporting a larger number of devices and spanning greater distances than twisted pair wire. Although it is very expensive, optical fiber has even higher potential, for it carries a larger number of devices, has light weight, small diameter and is more resistant to noise than the other two.

It is important to note that choices of transmission medium and topology can not be done independently. For instance, twisted pair wire is more suited to the star topology than coaxial cable or optical fiber. This is due to the fact that the star topology requires a single point to point link between each device and a central switch. The higher data rates of coaxial cable or optical fiber would overwhelm the switches available with today's technology.

5. THE ROLE OF MICROCOMPUTERS IN LAN DEVELOPMENT

The microcomputer (or personal computer) has pervaded all aspects of life in industrialized countries. Today one finds micros in the school room, on college campuses, corporate office, research laboratories and public libraries where they are provided free for patron use. When they were introduced in the early 1970s, micros were not taken seriously by information professionals. They were relegated to lobbyists ventures. Large reputable computer manufacturers were initially not interested until Apple Computer Corporation built easy to use commercially available Apple II series in the late 1970s. Realizing that the micro market was rapidly expanding the computer giant, Big Blue joined the gang in 1981 with its IBM PC. The microcomputer has continued to be popular among the traditionally non-computer experts. Their increasing domination of the layman's computing arena is a result the micros highly desirable characteristics compared to mini or mainframe computers.

First, the micro has so far proved to be more versatile than any other computer on the market. It has been used for entertainment, from playing computer games to accessing electronic bulletin boards. Education in general has been promoted by a multitude of programs developed on the microcomputer. Every facet of the work place is currently enhanced by micro based applications. In fact, there are very few areas of human society, if any, which have not been touched by the power of the micro.

Second, the microcomputer is characterized by simplicity which in computerese translates into user-friendliness. The age of the mainframe computer was very intimidating to the layman. Introducing minicomputers in the 1960s somewhat reduced the level of intimidation, nevertheless, the end-user was still served via a middleman, the computer consultant. The advent of the micro ended the log on procedures and computing power became instantly available to whoever had access to it. In addition, both systems and application programs became easier to master and use. In other words, it revolutionized the computing environment for the layman.

Third, the micro is extremely portable in contrast to other computers. It may be placed on the desk top; put on ones lap while sitting on a bus, a subway or even on the plane; and may easily be moved from one office to another within an organization. The use of diskettes makes sharing of simple data and software relatively easy contrasted to mini or mainframe operations. One must, however, stress the fact that software portability is in this case limited to microcomputer systems with compatible hardware and of course software.

Fourth, availability of abundant systems and applications software has characterized the micro market. The end-user of micros has been blessed by the enthusiasm with which software houses have developed appropriate software. Several types of new or revised editions are unveiled every day. The user's major problem lies in identifying software appropriate for his or her application. For common applications, it is imprudent to start inhouse software development without surveying the market, because the chances are one or more packages have already been marketed. If not completely appropriate, the existing software may need minor modifications, which makes it more cost-effective than starting from scratch.

Finally, another desirable characteristics of micros is the gradual upward growth into the mini and mainframe turf. The performance of the top of the line super micro like IBM PS/2 model 80 or some of Data Generals 32 bit super micros is higher than the lower end mini or mainframe, for instance the IBM 360s or Digital Equipment Corporations PDP 11 series. One may wonder how and why has this been possible. The answer partly lies in the evolvement of computer technology.

5.1 Underlying Technology

Microcomputer upward migration has come as a result of relatively recent developments in computer hardware and software, particularly in the 1970s and early 1980s. Computer circuit designers have successfully experimented with large scale integrated circuits (LSI) and later very large scale integrated circuits (VLSI)(3). Using LSI and VLSI technology, it is possible to compress more electronic circuits on a single silicon chip. These high density chips are used in creating microprocessors. Such microprocessors are in turn used as the building blocks for microcomputers and associated devices.

LSI and VLSI technology based devices are characterized by smaller sizes, large memories and faster response times. The tendency to miniaturize computer components which have more power is clearly manifest in the microcomputer memories. The earlier micros had main memories of 8K as standard memories. Memories have advanced to 64K, 128K, 256K and 512K. Megabyte (million bytes) memories are now standard for super micros. Word sizes have likewise progressively increased from 8-bit, through 16-bit to currently 32-bit for the super micros.

Concurrent improvement of microcomputer hardware and software has resulted in the marketing of sophisticated software packages. Such packages can perform a multitude of functions like accounting, word processing, data base management and communications. Due to the size of their memories, earlier microcomputers could not accommodate some of the modern packages. For instance Wordperfect which needs a minimum of 256K of main memory could not be used on earlier microcomputers. Similarly, Lotus 1-2-3 which requires a minimum of 128K of memory could not be used on some of the early micros.

5.2 Influence on Usage

Usage patterns for end-users have been greatly influenced by the increasing sophistication of the micro. When micros infiltrated individual offices in the early and mid 1980s, they were used mainly for relatively simple tasks like word processing and accounting. A number of developments have occured on the user scene since then. First, the simple micro has become a very sophisticated indispensable workstation in the work place. This is true in business and industrial environments, academic settings and libraries or information centers of all types. As the information appetite of desk top computer users get sharper, they realize that they must access common data banks locally or outside their institution. Inevitably several modems must be purchased as well as taking subscriptions to interstate, national or international communications vendors.

Second, to the information systems manager in organization X, what was initially applauded as desirable distributed processing becomes an insurmountable problem. Not only are users demanding access to common data, they also demand easy access to expensive devices like high quality printers and winchester storage systems. At the same time, some users may have under-utilized disk space and communication devices. Thus on some sites, there may be a lot of computing power, and yet it may appear to be inadequate to some users.

Finally, the LAN has come to the rescue to ameliorate both the user and information manager's problems. The LAN satisfies both the end-users need for independence and the information managers desire for co-ordination. The user can have proprietary files and at the same share common data and expensive peripherals(4). Similarly, the information systems manager will ensure that common data is not contaminated by unauthorized modification thus maintaining high data integrity. It may be safely said that the LAN is the logical by-product of microcomputer proliferation in organizations.

6. LANS AND THE ONLINE CONCEPT

Whereas the term online is commonly used in data processing, it attains a special connotation when used in libraries and information centers. Traditionally, information centers and libraries used hard copy resources to satisfy the basic information needs of most organizations. With the development of data banks like DIALOG, BRS, SDC and the Source, the librarian can by pass the conventional sources and obtain information instantly. Similarly, the creation of organizations like Online Computer Library Center (OCLC), Research Libraries Information Network (RLIN) and the Washington Library Network (WLN) has resulted in the provision of computerized services which aid the librarian in providing information quickly to library patrons. The latter group of organizations are sometimes referred to as bibliographic utilities. The two most significant funcations of bibliographic utilities are first to minimize original cataloging and processing of books by providing online standard bibliographic records which may be adopted by libraries. Second, by maintaining online library holdings at regional and national levels, they facilitate easy and speedy routing of inter library loan requests.

Many other internal library functions have been improved by computerization. The earliest library function to computerize was the item check out (or circulation) system. With this system, an item may be checked out quickly without either the library staff member or patron filling out check out forms. If necessary, a librarian can review online items checked out to see who has what and when it is due back in case some one else desires to use the same item. One of the most fascinating areas of library automation is the computerization of the catalog. In a number of libraries, the traditional card catalog has been replaced by an online public access catalog (OPAC). Using a computer terminal patrons can access the catalog online via author, subject or other access point.

Online is changing the way librarians and other information specialists do business. The hard copy printed document is gradually ceasing to be the major source of information. This is particularly true of current information. Most information providers in corporate information centers and large research and academic libraries resort to the computer as the first resource to search when faced with user questions demanding very current information. Thus online has meant simplification of repetitive routines and enhancement of library services for the benefit of patrons.

Local area networks optimize the concept of online in several ways. First, they facilitate online sharing of expensive hardware like high quality lazer printers, storage devices like hard disks, tapes and cassettes. Users are alternated among these devices using servers. Second, software can be shared online without physically transporting diskettes from one micro user to another, known in the popular press as the 'diskette derby.' In this case one LAN version of the software package is loaded on the server and may be accessed by any of the users on the LAN. Third, commonly used data can be conveniently shared online by microcomputers without going through larger computers (minis or mainframes). This may be administrative data, such as staff files to be used by the library management group. It may also be the conventional catalog data to be used by both the public and library staff. It has been demonstrated in the United Kingdom that OPACs can be designed to run effectively on LANs (5).

Fourth, LANs are used for sharing communications devices especially high quality powerful modems. Depending on usage ratio, frequency of use and capacity, a set of modems can serve a group of users who must access outside data banks and bibliographic utilities. This is again implemented on a LAN through a communications device server. Complementary to this, data downloaded from a data bank or a bibliographic utility may be stored on a common access disk and later be searched, reformatted or otherwise manipulated by any of the devices attached to the LAN. Uploading is equally enhanced. Data created on different micros may be stored in a file, on a common disk. When all the refinements are done on the common file, any of the micros on the LAN may issue a command online to upload it into a cooperative bibliographic utility. Checks and safeguards can be built into the LAN design to maintain data file integrity.

Starting from the mid 1980s, the term professional workstation has been commonly used by information professionals to refer to powerful desktop microcomputers. It is a workstation because such a micro may be designed to manipulate most of the programs that a given professional requires to effectively perform his or her duties. Report writing, accessing data banks and communicating to other professionals can be done online using the workstation. The corporate executive office, the scientific laboratory as well as libraries and information centers achieve higher levels of productivity by using a workstation on a LAN. Economies are realized through online sharing of resources and file and data quality can be achieved through careful planning.

7. THE CUNY STUDY

This section of the paper presents a summary of results of a study of microcomputer networking systems in American libraries and information centers which stressed LANs. The aim of the nation-wide study was to evaluate the relevance of currently available systems for library use. There were two major aspects to the study. First, using a representative sample (600) of United States libraries and information centers, it was intended to access library need for microcomputer networking. This was done by a combination of questionnaire, interviews and site visits. Second, it was intended to investigate a broad representation (200) of microcomputer networking systems manufacturers/vendors to identify systems which can be adapted/adopted for library applications. This was done by questionnaire, interviews, site visits and demonstrations. Only four sites were visited for demonstrations. The study which was funded by the City University of New York (CUNY) started in July 1986 and ended in December 1987.

In pursuit of the two basic aspects of the study, the main focus was on the following objectives:
1. To identify the variety of microcomputers currently in use in libraries and information centers in the United States.
2. To identify functions and services which require microcomputer networking as perceived by librarians and other information specialists.
3. To identify which libraries and information centers already use microcomputer networking systems.
4. To identify what microcomputer networking systems, if any, are currently in use and for which functions.
5. To investigate the availability of in-house developed microcomputer networking systems. If such systems exist, are they available for purchase or lease to other libraries.

6. To identify advantages/pluses or disadvantages of using microcomputer networking systems as perceived by librarians and other information specialists.
7. To identify microcomputer networking systems which can be adopted/adapted for library applications.
8. To appraise cost estimates for the relevant systems.
9. To appraise software and hardware features required for the suitable systems.
10. To produce a comprehensive report which can be used by librarians and other information specialists in evaluation and selection of microcomputer networking systems.

7.1 Research Results

Tabulation of field data indicated a number of interesting tendencies as demonstrated in tables 1 and 2. What follows is a summary of the findings. A full report of the CUNY Study will be published by Greenwood Press in 1988 in a full length monograph on local area networks.

7.11 Rationale for Networking Microcomputers

Librarians and information specialists are very keen on LANs. They have expressed frustration that several of their microcomputers cannot communicate with each other. Those who can transmit messages using PBXs think that this is somewhat limited and see LANs as one of the logical alternatives. The following have been given as the main reasons for networking microcomputers (see rows 1-5 respectively):

(1) To access common data, examples - online public access catalogs, acquisitions, and serials information.
(2) To share expensive devices, examples - hard disks, high quality printers.
(3) To share software (program packages) examples - Word Processing, accounting, communications.
(4) Electronic mail among departments and with patrons.
(5) Uploading and downloading to and from other systems, examples - OCLC, RLIN, DIALOG, the Source.

With 95.5% of the respondents agreeing, the research indicated that online access to common data is the single most important reason for networking microcomputers. Sharing software had 78.1% consent level indicating caution with regard to copyright provisions.

7.12 Current Usage of LANs

As indicated by row 6, the number of libraries and information centers which are already using LANs is relatively small (18.6%) Of the institutions surveyed, there was a marked concentration among academic libraries and few public or special libraries. However, as indicated by row 7 45.4% of the sample have definite plans to use LANs. A considerable number of institutions are in the middle of negotiations with vendors.

Some of the current users in the sample were:
Allegheny General Hospital, Health Sciences Library (Pittsburgh, PA)
AT&T Bell Labs Information Center (NJ)
California Institute of Technology (CA)
Dow Chemical Company Information Center (MI)
Ford Motor Company Information Center (MI)
Georgetown University Medical Center (Washington, D.C.)
Humboldt State University (CA)
Lexington Public Library (KY)
Massachusetts Institute of Technology (MA)

1.	ACCESS	FREQUENCY	PERCENT	CUMULATIVE FREQUENCY	CUMULATIVE PERCENT
		7	.	.	.
	N	16	4.5	16	4.5
	Y	341	95.5	357	100.0

2.	SHRDEV	FREQUENCY	PERCENT	CUMULATIVE FREQUENCY	CUMULATIVE PERCENT
		13	.	.	.
	N	77	21.9	77	
	Y	274	78.1	351	100.0

3.	SHRSOFT	FREQUENCY	PERCENT	CUMULATIVE FREQUENCY	CUMULATIVE PERCENT
		18	.	.	.
	N	84	24.3	84	24.3
	Y	262	75.7	346	100.0

4.	ELECMAIL	FREQUENCY	PERCENT	CUMULATIVE FREQUENCY	CUMULATIVE PERCENT
		9	.	.	.
	N	52	14.6	52	14.6
	Y	303	85.4	355	100.0

5.	UPDNLOAD	FREQUENCY	PERCENT	CUMULATIVE FREQUENCY	CUMULATIVE PERCENT
		10	.	.	.
	N	59	16.7	59	16.7
	Y	295	83.3	354	100.0

6.	PRESLAN	FREQUENCY	PERCENT	CUMULATIVE FREQUENCY	CUMULATIVE PERCENT
		4	.	.	.
	N	293	81.4	293	81.4
	Y	67	18.6	360	100.0

Table 1. Data Analysis I

7.	LANPLANS	FREQUENCY	PERCENT	CUMULATIVE FREQUENCY	CUMULATIVE PERCENT
		115	.	.	.
	N	136	54.6	136	54.6
	Y	113	45.4	249	100.0

8.	WANTREPT	FREQUENCY	PERCENT	CUMULATIVE FREQUENCY	CUMULATIVE PERCENT
		15	.	.	.
	N	74	21.2	74	21.2
	Y	275	78.8	349	100.0

9.	TOO_EXP	FREQUENCY	PERCENT	CUMULATIVE FREQUENCY	CUMULATIVE PERCENT
		337	.	.	.
	Y	27	100.0	27	100.0

10.	TOO_NEW	FREQUENCY	PERCENT	CUMULATIVE FREQUENCY	CUMULATIVE PERCENT
		354	.	.	.
	Y	10	100.0	10	100.0

11.	NO_ASESS	FREQUENCY	PERCENT	CUMULATIVE FREQUENCY	CUMULATIVE PERCENT
		278	.	.	.
	Y	86	100.0	86	100.0

12.	OTH_OBJ	FREQUENCY	PERCENT	CUMULATIVE FREQUENCY	CUMULATIVE PERCENT
		323	.	.	.
	Y	41	100.0	41	100.0

13.	NOT_APP	FREQUENCY	PERCENT	CUMULATIVE FREQUENCY	CUMULATIVE PERCENT
		146	.	.	.
	Y	218	100.0	218	100.0

Table 2. Data Analysis II

Monsato Company Information Center (MO)
New York University Library (N.Y.)
Northern Illinois Library System (IL)
Oregon State University (OR)
University of California, Los Angeles (CA)
University of California, San Diego (CA)
University of Kentucky (KY)
University of New Mexico (NM)
University of Virginia, Charlottesville (VA)

7.13 The Vendor Market

The market for LANs is in a state of flux and confusing. Whereas the potential for them in library automation is tremendous, the market has several sleek ads and aggressive salespeople. Extreme caution is needed to distinguish between genuine LANs products and products which vendors claim to be LANs but are in fact multi-user systems based on data switches.

As for the types of LANs currently in use in libraries/information centers, Ethernet appears to be the most popular so far. Most commonly cited vendors include: Corvus Systems, Nestar Systems, Novell, 3 COM and Ungermann-Bass. IBMs token-ring is receiving much attention due to the prestige of the vendor, but has relatively few installations. AT&Ts LANs are incorporated in campus-wide networking systems which are relatively few.

7.14 Current Problems

The basic problems center around the following:
(a) Estimating the workload of the library/information center.
(b) Designing the LAN, in collaboration with technical personnel.
(c) Identifying suitable LAN software and hardware.
(d) Selecting a reliable vendor.
(e) Lack of standards among currently available LANs.
(f) Maintaining data security after installation.

Some of the solutions to these problems, as revealed by the research findings, are discussed in detail in the Greenwood Press book mentioned earlier.

8. REFERENCES

1. Stallings, William. "Local Networks." Computing Surveys 16, No. 1, p. 4-5, March 1984.

2. Graube, Maris and Mulder, Michael C. "Local Area Networks." Computer 17, p. 243, October 1984.

3. Mead, Carver and Conway, Lynn. Introduction to VLSI Systems. Reading, Mass.: Addison-Wesley, 1980 1-50.

4. Puette, Robert. "Executive View of Microcomputers." Infosystems 33, No. 8, p. 28-30, 1986.

5. Mitev, Nathalie Nadia, et al., Designing an Online Public Access Catalogue: Okapi, a Catalogue on a Local Area Network. London: British Library, 1985.

OPTICAL MEDIA: CONVERTING HIGH-TECH LIBRARY NEEDS INTO MARKET REALITIES

Linda Joyce Kosmin, Johns Hopkins University Applied Physics Laboratory

Keywords: CD-ROM, Videodiscs, Libraries, Evaluation Criteria

Abstract: The purpose of this paper is to assess current optical media opportunities for scientific and technical libraries. An array of insights about currently marketed applications software is presented, as well as an analysis of targeted audiences. Most of the off-the-shelf CD-ROM packages that are being sold only modestly address high-tech library needs. Although optical media with their random access capabilities are capable of rivaling traditional collection formats, high-tech librarians continue to be forced to respond to most complex reference inquiries by using relatively outmoded resources that are available only in print, microfilm, or microfiche. The results of an informal opinion poll of 25 high-tech librarians are summarized, indicating some expectations for future optical hardware and software developments. Criteria for evaluating and selecting optical information products for libraries are discussed.

1. INTRODUCTION

Since first-generation CD-ROM drives were introduced into the marketplace in November 1984, more than 150 different software packages have become available from a variety of vendors. Most products of interest now offered to the scientific community tend to be subsets of existing on-line databases, replications of multivolume encyclopedic works, selective military data, other government data, business and financial information, and illustrated manufacturer's parts catalogs. They give hope to many librarians, who are anxiously awaiting the day when an abundance of off-the-shelf applications software will emerge to support high-tech research and development interests. Many high-tech librarians feel that they represent a substantial market that is ready and able to buy — even more so than some other markets — as soon as the right products are available for sale or lease.

The optical media industry needs to take more initiative in discovering what compact software is required by high-tech librarians to help facilitate library data retrieval. The industry should then make every effort to produce and market the needed products in a timely fashion. Most of the packages produced thus far tend to be geared toward public or general academic libraries, legal- and business- oriented markets, specific government agencies, and health science sectors.

In an age when the technology has already been developed to facilitate rapid automated and random access to the contents of highly sophisticated reference works, it seems a waste of time and effort for librarians to be forced to continue to respond to the bulk of complex scientific library inquiries using tools that are available only in such relatively outmoded formats as print, microfiche, and microfilm. There appears to be no single clear-cut rationale for such slow delivery of a wider selection of needed high-tech applications software. Delays have been attributed in part to unresolved issues such as costs, disc size, graphics, standardization, copyright compliance, product quality, and competition from magnetic media.

It has been said that some optical media producers are concerned about which hardware manufacturers will survive the short haul. On the other hand, many hardware developers seem to be hesitant about predicting which applications software will be bestsellers if the appropriate support equipment is delivered (Ref.1). Fear of copyright infringement has also contributed to CD-ROM product delays. Not only is there a real risk that an entire disc will be pirated, but publishers are concerned about seeing massaged portions of selected material from their discs being marketed as competitive products (Ref.2).

If a publisher is already making a substantial profit by selling information packaged in conventional formats, it may not be fiscally expedient to invest large amounts of time and money in developing repackaged products using optical technology. The trade-off is not always obvious at first glance, especially when it costs a minimum of about $1000 to convert one million printed characters into a machine-readable format. Optical media publishers may need to spend hundreds of thousands of dollars to fill one CD-ROM disc with newly converted information (Ref. 3). In addition, selling information that is also available in alternative formats is not always considered the wisest marketing strategy for an individual publisher. When a company puts two or more of its products in competition with each other, the possibility always exists that one product will produce average profits, while the competitors produce a substantial loss of revenue. To circumvent the problem, some companies are aiming specific formats toward regional markets. For example, one multimedia publisher concentrates its traditional print product in one geographical location while marketing only the CD-ROM version in another part of the world (Ref. 4).

2. CHALLENGES AND EXPECTATIONS

During the past four years, CD-ROM technology has overcome a wide range of obstacles. Software developers have successfully met such challenges as integrated graphics, increasingly smaller levels of text compression, windowed user environments, and hypertext browsing capabilities (Ref.5). Librarian wish lists are beginning to change as technology and production efforts continue to meet earlier demands. For example, the results of a 1986 survey of 25 librarians in the Washington, D.C., area indicated that most respondents thought that optical discs could provide better access to full-text contents of periodical backfiles than is now available on microfilm and microfiche (Ref. 6).

Today, full-text sci-tech journals on optical discs have become a reality. Many burdens associated with interlibrary lending and borrowing have been nearly eliminated or are greatly reduced. The pilot ADONIS project will attempt to show how this might be accomplished. The initial intent of this international endeavor is to supply on multiple CD-ROM discs the entire article contents of 219 biomedical journals. Periodicals published by 10 participants in 1987 and 1988 will be distributed to 11 centers around the world. The two participants in the United States — Information on Demand and University Microfilms International — as well as six output centers in Europe and others in Mexico, Australia, and Japan will use the CD-ROM full-text files to fill actual journal article requests until June 1989 (Ref. 7). Apparently, any research library can order an item from the ADONIS CD-ROM collection from the nearest distribution center and expect a high-quality reproduction by mail, telefacsimile transmission, or overnight courier delivery. "The original ADONIS concept was based on the hypothesis that if a new technology could be used to fulfill requests more cheaply than the current labor intensive photocopying procedures, the money saved could be shared with the copyright holders without substantially changing the price that the centers would charge for the supply of documents" (Ref. 8).

In an attempt to ascertain current interest as well as to strengthen support for optical products that might meet high-tech library needs, a second informal opinion poll was taken by telephone in November 1987 among the same 25 information professionals working in the Washington area. Results of that survey provide some interesting new insights:

- o Eighteen favored a single workstation configuration that would enable the end user to add information to a CD-ROM disc that already contained some replicated data.

- o Fifteen thought that smart discs incorporating features of expert systems would be advantageous in guiding decisionmaking.

- o Twenty-one wanted mixed-mode databases combining numerical data, full-text, graphics, sound, and analog- and digital-type images.

- o All 25 wanted the capability for simultaneous rather than sequential searching of both on-line and CD-ROM bibliographic files.

- o Sixteen felt that a compact type of jukebox mechanism for ease of CD-ROM disc changing would be a plus.

- o Eighteen respondents thought that networked CD-ROM systems would facilitate end-user access and eliminate single workstation queuing problems.

- o For a second year, all 25 reaffirmed their interest in seeing full-text product offerings of core sci-tech reference books, traditionally classified within the same subject categories — all on as few CD-ROM discs as possible and independent of publisher.

- o Twenty-two respondents continued to favor the concept of a multipurpose workstation with mixed-media drives that could handle an assortment of optical information formats including CD-ROM, 12-in videodiscs, WORM discs, CD-I, LaserCards, and multiple-sized floppy discs.

3. NEW APPLICATIONS SOFTWARE

There continues to be speculation about what will be the optical media industry's most effective propelling force for growth over the next five to ten years. Until now, it certainly does not appear to have been the vigor of competition but rather an apparent product pull attitude on the part of certain market segments. For high-tech librarians, confidence in the generic declarations of laser-disc technology has been strengthened by recent entries into the sci-tech marketplace.

For example, the scientific community has benefited recently by the production of McGraw-Hill's Science and Technology Reference Set on CD-ROM, which combines 4000 pages of text with scanned image graphics, permitting illustrations to appear in their appropriate context (Ref. 9). In addition, technical librarians are applauding four products being sold in CD-ROM format by John Wiley & Sons: the Kirk-Othmer Encyclopedia of Chemical Technology (24-volume set), the Mark Encyclopedia of Polymer Science and Engineering (19-volume set), the International Dictionary of Medicine and Biology (3-volume set), and The 1987 Registry of Mass Spectral Data (Ref. 10). Also, the long-awaited Science Citation Index was recently released by ISI on disc.

A commendable new product offering from the International Association for Scientific Computing is CD/BIOTECH. In addition to original articles and conference papers, this innovative optical disc product combines complete and condensed versions of NIH's Genetic Sequences Databank and the Protein Identification Resource compiled by the National Biomedical Research Foundation. Moreover, it includes the European Molecular Biology Laboratory's Data Library, which completes the initial CD-ROM collection of five databases (Ref. 11).

One hardware developer interested in seeing new applications software has adopted a useful approach as it enters the CD-ROM marketplace. Last summer, Apple Computer, Inc. announced that the company planned to provide both technical support and stimulus to existing optical software publishers interested in initiating products for use with Macintosh PCs and their Apple II product line (Ref. 12). We hope this innovative stimulus will lead to many new high-tech-oriented products.

4. EVALUATION CRITERIA

Development of criteria for evaluating optical media is as important to library collection development programs as applying conventional selection parameters to new acquisitions of publications in traditional formats. This is especially true for two important reasons. First, more and more optical media publishers are offering standard publications in this alternative format. Second, many new optical applications software programs are expected to be targeted for library markets.

There may be times when selecting compact discs for the library's collection may appear to be somewhat more complicated than merely choosing microfilm/microfiche over print editions of books and serials. For example, selecting those CD-ROM databases that compete with on-line files can significantly change the total work environment, affect areas of job responsibility, increase such service processing requirements as filling interlibrary loan requests for journal articles or conference papers not available on-site, and can cut initially into annual budget plans and allocations.

In developing criteria for selection, librarians need to consider seriously, but not be limited to, the following: storage capacity; quality, comprehensiveness, and updating of the information content; disc accessibility and retrieval speeds; initial costs; ongoing supplies and maintenance obligations; workstation configurations; ease of disc changing; system and disc security; and additional staff training and monitoring requirements (Ref. 13).

While fewer CD-ROM product alternatives confront today's librarian than other types of computer software products, criteria used to select other computer software packages on the market can be applied to optical media. The selection process should include advance planning, needs assessment at various levels, a detailed evaluation and comparison of products available or in prototype phases, estimations of the added value of one product over its alternative format, and cost/benefits/risk analyses. Getting input from library advisory committees and volunteering to serve as beta testing sites may be very constructive methods to use before making final purchasing decisions. It is always wise to involve early those who might be using the compact disc products.

Shelving space is gained. Compact disc storage arrangements foster collection resource expansion, while permitting the rededication of stack space for other functions. Also, disc use could mean a significant reduction in the need for remote storage facilities. Staff time and energy previously spent repairing torn pages, hunting for misshelved printed publications, shelving repeatedly, and reading shelves in a seemingly endless cycle might now be channeled in other, more productive directions. Replacement of worn books, lost or damaged microfiche, and need for multiple copies tends to take on a historical perspective (Ref. 14). On the other hand, while compact disc workstations do much to alleviate overcrowded dusty stacks, much of the available high-tech hardware definitely alters the historic library perspective of an inviting, cushioned, aesthetic ambience often traditionally associated with comfortable library reading rooms (Ref. 15).

One must consider ease of access if a patron is to use the newly installed technology comfortably. The number and type of workstation configurations, as well as the actual space allocated to the hardware, become important considerations. For many systems, a drawback of CD-ROM access has been that only one patron could access the machine at one time, a problem that is being resolved by a few vendors who have employed technological innovations that permit multiuser support. Unfortunately, most of these configurations can only accommodate up to four simultaneous system users (Ref. 16).

Commitment to a favorable technological development in one's vocational field is another important factor. Of course, while the inclination may be present, a lack of purchase power may constitute a major deterrent. Some libraries are committing substantial resources in support of optical media collections. For example, Vanderbilt University has taken a leadership role in this direction. As part of their Enhanced Information Access Project, which enjoys substantial grant funding support, library users have access to about 25 different optical disc titles. These span a broad range of subject disciplines (Ref. 17). Embracing the new technology with such fervor now appears to be the exception rather than the norm. Most private organizations continue to be cautious and hesitate to commit fully to an optical disc format, and many are only gradually sampling a few products. Curiosity seekers tend to overshadow real buyers. Direct sales are slow and carry a high cost per sale. "It is expensive to carry an entire system, including personal computer, CD-ROM drive, and cables, on the road, and salesmen often have to visit a client site many times before closing a sale" (Ref. 18).

Costs need to be considered from many different angles. For example, while many optical applications software products duplicate subsets of retrospective bibliographic databases that are searchable on-line, CD-ROM versions appear to be less expensive because they tend to eliminate computer connect fees and telecommunications charges. Whether or not fixed pricing for CD-ROM software is actually less expensive in the long run continues to be questionable. While heavily accessed CD-ROM files seem to benefit from pricing that is subscription-based, the additional licensing fees to hold on to and use certain retrospective discs may add to the annual costs. Also, the recent emergence of flat-rate dial-up database searching options (e.g., EasyNet's Answer Machine) offers a viable counterchallenge to the optical media industry (Ref. 19).

5. CONCLUSIONS

Most of the available CD-ROM and videodisc information packages are of interest to public or general academic libraries, health science sectors, and business-oriented markets. Products useful to high-tech librarians are emerging but not as rapidly as hoped. Many products being marketed duplicate or are subsets of databases sold in alternative formats. As more optical applications software products become available, librarians will need to develop and apply selection criteria to aid in purchasing decisions. Acquisition of optical media can be costly compared to traditional print and microform products. Moreover, many publications on disc can only be leased and may require licensing or other forms of contract negotiations. Competition from the magnetic media sector is emerging. Some on-line vendors are now offering flat-fee searching options, which makes their services very attractive from an immediacy standpoint. In contrast, most optical applications software packages tend to be updated only monthly or quarterly.

Many technical information specialists are looking forward to the day when an abundance of optical media will be available to assist them in responding to difficult reference inquiries. Results of 1986 and 1987 opinion polls in the Washington, D.C., area indicate that many high-tech-oriented librarians would like to see full-text product offerings of core sci-tech reference compilations accessible on CD-ROM. Respondents also favored multipurpose workstations, mixed-mode databases, inexpensive jukebox disc-changing equipment, and simultaneous (not merely sequential) on-line and disc-searching capabilities. In general, it was believed that the optical media industry needs to take more risks, talk to more high-tech librarians about their perceived needs, and make every effort to produce needed products in a timely fashion. On the other hand, librarians should be more vocal about their optical media requirements, state their expectations clearly, and make plans to evaluate and buy as soon as viable products become available.

6. REFERENCES

   1. Schwerin, J.B. "Optical Publishing: Microcomputer Technology Issues." Information Today, 4(9):25. October 1987.

   2. Hodgkin, A. G. "Publishing Dictionaries on CD-ROM." OPTICA '87:239. April 1987.

   3. Paisley, W. "Optical Publishing: The Fourth Revolution." Proceedings of the Optical Publishing and Storage'87 Conference:135. November 1987.

   4. Benscheck, W. "CD-ROM in a Publishers Multi-media Distribution Strategy." OPTICA'87 Proceedings:133;136. April 1987.

   5. Dow, D.G. "Indexing and Retrieval Software: Solving the Integration Puzzle." Proceedings of the Optical Publishing and Storage'87 Conference:31. November 1987.

   6. Kosmin, L.J. "Assessing Current Optical Media Opportunities for Scientific & Technical Libraries." Presentation at one-day institute entitled Laser Disk Systems in Libraries held at the Library of Congress, May 11, 1987.

   7. Stern, B.T. "The Status and Future of ADONIS." OPTICA'87 Proceedings:211;217. April 1987.

   8. "The ADONIS CD-ROM Biomedical Collection Available World-wide." CD DATA REPORT, 4(1):3. November 1987.

   9. Befeler, M. "Combining Image and Text Using a CD-ROM Document Delivery System." Information Times:12, January 1987.

10. "Wiley Announces Three New CD-ROM Databases." *Information Today*:12. June 1987.

11. *CD-ROM Librarian*,2(6):3-4. November/December 1987.

12. Herther, Nancy K. "The Silver Disk: Apple, Computers, and CDROM." *DATABASE*,10(6):91;94. December 1987.

13. Kosmin, Linda. "Criteria for Selecting Optical Discs for High-Tech Libraries." *Proceedings of Optical Publishing and Storage '87*:109-115. November 1987.

14. Connolly, Bruce. "Looking Backward — CDROM and the Academic Library of the Future." *Online*,11(3):59. May 1987.

15. Ibid.

16. McConnell, Karen. "Optical Technology: Interacting with Traditional Systems." *Wilson Library Bulletin*,61(10):22. June 1987.

17. Steffey, Ramona. "New Issues in Budgeting for Optical Publications." *Proceedings of Optical Publishing and Storage '87*:165-170. November 1987.

18. "CD ROM Gets Much Attention, But Sales are Slow." *Advanced Technology Libraries*,16(11):1. November 1987.

19. Quint, Barbara. "How is CD-ROM Disappointing? Let Me Count The Ways." *Wilson Library Bulletin*,62(4):32. December 1987.

DOD GATEWAY INFORMATION SYSTEM (DGIS) COMMON COMMAND LANGUAGE: A SUMMARY OF THE FIRST PROTOTYPING & THE DECISION FOR ARTIFICIAL INTELLIGENCE

Allan D. Kuhn, Defense Technical Information Center

Keywords: Common Command Language, C Language, Artificial Intelligence, PROLOG, DoD Gateway Information System, DGIS.

Abstract: Our first prototyping experiences in DGIS Common Command Language (CCL) are related. DGIS began its initial prototypes in C language with DIALOG, BRS, NASA/RECON, and DROLS. These prototypes in a third-generation algorithmic language brought to surface a number of problems and questions in dealing with the distinctions of information systems. The issues concern both the user approach and the development approach. Experiences, results, and conclusions in working with these systems are brought out. The decision to convert to and continue our CCL development with Artificial Intelligence tools is explained. Our effort is a merging of PROLOG and C capabilities, to provide the DGIS user an AI-based searcher assistant interface to make the human-machine interaction more human-like on DGIS.

1. INTRODUCTION

The Defense Technical Information Center (DTIC) of the U.S. Department of Defense (DoD) has sponsored development of a DoD Gateway Information System (DGIS) since 1982. The purpose of DGIS is to provide online, streamlined methods for identifying, accessing, searching and analyzing data from heterogeneous databases of interest to the DoD community [CGA85]. The following figure is the top menu of DGIS, and shows its core operations to achieve this purpose [KAD86]:

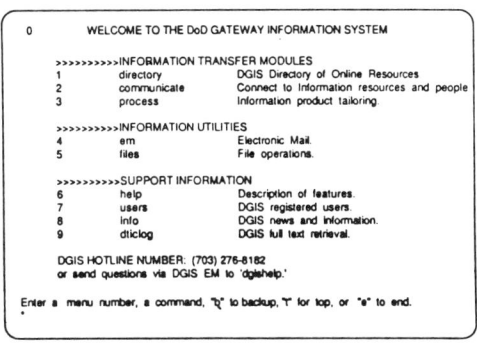

One of the barriers to searching diverse databases is the lack of a common command language set for retrieving in heterogeneous databases. To overcome this barrier, the Program Manager for the DoD Gateway Information System (DGIS) requested that a Common Command Language (CCL) design activity begin, and in April 1986 a team of three people was assigned the effort. The objective of the DGIS Common Command Language project was to determine, formulate, and structure a DGIS common access approach that facilitates access to multiple databases in as easy and rapid a manner as possible.

The operational premises we established for using CCL were:

    a. DGIS CCL is optional, at the discretion of the user; if the user so desires, native command language searching is available.

    b. Various CCL modes are to be explored; this includes:
        (1) Formulation of a CCL set for use in DGIS.
        (2) The ability to search any database system with the native language of a system already familiar to the searcher. In this case, the DGIS CCL serves as a transparent conversion mechanism.
        (3) Query languages, forms and methods provided by the fourth generation languages and artificial intelligence.

    c. The DGIS Common Command Language development will be compatible with developments of standards organizations, especially that of the National Information Standards Organization (NISO) and its Subcommittee G for Common Command Language for Online Interactive Information Retrieval to the extent possible.

2.   PROJECT CONCEPT MODULES

2.1   Concept Elements

As we developed the project concept the complexity of the activity became apparent. We organized it into a modular structure for easier management, as follows:
        Requirements Development Module
        Common Access Development Module
        CCL Standards Module

The Requirements and Access development modules evolved into distinct high activity environments. The Standards module evolved into a support role of periodic activity.

Requirements Development Module

The database sets of commonly used commands, i.e., those most frequently required the user community, were identified. This established a core set of common function commands. This module then entailed:

    a. Mapping the commands/functions of the initial DGIS-targetted databases:
        Defense RDT&E On-Line System (DROLS) (Dept. of Defense)
        Work Unit Information System (WUIS) (Dept. of Defense)
        Manpower and Training Information System (MATRIS) (Dept. of Defense)

DOE/RECON (Dept. of Energy)
NASA/RECON (National Aeronautics and Space Administration)
DIALOG
BRS
ORBIT

b. Designing a DGIS common command language structure. The design was to incorporate established standards. This activity was to define the syntax and semantics of a native command language, and to bridge it to the Common Command Language.

c. Designing command language translators. This was to be based on merging the mapping requirements with the DGIS UNIX operating system C language programming capabilities.

d. Designing the DGIS Common Command Language communication software for interacting with the target information systems.

Common Access Development Module

In this module we explored the potential applications of fourth generation languages (4GL) and artificial intelligence (AI). We identified their potential for creating uniform methods of searching in and retrieving from diverse databases. This included screens, utilities, menus, windows, query organizing, natural language, knowledge base systems, et al. Application of these technologies could provide the capability for true simultaneous searching in multiple databases. We partitioned this development into two phases:

Phase 1 (Near Term): Establishment of single database searching.

Phase 2 (Long Term): Establishment of simultaneous database searching.

CCL Standards Module

The intent of this module was to track national and international CCL standards for use in our DGIS CCL effort. We opted to follow the common command language standard adopted by the U.S. National Information Standards Organization (NISO).

2.2. Module Development

Standard CCL

We adopted the NISO Draft Standard to serve as the foundation of the CCL. The Standard was very useful because the online searching functions were labeled [NISO87]. With the standard selected as the basis for our CCL activity, the next task was to map commands from our target group of databases to the NISO standard.

Mapping

We learned very early that we were not dealing with commands, but with functions. Mapping involved identifying the functions, and making the bridge between the database function label and the CCL function label. We conducted intensive reviews of database functions, commands, and operating characteristics.

We partitioned the functions and their commands into three groups. Group assignment was made by criticality and frequency of use [BRL87]:

        Group I: Most commonly used, basic functions.
        Group II: Remaining common functions.
        Group III: Database Idiosyncratic functions.

Selection for Group I was based on the following criteria:
    a. Common to all databases.
    b. Essential for a complete search and retrieval session.
    c. Small enough group to that several working prototypes could be programmed within a reasonable length of time, e.g., four to six months.

The NISO commands START, CHOOSE, FIND, DISPLAY, and STOP were selected to form Group I. Since the DGIS already had automatic connects and disconnects established, only CHOOSE, FIND, and DISPLAY were left to analyze. The CCL elements associated with Group I are shown in the table below, from the perspective of the CCL user [KAD87]:

DGIS	NISO	Diverse Databases	
Automatic Connect	START	[Logon Routines]	
	CHOOSE	DIALOG:	b
		DROLS:	@s[database name]@
		ORBIT:	[file name]
		NASA:	b, bb
		BRS:	change/ [database name]
	FIND	DIALOG:	s, ss
		DROLS	@s[database name]@
		ORBIT:	[search term]
		NASA:	' s
		BRS:	..s
	DISPLAY	DIALOG:	t
		DROLS:	@dsr@
		ORBIT:	print
		NASA:	d
		BRS:	..p
<ESC><CONT>d	STOP	DIALOG:	logoff
		DROLS:	@term@
		ORBIT:	stop
		NASA:	signoff
		BRS:	..o

Table: Comparison of CCL and Native Command Language Examples.

The command function set for Group II was lengthy, but the primary objective was first to validate the working prototypes based on the Group I commands, and then add on the remaining functions. Group II, therefore, was comprised of (and informally broken down as):

(a)	(b)	(c)
SCAN	PRINT	EXPLAIN
MORE	REVIEW	HELP
BACK	SORT	SHOW
RELATE	SAVE	SET
	DELETE	DEFINE

Group III, idiosyncratic commands, are those peculiar to the individual systems and without a common command standard. Our 'pro tempore' solution for those commands was to allow the user to switch into database native command language mode; this decision is subject to further analysis.

Common Access

We made a preliminary review of Fourth Generation Language (4GL) capabilities. An important reason for this review was that the DGIS Directory of Online Resources [JCE86], a component of the DGIS software, is being developed on the INGRES DBMS. Through the Directory, users can search by subject for databases that are relevant to their queries. DGIS CCL eventually is to be interfaced with the Directory so that, once the relevant databases are determined by the Directory, the user's query is automatically filtered through the CCL capability to search those databases simultaneously.

We looked at INGRES 4GL features, such as query organizing, query-by-form, windowing, database building relative to CCL, forms generating, etc. We concluded that 4GL might be useful in advanced CCL versions but our initial emphasis was to develop a prototype CCL as quickly as possible. We decided, therefore, to concentrate on C language prototype programming with the purpose of validating simple prototypes and then pursuing more advanced features. The decision turned out to be fortuitous, for later we made the jump to artificial intelligence applications 'vis-a-vis' 4GL.

3. OUR FIRST PROTOTYPING DEVELOPMENT

Our initial effort to implement CCL involved selecting a simple approach, and trying to get several prototypes up quickly. Once in place, we could then experiment with them and learn from our experiences. Programming was done in C, merged with two UNIX utilities that were immediately adaptable to CCL needs. Those two utilities were LEX (generator of lexical analysis programs), and YACC (Yet Another Compiler-Compiler) [UNIXo1]. LEX was used for lexical analysis of the CCL prototype C programs, YACC for the syntactical analysis. C was used to implement all remaining semantic processing and miscellaneous tasks. [TDTpip]

Communications was a highly critical element. We needed some type of communications program to talk with databases. DGIS had NAM (Network Access Machine) software agents available in the DGIS software for connecting users to databases for native language searching. NAM provided a utility for:
    a. Establishing the connection.
    b. Validating user access.
    c. Logging on to the target database, including entry of the logon codes. The NAM agent was reviewed and found adaptable to CCL for communicating the command and response in searching the remote database system [TDTpip].

4. THE FIRST PROTOTYPES

Our first prototype, achieved five months after beginning the effort (August 1986), was DGIS CCL for DIALOG. DIALOG was chosen because it was a system with which many users in the DoD community are familiar, and find easy to use.

The DIALOG prototype was followed by BRS, NASA-RECON, and DROLS in fairly rapid succession. BRS was chosen because it was a another major vendor system with many databases, NASA-RECON because it was a Federal government database system, and finally DROLS, DTIC's database system.

The following, a BRS session, shows how the CCL BRS prototype works. Please note that at this stage, CCL is only a substitute for BRS native commands. Other than the commands, BRS must be addressed on its terms. The CCL invocations are indicated by the prompt 'CCL >'. The line following this prompt is the BRS command entry, which echoes the CCL entry:

```
* Connect brs
Attempting telephone connection at 2400 baud to TYMNET.
   [...etc.]
Login Completed

ENTER Y OR N FOR BROADCAST MESSAGE._:  n
ENTER DATABASE NAME_:

Starting up CCL filter

              *** Welcome to CCL ***

CCL > choose psych
..change/psych

*SIGN ON     11:22:50         10/31/86
PSYC 1967 - NOV 1986
BRS SEARCH MODE - ENTER QUERY
    1_:
CCL > find sleep
  ..search

BRS SEARCH MODE - ENTER QUERY
    1_:  sleep

       RESULT       6902 DOCUMENTS
    2_:
CCL > display au,ti 1-3
  ..print
```

```
USING SEARCH STATEMENT NUMBER 001.
BRS PRINT MODE - ENTER PARAGRAPH SELECTIONS._:  au,ti

ENTER DOCUMENT SELECTION._:  1-3

      1
AU KAVANAGH-KEVIN-T.   KAHANE-JOEL-C.   KORDAN-BERNARD.
TI RISKS AND BENEFITS OF ADENOTONSILLECTOMY FOR CHILDREN WITH DOWN
   SYNDROME.

      2
[...etc.]

END OF  REQUEST
ENTER DOCUMENT SELECTION._:
CCL > ^D
            ** Goodbye **

You are now back to NAM.
Logging off BRS.
*CONNECT TIME   0:01:02 HH:MM:SS     0.017 DEC HRS     SESSION  233
```

In addition to showing CCL command application, this session is also an example of the need to still know the individualistic operating characteristics of a database system.

5.   FIRST PROTOTYPE RESULTS

We terminated C-programming with completion of the four prototypes. The experience we gained was immeasurably useful. The following issues and features resulted from this first prototyping:

5.1. The Adaptation of the NAM Connection Agent

As mentioned NAM software for connecting with remote databases was already available. Once the sign-on is completed, the user is connected directly with the database. The user then invokes the CCL translator.

5.2. CCL Invocation

Currently, once one has accessed a database system through the NAM connection agent, one may invoke the CCL translator with a special key.

5.3. CCL Translators

The creation of prototype CCL translators taught us that each information system is individualistic and must be treated as such. The translator programming is totally dependent on the mapping requirements for each system. The programmer must also detect anything "hidden" in the target database system that is needed for a response. The CCL translator is a filter that is toggled on and off by a special key. Once activated, it intercepts all CCL commands from the user, translates the command, sends the translation (i.e., the target database native command) for execution, and brings the results back to the user [TDTpip]. The translator is deactivated by the conventional <CNTL>d (exit from a process).

5.4. Native Command Language Option

The option to use the native command language was necessary when we were prototyping only the basic commonly used commands (Group I already mentioned). The entry of a native command was made very simple: at the CCL prompt, one precedes the native command with a backward slash (\) to tell the translator that the native command is coming, e.g.,

  CCL > \s (for DIALOG 'select')

5.5. The CCL Prompt

The prompt 'CCL >' was incorporated as a reminder to the user that one has invoked the CCL utility.

5.6. CCL Command Verification

When the user invokes a common command, the translation of the invocation is echoed in the database system structure, e.g., for DROLS:

  CCL > find artificial intelligence and psychology

echo: @str@
    artificial intelligence
    and
    psychology
    end

    CCL: Searching...

The echo may also be turned off, currently with the command:
CCL> noecho.

5.7. Online Documentation

The HELP feature to show the user how to use the CCL. The documentation, in very abbreviated form, covers the CCL commands available. For example (DIALOG):

    CCL > help find

        CCL format
            find <term> ...
        DIALOG2 format
            select <term> ...
        DESCRIPTION
            Initiate a search.

5.8. Shell Spawning while in CCL

We incorporated the capability to exploit a UNIX shell, file, or utility while in the CCL. Use of the capability is at the user's discretion; for example, the user may want to list one's files as a review measure while searching a database. The signal to the CCL translator is an initial bang (!), e.g.,

    CCL > !ls   (for listing files)
    CCL > !w   (for seeing who is on the system)
      etc.

5.9. New Commands

In developing the DGIS CCL we found that the NISO standard did not cover several items that we deemed useful. Usefulness was based on the following criteria:
    a. Functions, prevalent in systems, that aided the user; an example is successive session cost display.
    b. Functions, not prevalent, seen as highly useful; e.g., listing the accession numbers of finds.
    c. Functions that we found were needed for an operative CCL; an example is cancelling the translation echo display at one's discretion.

The non-NISO commands that we incorporated under the first prototyping are:

    COMBINE Do Boolean operations (and, or, not) on previously created sets.
    COST   Display session cost thusfar.
    EXECUTE Execute a previously saved search strategy (in target database).
    LIST   List accession numbers of search results.
    NOECHO   Cancel native command function echo to CCL command function.

5.10. NISO Standard Common Commands Incorporated in the First Prototyping:

As we developed the four prototypes, we added on commands to enhance the prototype capabilities. We used, therefore:

```
    CHOOSE      (Group I)
    HELP        (for target database help)
    FIND        (Group I)
    DISPLAY     (Group I)
    RELATE
    MORE -- in NISO 86; changed to FORWARD in NISO 87.
    BACK
```
The standard START and STOP (Group I) are taken care of by the DGIS automatic connect and disconnect.

5.11. CCL System Menu Development

As we progressed through the four prototypes, the systems became more terse. We were exposed to many unique features. The programmer was totally unfamiliar with DROLS which is a terse, no-assist system with access limited to a strictly controlled user community. As a skillful programmer he was, therefore, an ideal person to look at DROLS and determine its appropriate functional CCL requirements.

The very terseness of DROLS (including the lack of a prompt) generated the need to experiment with menu sets to step the unfamiliar user through the database. These menus, basically, provide functional information the expert DROLS searcher knows, but is not on the system. CCL menu examples are:

When invoking CCL CHOOSE in DROLS without designating which database -

```
CCL > choose

  Select one of the following files :
        1. Current Reports
        2. Technical Reports
        3. New Accessions
        4. Work Units
  Please enter your choice (1-4) --> 2

  Technical Reports file is selected.

  CCL > find ...(etc.)
```

When invoking CCL DISPLAY for search results in DROLS without designating a display format -

```
CCL > display

  Select data type to be displayed:
        1.  Search Results.
        2.  Qualified Results.
        3.  User File.
        4.  Single Technical Report Number.
        5.  Single Current File Number.
        6.  Single Work Unit Number.
        7.  Available Files.
        8.  Information Log.
        9.  Order Log.
       10.  Inverted File.

  Please enter your choice (1-10) --> 1
  Please enter a field no (0 for end of field list) --> 3
  Please enter a field no (0 for end of field list) --> 21
  Please enter a field no (0 for end of field list) --> 23
  Please enter a field no (0 for end of field list) --> 0
```

```
CCL > (Sub command for display mode)

Select a display mode :
        1.      Item by item display.
        2.      Continuous display.
Please enter your choice (1-2) --> 1

--      1   OF      20
-- 1 -  AD NUMBER: P003929
-- 3 -     [etc.]
```

The inclusion of the menu sets aids the CCL user to navigate the unfamiliar system, and hopefully helps eliminate the need to totally rely on user manuals.

6.   MAJOR PROBLEM

Each prototype raised issues and problems which we used to refine the successive prototype. As the prototypes progressed, various problems in working with them lead to solutions such as HELP features and menus as mentioned above.

The major problem, however, surfaced as a result of our cumulative experience. We learned that creating "Common Command Language" was NOT a panacea. Programming a "standard" command language was in actuality only substituting one command language for another.

This was most apparent when the DISPLAY function is employed. Quite factually, if the one does not know the DISPLAY formats of an unfamiliar system, one cannot see results. A command with less knowledge requirements is the FIND function. Using FIND, the user is very likely to be able to enter the query and foment results. But any function involving a display is likely to be dead-ended in no display. Substituting CCL for the native command language simply does not obviate the need for referral to a system's user documentation, which gives instruction in terms of its native command language.

Another example is the CHOOSE function. Some systems identify databases by number, others by acronym. For BRS, one must enter CHOOSE NTIS; in DIALOG, CHOOSE 6. The hydra of options and formats keeps cropping up. Each system must be addressed individually, with the goal of having some central pattern program to draw upon. The crutch we have used for the C language-based CCL prototype is the menu.

The creation of a CCL is only one component of the "CCL-need" issue. A second component is creation of a CCL System that allows a user to search in unfamiliar database systems without needing to know that system's operating characteristics. A third component is identifying the critical purposes that a CCL system is to serve.

In the case of DGIS, the critical CCL purposes are defined by understanding the DGIS information processing operations, particularly in postprocessing downloaded files. A DGIS postprocessing requirement is to have a tagged citation for translation. Downloaded citations must be translated into the DGIS standard citation format before the automated processing routines can be applied.

This necessity is an example of a requirement for a DGIS CCL system. Additionally, the CCL system must include function default results for those users unfamiliar with a database, particularly for DISPLAY. The default, on simple invocation of DISPLAY, will provide the fully tagged citation. Other elements, such as menus and question prompts, e.g., "DISPLAY on last set? y/n," must also be incorporated.

The case of CHOOSE represents another problem environment. In DGIS the solution is the eventual integration of CCL with the Directory of Online Resources. When this is accomplished, the query will be forwarded automatically to the relevant databases through CCL.

The real demon for CCL has turned out to be the idiosyncratic operating characteristics of each database system.

7. THE DECISION FOR ARTIFICIAL INTELLIGENCE

7.1. The Cause

The rigidity and constraints of a straight algorithmic program-based CCL discovered during the prototypings lead us to exploring the potential of artificial intelligence. The natural language and expert system possibilities of AI were very appealing. The project's programming technical expert reviewed the main AI programming languages. His recommendation was to explore AI applications with PROLOG, a simple but powerful relational programming language based on the idea of programming in logic [BA-86].

The initial technical reasons for selecting PROLOG were [TDTpip]:

  a. The Reversibility of PROLOG: In determining object relationships, a program can be written establishing those relationships, with the inverse of the relationship inherent in the program.

  b. Its Database Capability: In that PROLOG has its own internal databases, this feature allows a PROLOG program to manipulate codes as relations that can be asserted or deleted. PROLOG incorporation in CCL includes extending to external databases, e.g., INGRES DBMS in the DGIS software, to achieve the flexibility of storing knowledge in both PROLOG internal databases and traditional external databases. This allows including more powerful database technology in the program system for greater performance and easier use of DGIS by the enduser.

  c. The Separation of Logic and Control: A PROLOG program amalgamates rules and facts, basically making one also the other. Although they are governed by a default execution control, the control can be easily supplemented or replaced by more powerful meta-rules also coded in PROLOG.

  d. Object Inheritance and Message Passing: These are two powerful features of object language methodology. Both are easily implemented and embedded in PROLOG. Both features are elemental for the more graceful functioning of CCL.

7.2. The Conceptual Restructuring Of CCL

Using C language programming, the basic CCL elements consisted of the user, the CCL, the database language processor,

and the database information accessed. The jump to PROLOG
opened new possibilities in which CCL now could be developed as
a knowledge-based system. The CCL conceptual structure now
became [TDTpip]:

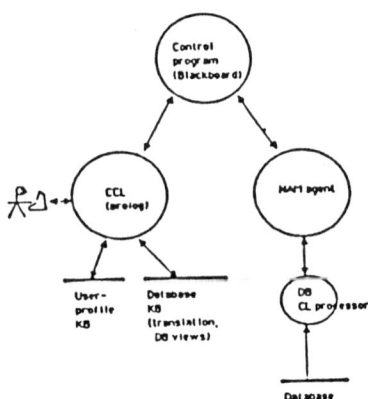

CCL as a knowledge-based system

To the DGIS user making use of CCL, the fact that CCL will be
PROLOG-driven is transparent. The PROLOG CCL, however, in
serving the user, will draw on the command language knowledge
base, and also a CCL-user profile knowledge base (still to be
developed). The user's query and profile data will be
controlled through the control program blackboard, which will
coordinate translation and communications in a continuous real-
time system mode [BA-86] through the NAM connection agent. The
NAM agent passes the communications to and from the target
database system's command language processor for searching on
the database information.

With the transition to an AI-based CCL System, the goals of
DGIS CCL have been re-constituted to incorporate AI-supported
capabilities as follows:
    a. One command language to communicate with all
bibliographic databases.
    b. Creation a CCL System that assists the user in
searching unfamiliar database systems.
    c. Provision of a user-friendly search session.
    d. Provision of an intelligent, user-useful search
session.
    e. Flexibility to adapt easily to changes and
enhancements.

7.3. Other Changes In The Activity

Because of the relative ease of learning PROLOG
programming, another effect of making the transition to PROLOG
was to transfer much of that programming from the technical
expert to the requirements expert. This change was made at the
suggestion of the technical expert. The requirements expert
took the training provided by the PROLOG vendor, and began
PROLOG programming under the tutelage of the technical expert.
This change gave her fuller control of the command requirements,

from command language researching to command language knowledge base building. This also allowed the technical person to concentrate on the knowledge base - database system connector programs, in itself a programming-intensive activity. The following is a small taste of the CCL knowledge base PROLOG programming, for the CCL DELETE command relative to DROLS:

```
%---------------------------------------------------------------
%       CCL to DROLS translation rules
%---------------------------------------------------------------
% Top level CCL
        ...
ccl_cmd         --> delete_cmd,         ( dbnl, dbnl ).
        ...
delete_cmd      --> "delete",
                    (
                        remember(delete),
                        del_cmd
                    ).
        ...

% Delete command
del_cmd:-       filename('CF'),
                cf_delete.
del_cmd:-       delete_menu(Dch),
                del_file(File),
                del_controlno(Control), scrnl,
                dbwrite(Dch), nl,
                scrwrite('File '), termwrite(File), nl,
                scrwrite('Search Control Number '),
                termwrite(Control).

delete_menu(Dch):-
                do_menu([
                'delete bibliography order',
                'delete document order'], 2, Choice),
                delete(Choice, Dch).
delete(1, '@ED@').
delete(2, '@ED@').

del_file(File):-
                scrnl, prompt(_, ' '),
                scrwrite('Please enter the last 6 digits of the file name'), scrnl,
                readln(File).

del_controlno(Control):-
                scrnl, prompt(_, ' '),
                scrwrite('Please enter the 6-character search control number'), scrnl,
                readln(Control).

cf_delete:-
                scrwrite('The delete(ERASE) function is not available'),
                scrnl,
                scrwrite('in the Current Technical Reports File').
```

7.4. Future Directions

Our next phase in CCL is a melding of PROLOG implementation, expert system building, and C supplementary programming. The PROLOG-based CCL has two parts [TDTpip]. One part is fixed, in compiled PROLOG code; the second is variable, in interpretive PROLOG code. The variable part loads and processes information from the two knowledge bases (KB), the command language KB and the user profile KB. Appropriate tools will be incorporated to maintain the KBs (adding, deleting, modifying information). We are currently (August 1987) procuring an artificial intelligence processor system and an expert system building software tool. The processor will be networked to the DGIS computer system, and will serve to both develop and maintain AI applications in CCL and other AI applications on DGIS [KAD87b].

We are investigating several schemes for KB organization. In general, we plan to couple PROLOG with a Relational DBMS (RDBMS) where large KBs (most of which are facts) will reside. The technical issue here is the interface between PROLOG and the RDBMS (likely INGRES). We intend to make this interface through

SQL (standard query language) so that it can work with any RDBMS, rather than only with INGRES. [TDTpip]
   Other CCL system factors are:
      a. CCL Integration with Other DGIS Functions: Other DGIS operations are potentials for AI applications, with which to link with CCL. One is the DGIS Directory of Online Resources, wherein a user's query resources are identified and communicated with automatically and simultaneously. Another is the DGIS postprocessing routines, with which the multiple resource responses are automatically downloaded, translated, merged, and processed (or tailored), based on a one-pass instruction entry with which the user invokes the whole process.
      b. Planning Capability: Includes the preliminary structuring of multiple queries and the combining of target databases' result sets.
      c. Learning Capability for CCL: Employing learning solution paths [BA-86] for optimizing the information added to the command language KB and the user profile KB.
      d. Migrate to Natural Language: The NISO and appended CCL will be the backbone of the DGIS CCL, but in migrating to Natural Language dialogue, will become transparent in a command language translation supporting role.
      e. Provide Simultaneous Database Access Capability: That is, true concurrent connecting with, searching in, and downloading of results from multiple systems.
   All this to bring about the resolution of, as the requirements expert states [BRL87]: "The problem of multiple command languages has plagued online searchers since the creation of the second online database."

ACKNOWLEDGEMENTS
Ms. Randy L. Bixby, Defense Technical Information Center, is the requirements expert on the project. Mr. Duc Tien Tran, Consultant, Control Data Corp., is the programming technical expert. Thanks is given to Ms. Sharon Karalus for reviewing and properly styling this paper.

REFERENCES
[BA-86] Bundy, Alan. Catalogue of Artificial Intelligence Tools. Springer-Verlag Berlin Heidelberg. 1986.
[BRL87] Bixby, Randy L. The DoD Gateway Information System (DGIS): Common Command Language Mapping. Defense Technical Information Center, Alexandria, VA. October 1987.
[CGA85] Cotter, Gladys A. The DoD Gateway Information System. Defense Technical Information Center, Alexandria, VA. October 1985, AD-A161 701.
[JCE86] Jacobson, Carol E., and Gladys A. Cotter. The DoD Gateway Information System Directory of Resources. Defense Technical Information Center, Alexandria, VA. August 1986, AD-A174 154.
[KAD86] Kuhn, Allan D., and Gladys A. Cotter. The DoD Gateway Information System (DGIS): User Interface Design. Defense Technical Information Center, Alexandria, VA. August 1986, AD-A174 150.
[KAD87] Kuhn, Allan D. Artificial Intelligence Developments Re: DoD Gateway Information System (DGIS), & Defense Applied Information Technology Center (DAITC). Defense Technical Information Center, Alexandria, VA. February 1987, AD-A181 101.

[KAD87b] Kuhn, Allan D. Toward an Artificial Intelligence Environment for DTIC: Proposed Tasks, Recommended Configurations, Projected Start-Up Costs. Defense Technical Information Center, Alexandria, VA. May 1987, AD-A181 103.

[NISO87] National Information Standards Organization (NISO), Washington, DC. American National Standard -- For Information Sciences: Common Command Language for Online Interactive Information Retrieval (DRAFT). [March 1987] ANSI Z39.58-198X.

[TDTpip] Tran, Duc T. DoD Gateway Information System (DGIS): Prototype Programming the DGIS Common Command Language. Consultant; Defense Technical Information Center, Alexandria, VA. Paper-in-progress.

[UNIXol] University of California-Berkeley. UNIX Programmer's Manual. LEX(1); YACC(1); NAM(1T). Online manual, UNIX Operating System BSD 4.2.

INSURANCE INFORMATION GOES ONLINE

Lynda S. Kuntz, Potomac Consultants

For many years, a publishing firm has been furnishing the latest developments, rulings, and regulations to insurance agents. This information is sold as a monthly printed bulletin service. Now the company wants to provide the current information in a more timely fashion. In addition, they want to enhance the service by providing retrospective searching of previous bulletins. The firm makes the decision to develop an electronic database. Access by the customer is to be via a microcomputer to microcomputer hookup. An employee of the firm is a "crack" dBASE III Plus programmer. The database development and searching programs are accomplished in-house. The communications interface is to be worked out by the author of this paper. The paper will present the processes of communications software selection, integration of the programs and implementation of the system. The final product is to be entirely command driven to include the installation. The target market for this product is the present users of the print version. To lure them to the electronic version, the system must be easy to operate. For the firm to realize a profit, development and materials costs must be reasonable.

This study concerned a data and forms publisher who wanted to develop or adapt present print products to the online medium. The basic requirements for this change were conversion, search and input programming, and the transmission of orders within the company. The product listing was to be converted from a paper to an electronic format. Programs were then written to allow for the searching of the listing database and the input of orders. The communications requirements included the host computer software and the transmission of orders through the production, shipping and billing departments. This case study illustrates the range of applications and advantages achievable through the use of online databases and electronic bulletin boards.

The subject business, a major publishing firm in the Northeast, furnishes the latest developments, rulings, forms, and regulations to insurance agents throughout the U.S. The information is sold as a monthly bulletin service by subscription. The Vice President of Information Services is also responsible for the incorporation of microcomputer technology to new and current products and services. The firm already utilizes IBM microcomputers in its general office activities such as accounting, inventory control, scheduling and management reporting.

The client wanted the system to improve current products by providing new information in a more timely fashion and to provide retrospective searching of previous bulletins. In addition, the client wanted to provide the customer with the capability to place orders for copies of forms, rulings, and regulations online. In turn this information would enter the printing, distribution and billing channels.

To implement these improvements and to provide new services, the firm began the conversion of its data and product listing into an electronic database. Since the staff of the Information Services included an experienced dBASE III programmer, the decision was made to develop the databases and searching programs in-house by the expert staff member. The opening menu appears below.

```
                  F O R M S    Q U E S T
:MMMMMMMMMMMMMMMMMMMMMMMMMMMMMMMMMMMMMMMMMMMMMMMMMMMMMMMMMM:
:OOOOOOOOOOOOOOOOOOOOOOOOOOOOOOOOOOOOOOOOOOOOOOOOOOOOOOOOOO:
:OOOOOOOOOOOOOOOOOOOOOOOOOO MAIN OOOOOOOOOOOOOOOOOOOOOOOOOO:
:OOOOOOOOOOOOOOOOOOOOOOOOOO MENU OOOOOOOOOOOOOOOOOOOOOOOOOO:
:OOOOOOOOOOOO:MMMMMMMMMMMMMMMMMMMMMMMMMMMMM:OOOOOOOOOOOOOO:
:OOOOOOOOOOOO:                              :OOOOOOOOOOOOOO:
:OOOOOOOOOOOO: [0] Exit System              :OOOOOOOOOOOOOO:
:OOOOOOOOOOOO:                              :OOOOOOOOOOOOOO:
:OOOOOOOOOOOO: [1] Enter a new Order        :OOOOOOOOOOOOOO:
:OOOOOOOOOOOO:                              :OOOOOOOOOOOOOO:
:OOOOOOOOOOOO: [2] Request New Order Blanks :OOOOOOOOOOOOOO:
:OOOOOOOOOOOO:                              :OOOOOOOOOOOOOO:
:OOOOOOOOOOOO: [3] System Configuration     :OOOOOOOOOOOOOO:
:OOOOOOOOOOOO:                              :OOOOOOOOOOOOOO:
:OOOOOOOOOOOO: [4] Reindex Data Files       :OOOOOOOOOOOOOO:
:OOOOOOOOOOOO:                              :OOOOOOOOOOOOOO:
:OOOOOOOOOOOO:MMMMMMMMMMMMMMMMMMMMMMMMMMMMM:OOOOOOOOOOOOOO:
:OOOOOOOOOOOO: [0] Enter Selection          :OOOOOOOOOOOOOO:
:OOOOOOOOOOOO:MMMMMMMMMMMMMMMMMMMMMMMMMMMMM:OOOOOOOOOOOOOO:
:OOOOOOOOOOOOOOOOOOOOOOOOOOOOOOOOOOOOOOOOOOOOOOOOOOOOOOOOOO:
:OOOOOOOOOOOOOOOOOOOOOOOOOOOOOOOOOOOOOOOOOOOOOOOOOOOOOOOOOO:
:OOOOOOOOOOOOOOOOOOOOOOOOOOOOOOOOOOOOOOOOOOOOOOOOOOOOOOOOOO:
:OOOOOOOOOOOOOOOOOOOOOOOOOOOOOOOOOOOOOOOOOOOOOOOOOOOOOOOOOO:
:MMMMMMMMMMMMMMMMMMMMMMMMMMMMMMMMMMMMMMMMMMMMMMMMMMMMMMMMMM:
```

Selecting 1 from the opening menu, gives the client the following possibilities.

```
                        F O R M S   Q U E S T
:MMMMMMMMMMMMMMMMMMMMMMMMMMMMMMMMMMMMMMMMMMMMMMMMMMMMMMMMMMMMM:
:000000000000000000000000000000000000000000000000000000000000:
:00:MMMMMMMMMMMMMMMMMMMMMMMMMMMMMMMMMMMMMMMMMMMMMMMMMMMMMM:000:
:00:                                                      :000:
:00:         [ 0] Return To Main Menu                     :000:
:00:                                                      :000:
:00:         [ 1] Personal Insurance Coverages            :000:
:00:                                                      :000:
:00:         [ 2] Personal Auto / Private Passenger Program :000:
:00:                                                      :000:
:00:         [ 3] Homeowners Policy Program               :000:
:00:                                                      :000:
:00:         [ 4] Simplified Commercial Automobile Program :000:
:00:                                                      :000:
:00:         [ 5] Simplified Commercial Lines Program     :000:
:00:                                                      :000:
:00:                                                      :000:
:00:MMMMMMMMMMMMMMMMMMMMMMMMMMMMMMMMMMMMMMMMMMMMMMMMMMMMMM:000:
:00:     [ 0] Enter Selection                             :000:
:00:                                                      :000:
:00:MMMMMMMMMMMMMMMMMMMMMMMMMMMMMMMMMMMMMMMMMMMMMMMMMMMMMM:000:
:000000000000000000000000000000000000000000000000000000000000:
:MMMMMMMMMMMMMMMMMMMMMMMMMMMMMMMMMMMMMMMMMMMMMMMMMMMMMMMMMMMMM:
```

When the client selects one of the above options, the list of available forms is displayed.

```
                Home=Top   / End=Bottom / PgUp=Page Back
                  PgDn=Page Forward  / Enter=Order
:MMMMMMMMMMMMMMMMMMMMMMMMMMMMMMMMMMMMMMMMMMMMMMMMMMMMMMMMMMMMM:
:Qty:UP & S No.:Bureau No.:  Form Title       :Code: Price   :
:MMMNMMMMMMMMMMMMMMMMMMMMMMMMMMMMMMMMMMMMMMMMMNMMMMMMMMMMMMMM:
: 0 : PI 100    :CPL-1     :Comp Pers Liab Bklt :  :  AT     :
: 0 : PI 100    :CPL-1     :Comp Pers Liab Bklt :  :  AT     :
: 0 : PI 100    :CPL-1     :Comp Pers Liab Bklt :  :  AT     :
: 0 : PI 100    :CPL-1     :Comp Pers Liab Bklt :  :  AT     :
: 0 : PI 101    :BFT-1     :Bd Frm Pers Theft   :  :  AS     :
: 0 : PI 101    :BFT-1     :Bd Frm Pers Theft   :  :  AS     :
: 0 : PI 101    :BFT-1     :Bd Frm Pers Theft   :  :  AS     :
: 0 : PI 101    :BFT-1     :Bd Frm Pers Theft   :  :  AS     :
: 0 : PI 101    :BFT-1     :Bd Frm Pers Theft   :  :  AS     :
: 0 : PI 101    :BFT-1     :Bd Frm Pers Theft   :  :  AS     :
: 0 : PI 101    :RG-1      :Res Glass Policy Frm:  :  AN     :
: 0 : PI 102    :RG-1      :Res Glass Policy Frm:  :  AN     :
: 0 : PI 102    :RG-1      :Res Glass Policy Frm:  :  AN     :
: 0 : PI 102    :RG-1      :Res Glass Policy Frm:  :  AS     :
:MMMMMMMMMMMMMMMMMMMMMMMMMMMMMMMMMMMMMMMMMMMMMMMMMMMMMMMMMMMMM:
:       [E]xit     [Q]uick Order      [V]iew Orders          :
:MMMMMMMMMMMMMMMMMMMMMMMMMMMMMMMMMMMMMMMMMMMMMMMMMMMMMMMMMMMMM:
```

The quick option inserts a window onto the above listing allowing the customer to list individual forms.

The order information is transferred back and forth between production, shipping and billing departments over a single IBM token ring network. Access by the customer is through a microcomputer to microcomputer hookup.

My contract was to evaluate various telecommunication programs which would allow this access by the customer. Initially the client was interested in the feasibility of interfacing a public domain or user supported package such as PC-TALK with dBASE III Plus. While the customer could use PC-TALK, the publisher would need a bulletin board system at the host site which was capable of patching the customer into the host's dBASE III programs. These dBASE programs are those that allow reading of current text files, searching for previous bulletins and placing orders.

Rather than combining at least three programs, i.e., PC-TALK, a BBS and dBASE III, the client wanted an evaluation of more specialized remote communications software. This remote software allows the customer to access the client's computer and directly read, search and order.

At that time, I identified the following communication packages: Remote, pcANYWHERE, Carbon Copy and Close-Up as allowing remote linking of two microcomputers. A call to the marketing representative of each firm explaining my purpose, i.e., evaluation for a client's use resulted in a mixed response. I received demo disks, promotional material and features and requirements listings from two firms. The other two sent promotional material only. The above products were reviewed in the September 1986 issue of PC World. I checked the current features as illustrated on the demos or in the promotional materials for each against that review.

Except for Remote, it is possible to run dBASE programs remotely with the above programs. However, each require a copy of the program at both ends. To work around the cost of duplicate programs, another breed of software was investigated. This breed is the "tools" or "add-on" type of software programs. To add communications capability to dBASE III Plus programming, a library of programs has been developed by SilverWare Inc. With the SilverComm library, the programmer can include communication functions as part of the application program already written in the dbase programming language.

The program comes in two versions, one for those who use Clipper and one for those who use dBASE III Plus alone or with dBXL, Quicksilver or FoxBase+. In the simplest of terms, SilverComm overrides the standard ROM-BIOS driver which normally controls the serial ports (COM1/COM2). SilverComm then operates the ports in the interrupt mode (asynchronous) rather than the normal polled mode. The interrupt routines run transparent to the application program.

By using this tool, the programmer is able to produce a final product which is entirely command driven. The client is now able to provide services online at a low cost with a system that is easy to operate.

THE RETRIEVAL AND DISPLAY OF PATENT IMAGES FROM OPTICAL STORAGE

Gary M. Kurtenbach, Chemical Abstracts Service

Keywords: Optical Storage, Patent Images, Image Retrieval, U.S. Patent and Trademark Office, USPTO, Automated Patent System, APS

Abstract: The United States Patent and Trademark Office has a paper file consisting of some 28 million patents which is searched manually by patent examiners when researching newly received patent applications. In April, 1984 the United States Patent and Trademark Office awarded a contract to automate its patent processing to Planning Research Corporation, with Chemical Abstracts Service as a major subcontractor. Chemical Abstracts Service is providing much of the software required for the automated system. The system is designed to store an estimated 30 trillion bytes of compressed, digitized image data for U.S. and foreign patents on optical media. Users of the system view patent images on high resolution, full-page display screens of customized workstations. The system also includes full-text searching of U.S. Patents, with the text search and image display capabilities integrated. The system design provides for patent images to be stored on two types of devices: storage units containing permanently mounted optical platters, and optical jukebox type units. The various hardware components of the system are connected by a high speed, ethernet-based local area network. Chemical Abstracts Service has developed software to retrieve patent images from the optical media across the local area network for display on user workstations. This paper discusses the status of the efforts to provide the capability to retrieve and display patent images as part of the Automated Patent System.

1. INTRODUCTION

The United States Patent and Trademark Office (USPTO) receives more than 125,000 patent applications per year. For each application received, a patent examiner must search the prior art in order to determine whether the application should be granted. The USPTO uses a classification system to support the searching of the prior art. The classification system breaks technology into roughly 400 classes, which are further broken down into approximately 115,000 subclasses.

Until recently, all searching for prior art was done manually, using a filing system that dates back nearly 200 years. The prior art (which consists primarily of U.S. and foreign patents) was maintained entirely as paper files. The patents are filed in trays (called "shoes" by the USPTO), organized by classification. To search the prior art, an examiner manually searches the shoes that contain patents in the same area of technology as the application being processed. Studies have shown that about 7% of the documents in the paper file are missing or misfiled at any given time, and this can exceed 25% in areas of high activity technology.

In 1980 Congress directed the USPTO to submit a plan for automating patent processing. As a result of this directive, the USPTO submitted an Automation Master Plan to Congress in 1982, and subsequently (in April, 1984) awarded a contract to develop the Automated Patent System (APS). The contract was awarded to Planning Research Corporation (PRC), with Chemical Abstracts Service (CAS) as a major subcontractor. The APS includes an image component which, when fully implemented, is designed to store an estimated 30 trillion bytes of compressed, digitized image data on optical media for U.S. and foreign patents.

2. APS SYSTEM OVERVIEW

The APS will convert the paper files currently used by the USPTO into an electronic, digital database, and make this information available to USPTO personnel through computer terminals. The heart of the system, from the patent examiner's point of view, is the search and retrieval capabilities. The system supports full text searching of patent data using the CAS developed Messenger(TM) software. Also, full page images of patents can be retrieved from optical storage media and displayed on customized workstations.

The automation of the patent processing operation will improve the accuracy of patent decisions and also reduce the amount of time necessary to make the decisions. The computerization of the paper files will provide for improved reliability, integrity, and accessibility of the prior art information that must be reviewed in order to decide whether a patent should be granted to the applicant.

The APS will also encompass a variety of other functions, including office automation, composition, and gateways to external databases. An overview of the architecture of the APS is shown in Figure 1.

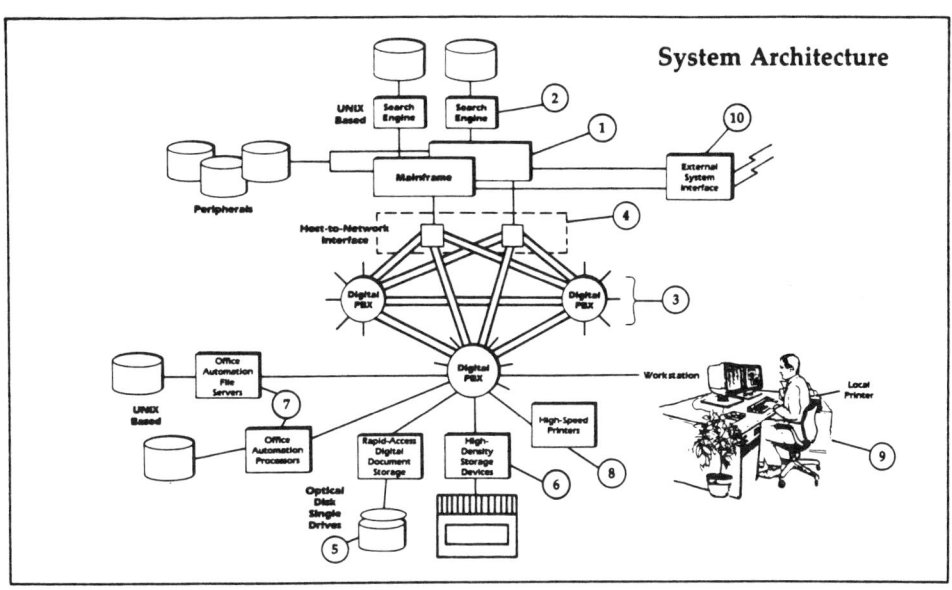

1. **Mainframe.** Two very large-scale mainframes provide indexes to approximately 30 terabytes storage capacity in a distributed system; support search and retrieval; manage system; maintain text and image data base.

2. **Search engines.** 40 or more microcomputers act as parallel processors for text and classification searches, using Boolean logic to locate word and symbol combinations and relationships in text data base.

3. **Digital PBX.** A network based on digital switches unites all elements of the system. Connections over the network are transparent to end users.

4. **Host-to-network interface.** Translates network protocol between the mainframe and the workstations and other devices connected to the mainframe via the network.

5. **Rapid-access digital document storage.** Single optical disk contains frequently accessed information, such as post-1970 granted patents.

6. **High-density storage devices.** Optical disk libraries, or "juke boxes" store a second copy of frequently used information and two copies of less frequently accessed information.

7. **Workstation servers.** Office automation file server allows user to store individual work. Office automation processor provides electronic mail delivery, spreadsheet capacity, calendar, word processing, etc. Latest software deliveries are stored in local storage devices, automatically update workstation software.

8. **Central and group laser printer.** Centralized printing provides 300 line-per-inch page images with each printer operating at more than 10 pages per minute.

9. **Workstations.** For use of examiners, paralegal, technical and clerical personnel, more than 1,800 workstations are the primary user interface with the patent processing system. Workstations provide access to the system for patent application processing and full office automation functions.

10. **External system interfaces.** Gateways that provide telecommunication with commercial data bases.

FIGURE 1: System Architecture for the Automated Patent System

3. IMAGE RETRIEVAL - PHASE I

The USPTO's implementation plan for the APS is divided into two major phases. The first phase involves using one of the 15 examiner groups to test the basic functionality of the system. Group 220 was chosen for this so-called "testbed" because of the broad range of applications processed by this group. Group 220 patent examiners will test the APS by using the basic search and retrieval capabilities of the system to support their routine application processing workload. The decision about whether to deploy the system to all of the examining groups depends on the results of this testbed.

As depicted in Figure 2, image retrieval and display in the APS involves 3 basic components: APS workstations, the mainframe, and Image File Servers. The hardware, software, and data being utilized for Phase I is described in more detail in the following sections.

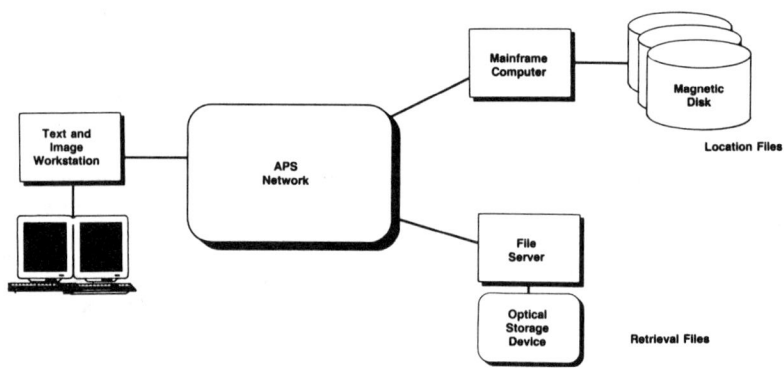

FIGURE 2: APS Image Retrieval and Display Components - Phase I

3.1 Hardware

APS Workstations

The APS workstations being supplied by Gould Inc.:

- o are built around a 68020 processor running the UNIX operating system, configured with 4 million bytes of memory
- o have dual-screen displays, each capable of displaying a full 8.5 x 11 inch patent page image
- o have a screen resolution of 150 dots per inch
- o are configured with 300 million bytes of local magnetic storage
- o include a keyboard and mouse for user input
- o have laser printers attached for hardcopy output

Mainframe Processor

For Phase I, the USPTO is using a NAS 9080 mainframe from National Advanced Systems, Inc. This dual processor machine is roughly equivalent to an IBM 3090 Model 180E in processing power.

Rapid Access Digital (RAD) Storage Devices

These devices serve as image file servers. RADs have the following characteristics:

- use a 68020 processor running the UNIX operating system, configured with 4 million bytes of memory
- are configured with 75 million bytes of magnetic storage
- each RAD is configured with 4 Optimem write-once 12 inch optical drives, and use 3M single-sided media with a capacity of 1 billion bytes per optical disk
- controllers for the optical drives were developed by Falcon Data Systems (the system integrator for this hardware device)

3.2 Software

APS users may request the display of patent images on an APS workstation in several ways. Retrieval may be requested by individual patent number, or by specifying a U.S. patent classification code. If a classification is entered, the system retrieves all of the patents currently assigned to that classification. Patent identifiers returned as a result of a full-text search may also be used to request the retrieval and display of the page images.

APS software has been developed to support the retrieval and display of digitized page image data. The retrieval of patent page images to an APS workstation is a two-step operation. First, the workstation communicates with the mainframe to retrieve index records for the patents to be displayed. These index records identify the location of the digitized page images on the image file servers (RADs). Second, the digitized image data is retrieved from the appropriate RAD. The retrieved patent page images are stored on local magnetic storage at the workstation. Workstation-resident software is then used to display the pages requested by the user.

In the APS architecture more than one workstation may be requesting image data from a single RAD at the same time. Therefore, the RAD retrieval software was designed to allow for multiple workstations to be connected to a RAD concurrently. The same is true of the mainframe index retrieval software (e.g. requests for index records from multiple workstations can be processed concurrently).

3.3 Data

Each examiner group has a hardcopy prior art search file, which includes the patents normally reviewed by that group as part of patent application processing. These patents are organized and filed (in the "shoes") by classification. For Phase I of the APS, the Group 220 prior art search file has been digitized and loaded onto the APS as page images. The file consists of approximately 150,000 patents. The average size of a digitized page image is approximately 85,000 bytes. The total size of the APS Group 220 image file, which is distributed across approximately 100 optical platters, is roughly 85 billion bytes.

4. IMAGE RETRIEVAL - PHASE II

The basic image retrieval functionality is implemented in Phase I of the APS. Phase II will fully deploy the system to all of the USPTO examiner groups. Thus, Phase II primarily involves the addition of data and hardware to support the much larger user base. When fully deployed, the APS image database will consist of approximately 5 million U.S. patents, 10 million foreign patents, and 1 million pieces of non-patent literature.

The projected size of the complete APS image database is in the area of 30 trillion bytes. Due to the very large size of this database, one additional hardware component is added in Phase II of the APS in order to support image retrieval. This new hardware component consists of optical disk jukebox devices (known in APS terms as High Density Digital (HDD) storage devices). The APS requirement is that all digitized page image data be stored redundantly to guarantee a high level of availability to the user. The APS strategy for the redundant storage of image data is:

- o frequently accessed data is stored on Rapid Access Devices (RADs), with a backup copy on HDDs
- o less frequently accessed data is redundantly stored on HDDs

From a user viewpoint, the difference between what device the image data is being retrieved from is strictly response time. Each platter on a RAD is mounted on an optical drive, making the data available for immediate retrieval. However, an HDD device contains many more optical platters than read stations. Thus, prior to being able to retrieve data from a platter located on an HDD, the platter may first need to be retrieved from its storage location (its "shelf"), moved to the read station, and "spun up."

The composition (formatting and printing) of newly issuing U.S. Patents is also scheduled for integration into the APS as part of Phase II. This will affect the way patent pages are displayed on APS workstations in two ways. First, for patents that have been composed in the APS, the display will be done using a combination of composed text and image data. In this case, only the drawings (i.e. non-textual data) in the patents will need to be stored in digitized, bit-image format. This will reduce the storage and network load requirements considerably for displaying these patents. Secondly, the plans are to use the same composed text and image data to display patents returned as answers to text searches. Therefore, text search answers will be displayed on APS workstations "as issued" (i.e. identical to the printed patent), with the search terms that caused the retrieval highlighted on the screen.

5. DISCUSSION

The USPTO required that the APS design provide for the display of patents "as issued" on APS workstations. Patent pages, which may consist of all text data, all graphical data, or a mixture of text and graphical data, must be displayable at high resolution on the workstations. These requirements dictated that much of the patent database be stored in digitized, bit-image form, which requires a large amount of storage.

The decision to use optical storage in the APS was influenced by the very large size of the patent image database. Another factor was the static nature of the data. Patents are legal documents that must be retrieved and displayed exactly as issued. For this reason, the "write-once" characteristic of the media actually becomes an advantage. Thus, optical storage was determined to be a more cost effective solution for this application than the more traditional magnetic media. Optical storage media also offers exceptional reliability (venders of the media typically quote a 10+ year lifetime for the media).

The choice of a distributed implementation utilizing multiple optical-based file servers connected to the APS network was dictated by the large number of users and the stringent performance requirements. Two different types of optical-based components are incorporated into the APS design: RADs and HDDs. This was done to provide the most cost effective solution to the storage and retrieval requirements. Data that will be retrieved frequently is stored on RADs, for rapid retrieval. Data that will be retrieved infrequently, and for which the retrieval response time requirement is not as stringent, is stored on the HDDs (optical jukeboxes).

The APS Phase I image retrieval hardware and software has been installed and tested at the USPTO. The Group 220 search file has also been loaded onto optical storage media, in page image form. The hardware and software was performing well enough for the USPTO to begin "production testing" on 12/14/87.

Some obstacles that have been encountered to date in implementing the APS patent image retrieval and display capability are as follows:

- o Data Load - Some data integrity problems were experienced with the digitized data received from the original data capture contractor. Also, the original APS image load hardware had insufficient error checking to verify that the data had been successfully written to the optical media. These data load problems were resolved by changing contractors for the image capture and by upgrading the optical drivers to include the needed error checking logic.

- o RAD Hardware - Problems have been experienced with the optical drivers on the Rapid Access Digital (RAD) storage devices locking up occasionally. This results in the data on a platter being unavailable for retrieval until the device is rebooted. The problem is being addressed by the hardware vendor.

- o Network Reliability - Due to poor reliability of the low-level protocols of the APS network software, messages and/or data have not always reached their destination successfully. Image retrieval places a heavy load on the network, because of the large amount of data that must be transmitted. To display a typical patent in page image form, approximately 500,000 bytes of data must be transferred across the APS network. These problems are being addressed by the vendor for the APS network software.

- o Responsiveness - In order for APS image retrieval/display to be effective in supporting the patent examiners in their work, the time spent waiting for a page to be displayed by the system must be minimal. Two aspects of response time for patent image retrieval are important: the time to display the first page of the first patent requested, and the "flip rate" (i.e. the time to display subsequent pages/patents retrieved as the result of an examiner's search/retrieval request). A variety of software and hardware enhancements have already been made to improve the system's responsiveness. Additionally, a comprehensive effort is underway to analyze the current performance in detail and identify additional areas for improvement.

The APS Phase I testbed involves only a subset of the data and user base that will ultimately need to be supported. Thus, while the majority of the image retrieval/display functionality is being evaluated currently, the throughput and reliability of the system for high volume use is still largely unproven. Also, one major hardware component, the optical disk jukebox devices, have not yet been incorporated into the system. Several components of the original target APS system are also currently being re-evaluated. These include the composition of patents for publication and the display of patents on APS workstations in composed ("as issued") text and image format. Changes in requirements in these areas would have significant impacts on the image retrieval/display capability in the final APS system.

6. SUMMARY

The United States Patent and Trademark Office (USPTO) is in the process of automating its patent processing. Phase I of the Automated Patent System (APS) has been developed and is currently being evaluated by the patent office. Phase I includes a patent retrieval component that provides for the retrieval of digitized patent page image data from optical storage media for display on high resolution workstation display screens. Overall experience to date with this component has been positive.

7. REFERENCES

1. U.S. Department of Commerce Request for Proposal PT-84-SAS-00349, October, 1983.

2. Hager, Peter, "System to Simplify Patent Searches", Government Computer News, August 1, 1986.

3. "U.S. Patent & Trademark Office Optical Disk System Proceeding", Optical Memory News, January 1987, p. 15.

4. Long, Janice R., "Patent & Trademark Office Tests New Phase of Computer System", Chemical & Engineering News, July 13, 1987, p. 16-19.

8. ACKNOWLEDGMENT

This paper describes a component of the Automated Patent System being developed for the U.S. Patent and Trademark Office (Department of Commerce Contract No. 50-SAPT-4-00319).

END USER ACCESS TO MEDLINE: THE ROLE OF CD-ROM

Donna Lee, University of Vermont

Keywords: CD-ROM, End-User Searching, Mediated Searching, Medline.

Abstract: Literature searches of the National Library of Medicine's (NLM) Medline database are available through several routes at the Charles A. Dana Medical Library of the University of Vermont. Mediated online searches via BRS, DIALOG or MEDLARS, end-user online searches on BRS Colleague, and end-user searches on Compact Cambridge CD-ROM have all proved to be popular. This paper describes the impact of CD-ROM on patrons and on the other services offered at the Dana Library.

The circulation, interlibrary loan, and reference departments have all been affected by CD-ROM, though not as dramatically as predicted. In the reference department in particular we anticipated a shift in our workload. We were prepared to spend more of our time training end users, and less time performing mediated searches. But the number of mediated searches requested did not decrease as much as expected.

Limitations of CD-ROM, ease of use, and patron satisfaction have been explored with the help of a survey of CD-ROM searchers. Although some patrons continue to pay for mediated searches, we were surprised by how many patrons were willing to spend time mastering what we librarians considered a cumbersome and inconvenient command language. In fact, so many patrons have been using the CD-ROM station that some have had to wait to access the database.

1. THE DANA MEDICAL LIBRARY

In the medical malpractice case Harbeson vs Park-Davis, Incorporated, three physicians were found negligent for prescribing the drug Dilantin to a pregnant woman. One of the points which contributed to the decision was the defendants' failure to review the literature. The court suggested, among other information retrieval methods, a Medline search. Medline contains citations to articles in health sciences journals. The fact that the court named the Medline database indicates how significant Medline has become.

Given Medline's prominence, it's no surprise that the Dana Medical Library at the University of Vermont has access to this database. What is revealing, is how many forms of access we have.

Before Medline, there was Index Medicus, a traditional printed index. The printed index is now produced from Medline computer tapes. The International Nursing Index and the Index to Dental Literature are also Medline spinoffs. The Dana Medical Library subscribes to all three of these indexes. Index Medicus, in particular, is heavily used.

Often, a Medline search is more appropriate than a search through the indexes. Our library offers Medline through several routes. The easiest approach for the patron is to choose a mediated search. Mediated searches are performed by professional searchers in response to search requests from patrons. Patrons receive the citations in a day or two, at a fee of between five and 24 dollars. University of Vermont students are allowed one free computer search each semester.

MEDLARS, BRS, and DIALOG all offer Medline. MEDLARS is usually the cheapest system, but BRS and DIALOG each have unique and powerful features that make them more useful than MEDLARS in certain situations. When a patron selects a mediated search of Medline, the searcher decides which vendor to use.

Patrons may search Medline themselves on BRS Colleague, an end-user online system designed to meet the needs of health professionals. We offer all of our patrons one hour of free online time through the library's Colleague password. If they choose, they may join our group subscription. Subscribers have their own passwords and must pay their online charges. The free hour is offered only in the library, while group subscribers may search from their home or office, as well as in the library.

In contrast to mediated and BRS Colleague searches, Medline on CD-ROM is free to patrons, no matter how much they use it.

Another major difference between the systems is the time periods they cover. The Dana Medical Library owns <u>Index Medicus</u> and its predecessors back to 1887. Online database searches, both mediated and end-user, can include literature back to 1966. Through our Compact Cambridge CD-ROM system, patrons may only search the literature back to January 1986.

Another time constraint involves updates. The National Library of Medicine updates the online and the print versions of Medline every month. Compact Cambridge updates their Medline CD's every quarter.

Our approach to training end users creates another difference between the end user online system and CD-ROM. To help patrons improve their searching skills and make cost effective use of their time online, we hold workshops and tutorials for Colleague, the online system. But we are afraid that by requiring training we were placing a barrier in the way of end-user searching. So we decided not to insist upon training for CD-ROM. Since the cost of CD-ROM remains the same no matter how long or often you use it, we were not worried about how much time patrons spent on CD-ROM. Also, the menu system for Campact Cambridge Medline provides more hints for the novice user than Colleague does. We did set up the CD-ROM system near the reference desk, with the intention of offering brief assistance.

2. EVALUATION

2.1 Staff Evaluation

By all accounts, patrons love the CD-ROM system. We librarians like it too, but we still have some reservations. Because one compact disc contains only one year of Medline, patrons must often switch the CDs. We could buy a player with a lock on it and require patrons to find a staff person when they want discs changed, but we bought Compact Cambridge Medline with the idea that it would be a way for patrons to search Medline on their own. So we let patrons change the discs.

We have had several small crises when we thought a disc had been lost. So far, these have been false alarms. We've experienced a scratched disc, but fortunately the disc was pronounced dead only two days before a new, updated disc arrived. If a disc is damaged weeks before the update is due, we will have to pay for a replacement disc and wait while the disc is shipped to us.

We've noticed that quite a few of our patrons have confused CD-ROM with LUIS, UVM's new online catalog. We tell patrons that LUIS is for books and the CD-ROM station is for journal articles, but, after all, one microcomputer looks pretty much like another microcomputer.

2.2 User Evaluation

We were concerned about the effectiveness of end-user searching so we asked our patrons to give us their opinion of CD-ROM. We distributed 100 survey forms during the first month we offered Compact Cambridge. Thirty-two survey forms were returned. The survey and its results are reproduced in the Appendix. Thirteen people were able to perform a search in under ten minutes. Seventeen people required up to 30 minutes to do a search. We were surprised by their perseverance. Only two potential searchers gave up.

We asked end users if they wanted further instruction, and if so, what kind? Nine searchers were satisfied with their ability to search, 15 people thought handouts might help them, six searchers wanted the option of attending workshops, and two people hoped that a librarian would be available to answer questions, should the searchers have any.

Searchers liked the added control they had over their searches. They appreciated the option of searching terms in titles and abstracts. Patrons were unahppy about the limited number of years available on Compact Cambridge, and they found the manuals unhelpful. In general, searchers wrote that CD-ROM was faster, easier, and more fun than either mediated searches or Index Medicus.

3. EFFECT ON SERVICES

3.1 Training

Through our experience helping CD-ROM end users we have become convinced that even end-user systems require some kind of training. Perhaps end-user systems in particular attract the kind of searchers who need the most help.

Patrons lack both computer skills and searching skills. People unfamiliar with computers do not know that a crooked arrow is a return or enter key, an arrow to the left is a backspace, and up arrows are shift keys. And what are those keys labelled Ctrl, Alt and Esc? What about the F keys? How do you get the paper out of the printer?

Patrons who could handle these details still had difficulty understanding the limitations of computers. One patron typed in MI, hoping to find documents discussing myocardial infarctions. Results which included research done in Kalamazoo, MI, puzzled him. The computer did not intuitively understand what he meant.

Other helpful hints to searchers include the difference between the Boolean operators AND and OR, and the ability to use previous search statement numbers in subsequent searches. We looked at several versions of Medline on CD-ROM and discovered that each system has its own unique difficulties. When searching Compact Cambridge Medline, for example, you must truncate a subject heading in order to retrieve occurrences of that subject heading with subheadings applied to it. If you don't truncate myocardial infarction, you miss articles which deal with therapy, diagnosis, rehabilitation, and prevention, to mention a few.

Because systems are changing so rapidly, manuals for CD-ROM systems are not good. But I'm not sure searchers would read the manuals even if they were more attractive and informative. BRS Colleague on CD-ROM offers an on-screen tutorial, but if novice searchers using the tutorial tie up the CD-ROM station, the database is not available for those people who actually want to search.

Librarians working at the reference desk try to help CD-ROM searchers when possible, but we don't always know who needs attention, and we don't always have time to do a thorough job. If patrons want more help, we make an appointment with them for a time when we are not scheduled to be at the reference desk. One of my colleagues has created a one page guide to Compact Cambridge searching, but it's not a substitute for help from a human being.

When we first offered BRS Colleague in the fall of 1986, we were concerned about the amount of time we might have to spend answering questions from searchers. Beginning in March 1987, we added a new category to our reference statistics. Along with directional questions, instruction, factual information, and mediated computer searches, we now record the number of end-user consultations we perform.

From March through August the number of end user consultations amounted to about 5% of all reference inquiries. After we introduced CD-ROM in September, the number of end user consultations jumped to 12% of all reference inquiries. The number of reference questions overall continues to climb.

Members of the library's circulation department have also fielded questions about CD-ROM. Circulation staff are often asked reference questions when reference librarieans are busy or when the reference department is closed. Eventually, we in the reference department realized that it would be wise to teach circulation staff how to boot CD-ROM, change discs, and perform basic searches. If end users can search, certainly our circulation staff should be able to handle it.

3.2 <u>Mediated Searches</u>

Having made such efforts to train searchers, the reference department hoped to be rewarded with a decline in the number of mediated searches requested. And indeed, we performed 10% fewer searches in 1987 than in 1986.

On the other hand, we actually spent 10% more money on mediated searches in 1987 than in the year before. This increase is partly due to a conscious decision by the reference librarians to take advantage of features available through the more expensive BRS system. I suspect that our decision to switch was influenced by the increasing complexity of the searches we've been asked to perform. Easy searches are disappearing-- end users can do them themselves. As patrons have become more knowledgeable, we've been prodded into searching a wider range of databases on a variety of systems.

When we add in the cost of online time for Colleague training and the free hour of online time we provide, the lease of compact discs, and equipment expenses, we see that our database searching expenses have almost doubled. But our goal in offering end user systems is not to save money. The University of Vermont intends to make computerized databases as available to its patrons as printed sources of information have been.

3.3 <u>Interlibrary Loan</u>

The availability of end user searching has not noticeably affected the number of publications our interlibrary loan department has been asked to obtain from other libraries, but this may be due to the relatively slow results ILL has been capable of.

As we watched patrons retrieve the citations they wanted in just a few minutes, it became obvious that the bottleneck in the flow of information had become interlibrary loan. The Dana Medical Library subscribes to about 1400 journals. Medline indexes over 3000. If a patron wants an article from a journal that we don't have, the ILL department will have a copy of the article mailed from a library that does own the journal. This procedure takes about a week.

In an effort to avoid the US mail, the library bought a telefacsimile machine. At the time this paper was written, we had just received the machine. It remains to be seen what effect telefax will have in our library.

4. CONCLUSIONS

As we continue to evaluate end-user searching, we've taken a look at what kind of information retrieval systems our patrons require, and how each version of Medline fulfills some or all of those requirements.

We would like to see undergraduates, medical students, grad students, professors, health professionals, and researchers find the information they need from journal articles as easily and cheaply as possible. If the topic under investigation is an _Index Medicus_ subject heading, printed indexes are the best possible sources.

If a question involves a number of _Index Medicus_ subject headings, a patron might prefer to combine terms in a computerized literature search. A mediated search presents the least difficulty, but the patron sacrifices the speed and control available through end-user searching.

For our library, CD-ROM versions of Medline provide the least expensive access to that database for end users. But there are still problems with CD-ROM. First, CD-ROM is only available to one person at a time, and that person must come to the library to search. We would like our patrons to be able to search at will, either in the library where we can help them, or in their offices or homes when convenient. Second, Medline is still only one database. Many other databases are available online.

So is our group subscription to BRS Colleague the answer? Not for patrons unwilling to shoulder the cost of online searching. Perhaps if the library were willing to provide unlimited free access to Colleague, our patrons would come to prefer it to CD-ROM. But that's just too expensive a proposition. End users spent over $7109.60 of their own money on Colleague in 1987. The library paid an additional $4514.54. The combined cost for end user searching through Colleague comes to $11,624.14. Imagine the total if the library had offered more free online time. By comparison, the cost of all of our mediated searches was only about $15,000.

We've concluded that CD-ROM has found a place, at least temporarily, in our library. But it remains an addition to our other services, not a replacement. Patrons still use _Index Medicus_, request mediated searches, and sign up for our BRS Colleague group subscription.

There are still improvements we would like to see in CD-ROM, particularly in the area of instruction and documentation. Multiple workstations and remote database access would be a big improvement. We'd like to be able to leave at night without worrying about what could happen to the compact discs. So far, our only reason for offering CD-ROM in addition to online systems is the high cost of online searching for end users. We are still looking for other, relatively inexpensive, ways to allow our patrons to search Medline.

5. APPENDIX

CD-ROM Survey Results

Question	Number of Answers

1. How long did it take you to do a search?
   - a) under 10 min. — 13
   - b) between 10 and 30 min. — 17
   - c) gave up — 2

2. How many citations did you retrieve?
   - a) more than expected — 13
   - b) fewer than expected — 8
   - c) same as expected — 10
   - d) don't know — 1

3. Did you want to limit or expand your search but didn't know how?
   - a) no — 29
   - b) yes — 3

4. Would you like more instruction?
   - a) yes — 19
   - b) no — 13

5. What kind?
   - a) handouts — 15
   - b) workshops — 6
   - c) other — 2
   - d) none — 9

6. Would you use CD-ROM rather than <u>Index Medicus</u>?
   - a) yes — 26
   - b) no — 3
   - c) both — 3

7. Would you use CD-ROM rather than pay for a computer search?
   - a) yes — 26
   - b) no — 4
   - c) both — 2

8. What do you see as the advantages/disadvantages of CD-ROM?

LEARNING MODES AND ONLINE BEHAVIOR OF NOVICE SEARCHERS

Elisabeth L. Logan, Florida State University

Keywords: Novice Searchers, Learning Styles, Online Searching

Abstract: Online searching behavior has been examined from a number of perspectives in the past decade. Among them have been studies by Woelfl, and Logan and Woelfl examining the relationships between online searching behavior and measures of learning style. The present paper reports findings from seventy-six novice seachers from Florida State University. Results show some consistent relationships between modes of learning measured by The Learning Style Inventory and online searching behavior. Novice searchers who rank in the Assimilation quadrant tend to spend longer online, enter more commands, complete more cycles, key more descriptors, and print more references during a search; those who rank in Accommodation quadrant tend to spend less time online, enter fewer commands, complete fewer cycles, key fewer descriptors, and print fewer references. While these measures do not attempt to evaluate the results of a search, there are implications for the selection and training of online searchers.

1. INTRODUCTION

    Several different studies in recent years have observed marked differences in the online searching processes followed by searchers. (1,2,3) There have also been attempts to identify some of the particular characteristics associated with online behavior. (4,5,6,7,8) Woelfl in her study of experineced MEDLINE searchers, (9) and Saracevic et al., (10) in their study of information seeking and retrieving behavior have documented substantial online differences among searchers of similar experience even when searching the same query.
    In a paper describing initial findings from a small sample of novice searchers, Logan and Woelfl, (11) reported some correlations between measures of learning style and the online searching behavior of beginning online searching students. The findings corroborate findings from Woelfl's MEDLINE study and suggest a possible relationship between learning style and search behavior regardless of the searcher's experience. The present study reports findings from a more extensive population of novice searchers. (12)

2. BACKGROUND

    The three measures of learning style used in the study are:
The Learning Style Inventory (LSI), a self-descriptive instrument used to measure preferences for four basic modes of learning, concrete experience, reflective observation, abstract conceptualization, and active experimentation. From the preferences indicated for these basic modes, cour styles of learning can be identified, convergence, divergence, assimilation and accommodation.(13)

The Remote Associates Test (RAT), a test evaluated as being closely related to verbal reasoning. (14) In Woelfl's MEDLINE study it is used as a measure of verbal inference, or the ability to infer a search strategy from a search query.

The Symbolic Reasoning Test (SRT), a test taken from the Employee Aptitude Survey. (15) It measures the ability to draw correct conclusions from symbolic statements. In Woelfl's study it is used as a measure on non-verbal reasoning or the ability to carry out the essential online task of performing Boolean operations.

The five measures of online behavior include:

Cycles, the number of iterations during a search.

Commands, the number of directives issued in response to the system prompt.

Descriptors, the number of actual terms for which the system is asked to search.

Connect Time, the total amount of time spent online during a search.

References, the number of records types or printed out during a search.

3. METHOD

The three tests of learning style (LSI, RAT, SRT) have been administered during the first class meeting of the beginning online searching course at the Florida State University Graduate School of Library and Information Studies each semester since the fall of 1985. These have been coded so that anonymity of the subjects is preserved throughout the course. The five measures of online behavior are applied to printouts from two searching assignments: a search for bibliographic information on two assigned topics; and a search initiated by the student from a client query.

After the completion of the course, and assignment of grades, scores are recorded form the LSI, RAT and SRT and from the measures of online behavior taken from the printout of the two assigned searches. For this study a data base of scores from all classes was compiled and the MINITAB statistical package used to evaluate the relationships. (16) Students who are not native speakers of the English language as well as some students for whom accurate data was not available were omitted from the study.

4. RESULTS

Scores from the Learning Style Inventory indicate that on the Learnint Style Grid, a large percent (45%) of this dataset falls into the Diverger quadrant and a considerably smaller percent (9%) into the Converger quadrant. As can be seem from Figure 1 the Accommodator and Assimilator quadrants contain roughly the same percents.

These distributions differ from the findings in Woelfl's first study which identifies a large proportion of the subjects as Convergers and from the engineering students in Borgman's study that closely resemble Woelfl's subjects in their distribution. (17)

FIGURE 1

LEARNING STYLES

	ACTIVE EXPERIMENTATION	REFLECTIVE OBSERVATION
CONCRETE EXPERIENCE	Accommodator 17 (22%)	Diverger 34 (45%)
ABSTRACT CONCEPTUAL-IZATION	Converger 7 (9%)	Assimilator 18 (24%)

The following table gives the relative numbers for each of three studies

Table 1

Quadrant Placement From LSI Scores - Three Studies

	LOGAN	BORGMAN			WOELFL
	Total	Total	Eng	Engl	Total
ACC	17	10	2	4	6
ASS	18	18	6	6	11
CON	7	18	10	4	25
DIV	34	16	0	10	1

Mean scores from the Remote Associates Test and the Symbolic Reasoning Test do not differ appreciably from those of the other two studies. Table 2 shows the scores.

Table 2

Comparison of Mean RAT and SRT Scores - Three Studies

	LOGAN		BORGMAN		WOELFL	
	Mean	S.D.	Mean	S.D.	Mean	S.D.
RAT	13.04	4.6	10.3	5.2	14.4	5.7
SRT	9.1	6.8	14.7	6.0	11.7	6.0

Using multiple regression techniques to examine the relationships between scores for the test of learning mode and the measures of online behavior, the results show little correlation among the individual measures.

Correlating composite scores from the LSI with measures of online behavior gives correlations well below ranges of significance, however they do exhibit a degree of consistency that may be worth noting. Looking at the correlations between the AC-CE scores which reflect the placement on the continuum between Abstract Conceptualization and Concrete Experience (higher scores indicate an "abstract" rating) and the measures of online behavior, there is a consistently positive relationship. Conversely, the correlation between AE-RO scores, which indicate placement on the continuum between Active Experimentation and Reflective Observation (higher scores indicate an "active" rating) and the measures of online behavior, there is a consistent negative relationship. Table 3 shows these relationships and the relationships for the RAT and SRT tests.

Table 3

Correlations Between LSI Composite Scores and Online Measures

	AC-CE	AE-RO	RAT	SRT
Cycles	.230	-.170	-.060	.088
Commands	.158	-.116	-.133	.029
Descriptors	.292	-.253	-.084	.061
Connect Time	.327	-.169	-.024	.048
References	.167	-.102	.090	.202

However, looking at the relationships between the five measures of online behavior and placement on the Learning Style Inventory Grid, the findings are considerably more interesting.

As can be seen in Figure 1, subjects ranking themselves as "high" in the areas of Active Experimentation and Concrete Experience are placed in the Accommodator quadrant. Accommodators are characterized as solving problems intuitively through trial and error, and having as their greatest strengths, doing things and generating enthusiasm in others.

High scores in Reflective Observation and Abstract Conceptualization place the subject in the Assimilator quadrant. Assimilators are characterized as using inductive reasoning, creating theoretical models, and assimilating much into integrated explanations.

Placement in the other two sections follows the same pattern. Convergers use deductive reasoning to solve problems, and tend to do well in situations where single correct answers are called for. Divergers view experience from many points of view and operate best in open-ended situations where many alternatives are needed.

The mean scores for each of the four quadrant groups of the LSI on the online measures is shown in Table 4.

Table 4

Mean Scores for Quadrant Groups

	Cycles	Commands	Descriptors	Connect Time	References
ACC	3.32*	23.88*	20.26*	.321*	17.15*
ASS	4.89*	32.59*	30.63*	.467*	33.47*
CON	3.45*	27.21	17.65*	.340	19.18*
DIV	3.74	25.41	23.58	.344	23.19

* Indicates a statistically significant difference from population mean.

Here it can be seen that Assimilators as a group, spend more time online, issue more commands, complete more cycles, key more descriptors, and print more references than any other group.

Accommodators, on the other hand, spend less time online, issue fewer commands, key fewer descriptors, complete fewer cycles, and print fewer references.

Recall that placement in the Assimilator quadrant depends upon high scores in reflective observation and abstract conceptualization and that placement in the Accommodator quadrant depends upon high scores in concrete experience and active experimentation. In fact the two quadrants are in opposite positions on the LSI grid.

Examining the ranges of individual scores for the five searching measures, observe the very great range between individual searchers. This would seem to corroborate results from other studies. Table 5 shows the minimum and maximum values for the five online searching measures.

Table 5

Minimum and Maximum Values for Five Searching Measures

	Cycles	Commands	Descriptors	Connect Time	References
MIN	1	5	4.5	.057	1
MAX	11	98	101	.983	113

All the maximum values are the scores of a single searcher. Four of the five minimum values are the scores of one other searcher. The searcher whose scores are all maximum values has LSI composite scores that place him in the Assimilator quadrant. The searcher whose score are four of the five minimum values has LSI scores that place her in the Accommodator quadrant.

Looking at the mean RAT and SRT scores for the different LSI quadrant groups, the highest mean score for the SRT appears in the Converger group and the highest mean score for the RAT appears in the Assimilator group. Table 6 shows these values.

Table 6

Mean Scores for RAT and SRT by LSI Groups

	Accommodator	Assimilator	Converger	Diverger
RAT	13.61	14.47*	10.3	12.75
SRT	9.77	10.63	11.12*	8.15

* The difference between this value and the population mean is statistically significant.

These results would appear to be consistent with the purpose for including these measures in the study. The Remote Associates Test is included as a measure of inductive reasoning. One of the characteristics of an Assimilator is the use of inductive reasoning. The Symbolic Reasoning Test is included as a measure of deductive reasoning; Convergers are characterized in part by their use of deductive reasoning.

5. CONCLUSIONS

The subjects of this study do not fall into the same LSI patterns as subjects of previous studies by Borgman and Woelfl. Although the placement of engineers in Borgman's Study does resemble that of the subjects in Woelfl's Study and the placement of English majors is similar to what we observe in this study. The large percentage of subjects in the Diverger category may reflect the large proportion of our students from social science and humanities undergraduate programs.

The lack of any real correlation between any individual test score from the LSI or from the RAT and SRT seems to indicate that patterns of online search behavior, at least in this case, are a result of more complex variables than can be measured by single scores. On the other hand, there are some encouraging results from relationships between quadrant placement as a result of LSI composite scores and measures of online behavior. Subjects placing in two of the opposing quadrants (Assimilator and Accommodator) appear to have demonstrated equally opposing modes of behavior online. Those subjects who placed in the Accommodator quadrant showed mean scores significantly lower than those of the population mean, whereas the subjects placed in the Assimilator quadrant showed mean scores significantly higher than those of the population mean. The subject with the highest scores on measures of online behavior identifies himself as an Assimilator; the subject with four of the five lowest scores on the searching measures identifies herself as an Accommodator.

Whether in the long run any definite conclusions can be drawn from this or related studies remains to be seen. We can say at this point, however, that for this study it appears that these subjects are able to evaluate themselves on the Learning Style Inventory in such a way as to be consistent with their behavior when online. It may be that this will have some real significance in the selection and training of people for online searching.

6.   NOTES

   1. Fenichel, Carol H. "Online Searching: Measures that Discriminate Among Users with Different Types of Experiences." JASIS 32 (1981): 23-32.

   2. Woelfl, Nancy N. "Individual Differences in Online Search Behavior: The Effect of Learning Styles and Cognitive Abilities on Process and Outcome." Unpublished PhD Dissertation, Case Western Reserve University, Cleveland, Ohio; 1984.

   3. Saracevic, Tefko et al. Experiments on the Cognitive Aspects of Information Seeking and Information Retrieving. Final report for National Science Foundation grant IST - 8596411 (Cleveland: Case Western Reserve University, September 1986).

   4. Bellardo, Trudi. "An Investiagtion of Online Searcher Traits and their Relationship to Search Outcome." JASIS 36 (1985): 241-250.

   5. Fenichel, Carol H. op. cit.

   6. Borgman, Christine L. "Individual Differences in the Use of Technology: Work in Progress." Proceedings of the American Society for Information Science. 22 (1985): 243-249.

   7. Woelfl, Nancy N. op. cit.

   8. Logan, E.L. and Woelfl, Nancy N. "Individual Differences in Online Searching Behavior of Novice Searchers". Proceedings of the American Society for Information Science 23 (1986): 163-165.

   9. Woelfl, Nancy N. op. cit.

   10. Saracevic et. al. op. cit.

   11. Logan, E.L. and Woelfl, Nancy N. op. cit.

   12. The conference presentation will include an additional 30 subjects from FSU and from UNC Chapel Hill.

   13. Kolb, David A. "The Learning Style Inventory". Boston: McBer & Co., 1985.

   14. Baird, Leonard L. "The Remote Associates Test". In The Seventh Mental Measurements Yearbook, edited by Oskar K. Buros. Highland Park, NJ: Gryphon Press, 1978.

   15. Ruch, Floyd L. and Ruch, Williams L. The Employee Aptitude Survey. Los Angeles: Psychological Services, Inc., 1957.

   16. Ryan, Thomas A. et al. MINITAB Student Handbook. North Scituate, Mass: Duxbury Press. 1967.

   17. Borgman, Christine. op. cit.

FULL TEXT NEWSPAPER RETRIEVAL IS HARD TO MANAGE: FACT OR FICTION?

Arlene Long, VU/TEXT Information Services, Inc.

Abstract: Online researchers have often found full-text newspaper databases more frustrating to search than subject-specific, bibliographic, or abstract files. Because newspaper databases contain a vast array of information with emphasis on immediate delivery, alternative research strategies are needed. This paper explores the myth that full-text newspaper retrieval is difficult to manage and suggests alternatives to searching subject indexes. Examples will be presented from three major vendors of full-text newspapers: VU/TEXT, NEXIS, and DataTimes.

1. INTRODUCTION

What makes full-text newspaper searching so difficult for some researchers? Is it the quantity of information, type of information, system design, training (or lack of training), prior search habits of researchers, or combinations of these elements? This paper explores how these issues relate to searching full-text newspapers databases vs. subject-specific, bibliographic databases, and offers suggestions to reorient the online researcher to full-text newspaper databases.

2. SO MUCH DATA, SO LITTLE TIME

Just how much information is available in a typical newspaper database? A mid-size newspaper might store 100-200 stories per day on weekdays, and 200-350 stories on a Sunday. Large metropolitan newspapers, Los Angeles Times or Philadelphia Inquirer, average 200-400 stories on a weekday, and 400-600 stories on Sundays. With some quick conservative computation, we estimate that in one year a smaller newspaper database contains a minimum of 46,500 documents, with 9,300,000 searchable words; larger newspapers store 220,000 documents or more, with a minimum of 55,000,000 words. Remember -- this is only for one year.

3. DIFFERENCES BETWEEN FULL-TEXT AND BIBLIOGRAPHIC DATABASES

Some differences between full-text newspaper databases and subject-specific, bibliographic databases effect the way the searcher structures the search strategy. The four most significant differences include:

3.1 Quantity of Free-Text Searchable Words

Obviously, full-text databases contain many more free-text searchable words than bibliographic ones. More importantly, this often results in retrieving more hits than expected or needed. The searcher needs to consider the relationship and proximity of search terms to each other. In full-text searching there is a greater need to use proximity connectors to avoid excessive hits.

3.2 Type and Variety of Information Stored

Since newspaper databases provide a vast array of information ranging from obituaries to international events, more consideration is needed when choosing appropriate search terms. An understanding of the available fields and segments, as well as the use of proximity connectors is essential.

3.3   Currency of Online Availability
Because newspaper stories are usually available online within 24 hours, there is little time for newspaper librarians to develop and apply hierarchical, permuted subject indexes as is usually done for bibliographic databases. Of course, the lag time for online availability for bibliographic databases is often 4-8 weeks, much longer than the 24-hour availability for most newspapers. Often, researchers need to do quick searching in newspaper databases for the most current data.

3.4.   Availability of Subject Indexes
Since the focus is on immediate availability of newspaper information, there is little time available for development of online subject indexes or classification codes that aid the searcher in the retrieval process. However, two of the larger newspapers, the Washington Post and the Los Angeles Times, are looking at the development of extensive subject indexes. Again, use proximity connectors and field searching to conduct subject searches. If possible, restrict subject searches to headlines or lead-graphs (see 6.2).

4.   HOW TO DEAL MORE EFFECTIVELY WITH FULL-TEXT NEWSPAPER SEARCHING

4.1   Think Like a Newspaper Reporter
Despite the belief that almost anything is grist for the media mill, not everything is newsworthy. Know what type of information is likely to be written about in a newspaper, and get a sense for the terminology that journalists use.

4.2   What's Likely to be Found in a Newspaper Database
Any local, national, or international event of significance or of human interest is likely to be reported. More specific to online versions, newspapers store the full-text of all news items, columns, feature stories, and editorials. Some newspapers do not store syndicated columns. All newspapers EXCLUDE weather reports, advertisements, calendar listings, horoscopes, and paid funeral announcements (also known as death notices).
The larger metropolitan newspapers tend to focus more on national and international issues with some coverage of local interest. (All metropolitan papers carry local sections.) Smaller newspapers tend to focus on local and national news with less in-depth coverage of international topics.

If it's not newsworthy, it's not there
If the information you need is extremely specific or of interest to a very small audience, it is probably not well reported -- if at all. For example, if you are doing a survey on course offerings at local colleges, this topic may not be well covered in the newspaper. It may not be possible to locate the "perfect article" you had in mind because it may not have been written. When you conduct a search such as this one, a response of zero hits or 1 hit is probably accurate.

The broader the topic, the harder the search
There are some very broad topics reported from many journalistic

slants including: economic forecasts, industry trends, effects of controversial legislation. These broad topics are often reported so frequently in the news that a quick search yields too many hits. (Another problem occurs when you are looking for a slant not well reported on the topic.) How do you get "the perfect article?"

First, you need to accept the fact that there may not be one or two perfect articles on your broad topic, there may be many. Therefore, you may need to gather information from several articles in order to get the whole picture. Also, rely on the strengths of the system to help you restrict searches as needed (see items 6-6.3)

4.3   That's What Toll Free Numbers Are For

A quick call to customer service will provide you with some advice on how to begin your research. Also, customer service can help you determine if you should try other databases for more targeted results.

5.   IT'S NOT JUST WHAT YOU SAY, IT'S HOW YOU SAY IT -- CONSIDER THE TERMINOLOGY REPORTERS MIGHT USE

Remember the writer's audience is the general public, not specialists using scientific or specialized jargon. Therefore, researchers need to include search terms the general public will recognize.

For example, if you are researching litigation or tort cases, reporters will more likely use terms such as: sue, suit, lawsuit, or trial. Or, when you are looking for articles providing forecasts, you might want to include words like outlook, prediction, survey.

Certain terms are more frequently used in news reporting than others. Example, organized crime is used more generally than a term such as mafia. Or use "aids" rather than acquired immune deficiency syndrome. Of course, you can always include all alternatives in your search statements.

6.   USE THE SPECIAL DESIGN FEATURES OF THE SYSTEM/VENDOR

Though most systems share similarities in conducting searches (boolean connectors, adjacency searching, and field or segment searching), each vendor has system strengths and weaknesses that differ slightly from others. Use system strengths to their fullest capacity. Identify weaknesses and develop strategies to avoid them.

I conducted sample searches in VU/TEXT, NEXIS, and DataTimes to identify some strengths of the particular vendors. The sample question below was selected because it is an actual question researched in newspapers, and because at least one modification was required before a final search statement was recommended. A little trial and error is the normal procedure for developing proper search strategies. Also, before I conducated my searches, I consulted the customer service departments for DataTimes and NEXIS. For VU/TEXT I relied on my own skills as a veteran VU/TEXT searcher.

The search question: How will tax reform effect real estate investing?

6.1   NEXIS

NEXIS' customer service suggested search statements that relied heavily on proximity connectors. There were no fields or subject indexes available that would have aided in this search, therefore, we conducted a free-text search. The results were quickly scanned for appropriate fit by using the KWIC command. KWIC, a decided strength of the NEXIS system, allows the searcher to view the search terms in context.

After two modifications, the final search strategy was: **tax reform w/25 (real estate w/15 invest!)**. Truncation is also handled very quickly in the NEXIS system.

6.2 VU/TEXT

My first statement in VU/TEXT was free-text and, similar to NEXIS, relied on proximity connectors to provide a tight relationship among the words. However, a modification using the headline and lead-graph fields restricted the search to the two fields most likely to contain the most significant information. (The who, what, where, when, and why of a story are usually contained in the headline and lead-graphs.)

The final strategy was: **@5,6 tax / reform and real / estate and invest(ing,ment,ments)**. Though truncation is available, VU/TEXT allows suffix searching. You select the exact word endings to fit your search. The system performs this function faster than a truncation.

6.3 DataTimes

DataTimes provides a unique twist to proximity searching. All search terms placed within quotation marks are immediately searched within one sentence. Therefore, hits tend to be targeted quickly, however, it may be too restrictive for some searches. You can further tighten the search by requesting all terms to occur only in the headline (perhaps too tight for this question). Set building (combining a previous search statement with proceeding statements) is another strong feature of the system.

DataTimes' representative suggested: **find "tax reform" and "real estate invest*"**.

7. ATTEND TRAINING OFFERED BY THE VENDORS

Yes, you are an experienced researcher on ABC, XYZ, and QRS systems. Your time is precious, and you don't feel it's necessary to attend another training. Wrong. Each vendor designs training geared toward getting the best out of its own system. A training seminar is where you can identify those strengths and weaknesses and can get tips on what works best for each system.

8. CONCLUSION

With a better understanding of the quantity, variety, and type of information likely to be contained in a newspaper, the researcher has a more realistic expectation of what can or can not be found in a newspaper database. Since every word (except stopwords) is free-text searchable, you are bound to find the data -- if it's there. Armed with good training and several weeks of hands-on experience in the full-text newspaper databases, searchers can quickly pick up the strengths of the vendors and use them appropriately to get what they want.

PROMOTING ONLINE SERVICES IN STATE GOVERNMENT

Kathleen Low, California State Library

Keywords: Online Search Services, Promotion, Marketing, State Libraries

Abstract: State libraries provide online search services to a varied group of users which includes members of the state legislature and their staffs, state agencies, and state employees. This paper discusses how the California State Library promotes both initial and repeated use of its online search service to its diverse user group. This paper will first examine the promotion of initial use of the service through the library's participation in appropriate state user groups, program presentations, publications and other activities, then focus on an overlooked promotion for repeated use, the rapid delivery of appropriate search results. The timely provision of search printouts and post-search services associated with the patron's initial use of the service can either encourage or discourage future use. The California State Library's online database search service policy, and database services, both commercial and noncommercial, accessible by the library, methods of accessing the service, and post-search delivery of documents are discussed herein. Since the provision of online search services varies from state library to state library, the paper concludes with a selective survey of online search services offered at other state libraries, and a look at their promotional techniques.

1. INTRODUCTION

Although our primary clientele consists of over 145,000 people spread out over 156,361 square miles, provision of the library's online database search service is not a problem. Promotion of the service is, however, a difficult task. This was the problem faced by the California State Library. This paper will examine both the problems and solutions facing the California State Library in the promotion of its online database search service, and how other selected state libraries promote their online services.

The California State Library first began offering online database searches in early 1973 with access to only two databases available through the DIALOG^{TM} system. Today the library has access to not only DIALOG,^{TM} but also Mead Data Central's$_{TM}$ LEXIS/NEXIS^{TM} system, BRS,^{TM} Pergamon ORBIT,^{TM} NEWSNET,^{TM} MEDLARS, VuText,$_{TM}$ DataTimes, the Council of State Governments' ISIS system, and the National Conference of State Legislature's LEGISNET system. Over 400 databases can be accessed covering just about every subject area.

The library provides online searches to members of the state legislature and their staffs, and to state employees working on state business. There is no charge to the patron or to their agency. Searches can be requested in person, by telephone, or by written request. Although no charges are associated with the service, it was not utilized by certain state employees and agencies who could have benefitted from the service. This was attributed to their lack of knowledge of the service due to its low visability.

2. PROBLEM: PROMOTION OF ONLINE SEARCH SERVICE

Two immediate problems faced the library. The first was to find a method of informing our clientele of the service. The second problem was finding a means of promoting repeated use of the service.

3. SOLUTIONS

The standard methods of promoting online services, such as demonstrations and brochures were not sufficient because the library resides in Sacramento and its user base encompasses patrons residing throughout the state, and in some instances out-of-state (for example the California State Franchise Tax Board office in New York) users. The State Library had to find the most effective method of reaching the largest number of patrons with as little disruption of its normal workflow as possible. To this end, the library solved the problem of informing patrons about the service through three approaches: participation in appropriate state user groups and organizations, special program presentations, and ongoing State Library publications and special state agency publications.

Inclusion of information on relevant online databases in ongoing library publications is an easy method of promoting online services which requires little time consumption. The California State Library produces a series of annotated bibliographies titled "Special Topics" which focuses on topics of interest to state government and includes information on relevant databases. For example, an issue devoted to groundwater protection included descriptive information on databases such as ENVIROLINE, and the Environmental Law Reporter Database. Inclusion of databases in these publications promotes the library's online service on an ongoing basis, and also brings important databases in the field to the attention of people who need the information.

Another method used to inform patrons about our online service was to have the service described in non-State Library publications which are distributed to our core user group. Two such publications, <u>California State Employee</u>, and also <u>Today's Supervisor</u>, produced by the California State Employees Association (CSEA) are distributed to all state employees. Both publications have carried articles describing the service. Various state agency publications, such as the state Department of Fish & Game's newsletter have also printed articles describing the service. Recently, the Assembly Office of Information Services put together a package of our materials on the service and distributed it to all Assembly committee consultants with a letter describing how the service could be of value to them. Needless to say, this type of promotion is invaluable to the library since use of the service is being promoted by the potential patron's colleague, at no expense or labor on part of the library.

Participation of library staff in appropriate organizations of state employees was also found to be an effective means of promotion. For example, some library staff members participate in the State Microcomputer User's

Forum, an organization established to promote microcomputer skills and knowledge. The benefits of participation in this group are twofold. Library staff have the opportunity of submitting articles about our online service for publication in the group's newsletter, and of actively promoting the service in the monthly meetings. At the same time, their participation in the organization will allow them to increase their microcomputer knowledge and skills.

State Library staff also participate in other organizations such as California State Agency Librarians, an informal gorup of librarians working in state agency libraries. This group meets regularly to foster the exchange of information and discuss common problems. State Library staff participating in this organization act not only as resource people, but also as a reminder that our online search service is a potential source of the information they may be seeking.

Program presentations, although time consuming, may well be worth the time spent in brining the service into the limelight. In 1987 the State Microcomputer User's Forum was asked by conference organizers to plan and present a series of programs at the Government Technology Conference to be held in Sacramento that May. Since a large percentage of the attendees would be California state employees, it seemed like a wonderful event in which we could promote our service. Because of staff participation in the Forum, the library was able to take the lead in planning a program on online information which included a presentation on the services offered by the California State Library. Although only a certain percentage of the total conference registrants attended the program, visibility of the service was increased due to the program description which appeared in the conference schedule.

Other program presentations have included talks to specific groups from various state agencies, or groups representing state agencies. The State Information Officers Council is one such group. A presentation on our online services not only educated the members of the group of the potential uses of the service, but also provided them with information they could in turn disseminate to employees within their respective departments.

Repeated use of the online service is promoted by delivery of appropriate search results and post-search services. With each search printout the library includes a cover letter which directs the patron to the appropriate library resource person should the patron have questions about the search results or if further searching on the topic is desired. The cover letter also informs the patron of how he can obtain the items cited on the printouts. Patrons can either personally search for and retrieve the items desired, or they can highlight the items desired from the printout and have library staff retrieve and check out the items for them. Library staff will also interlibrary loan items not found in the State Library should the patron desire. No limitations are placed on the number of items library staff will gather for the patron, or on the number of items to be borrowed through interlibrary loan.

The California State Library's promotion of its online search service has contributed significantly to the growth of the service. From fiscal year 1982/1983 to 1986/1987 the number of online subject searches performed the staff has increased 134.72%. In fiscal year 1986/1987 we performed 3664 subject searches. Approximately 54% of all searches performed were for members of the legislature and their staffs, and 45% for state agencies and state employees, and 1% for miscellaneous and other uses.

4. PROMOTION OF ONLINE SERVICES IN OTHER STATE LIBRARIES

The promotion and offering of online services varies from state library to state library. For example, the Oklahoma State Library provides online searches for elected officials at no charge. Every year they present an orientation to the library for new legislative staff members where they discuss the library's online services and the databases to which they have access.

The New York State Library, with access to nine different information services, also performs online searches for state employees and members of the state legislature at no charge providing the request pertains to official state business. Online searches are also performed for the public on a fee basis. To promote their service they actively hold informational workshops for their primary clientele, and publish a manual on the service annually. Flyers on the service are also published and distributed.

At the Oregon State Library the online database search service is totally integrated into their reference service. Online searches are not done upon demand, but as needed to fulfill the information needs of Oregon state employees, the state legislature, and school and public libraries. When a request does require an online search, it is performed without charge to the patron. Because online searching is not done upon demand, they do not promote their online service, but do promote the reference service in which it is integrated.

5. SUMMARY

Each state library differs in the level of online services provided, and the conditions under which the services are offered. The clientele can range from members of the legislature, to school librarians. And because of these variable, the libraries' promotion of online services ranges from continuing high priority efforts, to none.

The California State Library actively promotes its online database search service through a variety of methods. As a result of the promotion, use of the service has increased considerable. We expect to see the demand for the service continue to grow in the near future.

IMAGE PROCESSING: TECHNOLOGY/ OVERVIEW*

Lois F. Lunin, Herner and Company

Keywords: Image Processing, Image Processing Systems, Image Processing Issues, Image Databases, Image Processing Trends.

Abstract: Image processing is now a sophisticated and growing field that incorporates many recent computer software and hardware developments. The field has been estimated to be more than a half billion dollar market with a growth potential of 30-50% over the next few years. While attention is beginning to focus on building image databases, the problems in designing and handling these databases differ from bibliographic and numeric databases in kind, magnitude, and retrieval strategies. This paper outlines the elements of electronic images, image processing, and image databases.

1. INTRODUCTION

Although its history goes back several decades, only recently has image processing become a large and sophisticated field. The recent surge of activity in digital image processing is due to several factors including the importance of access to large numbers of digitized images, advances in computers, and the development of more sophisticated software. Recently, too, attention has been directed to image databases. Beyond the scope of this paper are computer generated graphics, three dimensional images, and color images.

Digital image processing, also called visualization, is a vast umbrella term. It includes optics, electronics, mathematics, photography, computer technology, and cognitive psychology. The field suffers from misconceptions, misunderstandings, and misinformation.

2. BASIC ELEMENTS OF ELECTRONIC IMAGES

2.1 Digitization

For purposes of this discussion, an image refers to the representation of a picture in terms of the binary 1s and 0s of digital computing. The picture--a photo, printed page, diagram--becomes a digital image by being digitized into picture elements or pixels. Another way to think of this process is mentally to place a fine mesh screen over a picture. Each open

---

* This paper is a condensation of the following publication: Lunin, Lois F.: Electronic Image Information, chap. 6 in Williams, Martha E., ed. Annual Review of Information Science and Technology, vol. 22. Published for the American Society for Information Science by Elsevier Science Publishers B.V., Amsterdam, The Netherlands, pp. 179-224.

space in the mesh is a pixel location. During digitization, the brightness of each pixel is sampled and a numerical value is assigned. This process generates a number that represents the brightness or darkness of the image at that point. When this activity has been completed for each pixel, the image is represented by a rectangular array of whole numbers. Thus, each pixel has a location or address and a number called the gray level. This digital data is now ready for computer processing. The computer reads the input image into storage. When output is requested, the computer operates on one or several of these lines of numbers and generates the image pixel by pixel.

Resolution and gray scale are associated with the quality of an image. The number of elements in an array, i.e., the number of pixels used horizontally and vertically, determines the resolution level of the image.

2.2 Gray Scale

The number of shades of gray represented by the pixels determines the gray scale of the image. For example, if only two shades are used--black and white--the result is a high-contrast image that has poor definition. However, if many shades of gray are used, there can be smooth transitions from light to dark. The number of pixels in an image is usually 256 x 256, 512 x 512, or 1,024 x 1,024, or based on standards such as the 525-line commercial television system. The gray levels are encoded in binary form. Eight-bit pixels provide 256 different gray values in black and white or 256 unique colors.

3. BASIC ELEMENTS OF IMAGE PROCESSING SYSTEMS

In general, an image processing system has five main components: 1) digitization or input, 2) storage, 3) processing, 4) communications (transmission), and 5) output.

3.1 Input

Scanners are the principal input devices for an image system. A scanner is a device that examines printed characters or graphics and represents them as electronic signals. Scanning devices generally scan one line at a time down the page; current scanning devices generally operate between 200 and 400 lines per inch.

During the scanning process each line on the document page is divided into thousands of pixels. If a page of print is being scanned, each pixel is interpreted as either a black or white point on the page--black for the part of the print character and white for the absence of print.

Scanning densities are usually measured by the number of pixels per inch on both the horizontal and vertical axes. A scan of 200 lines per inch is satisfactory for office correspondence and the body text of most printed matter.

Input systems also include the indexing process. The identifying entry for each document in the image system is usually created at this stage, with more complex index information added later.

3.2 Storage

Image information is stored differently from alphanumeric characters which are stored in ASCII code. For example, it might take 8,000 bits of information to represent the image of an A by analyzing it into its light and dark picture elements in contrast to 8 bits for an ASCII representation of an A.

3.3   Processing

Digital image processing covers a range of operations that manipulate the data to alter an image or to extract and refine meaningful information.

Digital image processing normally includes five processes: 1) enhancement, 2) restoration, 3) compression, 4) segmentation, and 5) description. In <u>enhancement</u>, pictorial information is improved for human interpretation and machine perception. <u>Restoration</u> deals with improving a given image by reconstructing an image that has been impaired or has deteriorated. <u>Compression</u> is used when it is necessary to reduce storage or transmission requirements. Image compression is a particularly important aspect of image processing and an active area of research. In <u>segmentation</u>, an image is subdivided into objects or regions of interest. Algorithms generally are founded on one of two basic principles: discontinuity and similarity. In <u>description</u>, features are extracted from an object for recognition purposes. Descriptors are usually based on shape and intensity.

3.4   Output

Because image processing data are bit oriented rather than character oriented, the resolution of both hard copy and terminal display devices must be very high. The higher the resolution, the greater the cost of the device. Generally a resolution of 100 x 100 lines per square inch is acceptable for workstation viewing and 200 x 200 lines per square inch is suitable for printing.

3.5   Communications

Because more information is contained in an image than traditional data networks handle, a communication network for an image processing system is a challenge. For example, an 8 1/2 x 11 inch page at 200 x 200 pixels per inch contains nearly 4 million bits of information. In contrast, the same page on a typical terminal screen contains 1,920 bytes (characters). Communications network designers have met these challenges by using several approaches, e.g., compression, separate networks.

4.   IMAGE PROCESSING ISSUES

A number of image processing issues and concerns have yet to be resolved. These issues include: cost, security, technology, immaturity, legal admissibility, standards, major vendor commitment, installed base, retention of documents, conversion, and organizational control.

5.   HARDWARE

A typical digital image system includes document scanning devices, image system controllers and processors, optical disk storage devices, printers, high-resolution workstations, and system software.

5.1   Scanners

As noted earlier, scanners examine the image and represent the pixels as electronic signals. Scanners include conventional cameras, optical digitizers, satellite scanners, and facsimile devices.

5.2   Image Controllers

Image controllers range from microprocessors to minicomputers. The controller provides image enhancement, compression and decompression of scanned images, conversion from analog signals to digital bit streams, and the physical routing of images throughout the system. In most configurations the scanners, terminals, and storage devices are linked together to the image controller.

5.3   Storage and Output

Recently the optical disk has interested potential users because of its storage capacity. Output devices are usually modified laser printers that range from slow conventional desktop units to high speed printers.

5.4   New Hardware Devices

Computing architectures and other new technologies are being designed and built for image processing and management. Recent efforts in research and advances in image information systems include: 1) high resolution scanners and 2) standalone image processors. There is also renewed interest in videodisk technology and in using microfiche for storage and retrieval of large quantities of images.

6.   SOFTWARE

Software for image systems consists of system and applications packages. Software for image processing has been hard to find and remains one of the major challenges in bringing more image systems to the market.

7.   IMAGE DATABASES

Image databases differ from conventional databases in many ways: characteristics of the data; acquisition; verification; data models; types of operations performed; input, processing, output, ordering, encoding, storage; queries and retrieval; hardware; software; communications; legality of data; users; user friendliness; applications; design complexity; and database design tools.

The term <u>image database</u> has been used in different ways in the literature. A collection of image data itself is sometimes called an image database; however, most authors define an image database as a system in which a large amount of image data and their related information are stored in an integrated manner with a management system. (Ref. 1)

The development of image database systems requires a huge amount of thought and effort. Examples of problems: How does one represent structural information in a database mode? Just what information is to be retrieved? Is the desired output a physical image, descriptive information, or just relevant information? What is a unit of an image entity? When are derivable image features computed? As yet there is no theoretical background in image database design. There appear to be two conceptual barriers (Ref. 2): 1) the discrete representation of continuous entities in conventional databases; and 2) the absence of total ordering in two dimensions. The similarities and differences of conventional databases vs. image databases have been compared according to 22 characteristics (Ref. 3)

The field appears ready for the application of concepts that will allow a unified structure to emerge from the details.

8.   APPLICATIONS

Pilot or operational image handling efforts are ongoing in several fields. The applications range from scholarly archival studies to life-saving events in hospitals. Areas of activity include: business; government; art libraries, museums, architecture; maps, cartography, geography; libraries;

and in medicine in areas where many images may be accessed quickly and easily. Common to all areas are the need to organize, manage, and communicate the image information.

9. PROBLEMS

The development of new subject access methods and languages specifically developed to retrieve images lags far behind the technology. A continuing barrier to rapid progress in image processing research is the lack of a universal method of transferring image data between different facilities. The proliferation of different image data formats has compounded the problem. The establishment of logical formats and standards for images and image data headers has been recommended as the first step. (Ref. 4)

10. TRENDS

While the lack of interface, resolution, and data-compression standards in image processing will continue to pose problems, technology keeps forging ahead. The personal computer has created a popular market for image processing, which is seen by experts as the second fastest-growing application in the microcomputer area, right behind desktop publishing. (Ref. 5) In effect, one industry is driving the other. When image processing is incorporated into publishing systems, users can combine images with text in one package. Windowing and providing simultaneous access to document images, word processing, and mainframe data are already a reality, although integration of all of these technologies has yet to be accomplished.

The number of scholarly and trade publications with articles on image information and the number of conferences and workshops on the topic are growing rapidly. Standards are being discussed. Yet one of the chief areas of concern remains how to represent structural information in a database mode. This calls for thinking in terms of spatial, continuous, gray-scale information--a realm far different from the databases and online systems familiar to most of us.

11. REFERENCES

1. Tamura, H. and Yokoya, N. Image Database Systems. A Survey. Pattern Recognition 171, No. 1, p. 29-43, 1984.

2. Nagy, G. Image Database. Image and Vision Computing 3, No. 3, p. 111-117, 1985.

3. Lunin, Lois F. Electronic Image Information, chapter 6, in Williams, Martha E., ed. Annual Review of Information Science and Technology, vol. 22. Published for the American Society for Information Science by Elsevier Science Publishers B.V., Amsterdam, The Netherlands, p . 179-224.

4. Prewitt, J.M.S., Selfridg, P.G.; Anderson, A.C. Name-Value Pair Specification for Image Data Headers and Logical Standards for Image Data Exchange. Proceedings of the Society of Photo-Optical Instrumentation Engineers. 515, p. 452-458. 1984.

5. Hicks, Patricia. PC Spurs Growth in Image Processing and Media Cybernetics. Washington Technology. 1, no. 8, p. 17, July 10, 1986.

IMAGE RETRIEVAL, DISPLAY, AND REPRODUCTION

Clifford A. Lynch, University of California

Abstract

A user typically searches an image database or requests documents from a digitized document storage system using relatively traditional query languages. It is only after images have been selected for use that the unique characteristics and problems of image databases become apparent to the end user. This paper focuses on issues involved in the transfer of images to an end-user workstation and the subsequent display and printing of these images by the end user. The emphasis is on network environments that include image database servers, although local image databases housed on optical media are also considered. Capabilities and limitations of currently available technology for image transfer, display, and printing are examined, including the use of computer networks for image transmission, data compression issues, bit-mapped displays, local storage requirements for workstations, and all-points-addressable laser printers.

1. Introduction

This paper explores technical issues involved in the transfer of selected images from an image database to an end-user terminal or workstation and the subsequent display or printing of the retrieved images. It is during these activities that the unique and demanding nature of image databases becomes apparent. While images can be selected using traditional query languages, the *movement* of a set of images from an image database raises qualitatively new design considerations that do not figure in the use of textual databases. In addition, displaying or printing high-resolution bit-mapped images imposes new requirements on both workstations and printers.

2. Image Database Access Architectures

Most textual databases are mounted on large host computers. End users retrieve and display information from such databases using simple character-oriented terminals connected to the host at relatively slow speeds (9600 bits/second or slower). When PCs are used as access devices, they normally run a program that emulates a character-oriented terminal. The processing capabilities of the PC are not used, except perhaps to record the online session for future reference or to aid the user in the formulation of queries. (CD-ROM databases attached to workstations are the exception and are discussed later. Access to image databases is not standardized in the same way, and the evolution of intelligent workstations has resulted in a complex range of system architecture alternatives based on distributed computing models. The architecture chosen to provide access to an image database largely determines the major design and performance issues for a given system. This section discusses several popular architectural models.

1. *The terminal model.* A dumb terminal with high-resolution graphics display is controlled directly by the host supporting the image database, much like traditional textual database systems. The major difference is that the host sends pixels rather than characters.

2. *The fully distributed computing model.* The user has a full-function workstation or personal computer. Selected images are transferred as *files* from the image database host to the local workstation. Subsequent manipulations, including display and printing of the images, are carried out exclusively on the workstation, without further interaction with the host. The user obtains an actual copy of selected images which can be stored on a long-term basis on the local workstation. In this model, the host supporting the image database acts as a *server*. The workstations function as *clients* to the image server.

3. *The local server model.* The local workstation runs a display *server* in this model. The central image database becomes a *client* of this display server by transmitting remote directives and data across the network. The workstation performs a significant amount of local processing, but in close and continued cooperation with the host supporting the central image database. Images are never formally transferred to the workstation or stored there; the central host transmits material that appears on the workstation screen via the display server software running in the workstation.

3. Bandwidth and Transfer Time Reqirements for Images

Raster images are several orders of magnitude larger than ASCII text; on a crowded page one might find 4,000 characters (4 Kbytes of data). The same page, digitized at a density of 300 pixels/inch, yields close to 800 Kbytes of information. In the following calculations, only simple black and white images, appropriate for digitized text, are considered. To transmit pictures in black and white, it may be necessary to use greyscale, which increases all numbers by perhaps 2 or 4 since 2 or 4 bits are needed to encode each pixel. To transmit in color, each pixel will be encoded in 4 to 24 bits, and numbers need to be scaled up appropriately. The following transmission times for a single page of information in both text and image forms over various telecommunications facilities give a sense of what image size means in practice. All transfer times are idealized and do not allow for protocol overhead or (in the case of the Ethernet) packetization and contention from other devices sharing the medium. Realistic measured transfer rates for bulk file transfer on an Ethernet are typically on the order of 50 Kbytes/second to perhaps 250 Kbytes/second, or 3 to 4 seconds per page.

Medium	Raw Transmission Rate	Time for 1 Page of ASCII Text	Time for 1 Page of Digitized Image
Dialup phone line	2.4 Kbits/second	16 seconds	55 minutes
Leased line	9.6 Kbits/second	4 seconds	14 minutes
Leased line	56 Kbits/second	1 second	2.5 minutes
Leased line (T1)	1.544 Mbits/second	negligible	4 seconds
Token ring network	4 Mbits/second	negligible	1 second
Ethernet	10 Mbits/second	negligible	1 second

Delivery of page images is feasible only in a high-speed network environment unless the size of the image is reduced. Most images have a high degree of redundancy and can be compressed significantly using well-known algorithms developed for facsimile transmission (the CCITT group 3 and group 4 compression algorithms) [3]. Images of text, in particular, have a high degree of internal redundancy. These algorithms can deliver compression rates from 8:1 to 20:1 or higher, depending on such factors as the amount of white space on a page. If greyscale images or color images are being compressed, more elaborate algorithms are required, and prediction of the compression rate becomes much more difficult.

Unfortunately, compression cannot be used easily in all image database access architectures. In the simple terminal model, compression cannot be used unless the hardware in the display device can decompress data; this is normally inconsistent with a simple, all-points-addressable display device. Compressed data can be transmitted as a file in the fully distributed model; decompression is simply a local process on the workstation. In the local server model, it may be feasible to decompress data prior to display if the display server software on the workstation is appropriately programmed, but this can be a delicate process.

The realities of image transfer time are crucial factors which must be considered, not just from the image database to the workstation, but whenever an image is moved from one place to another. Inside the workstation, the image must be transferred from processor memory to the display; for printing, the image must be passed from processor memory into memory in a laser printer attached to the workstation or independently connected to the network as a print server. If the image is retrieved locally from a CD-ROM attached to the workstation rather than from an image database across the network, the bandwidth of the CD-ROM-to-workstation interface becomes the limiting factor (on the order of 150 Kbytes/second for most current CD-ROM readers, though these numbers are steadily improving).

The bandwidth of display memory is not a major problem from a response time perspective, but it can introduce some important human factors considerations. If a user wants to switch between multiple images on the workstation display, it will often be impractical to regenerate the screen display. The solution is to keep multiple screens of display memory and to switch from one screen to another by moving a pointer.

The bandwidth on the workstation-to-printer interface is a potentially serious bottleneck, however. For example, printing a single bit-mapped image will take nearly an hour with a 9.6 Kbit/second serial interface. The ideal solution is a very high-speed parallel interface. In addition, the performance figures given in sales literature for most laser printers do not consider the amount of time it takes to load a full-page, bit-mapped image into the printer, but only the time needed to run the print mechanism. Figures of several minutes per page are common for printers that run at a nominal 6-8 page/minute rate when full-page, bit-mapped images are being generated. If the printer is a network print server, it will take as long to move the image to the print server as it originally took to move it to the workstation.

In the fully distributed image access architecture, the size of even compressed images (e.g., 80 Kbytes/page) gives rise to other design considerations. Since it is necessary to work with uncompressed images in workstation memory, approximately 1 Mbyte of memory must be available for each image that is to be manipulated in memory concurrently. Under these constraints, overall workstation memories in the 3-4 Mbyte range are often necessary, particularly if any local image processing is to be done. In addition, in the fully distributed access architecture, images are transferred to the workstation and stored there, requiring either magnetic or optical write-once storage in sufficient quantities to house the received images. An empty 20 Mbyte hard disk will house only about 200-250 images in compressed form; a 5.25-inch WORM disk will hold a few thousand compressed images.

4. Browsing and the Progressive Transmission Philosophy

A user may wish to browse a series of images that have been retrieved from an image database. The user may be seeking a known image that cannot be identified precisely through the descriptive indexing in the image database, or the descriptive indexing in the image database may not be sufficiently precise to distinguish among multiple similar images. As the figures for transmission time above have suggested, even in the best of environments it will be time-consuming and resource-intensive to transfer each image so that the user can glance at it and perhaps discard it. Further, a long wait will be particularly irritating for the user who wishes to browse. It may actually take longer to receive the image on the display than it will then take the user to evaluate it.

Several approaches can speed up image display. One simple approach is to recognize that most currently available display units offer far less resolution than the 300 dots per inch necessary for acceptable reproduction on a laser printer; 100 pixels per inch is typical of a good mid-range, bit-mapped display. The image database server can decimate the image from 300 dots per inch to 100 dots per inch prior to transfer, which will reduce the amount of data to be transferred (and thus the transfer time) by almost an order of magnitude. There are, however, a number of disadvantages to this method. First of all, the image database server must have enough computational capacity to perform high-speed decimation algorithms on images before transmitting them. If the user wants to zoom in on part of the displayed image to see greater detail, then that part of the image will have to be retransferred to the workstation at higher resolution while the user waits. This procedure also implies a more complex interface between the workstation and the image database server since the workstation must be able to request segments of an image at variable resolution. If the user wishes to print the image, then the entire image must be retransmitted to the workstation for passage to the locally attached printer, or to a print server. As an additional complication, different decimation algorithms may produce more or less satisfactory results depending on the actual contents of the image being decimated. Only the user can decide whether the current decimation algorithm is producing satisfactory results or whether a different decimation algorithm should be invoked. Such ad-hoc image processing is best performed locally at the workstation, rather than through repeated image transfers across the network.

A second approach to resolving the browsing problem is to use progressive transmission to transfer the image to the workstation [4]–[9]. With progressive transmission, the image is passed to the workstation in a series of successively more accurate approximations; as the approximations become more accurate, they require more bandwidth and thus longer transfer times. Even a fairly early approximation in the series may provide sufficient detail to permit the user to conclude that the image being transmitted is not of interest and that transmission should be aborted in favor of transferring a new image. Most work on progressive transmission algorithms has been oriented towards pictorial images rather than digitized text images, concentrating on the selection of major pictorial elements for transmission in the initial approximations. The same philosophy should be applicable to text images; the key "picture" elements that need to be transmitted in early approximations of text pages might include such features as:

- Any lines of text standing alone on the page, such as section heading.
- The first and last sentences of each paragraph.
- Captions and headings for any tables or illustrations.

This approach should make it possible to provide the user with a summary of the key information on a page of digitized text image with relatively little data transfer.

Implementation of progressive transmission is delicate in the context of the fully distributed image access architecture. Essentially, the image will arrive as a series of files, each of which should be displayed as soon as it arrives. Since each successive approximation builds on data in previous approximations, the current composite approximation needs to be retained in workstation memory, and the page image should not be written out to a file on the workstation until the entire progressive transmission has completed.

5. Conclusions

Retrieval and subsequent use of images stored in an image database introduces different engineering and human factors than are encountered in a typical text-oriented database. High-speed local networks are necessary. In environments where such networks are not available, it will be necessary to consider supplying local image databases published on optical media. Due to the relatively slow transfer rate of current optical publishing media, the issues that must be resolved when handling local databases on optical media are similar to those of image retrieval using high-speed networks.

Sophisticated display techniques such as progressive transmission offer major benefits, but also require close cooperation between the image database server and the workstation in a distributed environment. Substantial research is needed in appropriate heuristics for progressive transmission of text-oriented images. Research is also needed to explore the appropriate trade-offs between throughput and reliability in lower level network protocols that support progressive image transmission in lossy networks. As progressive transmission algorithms mature, consideration should be given to developing a standard file transfer protocol for progressively transmitted images so that workstations and image database servers can interoperate freely.

It should also be clear from the discussion in this paper, that raster images are not the best way to store pages containing predominantly text. Not only are these images large and consequently expensive to move or process, but advanced techniques such as progressive transmission require the use of complex heuristics to extract content from the image. As omnifont optical character recognition improves, it seems likely that the storage and transmission format for digitized pages will shift from raster images to an extended ASCII text representation that includes enough typographic encoding to reproduce the page that has been imaged [9]–[11]. Such a format is not only more efficient to store, transfer, and display but also lends itself to easy extraction of content. At present systems to perform such conversions are commercially available from vendors such as Palantir; they are immature, but evolving rapidly. Extended ASCII text/typographic representation can be used as a transfer format in all image access architectures except for the remote terminal model, and can be expected to significantly alter the design tradeoffs for image retrieval systems within the next five to ten years.

6. Acknowledgements

My thanks to Doug Henderson for his comments on an earlier draft of this paper and to Nancy Gusack for her editorial help. Thanks also to John Gale and Howard Besser for helpful discussions on these topics.

7. References

[1.] Schieffer, Robert and Gettys, Jim. "The X Window System" *ACM Transactions on Graphics* **5:2** (April 1986).

[2.] Sun Microsystems Corp. *Sun NeWS Preliminary Technical Overview* (Mt. View, CA: Sun Microsystems Corp., 1986).

[3.] Study Group VIII. *Final Report on the Work of Study Group VIII During the Study Period 1981 - 1984, Part III: Proposals for New and Revised Series-T Recommendations*, CCITT Document AP. VIII-37-E, Report R 11 (May 1984).

[4.] Knowlton, Ken. "Progressive Transmission of Grey-Scale and Binary Pictures by Simple, Efficient, and Lossless Encoding Schemes," in *Proceedings of the IEEE* **68:7** (July 1980), pp. 885–896.

[5.] Hill, F.S. Jr.; Walker, Sheldon, Jr.; and Gao, Fuwen. "Interactive Image Query System Using Progressive Transmission," *Computer Graphics* **17:3** (July 1983), pp. 323–330.

[6.] Sanz, Alberto; Muñoz, Carlos; and García, Narciso. "Approximation Quality Improvement Techniques in Progressive Image Transmission," *IEEE Journal on Selected Areas in Communications* **SAC-2:2** (March 1984), pp. 359–373.

[7.] Hofmann, William D. and Troxel, Donald E. "Making Progressive Transmission Adaptive," *IEEE Transactions on Communications* **COM34:8** (August 1986), pp. 806–813.

[8.] Blanford, Ronald P. "Adaptive Progressive Refinement," Technical Report #87-07-05 (Seattle, WA: Department of Computer Science, University of Washington, July 16, 1987).

[9.] Lynch, Clifford A. and Brownrigg, Edwin B. "Electronic Publishing, Electronic Imaging, and Document Delivery," in *Proceedings, Electronic Imaging '86* (1986), pp. 662–667.

[10.] Lynch, Clifford A. "Implications of the Electronic Manuscript Project for Libraries, Scholarly Publications, and Universities," *Electronic Publishing Business* **4:8** (September 1986), pp. 22–26.

[11.] Gale, John C.; Lynch, Clifford A.; and Brownrigg, Edwin B. *Optical Media Applications: Textual Retrieval and Networking Issues* (Alexandria, VA: Information Workstation Group, 1987).

MONITOR ONLINE SEARCH COSTS—AN EVALUATION

Katherine M. Markee, Purdue University Libraries

Keywords: Online Search Costs, Academic Library, Non-Profit Organization Search Service, Information Retrieval Costs, User Costs, Monitor Online Costs.

Abstract: Online Search Costs! What are the direct costs (computer connect time, telecommunications and citation display) and indirect costs (labor, hardware, software, marketing, training and system malfunction)? Have cost factors increased, decreased, or remained stable with personal computers and downloading? This paper reports on a study of search costs by users of online services at a large academic institution.

The location of any specific piece of information presents an extremely complex problem for the Library user, faced with the numbers of indexes, numbers of books, journals, and microforms. Access and usage can be overwhelming. It takes time to sift through these information sources. A scholar or scientist's ability to cope with the vast range of information, even if there is an interest in coping with it, has declined with the increase of available, but not readily accessible, resources.

For more than fifteen years online access to information has been available and accessible in Libraries and Information Centers within the United States and outside North America. User accessibility varies by the type of organization in which the user resides. Often the user is unaware of the cost incurred in providing this information.

Online search costs! What are the direct costs (computer connect time, telecommunications and citation display) and indirect costs (labor, hardware, software, marketing, training and system malfunction)? Have cost factors increased, decreased, or remained stable with personal computers and downloading?

The July 1987 Cuadra Directory of Online Data Bases lists 3487 databases, 1602 producers and 547 online services (Ref. 1). This can offer an organization a wide choice which, in most cases, will be scaled down to meet the information needs of the user's organization.

Purdue University Library began offering online services in 1975 with a single site and a single Librarian-searcher. The service has grown to thirteen sites and twenty-two Librarian-search analysts - all using microcomputers. All users are charged direct search costs plus an overhead for each request. For University requestors the minimum charge is $5.00; for non-University requestors the minimum is $7.00. Ready reference is excluded from this cost analysis. There is currently no subsidy for online search services in the Library's budget.

As with any educational institution, the community is constantly changing and the Libraries' Computer Based Information Service markets its information product on a continuing basis. An online search, as defined by Hawkins and Brown, is "an interactive access by computer to as many machine-readable databases as the searcher considers necessary to conclude the search" (Ref. 2). The request is the information needed to satisfy the user's information requirements.

The number of online searches done is a measure of an organization's computerized bibliographic retrieval search service. The costs incurred in providing this service is a measure of its usage and usefulness by users as well as for management in providing the search service. A strong and firm user base is desirable.

All Purdue University Librarians give lectures and demonstrations of the vendors' systems to schools and departments at the Lafayette campus. Frequently, users ask, "How much will this cost?" or "What is the average search cost?". An analysis of search costs and service activity is given at the 1988 National Online Meeting, covering fiscal years 85, 86, and 87.

Martha Williams at the 1987 National Online Meeting, said "it is difficult to sell intellectual products, pricing is tricky and it is hard to counter the free information mentality when the product is excellent and far exceeds the type of free service provided by public libraries. Information is certainly the most important product in the U.S. industry, but it is expensive and cannot be mass produced (Ref. 3).

Ten years ago, James Cogswell said "On-line, interactive searching of bibliographic data bases is here to stay in academic and research libraries. ...in a very few years, online searching will likely be as common in most libraries as conventional reference service is today (Ref. 4).

At Purdue University, our users continue to demand information by electronic means and the Librarians respond to these demands efficiently and effortlessly -- keeping the faculty and students at the forefront of today's high tech era.

REFERENCES

1. Directory of Online Data Bases, Cuadra/Elsevier, New York, Vol. 8 #3, p. v, 1987.

2. Hawkins, Donald T. and Brown, Carolyn P. Online. Vol. 4, No. 1, p. 17, January 1980.

3. Williams, Martha E. Highlights of the online database industry: assessing the status of the online industry. Proceedings of the 8th National Online Meeting, May 5-7, 1987, Medford, NJ, Learned Information, Inc., p. 4, 1987.

4. Cogswell, James A. On-Line Search Services: Implications for Libraries and Library Users. College & Research Libraries, Vol. 39, p. 274, July 1978.

DESIGNING AN ONLINE MEDICAL 'HYPERTEXTBOOK'

Bruce McClelland, BRS Information Technologies

Keywords: *Hypertext. Knowledge Bases. Medical textbooks. Gateways. Linking. Table of Contents.*

Abstract:

Hypertext technology has at last evolved to the point where its capabilities can be appreciated in the marketplace. The increasing availability of commercial hypertext software such as Hypercard suggests that hypertext applications will develop rapidly, as more and more texts are created in electronic form.

Clearly, the document-linking aspect of hypertext has strong implications for the online industry, especially in those cases where the reader of an electronic text needs to view documents or other materials which are conceptually linked to the document at hand.

In collaboration with San Francisco General and Columbia Presbyterian Medical Centers, BRS has designed two medical textbooks which are intended to be accessed entirely electronically. The fundamental advantage of designing 'textbases' solely for computer access is that it is possible to build in such features as a dynamic table of contents and explicit links between text segments. Ideally, such online textbooks should provide the reader with immediate links to references, other relevant chapters or topics, bibliographic citations, or even the full-text articles behind the references, either in local or remote databases.

With the millions of documents available online, mechanisms that eliminate existing constraints upon access and display are extremely desirable, and many of the features embodied in the concept of hypertext hold great promise for the online industry. Nevertheless, the availability of the technology is only the beginnning, inasmuch as hypertext itself opens up a large array of new problems, ranging from technical and cognitive to legal and ethical.

1. Introduction

Whatever else the term hypertext has come to mean between the time of its coinage and the present flurry of commercial applications such as Hypercard, it is clear that the concept represents a virtually inevitable extension of computer technology. Once the use of computers began to be extended to the processing of text, it was not long before the deficiencies of the new technology were shown up by the convenience and compactness embodied in a much older technology, the book.

Even today, a large portion of the texts that are available online first existed in a format and structure more amenable to conventional typesetting and book design. We all know that the computer potentially offers one enormous advantage over the book, namely immediacy of retrieval. However, in the comparing manual and electronic forms of information retrieval, the constraint of having to view linearly presented text on a single 80-column by

24-line monitor is an unacceptable technological limitation, which is not entirely offset by the speed gained through the use of the computer.

Hypertext, or more generically hypermedia, which in addition to text may involve graphics, sounds, films, or any other medium which can be represented or generated in digital form, attempts to overcome physical limitations by permitting the user to pass from one point to another electronically, without getting "lost in hyperspace." But this passing from point to point currently requires careful consideration of design constraints.

At BRS, where we spend a good deal of time converting text originally intended for print into online, full-text databases, we recognized that because these books were not originally designed to be accessed electronically, certain advantages of online availability were not being realized. We therefore embarked upon two pilot projects, each in collaboration with a team of physician-authors: the "AIDS Knowledge Base" (ASFG), written by doctors affiliated with San Francisco General Hospital, and another electronic medical textbook with no print counterpart (as yet), Cardinal Topics in Internal Medicine (CTIM), authored primarily by the staff at Columbia Presbyterian Medical Center in New York.

So far as hypertext is concerned, it is the latter project which was envisioned as a prototype in an online environment of many software features currently included under that rubric. The Cardinal Topics textbook, originally conceived by Dr. David Margulies and currently directed by Dr. Jonathan LaPook, would be written at several different style levels, for audiences ranging from patients to subspecialists. There was to be seamless transfer across these levels, so that one could pass from, say, the "General Textbook" level to some corresponding point in the "Specialist Level," with a keystroke or two. In addition to links across these levels, there would also be links (or more commonly, cross-references) from sections in the text to other (relevant) sections, which presumably would contain additional information about the topic at hand.

Finally, the design called for explicit links to bibliographic references (including abstracts), as well as to tables, charts, and eventually full graphic elements. Since the textbook was from the outset to be written solely for online access, certain features could be built in to the design that would make it easier to handle the full-text documents.

2. Dynamic Table of Contents

One of the most important elements of a technical book that is frequently either inadequate or else missing entirely from the online version is the table of contents. The ASFG Knowledge Base includes a dynamic table of contents incorporating two hierarchical levels, from which the user can select the desired (sub)chapter simply by entering a number.

Advancing from that design, the Cardinal Topics Hypertextbook will provide a dynamic, hierarchical table of contents for each style (patient, specialist, etc.) and sublevel within each style. Once the user has reached the appropriate level, he may elect to view all the text at that level.

3. Searching Within Levels

An obvious advantage of online browsing is the ability to perform keyword searches. This ability is utilized fully in the Cardinal Topics project: in addition to ordinary keyword searching across the entire database, the CTIM interface will permit searching only within a specified topic, chapter, or subtopic.

Thus, for example, while a search on 'BLEEDING' may be impractical when performed against fifty topics in Internal Medicine, confining the search to the subsection on the 'EPIDEMIOLOGY OF UPPER GASTROINTESTINAL BLEEDING' should provide a more manageable result set.

4. Structural Context

In searching for an index term in a textbook, electronic or otherwise, it is often useful to know which sections of the book contain the term, before actually turning to the text. Although with online systems, browsing "hits" is commonplace, it may not be as efficient for obtaining a specific piece of information as first viewing a list of sections or subsections containing the search term(s).

Hence, when searching a portion of the CTIM textbook, the user has the option of displaying the headings under which the term was found. To continue the example above, searching for 'BLEEDING' within the subtopic 'GASTROINTESTINAL BLEEDING' might produce a list of entries similar to the following:

Level: **3** *Topic:* **Gastroenterology** *Chapter:* **Gastrointestinal Bleeding**

1 **Upper Gastrointestinal Bleeding/Varices/Epidemiology**

2 **Upper Gastrointestinal Bleeding/Varices/Risk Factors**

---

5. Linking

The most important concept in the CTIM design was to permit linking both from level to level, and from text section to reference or other text section. It is this linking mechanism that more than anything qualifies CTIM as hypertext.

5.1 Executing a Link

In the first phase of the project, all executable links will be a) pre-defined, i.e. embedded within the text, and b) confined to text elements within the database. At a later stage, we hope to provide a number of methods whereby the user can define dynamic links between text elements, and by means of gateways, across databases. Eventually, linking from local workstations on networks to online databases or other services should prove to be a common arrangement for information retrieval and post-processing.

6. Problems

While a good deal of the technology required for hypermedia (or at least hypertext) to move into the online world already exists at least in prototype form, a number of difficulties have yet to be resolved, some technical, others legal, ethical, or simply administrative

6.1 Dynamic / Automatic Linking

The online searching process as currently implemented uses Boolean and relational operators as the primary means to establish relatedness, i.e. result sets arrived at by means of these operations are assumed to be somehow related to at least the query, if not to each other. However, the problem of creating links ('relations') between documents that have no explicit relationship other than being members of the same database (or worse, members of quite different databases) requires the development of some rather sophisticated techniques for generating those links at the user's discretion. Techniques from the domains of AI and Computational Linguistics, as well as Information Science, are being developed which will permit links to be actuated dynamically, by means of some interpretation of the data being displayed. In the absence of such developments, the millions of potential links between the millions of online documents will never be realized because of the cost of the effort to create the links in the editorial process.

6.2 Accounting, Copyright, Intellectual Property

It is all well and good to talk enthusiastically about the virtues of unlimited linking and how such unrestricted information flow might be beneficial, but the truth of the matter is, there are enormous accounting and royalty issues, even in a small-scale prototype such as the BRS/Columbia Presbyterian project. For example, linking from an online medical textbook (even in a controlled-network environment) to texts and citations in other public databases requires consideration of how to account for access. Obviously these issues will be resolved, but we are currently at a stage where even the fundamental standards required for seamless telecommunications and networking are not in place; much less developed are the procedures for allocating costs and profits among information providers.

6.3 Interface

At the recent Hypertext '87 Conference at UNC, it was widely supposed that hypertext/hypermedia technology would eventually become as transparent as, say, the word processor, if not the telephone or television. While such claims are valid, those of us in the commercial side of the information industry are acutely aware of the lack of standards and protocols for even the old fashioned command or menu-driven interfaces. Digitized graphics enviroments are becoming de facto standards for PCs, but at the same time, it is still difficult to find a telecommunications software package that works 100% of the time on every modem out there. The complexity introduced by hypertext demands that a good deal more attention be paid to solving interface standards within the online network.

7. Summary

At last, we seem to be moving away from total reliance upon the printed page. This movement could only occur after the development of technologies which could in some way compensate for the loss of the convenience inherent in the printed word, especially the book. The concept of hypertext, in which the user no longer must physically move from place to place to view related texts, but rather actuates such links electronically, goes a long way towards providing a greater degree of freedom for the reader. This should in turn result in much greater acceptance of the computer as a tool for reading and learning. The hypertextbook, which is designed for, rather than adapted to, the online environment, can provide a number of significant advantages over the book, primarily speed and centrality of access.

Nevertheless, while such hypertexts should prove immediately useful in some environments, such as a hospital or medical center, or in educational situations like Brown University, where the Intermedia system has been used to develop networked courseware, a large number of issues exist for the eventual importation of the concept into the online industry, where there are very large numbers of texts available from different producers, and where there are large numbers of users with different backgrounds, equipment, and information needs. We hope that the BRS/Columbia-Presbyterian project, and others like it, will go a long way towards changing the nature of the way electronic texts are utilized.

TEXTUAL INFORMATION MANAGEMENT SYSTEMS (TIMS): POWERFUL FULL-TEXT RETRIEVAL

Michael A. McDonald, Information Dimensions, Inc.

Abstract: In the early years computers were seen as efficient manipulators of numbers. It's not surprising that early Database Management Systems (DBMS) were primarily number oriented with textual information limited to codes, single words, names or short phrases. This trend in DBMS has reached its current zenith with Relational Database Management Systems (RDBMS) which are modeled as tables of information. Current systems in this class emphasize shorter numeric data which is easily presented in tabular format. In most offices today, typewriters are gone; replaced by computers which not only tolerate text but are in fact "word" processors. With this growing awareness of computers as important aids to text generation comes an expectation that they should also store and retrieve textual information. Textual Information Management Systems (TIMS) meet this expectation. They share many features of DBMS and RDBMS but their focus is on text. This paper discusses issues that distinguish TIMS from Database Management Systems and talks about some of the directions being taken by TIMS products.

1. TEXTUAL INFORMATION MANAGEMENT SYSTEMS

TIMS are a new category of systems which share many of the characteristics of Database Management Systems. Issues of data independence, data integrity, security, ease of access, and a host of others which serve to distinguish good DBMS's from poorer implementations can also be applied to TIMS. For example, it is important to a Pharmaceutical company that lab reports be readily accessible to researchers thus preventing "rediscovery" of reported results. It is equally important that their accountants have the most current and accurate accounts receivable information. In both cases integrity and security are critical. TIMS share many if not most of the characteristics of DBMS but I do not mean to imply that TIMS is a superset of DBMS. The differences in their emphasis have simply created "specialist" products. Firms which have implemented TIMS generally have DBMS products as well to manage more numeric applications.

TIMS is not a new product. It is a new category of product just being discovered by many companies. Companies whose major product is textual have already implemented TIMS. Law firms are an obvious example. Their major product is text based. Previous research results from the firm become a major asset. These firms also view TIMS as a competitive edge when they help organize the reams of documents generated by a major litigation. Highly regulated industries with extensive reporting requirements like the nuclear energy, drug and biotechnology industries use TIMS to track the text of regulations and to organize and track the required reports. Newspapers have automated their "morgues" via TIMS.

Demand from some new sources has recently been strong. Companies are seeing opportunities to reduce lag time between policy inception and implementation. Policy and procedure manuals are going on-line with all the benefits of accuracy and currency. Companies are also establishing on-line correspondence databases. These databases are becoming key central resources for large companies. They help the left hand know what the right hand is doing. The fact that one regional office has had contact with a vendor may be significant in helping another region to either contact or avoid the same vendor based on the experience of the first.

When a company makes the decision to allow on-line access to its text, it has two fundamental choices: store the documents in machine readable form (ASCII or EBCDIC Text) or store images of the documents. Using either method allows access to the document via indices that are maintained on-line using computer software. The documents could be retrieved by the title, author, date, etc. In addition, 'expert indexers' could read the documents and choose keyword descriptors to reflect the their subject matter. Systems are distinguished by their ability to access the document. Document Retrieval Systems or Records Management Systems typically store information about where the user can go to get the text of the document. This might be a central file number or a microfiche frame location. These systems can inform a user that a document exists but they cannot immediately access the document and display it on their terminal. Document Image Processors store an image or picture of the document in digital form on the computer. Thus, once these documents have been retrieved using the available indices, the user has the option to display the image of the actual document on the terminal. The fact that documents are immediately available for review even at remote locations is a key advantage over Document Retrieval Systems. Unfortunately, one of the key disadvantages of storing document images is the storage space they require. A page of text from a word processor requires approximately 2000 bytes of storage. An image of the same page of text would require approximately 30,000 bytes. While it may be true that a picture is worth a thousand words, it is also true that in the computer it takes more than 10 times the storage.

Textual Information Management Systems (TIMS) store the entire text of a document in ASCII or EBCDIC character form. Documents produced in-house on word processors are already in this form. Documents received from outside the organization may be converted to text via Optical Character Recognition (OCR) technology. Aside from the benefit of reduced storage requirements, TIMS offer decided advantages in many other areas. Since TIMS deal with standard text they generally require less expensive display terminals. The smaller storage required also results in much faster transmission of the document to remote locations. This is especially true when low speed voice grade lines are used. Transmission of a single uncompressed page image over 2400 baud lines would take up to 3 minutes. The same page transmitted in character form would take less than 10 seconds.

Storage of text as ASCII or EBCDIC characters is the most important advantage of TIMS over Document Image Processors or Document Retrieval Systems. This allows the computer to manipulate the full text of the document to facilitate retrieval and display. TIMS allows you to retrieve documents not only by author, title, date or keywords as do Document Retrieval Systems, but by any word or phrase that occurs anywhere in the document. This advantage is particularly important when documents are being used in a research environment. Researchers are paid for discovery. Part of that process is finding new patterns in information. If the documents have been through a "filtering" process of keyword selection, the ability to "see" the document based on new or unique thought processes can be severely hampered.

Another key advantage involves the display of the documents. Document Image Processors do not see text as characters and words but rather as pictures. This means that your display choices are limited to the page you wish to see. TIMS can manipulate the text and show you the document in ways that may facilitate your review. After you retrieve a document by searching for the word "pneumonia" the TIMS can take you immediately to the exact place in the text that mentions "pneumonia" regardless of the document's length. The word is highlighted in the display. If you think the passage is interesting you can scroll through the document or instruct the system to take you directly to the next occurrence of the word in this document. If you determine that a particular document is not of interest you can instruct the system to skip remaining occurrences of the word or phrase and move directly to the first occurrence in the next document. When dealing with long documents (several pages) it is easy to see the advantage of a system which can intelligently treat the text as something other than a "black box".

2. FEATURES OF TIMS

TIMS offer many distinctive features which separate them from either DBMS or Document Retrieval Systems. The following is a review of the most important aspects of TIMS.

2.1 The System Should Have No Practical Limit To The Amount Of Text Which Can Be Stored As A Document

Clearly the purpose of TIMS is to store textual information, thus the first aspect to consider deals with acceptable amounts of text. Systems which can store titles or abstracts of under 256 characters are not TIMS. It is useful to think in terms of printed 8½ x 11 inch pages when determining an acceptable amount of text. Using elite type (12 characters per inch) and one inch margins all around the page you can calculate the maximum page capacity as approximately 4000 characters. 2000 to 3000 characters may be a more reasonable estimate. 16,000 characters of text might represent between 4 and 8 pages. This might suffice for a lot of correspondence type databases (e.g., memo or electronic mail archives); but then again, although we would never admit to writing one, many of us have seen memos which exceed this limit. 64,000 characters (16 to 32 pages) would likely be sufficient for these applications until a complex contract or a business plan were stored. Of course you would have to have even more capacity for research reports, transcripts, or manuals.

Although systems which support 16-64,000 characters of text offer many of the benefits of TIMS in limited applications, they are analogous to the early days of DBMS when the number of records allowed in a database was restricted by many systems. Ultimately, the best systems essentially eliminated any arbitrary boundaries. When users could choose these systems and not have to gamble that their present and future applications would not exceed arbitrary limits, they quickly did so. TIMS should be as serious about text as DBMS are about data.

2.2 TIMS Should Handle Both Structured And Unstructured Data

Many documents have attributes common to each document. For example, typical memos have a date, an indication of who the memo is to, who it is from and a subject line. It is very useful for the system to be able to identify this recurring structural information and allow users to restrict searches to these areas of the document text. If the user can restrict a search to the "TO:" data of the memo, he can find memos addressed to him without retrieving memos that were either from him or mentioned his name in the body.

The term "structured data" is also applied to certain data which describe the document but may not actually occur in it. Examples include the creation date of a memo, the name of the typist, the name of the word processor file where the document is stored, the account number used to pay for the typist's time, etc.

TIMS should give a user the flexibility to define structured fields so that they can be queried, displayed, edited and otherwise acted upon individually, or in groups, as desired by the user. This usually has some ramifications for data entry. Structured data which occurs as part of the document must generally be tagged or entered separately from the document. Better systems will allow document layout to be defined and will locate structural information based on its spacial location and delimiting white space just as our eye finds the memo date because it is in the upper right hand corner of the memo.

Some standards are emerging for document tagging. AAP's suggested implementation of SGML is a good example of a tagging scheme to identify structure within documents. (Ref. 1)

2.3 TIMS Must Be Able To Search The Complete Document Text Using Special Text-Oriented Tests

The fundamental premise of TIMS is to allow access to documents based on any word or phrase contained in the document. If a system stores large amounts of text but only allows the documents to be retrieved based on structured data and a limited number of preselected keywords it is not a TIMS. Neither is it sufficient to use normal database operators such as AND when dealing with words in the text. Finding both the words "department" and "health" in the same 30 page document is almost no indicator that the document discusses the "health department".

TIMS require retrieval tests that can discriminate word distances. Finding "health" and "department" in the same sentence greatly increases the likelihood that the words are in fact being used to describe the concept that the searcher wants to retrieve. An even better test might require that the two words occur within three words of each other. The system would find "health department" or "department of health" but would eliminate "police department investigates reports of health hazards". Unfortunately, it might also eliminate "the city department responsible to ensure the health and well being of..." even though this seems to be discussing the city health department.

Such access to the entire text field is fundamental to the TIMS concept. Better systems will allow various aids to retrieval that help users select other words that may relate to the concept for which the user is searching. These aids include spelling checkers, singular/plural form generators, inflected form generators (e.g., automatically search for "adopts", "adopting", "adoption", etc. when the user asks for "adopted") and complete thesauri.

2.4 TIMS Must Recognize And Facilitate The Interactive Nature Of Full-Text Searching

Searching the text of a document in an effort to retrieve documents relevant to a given subject is an inexact science. In traditional DBMS, the data is highly structured and carefully filtered. The retrieval results are therefore very predictable. If you instruct a traditional DBMS to list all the employees in department 301, you can be sure that the list will in fact show all the employee records in the database associated with department 301. The structure may restrict the kinds of questions you can ask and the way you can ask them, but if asked properly the result is quite predictable. When searching the text of a document the situation is quite different.

If you ask the system to find all documents which contain the phrase "abuse of government contracts" you can rest assured that the system will find all occurrences of that phrase. Unfortunately the system did not retrieve the phrase "misuse of navy agreements" even though it seems to deal with the same idea. It is essential to the process that the searcher be able to easily refine and reapply a search since it is unlikely that the first search criterion will yield all of the satisfactory results. Studies have shown that the average number of queries against a full-text database prior to display can be 10 or more (Ref. 2). It is very important then that each result be located quickly and that new criteria can easily be added to prior search results in a refinement process. Another feature which aids the user is to display retrieved documents based on some heuristic determination of relevance to your search. If you search for a single word, the simplest example of relevance ranking would be to display the documents in decreasing order of occurrence frequency of the word. Seeing the most relevant documents first helps suggest new search terms and thus speeds the refinement process. TIMS should also provide help to users in suggesting alternate words to describe concepts. Word stemming and thesauri are important in this regard.

2.5 TIMS Should Retain The Original Format Of The Document If Desired

In some applications, the original format must be preserved. When citing legal precedence for example, it is essential that page and line numbers be referenced. Thus, it is required that legal researchers retrieve accurate reproductions of the reference material paper copies. In most applications, users will be more open to a TIMS if it displays the document in a familiar form.

Better systems will be able to output documents in a variety of formats. Report writers will have functionality which allows reformatting of text. Standard output formats will connect to various text processors.

2.6 Display Highlights Search Terms In Context And Allows Document Scrolling

After searching for any word in the text of a large document the user will want to go directly to the occurrences of that word within the document's text. By reading these selected passages, the user will determine the actual relevance of the document to the search. A search term may occur many times in a long document. After reading the passages that contain the first occurrence or two, the user can determine whether the document is useful. If it is not useful, the user should be able to skip any further occurrences in this document and move to the next.

Better systems will allow forward and backward scrolling among word occurrences and among documents. They will also display the documents in order by some user specified sort key, or based on some measure of relevance to the search. Better systems will also use structural information to allow the user to jump back to the start of the current chapter and begin to page forward.

3. FUTURE DIRECTIONS

   As is the case with most database vendors, TIMS vendors are all moving to make their product's more accessible. User interface is being rethought with movement away from commands and toward graphical interfaces. Most current TIMS vendors are concerned with at least three major areas that are specific to the needs of text databases:
   o   connection to document sources
   o   changing nature of a document
   o   retrieval aids

   TIMS are easiest to justify when the textual information to be stored is readily available in ASCII or EBCDIC form. Since this normally means data that was entered into an editor or word processor, TIMS vendors are anxious to ease the movement of text from these systems to TIMS. Users want the ability to take text from their TIMS and use it in new documents they create on their word processors. This means that the TIMS must store what is called "revisable form", the word processor's internal forms. It is responsible for the word processor's flexibility. In a single command, revisable form documents can be reorganized to match new margin settings. Final form documents must be reorganized line by line. Future TIMS will be able to accept, store, and return revisable form documents.

   Documents no longer consist only of text. Pictures, diagrams and tables are also important parts of most documents. The developers of TIMS recognize this and are beginning to offer solutions. Various document architectures have been proposed to deal with these requirements. IBM has DIA/DCA (Document Interchange Architecture/Document Content Architecture). Digital has DDIF (Digital Document Interchange Format). Wang has WITA (Wang Information Transfer Architecture). ISO is developing ODA (Office Document Architecture). TIMS vendors are watching these with great interest.

   Finally, a great deal of interest in the TIMS market place today is being focused on retrieval aids. These aids generally fall into three classes: Automatic Indexing, Alternate Word Generation and Relevant Document Evaluation. Automatic Indexing is an attempt to have the computer process a document as it enters the database and enhance it to make it more retrievable. Attempts have been made to have computers assign descriptors to documents as the expert indexers would. For the most part, results have been disappointing. As natural language processing becomes more sophisticated this may change. Natural language processing can now be used to solve some problems in text retrieval like pronoun usage. When a user attempts a search for a proper name and a word in the same sentence, he may be surprised to find that the name occurred 2 or 3 sentences earlier and that the sentence containing the other word of interest uses a pronoun (i.e., he) rather than the proper name. There are natural language processors which could enhance the text to include proper names in place of the pronouns that refer to them.

   Alternate Word Generation would suggest to the user who is searching for the term "abuse" to also try "misuse". Certain forms of word generation make use of a priori linkages between words that are a result of their use in natural language. Searching word roots is an example. Natural language thesauri are another example. The linkages are a result of the language rather than the subject matter. Another form of Alternate Word Generation is based on statistical analysis of words that co-occur frequently in a particular collection. The TIMS might suggest such words to the user and the user could decide which, if any, to use as alternate search terms.

   Relevant Document Evaluation is very much like the statistical analysis of co-occurrence mentioned above except that it looks only at a document or group of documents identified by the user as relevant to the search. Co-occurrence of words in these specific documents can be very different from co-occurrence in the larger document collection. For years successful searchers have examined relevant documents to suggest alternate terminology that might have been used in additional searches. This is essentially the same process. By building that process into the TIMS, textual databases become more accessible to users with little training in search methods.

4. SUMMARY

Traditional database systems are not equipped to handle the special problems of storing, searching, and displaying the full-text of documents. The computer industry is at work to make the full-text of documents available at very little cost. Many companies recognize this and are moving to implement full-text databases. Text Information Management Systems (TIMS) can handle this information. As advances in user interface continue, using TIMS for storage and retrieval of text will become a natural accompaniment to word processing.

5. REFERENCES

1. Reference Manual on Electronic Manuscript Preparation and Mark-up. Association of American Publishers, May 1986.

2. Cunningham, Julie A; Weinber, Bella Hass. "Search Strategy in the Field of Engineering: A Statistical Approach". Proceedings of the Sixth National Online Meeting, 1985: 117-123.

ABI/INFORM: A DATABASE OF MINI-DATABASES

Tim McDonald, UMI/Data Courier

Abstract

Keywords: Studies; Databases; Information retrieval; Searches; Online

Growth in the range of subject coverage of the ABI/INFORM business database for 1978-1987 was studied. Four subject areas (insurance, finance, economics and accounting) were examined using the ABI/INFORM classification code scheme. Changes in coverage patterns (illustrative of changes in the world business and economic environment) demonstrate how ABI/INFORM can be used as a "database of mini-databases."

1.0 INTRODUCTION

Predicast's PROMPT, IAC's Management Contents and UMI/Data Courier's ABI/INFORM constantly add records and like Alexandrian libraries nothing is ever eliminated. As these business files evolve into larger "superfiles" it is important to focus your search to retrieve only relevant records.

Each of these databases have methods to focus results, PROMPT has event codes; Management Contents utilizes the Standard Industrial Classification Codes; and ABI/INFORM contains four-digit classification codes.

ABI/INFORM has long been recognized as a solid source for business and management information and as problems, issues and emerging technologies affect the business world they are in turn reflected in the database. This paper introduces the searcher to a different way of viewing the ABI/INFORM file. We will explore ABI/INFORM as a database of mini-databases.

To illustrate the mini-database concept, I selected four areas on which to base this study. The growth patterns of the coverage of the insurance and finance industries as well as economic and accounting information will be analyzed in relation to the overall database. The manipulation of subject areas within the database will be discussed as well as new growth areas for ABI/INFORM.

2.0 THE METHODOLOGY

For the purposes of this study, three control elements were used:
- DIALOG system for gathering data
- The total number of record entries calculated annually from 1978-1987 inclusive
- The ABI/INFORM classification code scheme to focus on the four subject areas described.

The classification code scheme (Figure 1) was used to isolate the four areas of this study, because it is an objective method for searching these subjects. The ABI/INFORM controlled vocabulary could have been used for this purpose, but this would have required subjective selection of terms from the 6,000 term list.

With the ABI/INFORM classification code system, the four-digit codes are arranged hierarchically in five distinct areas.
- **Business environment codes** define economic conditions, international trade, and social and energy policy.

- **Management function codes** identify six areas common to most organizations, including planning, finance, accounting and human resources.
- **Industry and market codes** are assigned to articles focusing on any of 34 manufacturing, service, extractive or agricultural industries.
- **Article treatment codes** define article type, such as company-specific or product-specific.
- **Organization codes** focus on the type of organization being discussed; for example, non-profit institutions or small businesses.

Data Courier added the classification codes to the file in 1982 to enhance efficiency and precision in searching ABI/INFORM. The classification codes were based on the listing of subject headings used by the American Management Association in its <u>Index to AMA Resources of the Seventies 1970-1976</u> compiled by Elizabeth A. Keegan (AMACON, 1977), and <u>The London Classification of Business Studies</u>, Second edition by K. D. C. Vernon and Valerie Lang (Aslib, 1979).

Most often such enhancements are searchable only from the date of implementation. The management of Data Courier, however, believed this feature should operate throughout the database. Classification codes were assigned manually to the 1971 to 1977 segment of the file and computer assigned to the 1978 to mid-1982 segment. ABI/INFORM was reloaded on vendor systems once this process was completed.

In viewing the results, keep in mind that the ABI/INFORM indexers assign an average of two classification codes to each article, taking into consideration the author's focus and the intended audience. Codes are assigned at the most specific level; for example, when 8120 (Retail banking) is assigned, the more general code, 8100 (Financial services industry), is not.

To create broad subsets of the database, classification codes can be truncated to the code's root. For example, truncating after the second digit of 8100 (Financial services industry) searches 8100 as well as 8110

(Commercial banking services), 8120 (Retail banking services) and 8130 (Investment services) in one step.

3.0 THE RESULTS

At the beginning of 1978 there were 65,727 records in the entire database. By the end of 1987 this figure had grown to 383,652. Figure 2 illustrates the number of records entered into the database for each of the years from 1978 through 1987. Each year was searched using the PY= prefix on DIALOG combined with the four classification codes that pertain to the subject areas that constitute this study. For display purposes, the results from the years 1978 (figure 3), 1982 (figure 4) and 1986 (figure 5) are illustrated.

Let's take a look at figures 3, 4 and 5. As you can see, I searched the range of classification codes that pertain to the selected subject areas. I identified 1100 series of classification codes to search economics, the 4100 series for accounting, the 8100 series for the financial industry and the 8200 series for the insurance industry. To broadly search each of these areas I truncated after the second digit (please refer to figure 1).

The range of economics codes was applied to 20 percent of the records added to the database in 1978 with the gamut of financial and accounting codes being applied to nine and eight percent of 1978 records respectively.

Look at what happens to these numbers in figures 4 and 5. The economic codes change to 14 percent from 20 in 1982 and to 12 percent in 1986. As a block, the four areas were applied to 43 percent of the records in 1978 and 31 percent in 1986.

What happened during these years to change the results? Think back to the introduction section of this paper, as issues and problems affect the business world they in turn are reflected in the database. In 1978, this country was in a recession: double-digit interest rates, high unemployment and fuel shortages.

In 1982 and 1986 we had crossed the threshold of Reaganomics; things were getting better with interest rates dropping and the Dow climbing. Obviously this affects what is written in the journals and how articles are indexed. ABI/INFORM's focus had not changed, rather there were new problems and challenges in the business community such as foreign investment in the U.S., the flexing of the computer industry and let's not forget merger mania.

4.0 THE IMPLICATIONS

The preceeding paragraphs provide a background on the classification codes and highlighted four of them specifically. The classification codes afford the searcher a high degree of flexibility in manipulating the information in the database. The four areas illustrated here are very broad subject areas; however, any of them can be narrowed to provide highly focused information.

One of the areas that I searched in a broad manner was the financial industry (CC=81?). This search can be focused to create a mini-database; for example, containing information about interstate banking within the retail banking area. To accomplish this I combined classification code 8120 (CC=8120) with a controlled vocabulary term for interstate banking (INTERSTATE BANKING/DE). This is a very tight search yielding 65 citations, some titles are shown below.

- Interstate Banking Update: More States Continue to Open Their Doors
- Ohio Banks: Hitting the Interstate Acquisitions Road
- Research: The Saga of a Merger-Hot Sector.

The classification codes are specific enough to allow for the construction of a current awareness profile. For example, one could create a current awareness profile for marketing in the healthcare industry by entering classification code 8320 (CC=8320) and truncating after the first digit of the marketing code 7? (CC=7?). This search yielded 767 citations spanning the years of the database. However, for one week in January of this year, there were 13 citations fitting this profile. Some of those titles include:

- The Economics of Patient Satisfaction
- Physicians Compete for Market Share
- A Blueprint for Hospitals in an Aging Society: Position Your Hospital as the Powerful Hub of the Aging Network (Part 5)
- Dr. Blasts U.S. Health Care Priorities.

Furthermore, strength and flexibility is enhanced by using either the organization type or article treatment codes. Combining the classification code for GUIDELINES -- 9150 (CC=9150) and the code for ACQUISITIONS & MERGERS -- 2330 (CC=2330) locates articles concerning the "How to's" of an acquisition process.

- Good Acquisitions Fit a Pattern
- The Initial Stages of a Target Company Purchase: What to Look for and What to Expect of Counsel
- How to Spot a Takeover Candidate.

Also, specific trends and innovations can be tracked: CC=52? AND DIS?LESS WORKSTATION?

- ASICs May Lead to Future Application-Specific PCs
- Connectivity: 'Diskless' Computing
- 3Com 3Station Gets Good Beta Test Marks.

The preceeding examples illustrate how easy it is to create a mini-database within the ABI/INFORM database. To recap, a mini-database can be constructed by:

- Combining classification codes
- Combining classification codes with controlled vocabulary terms
- Combining classification codes with free-text terms.

5.0 CONCLUSION AND NEW DIRECTIONS

The ABI/INFORM file provides a wealth of information concerning business and management. As a trainer who has conducted many sessions for ABI/INFORM, I am amazed at the number of searchers who are familiar with the file but have not used the classification codes. While they do not represent the alpha and the omega of searching, they do, as you have seen, provided a powerful tool in the quest for information.

This year will be an exciting one for the ABI/INFORM database with expanded coverage. More than 100 new journals will increase the number of records for 1988 to 48,000. Three expanding areas are:

- Engineering management
- Computers and telecommunications
- Production and technology.

UMI/Data Courier remains committed to expanding journal coverage and the classification codes, when new ones are needed to identify growing industries. New advances in technology allow us to offer searches new delivery forms and faster, more efficient information products.

As database files continue to "grow" each has devised methods to separate the sets of pertinent records from the false hits.

We have shown you how ABI/INFORM focuses its mini-database, this can serve as a microcosm of how-to-precision search in the larger superfiles.

Figure 1

BUSINESS ENVIRONMENT

1100 Economics
   *1110 Economic conditions & forecasts
   *1120 Economic policy & planning
   *1130 Economic theory
1200 Social policy
1300 International trade & foreign investment (see also multinational corporations 9510)
   *1310 Foreign investment in the US
1500 Energy/environment
   *1510 Energy resources
   *1520 Energy policy
   *1530 Natural resources
   *1540 Pollution control

MANAGEMENT FUNCTIONS

2000 GENERAL MANAGEMENT
  2100 Administrative & management personnel
    *2110 Boards of directors
    *2120 Chief executive officer
    *2130 Executives
  2200 Managerial skills
  2300 Planning & strategy
    *2310 Planning
    *2320 Organizational structure (subsidiaries, decentralization, etc.)
    *2330 Acquisitions & mergers
  2400 Public relations
    *2410 Social responsibility
    *2420 Image
    *2430 Business-government relations
  2500 Organizational behavior
  2600 Management science/operations research
3000 FINANCE
  3100 Capital & debt management
  3200 Credit management
  3300 Risk management
  3400 Investment analysis
  3500 Foreign exchange administration (see also 1120)
  3600 Pension fund management
4000 ACCOUNTING, TAXATION, & LAW
  4100 Accounting
    *4110 Accounting firms & accountants
    *4120 Accounting policies & procedures
    *4130 Auditing
  4200 Taxation
    *4210 Institutional taxation
    *4220 Estate planning
    *4230 Personal taxation

  4300 Law
    *4310 Regulation
    *4320 Legislation
    *4330 Litigation
5000 OPERATIONS
  5100 Facilities management
    *5110 Office management
    *5120 Purchasing
    *5130 Maintenance management
    *5140 Security management
    *5150 Energy management
    *5160 Transportation management
  5200 Communications & information management
    *5210 Office automation
    *5220 Data processing management
    *5230 Hardware
    *5240 Software & systems
    *5250 Telecommunications systems
    *5260 Records management
  5300 Production management
    *5310 Production planning & control
    *5320 Quality control
    *5330 Inventory management
    *5340 Safety management
  5400 Research & development
6000 HUMAN RESOURCE MANAGEMENT (see also 2500)
  6100 Human resource planning
  6200 Training & development
  6300 Labor relations
  6400 Employee benefits & compensation
  6500 Employee problems
7000 MARKETING
  7100 Market research
  7200 Advertising
  7300 Sales & selling
  7400 Distribution
  7500 Product planning & development (see also research & development 5400)

INDUSTRIES & MARKETS

8100 Financial services industry
    8110 Commercial banking services
    8120 Retail banking services
    8130 Investment services
8200 Insurance industry
    8210 Life & health insurance
    8220 Property casualty insurance
8300 Other services
    †8301 Advertising agencies
    †8302 Software & computer services industry
    8310 Consultants (not elsewhere classified)

    8320 Health care industry
    8330 Broadcasting & telecommunications industry (not equipment)
    8340 Electric, water, & gas utilities
    8350 Transportation industry (not equipment)
    8360 Real estate industry
    8370 Construction & related industries
    8380 Hotel & restaurant industries
    8390 Retail stores, includes groceries
8400 Agriculture industry
8500 Extractive industries
    8510 Petroleum industry
8600 Manufacturing industries
    8610 Food processing industry, includes beverages & liquors
    8620 Textile & apparel industries
    8630 Lumber & wood products industries, includes paper
    8640 Chemical industry, includes rubber & plastics
    8641 Pharmaceuticals industry
    8650 Electrical, electronics, instrumentation industries
    8651 Computer industry
    8660 Metals and metalworking industries
    8670 Machinery industry (industrial, construction, farm, etc.)
    8680 Transportation equipment industry (cars, aircraft, shipbuilding, etc.)
    8690 Publishing industry

ARTICLE TREATMENT

*9110 Company specific/case studies
*9120 Product specific treatment
*9130 Experimental/theoretical treatment
*9140 Statistical data
*9150 Guidelines
*9160 Biographical treatment
*9170 Non-US
*9180 International

ORGANIZATION TYPES

*9510 Multinational corporations
*9520 Small businesses
    *9521 Minority- and women-owned businesses
*9530 Diversified companies
*9540 Non-profit institutions
9550 Public sector organizations

No asterisk - Searchable from 1971 to the present
Asterisk - Searchable only from mid-1982 forward
† - Searchable from mid-1986 forward

254

Figure 2

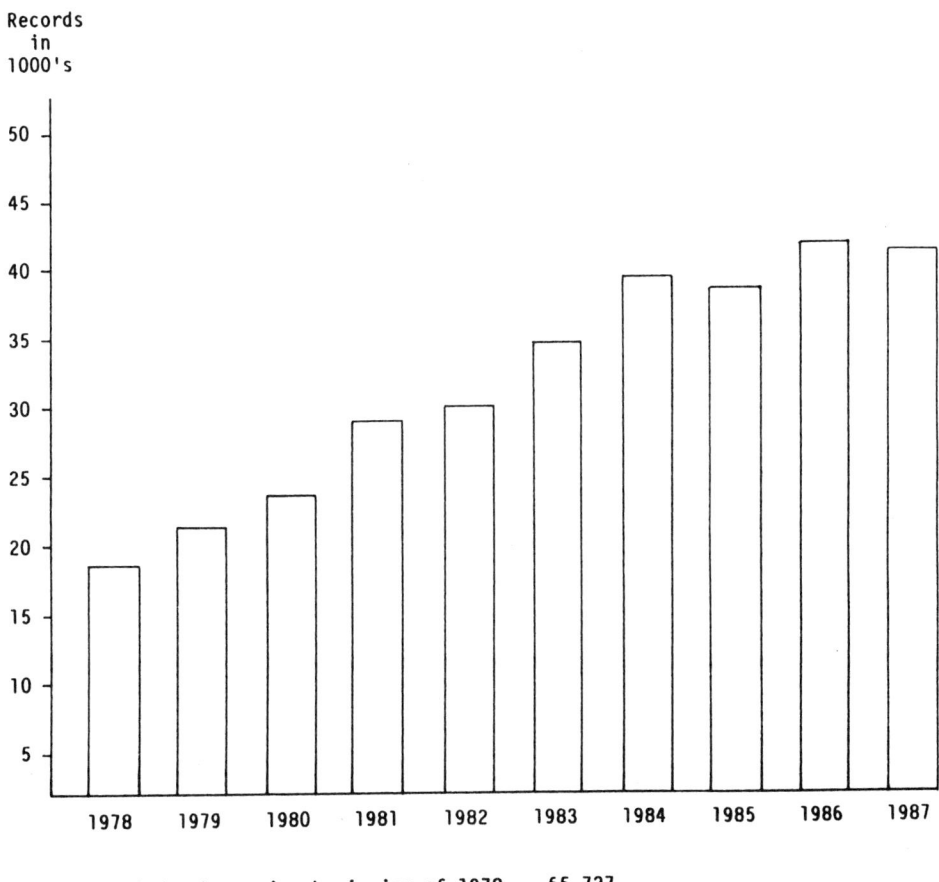

Total database size beginning of 1978 65,727
Total database size end of 1987 383,652

Figure 3

```
PY=1978        19,420 records

   CC=11?       3,904    20%
   CC=41?       1,538     8%
   CC=81?       1,757     9%
   CC=82?       1,151     6%
```

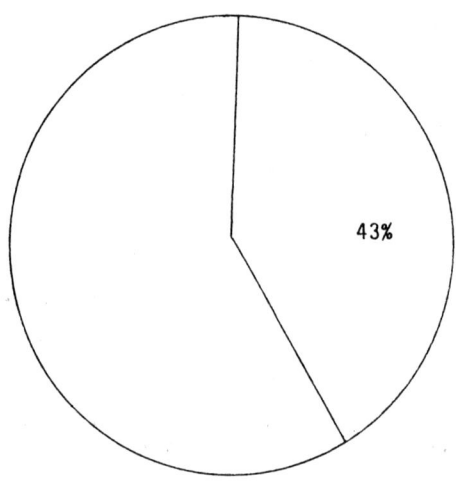

Figure 4

```
PY=1982   30,993 records

CC=11?    3,904      14%
CC=41?    1,229       4%
CC=81?    2,536       8%
CC=82?    1,839       6%
```

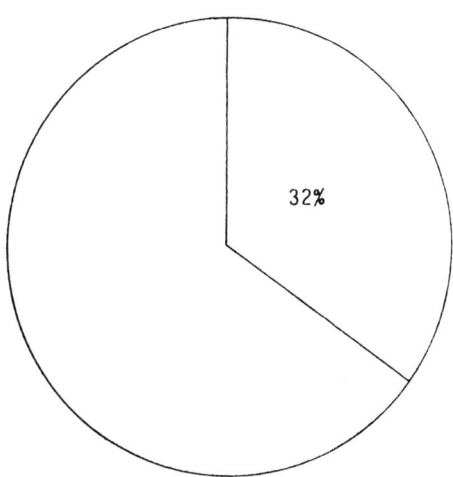

Figure 5

PY=1986   42,634 records

CC=11?	5,096	12%
CC=41?	1,389	3%
CC=81?	4,191	10%
CC=82?	2,778	6.5%

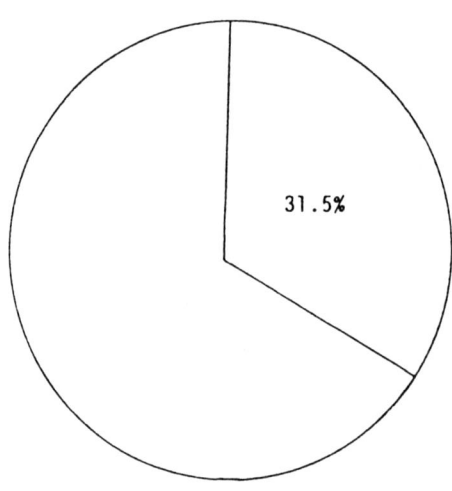

THE GEORGIA INTERACTIVE NETWORK FOR MEDICAL INFORMATION (GaIN)

Kimberly A. McInnis, Mercer University School of Medicine

Keywords: Networks, health information systems, end user searching, medical library, Georgia Interactive Network for Medical Information (GaIN), Bibliographic Access and Control System (BACS).

Abstract: In 1983, the Medical School Library at the Mercer University School of Medicine (MUSM) received grant funding for a three-year project from the National Library of Medicine to establish the Georgia Interactive Network for Medical Information (GaIN). GaIN responds to the AAMC Report on Academic Information in the Academic Health Sciences Center that challenged health science libraries to assume an assertive role in the management of computerized biomedical information systems and in the development of computer networks.
 The GaIN project involves networking on three levels: the physician's practice site, the hospital library or local information resource and the MUSM library which houses the central computer. Through cooperation on all three levels, information is provided directly to the person who needs it.
 GaIN offers a variety of information services to network members including: GaIN Medline, Electronic Messaging, On-Line Catalog, Continuing Education Bulletin Board, Information for Patient Management, Gateway to Remote Databases and Consultants' Registry.
 This paper will describe the network structure, services offered, patterns of use and future plans of this network. In addition, growth of the network from 1983 to the present will be discussed.

1. INTRODUCTION

 In September 1983, the Medical School Library at Mercer University received grant funding for a three-year project to establish the Georgia Interactive Network for Medical Information (GaIN). The GaIN project was designed in response to the Association of American Medical Colleges' report on Academic Information in the Academic Health Sciences Center that challenged health science libraries to assume an assertive role in the management of computerized biomedical information systems and in the development of computer networks. (Ref. 1)
 The purpose of this project was (and still is) to provide a mechanism to disseminate medical information into rural areas of Georgia where access might not otherwise be available. In addition, GaIN enhances the mission of the Mercer University School of Medicine (MUSM) which is to educate primary care physicians for practice in rural areas of the state. Students are taught the computer competencies necessary for effective information retrieval through workshops and siminars presented during their four years at MUSM. Currently, GaIN transmits medical information via telephone lines from a PDP 11/44 computer housed at the medical library, to network members which

include approximately 450 physicians and allied health professionals, as well as health care institutions across the state.

2. NETWORK COMPONENTS

The network is comprised of four major components. These are: 1) GaIN Medline; 2) The Post Office; 3) The Reference Desk; and 4) The Conference Center. The software controlling these components consists of the Bibliographic Access and Control System (BACS) leased from the Washington University School of Medicine (WUSM) and the Veteran's Administration Kernel and Filemanager software obtained from the public domain. The software runs on a Digital Equipment Company PDP 11/44 minicomputer using the Intersystems M11+ operating system.

The GaIN Medline component is a user-friendly database that allows the end user to search for citations dating 1984-present from over 400 journal titles. These journal titles reflect the holdings of the MUSM library and the network libraries. The user is presented a menu of options that allow him to perform a search, store an individual search or group of searches from which he may perform monthly updates, view the table of contents for a current issue of a journal, send a message to the reference department at the MUSM library or view extensive help screens on use of the system.

The GaIN Medline software, programmed in the MUMPS language, was designed by Dr. Simon Igielnik. Dr. Igielnik serves as the Director of Computing Facilities at the Washington University School of Medicine. The software is very flexible and was designed to meet a variety of needs. For example, the novice user may perform a search with little or no instruction while the advanced user enjoys such features as exact and truncated searching.

Searches are performed on GaIN Medline in a variety of ways. The user may search the title, author, journal source, medical subject heading (MeSH) or abstract by entering a response to any one or a combination of these fields. When the search strategy has been completed the user is prompted to select a print format. The print capabilities of GaIN Medline are very flexible. The user may elect to print any or all of the following fields: author, title, journal source, medical subject heading (MeSH) or abstract. For easier reading, the searcher may choose to have blank lines inserted between the fields printed. Another feature offered is the ability to receive a count of the citations retrieved from the search before printing. The database is updated monthly from tapes generated at the National Library of Medicine from a profile created at MUSM.

The value of this component of the network was confirmed by a survey conducted in August 1987 (Figure 1). Using a scale where 1 equaled not useful and 5 equaled very useful, the network institutions rated GaIN Medline 3.8 while the clinical practice sites rated it 4.5. In addition, the number of accesses for this component of the network is second only to the Post Office electronic mail component (Figure 2).

The next component of the system is referred to as the Post Office. The software for this component consists of the VA Kernel Mailman. Network members may communicate with approximately 450 individual and institutional members online. When the user selects the Post Office option from the master menu, he is presented with a sub-menu that allows him to receive new mail, read messages stored previously or send messages to other network members. If the network member has received any new messages since he last used the system, he is flagged with a banner when he logs on again notifying him of the number of new messages received. The user then selects the option to read the incoming messages. After reading a new message, the user may choose to take any of the following actions: 1) send a reply; 2) delete the message; 3) save the message in a specific basket created by the user; 4) query the list of recipients for that message and determine whether or not they have read it; 5) ignore the message by entering a return; 6) forward the message to another user; 7) print the message; or 8) terminate seeing any future responses to the message. When the user sends a message, he has the choice of sending it to an individual, a mail group or network-wide. Before sending a message, he may edit the content. The edit mode offers a variety of features such as adding, deleting or inserting text, searching for a string of characters, changing a specific string of characters to another each time it appears in the text and more. After completing the text of the message it is ready to be transmitted. Before the final transmission of the message, the user may choose any of the following actions: 1) go back into the edit mode; 2) scramble the message with a password; 3) request a confirmation when the message has been received or 4) cancel the message entirely. An additional feature of this software is the ability to assign surrogate users. This feature is especially useful for physicians or faculty members and their secretaries. The secretary can be assigned as a surrogate for their supervisor. The surrogate user may have reading privileges, sending privileges or both. Password security is maintained by simply making the surrogate privilege a menu option for those designated users. Any mail sent by a surrogate on behalf of their supervisor is automatically labelled as such by the system.

As expected, use of this electronic mail component of the network surpasses that of any other component. Approximately 75% of the total accesses on the network are accounted for by electronic mail (Figure 2). In the August 1987 survey, users rated the Post Office as 4 on a scale of 1 to 5 with 5 being the highest possible rating. Institutions place a high value on the electronic mail service due to a large volume of interlibrary loans being transmitted.

The Reference Desk is the third component of the network. This component is comprised of the Bibliographic Access and Control System (BACS) also programmed by Dr. Simon Igielnik at Washington University School of Medicine. Also included in this component are some special functions designed by the network staff and programmed by Dr. Igielnik. Upon selecting the Reference Desk option from the master menu, the user is presented the following list of options: 1) RT--Gateway to Remote Databases; 2) RL--List Output of Gateway Searches; 3) RF--Edit Output of Gateway Searches; 4) SP--Online Card Catalog; 5) RC--Continuing Education Announcements; 6) RD--Consultants' Registry; or 7) RE--Request Form for Library Search Service.

The online catalog is part of the BACS software mentioned earlier. It is the only portion of the software that is available for public use. The other BACS functions include library circulation, acquisition, periodical control and statistical reporting and are used only by the library staff. The BACS software selected to automate the library provides considerable flexibility. Initial modifications necessary in the software to suit MUSM policies were easily made. In addition, as changes in policy occur, most modifications are covered under a maintenance contract.

The online catalog contains records for materials housed in the MUSM library and most of the institutions on the network. The user may search for an item using any combination of the author, title, subject, series or date fields. The system responds with a listing that contains the brief title, call number and location for each item matching the search strategy entered. The user may stop there or choose to display the full bibliographic record and circulation data for an item.

The gateway to remote databases allows a user to make a connection to most any national database for which he has a password. The user conducts a search and returns back to the network where the option of storing the search is offered. If the decision is made to store the search, the user may also edit and list the results at any future time. This function also is used to answer requests for library search services. The user can request that a literature search be performed for him via a computer-generated request form. This request form supplies all the necessary information to the search analyst at MUSM. The search is performed via the gateway function and is stored on the system. The requestor is notified via the Post Office component that the search results are ready to be retrieved. The user then selects the Reference Desk option and prints the results of the search on his printer. It is entirely possible for a physician 200 miles away from MUSM to request and receive a literature search within an hour.

Other Reference Desk functions include continuing education announcements and a consultants' registry. The continuing education file contains listings of courses being offered across the United States. Information included in the record consists of title of the course, location, cost, contact person and the number of continuing medical education credits offered. The file is keyword searchable by any of those items.

The consultants' registry is also keyword searchable. This file includes the names, addresses and phone numbers of physicians who are willing to serve as consultants on specific medical problems. To participate as a consultant, the physician must submit his qualifications to, and be approved by, the GaIN Advisory Board.

The final component of the system is the Conference Center. This component consists of the Veterans Administration's teleconferencing software. While the software is fully implemented, applications for the software are still being explored. Possibilities include participation in conferences for continuing medical education credit and integrating the software into the individualized problem-based curriculum at MUSM.

3. NETWORK SERVICES

In addition to the services provided by the four network components, GaIN also provides interlibrary loan and cataloging services. Interlibrary loans are originated and received by the institutional network members via the electronic mail component of the system. Institutions may also choose to participate in a union catalog by having their books cataloged at MUSM for inclusion in the GaIN online catalog. A cataloger at MUSM catalogs the materials and provides the library with cards, book pockets and spine labels. Photocopy services are also provided. If a physician conducts a search on GaIN Medline and needs an article, he may request a copy of the article via the electronic mail component of the system. Reference services are provided to both individual and institutional members of the network on demand.

4. NETWORK GROWTH

Growth of the GaIN network since 1983 has far exceeded original estimates in the grant proposal. By the end of the grant period in August 1986, it was estimated that the membership would consist of 7 institutions and 15 physicians. Actual membership at that time consisted of 18 institutions and 172 individuals. As of December 1987, the membership had grown to include 20 institutions and 497 individuals (Figure 3).

5. FUTURE PLANS

To meet the needs of a continually growing user population, many plans for network development are underway. Interlibrary loan software programmed by the Veteran's Administration has recently been received and installed on the system. The online catalog will be enhanced to allow the user to view the collection(s) of one library, several libraries or the entire network. Teleconferencing packages are being evaluated for dissemination of continuing medical education courses. The possibility of implementing a drug database is also being evaluated. By having a network that evolves in an effort to meet user needs, it is hoped that GaIN will continue the phenomenal growth rate enjoyed thus far.

6. REFERENCE

1. Matheson, N.W. and Cooper, J.A.D. "Academic Information in the Academic Health Sciences Center: Roles for the Library in Information Management." J. Med. Educ. 57: Part 2, October 1982.

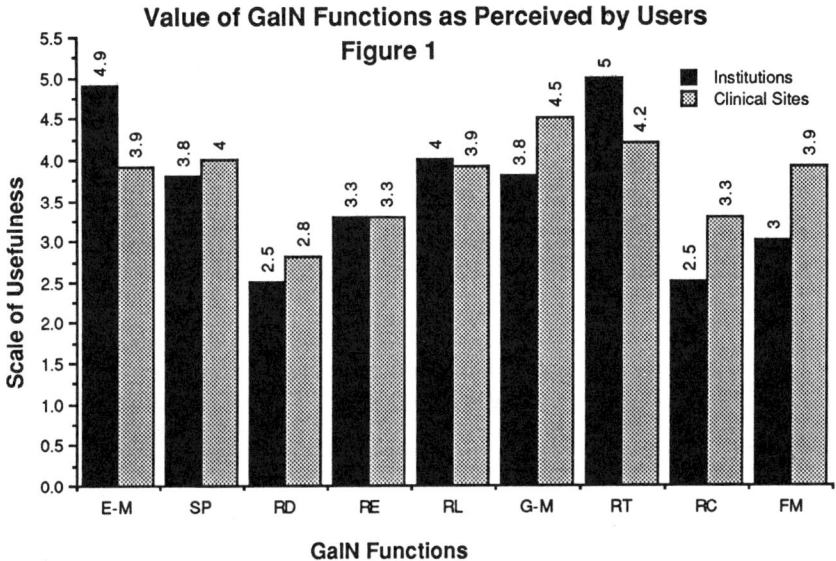

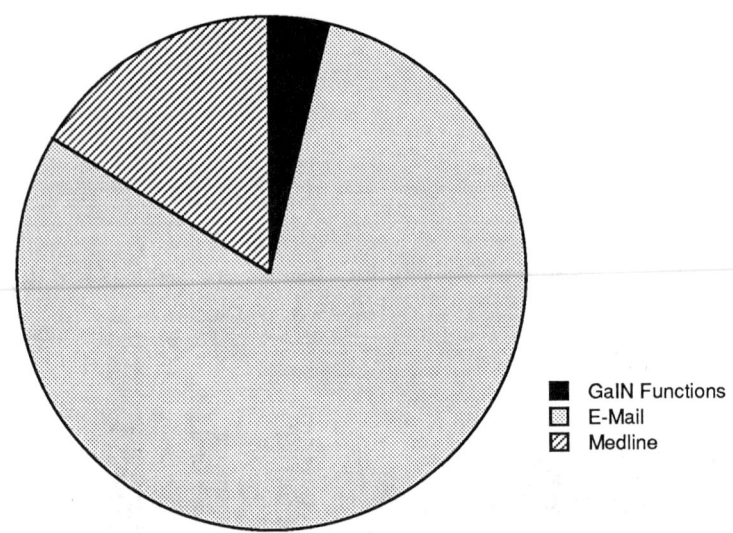

Number of Accesses
January, 1987 - December, 1987
Figure 2

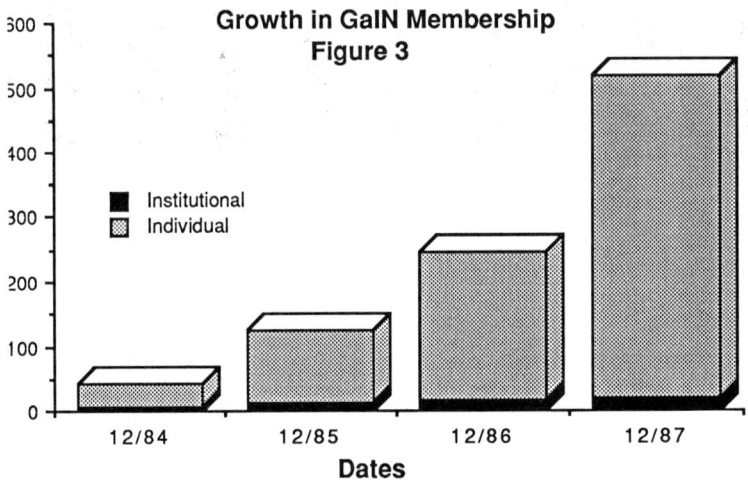

Growth in GaIN Membership
Figure 3

```
Institutional Members:  December 1984    5
                        December 1985   14
                        December 1986   17
                        December 1987   20

Individual Members:     December 1984   36
                        December 1985  110
                        December 1986  230
                        December 1987  497
```

DEVELOPING AN ELECTRONIC INFORMATION SERVICE

John F. McLane, Wilson & McLane, Inc.

ABSTRACT.

Because of the hazards, all electronic information services should be regarded as ventures. This paper focuses on approaches to reduce risk.

Wilson & McLane has developed new definitions to better understand issues; new techniques to develop services, estimate market demand, and define what will motivate a market to economically support a service. Other risk reduction elements include management styles and corporate cultures to fit the environment.

Information, as a resource is vital to the economic health of America, but the atmosphere is uncertain, especially for ventures upon which the emerging information economy depends.

Larger firms targeting growth in information businesses, are acquiring, not creating. Experienced seed investors are doing only LBO's. The perception of risks versus rewards will have to change to make investors become more long-term oriented.

Firms have failed because of their lack of marketing skills and their inability to adapt corporate cultures to a dynamic environment.

Services are best developed through stages, along with their markets. They never cease to evolve. Success requires: long-term investment; deep technical development; continued "production"; and marketing talent for reading markets and creating wants.

Many factors determine an information service's fit with its market including: content, delivery, and market momentum.

Using the proper techniques to orchestrate corporate resources, firms from industries beyond publishing, with the appropriate culture and vision, have a high probability of being winners. The rewards will be enormous.

1.   INTRODUCTION.

Five thousand years from now, when Egypt may be remembered for the pyramids, Greece for democracy and philosophy, and Rome for government, we believe America will be remembered for an information economy, and for marketing.

Tom Peters writes in his new book, <u>Thriving on Chaos</u>: "Niche markets may eventually be the only markets". With information, this is true today, and, the ultimate niche market is the individual.

Many think America's opportunity lies with technology. In the information field, technology has had a tremendous impact largely because it creates dramatic new economies of scale. If the automotive industry had tracked with the computer industry since 1955, a new Buick would cost $1.50, get 200 mpg, and fit in the palm of your hand.

But for the consumer, at the end of the value-added chain, technology, is a means, a facilitator, a "raw material". It must be focused and packaged toward specific consumer needs. Marketing is required to help potential consumers convert a need to a **want**.

A classic example of a missed opportunity because a want was not created:

> Picture the machine-gun salesman who called on Napoleon before Waterloo. An aide told the salesman that the Emperor didn't have time to see him.
>
> A better <u>salesman</u> might have been responsible for changing the course of history. Had the marketing department done its job? Research had identified a need; a product had been developed; price was not yet a factor. Was promotion adequate? Was the sales approach deficient? A want had not been created. How many of us can have empathy for this salesman -- for Napoleon?

This paper addresses some of the major elements involved in reducing risks when creating information services. It focuses on a process of understanding market needs and creating wants.

If the U.S. is to continue to be a world economic power, it must now utilize its resources very competitively.

The service economy has already evolved as large firms have streamlined and restructured. These firms must go to outside contractors, form strategic relationships, or develop new, creative ways to obtain functions previously performed by their own staffs. Opportunities exist for information services to assist in this effort. An information economy will begin to build from this foundation.

However, the trend, as elsewhere, is to buy information services, not to create them. International Thompson, TRW, and Dun & Bradstreet are acquiring, not creating. Experienced information investors like Welsh, Carson, Anderson, & Stowe are finding greater short-term returns with less risk in leveraged buy-outs of established companies.

But, many new information businesses and their services will be necessary for America to evolve into an information economy. How do we reduce the risks?

How are successful information services developed? If we examine many of the attempts over the last few years, the answer would be -- not very well!

1.1 WHY FAILURES?

Information company managers have had no generally accepted road map to follow to develop new services. Because of the early stage in evolution of most markets, the speed with which new services can impact markets, as well as the stage of most firms, companies providing information electronically are new ventures. This includes many which are recognized as relatively large businesses, including Quotron, Telerate, Mead Data Central, etc.

Most American consumer videotex ventures haven't had a chance. They have not been market oriented. The "**catchability**" wasn't there. (Catchability, relates to the installed base of terminal devices and consumers ready and able to use the service.) The pricing of the service and the cost of new equipment was high. The "pain" of the learning curve was high, even intimidating. The information content was available elsewhere, and the service had not been customized or made "tailorable" by consumers for electronic delivery. The market perceived no real economic value associated with the service.

GEMCO, a joint venture between McGraw-Hill and Citicorp, was formed to provide the oil trading community with a combination of transaction support, information, and financial services. It failed. It is our opinion that it was not because the oil industry was depressed, or because the services were integrated poorly. There was a need. But, a want was not developed. Traders are a unique breed, and new systems for trading require cultural change. Information and financial services continue to be offered separately. GEMCO did not understand the market or the business implications.

1.2 THE ENVIRONMENT.

The environment for electronic information services is full of uncertainty: change in markets and technology is rapid and unremitting; experienced managers are few and difficult to locate; regulatory restraints are baffling, constricting, inconsistent and often unpredictable; competition is escalating as more firms see opportunities. Utilities now entering information industries have historically survived because they were monopolies. What impact will they have, and how will they be impacted? All these add to risk.

The rules have changed and one firm's troubles signify another's emerging markets. Hundred year old firms are becoming ventures again! Many will not survive. AT&T defines its business as the movement and management of information. Other large firms are looking at this field. What will GM be doing? What will the environment be in five years?

How do we reduce the risks?

2. REDUCING THE RISK.

High-risk elements must be defined and addressed. They include: a new definition of old terms to understand issues, new management approaches, iterative development, market evolution by stages and, the use of "critical mass" principles.

2.1 DEFINITIONS.

We must establish a common foundation upon which to examine issues.

WEBSTER'S:

A **service** is a system of providing people with "something", as with electric power, water, transportation, mail delivery.

A **consumer** buys goods or services for his own needs -- not for resale.

A **business** is defined as the buying and selling of commodities or services; a commercial or industrial establishment.

Publishing is defined as making publicly known or issuing work such as books, newspapers, music.

And, **Information** is defined as facts, not necessarily accurate, gathered in any way, including news, and intelligence.

MODIFIED DEFINITIONS:

A **service** is an "intangible product". Its value disappears as it is created. It is created only as it is consumed -- but, it may be consumed many times.

A **consumer** buys goods and services for his own personal use ("consumer markets"), and to enhance his job function ("commercial or business markets").

It should be noted that the term consumer is applied in this article and not "user" or "end-user". These terms are overused and too often misapplied to the same individual. We are focusing here on the user of the information, not the system through which it was obtained.

A **business** is an entity which exists because it provides valued products and/or services to consumers.

Publishers have historically been merchandisers and promoters of discrete, tangible written or printed "products", produced (printed) and created (authored) by third parties.

Information is a misunderstood term that is over-used to broadly define everything from trivia to propaganda. We will use it strictly as defined by Webster; and differentiated from each of the following: **data**, which, once compiled may create information; **knowledge**, which is information once understood; and **wisdom**, which requires superior judgement <u>and</u> understanding -- much needed in the development of information services.

An **information service** is a business that provides enough economic value to motivate consumers to repeatedly utilize it.

Information services provide value in various ways. Value may be added to information by gathering, editing, interpreting, manipulating, delivering, integrating, and through other definable -- and manageable -- processes.

Individuals are becoming recognized as niche markets. Value-added information for one consumer will not be value for another. Whether created by the vendor or the consumer, we are in a stage of mass customization. Tailored information yields the highest value.

The most active markets for electronic information services are business consumers and resellers that add value. Significant personal consumer markets have not <u>yet</u> evolved in the U.S. This article is based on experience and proven concepts working with several information markets.

If implemented with only Webster's definitions in mind, information services will fail. This calls for another definition. **Marketing** is defined as that part of a business impacted by the consumer. Marketing arguably includes every discipline, even to a lesser degree, finance, law, administration, and production.

2.2   <u>NEW MANAGEMENT APPROACHES</u>.

Publishing has evolved significantly over the last 50 years, but the next 20 years will be revolutionary as information will be used more through electronic means. Electronic information services differ radically from traditional publishing. They require:

> Longer-term investment. Publishing has historically been an entrepreneurial, discrete risk, merchandising business with third parties frequently providing the product and the "manufacturing". This has not usually required large or long-term investment before payback.

> Where most American industry is oriented towards fulfilling the quarterly earnings forecasts of the securities analysts, some firms have matured in their outlook. The President of AT&T Bell Labs, Robert E. Allen, indicates: "We fund research with a long term view, not with our eyes on next quarter's earnings".

Continued technical investment and development in systems, software, communications, and daily operations and customer service.

A different corporate culture allowing freedom from old institutional constraints and politics, and proper incentives and performance rewards. All successful companies will be able to change directions rapidly. Decisions will be made at the lowest level by entrepreneurial managers. This ability is even more important for information services.

Full use of marketing skills. This includes: a different product development approach, uniquely edited content for more ability to add value through electronic delivery, a different sales approach, customer service and support, user guides, complex (bundled) pricing, different promotion, a focus on niche markets, and different channels of distribution.

Publishers' historical proprietary positions with some forms of information content and editorial expertise have represented only a part of the resources necessary for a successful information service, and not always a difficult hurdle for newcomers to overcome. Those with significant application skills or an information resource that was created for a different purpose may actually be better positioned over-all.

It is not surprising that the more successful early electronic services have come from outside the publishing arena. They had no momentum in the wrong direction. LEXIS was developed by a forest products company; COMPUSERVE, as an independent company, now owned by H&R Block, a service firm; TRW's information business was developed by an automotive and aerospace company; and DIALOG, from an aerospace company. These were all long-term developments, built on technical foundations, and their corporate cultures have enabled them to be flexible enough to evolve with their markets.

2.3 THE DEVELOPMENT PROCESS.

THE OLD WAY.

A large percentage of all new business developments have always been driven by instinct and intuition -- in all industry. Alan Kay, the father of the Macintosh, has said: "You forecast the future by inventing it". Many businesses started because they just started. They perceived a need. Most have failed. Some were lucky.

"OBAR", the Ohio Bar Association Automated Research Service, was started on a conviction and instinct. It created a prototype service from which skillful management later created LEXIS.

THE RIGHT WAY -- ITERATE.

It is said that New York will be a nice city when they finish it, but we have to use it in the interim. Information services are analogous. They are never finished. They are best developed through stages. Each stage is a deeper, more involved iteration of the one before it. An iterative cycle considers all aspects of the service and includes finance, management, research, planning, implementation, feedback, analysis, etc., and adjustment in varying degrees. A first stage (iteration) might be as follows:

A service concept is developed that is informed and objective.

Market research, generally the next step, will be by-passed for the first few iterations. These techniques will not work yet. Interviewees cannot effectively react, because they have not yet been exposed. This is true for questionnaires and most focus groups.

Market probes -- Early research should be done through many smaller qualitative as well as quantitative probes to define the characteristics (needs, wants, motives, and a perception of value) of niche markets. Environments, once understood, may disqualify a concept or qualify it for further work. Determining the evolving characteristics of a market niche requires expert interpretation. This includes "unthought-of need" identification, timing, and defining the need for later, more traditional market research. It requires unique qualifications: technical, marketing, professional, market specific, interpersonal, etc.

Internal resource analysis -- organization (people and management), capital, technology, current products/services, production capabilities, environment and culture, perception of market and opportunity, strategic relationships.

Strategic fit analysis (market/product/resource)

Marketing mix planning:

- Products/services
- Pricing
- Sales, channels of distribution, and customer support
- Promotion and advertising.

Adjusting the plan in "A service concept," above, considering information obtained.

Begin a new iteration.

The product aspect of the service may be <u>conceptualized</u> in the first iteration. After change it may be <u>designed</u> during the second iteration. During the third it may be <u>prototyped</u>, etc. This is more deliberate than the standard prototype, alpha, beta, gamma development cycles. The service evolves as the information from the market evolves. A service probably won't be used commercially by the market in the first several stages.

Luck is when opportunity crosses the path of preparedness. The "lucky firms" identify a need, then, estimate when the need will become a want in the culture of the market, or what is needed to impact the change. This process greatly increases the probability of long term success. It is analogous to playing stud poker. Players do not legitimately control their cards and may lose several hands in a row. To optimize returns, players will estimate the probability of success on each card (iteration) and bet (not gamble) for the "long-term". They limit their losses by folding losing hands early, and optimizing winning hands.

2.4   <u>MARKETS EVOLVE IN STAGES</u>.

First, potential consumers become aware of a service. If they perceive value, they try it, and struggle to learn it. Later, it becomes part of their daily life. Once comfortable with it, they will use it creatively. Creative use provides the highest value.

All aspects of a service should continue to evolve after being offered to the market as consumers learn about its features and value, and as the reliability of their opinions and feedback increases.

If a service or product has enough economic value, the market will find a way for it to evolve even if the original company does not or cannot take the necessary actions itself. This is done through both competitive and complementary ventures. An example is the new microcomputer <u>industry</u> with the family of clones, various software products, service organizations, etc.

Markets are affected by many factors: catchability, competition in the consumer's marketplace; consumer literacy factors (sophistication); etc.

Key to the over-all success of the service will be management's ability to determine the then current market potential and demand for each aspect of the service.

Historically, several firms have <u>managed</u> to increase the rate of evolution of a market. Not all have been high-tech. They increased client awareness and conditioned them to become use to their product/service. They created a "have-to-have" versus a "nice-to-have" value. Examples from the educational community include: IBM in the 1950's, for contributing to the development of computer programming and systems analysis at the university level; West Publishing, with research in law schools for decades; CCH in accounting; and LEXIS, with online research in law schools since 1969.

2.5   CRITICAL MASS.

Focusing on the market for information services requires an understanding of the concept of **critical mass**. Critical mass is defined by Webster as: "the minimum amount of fissionable material that can sustain a nuclear chain reaction under a given set of conditions".

Wilson & McLane defines critical mass as the minimum level of certain factors that will motivate a large enough percentage of consumers to economically support a service.

The combination of factors depends on the service and the characteristics of the market segment. Factors for an electronically delivered, professional information service may include:

Information content: breadth, how many topical areas; depth, with how much detail; history, how many years; and the editorial process, tailored for each form of delivery; etc.

Systems delivery features and function: catchability; tailorability or focus on the consumer's style; ease of use and training; ease of support; functionality; price; etc.

Market momentum: awareness; promotion and advertising; channels of distribution; sales activity; support activity; joint efforts and relationships; price; etc.

Critical mass for other services, which may provide information content but establish consumer value mainly through communications or transactions services, have additional factors of greater relative weight that must be estimated. These services, though related, are not the subject of this paper.

French videotex didn't have to match the initial service to the market. As a government monopoly, they could force the market to accept the service. However, they did a much better job of fitting with their market than the American videotex ventures did. It was simple and cheap. A special organization was created outside the mainline culture of the phone company. Content, tailored to the delivery media, added value. An entrepreneurial platform was established upon which information ventures might flourish. Critical mass was established. They led the horse to water, and the horse is drinking.

In the U.S. we cannot really force the horse. We have to <u>sell</u> him by creating a want. But, the same formula holds.

Critical mass equates with a market's **perceived value** at any given time. It changes as the market's characteristics change.

The questions are: 1) what percentage of consumer want is satisfied by what level of "service" -- and more importantly, 2) what percentage has to be satisfied to create enough value to support a service. The first question can be fairly well determined through interviews with prospective consumers, the second must be inferred through experience and expertise after the first.

The perceived value has to be some amount higher than the "**consumption cost**". This cost equates with the price the consumer pays to the service plus the dollar and time costs estimated for training, learning curve inefficiency, equipment, telecommunications, etc.

Factors considered in evolving market demand:

Critical Mass (The market's perceived value.)

Consumption Cost (The market's perceived cost.)

Literacy Factors (The market's ability to perceive.)

3. <u>CONCLUSION</u>.

Growth in our information resources are vital to the economic health of America. The perception of risks involved with new information ventures in the current environment doesn't encourage venture development as much as it will. There are successful methods, if used properly, that reduce risks and encourage confidence.

A new culture is emerging with the information revolution. New management techniques will become more widely adopted. Companies will become flexible, able to focus on multiple niche markets, more long-term oriented, and realize the prospective value of technological development to create quality services. Leveragable information "franchises" and application skills in specific industry operations may be found in unsuspecting places.

Using the proper techniques to orchestrate corporate resources, firms from industries beyond publishing, with the appropriate culture and vision, have a high probability of being winners. The rewards will be enormous.

ENSURING END-USER QUALITY CONTROL: AN ACADEMIC MODEL

Chris J. Miko, Bowling Green State University

Keywords: End-users, quality control.

Abstract: Through established efforts between the library and academic departments, end-user searching programs can be successfully implemented and maintained. A three phase approach, which systematically introduces the concept and practice of online searching to faculty and graduate students, helps ensure an acceptable level of quality control. The first phase involves the identification of an interested faculty member within the department. This individual receives an adequate level of computer database searching training. In-house training must be complemented by formal vendor or database producer seminars. Once training has been completed, the faculty member should begin accepting database searches from other faculty and graduate students in the department. For an initial period of time, a librarian should offer and provide appropriate assistance. The second phase involves the training of other interested faculty by their trained and experienced colleague. The third phase involves the integration of end-user computer database searching into graduate research methods courses. This instruction could be managed by either a librarian or by searchers within the department. Through this phase approach, training can be better controlled and monitored, thus maintaining search quality. Also, a wider population is ultimately exposed ot end-user searching.

    For a number of reasons, many academic libraries are today faced with the challenge and opportunity of introducing end-user online searching to research faculty and university students. Although database searching has historically been the responsibility of professionally educated and trained librarians, they are now sharing this responsibility with increasing numbers of academic discipline-specific end-user searchers. On campuses throughout the country, more and more research faculty and graduate students are conducting online database searches independent of the university or college library. Some information scientists and librarians encourage end-user searching. According to this group, end-user searching ultimately increases information access to wider populations. On the other hand, some other information scientists and librarians oppose end-user searching. According to this group, end-users are not information retrieval specialists. While these potential end-users are highly educated and respected in their own academic and research specialty, they lack the basic and continuing education required for effective and productive database searching.
    This author will not attempt to address this professional difference. This author will assume that end-user searching will continue at some given level. This author also assumes that end-user searching will continue in

academic departments independent of university libraries. Given these two stated assumptions, librarians must decide and determine the extent of their own responsibility toward end-user searchers. If a faculty member or an entire department commits itself to end-user searching, what should the library's response be? Should the library let them go it alone? Should librarians, partially because of other numerous responsibilities and commitments, assume unequivocal end-user searching competence and proficiency? This author believes if librarians fail to respond, we have failed our professional responsibility. This author again believes if librarians fail to train, guide, and consult end-users, we have neglected our basic and fundamental commitment to the principles and practices of bibliographic instruction. If an academic department decides to embrace the concept and practice of end-user searching, it is then the library's responsibility to help implement the program. It is also the library's responsibility to provide continuing education and training as well as quality control measures. Recognition of these responsibilities is consistent with accepted bibliographic instruction and library user education principles.

End-user computer database searching by departmental faculty can be efficiently implemented and supported by utilizing a systematic three phase approach. The first or initial phase involves the selection and training of one departmental representative. The selection process for this individual could parallel the selection process for other library related activities such as collection development. The faculty representative must commit the time and energy necessary to successfully implement the program in his or her department. This individual must also demonstrate an on-going interest and competency for online searching. The departmental representative will not only be central to the successful introduction of the program, but also to the maintenance of continued quality assurance.

The departmental representative will receive adequate database searching training. While this training would include sessions by on-site librarians, the training must include vendor based or producer sponsored training. In other words, the departmental representative must be formally trained. Just as librarians routinely receive vendor based or producer sponsored training, so must the departmental representatives. This formal training will also help institutionalize and solidify the representative's duties and responsibilities to his or her department and to the library. However, while it is common for librarians to be trained to search databases through a number of different vendors, this should not be necessary for departmental end-users. Given the subject specific nature inherent in most academic departments, training on one vendor should be sufficient to meet most research needs.

Once initial formal and informal training has been completed, the departmental representative should begin accepting database searches from other faculty and graduate students within the department. Depending on the observed proficiency and the expressed needs of the departmental representative, the librarian should offer and provide appropriate assistance. It is critical, at this stage, to establish scheduled, continuing contact with the departmental representative. As the representative becomes more proficient and comfortable with his or her role as database searcher, the contact with the library will tend, no doubt, to decrease over time. However, system changes do occur. Vendors and database producers constantly alter and improve searching software procedures. Librarians, through vendor and producer publications and professional literature, are continually alerted to these alterations and improvements. Concurrently, the departmental representatives must be informed. Regular meetings with the representatives must be established.

Through these meetings, the representatives will be informed of all vendor and database producer changes. Through these meetings, quality control will be established and maintained. Through these meetings, initial training will be enriched by continuous updates.

The second end-user computer database searching implementation phase involves the training of other interested and qualified faculty and graduate students. This training would be performed by the departmental representative. It is important to note that while initial training is performed by the departmental representative, the librarian should be prepared to respond with appropriate assistance. Also, those faculty and graduate students who demonstrate interest and qualification should have access to formal vendor or producer sponsored training.

The third end-user computer database searching implementation phase involves the integration of the practice into required graduate coursework. Part of the rationale for coursework integration is to introduce graduate students to computerized bibliographic searching and ultimately to end-user computer searching. The remaining rationale is to broaden the base of support and interest for computer searching within the department. As computer searching becomes institutionalized within the context of departmental curriculum, an active and continuing level of computer searching will be ensured. Just as with the training of other faculty and graduate students in phase two, the required exposure and training of every new graduate student will broaden the responsibility for computer searching away from the departmental represenative. As more people become interested and trained in computer searching, the responsibility for the continued success of the program will fall less and less to the departmental representative. While the representative will continue to play an important role, more and more individuals will contribute to the department's computer searching program. This broadened base of support and responsibility will prevent the demise of the program if the departmental representative should be forced to relinquish his or her responsibilities because of other commitments, a sabbatical, or departure from the university. The active inclusion of wider numbers of faculty and graduate students will provide a needed sense of program continuity. Therefore, the computer searching program would need not be totally reintroduced upon the absence or resignation of the departmental representative.

Academic departments may implement the third end-user computer searching phase by including the concept in the department's basic research methods course. This would be consistent with the trend toward the incorporation of general library research skills in this type of coursework. In many cases this course is designed and taught through the cooperation and expertise of the faculty of both the library and academic department. Along with lectures and materials addressing topics such as library services, the structure of scientific literature, and literature searching strategies, the librarian could present lectures and materials devoted to computer end-user searching. The graduate students would not only be introduced to computerized bibliographic searching, but also to end-user searching. Students would not only be exposed to the concept of computer searching, they would also be given hands-on experience. Ultimately, each student should select a topic, preferably within his or her research area, set up a search strategy, and actually perform the search. It should be stated, however, that the objective of the course is not to produce fully trained searchers. Rather, the objective of the course should be to provide an introduction to, and hands-on experience with, a wide range of library resources, including end-user computer searching in the context of scientific research.

Obviously, certain basic materials should be presented to the student before he or she conducts an online search. An initial overview of computer searching must be included. Computer searching should be compared to searching printed indexes. Advantages and disadvantages of searching online and printed indexes should be presented as well as the organizational structure of computer searching. Relationships between database producers, commercial vendors, and telecommunications organizations should be analyzed. Boolean logic should be thoroughly discussed as it is widely assumed that an understanding of boolean logic is fundamental to computer searching.

System specific and hardware specific procedures should also be included. Basic system protocol, sign-on procedures, and key commands should be reviewed. Descriptions of applicable and relevant databases must be included. Particular attention should be paid to those files containing subject parameters specific to the department offering the particular research methods course. Subject coverage of journal indexing within particular online files should also be discussed.

It may be advisable to require each student to perform a 'canned' search before they perform a search on their topic. The purpose of this 'canned' search would be to provide basic familiarity with the mechanics of online searching. The 'canned' search could be designed so that each student is exposed to the basic components of online searching. It is assumed that the need for this type of exercise varies among students. While many students are computer literate, many are computer illiterate. The 'canned' search would provide an initial exposure to the computer hardware in an unpressured situation. Also, basic boolean logic exercises could be included as demonstrations. The 'canned' search strategy would be designed to demonstrate an ideal search. Complications would be controlled as much as possible. While unexpected system and telecommunications interruptions could not be controlled, search results would be predetermined and designed to illustrate specific points. This particular exercise would be useful in demonstrating in real terms the theoretical concepts of boolean logic.

Before conducting the actual online search, students should have the opportunity to consult individually with the librarian. If needed, research topics would be adjusted and refined. Ultimately, each student's research topic would be translated into a computer search statement. Subsequently, each search statement could be broken down into subconcepts and search strategies would be established. Prior to the search session, each student should identify a research topic, construct an appropriate computer search statement, and prepare a probable search strategy. Following the completion of the online searches, each student should be required to analyze the search process and results.

Through the implementation and support of this three phase approach, vital end-user searching programs can be established and maintained in academic departments. More importantly, quality control will be monitored through close contact with the departmental representative.
As is true with most other library services and activities, the level and quality of cooperation between the library and those we serve will greatly determine the success of our efforts.

REFERENCES

1. Hansen, Kathleen. The effect of presearch experience on the success of naive (end-user) searches. Journal of the American Society for Information Science 37, No. 5, p. 315-318, September 1986.

2. Kirk, Cheryl L. End-user training at the Amoco Research Center.

Special Libraries 77, No. 1, p.20-27, Winter 1986.

3. Meadow, Charles T. User education for online information systems. Information Services & Use 3, No. 4, p. 173-177, August 1983.

4. Penhale, Sara J.: Taylor, Nancy Integrating end-user searching into a bibliographic instruction program. RQ 27, No. 2, p. 212-220, Winter 1986.

5. Poisson, Ellen H. End-user searching in medicine. Bulletin of the Medical Library Association 74, No. 4, p. 293-299, October 1986.

6. Trzebiatowski, Elaine End user study on BRS/After Dark. RQ 23, No. 4, p. 446-450, Summer 1984.

ARTIFICIAL INPUTS, NATURAL INTELLIGENCE: THE DATABASE AS MENTAL PERIPHERAL

Tim Miller, Gannett Center for Media Studies

Keywords: Online information retrieval, databases, digitized information, database applications, endusers.

Abstract: Although intelligent knowledge retrieval is still far from being realized, the computerized database in its present form can be used as a mental peripheral to extend our 'natural intelligence'. The 'artificial inputs' provided by the computer increase the quality of various building blocks of analysis, thus increasing the quality of the resulting mental product. The key to the effectiveness of the database is digitization, which breaks down barriers imposed by time, physical distance and delivery medium and makes possible a vast range of new opportunities to use information. Thinking about the unique properties of digitized information helps us forge new and creative applications for both commercial and in-house databases.

1. INTRODUCTION

As information becomes an increasingly large component of productivity it becomes more imperative that, as with any resource, we maximize its utility. And because we will get more and more of our information from computerized databases in the future, it is to our great advantage to consider the unique research opportunities made possible by digitization.

Considerable attention has been given in the past to the ability of computerized spreadsheets to enhance the analysis of numerical data; much less has been given to the somewhat parallel ability of retrieval software to manipulate textual data. By examining the ways in which digitization removes certain time, space and medium-based constraints, this paper attempts to create a new conceptual vantage point for generating database applications. Each property will be discussed briefly, application areas will be discussed and examples will be provided, most of them having been gathered from interviews with online users in business and the media.

2. DIGITIZED INFORMATION: A LIQUID ASSET

Digitized information is to print information what water is to ice. Digitization dissolves many of the crystalline structures imposed by traditional media. This 'liquified' data is much more readily transmitted over time and space and is more easily manipulated. Novel applications emerge and once-impractical applications suddenly become feasible. Our information use expands at the margins; our natural intelligence is enhanced by the 'artificial inputs' provided by the database.

For a simple example, look at the experience of an NBC television news producer in Chicago who recently was preparing a story about a local economic development organization. On a hunch he dialed up Mead Data's Lexis and ran the names of the organization's board members through the Illinois corporate registry (ILLSOS). Lo and behold, he found that several board members also were officers of companies that contract with the board. The information added a significant new conflict-of-interest angle to the story, an angle that competing news media didn't have.

Would he have gotten the information if it hadn't been online? No, said the producer. "I would have had to run to Springfield to get that and even then I wouldn't have been able to get at it like I did." Digital electronics not only allowed him to overcome the geographic barrier to getting information, but also, by providing mulitple access points, allowed him to use it in an entirely new way. His information use was extended at the margins with the result being a better product.

What follows is a discussion of some new opportunities for information use made possible - or practical - by the emergence of online information.

3. TIME STRUCTURES DISSOLVED

Not only does digitization allow real-time transmission of information, it also allows more ready access to the past. The archive is seamless, contained in a large digital 'vat' where only a few electronic pulses separate today's information from that of last year or decade.

3.1 Real-time Transmission

The immediacy offered by online systems increases one's ability to react quickly to take advantage of changes in markets, prices or technologies. For instance:

Get instant payoff: In what ways can use of breaking information immediately increase competitive advantage? Example: A breaking report from Nikkei Telecom allows U.S. subscribers to 'make a killing' in U.S. Treasury Bonds.

Increase marginal quality: In what key areas might a small time investment pay off disproportionately in the quality of analysis? Example: Nexis helps CBS scoop the competition with background about the checkered past of Pope John II's assailant.

3.2 The Digital Archive

The ability to go back into an archive where information can be ordered chronologically opens up a number of new possibilities for analysis. For example:

   Create custom chronologies: How might assembly of information over time help expose patterns? Example: General Foods researchers go online to create new product 'histories' of competitors - then examine them for patterns.

   Spot content change: How can changes over time help indicate important shifts in emphasis or strategy? Example: A newspaper editor pulls up a decade's worth of George Bush policy statements to find shifts in thinking.

   Spot change in placement: How can change in placement over time convey meaning? Example: A business researcher interested in a competitor's commitment to a given product goes back through annual reports to see how the product is 'played'. Online allows almost infinite extension of this method.

   Follow trails: How can retracing 'word paths' help track the evolution of a concept or product or shed light on associations among particulars? Example: An investigative reporter, given a code name for a military technology, tracks it back through Nexis to find new associations which, when also traced, provide vital clues as to the nature of the technology.

   Recreate context: In what ways can recreation of context for a certain event in time help reveal meaning? Example: A business researcher is curious to know why two executives had resigned several years ago. Using news and business databases, she reconstructs the scenario of that time - and surmises that the resignations were related to loss of a critical contract.

   Extended memory: In what ways can one exploit the ability of the database to serve as a vast extension of the memory? Example: When a large team of reporters at Newsday put together a book-length series of articles on waste disposal, they used an in-house database of notes, captured searches, memos and documents to serve as their collective memory. The ability to synthesize data was greatly improved.

4.   REMOVAL OF PLACE BARRIERS

   With online systems, the information we need is no longer place-bound. This implies a new ability to use distant or specialized information that was once out of pratical reach.

4.1   Transcend Geographic Boundries

   New information from new places might shed new light on events and issues. Some possible applications:
   Make use of the global village: What kinds of international information might be of use now that it is accessible? Example: Bank of America uses Australian Financial Review abstracts on Textline to help qualify a loan applicant from down under.
   Visit the 'local village': What new kinds of regional information might be of use now that it is more readily available? Example: An East Coast athletic shoe maker buys an Oregon firm and competitors immediately go to the full text of the Portland Business Journal on Business Dateline for a richly detailed profile.
   Uncover megatrends: In what ways can the growing mass of news and information be used to point out trends or patterns? Example: An editor uses Nexis, Vu/Text and DataTimes to find national trends in such things as drug smuggling in container

ships.

4.2 Transcend Disciplinary Boundries

Online systems allow us to break out of our narrow information world and invade the once-remote world of the experts. Our analysis is given more depth. Some examples:

Visit the specialist's domain: How can the specialist literature be used to give depth to an analysis? Example: Within an hour of the space shuttle's failure NBC researchers in Chicago were searching NTIS database on Dialog for information about temperature fluctuations and rocket failures.

Compare across disciplines: How can different emphases across various publications be of significance? Example: With the help of online data, a researcher quickly juxtaposes an executive's quotes from the Wall Street Transcript with those from Chemical Week. From the differences he can infer the executive's strategy.

5. EROSION OF BARRIERS IMPOSED BY A MEDIUM

Digitized information frees the searcher from the rigid structures forced on it by chapters, pages, titles, indexes, subject headings, even sentence structure. Database software acts as a 'textual spreadsheet' to expand greatly the kinds of 'calculations' that can be made.

5.1 Increase Selectivity

Although the digital database 'liquifies' information, it also allows it to be recrystallized in virtually any way we like. The possibilities for retrieval are as varied as fingerprints. Some examples:

Fish for single terms: How can a quick perusal of a single term or name possibly yield a big payoff? Example: A wire service reporter uses a quick Nexis search to uncover the checkered past of a child abuse consultant recently hired by the state.

Dig out novel concepts: How can a search string of distinctive words root out embedded concepts that elude the grasp of traditional indexing methods? Example: USA Today uses databases to find stories about a youth fashion fad that involves wearing unlaced sneakers.

Sift out novel phrases: How might a database easily help recover a specific comment or quote that will enhance the quality of a report or analysis? Example: News reporters add to the depth of a story by tracking down an exact quote in a database.

Cull by field: How can I use data fields to make new uses of information? Example: Librarians at the St. Petersburg Times limit their search to photo cutlines in order to find certain pictures - of the ill-fated Titanic for example.

5.2 Increased Ability to Compare

The fluidity of the database allows much more juxtaposing, comparing and contrasting. In so doing it allows more depth of analysis. For instance:

Cross examine: In what ways can a search across material pull out key webs of information? Example: Reporters at a New Jersey daily use Disclosure online to find interlocking directorates held by corporate executives.

Create patterns: In what ways can online information be massaged to reveal regular occurrences that shed light on a problem? Example: Congressional Watergate investigators digitized the phone records of the alleged conspirators and used computers to spot patterns of communication among them.

Create novel uses of fields: How can non-traditional use of database fields help to establish patterns? Example: Marquis Who's Who is used to assemble lists of university alumni.

5.3 New Ability to Count

The database's multiple access points provide an unprecedented opportunity for one to treat a mass of text as a source of primary research. Some examples:

Word counts: How might simple number of occurrences of a word or phrase shed light on a subject? Example: National Journal editors used Nexis to count the most voluble public figures. Henry Kissinger won with 10,187 cited quotes since 1977.

Word associations: How might change in pattern of word co-occurrences give hint of change? Example: A search was made of Tass to see if there is any change in the association of "imperialist" with "United States".

Content analysis: How does the ability to count word patterns aid in evaluation of text? Example: A Miami Herald editor uses his online newspaper archive to grade reporters on their use of such shopworn phrases as "gave chase".

6. DATA FUSION: WHEN IT ALL COMES TOGETHER

The true value of the database does not come from just one 'artificial input' but from combinations of many. By expanding our information use at the margins and by forging new uses for information we enhance the quality of the 'bits' of information that when combined and organized, form a whole that often is greater than the sum of its parts. It is not this process of inference that is new - what is revolutionary is the ability of electronic information technology to improve each input and in so doing enhance the overall clarity of the resulting mosaic.

Hopefully this discussion will encourage users to generate new ways to extend their natural intelligence with artificial inputs. There are many questions to be asked: How can we more fully exploit the interactive quality of databases, the transmission capabilities offered by data communications or the growing ability of the computer to 'learn'? These are important questions if we consider the fact that information - and the systems that deliver it - will become an ever-more-important part of our lives at work and home.

FACTORS USED IN SELECTING ONLINE DATABASES

Judith E. O'Dell, Central Michigan University

With the increasing number of vendors, gateways, and front end software available for searching the same databases what are the factors one uses in making a choice? This includes deciding on contracts and purchases which make sources available to the searcher, and choosing the most appropriate source for completing a given search once an institution makes options available. The three most obvious concerns include cost, efficiency in search strategy, and ease of access; which are influenced by the purpose of the search and the expertise of the searcher. Each of these considerations affects the quality of the search and the value to the end user. To make such decisions about contracts and purchases each institution must try and predict who the end users will be, the sophistication of the requests, and the type of information that will be needed. If an institution makes more than one method available to the searcher, the person must then evaluate the needs of the patron, or their own needs if the end user does the searching, using these same criteria. While each of the above considerations is important to the outcome of the search, the factors are not mutually exclusive and have an effect on each other (e.g. an inefficient search can take longer which affects cost.) The result is a complex myriad of concerns which must be viewed in connection with each other. It is my intent to look at each of these factors, how they affect each other, and ultimately how they affect the outcome of the search.

INTRODUCTION

When an organization decides to provide online services for its patrons there are a series of decisions that must be made about what information will be accessed and how that information will be accessed. These decisions start with the determination of what databases will be offered, the decisions continue with the determination of appropriate vendors, and end with the searcher's determination of what databases to access if given a choice. The following is a discussion of the factors affecting these decisions, the interaction between the factors, and their effect on search results.

WHICH DATABASES TO OFFER?

Deciding what databases to have available for online searching is a two part process. The first question being, what information is needed? This question must be answered both in terms of the disciplines for which online access is needed, and the specific types of information needed within each discipline. The initial concern, deciding on the appropriate disciplines, may seem like an easily answered question by saying the information that conforms to the needs of the patrons. But one must ask if each of the informational needs is great enough or important enough to justify the cost of online access, the cost being the price of obtaining access to the databases and the overhead expenses. While pertinent to all organizations, this question is particularly acute for those organizations that use a wide array of subject matter. Should online access be available on all subjects or only a few? Once the discipline/s have been established the need for specific types of data must be considered. If one were looking at legal information the issue might be the need for primary vs. secondary sources or full text vs. citations. If the discipline were business the considerations might include the need for statistical vs. textual data, full text vs. bibliographic data, or more than one type. Each discipline includes its own set of variables as to what specific type of information might be useful. The answer to all of these questions can be obtained by considering who will be using the information and the purpose for which it will be used.

While in many situations it is impossible to know with absolute certainty exactly who and how the information will be used, one can make reliable predictions based on knowledge of the intended users. Professionals, faculty, graduate students, or other researchers are likely to need access to technical or in depth sources of information and are likely to be less satisfied with databases which provide only bibliographic data. Of course this latter assumption may not hold true if the sources cited in bibliographic databases are readily available in print. In contrast many students or other casual users often only want an easy way to start their research and are more likely to be satisfied with obtaining bibliographic data online, then locating the documents manually. Once the needs for each discipline have been evaluated efforts can be directed at the second question involving availability, what databases exist to satisfy these needs? Although answering this question may be a time consuming task, it is one which is easily described in that it simply requires searching various directories and other sources for lists and descriptions of databases that satisfy the organization's requirements.

WHAT VENDOR TO CHOOSE?

Today most online publishers offer their databases through more than one vendor and some offer front end software for using many of these databases. It is at this point that the decision-making process can become complex. If a particular database is only offered by one vendor, the need to choose is eliminated; but issues of cost and ease of access are still relevant in deciding whether the database should be used at all. Even when a vendor offers the database on a pay-as-you-go basis the price can be high enough that the organization may need to consider some form of reimbursement from the user. The issue then becomes whether the users can and will accept charges. Some vendors require subscription fees in addition to usage fees which can further increase the cost of searching the database. The organization then has to decide, if charging the patron, whether to absorb the subscription fee or create some complex method of allocating it to each search. Other vendors have eliminated usage fees and charge high subscription fees which provide a certain number of hours of searching. With this system the organization has to predetermine if the usage will be high enough to justify the initial expenditure. To combat some of these problems there are vendors that give some types of institutions, such as universities, a choice of payment methods but they still generally require a high monetary commitment. After all of these considerations have been analyzed, the organization has to be concerned with the ability of the intended user to access the data.

While it is becoming commonplace for databases to be designed as user friendly systems, most databases still require some if not a significant level of training to be used effectively. If the system is menu driven, the user can do his or her own searching. But even menu driven systems often require someone who can help users get started, which may have staffing and cost implications for the organization. If the system is not menu driven, the organization needs to commit personnel to do the searching unless the users are a small group of intensive searchers who will in time learn the intricacies of the system.

If the process of identifying vendors results in a choice, the organization must make further decisions affecting cost and ease of access. In this case costs include the producer's fees, the vendor's fees, and the communication charges. The producer's charges will normally be the same for the same information, but the organization must be sure each vendor is actually providing the same database. The F & S Indexes on BRS include citations in the Prompt database (Ref. 1) but this is not the case on Dialog (Ref. 2). These discrepancies make cost comparisons rather difficult and are rarely noted in database directories. Even when the information in the databases are the same, vendors will often charge different access fees and have different communication charges. Access fees not only vary in terms of cost per minute of searching but can also vary in the way they are computed. Some vendors, in addition to per minute costs, charge for data points or data elements, or CPU's (computer processing units) used which adds to the frustration of predetermining the cost of using the system. The choice of a vendor also determines the amount you will pay for communication charges. Although most vendors allow access through the major systems such as Telenet and Tymnet, not every vendor allows access through all systems and the charge for using the same system can vary. If an organization does not have local access to the system in use, a long distance or Watts charge must be added into the cost of searching. But finding the cheapest database is not necessarily the solution. Consideration needs to be given to the efficiency of conducting a search on a given system.

The determination of a system's level of efficiency involves at least three concerns. First is the question of searching the system with certain types of input. Using Dialog it is impossible to search PsycInfo by the accession number, but on BRS the accession number is searchable. If this capability were important to the searches an organization expected to conduct, it would make BRS the more efficient system. Second there is the question of whether specific segments of data can be obtained without printing larger segments of data. Although access to Disclosure has been offered for years by many vendors, until recently it was only possible on systems like ADP to obtain segments of data such as the management statement without printing a major portion of the total record. Having to print significantly more of a record than is needed could increase the cost of doing a search and possibly result in a reluctance to use the system. Therefore it is necessary to look at the forms in which output is received on a given system, to measure its effectiveness for a given purpose. The third issue is the ability to manipulate the data while conducting a search. It is a common occurrence to start a search by putting in a series of terms then find that the terms need to be related using different proximity or Boolean operators, or that some terms need to be eliminated. Dialog offers a relatively simple method for doing this if the terms have been set up in "steps," because each term receives its own set number which can then be rearranged. In contrast some systems are structured in a manner that makes this process difficult or necessitates retyping the search statement. The result can be the use of more online time to complete the search which in turn can make the search more costly, even if the per minute charge is less. Each of these issues affects the desirability of using a particular system and should be considered when selecting a vendor. When organizations make these decisions for many databases they may find that they are contracting with a number of vendors which raises the question of how a searcher is going to master the various systems.

Some vendors have answered the question of searching multiple systems with front end software which is designed to make access easier. But this creates its own set of problems which affect cost and efficiency. Some front end software such as Wilsearch is designed to help search the databases produced by one company while others such as Prosearch are designed to allow searching many systems with one set of input. The purpose of front end software is to allow searching without the person learning complex multiple command systems, in essence it makes searching easier. But doing this reduces the specificity of the output increasing the amount of irrelevant information obtained. The result being a trade off between ease of access and effective search results. To compensate for the less efficient system which requires less sophisticated programming, the cost of using the system is reduced. While this may be a satisfactory answer for the casual end user who does their own searching, it may increase the problems for the serious searcher. Even if a person finds that front end software satisfies some of their needs, most serious searchers will at times find the need to be much more specific to adequately complete many searches. Therefore, they will still need to know the more complex strategies. The result being that they will have had less experience using them if they have relied primarily on front end systems, and the front end techniques simply become one more system to learn. While front end systems can help in certain situations and may encourage some people to search that might otherwise be reluctant, they have definite limitations and may ultimately be just another option allowed the searcher rather than a relief from the complexities of searching.

WHICH SYSTEM TO SEARCH?

Once an organization has selected the vendors and possibly the front end software they are going to use, the situation may occur where a searcher has a choice of systems in gaining access to a particular database. This decision may include a choice of direct access among various vendors, of using front end software, or of using gateways which vendors are often providing to allow quick and easy access to the systems of other vendors. These issues involve the same concerns of cost and ease of access which were relevant to contracting with specific vendors. The burden of making the decision is simply shifted to the searcher, with the added concern of whether to use a gateway. The main advantages of using gateways are eliminating the need to completely sign off and sign on another system, and retrieving data from two or more systems in similar formats. The question of signing off and on can provide some measure of convenience, but with communication packages providing automatic sign on this is of limited benefit. The second issue of retrieving data in like formats is similar to the use of front end software in that it reduces the variety of formats encountered, but differs in that gateways eliminate variation in output while front end systems eliminate variation in input. But like front end software this might not be the most efficient or effective method of searching a particular system.

A searcher who has access to Dialog and Westlaw would have the choice of searching Dialog directly or using Westlaw's gateway to Dialog. When searching directly, responses from the system scroll across the screen and into the printer or another form of storage selected. In contrast when Dialog is accessed through Westlaw's gateway service, the data is received page-by-page and must be printed accordingly, requiring more online time. While this page-by-page method of retrieval may be an efficient way to search the full text Westlaw database allowing the searcher to view the results, it is often an inefficient method of accessing Dialog's many bibliographic databases which do not require viewing. Therefore the searcher must make another decision between cost and ease of access in deciding which method is best for a given search. To ease the burden of the searcher having to weigh these factors each time they search, an organization might want to predetermine how a given database or system will be accessed. Of course doing so limits the flexibility a searcher has in determining what is best for a given search.

CONCLUSION

The issues discussed in this paper are presented with the intent of giving the reader an overview of the many factors that affect the selection of databases. While many of these concerns are appropriate to the selection of other forms of technology such as compact disk, the focus is on the selection of online systems. The process of examining each of these factors should provide a basis for the decisions necessary to an orderly and thorough determination of an organizations needs. The intended result being more efficient and effective use of resources, and ultimately better service to patrons.

1. BRS Information Technologies. _PTSP Database Guide_. Latham, New York: BRS Information Technologies, October, 1986.

2. Dialog Information Retrieval Service. _PTS F & S Indexes: Bluesheet_. Palo Alto, California: Dialog Information Retrieval Service, September, 1986.

PROMOTING MEDICAL LITERATURE DATABASES TO THE PHYSICIAN END-USER

Christine A. Olson, Chris Olson & Associates, Karen Hackleman, University of Maryland, and Robert E. Kristofco, West Virginia University

Keywords: Marketing Research, Educational promotion strategies, Physician end-user, Online training, MEDLINE, West Virginia, Medical literature databases.

Abstract: The physician market segment promises to be a lucrative one for database producers seeking to develop new customer bases for their online products. Developing a marketing program for promoting medical literature databases to physicians requires an understanding of the physician's knowledge of computers, databases and willingness to learn and utilize searching techniques to locate patient care information.

In 1987, The National Library of Medicine's Southeastern/Atlantic Regional Medical Library Service (SE/A RMLS), sponsored by a coalition of West Virginia healthcare organizations, conducted a study to determine an effective way of introducing physicians in West Virginia to seven medical literature databases containing MEDLINE. Three different educational promotion sessions; a one- and-a-half hour overview; a half-day briefing; and a full-day session featuring hands-on practice, were conducted by librarians in four geographic locations within the state. Through observation, questionnaires, telephone interviews, and phone inquiries to a toll-free telephone number, each of the three session designs were tested to determine which would generate the greatest response by attending physicians and be the most effective in introducing medical literature databases to practicing physicians.

The presentation will include the study design, data collection protocols, evaluation methods, and the roles of librarians as educators. Outcomes of the study will be summarized and recommendations for marketing medical literature databases to physician end-users in a state such as West Virginia.

1. BACKGROUND

This study was follow-up to the 1986 Continuing Medical Education (CME) survey conducted by the CME offices of West Virginia University and Marshall University schools of medicine (Ref. 2). The 1986 study identified CME practices, preferences, and utilization patterns of West Virginia physicians, and included two questions related to learning resource preferences and uses of computers. Of the approximate 3,000 physicians in West Virginia, over a third (1,211 physicians) responded. Over 79% ranked medical journals as their first learning choice, while current medical textbooks ranked second (64%). More than 51% of the CME study respondents said that they used no computer equipment in any aspect of their office/clinical practice. Interest in computer searches of the medical literature (36.8%) and the availability of computerized national data bases (28.6%) ranked well below the first two traditional forms of literature research.

The results of the CME survey sent a clear message: although national medical initiatives point to increased reliance on computerized access, West Virginia physicians, as a group, were not following the national trend. If the majority of the state's physicians continued to rely on the printed page for information in a medical profession rapidly converting to computer-based information transfer, there could be serious implications for the quality of future health care in West Virginia.

One outcome of the CME survey was the realization that an in-depth study would be needed before any state-wide corrective plan could be initiated. The West Virginia healthcare organizations needed to understand the best ways to interest physicians in computerized access to information. This paper is a report on the follow-up study to the CME survey. The study was designed to provide practicing West Virginia physicians with an awareness of the variety of medical literature data bases available in today's marketplace, as well as to identify effective methods of introducing physicians in West Virginia to computerized literature data bases.

2. DESIGN

The 388 physicians who requested individual follow-up on the 1986 CME survey became the target population for determining an effective way of introducing physicians in West Virginia to seven medical literature data bases. The National Library of Medicine's (NLM) MEDLINE was the common link among all the database systems introduced to physicians. The study tested three different CME educational promotion sessions: one-and-a-half hour, half-day, and full-day (six hours). The shortest session gave a brief overview of all seven database systems. The half-day session not only gave this brief review, but also provided examples of actual searches conducted on each system. The full-day session also included hands-on experience with the different database systems.

3. OBJECTIVES AND HYPOTHESES

This study's primary objective was to identify an effective method to introduce West Virginia physicians to computer-based literature data bases. Other complimentary objectives included: (1) to reveal logistical strengths and weaknesses of conducting a session to introduce such databases to physicians; (2) to predict the response of physicians to such educational offerings; (3) to develop effective promotional messages to announce computerized access to data bases; (4) to lay the groundwork to make West Virginia's medical librarians more knowledgeable of such database systems; (5) to increase primary care physicians' awareness of the value of database systems in the delivery of health care; (6) to identify market penetration projections; (7) to outline resources needed to conduct a state-wide promotion of computer-based information services; and (8) to identify roles West Virginia healthcare partners can play in this promotion.

We also developed a number of hypotheses to further guide study design parameters and test results from the 1986 CME survey.

4. APPROACH

We developed a matrix that outlined the three different educational promotion sessions and their geographic distribution around the state. Figure 1, Educational Promotion Study Matrix, shows the final session matrix, listing the three sessions, their times, and their locations in West Virginia.

Because the NLM's MEDLINE is probably the most well-known medical literature data base in the healthcare community, we decided that MEDLINE should be the common link among all the systems introduced to physicians in study sessions. Seven database systems were covered in all study sessions: NLM MEDLARS, DIALOG Medical Connection, BRS Colleague, Grateful Med, EasyLink's Medscan, PaperChase, and AMANET. The database systems reviewed during study sessions provided a variety of access and interaction examples.

```
                  Martinsburg  Clarksburg  Charleston  Princeton
          (Test Site)
-----------------------------------------------------------------
#1. Briefing      6/5 Fri     6/18 Thurs  6/19 Fri    6/20 Sat
8:30am - 10:00am
-----------------------------------------------------------------
#2. Half-Day      6/5 Fri     6/18 Thurs  6/19 Fri    6/20 Sat
    Workshop
8:30am -12:00
-----------------------------------------------------------------
#3. Training      6/6 Sat     6/18 Thurs  6/19 Fri    6/20 Sat
    Seminar
9:00am - 3:00pm
-----------------------------------------------------------------
```

Figure 1.   Educational Promotion Study Matrix

We developed an information folder to distribute at the beginning of each session. In addition to containing general information (the participant's profile questionnaire, glossary of computer terms, description of microcomputer equipment, and a graphic illustrating boolean logic), the folder also contained an agenda of the data bases to be discussed, as well as a one-page fact sheet and sample search on each data base. Each database system was introduced by using its one-page fact sheet description. The fact sheets provided the following information about each system: (1)brief description, (2) equipment needed, (3)basic costs, (4)special features, and (5)available training.

We conducted sample searches on each data base to show the differences between search strategies and end-user interaction with each system. The topic of the sample searches was "current treatment of peripheral vascular disease." Each data base was allotted equal in-session time and subject coverage. At the end of each session, participants were given promotional pieces, provided by individual vendors.

Originally, we thought that the sessions would be led by librarians who were experienced in teaching on-line database seminars. However, after careful consideration, we decided to abandon this approach in favor of utilizing practicing West Virginia librarians. There were several reasons for adopting this approach. First, we hoped to strengthen the bond between the librarians and physicians. Second, although the librarians in West Virginia were familiar with on-line database searching, their knowledge usually spanned only one or two systems. If the librarians learned to lead the study sessions, they would have an opportunity to broaden their knowledge of available systems. Finally, bringing the librarians together would help to foster and strengthen the West Virginia medical library network.

In an attempt to maintain contact with the study participants, to answer their questions, and monitor their progress toward adopting computers and access to literature data bases, two sets of telephone interviews were conducted. They monitored the progress of the physician, thus facilitating the evaluation and prediction of effective methods of introducing physicians to computerized medical literature data bases.

To create opportunities for answering questions, establishing personal network links, and encouraging physicians to utilize computerized literature data bases, we made a toll-free telephone number available to all study participants through the offices of SE/A RMLS.

5. STUDY ACTIVITIES AND RESEARCH TOOLS

The study sessions were scheduled in early June of 1987. The invitations were mailed to physicians in the middle of May, and another mailing followed several weeks later. Additionally, an announcement urging attendance appeared in the journal of the West Virginia Medical Society. Of the 62 physicians who signed up for the sessions, 35 actually participated.

A 24-question survey instrument established baseline profiles of the physicians who participated in the study. A Quick Status Check Evaluation Form was administered to session attendees immediately after each session. With this "Quick Status Check" we sought to measure the intended actions of physicians and obtain immediate feedback on the sessions. This information supplemented that gathered from the two sets of follow-up, status-check telephone interviews that were conducted six weeks and six months after the sessions.

6. FINDINGS

One unexpected outcome of the sessions was the large number of other healthcare professionals who received information from the physicians who attended the sessions. Of the 35 attendees, 19 passed information to 99 others, including nurses, office managers, physicians, librarians, and hospital administrators.

Of the three time durations offered in this study, the half-day session consistently proved the least popular.

Proximity to physicians' homes or offices contributed to their willingness to participate in learning sessions.

Physicians needed criteria for selecting database services. The lack of criteria prohibited some physicians from purchasing computer equipment and accessing database systems.

This study attracted a significant number of physicians who did not utilize computers, but found the subject of interest.

Approximately 97% (34) of the respondents stated a belief that information obtained from medical literature data bases, such as the ones they learned about in this study, could impact the quality of care provided to their patients.

Five physicians began subscriptions to medical literature database systems as a result of this study. Of the 16 physicians who did not own a computer in June, but said they were going to purchase one, 11 made such a purchase within six months.

In the six months after attending the study sessions, 57% of the participants requested medical literature database searches.

Video tapes were the learning method of choice among study participants. The least preferred learning methods were TV segments and audio tapes.

7. RECOMMENDATIONS

We made a number of recommendations to West Virginia healthcare organizations as a result of this study. Of these, we considered the following five to be critical to the success of future medical information network development activities in West Virginia. They can be applied to states with similar geographic and physician population characteristics.

Recommendation 1. Develop profile notebooks or information packages containing reprint articles, reviews, comparisons and purchase information on computer systems and medical literature data bases. Offer these directly to interested physicians and through medical libraries.

Discussion: We found that many physicians were not familiar or comfortable with computer jargon, medical literature data bases, or telecommunication procedures. Several of the physicians who participated in this study made unsuccessful attempts to obtain information from local computer dealers. Many of the phone calls received on our toll-free telephone line were requests for comparative data to facilitate the physician's decision-making. Physicians consistently expressed frustration regarding their lack of time to learn about the details of computerized access to the literature.

Recommendation 2. Identify the target market segments to receive promotional messages on computers and medical literature data bases. Develop promotional messages directed to each market segment, taking care to address that segment's specific information needs and interest level, based on knowledge and interest characteristics.

Discussion: At the conclusion of the study, we realized that physicians, as a group, were at different points on the computer and medical literature database learning curve. It is not worthwhile to initiate a promotional effort without considering these differences. Vendors, medical librarians, and organizations seeking to penetrate the physician marketplace need to segment the market into knowledge groups, and then develop their messages based on the physicians' knowledge levels.

Recommendation 3. Establish more telecommunication nodes in the state.

Discussion: One of the drawbacks to accessing computer data bases was the lack of telecommunication modes in West Virginia. During this study at least one physician signed up for a vendor service and later dropped it because his closest telecommunication node required a long-distance telephone call. Other states with large rural areas may face the same dilemma.

Recommendation 4. Offer video learning tapes to interested physicians, hospital staff and medical librarians.

Discussion: Although a large number of physicians enjoyed personal database demonstrations, the majority of physicians, when provided the option, preferred to learn about computers and database systems by viewing video tapes in their office or home. This preference complimented the study's findings that many physicians were unable to attend educational promotion sessions due to prior commitments and time constraints. Video tapes would provide learning opportunities at each physician's convenience.

Recommendation 5. Establish a medical computer users' network, working group, or special interest group.

Discussion: Several physicians in this study were identified as being individuals who could organize user networks and who other physicians would respect and seek out for advice and information. Establishing a support network database users appears to be a cost-effective way to provide continuing support for the various market segments throughout rural states like West Virginia. The network also would permit timely distribution of database enhancements and would facilitate product testing.

8. CONCLUSIONS

While we recognize the study's limitations, it is apparent to us that educational promotion strategies should assume characteristics found in our study in order for the promotion to be successful with similar physician populations. We believe our study findings provide valuable baseline data for initiating a plan of action aimed at introducing West Virginia physicians to medical literature data bases. We also believe the study parameters are portable to other medical information settings where there is a need to know the best way to introduce medical online capabilities to a population of healthcare providers.

9. NOTES

1. Ms. Hackleman was formerly a Coordinator with Southeastern/Atlantic Regional Medical Library Service.

2. This study was conducted under the auspices of SE/A RMLS, one of seven regional medical library programs administered by the NLM. Funding for this study came from the following sponsors: West Virginia State Medical Association, West Virginia University School of Medicine Office of Continuing Medical Education, Charleston Area Medical Center Office of Continuing Education, West Virginia Hospital Association, University Health Associates and SE/A RMLS (Region 2). Facilities, technical resources and expertise were provided by City Hospital in Martinsburg, United Hospital Center in Clarksburg, Charleston Area Medical Center in Charleston, and Princeton Community Hospital in Princeton, West Virginia.

A PROTOTYPE CLUSTERING PROGRAM

Miranda Lee Pao, The University of Michigan

Keywords: software design, software development, clustering retrieval

Abstract: An integrated front-end system is planned for the enhancement of online database retrieval. A merger program has been developed to merge records from downloaded files from SCISEARCH and MEDLINE. Another program is also under development. The objective of this software is to develop a clustering program to be used as a back-end add-on to the merger program. An early version of the program used on an IBM-PC has been shown to cluster a set of documents according to the co-occurrences of content-bearing words found in the titles. As a result, the output from the program consists of groups of records whose content shows more subject similarity. It is therefore possible to form a partial cluster hierarchy so that a list of records ranked according to their probability of relevance may be displayed as eventual output. Various constraints and design considerations are discussed.

1. INTRODUCTION

As part of a larger research project, a front-end merger program has been developed such that for the same query, a searcher could merge two retrieved sets derived from SCISEARCH using relevant citation searching and from keyword searching from databases such as MEDLINE.[1] On demand from the searcher, the program is able to present the union and/or intersection from the two searches. Preliminary results showed that the union and intersection could provide improved recall and precision respectively.[2] At the moment, an experiment is underway to learn more about the relative retrieval characteristics resulting from using terms and from using citations in subject searching in operational settings. Since increased recall is often accompanied by larger number of retrieved items, a logical extension is to build a ranking algorithm so that documents in the retrieved set could be ordered by some probability of relevance to the originating query. This paper presents the rationale and design for the development of one such ranking program.

All operational retrieval systems are based on Boolean search logic and with only a few exceptions, documents are represented by subject terms in most systems. The retrieved set must contain only those documents with representations matching exactly the specified representations from the query. Although the file structure design is simple and retrieval is efficient, defects of the Boolean model is well-known. The recent chapter appearing in the Annual Review of Information Science and Technology by Belkin and Croft [3] reviews the problems of retrieval techniques which are based on the principle of exact match of the query representations with that of the documents. They state that the simple exact match:

1. misses many relevant documents whose representations only partially match those of the query;
2. does not rank the output set;
3. cannot incorporate the relative importance of concepts found in either the query or the documents;
4. requires complex query formulation; and
5. demands the use of a common vocabulary between the searcher and the indexer.

2. THE BASIS OF RANKING TECHNIQUES

In spite of the lack of precision in systems evaluation, there is common agreement that almost all techniques using some partial match mechanisms produce far superior retrieval results than strictly Boolean retrieval. Belkin and Croft [3] provide a comprehensive classification and a systematic survey of retrieval techniques based on partial matching principles. The basis of partial matching of query with document representatives is that a more relaxed requirement is imposed on the retrieved set. The representatives for the candidate document need not match exactly those of the query in order for the document to qualify as a member of the retrieved set. The result is a set of documents with varying degrees of relevance to the query. Since the matching procedure must monitor the level of relevance associated with each document with respect to the query, the relevant data could also be used to rank the document set. This basic principle is at the heart of probabilistic retrieval. In other words, the larger the overlap, the higher the probability of relevance between the query and the document. Obviously for the same query, the set resulted from an exact match retrieval technique is a proper subset of the output from a partial matching algorithm. Thus, an ordered list may be produced such that the most relevant items could be displayed first. Such a ranked output enables the user to control both the quantity and quality of items to be used.

Based on the above principle, a ranked order may be implemented by using a number of different characteristics. Two categories are distinguished by Belkin and Croft. The first group of techniques is based on a direct comparison of the attributes of the document with those of the query. The second relies on a subject structure of the document collection. Documents are connected to other documents in the collection on the basis of their shared content attributes. Thus, a network-like structure may be defined on the collection in which each document represents a node and each linkage between two documents is an edge. Retrieval means initially finding one or more documents which could then lead to other similar documents via linkages found in the network structure. There are a variety of actual ranking techniques implementing such document structure for retrieval purpose.

Although probabilistic retrieval is theoretically sound, thus far its implementation has yet to be realized. The main obstacle involves considerable data manipulations and processing either at the indexing or the retrieval stage. For example, the single link or one-way connection between two documents commonly used to calculate the similarity between documents involves the comparison of every other pair of documents in the file. For a collection of n items, this means a total of n x n comparisons. For even a moderate collection size, a staggering amount of computation is needed. Additionally, an enormous workspace in the computer is required and it would also necessitate massive storage requirements. Although very few studies have ever reported the response time of probabilistic searching, near instant turnaround time is expected by searchers today. It is understandable that most of these partial matching techniques have been demonstrated with small samples. On the other hand in almost all cases, these experimental efforts have been shown to produce much improved retrieval. Thus, problems of implementation should not invalidate the soundness of these approaches.

To overcome some of the requirements needed for operational applications, some researchers have proposed ways to modify the computationally intensive procedures. In recent years, some have also advocated that not only further experimental efforts should be made, but interim solutions should also be found to improve operational retrieval systems. Two outstanding examples in this latter direction are the ZOOM facility on the ESA-IRS system [4] and the SIRE retrieval system developed by the research team formerly associated with Syracuse University.[5] After an initial search, the ZOOM feature allows the seacher to display a frequency ranked list of descriptors in the retrieved set. Further improvements have been reported recently.[6] ZOOM is now incorporated into AUTOSEARCH which can perform frequency analysis of defined fields found in a set of records with various display capabilities. Such a word list could suggest other semantically related terms for the refinement of the initial search. Although AUTOSEARCH does not produce ranked output, in bringing the searcher closer to the vocabulary of the indexer, it could improve both recall and precision. SIRE is an operational system which provide a ranked list of retrieval output based on their probability of relevance to the incoming query. It is implemented on the microcomputer. An ordering function is defined on the document set based on the frequencies of term occurrences of records in the retrieved set. Although the exact algorithm is not entirely clear from the documentations, it is the only operational system with the ranked output capability.

3. A CLUSTERING TECHNIQUE

The ranking technique developed for the present project is designed for the union set derived from term and citation searching in order to achieve a meaningful order of the retrieved items. One can expect no more than 400-500 items in an average retrieved set. As a result, the problems of large-scale storage and intensive computation need not be a concern. A cluster-based approach to probabilistic retrieval is used.[7] Basically, the set is partitioned into groups with similar content. To generate any cluster configuration requires knowledge of each member of the set so that linkages can be set up between related members. Conceptually, this usually means the construction of a matrix so that the level of linkage between every member with every other member in the set may be kept. The strength of linkage is known as association or similarity measure. Fewer clusters of larger size may be formed if the requirement for membership is a minimal similarity value. On the other hand, many clusters, each with fewer members, may be formed if the criterion for membership is a higher degree of similarity. An arbitrarily determined level of similarity required of all documents for membership in clusters is sometimes known as the threshold value for the cluster configuration. Thus, successive partitionings of the same document set can be conducted starting with a low threshold value of zero, and ending with the highest possible threshold value of one which would then split the set into document cluster groups of single membership. If larger clusters are successively split into smaller and smaller groups, obviously a partial cluster hierarchy could be automatically formed.[8]

One of the first decisions was to select an appropriate similarity measure. In theory, it is possible to generate this value on the basis of co-occurrences of any content indicators such as common citations, references, index terms, or title words between every other pair of documents. In fact, the degree of similarity between every other pair of document could even be subjectively decided upon, although the task would require an inordinate amount of human effort. If an algorithm is to be used, the chosen content indicator must be present in all the bibliographic records of the set. Index terms could not be used since SCISEARCH does not include descriptors in its bibliographic citation output. To compute the similarity measures based on co-citations requires additional online searching. Data required for bibliographic coupling, which is a term denoting the measures of co-references, could not be obtained on the SCISEARCH file on the DIALOG system. For testing and demonstration purposes of the biomedical data from SCISEARCH and MEDLINE, content-bearing title words were used to test the prototype system.

4. DESIGN CONSIDERATIONS

Although several programs have been written to perform clustering, all have been developed for specific experiments using either a mainframe or minicomputer, such as the one used by Garland.[8] None are able to accept raw data directly. Turbo Pascal has been selected as the programming language for this project. Since Turbo Pascal has been used for the previous merger program, it was easier to continue the developmental work using the same language. It is also one of the best programming languages for the PC due to its elegance, its speed, and its ease of use. It is also widely known to programmers. Additionally, since a compiled version could be used on the IBM PC, it would be possible to test the system on various sites. The set of program has been developed for use on an IBM PC. An array is used to store each document. Linked list is the chosen data structure to represent the matrix of similarity measures. Documents are linked to each other by pointers. Since many cells are left with no values, this data structure is efficient in conserving unused space. At the specification of a threshold value, the program is able to produce a set of mutually exclusive clusters of documents. Members of each cluster are identified by their numeric document identifiers.

The program is able to accept data in two coded formats:

1. All documents in the set must be coded as integers. The first

column contains all coded document identifiers. For example, the first document would be represented as "1". Associated with each document identifier is a list of numbers. The first number represents the total number of unique content-bearing words found in the title of document # 1. The rest of the list consists of pairs of integers. The second of each number pair is the document number with which the document # 1 has at least one common title word. The first of each pair is the number of common words found between the document pair. A zero marks the end of the list of numbers associated with the original document.

2. In the second coded format, all documents in the set must also be coded as integers. The first column contains the coded document identifiers. In this format, the similarity measure between every other pairs of document must first be computed. Associated with each document identifier is a list of numbers which comprises several sub-lists. Each sub-list is headed by a similarity measure represented by a real number, for example, 0.40, which is followed by a series of integers which are the document identifiers representing those documents which have been found to associate with the original document at the specified similarity level of 0.40. Again, a zero marks the end of the series of sub-lists for the given original document.

The program has been tested on a collection of 400 bibliographic records. It is able to produce:

400 clusters at the 0.90 threshold level, (3 clusters of 2 members, and 397 clusters of single membership),
214 clusters at the 0.50 threshold level,
121 clusters at the 0.40 threshold level,
100 clusters at the 0.38 threshold level,
 46 clusters at the 0.00 threshold level, and so on.

By clustering the set at several threshold levels, a ranked list emerges. The response time to cluster 400 documents is slow. At the moment, one must refer to the bibliographic citations by their numbers. Moreover, the program cannot accept data input in bibliographic record format. However, future plan calls for the full capability to automate the computation of similarity measures between any pairs of bibliographic records based on their common title words. A sub-routine could accept the bibliographic records as input data. It will proceed to assign consecutive numeric document identifiers, and incorporate a checking procedure to eliminate a list of trivial words.

ACKNOWLEDGEMENT

The publication is supported in part by NIH grants R01-LM-04677 and K04-LM-00078 from the National Library of Medicine.

REFERENCES

1. Pao, M.L. "Developing a Front-end Integrating Keyword and Citation Retrieval," Proceedings of the 8th National Online Meeting, 379-386, 1987.

2. Pao, M.L. and D.B. Worthen. "Retrieval Effectiveness by Semantic and Pragmatic Relevance," Journal of American Society for Information

Science. (to appear)

3. Belkin, N.J. & W.B. Croft. "Retrieval Techniques," in Annual Retrieval of Information Science and Technology, edited by Martha Williams, Volume 22. While Plains, Mew York: Knowledge Industry Publications, Inc. for the American Society for Information Science, 1987. p.109-145.

4. Ingwersen, P. "A Cognitive View of Three Selected Online Search Facilities," Online Review, 8(5):465-492, 1984.

5. Koll, M.B., Noreault, T. and M.J. McGill. "Enhanced Retrieval Techniques On A Microcomputer," Proceedings of 5th National Online Meeting, 165-170, 1984.

6. Martin, W.A. "Autosearch: A Proposed Clustering Procedure for the Automatic Searching of Online Information Retrieval Systems," Proceedings of 7th National Online Meeting, 295-305, 1986.

7. Goffman, W. "The Indirect Method of Information Retrieval," Information Storage and Retrieval, 4:361-373, 1968.

8. Garland, K. "An Experiment in Automatic Hierarchical Document Classification," Information Processing and Management, 19(3):113-120, 1983.

PICTURE PERFECT

Allen W. Paschal, DataTimes

"Picture Perfect" is about emerging trends and technologies available for storing images in high resolution retrievable formats, and how you and I might be routinely retrieving photos and graphic displays from stored archives in the same manner we retrieve full text or abstract information from today's online providers.

To understand my presentation, you must understand my perspective. "Picture Perfect" is about the potential for stored image archiving in the newspaper and magazine publishing environment.

Today, DataTimes automates the old manual clip and file systems commonly found at almost all metropolitan daily newspapers. Text is captured from an editorial system and electronically copied and stored with little human manipulation. This same text can be retrieved and displayed in full text form in a matter of seconds from almost any computer terminal, anywhere.

DataTimes provides these automated library and archiving systems to newspaper/magazine publishers throughout the world. In addition, DataTimes resells this electronic archive information to commercial businesses for competitive and daily decision research needs.

Why are pictures important? If you read an article which describes the fireworks display and celebration surrounding America's Bicentennial several years ago, an article would tell you about the display of light and fireworks in the sky with the Statue of Liberty in the foreground, while celebrating revelers and patriotic themes abound. Those words are very descriptive. However, the old saying is still good, "A picture is worth a thousand words".

A photo of the fireworks display of the Statue of Liberty tells all instantaneously. It evokes emotion and relays the colorful and patriotic moment of the day.

Today we can only retrieve the factual; the words. In the future we hope to retrieve the emotion; the images. The industry's goal is to provide retrieval of the factual and the emotion through a combination delivery of words and images.

The storage of old clipping files was begun to serve the editorial research needs, and to preserve history. Today, those efforts are enhanced through the automated archiving of information. No longer will clipping files turn crusty and disintegrate. The same is true of photos and images. The need to preserve history and to make it more accessible and useful is the challenge we face.

Not only do we have the need to satisfy the emotion and message delivered by images, but there are more tangible and compelling reasons why newspaper and magazine publishers will ultimately be the

first to incorporate a daily image archiving solution in their businesses. There are administrative and economic reasons why stored images will quickly be incorporated into their environments.

Presently, archival images are hard to get to. They have been filed over the past 100 years by multiple different librarians under multiple different categorizing systems. Often it takes hours or days to find a specific photo filed in over 80 or more file cabinets. In some cases, these file cabinets will become so large and so numerous that they can actually be housed on different floors in publishers buildings; which brings up the issue of space. Filing cabinets take space; precious space. In a society which experiences the growth we have seen over the last several decades, space in urban buildings is a prime consideration. Most metropolitan publishers are located in the head of these crowded urban centers. Photo and image filing cabinets takes up precious space.

And finally, the administrative issues of deterioration of stored images in a paper form, and the ability to lose this information can damage the quality of the historical archives.

But far beyond any administrative (and perhaps sometimes intangible) reasons why publishers will incorporate this technology, and incorporate it soon, is the development of the electronic still camera. Papers are being driven to incorporate the electronic camera in their daily operation. The economics of moving away from metal based film operations are tremendously favorable. Publishers will not necessarily choose to incorporate the electronic still camera, but they will be driven to it by economics.

Publishers will thus be driven to electronic archiving. If they have an electronic still camera, they almost have to have electronic archiving. It doesn't make much sense to go from an electronic format back to a paper format.

How many times is an image or photo reused at a typical daily newspaper? What's the maximum number of times a photo is republished? We did some surveys and found that even a small metro paper could reuse 33 photos per week. Some photo could be reused as often as 7 times. I think these figures would surprise almost any layman.

The entire production of a newspaper/magazine is going electronic. The handling of images has been following that trend, but has yet to be perfected. Associated Press and other wire services are already experimenting with digital transmission of images. Pagination systems, the ability to maneuver an entire page with text and images on a screen, are being tested in many large metropolitan newspapers. And finally, scanning capabilities and new high resolution cameras allow electronic storage of images as they are produced on a daily basis.

It is anticipated that image archiving solutions will be mostly adapted to WORM technology. CDROM has the capability to compress more data, but in the daily environment for newspaper/magazine publishers, the turnaround time to press and produce a CDROM is unacceptable. The ability to transfer from paper or digital means from the production system directly into the archive on a real time basis is critical.

Other interesting questions revolve around resolution and re-use of the stored image. Resolution quality continues to improve. USA

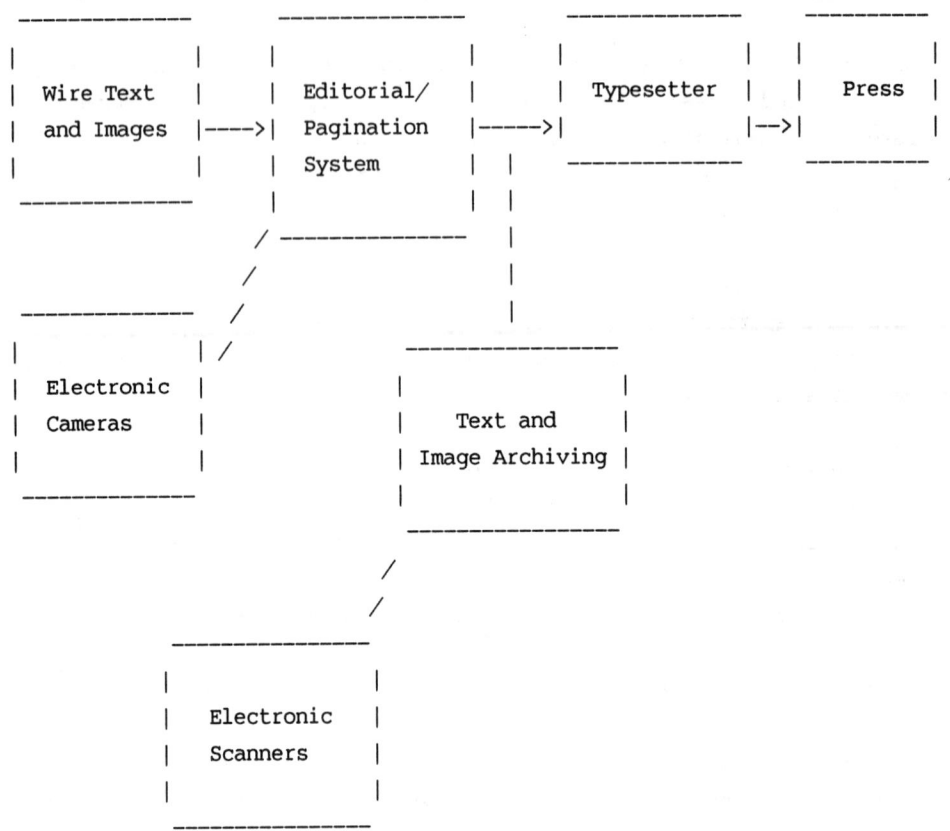

TODAY, reproduces images or photos at 133 lines of resolutions. We currently have the capability to store images at 500 lines, but only reproduce them at somewhere around 300 lines of resolution.

But another question is created by resolution. If we store with current technology at 500 lines of resolution, are we always committed to reproducing at 300-500 lines, or will we be able to reproduce at greater resolutions as new technologies emerge in the future?

It is evident that the electronic production of newspapers and magazines, and the introduction of the electronic still camera with its compelling administrative and economic reasons for its quick adaptation in the publishing environment, will force the technology of image archiving.

CD-ROM AND OPTICAL TECHNOLOGY: THE USER INTERFACE

Charles Peters, University of Arizona

Keywords: Graphics, User Interfaces, Interactivity, Libraries, Library Instruction, Graphic Displays.

Abstract: User interfaces that facilitate use of databases contained on CD-ROM are needed to increase the market for this alternative medium for dissemination of information. Interaction with the end-user is attained through instructions placed on the CD-ROM disc. This information is brought to the attention of the user through the interactive attributes of random access and still-framing of the CD-ROM drive while under personal computer control. Graphic displays are needed to simplify instruction to end-users in how to use both the computer hardware and in how to search for information embedded within the CD-ROM database. Graphic operating environments replacing the software supplied with personal computers which governs the CD-ROM drive are described. The assistance which graphics displays can give to end-users also enhances the acceptance of databases on CD-ROM in libraries.

Introduction:

The interactive attributes of optical discs such as CD-ROM are their best selling points to librarians. This interactivity is attained in CD-ROM optical technology because of the random access and still framing capability of the drive while under personal computer control. These features give designers the ability to offer simplified searching interfaces needed for the wide variety of end-users targeted as the primary market for the information contained with a CD-ROM disc. Similar types of users will also be encountered in an institutional setting such as a library.

User Interfaces for CD-ROM Databases:

Graphical user interfaces are desirable to use in conjunction with CD-ROM because of their ability to show the technical details of gaining access to the information contained within a particular database. A screen display of the function keys along with icons which illustrate their use on the specific personal computer governing access to the CD-ROM database can assist librariarns in introducing this technology into the reference area of a library.

Icons are useful in graphic displays because they are a symbol of the processing option they are meant to represent. Such visual and mnemonic devices are also useful in refreshing the searching skills of occasional users of the library in utilizing databases contained within this type of personal computer technology.

Use of Graphic Displays:

Computer-graphic displays can be used to highlight information which is needed to draw the attention of the user to the proper area on the keyboard or other input device utilized to gain access to the information contained within the CD-ROM database. The display monitor or CRT (cathode ray tube) connected to the personal computer hardware system is the primary candidate for the hardware devices needed to gain access to the database. The advantages which accrue in using icons within such a display are that they are more easily understood and take up less screen space than a textural description of their corresponding functions.

Ancillary instructional devices such as flip charts, loose-leaf books or instruction sheets posted on the machine are poor substitutes for direct instruction via the CRT in the use of databases embedded within CD-ROM technology.

Examples of Graphic Operating Systems:

There are many competing graphic operating system environments in existence at this time. Two which seem to be gaining acceptance are GEM (Graphics Environment Manager) from Digital Research and Microsoft Windows from the Microsoft Corporation. This latter company is also the developer of the MS-DOS and PC-DOS operating systems. The MS-DOS operating system is the one used in IBM compatible personal computers and the PC-DOS system is used in IBM personal computers.

Microsoft is doing much of the work in bringing out the operating system software which will be used in the new family of personal computers currently being introduced by IBM. These utilize a more propietary computing technology than has been the case to date in their existing systems. IBM PS/2 computers will have enhanced features for graphic displays over the ones now in use. It remains to be seen if integration of the variety of CD-ROM databases that is presently being accomplished with IBM compatible computers will present another set of challenges for librarians to overcome in introducing the new features of the PS/2 class of machines to end-users in the library. The Microsoft Windows operating environment will have compatibility with the operating system on this new IBM line of personal computers. This will do much to alleviate librarian's concerns about yet another system on which to offer instruction in database searching.

Apple Computer has done much work in enhancing the original concept of a graphical system for implementing a visually cued operating system environment for personal computers. However for a variety of reasons Apple class machines do not seem to be the medium of choice for system integrators to use in making database systems available with CD-ROM. The market impetus to developers to design independent hardware and software mechanisms for the Apple system of computers is smaller in relation to that for MS-DOS or PC-DOS class machines at this time.

Atari personal computers which received excellent reviews for the quality of their CRT monitors and use of graphic displays in its operating system does not seem to have received the market acceptance that MS-DOS class machines did for use with CD-ROM players. The Atari ST computer was marketed with the Grolier Encyclopedia on CD-ROM but this system did not attain the widespread consumer acceptance originally predicted for it.

High Sierra Group Standard for CD-ROM:

There is no existing standard for compatibility between user interfaces at the application level within personal computing operating systems. Even within the family of personal computers that can be accessed by MS-DOS class machines widespread variations can appear in CD-ROM databases. The types of interfaces used to access databases can range from command-driven systems emulating those used by the online systems to menu-driven systems with only a limited number of choices displayed on the monitor which the user needs to know.

The Graphic Environment Manager and Microsoft Windows:

The Graphic Environment Manager and Microsoft Windows facilitates the use of personal computers for novices to the use of such technology. This type of system replaces certain commands in the disk operating system (DOS) supplied with the personal computer. Software developers do this in order to design an easier method for mastering the commands necessary to use CD-ROM database contained within a given personal computer operating system.

Commands can be entered via a variety of standard input devices. Some of these devices are the computer keyboard, light pens, touch-screen panels, joysticks, mice and trackballs. The mouse is one type of pointing device widely used in different personal computer graphic display applications. It is a small hand-held device on wheels or rollers that records the amount and direction of motion applied by the user and converts it to a corresponding movement of the screen cursor. Switches on the top of the mouse are used to execute instructions from the user. Such instructions are given in menu form in a window or corner of the CRT and usually have a graphic display or icon of the task to be performed associated with them.

This type of graphic display allows users to intuitively grasp the tasks needing to be performed in order to attain the desired results from the CD-ROM database. It also allows bibliographic instruction in the use of the whole system of personal computer hardware needing specified tasks to be displayed such as printing bibliographic citations or full-text from the CD-ROM databases or downloading of the information in some other format.

Libraries and CD-ROM:

Bibliographic instruction in the use of the vast amount of full-text and other types of bibliographic databases to the wide variety of users encountered in a library is a major task for the librarian. The 550 to 640 megabyte storage capacity of an individual CD-ROM disc gives to publishers yet another means for dissemination of their information products. They now have the ability to publish and sell databases in an interactive format that emulate publication in electronic form by the online systems along with the information density attained by the printed page but with several more value-added features.

Publication of databases in personal computer format containing the huge amount information that a CD-ROM disc can store makes this technology a useful one for librarians to investigate as an another alternative to using printed books and online information services for dissemination of bibliographic information to a library's clientele.

The library is a large information storage and retrieval system as varied as it is complex. End-users of the databases being published within the CD-ROM technology arrive at the library with varying levels of computer literacy. Instruction to such users needs to be done by various methods. Such teaching can range from individual instruction in how to use a personal computer to advice on how to do a serarch involving logical operators with proximity operators for context searching in an abstracts database.

The content and compact storage format of databases in CD-ROM give the librarian attractive reasons for their purchase. Giving the end-user easy access to the huge amount of information stored on the CD-ROM disc will allow this format to achieve the consumer acceptance predicted for it. This popularity will give librarians even more reasons for purchase of databases and other products appearing in this interactive format.

Database producers using interactive programs as an alternative medium for dissemination of their products need to embed human factor research into them. The databases presently available in CD-ROM are using techniques taken from online technology through placement of both command mode menu-driven software in these products. The command mode allows professional searchers to access the data in a familiar environment while menu-driven software introduces interactive searching of databases under microcomputer control and allows for instruction to novice users.

Graphic interfaces, such as that used in the Apple Computer line of products, have done much to facilitate instruction in the use of microcomputers to novices. The MS-DOS class of machines now have Windows available to allow this type of graphical access also. Many other developers are bringing out interfaces for specialized uses. These graphic interfaces use different standards for interactive control over the content of the data embedded in the CD-ROM disc. The products presently available in CD-ROM utilize some techniques taken from these interfaces which allow new or infrequent users to intuitively search such databases.

Databases on CD-ROM with graphic interfaces that would easily allow the introduction of this technology to users would facilitate its acceptance in libraries. Enhancements such as placement of a map of the function keys on the screen and simulating an online search do assist the user in utilizing this technology. Further work in this area is needed in order to make CD-ROM information products more accessible to end-users. The developers of this technology have brought out many products that are being used in libraries. Further enhancements need to be done on the user interface to allow wide-spread consumer acceptance in order for CD-ROM technology not to founder on hardware and software issues in libraries.

USE OF A PC TO SEARCH IN JAPANESE ONLINE DATABASES

Wolfgang Pilch, INPADOC International Patent Documentation Center

Keywords: Kanji Alphabet, Communication Software, Automatic Translation, PATOLIS Database, INPADOC.

Abstract: PC's are a well established tool as workstations in searching online databases. They store and perform complicated LOGIN operations and search strategies, they even form convenient user interfaces to different database languages.
The power of these machines can be used in a much wider range. They can help to display and to print information even from online databases in Japanese language and they can assist the user of this information by translating basic Japanese phrases automatically into English.
Japanese hardware with all the options to display Kana and Kanji characters is not used outside Japan on a broad basis. Therefore it is necessary, that the software involved works with hardware which is generally accepted as a standard in Western countries.
Display of printouts of online information in Japanese language has to be passed on to the interpreter, if textual information is necessary.
For highly standardized texts, like the detailed bibliographic data shown in the PATOLIS database of JAPIO, the PC is a good translation tool. Phrases and bibliographic facts are sent from the database in Kanji characters, but are translated by the PC into English. In this Japanese patent database searches for bibliographic data and for the legal status of a document can be carried out even by people who cannot speak and read Japanese.

1 The impact of research and development

Recent studies (Ref. 1) show, that Japan becomes more and more "technological independent". Already in the early 1970 the balance for newly concluded license contracts was positive for Japan . Only the total balance taking into account earlier concluded contracts was negative until 1984.

As a consequence using the broad OECD indicator of output of highly research and development intensive industries the United States went into the red in 1984, whereas the more sophisticated national high-tech products indicator shows the first deficit in 1986.

These figures show, that there is knowledge in Japanese industries as a result to research and development which is worth looking into. A lot of this knowledge is documented properly in patent documents.

2 The impact of Japanese patent information

Patent documents are rated as the most complete source for technical knowledge. The Libesny study (Ref. 2) showed, that only a fraction of the information stored in patent documents also can be found in other forms of literature.
Japanese research catches up with Japanese productivity and the basis of Japanese products sold all over the world can be found in a well documented form in patent documents.
The number of Japanese patent documents issued every year is still increasing.

Year	Published Patent Applications
1983	225.800
1984	233.100
1985	264.400
1986	297.200
1987	>> 300.000 (estimated)

Due to the nature of the patent laws, translations of those applications are printed, when Japanese inventions become patents in other countries. However there is still a great number of domestic applications which don't get published in completely translated form. For those cases the patent community relies on well established abstract services like Chemical Abstracts or DERWENT.
The Japanese themselves prepare abstracts of the Japanese patent applications and sell those abstracts in printed form. The same abstracts prepared by JAPIO (Japanese Patent Information Organization) are made available online by Pergamon Orbit Infoline.
INPADOC (International Patent Documentation Center) in Vienna collects the bibliographic data of Japanese documents and makes them available online in the INPADOC file via ORBIT.

The consequence is, that most users don't try to get hands on the original data. The services mentioned above have their drawbacks, if you need extreme actuality or if you are interested in the status of a patent. It takes some months until abstracts are available and in the meantime only the original Japanese information is available. The legal status of a patent, namely informations concerning the granting process or information with regard to the validity of a patent after infringements or with regard to yearly fees cannot be found in Western languages.

3 Japanese patent online information

JAPIO runs its own online service covering Japanese patent and utility models as well as designs.
There is an international file delivered by INPADOC and a national Japanese file produced by JAPIO. This latter service called PATOLIS makes available bibliographic details including abstracts, as well as legal status information in Japanese language. It is even possible to printout facsimile copies of the

main drawing. In Japan this can be done online, whereas for other countries an offline printout of figures is possible. The start menue of the system, giving the coverage of the database is a good example of the different alphabets used:

```
*** PATOLIS ONLINE SERVICE ***      19:09:18
サービス： 日本特実   データベース蓄積期間, 件数
A： 公開特許  昭 46.07.01 - 昭 62.11.30   2942210
B： 公告特許  昭 30.01.01 - 昭 62.11.30   1242860
U： 公開実用  昭 46.07.01 - 昭 62.11.30   2700321
Y： 公告実用  昭 35.01.01 - 昭 62.11.30   1192980
審査経過は特許庁で昭 62.12.11 入力分迄
処理項目 [ 1:検索 2:照会 3:番号リスト ]
あなたの受注番号, ユーザーコード, 処理項目を入力して下さい
```

Fig. 1

Later we will se a PC generated translation of this table. PATOLIS covers the following data:

Unexamined Patent Applications 1971-   2,500,000 citations
Examined Patent Applications   1955-   1,200,000 citations
Legals Status Information   1964-

Additionally data concerning utility models, designs, trademarks and industriual property trials are stored. The system is well designed for Japanese needs and interacts with Japanese hardware handling the more than 4.000 characters of the Japanese Kanji alphabet.

4 Processing of Kanji-characters on a PC

Japanese writing is based on several alphabets. 500 A.C. Chinese pictographs were imported to Japan. This alphabet is called Kanji and forms the most important part of standard texts. The Japanese developed between 800 A.C. and 1100 A.C. a special alphabet, called Katakana, to express grammatical specialities of their language.
At the same time Japanese woman developed their own writing called Hiragana. Later Hiragana took over the original task of Katakana and Katakana was used to express Western words. Western technology was imported to Japan together with the Western words for said goods. Additionally the Japanese use Latin characters and arabic numbers as a subset of their writing.
Terminals and printers communicating with national Japanese databases therefore have to handle those three types of characters mentioned above.
ASCII characters (the normal alphabet) are no problem at all, but already the characters with numbers greater than 127 provide problems. IBM compatible equipment produces a special set of semigraphic characters, whereas Japanese equipment uses those characters for printing of Kana characters.
Kana characters as well as Latin characters are contained a second time in the character set which is used by Japanese databases. This set is based on the Japanese standard JIS C 6226 (now

JIS X 9051). This standard defines a square matrix (94 columns with 94 rows, i.e. 8.836 cells) which can be used to define characters with a two character code.
For standard texts only the first 47 rows are used. Within this subset 2.966 Kanji characters are defined.
Kanji characters are pictograms derived from the Chinese writing, which was developed more than 3.500 years ago. These characters are used now in a modernized style, but they need a higher resolution than our alphabet.
Simple printers use only 5 x 7 dots to display Western characters, whereas 16 x 16 dots are necessary to display Kanji characters.
As a standard PC has a character generator for Latin characters (ASCII character set) only, Kanji characters must be generated in graphic mode. Standard graphic mode works with 320 points per line, therefore only 20 characters with 16 points can be displayed. The Enhanced Graphic Adaptor (EGA) mode works with 640 points. Using this graphic mode a program can write 40 characters per line with 16 points width per character.

Printers can print such 16 x 16 characters, if they work in graphics mode. Even 8 dot needle printers as well as laserprinters are suitable for that purpose.

The input of texts into a Japanese program is quite a different problem. Kana characters can be typed on a normal ASCII keyboard if you toggle the input mode with the SO SI sequence. The different approaches to the keyboard problem are explained in (Ref. 3).
The input of Kanji itself can be done by special keyboards or with a selection method. A syllabel is input in phonetic form and different options are offered by the software. This method is used by Japanese word processors (Ref. 4). An approch to input the radicals of Chinese characters was described in (Ref. 5).
Luckily the PATOLIS database does not need Kanji input, it only produces Kanji output.

5 Language barriers

Japanese is one of the most complicated languages to master and translation capacity normally is rather limited in a company or in a patent department.

External translations from Japanese into English are expensive and it pays if you reduce your translation needs to a minimum. There are the following possibilities to reduce the working load for the translator:

* An online specialist and not the translator should run the search and should, if necessary hand over the printout for professional translation.

* Only those parts of the printout which are needed for professional working should go to a translator. It is not neccessary to translate standard headings or abbreviations.

* Special patent bibliographic terms should be handled by the patent specialist and not by the translator.

Complete machine translation would be the ideal means to reach those goals, but at present there are no Japanese-English translation programs available within the framework of a department budget.
We shall investigate now, which of the goals can be achieved using a PC when we access the PATOLIS database.
If you work with the PATOLIS patent database you have to read commands or prompts, which are given in Kanji. In response to this commands you have to key Latin, in most cases numeric input.
As a response you get standard headings in Kanji and Kana, as well as free texts (like titles and abstracts) in Kana and bibliographic details. Those details are mostly calendar dates, serial numbers and codes. The codes referring to the legal status are given in Kanji as well as in a numeric code established by JAPIO.

Even an easy question like: "Is a certain patent still valid ?" can only be answered if the user of the online system can navigate using Kanji prompts, can translate standard headings and knows the legal status code of JAPIO.
These barriers exclude most of the community from this comprehensive and most up to date database.

6 How can a PC help to read Japanese patent data?

Personal computers help to make some work easier, like text editing, but they also open possiblities, which are not available on a mainframe computer.
Personal databases, spreadsheets and personal publishing are fields which have been established by the PC.
For the user of online databases the computing power of the PC can also open new possibilities. Automatic login, downloading and offline preparation of searches are possibilities offered by standard communication packages.
The PC can solve the problems outlined above, creating an English language interface to a Japanese database like PATOLIS.

7 Technical considerations

If we want to use our PC as a Kanji terminal emulator we have to check the technical specifications. Generally speaking it is possible to work with a normal PC without graphics card and standard printer, if we only want to handle the information which can be translated by the system. If speed is crucial and Kanji information is needed, more sophisticated equipment is necessary.

7.1 Resolution

For display of Kanji characters on a screen with 40 characters per line we need an EGA (enhanced graphics adapter) card and the matching CRT.
Quite recently laptops were offered having a 640 x 400 points plasma display. Those machines are also useful for our task as well.
Printer resolution is no problem, as long as a graphic mode exists. For a needle printer the characters are produced by printing two lines with 8 dots each and no distance between

those half lines.
Laser printers can be operated with 75 or 150 dots/inch. The higher resolution gives a medium sized, but well legible print, whereas the lower resolution shows oversized characters, which look a little clumsy.

7.2 Speed

As all programs discussed work in a standard DOS environment, they have to paint the characters pixel by pixel. This is done using rather quick routines in C-language, nevertheless an AT compatible machine is recommended.
The code is efficient enough to handle the Kanji display, online printout of Kanji, the translation, the display and printout of the translations as well as the storage of the dialog on hard-disc for later editing when 300Baud lines are used (PATOLIS is not available on higher Baud rates outside Japan).

7.3 Memory

It is possible only to load the translation table with approximately 600 phrases in RAM and to use the character file from a hard disc.
The translation table needs 21kB and the character table for Kanji needs 140kB. If the characters are loaded in RAM, the speed goes up, but in that case 640kB RAM machines are necessary.

8 Examples of an online search in the PATOLIS database

The PATOLIS file at JAPIO is taylored to the Japanese needs. Due to the specialities of the language the systems is based on a fixed dictionary which works with codes instead of free keywords.
Special features of the file are the possibility to print drawings and the possibility to order data on CD-ROM. Login and general usage works similar to western systems.

8.1 Using a PC as a Kanji terminal emulator

The PC acts as a terminal emulator. It takes input either from the keyboard or from prepared files with storted search strategies.
The data are sent via a resident program to the communication interface (COM1 or COM2) and data are received from the same interface. The incoming data are stored in a logfile and displayed on the screen.
The data arrive in packets. Each packet starts with an escape-sequence, which identifies the type of characters. They are either Kanji data and arrive in pairs of bytes or normal data. Kanji packets consist of two ASCII characters per Kanji, whereas standard packets have one ASCII character per output character. Within the standard packets SO and SI characters toggle between Katakana and ASCII characters.
The dialog can be printed already during the online session, but editing of the text and printout with a stand-alone program is also possible.

The complete bibliography of a document (without abstract) looks like this:

```
*** 照会回答 ***  [特実] 様式(C) 受注番号(99999999)  88.01.26   順位 0000001
*** 特開 54- 81275 [54.06.28] 請求 (1) ***
出願 52-121285 [52.10.08] 公告   -      [ .  . ] 登録         [ .  . ]
公開名称    N-（２-クロル-４-ピリジル）尿素類及びその製法並びに植物生長調
            節剤
要約        （新規物質）（用途）植物生長調節剤。細胞分裂促進作用，苗条形成促進
            作用及び収穫増加作用を有し特にマメ科，ナス科，セリ科，イネ科等に有
            効。
キーワード   クロル ピリジル 尿素，植物 生長 調節剤 細胞 分裂 促進 作用
            , 苗条 形成, 収穫 増加, クロル アミノ ピリジン, フェニル イソ
            シアナート
公開出願人 141     岡本 敏彦, 131     磯谷 遥, 141     首藤 紘一,
           131     佐藤 進
発明者      岡本 敏彦, 磯谷 遥, 首藤 紘一, 高橋 惣四郎
優先権
公開ＩＰＣ  *C07D213/00 ,    A01N 9/22 ,
公開ＪＰＣ  * 16  E431.    30  F371.221.   30  F932.
広域        141,111,144
代理人      通常 (6334)  他(1)  出願人数 (04)  発明数 (03)  優先権数 (00)
出願種別  （通常） 原出願番号 ( - )       原登録番号 (         )
基準日 (出願日 ) [52.10.08]  遡及日 [ .  . ]  部門 (2-2) PAGE数 (0009)
権利譲渡の用意 ( )   実施許諾の用意 ( )
関連出願 (分割)(1) (特許)(55-107924)   (分割)(1) (特許)(55-107925)
異議数 (00)  査定種別 (拒絶) [61.01.28]   最終処分 (       ) [ .  . ]
審判   (審判  ) (61- 2894)[61.02.27]  審決   (拒絶審決 ) [62.01.05]
中間記録           (審査請求81,530920,28000) (自発補正52,530920,00000)
(自発補正52,531211,00000) (上申物件78,531211,00000) (不受理 99,540323,1211 )
(上申物件78,540329,00000) (拒絶理由13,540724,71388) (自発補正52,540830,03000)
(自発補正52,540911,00000) (不受理 99,541130,0911 ) (拒絶理由13,550701,71384)
(自発補正52,550807,00000) (意見書 53,550807,00000) (手続補正29,551111,0013 )
(自発補正52,551118,00000) (拒絶理由13,570413,71442) (意見書 53,570513,00000)
(補正却下19,570921,7144) (補正却下19,570921,7144 ) (補正却下19,570921,7144 )
(補正却下19,570921,7144) (戻し 34,580225,      ) (拒絶理由13,580614,71444)
(自発補正52,580721,00000) (意見書 53,580721,00000) (手続補正29,580816,0013 )
(不受理 99,580830,0721 ) (自発補正52,580906,00000) (意見書 53,580906,00000)
(補正却下19,590306,7144) (拒絶査定A2,610128,7144 )
 引用文献 (19,540623,2441  )
         (19,550526,24    )
         (19,570216,04    ) (04,JA, 特許公開,52-43669)
                            (04,US, 特許公告,3469965)


                            Fig. 2
```

8.2 Using a PC as a translation help additionally to Kanji

We can now switch on the translation module of the terminal program and when we process the same search a second time, we get a result, which is much more easy to understand.
In this mode the Kanji characters are displayed on the screen and after a Kanji packet is finished the program uses a table-lookup module to find a translation for the phrase. If the search is successful the translation superseeds the original text on the screen. In the printout successful translations are given, parts like title and abstracts, which cannot be found in the translation table, are printed in Kanji.

The system prompts and the standard headings are translated. As an example the statistics at the beginning show now the coverage for different types of documents.

The first screen is an open message in Latin characters. Already the second screen after starting the PATOLIS data base is not clear unless you know a little Japanese. We have seen before the original version and we look now at the computer translated version.

```
        *** PATOLIS ONLINE SERVICE ***      19:09:18
        Service  : Pat & Ut *** Covered Period. Documents
        A : Pat. unx: YS 46.07.01 - YS 62.11.30   2942210
        B : Pat.  ex: YS 30.01.01 - YS 62.11.30   1242860
        U : Ut. unx:  YS 46.07.01 - YS 62.11.30   2700321
        Y : Ut.  ex:  YS 35.01.01 - YS 62.11.30   1192980
        Legal Status cutoff: 62.12.11  in JPO
        Search Type[ 1:Bib.  2:DcNo  3:Numb. List ]
        Please enter your OrderNo, User Code and Search Type
```

Fig. 3

Naturally the effect is far more impressive, if we run into messages like this:

```
*** 出願 昭41-060122
***********************************************************
     *  御照会されたデータは、現在のマスターには蓄積されておりません。  *
     *  詳しくは、特許庁 備えつけの原簿を御参照下さい。                *
***********************************************************
     *続き有り*
```
Fig. 4

Which also can be translated easily:

```
*** App. YS41-060122
***********************************************************
     *  The requested data are not contained in the current Master File  *
     *  For detailed information please look the original file in the JPO*
***********************************************************
     *Continue*
```
Fig. 5

The program uses a table of more than 630 translations of phrases and codes. In the next example we shall see the effect on the patent bibliography.
If we look now into the bibliography we find, that the structure of the document is quite clear, but that abstract and title still need professional manual translation.
The legal status information now is easy to understand and we see that the application 52-121285 was refused.

```
*** DcResult ***    [P&Ut] Form(C) OrderNo:(99999999)  88.01.26   No.: 0000001
*** unxP 54- 81275 [54.06.28] Reg. (1) ***
        App. 52-121285 [52.10.08] ePub  -   [ . . ] Reg.      [ . . ]
        Tit. unx:    N-(2-クロル-4-ピリジル)尿素類及びその製法並びに植物生長調
                     節剤
        sSum         (新規物質)(用途)植物生長調節剤。細胞分裂促進作用、苗条形成促進
                     作用及び収穫増加作用を有し特にマメ科、ナス科、セリ科、イネ科等に有
                     効。
        Keywords:    クロル ピリジル 尿素、植物 生長 調節剤 細胞 分裂 促進 作用
                     、苗条 形成、収穫 増加 クロル アミノ ピリジン、フェニル イソ
                     シアナート
        Appnt unx:  141     岡本 敏彦, 131     磯谷 遥, 141     首藤 紘一,
                    131     佐藤 進
        Invtr:              岡本 敏彦,磯谷 遥,首藤 紘一,髙橋 惣四郎
        Prio.:
        Unx. IPC: *C07D213/00 ,      A01N 9/22  ,
        Unx. JPC: * 16  E431.      30  F371.221.     30  F932.
        JCl:     141, 111, 144
        Agent    norm (6334)  Ot(1)    Appnt # (04)    Inv. # (03)   Prio. # (00)
        Kd App.  (norm)   Or. App. No. ( - )        Or. Reg. No. (       )
        Bas Dt (App. Dt ) [52.10.08]  RactDt [ . . ]  Sect (2-2) PAGE # (0009)
        Right transfer ( )    Enforcem. Cons. ( )
        Rel. App. (Div.)(1) (Pat.)(55-107924)    (Div.)(1) (Pat.)(55-107925)
        Opp. # (00)  Kd Dec. (Rej.) [61.01.28]   Fin. Dec. (      )[ . . ]
        Tria  (Trial ) (61- 2894) [61.02.27]   TrDe  (Rejection ) [62.01.05]
        PRS INFO              (PRS Code81, 530920, 28000) (PRS Code52, 530920, 00000)
    81 Request for Examination
    52 Amendment
      (PRS Code52, 531211, 00000) (PRS Code78, 531211, 00000) (PRS Code99, 540323, 1211 )
    52 Amendment
    78 Miscellaneous Documents, Petition and Submission of Document
    99 Non-Acceptance
      (PRS Code78, 540329, 00000) (PRS Code13, 540724, 71388) (PRS Code52, 540830, 03000)
    78 Miscellaneous Documents, Petition and Submission of Document
    13 Notice of Reason of Rejection
    52 Amendment
      (PRS Code52, 540911, 00000) (PRS Code99, 541130, 0911 ) (PRS Code13, 550701, 71384)
    52 Amendment
    99 Non-Acceptance
    13 Notice of Reason of Rejection
      (PRS Code52, 550807, 00000) (PRS Code53, 550807, 00000) (PRS Code29, 551111, 0013 )
    52 Amendment
    53 Argument
    29 Action for Amendment
```

```
 (PRS Code52,551118,00000) (PRS Code13,570413,71442) (PRS Code53,570513,00000)
52  Amendment
13  Notice of Reason of Rejection
53  Argument
 (PRS Code19,570921,7144 ) (PRS Code19,570921,7144 ) (PRS Code19,570921,7144 )
19  Decision of Dismissal of Amendment
19  Decision of Dismissal of Amendment
19  Decision of Dismissal of Amendment
 (PRS Code19,570921,7144 ) (PRS Code34,580225,     ) (PRS Code13,580614,71444)
19  Decision of Dismissal of Amendment
34  Sending back (no response to Action 14 OR 19)
13  Notice of Reason of Rejection
 (PRS Code52,580721,00000) (PRS Code53,580721,00000) (PRS Code29,580816,0013 )
52  Amendment
53  Argument
29  Action for Amendment
 (PRS Code99,580830,0721 ) (PRS Code52,580906,00000) (PRS Code53,580906,00000)
99  Non-Acceptance
52  Amendment
53  Argument
 (PRS Code19,590306,7144 ) (PRS CodeA2,610128,7144 )
19  Decision of Dismissal of Amendment
A2  Decision of Rejection
   Cit.Ref: (19,540623,2441 )
            (19,550526,24   )
            (19,570216,04   ) (04,JA. Pat. unx,52-43669)
                              (04,US. Pat.  ex,3469965)
  * E. o. D. *
```

Fig. 6

8.3 Using a PC in text mode

If the PC does only work in textmode and not in graphics mode, we nevertheless are able to run a search now. The display of the prompts is in English on the screen and so is a lot of the information which is sent by the database.
This display allows an exact rating of the legal status.
If a complete printout of the Kanji texts is necessary, we can print the stored dialog with a special program which works with needle printers and has compatible graphics mode. Also laserprinters are supported.

8.4 Conclusion

Japanese patent documents are an important source of knowledge about the results of Japanese Research & Development. This source can be utilized by several online databases. The most comprehensive one is the PATOLIS database produced by JAPIO (Japanese Patent Information Organization). This database uses Kanji characters. It is technically possible and economically feasible for Western companies to acces this database via a terminal emulator which is running on a PC and forms a English language interface.

8.5 References

(1) STI Indicators Newsletters No. 10 1987
    Scientific, Technological and Industrial Indications Newsletters

(2) Libesny, Hewitt, Hunter, Hannah
    The Scientific and Technical Information Contained in Patent Specifications - The Extent and Time Factors of its Publication in Other Forms of Literature.
    The Information Scientist 1974

(3) Big Blue goes Japanese
    Richard Willis
    Byte the small systems journal. November 1983

(4) Computerchinesisch
    COM Siemens Magazin 4/87

(5) A new Chinese character coding system for computers
    Yili Zheng and Chunpei He
    Proceedings of the Seventh National Online Meeting New York 1986

F-TAS: A FULL-TEXT ACCESS SYSTEM

Michael J. Prasse, Martin Dillon, Martha J. Gordon, Bruce Mortland, and Anthony Repka, OCLC Online Computer Library Center

Keywords: Full text retrieval; human-computer interaction; user interface; interface design; human factors.

Abstract: This paper describes a mouse-controlled, full-text access system (F-TAS) that integrates general interface design principles with the results of studies of perceiving and comprehending text. F-TAS is discussed within a framework of three categories of interface-design issues for full-text retrieval: 1) general interface issues, 2) perceptual issues relevant to reading, and 3) cognitive issues such as displaying paragraphs as "cognitive units." F-TAS users may access a document at the page or word(s) level. Pressing the left or right mouse button, respectively, pages forward or backward throughout the document. The middle mouse button can be used to select: 1) icons representing the first or last page of the document, 2) locations on a scrollbar relative to the first or last page, 3) icons to display the table of contents or the index, 4) page numbers from the table of contents or the index, or 5) bookmarks established by the user. At the word level, a user can use the mouse to select search terms from the displayed text or enter terms from the keyboard. The locations of paragraphs containing the search term(s) are indicated by icons displayed below the scrollbar, and special icons indicate whether the search term appears in the table of contents or index. These icons may be selected with the mouse to display the corresponding area of text with the search term(s) highlighted. A first-time user can use the system without training by reading the introductory help screen and requesting additional help screens if needed.

F-TAS can be described within a framework of three categories of interface-design issues: 1) general interface issues that apply to many types of interfaces; 2) perceptual issues that are specific to screen presentations of full-text; and 3) cognitive issues that are particularly important for interfaces that provide access to long full-text documents. Each of the following sections summarizes how recent research results in one of these areas were applied during F-TAS design. Many of the issues overlap across the areas, but each issue is discussed only once. F-TAS is part of the D interface-design language project (Ref. 1), which allows rapid prototyping of interfaces for information-retrieval systems. Both F-TAS and the D language are implemented on a SUN 3/50 workstation with a 19" screen.

1. GENERAL INTERFACE ISSUES

    As Shneiderman has noted, recent research indicates that users, particularly novice or infrequent users, accomplish their tasks more easily when commands are visually represented than when the commands must be entered via the keyboard (i.e., when a direct-manipulation rather than a command-language interface is used) (Ref.2). Consequently, in contrast to many full-text retrieval systems, the F-TAS interface is primarily controlled by mouse input. However, keyboard entry may be used for search terms, allowing the user to search the text unconstrained by a controlled vocabulary. Two of the windows in Figure 1 illustrate these aspects of the F-TAS interface. In this example, the user has selected the document (book) to be searched, requested that the introductory screen be displayed as a help screen, and requested that the system search for the word "newspaper". The left window in Figure 1 contains a help screen that provides instructions about how to use the mouse. The user has to remember only three input commands: 1) the left mouse button displays the previous screen, 2) the right mouse button displays the next screen, and 3) the middle mouse button is used to select any other function when the mouse cursor is placed on the appropriate icon. (Selecting locations on the scrollbar icon is discussed in detail in Section 3.)

The small window at the bottom right of Figure 1 illustrates how keyboard input is integrated into the direct manipulation interface. The user opens this window by clicking the middle mouse button while the mouse cursor is over the FIND icon. The user then types in the word or words that are to be used for the search (e.g., "newspaper"). This allows free word searching of the full-text document; Boolean operators may be used to broaden or narrow the search.

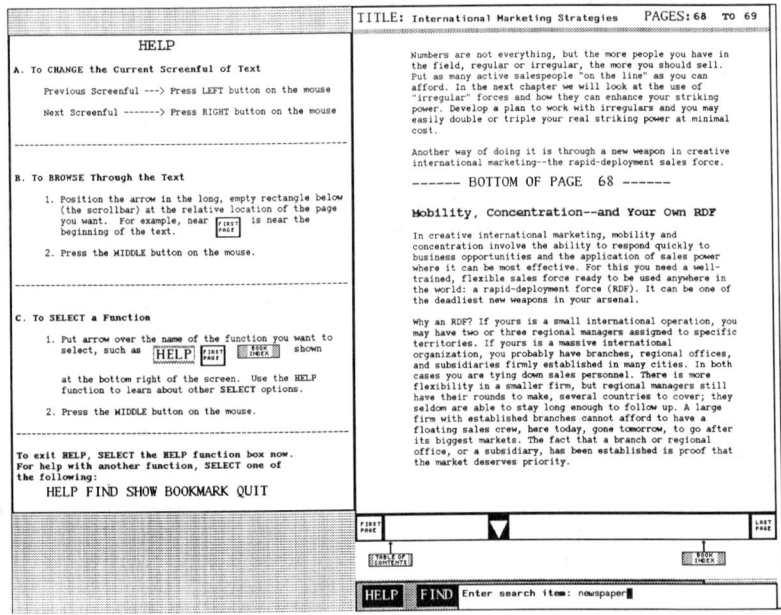

Figure 1.   A sample screen from F-TAS showing the introductory help screen in the left window, general information (i.e., title and page numbers displayed) at the top right of the screen, a screen of text in the right window, and icons that may be used to activate functions (with the FIND window open) at the bottom right of the screen.

2. PERCEPTUAL ISSUES FOR FULL-TEXT RETRIEVAL

The primary perceptual issue for full-text interface design is difficult to identify; however, the primary factors can be subsumed under typography (e.g., font) and layout (e.g., organization of the text on the page). Several guidelines have been suggested for typography (Refs. 3, 4). We used an 11 pt. font (Ref. 5) in a courier style, and monospaced rather than variable character width (Ref. 6). Chapter and subsection names were displayed in a larger and bolder font for easy discrimination. For page layout, we used 1) a left margin of one inch (about one-eighth of window width; Ref. 7), 2) a ragged right margin (Ref. 8), and 3) single spacing within paragraphs and double spacing between paragraphs (Ref. 3). The bottom of each document page was marked by an optional "end of page" delimiter.

3. COGNITIVE ISSUES FOR FULL-TEXT RETRIEVAL

One important cognitive issue is how to define and display "cognitive units" of the text so that the text is easy to understand. For F-TAS, a cognitive unit was defined as the smallest unit of text about a single topic, and thus F-TAS treats each paragraph as a cognitive unit. Consequently, screens are formatted as they are requested and they begin and end with complete paragraphs to increase comprehension (Ref. 9). Complete paragraphs also allow the user to integrate all of the information within a particular paragraph without having to request another screen; research in the psychology of discourse processing indicates that this should decrease the demands on the user's cognitive resources such as short-term memory (Refs. 10, 11). The only exception to the display of complete paragraphs is when a user requests a particular page number; in that case, the top of the page is displayed at the top of the screen, regardless of the intra-paragraph position of the first word displayed.

Another salient cognitive issue in the presentation of a book-length document on a CRT is how the user can navigate through the document (Ref. 12). The ability to efficiently navigate depends on the user's understanding of the logical structure (organization) of the document. Three views of this structure may be used for navigation: 1) the physical structure of the document as an ordered collection of pages; 2) the structure of the text that was expressed by the author in the table of contents, chapters, etc.; and 3) an idiosyncratic organization of the text that is imposed by the user and that is based on relevance to the user's goals (cf. Ref. 13).

In a book, one common method of navigation is to use the table of contents or the index to identify the pages that contain the desired information. A reader may use his or her fingers to mark the table of contents and/or index (or the current page of text) while checking the pages that are referenced. This awkwardness is avoided in F-TAS by allowing the user to display a page from the table of contents or the index (or the current page of text) in one window while any other page is displayed in the other window. Users may use several different methods of selecting which page will be displayed; these methods are discussed in the following paragraphs.

SCROLLBAR: The results of previous research indicate that giving a user a mental model for a task can improve understanding and performance (Refs. 14, 15). Spatial metaphors are often good ways to communicate mental models (Ref. 16). In F-TAS, a long, horizontal window, which acts as a scrollbar, is used to spatially represent the physical structure of the book. The beginning and ending of the text are demarcated by icons at the ends of the scrollbar that are named "FIRST PAGE" and "LAST PAGE," respectively (Figure 1). Selection of the FIRST PAGE icon will display the first page of text in the right window; similarly, selection of LAST PAGE will display the last page of text. Alternatively, the user can locate the mouse cursor in an intermediate location in the scrollbar, and the page that corresponds to that relative text position will be displayed in the right window. Whenever a page is displayed in the right window, an arrow is located in the scrollbar at the appropriate location for that page.

TABLE OF CONTENTS AND INDEX: If the author has provided a table of contents and/or an index, either of these may be used as navigational aids, and each may be displayed in either the left or the right window. To display the first page of either in the left window, the user selects the SHOW function, which causes a menu to appear with the options "table of contents," "index," and "current page." If "table of contents" is selected, the first page of the table of contents is displayed in the left window. Similarly, the first page of the index is displayed when "index" is selected (Figure 1). If "current page" is selected, the page that is currently being displayed in the right window is then also displayed in the left window. The user may then page forward and backward in either window whenever there are following or preceding pages.

There are two different ways in which the mouse may be used to display the table of contents or the index in the right window (for example, when the user has a help screen displayed in the left window). In one method, the user may page to the table of contents or the index by pressing the appropriate mouse buttons to page forward or backward through the book. In the other method, the user may directly "go to" (display) the first page of either the table of contents or the index by selecting either the TABLE OF CONTENTS or INDEX icons as shown under the scrollbar in Figure 1.

PAGE: The user may display a particular page in the right window with either mouse or keyboard input. When a page from the table of contents or the index is displayed, the user may select any page number on that page by placing the mouse cursor over the number and pressing the middle mouse button. The selected page number is highlighted, and clicking on the FIND icon causes that numbered page to be displayed in the right window. When the desired page number is known but is not present on the screen, a user may request a particular page by selecting the FIND function and then typing the desired page number (in place of the word "newspaper" in Figure 1). The requested page number is then displayed in the right window.

BOOKMARK: Users may "mark" particular pages to create their own navigational aids by selecting the BOOKMARK icon shown at the bottom right in Figure 1. A miniature BOOKMARK icon (as shown in Figure 2) then appears below the appropriate location on the scrollbar. Users may then at any time return to any marked page by selecting its appropriate miniature BOOKMARK icon.

WORD SEARCH: Users also may create their own navigational aids by searching for any word, phrase, or Boolean combination of words. For example, Figure 2 shows how the screen may appear after the system has completed the search for "newspaper" that was requested in Figure 1. The same search would have been done if the user had 1) selected (clicked on) the word "newspaper" when it was shown on any page displayed in the right window, and then 2) selected the FIND function.

The ITEM icons below the scrollbar in Figure 2 indicate the location of each paragraph in the text that contains "newspaper." Notice that the last item icon on the right contains the word "index" to indicate that the word appears on a page in the index. To display any of the paragraphs containing "newspaper," the user selects any of the item icons with the mouse. The page containing the selected paragraph is then displayed in the right window. The user can then browse through nearby pages by using the mouse buttons to move forward or backward through the text. The search term ("newspaper") will be highlighted whenever it occurs. The positioning of the item icons allows the user to quickly see where the search term is frequently used in the text and to easily retrieve and browse areas of the text that are likely to be highly relevant to the user's goals.

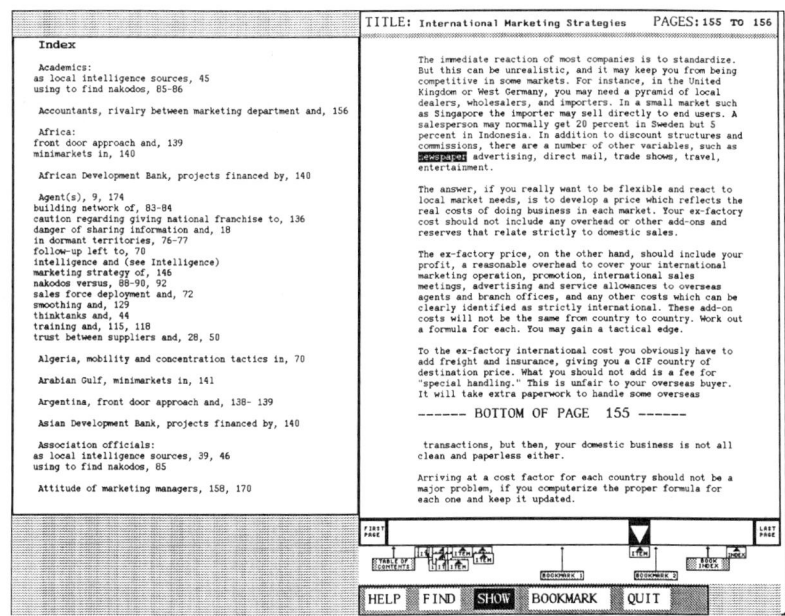

Figure 2. A sample screen from F-TAS showing the first index page in the left window, the same general information as in Figure 1 at the top right of the screen, a screen of text in the right window with the search term highlighted, bookmark and item icons at the appropriate locations on the scrollbar, and various functional icons at the bottom of the screen.

4. SUMMARY

F-TAS provides the user with an easy-to-use method of accessing and reading text presented on a CRT. This was achieved by 1) minimizing the amount of cognitive effort necessary to use the system and understand the text, and 2) maximizing the degree of correspondence between a user's "book reading" expectations and their realization in F-TAS. Although in a state of continual refinement, the initial implementation of F-TAS described in this paper provides capabilities of both reading and researching online full-text documents easily and rapidly. As the functionality of the system is expanded (e.g, linked records of user input analogous to "margin notes"), the best of both worlds, books and computers, could be combined in a single system.

5. REFERENCES

1. Dillon, M., Mortland, B., & Repka, A. (1987). D: A design language for retrieval system interfaces. In Proceedings of the Eighth National Online Meeting, (pp. 111-117). Medford, NJ: Learned Information, Inc.

2. Shneiderman, B. (1987). *Designing the user interface: Strategies for effective human-computer interaction.* Reading, MA: Addison-Wesley.

3. Smith, S. L., & Mosier, J. N. (1986). *Guidelines for designing user interface software.* Boston, MA.: The MITRE Corporation.

4. Beldie, I. P., Siegmund, P., & Schwartz, E. (1983). Fixed versus variable letter width for televised text. *Human Factors*, 25(3), 273-277.

5. Gould, J. D., & Grischkowsky, N. (1986). Does visual angle of a line of characters affect reading speed? *Human Factors*, 26(3), 323-337.

6. Gould, J. D., Alfaro, L., Finn, R., Haupt, B., & Minuto, A. (1987). Reading from CRT displays can be as fast as reading from paper. *Human Factors*, 29(5), 497-517.

7. Galitz, W. O. (1985). *Handbook of screen format design.* Wellesley Hills, MA: QED Information Sciences, Inc.

8. Trollip, S. R., & Sales, G. (1986). Readability of computer-generated fill-justified text. *Human Factors*, 28, 159-163.

9. Frase, L., & Schwartz, B. (1979). Typographical cues that facilitate comprehension. *Journal of Educational Psychology*, 71, 197-206.

10. Kintsch, W., & van Dijk, T. A. (1978). Toward a model of text comprehension and production. *Psychological Review*, 85(5), 363-394.

11. Just, M. A., & Carpenter, P. A. (1980). A theory of reading: From eye fixations to comprehension. *Psychological Review*, 87(4), 329-354.

12. Kerr, S. T. (1986). Learning to use electronic text: An agenda for research on typography, graphics, and interpanel navigation. *Information Design Journal*, 4(3), 206-211.

13. Bernstein, L. M., & Williamson, R. E. (1984). Testing of a natural language retrieval system for a full text knowledge base. *Journal of the American Society for Information Science*, 35(4), 235-247.

14. Bransford, J. D., & Johnson, M. K. (1972). Contextual prerequisites for understanding: Some investigations of comprehension and recall. *Journal of Verbal Learning and Verbal Behavior*, 11, 717-726.

15. Jamar, P. (1986). Lost in computerland: Functional model-enhanced training and interface designs. *Proceedings of the Human Factors Society 30th Annual Meeting*, Vol. 1 (pp. 497-501).

16. Johnson-Laird, P. N. (1983). *Mental models: Towards a cognitive science of language, inference, and consciousness.* Cambridge, Great Britain: Cambridge University Press.

PSYCH/NEURO CORE CONCEPT DATABASE: A QUALITY-FILTERED DATABASE

W. Jean Pugh and Gary Moore, Johns Hopkins University

Keywords: Database Development, Quality Filtering, Knowledge Base, Core Concept Database.

Abstract: The Librarian of the Psychiatry/Neurosciences Library (PNL), a distributed service site of the William H. Welch Medical Library, the Johns Hopkins University, and the Assistant Director for Computer Systems, also from Welch, collaborated with the faculty and house staff of the Departments of Neurology, Neurosurgery and Psychiatry to develop a Psych/Neuro Core Concept Database. This database provides a knowledge base of recommended citations with brief annotations to core materials that support clinical education in the subject areas of psychiatry, neurology and neurosurgery. The annotations were written by Hopkins subject experts. The purpose of the database was to create a system which filters subject literature and provides immediate access to quality materials at the location of need. In addition to the Psych/Neuro Core Concept Database, a companion database, entitled the Core Experts Database, includes the names of the Hopkins specialists who contributed to the Psych/Neuro Core Concept Database, thus formalizing the invisible college common to most academic institutions. Both databases primarily serve medical students, house staff, nurses and clinical staff. The databases are loaded on a Welch Library minicomputer and are accessible through common search software for all the Library's bibliographic databases (WELMED). Remote access is available twenty-four hours a day, seven days a week.

1. BACKGROUND

Librarians are well aware of the information explosion that is bombarding today's researchers, clinicians and students. The scientific literature has included statements expressing the need for a filtering mechanism which would "save precious working years for the scientific community, which now faces the options of being flooded by unneeded information, devising its own ad hoc filters as the system spouts out its publications (or lists of references), arbitrary skimming of the endless pulp, or ignoring it altogether." (Ref. 1)

The William H. Welch Medical Library, in expanding its traditional library role to include the creation and maintenance of databases, has developed one solution to this quality-filtering need - a Psych/Neuro Core Concept Database. The database is the result of a cooperative project between the librarian of the Psychiatry/Neurosciences Library, a distributed service center for the Welch Medical Library, Welch's Assistant Director for Computer Systems, and the faculty members and house staff of the Departments of Neurology, Neurosurgery and Psychiatry. The Psych/Neuro Core Concept Database provides a knowledge base of recommended citations with brief annotations to core materials that support clinical education in the subject areas of psychiatry, neurology and neurosurgery. The content of the database was contributed by the faculty members and house staff of the Johns Hopkins School of Medicine and the Johns Hopkins Hospital. This paper describes the database's structural content as well as its development process.

2. DATABASE DESCRIPTION

The database consists of two separate files: 1) the citation database which contains approximately 1,300 records of citations to books, chapters in books, journal articles and audiovisuals and 2) the experts database containing approximately 125 name and address records for individuals willing to serve as expert consultants in a given subject speciality. Users of the Psych/Neuro Core Concept Database can enter the Core Expert Database file to obtain a telephone number of an expert on a subject of interest in order to contact the expert for additional information.

Records in the citation database include the following fields: author/editor, title, source, publication information, edition, series, annotation, abstract/call number and library location, subject, identifier, notes, expert name, document type, accession number, entry date, the date expert submitted citation, and a record update date. The database can be searched by author, title, subject, keyword, journal title, publication date, document type, expert name or series. Search sets may be combined with Boolean logic. Citations may be displayed or printed one at a time or continuously. Three display/print formats are available. All materials cited in the database are located within the Psychiatry/Neurosciences Library or the Welch Medical Library.

The companion Core Experts Database contains the following record fields: expert's name, Hopkins address and telephone number, department, and subject specialties. It can be searched by the experts' names and subject specialities. Only one display/print format exists.

3. AUDIENCE

The database was created mainly for medical students, house staff, nurses, and clinical staff. However, it may also be used by faculty who are not specialists in order to enhance their knowledge of the subjects.

4. THESAURUS

The subject headings used in the Psych/Neuro Core Concept Database correspond with those contained within the National Library of Medicine's Medical Subject Headings - Annotated Alphabetic List.

5. TECHNICAL ASPECTS

The Psych/Neuro Core Concept Database files are mounted on a Data General MV-8000 minicomputer using the MIIS operating system. It is one of the databases that comprise the Library's WELMED system. WELMED is a general purpose bibliographic database management system which provides a common search interface to bibliographic databases developed in-house, as well as to databases produced elsewhere but mounted locally, e.g. a MEDLINE subset. The core WELMED applications software was originally developed by the Specialized Information Services (SIS) Division of the National Library of Medicine for its TOXNET files available online as part of its Toxicology Information Program. The Health Sciences Library of the University of Maryland and the Welch Medical Library have been working in cooperation with SIS over the past several months to develop an easy to use menu system for the Elhill command interface emulation software used for searching TOXNET.

6. <u>DATABASE ACCESS</u>

Access to the database is provided by library terminals located throughout the Welch Library System. It is also accessible remotely through the Johns Hopkins Medical Institutions (JHMI) local area network or by 1200 and 300 baud telephone dial-up. Except for 4 hours downtime for file back-up each week, the database is available twenty-four hours a day, seven days a week. Any person who obtains a Welch Library registration card may use the database.

7. <u>DATABASE DEVELOPMENT</u>

The first step in the development process was to identify the subjects that would be included in the database. To do this, the table of contents of standard textbooks within the disciplines of neurology, neurosurgery and psychiatry were consulted. In addition, the relevant Medical Subject Headings' tree structures were also reviewed. A list of approximately forty-five subjects per discipline was presented to each of the three department's chairmen and chief residents. They were asked to identify experts for each of the subjects.

Analysis of the medical school catalog, which highlights departmental faculty research interests, and a research directory published by Hopkins also helped to identify experts. In addition, the most recent PNL faculty publications were examined.

The experts were contacted either in person or via a package of information which included a cover letter describing the database, a sample annotation, workforms for each material format outlining the various fields for that format and a list of subjects. An expert information form was also enclosed asking for the information to be included in the Core Experts Database and an agreement that the expert could be consulted by users of the database if additional information was needed. Similar packets were given to all the house staff of the three departments. The experts were asked to contribute about ten citations for each subject including an annotation which explained the value of the cited material.

All contributions were verified against Welch's Online Catalog, or if they were journal articles, checked against databases offered by a commercial vendor for accuracy and to obtain subject headings. The original article or book chapter was consulted for citations not found within a commercial system.

Record content and formats were established. Policies were then formulated for record entry, indexing, and updating. The record entry policy outlines such items as date formats, authority control for authors'/editors' names, and standards for the various fields. The indexing policy records the fields indexed for each search key, stop words and the subject heading thesaurus. The updating policy states the frequency and method for updating the database as well as the projected growth rate of the database.

Database records were keyboard entered and edited using full screen text editing features of the WELMED software. After 150 records were entered, a pilot test was conducted to confirm that the proper fields were being included for the search keys. Modifications were made to the record design such as the rearrangement of the order of the fields within a record. Also, display/print formats were determined. A second test was conducted by patrons of the Psychiatry/Neurosciences Library. Modifications were made based upon their recommendations. The rest of the records were entered and a final test was conducted.

Documentation for the database was written as separate chapters within the two manuals created for the entire WELMED system; a public search reference manual and an internal maintenance manual.

The database was promoted through mailings to all registered departmental faculty, house staff and medical students. Brochures were also placed at strategic locations within the Welch Library and its four distributed service centers. Announcements appeared in campus and library newsletters. Personal contacts were made with the departmental chairmen and chief residents asking for their cooperation in announcing the database to their colleagues. Signs were also placed within the libraries of the Welch Library System, and library staff encouraged database use.

The database will be evaluated mainly upon users' suggestions, comments or criticisms. Changes will be made as needed. Statistics regarding use will also be analyzed.

8. CONCLUSION

Several benefits of the Psych/Neuro Core Concept Database have been realized. The database is an exemplification of the Library's objective to expand its role in creating and maintaining databases. The database provides state-of-the-art service to patrons by providing online information at the location of need, and it serves as a prototype for replication to other departments served by Welch. It is an excellent way for Hopkins experts to transfer their knowledge to fellow colleagues, thus formalizing the invisible college, and to improve the quality of patient care.

As for future developments, several new features designed to strengthen the database will be added over the coming months. These include a Medical Subject Heading vocabulary browser, the ability to cross database search, and a document delivery requesting option.

9. REFERENCE

1. Etzioni, Amitai. The Need for Quality Filters in Information Systems. Science 171, No. 3967, p. 133, January 15, 1971.

BUSINESS USES OF SCIENTIFIC AND TECHNICAL DATABASES

Carol L. Rich and Edward W. Badger, Chemical Abstracts Service

Keywords: Business Information, Online Searching, Scientific Information, Information Retrieval, Marketing Intelligence, Strategic Planning, Competitive Analysis, Investment.

Abstract: Online files containing scientific and technical information can have a variety of uses--not all of them restricted to extracting scientific or technical data. Chemical, engineering, biological, materials science, energy, and many other databases can be searched for important business applications. These files frequently include essential research, author, patent, and corporate data that can be used in nontraditional ways. Many types of businesses can use scientific files to aid in long and short range planning; the databases contain information useful for accurate projections. Many files can be used by businesses to monitor competitors' activities. Companies can also use scientific files for marketing purposes, to identify potential clients. Investors can extract data on scientific developments and use this information, before it is known by the general public, to guide investment decisions.

1. INTRODUCTION

With the smorgasbord of database choices offered by the information industry, online searchers can pick and choose to find exactly the database that matches their searching needs. The variety of databases offered is immense. Searchers looking for answers to legal questions can key in to Lexis; for questions on chemistry they can turn to CAS ONLINE; for searches on medicine they can use MEDLINE; for education information, ERIC; for technical data, NTIS; and so on. However, sophisticated information specialists (and some occasional searchers) have found that databases containing comprehensive information on one subject generally contain information on several other, less obvious, topics.

Online files containing scientific and technical information can have a variety of uses--not all of them restricted to extracting scientific or technical data. Chemical, engineering, biological, materials science, energy, and many other databases can be searched for important business applications.

2. USEFUL BUSINESS INFORMATION IS STORED IN SCIENTIFIC AND TECHNICAL FILES

As searchers in a variety of industries already know, bibliographic and full-text scientific files often contain highly useful business information. Marketing directors, publishing executives, securities firm staff, sales representatives, business analysts, insurance staff, accounts payable managers, trademark analysts, investment bankers and independent investors have all searched scientific and technical databases to retrieve business information.

Sometimes these files feature business data displayed prominently with the scientific data. Databases dealing with the business of science, such as Chemical Industry Notes (CIN), Chemical Journals Online (CJO) MarketSearch, and BIOBUSINESS are all sources for such information as sales, prices, capacity, appointments, stock offerings, acquisitions, plant expansions, reorganizations, subsidiaries, joint ventures, and management strategies.

Frequently, comprehensive scientific files such as COMPENDEX, INSPEC, INPADOC, SCISEARCH, and ENERGY contain useful business information which is presented inconspicuously. Scientific and technical files mainly include essential research activity, author, patent, and corporate data that can be used in nontraditional ways. Searchers can successfully obtain business information by identifying their searching needs and then learning how to apply these needs creatively to likely databases.

The business uses of scientific and technical files for business purposes break down into four broad categories: planning, marketing, monitoring competition, and investment. Files containing scientific and technical research information frequently contain references to breakthrough studies that show market trends while pinpointing advances being made by individual companies and organizations. Also, these files include references to individuals who are actively performing research in specific areas. All of these facts can be used to support business activities and decisions.

3. BUSINESS PLANNING THROUGH SCIENTIFIC SEARCHING

A variety of businesses use scientific files to aid in long- and short-range planning. Scientific databases contain information useful for making accurate projections since they contain clues to factors which guide future growth.

Marketing, sales, personnel, long-range planning, operations, and business departments can find helpful planning information by observing areas of particularly active research through bibliographic searches. Examining research trends is one means of devising future strategies. For example, an increase or decline in patents filed in a particular area might affect planning decisions for research and development expenditures.

In the short-term, planners can respond to information received through specific searches. For example, a company may decide not to fund research on a particular product if a search reveals that similar products are already patented or in the public domain. Also, through bibliographic searching planners can estimate what other companies have spent to solve particular technical problems and compose estimates for themselves, while using the information revealed to circumvent problems that others have already solved.

Companies that market technical or technically-related products, such as pharmaceuticals, scientific instruments, or engineering services, can use technical files to monitor trends in their industry. During planning, expenditures and staff time can be proportioned accordingly. For example, a manufacturer of chromatography equipment can monitor CA or INSPEC to determine trends in supercritical fluid chromatography and to stay current on their competitors' products. The manufacturer might note the number of supercritical fluid chromatography citations and compare them to the number of citations in past months. Industry trends can be easily monitored by creating an SDI (Selective Dissemination of Information) that searches relevant keywords. By monitoring the use of their own instruments and the status of competitors' products, the manufacturer can plan to spend its resources accordingly, for production, advertising, or product development.

Another firm might want to track the usage patterns of the medical instruments they currently produce, or might want to produce in the future. By performing an online search in a database such as MEDLINE, company planners will be able to examine reported use and forecast the market for similar products. To look for this information in MEDLINE, a searcher can make use of the /IS (instrumentation) subheading, linking it to particular tests or testing procedures to determine the current "state of the art" for a particular sort of instrument. For example, a search for instruments used for echocardiography (ultrasound examination of the heart) appears as example 1. Planners can predict trends toward or away from a particular technique by examining the number and content of citations retrieved when searching on that technique. Potential competition for a particular instrument can be detected by searching terms concerning a disease and its detection or therapy. Most clinical papers identify all instruments and products used by manufacturer and model number.

To plan possible mergers or acquisitions, a company will first want to pinpoint firms that are active in compatible or complementary areas. By searching technical files to discover firms reporting research, company executives can find appropriate firms to consider. For example, a company interested in expanding into the manufacture of supercritical fluids could find organizations who are studying or patenting supercritical fluids technology.

4. SCIENTIFIC DATABASES AS A MARKETING RESOURCE

Scientific and technical databases present clear indicators of which organizations are interested in particular topics. To locate the companies and individuals, a search is performed, and the authors and their affiliations determined; most scientific databases contain fields denoting the author's affiliation. By compiling authors' affiliations, marketing can easily create a list of organizations with active interests in any particular field of scientific research. Marketing staff can use this list to target their direct mail advertising campaign. By selecting organizations with proven interest in a subject area, they will have much higher response to advertising for specific products and services.

Sales, advertising, and direct marketing departments can make particular use of such a list not only to identify potential client companies but also to locate the end users of technical products within each company. For example, a company marketing molecular modeling software could perform an online search to find companies and universities interested in acquiring such software. Example 2 demonstrates how a list of authors and corporations can be generated from the CA file by examining recent papers containing keywords related to computer programs and molecular modeling. Also, while performing online searches concerning a specific product, a company may discover a new way in which the product is being used (or figure out a new idea for product use). In addition, sales staff can find fresh leads by matching this list against their existing client list.

CSCHEM and CSCORP are examples of files that can be used as sales tools. These catalog files contain information on chemical products and chemical product suppliers (CSCHEM) and addresses of companies that supply chemicals and chemical products (CSCORP). This information can be used creatively by chemical companies' sales departments. For instance, sales staff can locate competing suppliers for commodity chemicals. Raw materials producers can seek out fine chemicals manufacturers as potential customers.

Companies can search online scientific files in their area of interest to find the names of authors whose research fits their needs. Conversely, consultants can find potential customers. Companies can also employ this method to find conference or symposium speakers or participants. In addition, companies looking for partners or distributors in a particular geographic area can look for companies with complementary research interests. For example, an American pharmaceutical company seeking European distributors for a particular medication could find international companies through Excerpta Medica. By searching for keywords relating to a particular therapeutic area and limiting retrieval to non-U.S. published material, a searcher can compile a list of companies already manufacturing complementary product lines.

5. MONITORING THE ACTIVITIES OF SCIENTIFIC COMPETITORS

Performing online searches to monitor competitors' activities is probably the most frequent nontraditional use of scientific databases. Questions relating to which company is researching what subjects are readily answered through the scientific and engineering databases. A tire company investigating new polymers would install an SDI containing search terms about their monomers, catalysts, or techniques. The resulting updates would show the company exactly which other companies were publishing (and by inference investigating) research in the same areas, while keeping them current on industry trends.

Competitors can also be tracked through online searches. A pharmaceutical company may ask, "What companies hold recent patents on nifedipine?" This question is easily answered by searching for the drug by its CAS Registry Number in CA and by limiting retrieval to patents.

Individuals who are "hot" in a particular area can be tracked through their publications; searchers can watch both ideas and careers develop. Companies can be tracked through observing changes in the topics of the publications they sponsor. For instance, a drug company may suddenly sponsor a series of papers in a particular therapeutic area. This is an indication that they have either received patent protection in that area, or they are discontinuing research and no longer feel the need to keep the publications confidential.

6. INVESTMENT OPPORTUNITIES DISCLOSED BY SCIENTIFIC FILES

Investors with both a knowledge of online searching and of science can use scientific databases to extract data on economically important scientific developments and use this information before it is widely known to guide investment decisions.

If an investor has a clear idea of a scientific advance that he or she thinks will be profitable, then the investor can do online patent searches. Searching a patent file such as DERWENT or CLAIMS, or a current-awareness file that contains patent information, such as CApreviews, should give investors up-to-the-minute information that can be applied toward profitable investments. In addition, NTIS contains information on patents that will become available for licensing from the government. By searching NTIS, then following the Federal Register NTIS section, an investor can learn when a patent was licensed and to whom.

Example 3 shows how the above theory can be applied. An investor would like to invest in companies working on a drug that could treat migraine headaches. Logically, stock in one of these companies would be an attractive investment, particularly if the investor were able to find a company with early patent protection on such a drug before the patent were generally known and the knowledge sent stock prices up. The investor could search the CA file, using a query combining migraine with (drug? or pharm?) to determine which companies are actively seeking patent protection for these potential medications.

7. CONCLUSION

Scientific databases can be used successfully to find valuable business information. While the data may not be presented as the file's main subject, it is there nonetheless. The business areas of marketing, sales, research, and finance can all find useful -- and sometimes critical -- information in these nontraditional sources.

EXAMPLE 1

```
File 154:MEDLINE 80-88/FEB

    Set  Items  Description
    ---  -----  -----------
?s echocardiography(l)is
         11527  ECHOCARDIOGRAPHY/DE
         50361  IS/DE
    S1     183  ECHOCARDIOGRAPHY(L)IS
?limit s1/maj
    S2      51  S1/MAJ
?sort s2/all/py,d
    S3      51  S2/ALL/PY,D
?t3/7/1
```

3/7/1
06101166   87075166
  Intraoperative high-frequency epicardial echocardiography in coronary revascularization: locating deeply embedded coronary arteries.
  Hiratzka LF; McPherson DD; Brandt B 3d; Lamberth WC Jr; Marcus ML; Kerber RE
  Department of Surgery, University of Iowa Hospitals and Clinics, Iowa City 52242.
  Ann Thorac Surg (UNITED STATES)   Dec 1986, 42 (6 Suppl) pS9-11, ISSN 0003-4975   Journal Code: 683
  Contract/Grant No.: HL 32295; HL 14388
  Languages: ENGLISH
  During coronary revascularization, the precise location of major coronary arteries may be obscured by overlying fat, myocardial bridging, or epicardial scarring. High-frequency epicardial echocardiography can be used intraoperatively to quickly image and locate such arteries and eliminate the need for time-consuming epicardial exploration or potentially deleterious retrograde probing of distal coronary artery branches. This technique can be applied using commercially available equipment and the aid of a skilled technician.

EXAMPLE 2

```
FILE 'CA' ENTERED AT 14:40:16 ON 21 JAN 88
COPYRIGHT (C) 1988 AMERICAN CHEMICAL SOCIETY

FILE LAST UPDATED:  9 JAN 88 (880109/ED)   VOL 108 ISS 2

=> s (computer(w)program?)/ab,bi
        58159 COMPUTER/AB
        50756 COMPUTER/BI
        56162 PROGRAM?/AB
        33648 PROGRAM?/BI
L1      27976 (COMPUTER(W)PROGRAM?)/AB,BI

=> s (molecular(w)model?)/ab,bi
         2400 MOLECULAR/AB
       298934 MOLECULAR/BI
       399257 MODEL?/AB
       201625 MODEL?/BI
     L2        639 (MOLECULAR(W)MODEL?)/AB,BI

=> s l1 and l2
L3         34 L1 AND L2

=> dis l3 all 1

L3  ANSWER 1 OF 34

AN  CA107(26):243058g
TI  Molecular modeling system TDAMA
AU  Abe, Shoukichi
CS  Fac. Educ., Yamagata Univ.
LO  Yamagata 990, Japan
SO  Kaiho - Kagaku PC Kenkyukai, 9(2), 29-41
SC  65-5 (General Physical Chemistry)
DT  J
CO  KKPKDI
PY  1987
LA  Japan
AB  A microcomputer assisted system TDAMA for mol. modeling is described.
    Its BASIC source listing is given.
KW  mol modeling computer program; structure mol computer program
IT  Computer program
        (for mol. modeling)
IT  Molecular structure
        (modeling of, computer program for)

=> dis l3 au,cs,lo 2-34


L3  ANSWER 2 OF 34

AU  Nakano, Hidehiko; Danbata, Hideyuki; Kaneko, Masao; Sangen, Osamu
CS  Dep. Appl. Chem., Himeji Inst. Technol.
LO  Himeji 671-22, Japan
```

L3   ANSWER 3 OF 34

AU   Nakata, Yoshiro
CS   Fac. Gen. Stud., Gunma Univ.
LO   Maebashi 371, Japan

L3   ANSWER 4 OF 34

AU   Brickmann, Juergen; Waldherr-Teschner, Michael; Demuth, Reinhard
CS   Inst. Phys. Chem., Tech. Hochsch.
LO   Darmstadt 6100, Fed. Rep. Ger.

L3   ANSWER 5 OF 34

AU   Kihara, Hiroshi; Mukai, Kunihiko; Nakano, Hidehiko
CS   Hyogo Univ. Teach. Educ.
LO   Hyogo 673-14, Japan

L3   ANSWER 6 OF 34

AU   Vinter, J. G.; Davis, A.; Saunders, M. R.
CS   Smith Kline and French Res.
LO   Welwyn/Herts AL6 9AR, UK

L3   ANSWER 7 OF 34

AU   O'Donnell, T. J.; Mitchell, K. D.
CS   Abbott Lab.
LO   Abbott Park, IL 60064, USA

L3   ANSWER 8 OF 34

AU   Ricketts, David M.
CS   Phys. Chem. Lab.
LO   Oxford OX1 3QZ, UK

L3   ANSWER 9 OF 34

AU   Cole, Gregory Michael
CS   Texas A and M Univ.
LO   College Station, TX, USA

L3   ANSWER 10 OF 34

AU   Lejeune, J.; Michel, A. G.; Vercauteren, D. P.
CS   Lab. Chim. Mol. Struct., Fac. Univ. Notre-Dame de la Paix
LO   Namur B-5000, Belg.

L3   ANSWER 11 OF 34

AU   Lah, Myoung Soo; Lim, Byung Chul; Koo, Chung Hoe; Shin, Whanchul
CS   Coll. Nat. Sci., Seoul Natl. Univ.
LO   Seoul 151, S. Korea

L3   ANSWER 12 OF 34

AU   White, David N. J.; Pearson, John E.
CS   Chem. Dep., Univ. Glasgow
LO   Glasgow G12 8QQ, UK

L3 ANSWER 13 OF 34

AU White, David N. J.; Tyler, J. Kelvin; Lindley, Matthew R.
CS Chem. Dep., Univ. Glasgow
LO Glasgow G12 8QQ, UK

L3 ANSWER 14 OF 34

AU Cho, Seikichi; Takizawa, Reiko; Taguchi, Masahiko; Hoshino, Junichiro
CS Fac. Educ., Gunma Univ.
LO Maebashi, Japan

L3 ANSWER 15 OF 34

AU Connolly, Michael L.
CS Res. Inst., Scripps Clin.
LO La Jolla, CA, USA

L3 ANSWER 16 OF 34

AU Jefford, Charles W.; Mareda, Jiri; Combremont, Jean Jacques; Weber, Jacques
CS Dep. Org. Chem., Univ. Geneva
LO Geneva CH-1211/4, Switz.

L3 ANSWER 17 OF 34

AU Muramatsu, Takashi; Hanaya, Kaoru
CS Miyagi Univ. Educ.
LO Sendai 980, Japan

L3 ANSWER 18 OF 34

AU Cory, M.; Bentley, J.
CS Wellcome Res. Lab., Burroughs Wellcome Co.
LO Research Triangle Park, NC, USA

L3 ANSWER 19 OF 34

AU Nagoa, Teruo
CS Hakodate Tech. Coll.
LO Hakodate, Japan

L3 ANSWER 20 OF 34

AU Sato, Mitsunobu; Nakano, Hidehiko
CS Dep. Eng., Natl. Sci. Mus.
LO Tokyo, Japan

L3 ANSWER 21 OF 34

AU Marsili, Mario; Floersheim, Philipp; Dreiding, Andre S.
CS Inst. Org. Chem., Univ. Zurich-Irchel
LO Zurich 8057, Switz.

L3 ANSWER 22 OF 34

AU Murray, K.; Linder, P. W.
CS Dep. Chem., UWIST
LO Cardiff CF1 3NU, UK

L3 ANSWER 23 OF 34

AU Yurchenko, A. G.; Kulik, N. I.
LO USSR

L3 ANSWER 24 OF 34

AU North, A. C. T.
CS Astbury Dep. Biophys., Univ. Leeds
LO Leeds, Engl.

L3 ANSWER 25 OF 34

AU Takenaka, Akio; Sasada, Yoshio
CS Fac. Sci., Tokyo Inst. Tech.
LO Tokyo, Japan

L3 ANSWER 26 OF 34

AU Sakurai, Toshio
CS Inst. Phys. Chem. Res.
LO Wakoshi, Japan

L3 ANSWER 27 OF 34

AU Smith, Graham M.; Gund, Peter
CS Merck Sharp and Dohme Res. Lab.
LO Rahway, N. J., USA

L3 ANSWER 28 OF 34

AU Odeyanko, B. N.; Nigmatullin, R. S.
CS Inst. Tochnoi Mekh. Vychisl. Tekh.
LO Novosibirsk, USSR

L3 ANSWER 29 OF 34

AU Warme, Paul K.
CS Dep. Biochem. Biophys., Pennsylvania State Univ.
LO University Park, Pa., USA

L3 ANSWER 30 OF 34

AU Stilbs, P.
CS Chem. Cent., Lund Inst. Technol.
LO Lund, Swed.

L3 ANSWER 31 OF 34

AU Kuznetsov, M. A.
CS Leningr. Gos. Univ.
LO Leningrad, USSR

L3 ANSWER 32 OF 34

AU Still, W. Clark; Lewis, Arthur J.
CS Dep. Chem., Columbia Univ.
LO New York, N. Y., USA

L3 ANSWER 33 OF 34

AU Gavuzzo, E.; Pagliuca, S.; Pavel, V.; Quagliata, C.
CS Ist. Chim., Univ. Roma
LO Rome, Italy

L3 ANSWER 34 OF 34

AU Hilderbrandt, R. L.
CS Cornell Univ.
LO Ithaca, N. Y., USA

EXAMPLE 3

```
FILE 'CA' ENTERED AT 14:09:53 ON 21 JAN 88
COPYRIGHT (C) 1988 AMERICAN CHEMICAL SOCIETY

FILE LAST UPDATED:  9 JAN 88 (880109/ED)   VOL 108 ISS 2

=> s migraine?/ab,bi
         412 MIGRAINE?/AB
         480 MIGRAINE?/BI
L1       559 MIGRAINE?/AB,BI

=> s l1 and p/dt
     1256996 P/DT
L2       121 L1 AND P/DT

=> s l2 and (drug? or pharm?)/ab,bi
      116555 DRUG?/AB
       89861 DRUG?/BI
       51037 PHARM?/AB
      111560 PHARM?/BI
L3        66 L2 AND (DRUG? OR PHARM?)/AB,BI

=> s l3 range=(1987,)
       10828 DRUG?/AB
        7088 DRUG?/BI
        5561 PHARM?/AB
        8687 PHARM?/BI
L4        14 L2 AND (DRUG? OR PHARM?)/AB,BI

=> dis l4 ti,au,cs,lo,pi,ai,py 1-14

L4   ANSWER 1 OF 14

TI   Preparation of 1-imidazolylalkyl-, 2-triazolylalkyl-, or
     3-pyridinylalkyl-1,2,3-benzotriazin-4(3H)-ones as cardiovascular
     agents and antithrombotics
AU   Wright, William B., Jr.; Tomcufcik, Andrew S.; Marsico, Joseph W.,
     Jr.
CS   American Cyanamid Co.
LO   USA
PI   U.S. US 4680293 A, 14 Jul 1987, 9 pp.
AI   Appl. 835501, 3 Mar 1986
PY   1987

L4   ANSWER 2 OF 14

TI   Preparation of [[(p-fluorobenzoyl)-piperidino]alkyl]theophyllines as
     antimigraines, bronchodilators, allergy inhibitors, and bradykinin
     antagonists
AU   Thiele, Kurt; Geissmann, Felix; Zirngibl, Ludwig; Jahn, Ulrich
CS   Siegfried A.-G.
LO   Switz.
```

PI U.S. US 4668786 A, 26 May 1987, 4 pp. Cont.-in-part of U.S. 4,603,204.
AI Appl. 813439, 26 Dec 1985; CH Appl. 81/4739, 20 Jul 1981; US Appl. 474230, 11 Mar 1983
PY 1987

L4 ANSWER 3 OF 14

TI Preparation of 5-[2-(acylamino)ethyl]tryptamines as antimigraine agents
AU Mills, Keith; Eldred, Colin David; Oxford, Alexander William; Coates, Ian Harold; Bays, David Edmund; Webb, Colin Frederick; Dowle, Michael Dennis
CS Glaxo Group Ltd.
LO UK
PI Ger. Offen. DE 3700408 A1, 9 Jul 1987, 25 pp.
AI Appl. 3700408, 8 Jan 1987; GB Appl. 86/397, 8 Jan 1986
PY 1987

L4 ANSWER 4 OF 14

TI Preparation of 5-(2-aminoethyl)tryptamines as antimigraine agents
AU Mills, Keith; Coates, Ian Harold; Bays, David Edmund; Webb, Colin Frederick; Dowle, Michael Dennis
CS Glaxo Group Ltd.
LO UK
PI Ger. Offen. DE 3700407 A1, 9 Jul 1987, 17 pp.
AI Appl. 3700407, 8 Jan 1987; GB Appl. 86/398, 8 Jan 1986
PY 1987

L4 ANSWER 5 OF 14

TI Tetrahydroisoquinoline derivatives, their preparation and formulation, and their use for treating cardiovascular diseases susceptible to treatment with calcium channel blockers
AU Clark, Robin; Muchowski, Joseph M.; Chiu, Fang Ting; Gardner, John O.; Berger, Jacob
CS Syntex (U.S.A.), Inc.
LO USA
PI U.S. US 4667038 A, 19 May 1987, 34 pp. Cont.-in-part of U.S. 4,613,606.
AI Appl. 909659, 22 Sep 1986; US Appl. 830464, 2 Dec 1985
PY 1987

L4 ANSWER 6 OF 14

TI Preparation and formulation of quinuclidine derivatives having gastric motility enhancing and/or antiemetic activity
AU King, Francis David
CS Beecham Group PLC
LO UK
PI Eur. Pat. Appl. EP 221702 A2, 13 May 1987, 16 pp. Designated States: BE, CH, DE, ES, FR, GB, GR, IT, LI, LU, NL, SE
AI Appl. 86/307958, 15 Oct 1986; GB Appl. 85/25844, 19 Oct 1985
PY 1987

L4 ANSWER 7 OF 14

TI Pharmaceutical tablets for easy administration of pellets and their use

AU Deboeck, Arthur Marie; Fossion, Jacques Jean; Brusselman, Joseph Yvon; Baudier, Philippe Raymond
CS GALEPHAR S. A.
LO Belg.
PI Eur. Pat. Appl. EP 207041 A2, 30 Dec 1986, 31 pp. Designated States: AT, BE, CH, DE, FR, GB, IT, LI, NL, SE
AI Appl. 86/870080, 5 Jun 1986; LU Appl. 85943, 12 Jun 1985
PY 1986

L4 ANSWER 8 OF 14

TI Preparation of 1,3,4,5-tetrahydrobenz[cd]indole derivatives as pharmaceuticals
AU Somei, Masanori
CS Kissei Pharmaceutical Co., Ltd.
LO Japan
PI Jpn. Kokai Tokkyo Koho JP 62/63567 A2 [87/63567], 20 Mar 1987, 11 pp.
AI Appl. 85/203888, 13 Sep 1985
PY 1987

L4 ANSWER 9 OF 14

TI Preparation of pyridazinylbenzimidazoles for prophylaxis and treatment of migraine
AU Van Meel, Jacques; Trach, Volker; Austel, Volkhard; Heider, Joachim; Eberlein, Wolfgang
CS Thomae, Dr. Karl, G.m.b.H.
LO Fed. Rep. Ger.
PI Ger. Offen. DE 3536030 A1, 9 Apr 1987, 10 pp.
AI Appl. 3536030, 9 Oct 1985
PY 1987

L4 ANSWER 10 OF 14

TI Azabicylcoalkanes procedure for their preparation, and their use a spharmaceuticals
AU King, Francis David; Joiner, Karen Anne
CS Beecham Group PLC
LO UK
PI Eur. Pat. Appl. EP 214772 A1, 18 Mar 1987, 36 pp. Designated States: BE, CH, DE, FR, GB, IT, LI, NL
AI Appl. 86/306221, 12 Aug 1986; GB Appl. 85/20616, 16 Aug 1985
PY 1987

L4 ANSWER 11 OF 14

TI Preparation of dihydropyridine compounds as pharmaceuticals
CS Ciba-Geigy A.-G.
LO Switz.
PI Jpn. Kokai Tokkyo Koho JP 62/39569 A2 [87/39569], 20 Feb 1987, 35 pp.
AI Appl. 86/189711, 14 Aug 1986; CH Appl. 85/3504, 14 Aug 1985
PY 1987

L4 ANSWER 12 OF 14

TI Therapeutic (.+-.)-4-amino-5-chloro-2-methoxy-N-(4-[1-aza-bicyclo[3.3.1]-nonyl]) benzamide and related compounds
CS Beecham Group PLC

- LO UK
- PI Jpn. Kokai Tokkyo Koho JP 62/424 A2 [87/424], 6 Jan 1987, 6 pp.
- AI Appl. 86/144677, 20 Jun 1986; GB Appl. 85/15845, 22 Jun 1985
- PY 1987

L4 ANSWER 13 OF 14

- TI Tetrahydroisoquinoline derivatives, process and intermediates for their preparation and pharmaceutical compositions containing them
- AU Kaiser, Carl; Kruse, Lawrence Ivan
- CS SmithKline Beckman Corp.
- LO USA
- PI Eur. Pat. Appl. EP 210828 A2, 4 Feb 1987, 17 pp. Designated States: AT, BE, CH, DE, FR, GB, IT, LI, LU, NL, SE
- AI Appl. 86/305637, 22 Jul 1986; GB Appl. 85/18635, 23 Jul 1985
- PY 1987

L4 ANSWER 14 OF 14

- TI Pharmaceutical 9,10-dihydrogenated ergot alkaloid-containing compositions
- AU Zuger, Othmar
- CS Sandoz A.-G.
- LO Switz.
- PI Brit. UK Pat. Appl. GB 2170407 A1, 6 Aug 1986, 11 pp.
- AI Appl. 86/2602, 3 Feb 1986; GB Appl. 85/2889, 5 Feb 1985; GB Appl. 85/17604, 12 Jul 1985
- PY 1986

TRAINING THE END USER IN A CAS ONLINE ACADEMIC ENVIRONMENT

Johanna C. Ross, University of California

Keywords: End User Training, CAS Online, Remote Access, Online Searching, End User Profiles, Academic rates, Chemical Abstracts.

Abstract: The Physical Sciences Library at the University of California at Davis has participated in the Academic Rate program offered by the Chemical Abstracts Service, almost from it's inception. The Graduate Division has supported library efforts both by subsidizing database costs during the initial 16 months of service and by enabling access to the database from the campus Computer Center, or from any campus location with connections to the Computer Center data switch. Faculty and graduate students interested in searching the database may register for free training classes. After training, they may search by using the remote access microcomputer connected to the Computer Center data switch, they may use their own departmental accounts if they have one; or they may choose to continue to have their searches done by a librarian intermediary. After four years of participation in the Academic Program and offering end user instruction, approximately 40% of searches are performed by end users.

1. BACKGROUND

When the Chemical Abstracts Service (CAS) announced that they would make a flat rate fee of $500 per month during non prime hours available to academic users in late 1983, it was immediately recognized that this would be of great benefit to the campus community. Because the rate must be paid in advance, and the library budget did not have the funds to gamble on a recharging scheme to recoup our direct costs, a grant was requested from the Graduate Division.

Fortunately, the Dean of the Graduate Division was quick to recognize the value of the database and immediately granted our request for a years prepayment of online charges. In addition, he requested that the Computer Center make direct connection to a microcomputer which was to be housed in the Physical Sciences Library (PSL). Anyone who had remote or direct access to the Computer Center, which is virtually the whole campus, could ask at the Computer Center Develcon switch connection for CAS. This would shunt the call to PSL. The Library would already have entered a user code and password on the microcomputer for that individual. After these had been entered, the microcomputer would autodial the CAS computer in Columbus, Ohio and connect the user to the CAS Online computer. The microcomputer in PSL would keep a log of which PSL assigned password was using the system. If downloading was required and the user was using a dumb terminal, a command would result in the search results being downloaded on the PSL microcomputer to be printed out on request the following day. After recharging was initiated, the log was matched to the CAS bill for recharging.

In addition to paying for the first year of online service, the Graduate Division would pay for the microcomputer, arrange for the computer program to perform the above operations to be written, and pay for the cable connection from the Computer Center to the Physical Sciences Library.

By March 1984, the paperwork had been processed through channels and the CAS Online password was ready for use. As yet, no formal training of librarians on the use of the system had been taken and none could be scheduled for another two months. Several librarians in the Physical Sciences Library and the Biological and Agricultural Sciences Department of the Main Library were experienced searchers so it was decided to go online in March 1984 using the bibliographic file. We would wait for training before using the structural search capabilities of the registry file.

The remote access microcomputer program had not been written (and would not be available for a year) so search station equipment at the two library service desks would be the principal access points with additional access available during evening hours to those graduate students and faculty members who had access to search terminals or microcomputers. Because California is on the west coast, the system was available from 11:00 A.M. in the morning, Pacific Standard time. The regular work hours were divided between the two reference points so search demand could be more efficiently serviced while those with equipment could use the evening and early morning hours. It was expected that initial demand would be heavy but in two to three months usage would stabilize at a level somewhat higher than the full charge service had been.

2. INITIAL PERIOD OF SERVICE WITH NO RECHARGE

The first few months of usage can only be described as chaotic. Instead of demand slackening, it continued unabated. Instead of waiting for training to use the structural search capabilities, a synthetic organic chemistry professor wanted to use the system immediately.

Users quickly learned the scheduled hours of service and would drop by to see if a "quick one" might be sandwiched into that day's schedule. One department learned that the library divided the available search hours and split a systematic search of the literature on more than a hundred compounds between the two library search points in order to get the project completed.

To satisfy the demand for structure searches, that portion of the search manual was perused at length. The professor would come by with the structure to be searched and we would work together and test the system. After a few calls to the search desk we were doing structural searches with some regularity. A search process which had been expected to be difficult proved to be surprisingly simple. The professor was also acquiring a great deal of competency.

For those who wished to search during evening hours, when no assistance was available, training was required. It soon became apparent that a more structured approach to training was required. Several prospective end users would be scheduled for training at the same time rather than giving minimal directions on a one to one basis. The search manuals were summarized into a few pages of salient features and given to prospective end users. A class for the faculty in the Chemistry Department was held.

The system continued to be used almost every available minute during regular working hours. Other academic institutions were also using the system heavily. The demand on the computer at Columbus resulted in the non prime hours being cut from 11:00 A.M. to 5:00 A.M. Pacific time to 2:00 P.M. to 5:00 A.M. Pacific time, which further complicated our ability to meet demand during regular working hours; although the response time improved dramatically.

3. WORKING FOR A BALANCE, FORMALIZING TRAINING

Several new developments eventually eased the workload in the Physical Sciences Library although campus demand has remained at a much higher level than originally anticipated. First, offline prints were made available at the reduced rate. Long printouts could be ordered instead of being printed online. Second, the flat fee rate was changed to a percentage rate: 10% of commercial charges, which after July 1985, the user paid. Concurrently, more than one password could be obtained. This meant that each library service point could search at the same time and thus each could utilize the non prime hours during the regular work day. Third, campus departments could obtain their own passwords and not use the library password. Fourth, registry file searching was expanded by CAS to permit searching by molecular formulas, element counts, and chemical common names. The need to search by structure dropped significantly.

Since the promised computer program was slow being written and not ready for use until approximately one year after the introduction of the academic rate, the Graduate Division extended the grant for online time through the fiscal year, until June 30, 1985. In addition, for the next fiscal year, they funded 25% of a librarian's salary to provide training on the system to Graduate Students. Since the funding was from the Graduate Division, faculty and staff could only be admitted on a space available basis. The following year they were admitted on request. Approximately 12% of those taking online training are faculty or staff.

Initially, instruction was divided into bibliographic file and registry file instruction. The registry file was further divided into structural and nonstructural sections. Each class was one and one-half hours long. In addition, each student received $10 credit for online searching for each class attended. A very small amount of class time demonstrated using the system but familiarity would be primarily obtained through using credits. Formalized handouts to serve in lieu of a search manual were prepared and given to each student.

During the 1986/87 academic year the classes were restructured into basic and advanced classes. The two core classes teach the basic techniques of the bibliographic file and how to obtain registry numbers from the registry file without doing a structural search. The relation of the one file to the other, with file crossover, is presented. More than 90% of the class time is devoted to file content, with boolean logic knowledge assumed. Particular emphasis on display and analysis of index terms is made, so users will know if they have done a good search.

For those wishing to achieve advanced competency, an advanced bibliographic class is offered. This class is designed to analyze search questions and to recognize the different approaches different types of questions require. Because few register for any advanced classes, this class was combined into the searching laboratory class this year. This not only provides the opportunity to learn theoretical models of searching, but to actually practice on the system using the techniques.

Few students register for the class on chemical structure searching. In a 90 minute class it is difficult to do more than illustrate the theory of structural searching and it is suggested that those who truly wish to do their own structural searching register for the advanced class.

4. PROGRESSING TO MATURITY

The first year, 92 students enrolled in one or more classes for a total of 176 class registrations. The second year, there were 208 student class registrations. It is anticipated that registration will stabilize at between 150-200 class registrations per year. Most students take only the two basic classes; they account for more than 80% of total registration.

After almost four years of participation in the academic rate program offered by CAS and after two and one-half years of formal training to faculty and graduate students in the use of the system, the usage patterns are beginning to stabilize. Five departments have obtained their own accounts; each account can accommodate five different passwords. In addition, one of the PSL passwords is assigned to the microcomputer. The use of the PSL microcomputer continues to be high. When it became possible to obtain multiple passwords, it was expected that usage would drop so low as to make the microcomputer obsolete, just after the program had been written. It has not happened.

Usage in several departments remains minimal. A notable exception is the Chemistry Department. It should be remembered that the library continues to offer the option of the librarian performing the search for the user. Because of the superior skill of the librarian, having a search done will almost always cost less than the end user doing it himself since no surcharge is added by the library.

Many students continue to have the librarian perform their searches. If a student wishes to use class credit, however, that student must use the keyboard although liberal prompting by the librarian may be made. These hands on sessions are invaluable in putting the theory learned in class into practice.

A significant benefit of training, even when the librarian continues to perform the search, is the educated user. Students come to the search session with registry numbers already in hand and a clear concept of what the system will do. It is almost routine for them to express appreciation for what the system can do in so little time and for such a small cost.

A very significant change in the way the Chemistry Department does their work is apparent, both in the statistics of departmental use and in library use patterns. The faculty member who wanted to learn structural searching immediately had been a frequent library user, coming in to use the printed Chemical Abstracts, sometimes several times a day. He rarely comes to the library anymore. After purchasing his own office microcomputer he can do it better and faster as an end user.

Sometimes faculty and students try to do a search and encounter problems. The librarian has assumed the role of a consultant. It is very gratifying to be able to show a better way to structure a search, or to demonstrate techniques which will enable a structural search to run when it exceeded search limits for the faculty member.

Training the end user not only assists the researcher in doing his/her work in a more expedient fashion, it also teaches a respect for the information professional. This includes not only the one doing the searching, but those who index the information in so detailed a fashion as to make it available to the user.

CHEMICAL ABSTRACTS ONLINE USAGE

1984 ALL USERS

	CAS Hrs.	CAS $	Reg Hrs	Reg $
Mar-June 1984	106.54	11,003	44.19	15,717
July-Dec 1984	150.98	19,227	66.01	25,529
Totals	257.52	$30,230	110.20	$41,246

1985-87 Librarian Mediated Usage

Physical Sciences Library

	CAS Hrs.	CAS $	Reg Hrs	Reg $
Jan-June 1985	94.26	16,756	56.70	16,756
July-Dec 1985	54.01	6,037	24.58	3,763
Jan-June 1986	67.58	5,327	9.12	662
July-Dec 1986	50.83	6,596	8.15	692
Jan-June 1987	58.08	11,865	9.75	988
July-Dec 1987	50.75	9,813	5.47	883
Totals	375.51	$56,394	113.77	$23,744

Biological and Agricultural Sciences Reference Dept.

	CAS Hrs.	CAS $	Reg Hrs	Reg $
Apr-June 1985	12.52	1,179	0	0
July-Dec 1985	23.03	3,771	.09	7
Jan-June 1986	27.53	4,346	.73	66
July-Dec 1986	15.28	2,845	3.63	658
Jan-June 1987	25.61	4,670	.17	14
July-Dec 1987	17.27	3,445	.05	3
Totals	121.24	$20,256	4.67	$748

End User Usage

Remote Access via Computer Center Switch and PSL Microcomputer

	CAS Hrs.	CAS $	Reg Hrs	Reg $
Jan-June 1985	0	0	0	0
July-Dec 1985	30.22	3,443	2.25	392
Jan-June 1986	53.69	9,367	8.50	1,639
July-Dec 1986	67.27	7,235	10.19	660
Jan-June 1987	47.72	8,610	18.50	3,208
July-Dec 1987	40.49	6,634	2.80	785
Totals	239.39	$35,289	42.24	$6,684

Chemistry

	CAS Hrs.	CAS $	Reg Hrs	Reg $
July-Dec 1985	18.61	2,103	6.99	849
Jan-June 1986	39.98	5,558	9.15	1,308
July-Dec 1986	21.99	3,364	9.99	2,140
Jan-June 1987	29.67	4,291	12.92	3,105
July-Dec 1987	24.90	3,734	9.48	2,485
Totals	135.15	$19,050	48.53	$9,887

Viticulture and Enology

	CAS Hrs	CAS $	Reg Hrs	Reg $
July-Dec 1985	9.12	884	1.43	84
Jan-June 1986	9.10	1,121	.52	38
July-Dec 1986	8.12	1,059	1.39	104
Jan-June 1987	4.66	872	.27	23
July-Dec 1987	5.1	938	.42	31
Totals	36.10	$4,874	4.03	$281

Environmental Horticulture

	CAS Hrs	CAS $	Reg Hrs	Reg $
July-Dec 1985	n/a*	243	0	0
Jan-June 1986	n/a	679	0	0
July-Dec 1986	n/a	826	0	0
Jan-June 1987	n/a	1,007	0	0
July-Dec 1987	n/a	302	0	0
Totals		$3,057		

Biochemistry & Biophysics

	CAS Hrs	CAS $	Reg Hrs	Reg $
Jan-June 1986	n/a	984	0	0
July-Dec 1986	n/a	921	0	0
Jan-June 1987	n/a	681	0	0
July-Dec 1987	n/a	52	0	0
Totals		$2,638		

Animal Science

	CAS Hrs	CAS $	Reg Hrs	Reg $
Jan-June 1985	0	0	.48	118
July-Dec 1985	.56	56	0	0
Jan-June 1986	1.41	359	0	0
July-Dec 1986	1.10	211	0	0
Jan-June 1987	.18	30	0	0
July-Dec 1987	.22	48	0	0
Totals	3.47	$704	.48	$118

Total Usage January 1985-December 1987

	CAS Hrs	CAS $	Reg Hrs	Reg $
Library	496.75	$76,650	118.44	$24,492
End Users	414.11	65,612	95.28	16,970

* n/a=not available

MEDICAL INFORMATION ON CD-ROM

Peter B. Schipma, I.S. Grupe, Inc.

This paper postulates that the next major advance in information storage and retrieval may be engendered by the availability of inexpensive computational power, provided by the Personal Computer, together with the phenomenal storage capacity of recently introduced optical disc technology. Processing capability was the major constraint for many centuries, limiting information retrieval to single order classification arrangements of the primary material. The advent of the digital computer provided the power to permit information retrieval based on content of the materials or their surrogates, but the cost of the processing and storage hardware was such that databases had to be shared, giving rise to the online systems in widespread use today. Microcomputers have greatly reduced the cost of raw processing power, and optical discs show a similar promise for the cost of storage, making a new generation of retrieval systems, at the personal level, possible. The potential for such systems is described in this paper, and such systems are compared to the state-of-the-art online methodology. The supporting technologies are discussed in lay terminology. Optical media and devices are considerably different from the magnetic technology that underlies the previous generation of systems, requiring novel considerations in the design of these systems; the paper summarizes design considerations for generating such a system. Finally, an operational system in the medical field, based on the microcomputer and optical disc, is detailed.

1. INTRODUCTION

For many centuries, information retrieval was restricted to manual search through sets of printed materials, with individual information collections, typically books, organized according to one classification system or another. Early in this century, some semi-automated methods were developed which permitted a rudimentary level of concurrent searching, but the advent of the digital computer heralded the arrival of true information retrieval from an information collection, a database. The first systems were somewhat cumbersome and quite slow, but evolved to the reasonably powerful systems in use today that combine the power of mainframe computers with large shared data collections; these are called online information retrieval systems. Online access to databases is generally regarded as the current state-of-the-art in information retrieval technology. Although it has greatly increased the availability and reduced the cost of information, it still has some drawbacks. Online access is fairly expensive, requiring the user to pay for telecommunications charges and for use of the host computer/database. Since voice-grade telephone lines permit only low bandwidths, users typically operate at 1200 baud which transfers only about 100 characters per second. The user must have a terminal, modem, telephone line, and, optionally, a printer. It is not uncommon for the problems related to configuring the equipment and using the logon procedures to pose barriers to use. Online users are aware that "the meter is running" while a search is being performed, which may cause them to hurry or to limit their search strategy development. Some users are anxious about taking improper actions which may result in extra charges.

I. S. Grupe (ISG) has recently completed development of an information access system based on the CD-ROM (Compact Disc Read-Only Memory) storage technology and the Personal Computer (PC). Such a system is a radical departure from online technology, since it puts the retrieval mechanism and the databases under the direct control of the user. This paper describes the technologies that make such a system possible, indicates the design considerations followed in its generation, and discusses an application of such a system in the provision of medical information.

2. **PERSONAL COMPUTER EVOLUTION**

Advances in computer technology have been rapid and astounding. (To put this statement in perspective, consider: had aircraft technology increased at a comparable pace in the last quarter century, today's airliners would carry 1000 people around the world in an hour on $2 worth of fuel.) The current representative of these advances is the PC, a device having the computational power of a 1970's mainframe, 100 times the memory capacity, and high capacity rotating magnetic storage. And the cost of such a machine is within the reach of high school students. Though, for the sake of brevity, we will not dwell on this topic, and assume that readers are well aware of it, PC technology is a truly remarkable and unprecedented phenomenon. With suitable software, the PC has sufficient computational power to permit searches of multi-megaByte databases, using complex queries, in times very similar to those experienced using a mainframe in a typical online system.

3. **CD-ROM EVOLUTION**

3.1 **Derivation**

CD-ROM is one member of the family of Compact Discs. The first product in this family was the Digital Audio Disc (DAD), now called simply CD. The rapid growth of CD products has had an important effect; it has driven the cost of disc replication and the cost of players down. Retail prices for players have fallen from $500 to $88 in less than two years. Audio information is stored on CD in digital form, as discrete time samples of the waveform representing the music. Many samples are required to represent the waveform accurately, but the storage density of CD is high, and a 120mm diameter disc can hold about 73 minutes worth of audio information.

Only an extension of digital audio was necessary to generate CD-ROM, since information was already stored as digital (binary) data. A CD-ROM stores ASCII code comprised of 0's and 1's, providing information in a form typically used for machine data processing. The storage density translates to a capacity of 550mB (550 million characters) per disc. This is very high in comparison to other media. A floppy disk (magnetic) typically stores some 360kB, so one CD-ROM has the storage capacity of 1,500 floppy disks. The hard disks sometimes found on personal computers range in size up to 30mB; one CD-ROM is the equivalent of 18 30mB disks. In terms of a more common medium, one CD-ROM holds the equivalent of over 270,000 typewritten pages (a 45 foot stack of paper).

3.2 Mechanism

All types of CDs use reflective laser optical technology. This technology was postulated as early as the 1920's, and some patents were issued then, but the technology was not successfully introduced until the advent of laser videodiscs in the 1970's. Laser reflective optical media consist of a rigid aluminum or plastic substrate coated with a very thin layer of a highly reflective material all encased in a protective transparent coating. The thickness of the information-containing material is crucial. It must be very uniform and as free as possible of any defects, because a tiny pinhole would wipe out much information due to the high storage density.

Optical discs are replicated by a stamping process. The master is made by using a high-powered laser to ablate material forming very small pits about a micron long. A mold is made from the master, and from this mold stampers are made; these are used to generate replicates. The material cost is quite low - cents per disc, but the mastering cost is high. Since replicates can be stamped out inexpensively the unit cost is very volume dependent, making optical disc manufacture very similar to printing. It costs a lot to set up the press, but copies are inexpensive, so the larger the run, the lower the unit cost. For CD-ROM in quantities greater than 1000, unit manufacturing cost drops to about $15. This is much less than the cost of any other storage medium, even print on paper, yet the data on a CD-ROM are accessible by computer.

A low power laser or a laser diode is used to read an optical disc. The thickness of the information carrying film is one-fourth the wavelength of the laser light used in reading. Therefore, when the light enters a pit, its reflection is destroyed by interference. In the absence of a pit, light is reflected to a photosensor. Though the level of technology is high, and extremely precise positioning and light sensing are required, modern electronic manufacturing techniques have made the reduction of this complex mechanism to practice quite inexpensive. Optical disc players are accurate, rugged, reliable and cheap.

4. SYSTEM DESIGN CONSIDERATIONS

CD-ROM is different than magnetic media. There are only a few parameters that the designer has to worry about, but they significantly impact on the design of a CD-ROM retrieval system. The first is that CD-ROM is a Constant Linear Velocity (CLV) medium rather than a Constant Angular Velocity (CAV) device. CAV discs rotate at a constant speed, which makes the drive mechanism fairly simple, but requires that data be more closely packed near the center of the disc. CLV discs have a constant storage density, with pit spacing the same on outer tracks as on inner ones. Although this makes the drive mechanism more complicated, the reading optics can expect data of constant format at constant delivery rate.

Another consideration is that CD players have a slower access (seek) time than do the drives for magnetic discs. The values are 500 to 1000ms for CDs and 50ms or less for typical Winchester drives. This is due to the fact that data are more closely packed on the CD, requiring more precise head positioning, and to the CLV nature of CD. Because the reading is done optically, however, seeks to nearby positions can be done very quickly, since the mirrors on the head can be rotated slightly in such a case rather than requiring a head movement. So, seek times can be minimized if related data are kept in close proximity.

One must also take into consideration the data transfer rate of a CD-ROM drive, which is also slower than magnetic media drives (about 150 kBytes/s as opposed to 100-300 kBytes/s). This data transfer rate is quite comparable to that of a floppy disk, but only about half of what can be achieved with Winchester technology. Thus, though storage density of a CD-ROM is very high, there are penalties in both seek time and data transfer rate.

The final difference is extremely important. CD-ROM is a read-only storage medium. While this implies real restrictions in terms of the overall utility of the medium as a one-for-one replacement for magnetic media, it is a true advantage in the use of CD-ROM for storage of databases, because the designer can capitalize on the read-only nature by the way he organizes data, in confidence that the organization will remain unchanged.

In light of the advantages (incredible storage capabilities) and the disadvantages (slow access and average transfer rates) outlined, the designer of a CD-ROM retrieval system must spend a great deal of time deciding on the format of his data. Regardless of the data structures decided upon, the following points apply.

- o-Minimize Seeks - typically accomplished through multi-level shallow indexes, hashing and data encoding.

- o-Transfer Large Amounts of Data - typically accomplished through use of large RAM buffers (and, fortunately, PC memory is very inexpensive) and cacheing on a Least-Recently-Used basis.

- o-Store Related Data Proximally - typically accomplished through extensive pre-processing that employs all available knowledge on the content and projected usage of the data.

5. A MEDICAL APPLICATION

The application described below is a PC/CD-ROM system for oncologists (cancer specialists). It uses a proprietary information retrieval system, SearchLITE, developed by ISG, to access medical information from a number of databases stored on a single CD-ROM. It is meant to be used in active clinical practice, and contains current treatment information, the broad knowledge base underlying that information, and the related research literature that supports the knowledge base.

5.1 SearchLITE

SearchLITE (Search via Laser Information TEchnology) is a retrieval engine consisting of three major modules: relational information retrieval, text retrieval and overseer. It is optimized for the CD-ROM storage medium, though it will work perfectly well with data stored on conventional magnetic media. This optimization includes intensive use of the full memory of the host system and the fewest possible number of disc accesses, since long seek time is the most serious disadvantage of CD-ROM technology. SearchLITE performs information retrieval as well as the best of the online systems. It has similar functions and responds very quickly to user entries. However, it has considerably more power than the typical online system. While searching for treatment instructions, for example, the user can transfer to a textbook to check on the basis for a treatment parameter; if the textbook passage mentions an illustration, a single keystroke will bring that to the screen; when the user returns to the treatment database, she/he finds that her/his place has been saved. SearchLITE is written in the C language to make it as portable (transferable among differing hardware configurations) as possible. We have implemented it on the DEC VAX family and the IBM PC/XT and PC/AT. It can easily be ported to other hardware which supports a C compiler.

5.2 OncoDisc

The CD-ROM mastered by ISG is called the OncoDisc, and contains three major information collections. The first application on the OncoDisc is Physician Data Query (PDQ), the cancer treatment infobase generated by the National Cancer Institute (NCI). PDQ contains a directory of over 14,000 physicians who treat cancer, a listing of over 1,000 organizations at which cancer treatment is provided and both standard and investigational treatment protocols in full detail for nearly all forms of cancer. The CANCERLIT database, also produced by NCI, covers the research literature that underlies the treatment information contained in PDQ. CANCERLIT now contains over 600,000 citations going back to 1965. Citations are provided from the journal literature, meetings and symposia, doctoral theses, monographs and letters-to-editors. Abstracts are present for nearly all the citations, and, since 1981, all have been indexed with MeSH terminology. The final component of the OncoDisc is the full text of major references. Since the capacity of a CD-ROM is large, it is possible to include, along with the PDQ infobase and the CANCERLIT database, a selection of seminal references in full-text form. This permits the health professional to have a single source for the most pertinent treatment and reference information, instantly available. ISG generated the first OncoDisc to demonstrate the feasibility of this type of new information retrieval system. SearchLITE and various combinations of databases are now available from different publishers to whom ISG is a supplier.

REMOVING THE MYSTERY: TRAINING THE END USER TO SEARCH

Maxine Leeds Snow, Loyola University Library

Abstract: Loyola University has offered online database searching and bibliographic instruction for many years. Through a class for graduate education students, these two programs merged. This paper discusses the end-user training project, including reasons for designing the class, a description of the program, and the result of our efforts.

The foremost reason for initiating end-user instruction was to give students greater independence. Database searching had in many cases encouraged passive use of the library. Online generated bibliographies appeared magical to students. Yet the library's philosophy had always been to encourage students to make their own choices. Teaching students about the process of online searching was a natural extension of our course-integrated research skills classes.

At academic libraries one can find models of database instruction ranging from well-funded labs to programs where students do no actual searching. Costs, staffing and a consideration of our goals led us to choose a middle ground. Online searching instruction was integrated into a research course. Each students was required to develop a search strategy and perform a search.

After the course, students returned to having their searches done by librarians. Their requests were informed by an awareness of the search process and a sensitivity to its complexity. Student and faculty response was enthusiastic and the program will be a regular part of the curriculum.

1. INTRODUCTION

Loyola University library in New Orleans has been providing database searches for our students and faculty for over a decade. Online searching is the service that makes us look like wizards. At the beginning of the spring semester, this year, I addressed a group of new students in the MBA program. They stared politely as I tried to impress them with visions of hundreds of thousands of books and the vast system of inter-library loan, but when I described instant customized bibliographies, arriving in bright orange letters on a monitor, I saw their faces light up.

Even students and faculty members accustomed to having searches performed have only vague conceptions of the sources of those fabulous printouts. Some refer to all databases as ERICS and most gratefully accept any results as long as the price is right and the search fruitful.

The library also has a long-standing commitment to bibliographic instruction. In tours and lectures we teach students research strategies and spread before them an array of enticing reference sources to develop enthusiastic, informed, and independent library users.

Over the years database searches have been mentioned in library tours. Sometimes online services are introduced when we speak about indexes, to show the relationship between print and electronic reference tools. In other classes the database search service is described in a flurry at the end of a lecture which has up to that point covered traditional print resources. In those instances the subject is thrown in to rouse interest and to teach the students enough about online services to lead them to ask for a search in the future.

When the subject of databases is given five to ten minutes of a tour, we are fulfilling two of the three aims of our bibliographic instruction program. We hope we are stimulating students' interests in research and we are informing them about a service. The students in such classes are not being given greater control over their own research. By introducing them to the idea of online services we encourage them to be more dependent upon librarians. There is always a balance in library instruction between education and promotion of library services. In order to accomplish more teaching we looked for ways to devote more time to the description of online services. We wanted to move beyond dazzling them and provide an opportunity for more in-depth understanding.

This desire led the reference librarians to begin devoting half or more of the time in some library lectures to a search demonstration. In these classes students are invited to crowd around a microcomputer to view a live search. These demonstrations teach more about searching than a short description can teach. Students are fascinated by the live interaction and we succeed in lifting the veil of mystery which hid the mechanics of online searching.

2. MODELS OF END-USER TRAINING

Ralph Alberico, who was until 1986 Head of Reference Services at Loyola, took online instruction a step further. He taught a workshop to faculty members on electronic database searching. Many of the attendees attempted their own practice searches following the workshop. He planned to expand that program and teach some students to search, but in the summer of 1986 Ralph left Loyola to accept a position at another library.

I became Head of Reference Services and with the promotion I inherited Ralph's goal of end-user instruction and a microcomputer which had been ordered largely for that purpose. That was the sort of challenge I was looking for when I accepted the promotion, but when the microcomputer arrived I convinced myself that I was too busy to open the box. When at long last I pried open the carton I saw that the microcomputer had received a fatal blow in transit. Its board was concave. "What a disaster!" I said with a good measure of relief. I'd been given some time to figure things out. I read and read.

And there was a lot to read (Refs. 1, 2). I found description of end-user projects of all sizes. University of Pittsburgh and the University of Ottawa had developed impressive programs which enabled large numbers of students and faculty members to search fairly independently (Refs. 3, 4, 5, 6). At Earlham College in Richmond, Indiana online searching was incorporated into course integrated bibliographic instruction classes (Ref 7). Experimental projects at the University of Wisconsin at Stout, Saint Xavier College, Stanford University and San Jose State have been described (Refs. 8, 9, 10).

These programs show great variety. Each institution found its own way to guarantee password security, and to provide the funding, staffing and equipment required by an end-user program. At Stanford, password security was achieved by remaining continuously connected to a system for the entire period of a group practice session. Students at other institutions logged on using masked passwords. Psychology students at San Jose State received instruction and then developed search strategies which served as bases for searches performed by librarians. In that experiment the mechanics of searching and the problems of password security were bypassed, leaving the focus of instruction on the critical and creative processes of searching (Ref. 11).

3. GOALS OF THE PROJECT

Having surveyed the literature on existing programs, I began to develop one which could be successful at Loyola given our students, budget, and staff. Before shaping the project I considered its possible goals. Was I attempting to provide information? That was clearly not the prime motivation for undertaking this task. Mediated "wonder" searches had been providing students and faculty with helpful bibliographies for years.

Would reference librarians have more time for other activities if students conducted their own searches? Everything I had read and heard suggested the opposite was true. Training students to search takes time. New searchers need continued coaching. In addition, library users who know more about searching request more mediated searches. Nowhere did I read of librarians conducting fewer searches after the initiation of end-user instruction. In fact, building the demand for mediated database searches was an aim of the project at Loyola.

The primary goal was to end the extreme passivity of our search customers, to develop students who were sophisticated enough to participate in the development of searches, to know when and when not to use online databases, and to understand the source's strengths and limitations. The goal was to foster a more active, if not independent, use of our services.

4. AN ONLINE SEARCHING CLASS

The shape the project was going to take was clearer once its goals had been defined. Practical restrictions also guided my choices. Practice time for searching had to be scheduled during the day. We opted to use DIALOG's Classroom Instruction Program. I considered whether to offer a non-credit open workshop through the library, or to provide individual training by appointment or to integrate the instruction into a course.

Open tours that have been offered by the library in the past would usually result in one very fidgety student being led through the library by an embarrased and disheartened librarian. These experiences taught me that students are only enthusiastic about library instruction which is very closely tied to classroom assignments. I assumed that this would be true even if the content of the library instruction session was technology.

I searched Loyola's catalog for a first test class. Methodology of Educational Research, a graduate course taught by a member of the psychology faculty, was chosen. The professor had been a frequent customer for database searches, requesting primarily ERIC, Psychological Abstracts and Dissertation Abstracts searches. He also incorporated bibliographic instruction, taught by a librarian, into his courses. The assignments he gave his students required substantial library use. A member of the faculty who was committed to both database searching and bibliographic instruction was the ideal person to work with in starting an end-user program. When approached about incorporating search training into his class, he enthusiastically accepted.

My plan was to teach the students how to search one database, (ERIC), through one vendor, (DIALOG), while also making them aware of the variety of choices available. Each student was required to develop a search strategy and perform a search.

The database lecture was scheduled early enough in the semester so that students would be able to use their bibliographies to work on their final research papers. It was presented during one long three hour evening class. I tried to keep things lively, jumping around, handing out printed examples, and using overhead projections. Fortunately the novelty of my topic helped and the class remained valiantly alert. DIALOG was very helpful by providing multiple copies of booklets to distribute.

Students had been asked to read two articles to prepare for the lecture, "How to Prepare for a Computer Search of ERIC: A Non-Technical Approach" (Ref. 12), and "Faults and Failures - 25 Ways That Online Searching Can Let You Down" (Ref. 13). My checks with the reserve desk before the lecture indicated that these were not hot items. In other words, I doubt that one person read either of them.

The students were well prepared in another sense. Their professor had instructed them in the use of the print version of ERIC. I had only to introduce them to the automation of reference tools they were already familiar with.

The lecture began with the origins of bibliographic databases and their development from batch mode to interactive systems. After that we discussed advantages and disadvantages of searching online. In order to apprise them of the wide range of options open I described the major vendors of interest to academic users.

Having provided them with a broader context for understanding databases, I focused on the techniques of searching ERIC through DIALOG. We began with a question: "Are poor reading scores the result of overcrowded classrooms?" I said that a computer can not respond to a question in that form. It can match words and it can perform logical operations. The essense of search technique is translating the question into the language of the database and doing it as unambiguously as possible.

Logging on was covered briefly. I let them know that every step of that process was printed on a handout that they would receive at the search session. The masked password was loaded onto a function key.

I spent a good deal of time going over the commands and their functions. I concluded the workshop by having the students formulate a search strategy using our initial question. We did this by answering all the questions in a worksheet that had been developed for the class. It moved from a general description of the topic to the use of controlled vocabulary, Boolean operators, parentheses, suffixes, limits and print formats. The form was designed to remind the students of all the features available to them.

The students were instructed to develop topics in consultation with their professor. Using the ERIC thesaurus, DIALOG documentation, and the worksheet they were to create a search strategy. I went to Mexico for a week.

After a week at the beach, I was rested and ready to provide the moral support students need when they make the leap to independent searching. As with any academic task, students displayed different levels of comprehension talent and preparation. With the exception of one or two, all of the students came to their appointments with well defined topics and workable, if not sophisticated, search statements. With the exception of one or two cases, I made suggestions for refining the search statements.

Each appointment lasted about forty minutes. The student did the actual search while I sat at his or her side giving assurances. For two weeks, search appointments filled my day. I rarely have seen such exhilarated library users.

Database searching will be incorporated into future Methodology of Education Research classes. The model of instruction can be adapted for other courses. We will only reach a miniscule number of Loyola's students. The goals are quite modest. By leading them through the process of performing one search we hope to develop more knowledgeable clients.

5. CONCLUSION

If I return to the aims of traditional bibliographic instruction - to create knowledgeable, enthusiastic, and independent library users - I can say that the end-user project partially succeeds. We imparted some knowledge, stirred up by lots of enthusiasm, and broke through some of the dependency. Most students who perform one search will continue to request searches from librarians. We hope they will work with the librarian in developing a search strategy and will have a better understanding of the results. Their requests will be informed by an awareness of the search process and a sensitivity to its complexity.

Exceptional students may pursue searching on their own through one of the options designed for occasional users. Information about those systems, particularly those designed for classroom teachers, was provided in the lecture.

The number of ways databases are being brought to the public is growing. CD-ROM products and laser discs are   the best solutions for heavily used databases. These products allow novices the luxury of learning to search and using the database without fear of cost.

I have no doubt that librarians will continue to search the majority of databases in the online mode. The cost of CD-ROM systems prohibits libraries from subscribing to systems which will not be frequently used. Since online searching will remain a major means of providing information, the library will continue to educate students about online systems. We will seek ways to teach and not be satisfied with simple promotion of our services.

6. REFERENCES

   1. Lyon, Sally, "End-User Searching of Online Databases: A Selective Annotated Bibliography." Library Hi Tech, No. 2, p. 47-50, 1984.

   2. Dantin, Doris B., "End User Searching of Online Databases." Library Instruction Round Table News, Vol. 9, No. 1, p. 7-10, September 1986.

   3. Brody, Fern; Whitmore, Marilyn; and Greg McCormick, End-User Searching: An Experiment at the University of Pittsburgh. (Pittsburgh, PA: University Library System, University of Pittsburgh, 1986).

   4. Janke, Richard, Online After Six: The University of Ottawa Experience with BRS/After Dark. ED 241 027, October 31, 1983.

   5. Janke, Richard, "Online After Six: End User Searching Comes of Age." Online, p. 15-29, November 1984.

   6. Janke, Richard, "Presearch Counseling for Client Searchers (End-Users)." Online, p. 13-26, September 1985.

   7. Penhale, Sara J. and Nancy Taylor, "Integrating End-User Searching into a bibliographic Instruction Program." RQ 27, No. 2, p. 212-220, Winter 1986.

   8. Trzebiatowski, Elaine, "End User Study on BRS/After Dark." RQ 23, p. 446-450, Summer 1984.

   9. Steffen, Susan Swords, "College Faculty Goes Online: Training Faculty to Search in a Liberal Arts College." Online 84 Conference Proceedings, Weston, CT: Online, p. 232-238, 1984.

   10. Ward, Sandra N. and Laura M. Osequeda, "Teaching University Student End-Users about Online Searching." Science and Technology Libraries 5, No. 11, p. 17-31, 1984.

   11. ibid

12. Laubacher, Marilyn R., How to Prepare for a Computer Search of ERIC; A Non-Technical Approach. Revised and updated, ED 237 100, May 1983.

13. Pemberton, Jeff, "Faults and Failures - 25 Ways That Online Searching Can Let You Down." Online, p. 6-7, September 1983.

FRONT-END SOFTWARE: THE EFFECT OF THEORY ON REALITY

Lisa M. Staggenborg, STN International/Chemical Abstracts Service

The emergence of personal computers has led to the availability of numerous "front-end" software packages targeted at online searchers. These packages have attempted to simplify and automate logon procedures, file selection, the development of queries, search and retrieval mechanics, and post-search processing of results. For frequent online searchers, many of whom are information professionals, front-end software packages have been labor-saving devices that systematize tedious, repetitive procedures. For infrequent online users, software packages have attempted to simplify the mechanical process of online search and retrieval, often by creating a menu-driven interface between the user and the more complex online system protocols.

Can a single software package satisfy both the frequent and the infrequent searcher? Can a software package support both ease of use and development of comprehensive search strategies? What are the advantages and disadvantages of front-end software packages being produced by an online vendor, database producer, or independent organization? What effect do the developer's answers to these theoretical questions have on the reality of packages in the marketplace? These and other considerations regarding front-end software will be presented.

The emergence of personal computers has led to the availability of numerous "front-end" software packages targeted at online searchers. These packages have attempted to simplify and automate logon procedures, file selection, the development of queries, search and retrieval mechanics, and post-search processing of results. For frequent online searchers, many of whom are information professionals, front-end software packages have been labor-saving devices that systematize tedious, repetitive procedures. For infrequent online users, software packages have attempted to simplify the mechanical process of online search and retrieval, often by creating a menu-driven interface between the user and the more complex online system protocols.

Front-end interfaces offer a great deal of promise in enhancing and extending the capabilities of online systems. But what effect do developers' answers to theoretical questions have on the reality of packages in the marketplace?

My goal in this paper is to begin to make you aware of some of the issues facing developers that have a very real impact on the front-end products available for you to purchase and use. Throughout this paper I will draw on my experience in developing STN Express, the new front-end software from STN International, to provide examples and insights.

I am making several underlying assumptions:

o There are finite resources available to develop any software, including the amount of time, money and the target computer the software is to run on.

o The issues and tradeoffs faced by developers affect the final product available for market.

o Understanding the types of tradeoffs faced by developers will help you better evaluate what package, if any, will be most useful to you.

There are many issues to be faced when developing front-end software, including:

o Who is expected to be the "user" of the software? A frequent or an infrequent user? An established user or a new user?

o What constitutes ease of use? How important is comprehensiveness of search strategies?

o Who is in the best position to develop software? A software vendor? A vendor of online services? A database producer?

o What type of computer should the software be run on?

1. WHO IS THE USER?

This is probably the single most critical question to be asked when developing software.

The decision of who is the primary user has a critical effect on the final user interaction of the software. The user interaction is strongly influenced by the view of the user of the system. The orientation for novice or infrequent users will heavily emphasize a system that is easy to learn. The orientation for an experienced or expert user will often emphasize flexibility and control. Also, the specific features implemented will vary to some degree for an infrequent user and for an expert. Although in theory it may be possible to design a system that is all things to all people, practical limitations on the amount of software that can be developed or run on a computer do not allow for this in reality.

In the area of personal computers, another issue that must be addressed is: How experienced is the user in use of the computer itself? An expert online searcher is not necessarily an expert computer user.

If you are evaluating a package, be sure to look for features that speak to those who will actually be using the software. Look for patterns in the types of features available. It's reasonable to assume that the same general trend in new features will continue.

2. EASE OF USE

Many people are interested in making online systems "easier to use" through front-end interfaces. But if you ask users what is meant by "easy to use" you are likely to get very different answers, depending on the user answering the question. Often, infrequent users give answers in terms of what is easy to learn, which often results in the system making many choices for the user. However, frequent users often request capabilities to give them more control over the system.

For example, new or infrequent users are often interested in a menu-driven approach to providing information. Menus are typically easy to learn. However, more expert users often become tired of such an approach, partly because they have learned what is coming and want to speed the process, and partly because of the limited number of choices available on a menu. To some degree, both audiences can be satisfied with a menu approach, if response time is quick and if shortcuts (such as function keys) are provided for the most common functions. Providing defaults which can be overridden allows an expert to exercise control, but also allows the system to make choices for novices. Another approach is to have separate functions, some that address the "novice" and others the "expert."

If you are evaluating a package for use by an expert, don't immediately rule out a menu-driven system. Be sure to find out what features, such as shortcuts and defaults, have been provided.

3. WHO SHOULD DEVELOP THE SOFTWARE?

Online search systems typically result from a combination of expertise in a number of areas. In some cases, these may be combined in a single organization.

- o The software creator
- o The online vendor
- o The database producer

Having front-end software created by any of these has advantages as well as disadvantages.

For example, if an independent software vendor creates front-end software, the software package will often access several online vendors. Additionally, such a developer has an "outside perspective" that is less tied to an existing system. The advantage is that you are likely to see a consistent approach to a variety of systems. However, if the developer is not careful, the software may include the "least common denominator" from each system. Additionally, the developer may have little incentive to ensure that the software is kept up to date with evolving online systems.

An online vendor is most likely to be able to keep front-end software synchronized with the online system and to be sure that the front-end does not screen out important capabilities of the online system. Also, the online vendor has a vested interest in ensuring that you can use the online system and is motivated to provide support and compatibility with online changes. However, the software from an online vendor will, typically, only address a single online system.

Database producers will often focus on the content of specific databases and provide the most in-depth content assistance. In complex areas such as chemical structure searching, this can be important.

Typically, organizations will play to their strengths. If you decide which of these issues are most important to you, it will help you to most effectively evaluate software products from various organizations.

4. WHAT TYPE OF MACHINE TO RUN ON?

Another important consideration is the type of machine that the software will run on. The first level of consideration is "whose computer"? Should the front-end software be located on a machine operated by the front-end software vendor? Should it be run at the user's site? What type of computer does the software developer have expertise in developing software for?

Again, each of these alternatives presents advantages and disadvantages. Computers not at the user's site have the advantage that the user does not need to invest in hardware. Updates to the software are handled by the software developer. However, the user will typically pay some fee for each use. Also, line noise and other connection problems associated with online use are not alleviated.

If a machine at the user's site is selected, the connection problems are minimized. Also, menu and mouse interaction is easily and effectively supported at a local computer. However, additional issues arise. What type of machine does the user have? Are there a variety of machines that must be supported? How much of the capacity of a computer is a user willing to devote to the software? Is the user willing to invest the time to install and update the software?

From my experience, the speed and user interaction provided at a personal computer is excellent. However, users are interested in minimizing the resources required to run the software; for example, the amount of memory and disk space required. Unfortunately, features "cost" in both the development and the amount of resources required. Personal computers are small computers. They have limited memory and limited space. Another issue is the actual computer to be supported. Two of the major personal computers are the IBM PC and the MacIntosh. Unfortunately, it is not a simple job to support both of these machines! "Portable code" helps, but the operating systems are substantially different; additional development is required. Also, there are a number of user interaction questions. Is it better for a given piece of software to have a consistent interaction across machines? Or should the software adapt to the MacIntosh style of interaction versus the IBM PC style of interaction? Even simple things like the use of a mouse differ. For example, on a MacIntosh the mouse button is held down; on an IBM PC it is clicked.

Again, it is important for you to look at the value to you. Are you willing to invest in hardware if you do not already have it available? Are you willing to install and update software yourself?

5. CONCLUSION

In this paper I have tried to outline a few of the issues faced by developers of front-end software, in the hopes that raising these issues can make you a more effective purchaser and/or user of this type of software. My belief is that no one package can solve every problem. Just as developers are forced to prioritize, you must also prioritize your interests and see where the best "fit" is.

PROVIDING FRONT ENDS FOR MARKETING EXECUTIVES

Ruth E. Stanat, Strategic Intelligence Systems, Inc.

PROVIDING FRONT ENDS FOR MARKETING EXECUTIVES

During the past few years marketing and competitive intelligence have become key buzzwords in corporations. As a firm which specializes in the development of marketing and competitive information and systems for corporations, we have experienced the evolution of these changing needs. Specifically, we have found that organizations are faced with an "infoglut" of both internal and external information. Moreover, a number of internal departments are attempting to sift through this information and organize the information in a way that is useful and has a "bottom line impact" on the company. This paper will discuss a methodology for the development of front ends for marketing executives and will contain two case studies which involve a major food company and a consumer products company.

OVERVIEW

Until a few years ago, competitive intelligence entailed the informal gathering of facts and figures from competitive financial reports and/or the subscription to marketing studies which surveyed the major competitors' strengths and weaknesses vis-a-vis the industry's growth. Currently, with the advent of the personal computer, the hard disk, and innovative text retrieval software, corporate executives have access to competitive intelligence systems which allow them to capture and track industry and company specific events.

At SIS, we believe that some of the most valuable intelligence comes from the field or from sales and marketing reps who are in constant contact with customers, suppliers and distributors. As such, we develop systems or front ends for corporations which encompass a methodology for the capturing of this information and distribution of the information throughout the organization.

Competitive and marketing intelligence systems also serve as "early warning indicators" which allow management to formulate strategies and position themselves in a proactive mode, rather than a reactive mode. Environmental scanning captures social, economic, technological, and political trends which impact industry segments. Competitive intelligence, on the other hand, is more focused, zeroing in on competitor profiles, legislation, new product development activity, etc.

Environmental scanning covers a wide range of information sources, including periodicals, newspapers, TV media, issue management meetings/debates, economic roundtables, etc. Information sources for competitive intelligence systems can include the following:
- Annual Reports, 10K's, Financial Disclosure Statements
- Industry Periodicals (Both Horizontal and Vertical)
- R&D Internal Reports
- Manufacturing Competitve Monitoring Activity
- Field Sales Force Competitive Monitoring/Tracking Activity
- New Product Development Competitive Monitoring Activity
- Commercial Databases
- Organized Competitive Scanning Programs
- Purchased Market Research and/or Consulting Studies
- Field Collection of Competitive New Product Announcement Literature
- Subscription to Databases Which Track Merger and Acquisition Activity.

The development of marketing front ends involve the integration of synthesized, analyzed, relevant information from both internal and external information sources. Clearly, much of this information resides within the organization and in several departments (e.g., Strategic Planning, Market Research, Research and Development, Sales, Marketing, Business Development, and Finance.) The challenge is to capture this information from these various departments, organize it, and incorporate it on an ongoing basis into a dynamic competitive intelligence system. More importantly, the internal competitive intelligence material must be merged with the information from external sources.

Specific internal sources include documents from the following:
- Corporate and Functional Libraries
- Internal Memoranda and Position Papers
- Summaries of Staff Meetings
- "News Clippings" Within Staff Departments
- Published Speeches
- Monitoring of Competitive Advertisements and New Product Introductions
- Legal Department Tracking of the Implication of Legislation on Competitive Activity
- Internal Documents Which Contain Focus Groups, Attitude Testing, and Qualitative and Quantitative Surveys.

The ideal is to develop marketing front ends which maximize the utility of the documents to the organization and provide a return on the organization's investment in the information. The remainder of this paper will discuss two case studies: one of a major food company whose objective was to develop a competitive intelligence system that captured both relevant internal and external competitive information and the second is a major consumer products firm whose objective was to capture on a worldwide basis, their marketing research reports and integrate this internal corporate information with our external competitive intelligence databases.

CASE STUDY I: The Development of a Marketing Front End
Using Internal Documents

One of the major elements in the development of a corporate competitive intelligence system is diagnosis of end users information needs in addition to the design of the database and information format. Our firm held numerous meetings with market research, strategic planning, sales, and other personnel from the client firm to determine how they "viewed" the information and the relevance of the material. We needed to understand the experiences, functions, and expectations of the people who would be the end users of the system. Gathering this information was not an easy process, but it allowed us to develop the conceptual design for the database, and would eventually pave the way for the technical design.

At SIS, we design and develop competitive intelligence systems on a prototype basis for organizations. We find that prototyping offers the following advantages:
- --Avoids initial costly mainframe development
- --Accelerates development time
- --Allows the users to use the system at an early stage of the project
- --Allows for changes in the conceptual and technical design.

A prototype using a PC-based text retrieval package was developed after about three weeks which allowed management to evaluate the design and ease of use of the system. The initial prototype was very helpful in allowing the users to make recommendations for changes.

In this case, several other departments were simultaneously interviewed for their competitive intelligence input and needs. Our objective was to develop a cost-efficient, useful personal computer-based system for the original end users. Longer term, as the system grew in complexity and usage, alternative methods of distribution would be developed and implemented. Specifically, this involved the migration of the PC-based system to either a mainframe environment of distributed network with the company.

Our first phase of the project involved planning. Given the division's objectives, internal documents were identified based on their utility to the organization in addition to their focus on the competitive environment. Some of these documents included:
- --Multiclient Studies which Tracked Competitive Products and Pricing
- --Custom March Research Reports
- --Strategic Planning Documents
- --Selected Reference Books and Journals
- --Internal Memoranda which Summarized the Implications and Findings of the Research
- --Field Reports from Sales Personnel.

Phase I of the project focused on capturing the relevant information in a one-page or one-screen summary. As a result, our team of document analysts analyzed and systhesized their documents and extracted the following information elements.

Example: One Screen "Market Intelligence" Front End

```
Code #

Title

Author/Sponsor

Summary
--Key Findings:
--Implications:

Cross Reference/Key Words:
```

Our plan for the document analysis and data entry always depends on the internal resources available for the project. In this case, our organization worked closely with the client in the analysis of their documents. In some cases, the client's own staff analyzed the documents in conjunction with our staff's development of the database design and format. During Phase I, approximately 1500 documents were analyzed and input into the system during a period of 90 days. It should be noted that this 90-day period also included a two-week period for database design. The system was built for a PC system and the design allowed for growth of the database.

During the next 30 days, end users evaluated the system and hard copy of the material. Phase II then involved the selection of full-text executive summaries (1-3 pages) in support of the one-screen document summary. To this end, automatic document reading equipment was evaluated to input the necessary executive summaries.

Phase III of the project involves migration of the system for a distributed users network. Since this project was initiated on the divisional level, this project will serve as a prototype for the development of a corporate-wide system, using the same development methodology.

With prototyping and a phased approach, this major food company enjoyed the increased utility of having their documents in a database, while achieving a better understanding of their competitive intelligence needs without additional expenditures.

External Competitive Market Intelligence

To complement this custom-developed competitive intelligence system, SIS developed for this major food company a series of market and product competitive intelligence databases which tracked the relevant secondary information sources and trade journals. These databases were developed and are authored by our staff on a daily and monthly basis. The information is then organized by industry trends, issues, legislation, key competitor profiles, financial performance, new product development activity, merger and acquisition activity, and so forth. More importantly, the information is integrated with the internal information data base to maximize the utility of the information to the corporation. In short, we have provided a marketing front end which captures the relevant information and provides it in one place. This reduces duplication of effort within the corporation and between departments.

We have now taken this system for a major food company one step further. On a quarterly basis, we synthesize and analyze the information and develop value-added quarterly competitor profiles. This additional layer of intelligence enables mid-senior level managers to obtain a pulse on their competitor's activity over a 90-day period.

With this marketing front end, this food company is now able to access competitive intelligence which is updated monthly and integrate this information into their internal competitive intelligence database. Moreover, their investment in the capturing and cataloguing of internal information was justified on the basis of the following:
- --Avoids "reinventing the wheel"
- --Facilitates the capturing of the knowledge of their experienced professionals
- --Allows for end user input into the system and for dynamic updating of the database.

The next section will discuss the evolution and distribution of the databases.

Distribution

Following a six-month evolution of the system through end-user feedback, the need arose to provide distribution of the databases throughout the organization and to regional locations. Consequently, we reviewed several alternatives including porting the databases to the mainframe, using their minicomputer UNIX system, and networking of PCs. Given their need for distribution of "macro" competitive intelligence to their regional locations and the need to capture and input regional competitive intelligence into the system, the organization decided to pursue the option of a remote dial-up capability. Therefore, we located user-friendly, menu-driven text retrieval software with key work search capabilities for distribution of their databases. This program was accompanied with a communications and education program, along with specific user training.

CASE STUDY II: The Development Of A Market Research Competitive Intelligence Front End System

For a major consumer products company, Strategic Intelligence Systems, Inc. (SIS) has developed a proprietary database which contains, on a worldwide basis, summary reports of market research studies and local market and sales intelligence. To develop this system, SIS worked closely with the Corporate Market Research department to define the scope of the of the project and the design of the database. More importantly, SIS worked closely with the internal system administrator to define what was "actionable" or "value added" information.

Given the complexity of the industry and multiple product categories, we developed a design of the database which would allow for the input and access of a large volume of reports by country, by category and a series of other variables. In addition to market research summaries, SIS added budget information and a wide range of other critical documents which will enable this consumer products company to gain a significant edge with their sales force. More importantly, SIS receives field reports from over 50 countries worldwide which report competitive new product activity. As such, we input these reports and integrate the information within their marketing front ends.

Subscription To External Industry Competitve Intelligence Databases

To complement their internal information, this consumer products company subscribed to the SIS competitive intelligence databases in their specific market segments and product categories. Subscription to these databases was justified on the following benefits:
- Saves time of internal marketing staff of scanning and clipping of journals and news reports
- Increases efficiency of a "centralized market intelligence database" and reduces duplication of effort between departments
- Allows for the integration of domestic information and international information by product category in one database
- Provides focus for market and product planning
- Serves as a monitoring system of their competitive environment
- Provides information on market segments which are under consideration for acquisition or divestiture.

Clearly, the development of this corporate intelligence database which captures the intelligence from internal documents and integrates this information with our domestic and international databases will give this company a competitive edge in their product categories.

SUMMARY

Front ends for marketing executives are end-user based systems and should be customized to the end-user department. Internal documents are a rich source of competitive intelligence which are often passive and not dynamically accessed by key executives. To realize the full potential of the documents, we believe it is necessary to add the value of synthesis and analysis to them.

The ultimate goal of most organizations is to have rapid access to both internal and external environmental competitive intelligence via cost-efficient delivery mechanisms. Planning and prototyping is essential for the design, development and execution of these systems.

THE SOFTWARE JUNGLE: TO GUIDE OR NOT TO GUIDE

Sue E. Stigleman, University of North Carolina at Chapel Hill

Keywords: Bibliography Formatting Software, Evaluation.

Abstract: A rapidly developing segment of the software market is producing a growing number of information management products. These products perform such tasks as formatting bibliographic citations, searching national online databases, and creating and searching personal databases, both bibliographic and full text. Because of the obvious similarities between these software programs and a number of typical library services, such as online searching and cataloging, library staff are often asked to recommend or choose software for library users.

At UNC-CH, the Health Sciences Library was asked to recommend bibliography formatting software programs as candidates for official support by the campus Microcomputing Support Center. After evaluating the existing programs, two were recommended and are now being supported on a university-wide basis.

The process raised a number of issues which people encountering similar requests may want to consider, including 1) selecting and communicating criteria for evaluation; 2) knowing users' needs: expanding your perspective beyond the library; 3) working with software producers; 4) establishing responsibility and limits for supporting the chosen software.

1. INTRODUCTION

In common with many libraries, we at the Health Sciences Library have kept a particularly close eye on two types of software: end-user searching software and bibliography formatting software. We have offered workshops in end-user searching and reprint file management for several years, and the microcomputer component of these workshops has become increasingly important. In 1986, I began taking a thorough look at the existing bibliographic programs with the intention of settling, at least for the next few years, on a single program to use in the reprint filing workshops. Concurrently, the library was having discussions with the campus Microcomputing Support Center about various issues involved in providing campus-wide user support for this type of software. The Microcomputing Support Center was interested in providing support, but wanted to narrow down the field rather than trying to support all of the programs. We were asked to recommend two programs, at least one of which should be relatively inexpensive for student use.

I would like to share observations and suggestions about the process of recommending software for widespread use. I know from experience that it's easy to overlook some things that will result in a successful recommendation. For each of four areas I will describe what we did and how well it worked. I will finish with some overall observations on the evaluation project and with a recommended set of steps to use.

2. SELECTING AND COMMUNICATING CRITERIA FOR EVALUATION

A whole talk could be given just on criteria for evaluating bibliographic software. Briefly, the criteria I used were:

-- Hardware used: The Health Sciences Library and Microcomputing Support Center were interested only in software for the IBM and Macintosh families of microcomputers, so we ignored the other main families, such as the non-Macintosh Apples.

-- Reasonably large size limitations for the maximum number of fields per record, maximum number of records per file, and the maximum characters allowed for the various elements of a bibliographic record. One program was eliminated because it allowed a maximum of 10 unique keywords in the entire file.

-- Flexibility in document types, including support for more than just journal articles and books.

-- Full-screen data entry and editing.

-- Reasonably powerful searching features, such as Boolean operators, truncation, nesting, field qualification, and proximity searching.

-- Flexible sorting, including multiple levels and user selected fields.

-- Support for several citation styles and the ability to define additional formats.

-- Ability to scan a word processor manuscript and automatically generate a bibliography of the references cited in the manuscript.

-- The ability to import and export data. People may later need to switch to a different program.

-- The ability to import downloaded online search results, since, among other considerations, this is the most efficient means of data entry.

-- Ease of use.

-- Vendor reliability and support.

-- Price.

After evaluation, the major contenders for the high end programs were Pro-Cite, Sci-Mate, and Reference Manager. Notebook II, along with its companion program, Bibliography, was the only serious low-end contender. After considering all of the factors, I recommended Pro-Cite and Notebook II/Bibliography. The Microcomputing Support Center also later added support for Reference Manager.

None of the programs are perfect, all of them possessing some major limitations. As a result, I had to balance the programs' various strengths and weaknesses against each other. For a given user the criteria may be different, and almost certainly the relative weight of the different criteria will differ.

I particularly tried to avoid what I felt was likely to be a built-in bias towards the health sciences part of our campus, a bias due to four factors:
  (1) I work in a medical library;
  (2) a great deal of the interest in bibliographic software on our campus was in health sciences;
  (3) almost all of the end-user searching at UNC appeared to be done in health sciences;
  (4) the most commonly searched database on campus is MEDLINE.

I felt since I was evaluating for general campus-wide support I should try to recommend software usable by a large number of diverse types of people.

Regardless of the criteria used or the weights assigned to them, a difficult task in software selection is communicating criteria for evaluation so that users will understand them. I've observed that this is true for all software, but it's very noticeable for bibliographic software. Many people have never actually used this type of software before, and consequently have a very limited view of what the software can do or what they want it to do. Even people who have used the software won't always understand the criteria you use in the selection. The training coordinator at the Microcomputing Support Center observed: "In our attempt to locate trainers, I found that most users have a fragmented idea of a given package's capabilities. While they tend to be very competent in presenting aspects used with their projects, they are often wholly unaware of other features."

How well did the criteria work?

One faculty member disagreed vigorously with my recommendations. His comments illustrate clearly the difficulties in weighing the criteria when none of the programs fully satisfies them. A longtime user of Reference Manager, he believed that Reference Manager should have been chosen over Pro-Cite. He argued that the single most important task that this type of software performs is the one of scanning a word processor manuscript and automatically generating a bibliography of the references cited. In his view, the program that does this one function the best is the one that should be chosen. He is right that Reference Manager does do this task better than Pro-Cite. I disagreed with his assumption that his needs are the same as those of all of the potential users of the software.

The faculty member also downplayed the idea that anyone would actually use document formats other than journal articles and books, and he felt that my viewpoint represented some kind of idiosyncratic view of what libraries want for their own use, rather than genuine user needs. The philosophy underlying these comments is that a software choice should be based on the most common user profile. My philosophy was also to be concerned about the user who has more unusual needs, a factor which ended up favoring Pro-Cite over Reference Manager. Either of these viewpoints can be used -- the choice will vary in different situations.

3. <u>KNOWING USERS' NEEDS</u>

Because of my familiarity with bibliographic programs and with some of the tasks this software performs, such as searching and formatting citations, I relied heavily on my own expertise in developing the evaluation criteria. I used conversations I had had with people who had come to the library over the past few years to talk about their needs and/or their experiences with the programs. I also drew on the work of people in other libraries, most notably Abigail Hubbard at the Academy of Medicine Texas Medical Center and Joe Wibble at Stanford. There were relatively few existing users of the software on campus, and no identified experts. Neither the other campus libraries nor the Microcomputing Support Center had become involved in using or evaluating the software.

How well did this approach work? It worked well for the actual evaluation itself. My background is broad enough that I feel I took a thorough and objective look at the programs. The difficulties, as I have said before, came with the problems in weighting the different criteria. Although I had a fairly good idea of the likely user needs, more actively soliciting user input would have helped in two ways.

First, it would have had a psychological effect in assuring people that their viewpoint was being considered in the evaluation process.

Second, it would have given me a broader profile of the current and potential users, which would have been useful in weighting the criteria.

In preparing this paper, I asked for feedback from various people who had been involved with the evaluation process. One of the people from the Microcomputing Support Center observed that evaluations can be obtained from magazines. She felt that three things needed to be tied together for a successful evaluation: objective evaluations, reactions from current users of the software, and considerations of the specific applications in use or planned on our campus.

4. WORKING WITH SOFTWARE PRODUCERS

In this evaluation project, we didn't work with the producers in a systematic way. Because we were using Pro-Cite in the library, I had frequent conversations with the company and knew about their plans for the next version. I didn't have that level of knowledge of the plans for other software programs.

If I were doing the evaluations again, I would contact the companies of the most likely candidates and ask them for their plans for their next release, including both features and timetable for release (checking with current users of the programs to find out how reliable the information from the company usually is). I would also provide the producers with the results of my evaluation and ask them to address the areas that I perceived to be their programs' major weaknesses.

How much should you base your selection on the programs as they exist at that moment, and how much should you find out or rely on plans for the future? If a new version that corrects a major flaw is being released in two months, I would consider it strongly. However, it would be doing a grave disservice to future software users to base a decision on supposed improvements that turn out to be "vaporversion" -- an upgrade talked about but never actually released.

Another note: I didn't negotiate the volume purchasing agreements, but my sense is that the competitiveness created by looking seriously at more than one package helps reduce the prices offered by the producers.

5. ESTABLISHING RESPONSIBILITY AND LIMITS FOR SUPPORTING THE CHOSEN SOFTWARE

What happens after the recommendation? At UNC, the Health Sciences Library didn't have the resources to offer day-to-day support for the programs. In a series of meetings including people from the Library and the Microcomputing Support Center, we negotiated a division of labor.

> The Microcomputing Support Center:
>   made the final selection of programs to support;
>   supports the chosen software, including negotiating site
>   licenses and volume purchase agreements, assisting

> users in choosing a program, providing walk-in or phone-in user support services, and teaching the use of the programs;
> negotiates volume purchase agreements or site licenses;
> creates and collects citation styles for public distribution (not yet being done);
> provides evaluation copies of bibliographic software programs through its software library.

The Health Sciences Library:
> taught the first campus-wide short course;
> taught a training session for Microcomputing Support Center user support staff;
> evaluates new versions of all of the bibliographic programs and makes evaluations available through the Microcomputing Support Center;
> provides specific applications workshops using the software (not yet being done).

How well has this worked? The Microcomputing Support Center's experiences with user support have been tough. The Microcomputing Support Center trainers and staff don't use any of the programs in their daily work. The number of questions from users haven't been frequent enough to really get the user support staff trained. The staff must refer to the manual for every question. Some calls get referred to the library for resolution.

The division of responsibility has generally worked out well for the Library, although we have been unable to offer the workshops due to staffing shortages.

6. OVERALL OBSERVATIONS

The Microcomputing Support Center has been very pleased with the reactions to the evaluation project. They didn't have the time or the expertise to do the evaluation and appreciated the Library's willingness to step in and help them make a decision about which programs to support. Their one suggestion for improvement was to be more aggressive in soliciting user input.

Reactions to the selected programs overall are positive. People seem pleased at having support for two well-known programs, each with a base of users. Reference Manager and Pro-Cite are both popular, with Reference Manager generally being used more in the health sciences and Pro-Cite used more in Academic Affairs.

Notebook, the low-end program we hoped would be used by students, hasn't proven popular. Student use is low, possibly because students don't want to learn another piece of software in order to do their theses or dissertations. It may still cost too much for students. We may need to lower our standards in order to find a limited but cheap program as a starter package.

Reactions to bibliographic software in general can be summed up in this quote from the director of training at the Microcomputing Support Center: "Users seem largely unaware of how to apply these packages to their bibliography needs and are also relatively ignorant of the effort required to use them effectively. It is tedious and expensive to utilize the full power of the software."

7. RECOMMENDED STEPS

Finally, to summarize, here are a series of suggested steps to consider using if you undertake a similar evaluation process:

-- Publicize the fact that the evaluation is being initiated. Both the Microcomputing Support Center and I neglected to do this, with the result that the evaluation came as a surprise, and was perceived to be a fait accompli.

-- Actively solicit input from users. I suggest an open meeting for people interested in the type of software to discuss what applications they have in mind, what program(s) they are already using, and how well the programs work.

-- Arrange software presentation by users and vendors, trying to balance the perspectives.

-- Visit a few active users of some of the programs. This is not solely to get reactions to a specific program, but also to see how they use the type of software in their work.

-- Develop and articulate the evaluation criteria.

-- Conduct structured evaluations of all of the software being considered. Document the results.

-- Make the selection and advertise it along with the evaluation criteria and a description of the evaluation process.

-- Solicit feedback from users on an ongoing basis.

-- Continue to monitor new versions and new programs, comparing them to your original choice(s) and user feedback.

ONLY THE NEWS THAT YOU CAN USE

Stanley Stillman, Access Publishing Company

The New York Times motto "All The News That's Fit To Print," expresses the goal of all news organizations. While hard copy publications like newspapers, newsletters and magazines have been the media choice to date of print oriented news organizations, a new option is finally emerging: electronic-mail news services. Other terms have been coined before to describe news information conveyed in point images; electronic-mail news services best conveys the opportunities emerging in this field:

- for distribution networks to increase the data they transmit;

- for print oriented news organizations to widen the range of media they use; and

- for users to enhance the way they keep informed.

Non-entertainment publishing can be divided into news and reference publishing. Similarly the functions performed by various media technologies can be divided into point-to-multi-point broadcast and point-to-point interactive. Whether employing publication or electro-magnetic wave technologies, news is broadcast on a point-to-multi-point basis. Applying the newest electronic technologies to the traditional six-step news publishing editorial process are electronic-mail news services. A surprising number have been launched in recent years, among them First Call, OTC Alert, Online Today/IBM Forum, Tele/Scope, Presidential Campaign Hotline, Oxford Analytica Daily Brief, McGraw-Hill News and USA Today. They represent a dynamic new market for distribution networks, a fresh new medium for print oriented news organizations and a productive new source of news for users.

1. THE NEWS MISSION

Every day of the year, in a box in the upper left hand corner of its front page, a preeminent news source we all know well and admire proudly proclaims: "All The News That's Fit To Print." While identified with The New York Times, this motto properly expresses the goal of all news organizations. Each picks an audience to serve, defined by some profile of geographic, business, professional and leisure interests; selects an appropriate medium and frequency with which to reach that audience; and then in various ways and with varying degrees of success, covers all the breaking events and developments that fit the defined profile.

1.2   Terminology

With a few notable exceptions, hard copy publications like newspapers, newsletters and magazines have been the media choice to date of print oriented news organizations. While slow in arriving, a new option is finally emerging: electronic-mail news services. The technological revolution in data processing and communications is making it possible. One benchmark statistic, perhaps better than any other, dramatizes why: the estimated 25 per cent compound rate of improvement per year in the price to performance ratio of electronic delivery. All of us in this room, concerned in one way or another with the management of online information, have been touched by this revolution. It is now beginning to sweep into the field of print news as well.

Industry and user opportunities

At this point, some of you may legitimately ask if yet another term is required to describe the distribution of information online. Others of you, recalling the vain efforts of the Knight-Ridder Viewtron, Time Inc. Teletext and Times Mirror Gateway projects, may scoff. A few of you, if of a particular political proclivity, may even wonder if we don't already have enough news media. Before I am finished, however, I hope to convince you that this term, electronic-mail news services, best conveys the opportunities emerging in this field:

- o   for distribution networks to increase the data they transmit;

- o   for print oriented news organizations to widen the range of media they use; and

- o   for users to enhance the way they keep informed.

Personal perspective

Let me start by explaining where I come from. Before founding my own firm, Access Publishing Company, I was a correspondent for TIME magazine. Since 1979, I have been engaged in electronic information services. Initially Access launched and published a prototype electronic-mail news service. Since the suspension of that service, we have undertaken a variety of market research and development assignments for such clients as Ashton-Tate, Citibank, Value Line - and, closer to the focus and ken of those attending this conference, Dialog. Given this experience, my primary concern in electronic information has been with the inter-active retrieval of textual data over two-way telecommunications networks.

1.2   News and reference publishing

My professional career thus includes experience in both ends of the non-entertainment publishing business, news publishing on the one hand and reference publishing on the other. This is a distinction not often drawn about the industries dealing in information. Usually they are referred to collectively as the media industries and thus are classified by technology: Newspapers, Information (a pot pourri of non-traditional media in which most of us in this room are involved); Television; Periodicals; Books; Radio; and Basic Cable. But the non-entertainment product distributed by these media can just as easily be divided into news and reference information, and each of these then into print and audio-visual images. In discussing electronic-mail news services, I am concerned here with news information conveyed in print images.

Broadcast and interactive functions

Given this concern, I then prefer to divide the functions performed by various media technologies into point-to-multi-point broadcast and point-to-point interactive. This is yet another distinction not often drawn. In today's world, most people instinctively associate the word broadcast with radio and television - the so-called broadcast industry. But before the days of radio frequency technology, they associated it, for example, with farmers "broadcasting seed," with gossipers "broadcasting rumors," and town-criers "broadcasting news." While never a farmer and I hope never at least a malicious gossiper, I have as a newsman always identified with and tried to play the role of the town-crier. As such I have been concerned with whatever allowed me to reach my target audience.

Media technologies

You may never have thought of any of the hard copy media serving the same function as the radio frequency media. But consider the following diagram:

BROADCAST: One-way, point-to-multi-point	INTER-ACTIVE: Two-way, point-to-point
PUBLICATIONS: newspaper, newsmagazines, newsletters	PUBLICATIONS: Books, microfiche
ELECTRO-MAGNETIC WAVES: tower, cable, satellite	ELECTRO-MAGNETIC WAVES: telecommunications switch network
NEWS: producer initiative to alert users to information on periodic basis	REFERENCE: user initiative to request information from producer when needed

2.   THE NEWS MEDIA

Viewed from this perspective, certain hard copy media, for example, newspapers, newsmagazines and newletters, perform the broadcast function as well as radio towers, cable systems and satellites. They are just as one-way, or point-to-multi-point in broadcast jargon, as their radio frequency brethren. Ultimately both forms of communication are best categorized as news media, whether employing publication or electro-magnetic wave technologies.

2.1 Electronic News

News defined this way has been delivered in electronic form for over a century. The first such service, the New York Stock Exchange ticker, employed a wire network the management of which Western Union eventually assumed. Primarily numeric in form, it was followed in the 1890s by the Dow Jones Broad Tape and in the years since by such other textual news-wire services as the Associated Press and United Press International. Given the cost, the market for such services was almost exclusively institutional. Given technology, the networks for them were based on wireline telecommunications.

Electronic Mail

Because of the plummeting cost of electronic distribution in recent years, the market conditions for print news are now changing rapidly. The use of radio frequency technologies, such as microwave links in telecommunication networks and satellite, FM sideband and television and cable vertical blanking interval transmissions, partially explains why. As a result, a broadening range of individual business, professional and even some consumer users are finding it economical to subscribe to what I believe are best described as electronic-mail news services. Not that such services haven't existed before. But for the first time, costs permit distribution to smaller and smaller niche markets and thus more and more to individual users. In this context, electronic mail as a term, in suggesting direct communication to individuals rather than institutions, seems to capture the essence of this change. In this sense, it serves the same purpose in relation to news services that the term personal computer does to computers.

3. THE EDITORIAL PRODUCT

If news information conveyed in print images is so important to the future of online information, what is it and how is it produced? Each of you, no doubt, has your own answers to these two questions. From a newsman's perspective, allow me these insights.

3.1 Content

First, news covers the leading edge, the 1% or less of human knowledge which is changing. It ranges from intra-day pricing information on commodities, currencies and fixed income and equity securities to natural disasters and political campaigns to the arts and sciences.

Second, news comes in both numeric and textual forms. Easier to computerize and transmit and more universally understood, the former has been distributed by electronic networks the longest. The latter is now coming into its own.

3.2 User Relationship

First, in marketing terms, the relationship between publisher and user is characterized as a continuing subscription instead of a one-time sale.

Second, in editorial terms, the initiative in distributing information begins with the editor instead of the user. On some periodic basis (online and realtime in the case of the wire news services, several times a day in the case of radio and TV, daily in the case of newspapers, weekly in the case of newsmagazines), newseditors alert their audiences to what's new in the different fields of human knowledge, instead of responding to information requests on demand.

In this sense, the editorial process in news publishing exactly mirrors the technological characteristics of the various broadcast media.

3.3 Process

Thus defined, the news requires at least three and as many as six steps to produce:

1. collecting from on as broad a range of reliable sources as possible;

2. discerning from the information supplied by these sources what is really new and really relevant;

3. anticipating how user interests will change as a result of being informed;

4. organizing the result of the first three steps by subject matter;

5. composing the final reports distributed to subscribers in a concise and even entertaining fashion; and

6. presenting them with appropriate headlines, key words and graphic aids to alert subscribers to their content.

4. ELECTRONIC-MAIL NEWS SERVICES

Refining this editorial process, employing the newest technologies, is the category of news publishing I refer to as electronic-mail news services. In generic terms, their operations are depicted in the following diagram:

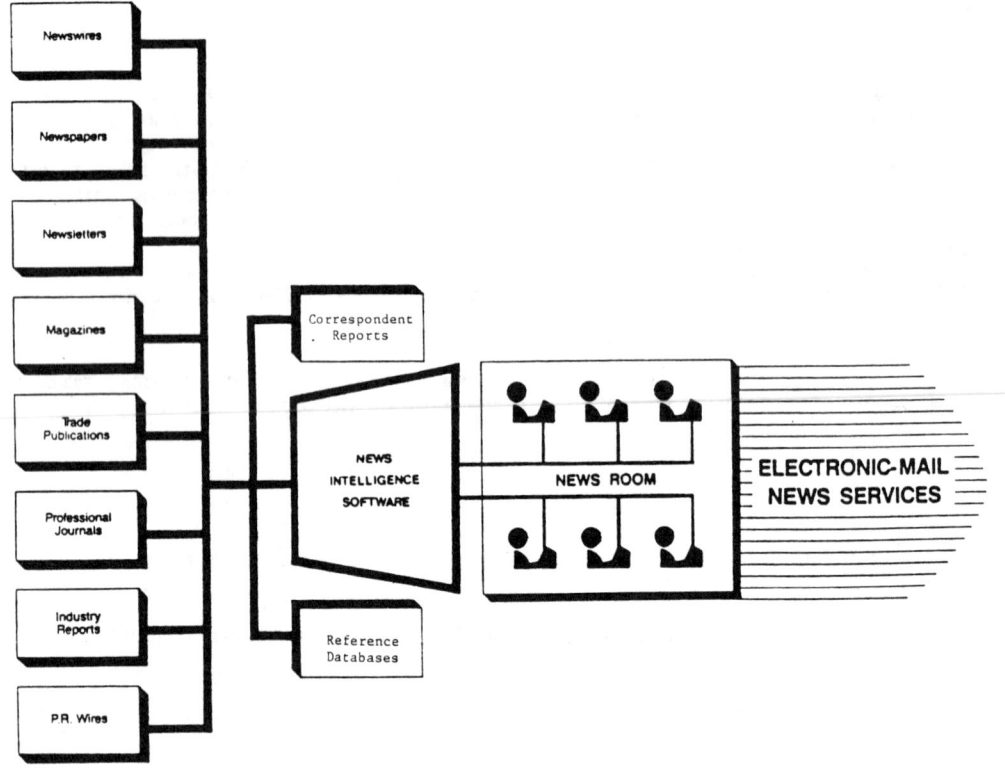

4.1 Diagram

Depicted on the left are a representative if not comprehensive selection sources to be drawn on in the first step; in the left center, news intelligence software to assist in steps two through four; in the right center, a news room of editors to apply live intelligence to steps two through four and to perform steps five and six; and finally on the right, electro-magnetic media to distribute the end-product to users.

4.2 Producers

In the past few years, a surprising number of electronic-mail news services of the kind depicted here have been founded. They come in many shapes and sizes and serve just as many different markets.

Investment community

From my perspective, the most enterprising and successful thus far focus on the needs of the investment community.

    Dow Jones Professional Investor Report
    First Call

Market News Service
OTC Alert

Data processing and communications industry

Developing rapidly are services aimed at the data processing and communications industry:

BYTE Information Exchange
Online Today/ IBM Forum
SearchLink
Tele/Scope

News and political organizations

Just emerging are a variant on the traditional services aimed at news and political organizations:

Federal News Service
Presidential Campaign Hotline

Multinational organizations

At a very high end of the market are services aimed at multinational organizations:

Global Analysis Systems Daily Risk Monitor
Global Report
Oxford Analytica Daily Brief

Multiple markets

Searching for a broad base are services aimed at multiple vertical markets:

McGraw-Hill News
NewsGrid
USA Today
X*Press Information Services

5. SIGNIFICANCE

5.1 Distribution Networks

5.2 Print Oriented News Organizations

5.3 User

GATEWAYS: THE USER HAS RESPONSIBILITIES AND RIGHTS TOO

Betty Unruh, National Federation of Abstracting and Information Services

Abstract: Gateways abound. Information producers, distributors, and users alike stand ready to reap the rewards. While these rewards are easily identified, the corresponding responsibilities are, perhaps, less so. To encourage all participants in the information distribution chain to acknowledge their obligations, the National Federation of Abstracting and Information Services (NFAIS) developed a Code of Practice for Gateways in 1987. The purpose of the Code and the guidelines contained therein was to help gateway participants -- the producer, the vendor, and the gateway -- avoid upsetting the delicate balance among the special interests involved. What are the obligations of the gateway participants? and Why is it the user's responsibility to help ensure that these obligations are met?

Since the early 1970's, database producers, online vendors, and electronic information users have operated in a business relationship based on a variety of bilateral contracts or agreements. The producers and the vendors negotiated contracts that protected the producer's ownership rights and guaranteed that the vendor would receive data in a timely manner and usable format, among other items. The vendors, in turn, required that each new customer to their service sign a contract that stipulated the terms of usage for both the system and the databases on it. It was quite clear who was obligated for what to whom --it was also clear who had what rights.

In the mid 1980's a new player entered the scene -- the gateway. Gateways can be nothing more than agreements between/-among online vendors, but they can also be an entry point to a variety of systems offered by an individual company that may be neither a producer nor a vendor. Regardless of the corporate "form" the gateway takes, the gateway's position in the information distribution chain between the vendor and the user has the potential to tip the delicate balance of understanding among the traditional members dating from the 1970's. That understanding provided prescribed methods for sharing of information. It is critical that those methods continue to function for the rights of all participants in the distribution chain to be preserved, including the users.

The National Federation of Abstracting and Information Services (NFAIS), an association of information producers, vendors, and users, recognized that gateways could present as much peril for its membership as promise. In an attempt to protect the property, efforts, and rights of its membership, NFAIS created and distributed, in 1987, the NFAIS Gateway Code of Practice. The principles and guidelines contained therein were intended to assist any participant in a gateway agreement.

The underlying motive for NFAIS to clarify roles, rights, and privileges by developing this Code was the possible eclipsing of bilateral contracts between the producer and vendor. The critical requirement was that the vendor convey certain sets of information to its users, thereby both protecting and informing them. The positioning of the gateway between the vendor and the users, however, can eliminate all or part of that trail of notices, warranties, and restrictions. Should that happen, clearly understood contractual obligations would become ambiguous or lost. The Code has ten points; each is a right or obligation for each participant. They bear a closer look.

1. **POINT ONE: IDENTIFICATION OF OWNERSHIP**

   Producers expend time, resources, and intellectual effort in creating and generating their products; many copyright these databases as protection against unacknowledged and/or uncompensated use/reuse. The copyright notice protects the producer. It also protects the users from unknowingly misusing the data retrieved.

   Ownership information, therefore, must be distributed throughout the gateway distribution chain -- ownership status must be readily accessible, publicly available, and automatically conveyed to the users. It is the right of both the producer and the users to have this information disseminated. The vendor and gateway are obligated to do so.

2. **POINT TWO: IDENTIFICATION OF THE USER**

   Database users are an identifiable and valuable group -- both producers and vendors will realize continued success only if they can reach this market. In order to do so, each needs to know where the usage has been, i.e., who has been using their services or products. This is especially true with gateways, which, by their definition and stated raison d'etre, open markets unknown or untapped by producers or vendors in the past.

   This data collection starts with the users who enter a unique code or otherwise identify themselves. That responsibility (and system requirement) having been fulfilled, the obligation passes to the gateway, then to the vendor, with the right resting finally with the producer. Any break in that distribution is damaging to the participants above the break; their marketing efforts and growth potential are severely curtailed.

And the wealth of information the users might have gained is blocked.

In the absence of an agreement to share data, the vendor and/or gateway needs to provide willingly a method for sharing this information, information of ultimate benefit to the users. Without cooperation in this area, the users suffer as much as the producer or the vendor.

3. <u>POINT THREE: IDENTIFICATION OF THE VENDOR</u>

The producer and vendor have the right to know which (other) vendors are participating in a gateway in which they, themselves, participate -- and know <u>before</u> the agreements are public. We must not lose sight of the fact that electronic information production and delivery are a business. And, as a business, the "partners" have their own individual interests to protect. Some producers have usage restrictions on their databases -- a gateway may offer distribution they choose not to accept. Vendors have competitors; they also have obligations to the producers to guarantee their terms and conditions regarding use as well as distribution. Vendors may, therefore, choose not to participate in a gateway in which another system participates or they may be forced, by their contracts with the producers, not to participate (at the worst) or to block access to that particular database (at the best). Regardless of the degree of importance of this aspect to the participants, the point is that all participants must be informed as to what vendors are involved in the complete gateway structure. The users, as well, should know which online systems can be accessed via the gateway being used.

4. <u>POINT FOUR: IDENTIFICATION OF DATABASES ACCESSED</u>

Producers devote too many resources to develop and create their products to accept anonymity. They expect identification and have the right to do so. New searchers, who many initially be led to a database via a gateway's menu selection, will one day, hopefully, be making their own database selection decisions. It would be a disservice to those users to help them develop to that point only then to discover that product identification had not been part of the training. The producer has the right to expect that the vendor and the gateway will, each in turn, identify the databases being accessed. The users have the right to know what products they are using; the information must be displayed clearly and conveyed consistently to them.

5. <u>POINT FIVE: DESCRIPTION OF GATEWAY COMPONENTS</u>

A gateway is a technological capability that requires promotional, informational, and publication efforts. Its menu of databases and systems -- unbound by the confines of a single system or a single contract -- is the advantage, indeed major selling point, of a gateway. Yet the gateway will probably have an agreement only with the vendor; nothing is required or sought with the producer, the owner of the very items gateways will "promote" in their sales and promotional efforts.

It is the responsibility of the gateway, therefore, to solicit data and portray it accurately in its own materials about both the databases and the vendors. Inaccuracies, mistakes, or flirtations with the truth benefit no one. Misrepresentation of fact, in favor of marketing rhetoric, is both a danger and an injustice -- for all so described and all who read and rely on the description.

6.   **POINT SIX: CHANGES IN GATEWAY COMPONENTS**

A gateway creates one product from separate entities, most of which have no business relationship with each other. These separate entities -- the database producers and vendors -- actively engage in their own line of business, however, modifying and improving their products. Document types, languages, data fields are added to and deleted from databases. Contracts are renegotiated generating new requirements, restrictions, disclaimers, or deliverables. Vendor search software is upgraded and improved; databases are added to or removed from vendor systems. Changes, whether major or minor in scope or impact, are occurring constantly.

Rarely will a change having an impact on the user of a gateway actually involve the gateway, itself. It is vital, therefore, that the party making the change notifies the other parties; conversely, each gateway participant has the right to receive such updated information. Failure to communicate in this manner deprives those having to "deal" with the changes. The users, in this case, are the ultimate losers in that what is being described may well not be what is being offered.

7.   **POINT SEVEN: ACCURACY AND QUALITY OF DATA SERVICES**

Each participant in a gateway has its own standards for accuracy and quality that it publicly announces. The data and services, therefore, provided by each participant in the gateway must continue to meet the publicly announced standards. It is the obligation of each party to do so as well as the right of each party to expect the others to maintain these standards.

At the same time, each participant must take care not to attribute to another participant statements of accuracy or quality not initially made by that participant. Only the party able to control, monitor, and deliver the accuracy and quality of the data/services can set the standards and initiate any public statements to that fact. Anything to the contrary amounts to customer deception.

8. **POINT EIGHT: UPDATING**

Database producers and vendors, in negotiated agreements, establish schedules for data delivery and file loading for public access. Both the producer and the vendor, therefore, have the obligation to provide to the gateway and the user timely access both as predetermined and as offered to their own customer bases. The database producer and the vendor have the right to expect each other to deliver the data or service in accordance with the agreed-upon schedules.

9. **POINT NINE: PRIVACY**

System accounting programs require collection of certain data: the identification of the users and the number of hours of database access, of records viewed, and of records requested for offline delivery. Beyond these unit tallies or user account data, no further information about the search content, strategy, or retrieval may be disclosed. Failure to comply with this point would threaten the users of online information and the future of the technology, itself.

The vendor and the gateway, both in a position potentially to know the content of a search, have the obligation to maintain the privacy of the users. The users, conversely, have the right to expect the gateway and the vendor to capture and reveal only those data necessary for accounting/reporting purposes.

10. **POINT TEN: USES OF INFORMATION**

The database producer determines the acceptable uses for the data retrieved from its database(s), including any limitations or restrictions. The vendor, through contract provisions, agrees to distribute to its users the terms and conditions of authorized use.

With gateways, the vendor and the gateway share the obligation to make these disclosures to the users. The users are obligated to abide by the terms and conditions as stated. At the same time, it is the right of both the users and the producer to expect that the vendor and the gateway will fulfill their obligations.

It is true that the NFAIS Gateway Code of Practice approaches the issues primarily from the database producer's perspective -- that reflects the focus and the mandate of the Federation. It is not true, however, that interests of the other parties in the gateway relationships are ignored. On the contrary, in almost each of the ten points, the users have the right to expect that the other participants will conduct that facet of the business properly. It is having that right that makes the users critical participants in a gateway -- and that right carries with it a responsibility.

Online information is a business. Gateways are a business. The business will succeed only if the product is accepted, i.e., used. The user can determine which of the gateways being introduced will succeed by being demanding and selective. Informed, sophisticated users can do that better than anyone. Ask questions -- Are you receiving the information about the databases and vendors that you need? Are the products being offered via the gateway being fully and properly identified? Has the gateway shared with you the terms and conditions of use of the product? Do you know what is allowed and what is not? Have you received that information "automatically," or did you have to seek it out? Is the gateway accurately representing the products that you know? If it is not, you need to speak up. When changes to a product are announced in the information press, do you receive notification of those changes from the gateway? Do you notice the changes being accommodated in their support documentation or system software? Are you assured that the gateway recognizes and respects the privacy of your searches? Have you inquired as to whether they can capture or whether they monitor searches and their content?

In any relationship, the participants tend to look out for their own needs first. That is both natural and expected. And it holds true for the gateway business as well. You, as the users, have a substantial list of rights -- expectations -- deliverables due you from the producers, vendors, and gateways. It is, therefore, your obligation and responsibility to see that your rights are respected -- that the other gateway parties are doing so.

The NFAIS Gateway Code of Practice was created to draw attention to the new fragility of historically sound contractual agreements under the weight of gateway distribution. The NFAIS Gateway Code of Practice was also created to highlight the point that no participant in a gateway arrangement is without obligation -- each has expectations and each has responsibilities. It is vital for all participants to recognize that their actions will have an impact on more than the one fellow participant with which they are negotiating or conducting business.

It was, and continues to be, the hope of the NFAIS Task Force that developed the Code and of NFAIS, itself, that vendors that "gateway" and gateway organizations, themselves, will read the Code, understand the guidelines offered therein, and publicly state their acceptance of the principles listed.

Doing so will demonstrate to their customers -- you, the users -- and their business partners alike that they recognize the importance of maintaining a balance among the participants and will conduct their business with an eye toward ensuring both that the balance not be tipped and that each participant enjoy the rights to which it is entitled. You, as the users -- the customers -- must demand no less.

THE SEARCH PERFORMANCE OF END-USERS

Geraldene Walker, State University of New York at Albany

Keywords: Online Searching, End-Users, Evaluation, Performance Measures.

Abstract: Report of a study to evaluate the performance of untrained end-users on the BRS/After Dark system, based on a self-selected user population in an academic environment. Two searches were performed for each query, one by the information-seeker in person, and the other by a trained intermediary. Performance measures are based on a comparison of the two search outputs, relying on user judgments of relevance. These comparative measures provide an evaluation in terms of both effectiveness (recall and precision) and efficiency (time and cost-effectiveness).

No significant differences between the two groups of searchers were found for either precision or recall, though the results for both groups varied widely. Significant differences were found, however, on both the efficiency measures, since end-users took over twice as long as intermediaries to perform their searches. As the cost-effectiveness measure is a function of the relationship between time and the performance measures, it also showed significant differences.

Data of this type, which attempts to quantify end-user search effectiveness, can be used to assist decision-making regarding proposed moves from mediated to end-user searching, and for the allocation of resources between online and CD-ROM files.

I. BACKGROUND AND RESEARCH OBJECTIVES

The last decade has seen a proliferation of online systems and databases, and a corresponding diversification of modes of access to online information. Menu-based frontend interfaces have simplified both access protocols and the search process itself, and many libraries have started using these systems to provide end-user online searching as an option within their traditional reference service.

Early reports of such end-user searching have concentrated on the mechanics of implementing the systems (Ref. 1, 2), the training of the end-user searchers (Ref. 3, 4, 5), and the way in which such a move might affect the role of the intermediary searcher (Ref. 6, 7, 8). Although user response has been enthusiastic and high levels of satisfaction are widely reported (Ref. 9, 10), the overall picture is somewhat confusing. Some writers have expressed reservations regarding the likely response of users (Ref. 11), and some libraries offering such a service have found only small numbers of users to be willing to make the commitment of time and effort necessary to learn to search (Ref. 12). On the other hand, other libraries have found it necessary to set strict time limits for each search in order to prevent being overwhelmed (Ref. 13), and some have found it almost impossible to meet the demand (Ref. 14).

Although much has been written on the topic of end-user searching in the last few years, most of it is subjective and qualitative. The most important question raised by the move from mediated (intermediary) to direct (end-user) searching - how it will affect levels of information provision - has remained unaddressed. The increasing availability of databases on CD-ROM in many libraries will undoubtedly accelerate the trend towards direct user access to online files of bibliographic information, and makes the clarification of end-user search effectiveness particularly vital as an aid to the effective allocation of resources. This research is a first attempt to quantify the likely change in levels of search effectiveness to be expected as a result of such a move in libraries.

2. RESEARCH DESIGN ISSUES

The empirical nature of this investigation involved some complex design considerations which are discussed in some detail in order to assist future research design.

- Both the search system used (BRS/After Dark) and the operating search environment (the University library at SUNY Albany) are considered to be fairly representative of their types.

- In order to maintain realism participation in the study was voluntary, with end-users searching their own real-life queries. Due to the expectation that numbers of such searchers would be small, a random sample was not deemed appropriate. The research population is thus the total population of end-user searchers taken over time (Oct. 1986 through March 1987). Trained intermediary searchers searched the same query.

- Because it was considered important to guard against the possibility of an interaction between the paired searches for the same query, intermediary searches were based on a written expression of the information need provided by the user. Although this was recognized as not being an ideal method of query negotiation, it was considered a necessary limitation of the research situation.

- Despite the fact that they are not entirely satisfactory as measures of search performance, it was decided to use the standard precision and recall ratios. Because they are well-tested and widely-accepted, they have the advantage of providing comparisons with results from other research.

- Relevance was judged by the end-users themselves at two different levels - highly relevant and possibly relevant - though the two were telescoped for final analysis. The outputs from the two searches were presented for relevance judging as a single set in random order, with duplicates eliminated.

- The total relevant retrieved by the two searches provided the denominator of the recall equation. Since the real total of relevant citations in an operating situation is unknown, the question of how to provide additional documents for the recall 'pool' had to be addressed. This can be tackled in a variety of ways - sampling, planting source documents or additional searching - none of which is entirely satisfactory (Ref. 15). This research adopted Lancaster's preference for the use of comparative recall as the most efficient way of coping with this problem (Ref. 16).

The application of these considerations resulted in a research design which provided a population of 100 searches (50 end-user and 50 intermediary) and 50 queries, of which 45 proved usable.

3. STUDY FINDINGS

The research findings for these 45 pairs of searches are discussed here in comparative terms using the four performance variables - precision, recall, time and cost-effectiveness.

3.1. Precision

Standard precision ratios were calculated (relevant retrieved over total retrieved for a single search multiplied by 100) combining the two levels of relevance. It had been expected that end-users would perform well in terms of precision, since previous research had reported a typical pattern of high precision combined with low recall (Ref. 17), regardless of searchers' levels of experience. This expectation was confirmed, since precision scores for intermediaries were not significantly higher than those for end-users (see figure I).

	Mean	Standard Deviation	n
End-user	64.4%	21.4	45
Intermediary	67.5%	23.2	45

$t = -0.94$, $df = 44$, $p = 0.3502$, power for a large effect size = 0.96.
R : alpha = 0.05, $t \geq 2.021$ (i.e. not significant).

Figure 1: Matched pairs t-test, N = 45, for Precision ratios

Earlier research had reported wide variations of performance among intermediary searchers (Ref. 18), and several writers have also identified two distinct types of intermediary search style (Ref. 19, 20). It would appear that similar patterns, possibly at an exaggerated level, also exist among end-users.

3.2 Recall

Recall was measured as a comparative ratio of relevant retrieved by one search over total relevant retrieved by both searches multiplied by 100. The literature had suggested that 'recall is a more difficult goal and a more valid measure of searcher skill than precision' (Ref. 21), so it was expected that intermediaries would perform significantly better on this variable. However, recall ratios were not found to be significantly higher for intermediaries (see figure 2).

	Mean	Standard Deviation	n
End-users	54.4%	21.8	45
Intermediaries	64.0%	21.4	45

t= -1.75, df = 44, p = 0.0873, power for a large effect size = 0.96.

R : alpha = 0.05, t ⟩= 2.021 (i.e. not significant).

Figure 2 : Matched pairs t-test, n = 45, for Recall ratios

It is a possibility that recall figures may have been enhanced somewhat by the method used to calculate recall (i.e. using the number of citations retrieved by the two searches as the denominator for the recall equation), though it is difficult to see how such a procedure could have affected the differences between the two groups.

Although the groups were significantly different in terms of the numbers of most highly relevant documents retrieved, neither precision nor recall ratios calculated using these results showed significant differences. This finding is consistent with recent reports of a small study at Earlham College (Ref. 22), and the intermediary recall and precision ratios reported here are also consistent with previous findings (Ref. 23). This suggests that there is no reason to believe that these intermediary performance measures are other than normal and that a failure to find significant differences must be attributed to the excellence of end-user performance.

But average figures can be misleading. To gain a more comprehensive picture of search performance individual pairs of recall and precision ratios were plotted together, though the resulting graphs failed to demonstrate any obviously identifiable patterns. This variability confirms the opinion of Lancaster, who has pointed out that:

> "few, if any, of the individual performance figures fall exactly on the average performance curve, in fact, the individual results scatter widely. There are some very good results (top right-hand corner), some very bad results (bottom left-hand corner), some high recall and low precision results, some high precision and low recall results, and some middle-of-the-road results." (Ref. 24)

3.3 Time

The greatest difference between end-user and intermediary performance was found in terms of connect time. These results are presented as decimal fractions of an hour, since decimals are easier for the computer to manipulate in formulae (see Figure 3).

	Mean	Standard Deviation	n
End-users	0.44 hrs.	0.19	45
Intermediaries	0.24 hrs.	0.11	45

t= 7.74, df = 44, p = 0.0001, power for a large effect size = 0.96.

R : alpha = 0.05, t ⟩= 2.021 (i.e. significant at alpha = 0.05).

Figure 3 : Matched pairs t-test, N = 45, for Connect Time

End-users took on average twice as long as intermediaries to perform a search for the same query, so that these differences are highly significant. It is the largest difference found between the two groups and confirms earlier findings relating connect time to training and experience (Ref. 25). In fact, it is probably not only a reflection of experience, but also of a more informed awareness of cost constraints. These poor user search times also confirm early reports from tests of student use of CD-ROM databases, where search times as long as five hours were reported (Ref. 26).

3.4 Cost Effectiveness

Cost-effectiveness is a compound measure relating recall and precision measures to connect time. It is calculated in terms of time per relevant document retrieved for total relevant. Because of the relationship of this measure to connect time, end-user and intermediary differences were again significant (see figure 4).

	Mean	Standard Deviation	n
End-users	0.024 hrs.	0.025	45
Intermediaries	0.009 hrs.	0.006	45

t= 4.43, df = 44, p = 0.0001, power for a large effect size = 0.96.

R : alpha = 0.05, t $\geq$ 2.021 (i.e. significant at alpha = 0.05).

Figure 4: Matched pairs t-test for Time per relevant document

4. SUMMARY OF PERFORMANCE

The findings for all the performance variables are summarized in figure 5.

Variable	Means User	Inter.	Std. Dev. User	Inter.	t	p-value
#total relevant	29.8	33.4	0.8	19.7	-0.98	0.3313
% precision	64.6	67.5	21.4	23.2	-0.94	0.3502
% recall	54.4	64.0	21.8	21.4	-1.75	0.0873
#highly relevant (relevance 1)	8.3	12.3	7.3	12.9	-2.05	0.0460*
% prec. (rel. 1)	34.1	37.0	21.5	20.6	-0.99	0.3265
% recall (rel. 1)	44.3	55.7	19.3	19.3	-1.98	0.0536
connect time (hrs)	0.444	0.226	0.2	0.1	7.74	0.0001*
time per rel. doc.	0.024	0.009	0.02	0.006	4.43	0.0001*

*significant at alpha = 0.05

Figure 5: Summary of Performance Measures, N = 45

Overall these performance figures confirm earlier reports of large within group differences linked to small between group differences for both precision and recall (Ref. 27). That is, precision and recall figures vary so widely for both groups, that they mask the differences between the groups. Since intermediary precision and recall ratios in this study fall within normal ranges previously reported (Ref. 28) and are still not significantly higher than those for end-users, one can conclude that end-users appear to perform very well in terms of these effectiveness measures.

Speed is obviously the performance measure where critical differences exist between the two groups. End-users took almost twice as long as intermediaries to achieve very similar results. This difference is reflected not only in connect time itself, but also in the other time-related variable, cost-effectiveness, with cost per relevant citation retrieved being significantly lower for intermediary searchers.

5. CONCLUSIONS

These results suggest that a move from mediated (intermediary) to direct (end-user) searching in libraries will have a minimal effect on the levels of information provided (recall and precision). The significant differences in search time, however, have important implications for the management of search services in libraries. They provide indications which can be used to help decide on the division of resources between mediated and direct search services, and on the acquisition of CD-ROM databases for in-house searching. Individual information-providing agencies may come to different conclusions in light of the resources which they have available and the subject areas of primary concern to their patrons, but this finding that the average end-user can search as effectively on the user-friendly systems as a trained intermediary must provide food for thought among both system managers and professional searchers.

6. REFERENCES

1. Janke, Richard V. BRS/After Dark: the birth of online self-service. Online 7, No. 5, p. 12-29, September 1983.

2. Slingluff, Deborah, Yvonne Lev and Andrew Eisan. An end user search service in an academic health sciences library. Medical Reference Services Quarterly 4, No. 1, p. 11-21, Spring 1985.

3. Snow, Bonnie. Making the rough places plain: designing MEDLINE end user training. Medical Reference Services Quarterly 3, No. 4, p. 1-11, Winter 1984.

4. Steffen, Susan Swords. College faculty goes online: training faculty end-users. Journal of Academic Librarianship 12, No. 3, p. 147-151, July 1986.

5. Friend, Linda. Independence at the terminal: training student end-users to do online literature searching. Journal of Academic Librarianship 11, No. 2, p. 136-141, July 1985.

6. Neilsen, Brian. Online bibliographic searching and the de-professionalization of librarianship. Online 4, No. 3, p. 215-224, May 1980.

7. Walker, Geraldene. End-user searching: the beginning or the end? Reference Librarian No. 14, p. 39-51, Spring/Summer 1986.

8. Suprenant, Thomas T. and Claudia Perry-Holmes. The reference librarian of the future: a scenario. RQ 25, No. 2, p. 234-238, Winter 1985.

9. Janke, Richard V. Online after six: end-user searching comes of age. Online 8, No. 6, p. 15-29, November 1984.

10. Trzebiatowski, Elaine. End-user study on BRS/After Dark. RQ 23, No. 4, p. 446-450, Summer 1984.

11. Tenopir, Carol. Systems for end-users: are there end-users for the systems? Library Journal 110, No. 11, p. 40-41, June 15, 1985.

12. Janke, Richard V., 1984. op. cit.

13. Sweetland, James H. and Wilfred W. Fong. Academic end-user access to databases. Paper presented at ASIS Mid-year Meeting, King's Island, OH., 17-20 May 1987. Not published.

14. Jaros, Joe, Vicki Anders and Geri Hutchins. Subsidized end-user searching in an academic library. Proceedings Seventh National Online Meeting, New York, 6-8 May 1986, p. 223-229.

15. Elchesen, D.R. Cost-effectiveness comparison of manual and on-line retrospective bibliographic searching. Journal of the American Society for Information Science 29, No. 2, p. 56-66, March 1978.

16. Lancaster, F. Wilfred. Information retrieval systems: characteristics, testing and evaluation. 2nd ed. New York: Wiley, 1979.

17. Fenichel, Carol H. The process of searching online bibliographic databases: a review of research. Library Research 2, No. 2, p. 107-127, Summer 1980-81.

18. Fenichel, Carol H. Online information retrieval: identification of measures which discriminate among users with different levels and types of experience. Ph.D. dissertation, Drexel University, 1979.

19. Fidel, Raya. Online searching styles: a case-study-based model of searching behavior. Journal of the American Society for Information Science 35, No. 4, p. 211-221, July 1984.

20. Rholes, Julia M. and Judith B. Droessler. Online database searchers: cognitive style. Proceedings Fifth National Online Meeting, New York, 10-12 April 1984, p. 305-311.

21. Bellardo, Trudi. Some attributes of online search intermediaries that relate to search outcome. Ph.D. dissertation, Drexel University, 1984.

22. Penhale, Sara J. and Nancy Taylor. Integrating end-user searching into a bibliographic instruction program. RQ 27, No. 2, p. 212-220, Winter 1986.

23. Fenichel, Carol H., 1979. op. cit.

24. Lancaster, F. Wilfred, 1979. op. cit. p. 134.

25. Wanger, Judith. Evaluation of the online search process: a preliminary report. Proceedings Third International Online Meeting, London, 4-6 December 1979, p. 1-11.

26. Sweetland, James H. and Wilfred W. Fong, 1987. op. cit.

27. Fenichel, Carol H., 1979. op. cit.

28. Fenichel, Carol H., 1980-81. op. cit.

THE DESIGN OF ONLINE THESAURI

Bella Hass Weinberg and Julie A. Cunningham, St. John's University

Keywords: Online Thesauri, Thesaurus Structure, DIALOG, BRS, MeSH, NLM, ERIC, Search Preparation, Online Displays.

Abstract: The formats of online thesauri are compared with those of corresponding printed tools, and commands for searching online thesauri on various vendor systems are reviewed. The major online thesauri compared with their printed versions are ERIC and Medical Subject Headings. The vendor systems examined include DIALOG, BRS, and NLM. Although postings data are clearly more up-to-date in online thesauri, it is felt that the display of a given thesaurus online is often inferior to that of its printed counterpart. In DIALOG, indentation which is indicative of hierarchical structure is absent; statistics on "related terms" that cover use references, narrower terms, and broader terms are felt to be confusing; and certain data elements present in printed thesauri, e.g., term history, are missing online. BRS has no online thesaurus, only one specialized vocabulary switching database. NLM's MeSH vocabulary file contains complete records for individual terms, but the full tree structures are not displayable online. As the poor display of online thesauri and even worse documentation may explain in part the lack of use of controlled vocabulary in searching, recommendations for improving and clarifying the format of online thesauri as well as directions for further research conclude the paper.

1. INTRODUCTION

"The Great Vocabulary Debate" was the theme of a session held at the 1987 ASIS Annual Meeting (Ref.1). The consensus of speakers on both sides of the issue was that thesauri are necessary for online searching whether or not controlled vocabulary indexing is done before a database is loaded because the burden is on the searcher to think of synonyms and related terms in free text searching. Search preparation as taught in library schools typically involves consultation of printed thesauri to minimize online charges. As part of question-negotiation with the user, descriptors may be selected from the thesaurus, and depending on user information needs, plans for broadening or narrowing the search may be made before going online.

A number of researchers that have analyzed search logs have shown that thesaurus terms often are not used, even when free terms are identical with descriptors (Ref. 2 - 4). It is our belief that non-use or underutilization of controlled vocabularies may be explained, at least in part, by the following:

1) A lack of understanding on the part of searchers and even online trainers of the structure and format of printed thesauri, many of which are poorly designed. (Experience by the primary author in teaching indexing has shown that the most complex concept is translation of thesaurus structure (Ref. 5).)

2) The lack of access, especially in small libraries, to printed thesauri, especially for databases not searched regularly. This would make a case for online thesauri, which leads to our next reason for non-use of controlled vocabulary.

3) The poor display of online thesauri, even where the printed source is adequate.

It is the purpose of this paper to focus on the latter aspect of thesaurus design, which has received little attention in the literature. Svenonius has written "Unanswered Questions in the Design of Controlled Vocabularies," but does not deal at all with the design of their online display (Ref. 6). New editions of thesaurus construction manuals by Lancaster and Aitchison have recently appeared, again, with little attention to this topic (Ref. 7, 8). Dubois considers the reasons why so few structured thesauri are available online, but does not address the question of their display format (Ref. 9).

2. STANDARD FORMAT OF PRINTED THESAURI

The standard printed thesaurus, as exemplified by the Thesaurus of Engineering and Scientific Terms (the grandfather of them all) and the Thesaurus of ERIC Descriptors , has a basic alphabetical display of authorized terms with cross-references from non-preferred terms (Ref. 10,11). Under descriptors, we find the reciprocals of use references tagged UF, as well as links to broader (BT), narrower (NT), and related (RT) terms. This thesaurus format is recommended by the American National Standards Institute, but the ANSI standard on thesaurus construction will soon undergo revision (Ref. 12).

Some thesauri have, in addition to an alphabetic list, a permuted or rotated display, which provides access to every word in multi-word descriptors and, in some cases, to words in cross references. Permuted lists serve the same function as inversions of multi-word headings integrated into the main alphabetic display as use references. Most thesauri have some sort of hierarchical display of terms, but in many cases, this is limited to broad groupings of descriptors, e.g., in the Thesaurus of Psychological Index Terms (Ref. 13). Some thesauri, such as the UN's Macrothesaurus have several types of hierarchical display - broad classes as well as a full hierarchy - in addition to the BT/NT information in the alphabetic display (Ref. 14). This is felt to be confusing to the user (Ref. 15).

An alternative format which we find preferable is exemplified by the MeSH (Medical Subject Headings) vocabulary (Ref. 16). No hierarchical information is found in the alphabetic portion of the list; instead, all levels of broader and narrower terms are in the tree structures, to which one is led by an alphanumeric code (Ref. 17, 18). The effectiveness of this structure - which permits one to "explode" a tree number in searching, automatically ORing terms narrower than the desired concept - is evidenced by the fact that MEDLINE's major commercial competitor, Excerpta Medica's EMBASE, has recently announced plans to implement EMTREE, a similar hierarchical display of controlled terms (Ref. 19).

3. ONLINE THESAURI

The term "online thesauri" - interpreted broadly - encompasses all types of name and subject authority files with links between headings, and even the thesaurus of Chinese, Japanese, and Korean characters available on RLIN (Ref. 20). The scope of this paper is, however, limited to online versions of controlled vocabularies used in subject indexing. The Library of Congress has recently changed the format of its subject heading list to a standard thesaurus format, but this is used only in the microfiche version, while the online file uses MARC tags

(Ref. 21). In this paper we concentrate on the online thesauri of abstracting and indexing services as loaded by the major vendors rather than cataloging networks.

Having analyzed online thesauri, we feel that the most effective way to present our findings is in terms of vendor systems rather than comparing the format of a given thesaurus on different systems. First, we document DIALOG's display format for online thesauri, comparing them with printed counterparts. Second, we evaluate access to controlled vocabulary in BRS, which does not actually have individual online thesauri, only one specialized vocabulary switching file. Finally, we describe the National Library of Medicine's online MeSH vocabulary file and the commands for displaying the hierarchical information contained in its tree structures.

The information we present is based on analysis of current searches and review of publicly available documentation, rather than on first-hand knowledge of vendor methods for loading thesauri.

3.1   Thesauri on DIALOG

On the simplest level, DIALOG provides access to controlled vocabulary terms through the "expand" command, which displays alphabetically adjacent terms in DIALOG's basic index or dictionary file. The latter includes single word free terms, descriptors and identifiers as well as multi-word descriptors and identifiers. The number of postings for single words includes both descriptor and free term occurrences. To limit a search to descriptor postings, the qualifiers /DE and /DF may be used. /DE shows the number of documents in which a term occurs as part of a multi- or single-word descriptor; /DF reports on the use of a single word as an assigned descriptor.

In this display of the dictionary file, DIALOG tags thesaurus headings and non-preferred entry terms in the column headed "RT," discussed further below. Inputting the command "expand" followed by the line number of such a term calls up the thesaurus display.

Online thesauri can also be called up directly on DIALOG for certain databases. A list of these is printed out in response to the command "?thesauri." The display format of these thesauri is standardized and does not mirror that of the corresponding printed thesauri. The command "expand" followed by the desired term in parentheses yields a display of the requested term plus eleven subsequent lines from the printed thesaurus, all aligned. Term history and scope notes found in the printed thesaurus are not generally given online, except for dates and qualifying terms in parentheses.

Each descriptor is assigned a reference number, which is followed by postings data under the heading ITEMS. Some printed thesauri, such as ERIC, include postings data, but this information is clearly more up-to-date online. Furthermore, the printed thesaurus gives postings data for the main heading only, while DIALOG indicates the occurrences of narrower, broader, and related terms. For single word terms, the statistics include free text occurrences.

The next column in DIALOG's online thesaurus display, headed TYPE, features single-letter codes that reflect the syndetic structure of the thesaurus. According to DIALOG's latest search manual, synonyms are linked through the codes F and U. in the words of the documentation, "F = Use For (prefer this term to the term EXPANDed)" and "U = Use (use the term EXPANDed as preferred term)" (Ref. 22). Although the manual instructs searchers to "Check the database chapter to determine the exact relationships used", we find the fact that these codes are used interchangeably and inconsistently across databases confusing. For example, a search on ERIC's preferred term EDUCATIONAL ENVIRONMENT revealed U [i.e., Used for] Academic environment, while a search on the latter term brought up the display Academic Environment U [i.e., use] EDUCATIONAL

ENVIRONMENT. In PsycINFO, we expanded (attitudes) and were shown F BELIEFS (NONRELIGIOUS); i.e., used for in the standard thesaurus sense - the opposite of the manual's explanation. Another variation in DIALOG's handling of see references is the use of X in MEDLINE to designate non-preferred terms.

DIALOG indicates hierarchical and associative relationships through the codes N (narrower term), B (broader term), and R (related term), which are shortened versions of the standard thesaurus codes NT, BT, and RT. The order of these is not standardized. B sometimes precedes N and vice versa. We think the former sequence is preferable.

DIALOG uses RT as the heading for the next column in its online thesaurus display, with a totally different meaning. The number of so-called "related terms" refers to the total number of synonyms (UF references), broader, narrower and related terms listed in the thesaurus for a given descriptor. In our view, this is a misleading and perhaps even useless piece of information. Multi-word synonyms have zero postings, and a searcher generally wants to either broaden or narrow a search, not both simultaneously. We recommend that a plus sign next to terms indicate that further information is available. If the RT column is necessary at all, it should be moved to the left of TYPE, as indication of the relationship of the term to the requested heading is more important to the searcher.

The absence of indentation is another disadvantage of DIALOG's online thesaurus display. Although improvements in thesaurus format were announced in DIALOG Version 2, the only change was a shift in the position of the column headed RT. We recommend that the requested term be centered, broader terms be pushed left and narrower terms indented right.

DIALOG also provides access to the rotated display of selected thesauri, which brings to the fore words in secondary or tertiary position in multi-word terms. The command that calls up this display is "expand ZZ=" followed by the desired word. The Blue Sheets indicate databases for which this is available, but the command is not explained in the new search manual. We compared DIALOG's online rotated display for the descriptor ENVIRONMENT in the ERIC database with the corresponding portion of the printed thesaurus. The first difference is the lack of indentation in the online version; the terms are not displayed in context, i.e., in direct order- they are all inverted. Next, we found that the online rotated list contains fewer terms than the printed one. The term ENVIRONMENT within a parenthetical qualifier is not picked up by DIALOG, nor are discontinued terms or terms in use references. DIALOG's rotated descriptor display thus contains only terms with postings and is less complete than some printed rotated displays which include old or non-preferred terms.

The number of postings for all the multi-word terms containing the desired descriptor plus the number of its occurrences as a single word term should logically equal the number of postings for the single word qualified with /DE, as the latter reflects DIALOG's "double posting" (Ref. 23).

We tested this assumption by examining the term ENVIRONMENT in ERIC. Unqualified, the word has 40,455 postings, which includes free text occurrences. With the qualifier /DF, there are 3246 documents. The total number of postings for all the rotated descriptors including the word ENVIRONMENT, ORed to delete documents that have two such terms assigned, is 19,389. ORing this with the single word set yields 22,374; however, searching ENVIRONMENT/DE gives a system response of 27,083. How can this discrepancy be explained? We hypothesized that the descriptors omitted from the online thesaurus display might account for the difference. We then searched these individually, ORed the resulting sets and got 5394 postings, a rather significant number. Combining this set with ENVIRONMENT/DF and the rotated terms that had appeared online yielded the expected total - 27,083. Thus, the postings data in DIALOG for a term qualified /DE may not exactly correspond to the logical sum of the postings in its rotated descriptor list because of the terms missing from the online display.

Hierarchical displays are not given in DIALOG for any thesaurus, although individual or ranges of classification numbers may be searchable. In the case of MeSH, tree numbers may be "cascaded" in DIALOG (the equivalent of NLM's "explode"), but the hierarchy cannot be examined online. A search on a tree number or, in DIALOG's terms, a <u>descriptor code</u> (DC), yields a display of tree numbers without feature headings explaining their meaning - which is essentially useless. The searcher must use the printed tool to survey the complete hierarchical structure of the vocabulary. One level broader and one level narrower than a given MeSH term may, however, be viewed via the regular "expand" command with DIALOG's thesaurus notation.

3.2 Online Thesauri on BRS

BRS does not offer online access to the thesaurus of a database, but only to descriptors in its dictionary file. This is accomplished through the use of the "root" command which is analogous but not identical to DIALOG's "expand" command. The display which results from using the "root" command followed by the desired word is arranged in column form. The first column lists R numbers which can be used in the subsequent search strategy until the next "root" command is executed. The second column lists terms in the dictionary file alphabetically in the following order: the "root" word, followed by multi-word descriptors beginning with the root word and then by a list of free text phrases whose words are separated in the document record by a forward slash. For example, BEHAVIOR/SOCIAL appears in the abstract in just that form. This part of the display may be confusing to searchers used to the double slashes in the rotated display which results from DIALOG's ZZ command. Finally, although paragraph qualification to the descriptor field (.DE. and .DF.) can be used post hoc to reduce the number of postings, it cannot be used with the root command to limit the display only to thesaurus terms.

The display which is called up by the "root" command does not provide syndetic information from thesauri. Narrower, broader and related terms are not indicated, nor is the searcher informed that they may exist. Term histories, use references, and scope notes are also missing.

"Pref" is BRS' rough equivalent to DIALOG's "expand ZZ=" command, except that it displays multi-word terms in context, without inverting them. It differs from a standard KWIC index in that the keywords are not aligned. Like "root," "pref" displays portions of the dictionary file, in this case for terms <u>ending</u> with the requested word or stem. The "pref" command is logically equivalent to automatic prefix stripping or left-hand truncation for single words. BRS uses $. for the latter search command, but "pref" displays the terms retrieved, not just the number of postings for the entire set. For example, a search on "pref ATTITUDES" or $. ATTITUDES picks up NONATTITUDES as well as typographical errors such as OFATTITUDES.

"Pref" is not available in all databases, and where available, suffers from the same limitations as "root" in that one cannot restrict the display to thesaurus terms. Another limitation of both "pref" and "root" is that (unlike DIALOG's ZZ) they do not call up words in medial position, e.g., ALCOHOL <u>DRINKING</u> ATTITUDES.

Although BRS does not have an online thesaurus for individual databases, it does have a vocabulary switching file called TERM that applies to six databases: ERIC, Family Resources, MEDLINE, NCMH, PsycINFO, and Sociological Abstracts. Designed to complement rather than substitute for the database producers' thesauri, it does not, however, include all the descriptors in those thesauri and "contains very few related terms" (Ref. 24). Besides descriptors, TERM includes identifiers, free text and "near" synonyms, as well as numerical, classification, category, and publication type codes.

TERM can provide a starting place for searchers who wish to search these and other related databases which use the same thesauri by providing information not available by using "root" or "pref" in the individual databases - particularly narrower terms and free-text hedges, i.e., lists of synonymous words and phrases "for searching frequently used, difficult concepts or concepts lacking descriptors" (Ref. 25). The information is displayed, however, in a manner which is difficult to assimilate and use while online. BRS itself suggests offline use of the free text paragraph: ". . . it is often a good idea to let the end user scan the field contents and underline the words and phrases which are wanted in the search "(Ref. 26).

A TERM record for each concept or "title," consists of fields which contain descriptors for the individual databases, free terms, codes, and narrower and broader terms. Searching a single term in the database can yield many records that are dense and overwhelming to read by the screenful. A searcher may eliminate irrelevant information and some screen clutter by displaying paragraphs selectively. But even this produces a lot of information which is difficult for the searcher to digest while online and requires further investigation either online or offline.

Various other search strategies may be used to produce a smaller, more relevant set of documents. The key points here, however, are that while TERM may be useful in certain contexts, it is a separate database rather than an online thesaurus linked to a bibliographic database and it does not tell the searcher how many documents are posted to each term. In addition, it is not complete, it is rather complicated to use effectively, the online display requires time to digest, and for lengthy displays probably requires a printout for further examination and search strategy development. Finally, the terms retrieved cannot automatically be searched on another database.

3.3   MeSH Vocabulary on NLM

In NLM databses, controlled vocabulary is the default option, i.e., in searching a single-word term without qualification, only descriptor postings are given, and one must specifically request free term occurrences through qualifiers. NLM has a separate database called MeSH, the printed counterpart of which is <u>Medical Subject Headings: Annotated Alphabetic List.</u> This is not to be confused with BRS' file called MESH, which contains the MEDLINE database.

The documentation for NLM's MeSH file is contained in Chapter 6 of its <u>Online Services Reference Manual</u> (Ref. 27), which indicates that thesaurus records may be printed out in varying degrees of detail. The most detailed record includes everything in the Annotated Alphabetic List, including scope notes as well as the number of postings in each of the MEDLINE backfiles.

Printed MeSH is not liberal with cross references, and the published permuted list compensates for this by providing access to every word in authorized headings and cross references (Ref. 28). Online, by adding the qualifier (TW) - <u>text word</u> - a display equivalent to that of the permuted list is achieved, with the additional advantage that the full records of terms can immediately be printed.

The most powerful feature of the MeSH vocabulary is its tree structures, and the "explode" command in the MEDLINE database has been discussed above. If an exploded term occurs in multiple trees, one may "expand" it and be shown the broader terms. In the MeSH database, the explode command may be used only with tree numbers, not with terms; the command yields a list of terms on a variety of levels in alphabetical order, rather than the hierarchical display one would expect. The manual does not provide a clear example to illustrate this point.

For the searcher who does not have printed MeSH handy, it would be desirable to have the tree structures displayed online. A TREE command may be used in NLM databases on either a term or a tree number, but the resulting display does not mirror that of the printed tree structures. Only one level above and one level below the desired term are shown online, which is equivalent to the BT/NT display in standard printed thesauri. Unlike DIALOG's online thesauri, NLM features indentation for these. A plus sign appears next to headings that have additional narrower terms, and one may repeat the TREE command to view these.

No reference to the TREE command is found in NLM's chapter on the MeSH vocabulary file, although the command may be used within this file. The MEDLINE chapter mentions it, and the index to the two-volume set leads one to Chapter 4 of the Online Services Reference Manual, which lists TREE among general commands for searching NLM databases. The MeSH pocket guide does, however, bring together all commands related to the display of the controlled vocabulary.

4. CONCLUSIONS AND RECOMMENDATIONS

We conclude from our examination of the online thesaurus display of three major vendors that none provides all the elements we consider desirable in such displays. We believe that the poorly placed, misleading, and/or incomplete information found in these online displays - particularly in comparison with their printed counterparts - all contribute to searchers' underutilization of controlled vocabularies. Where useful features exist, their frequent and effective use is sometimes discouraged by poor print documentation.

Based on these observations, we recommend that the following features be included in online thesaurus displays on vendor systems where they do not already exist:

1. Use references, not just postable terms, should be included in the basic index to lead the searcher to preferred terms.
2. Within thesaurus displays, postings should only reflect indexer assignment and not include free term occurrences.
3. Provide term histories, i.e., dates in which terms entered the vocabulary as well as older terms to be used in searching.
4. Given double posting of multi-word thesaurus terms online, it should be possible to create rotated descriptor lists in each database even where one does not exist in the printed source.
5. Searchers should have online access to broader, narrower and related term information from printed thesauri.
6. Use indentation to clarify the hierarchical relationship between terms.
7. Searchers should have the option of calling up a full hierarchical display, minimally where the print thesaurus contains one. It should also be possible for online vendors to generate a hierarchical display from the hidden classification of standard thesaurus format by following the BT and NT codes.
8. Thorough documentation should be provided for all online thesaurus protocols. This should be included with the basic information sheets for each database.

We also recommend additional research on user comprehension of online thesaurus displays and the testing of alternative formats in actual searching situations. Considering the interest of artificial intelligence researchers in syndetic structures of words, findings on the way the mind organizes hierarchical and associative information on words may also be brought to bear on the design of online thesauri (Ref. 29).

6.   ACKNOWLEDGMENTS

This paper is based on work done under NSF Grant IST-8217400. A research grant of online search time from DIALOG Information Services, Inc. is also acknowledged. The authors thank Prof. Gloria Kelman for expert online assistance.

7.   REFERENCES

1. Leide, John. Annual Meeting SIG/CR Session Reviews. SIGnews - American Society for Information Science, p. [3], January, 1988.

2. Markey, Karen; Atherton, Pauline; Newton, Claudia. An Analysis of Controlled Vocabulary and Free Text Search Statements in Online Searches. Online Review 4, No. 3, p. 225 - 233, Sept. 1980.

3. Cunningham, Julie A.; Weinberg, Bella H. Search Strategy in the Field of Engineering: a Statistical Approach. National Online Meeting, 6. Proceedings, p. 117 - 123, 1985.

4. Fidel, Raya. Controlled Vocabulary and Free-text Searching: Searchers' Selection of Search Keys. Proceedings of the ASIS Annual Meeting 24, p. 71 - 73, 1987.

5. Weinberg, Bella H. Indexing Concepts Which Students Find Complex. Proceedings of the ASIS Annual Meeting 22, p. 373, 1985.

6. Svenonius, Elaine. Unanswered Questions in the Design of Controlled Vocabularies. Journal of the American Society for Information Science 37, No. 5, p. 331 - 340, Sept. 1986.

7. Lancaster, F. W. Vocabulary Control for Information Retrieval. 2nd ed. Arlington, VA: Information Resources Press, 1986.

8. Aitchison, Jean; Gilchrist, Alan. Thesaurus Construction: a Practical Manual. 2nd ed. London: Aslib, 1987.

9. Dubois, C.P.R. The Use of Thesauri in Online Retrieval. Journal of Information Science 8, No. 2, p. 63-66, March 1984.

10. Thesaurus of Engineering and Scientific Terms. New York: Engineers Joint Council, 1967.

11. Thesaurus of ERIC Descriptors. 11th ed. Phoenix, AZ: Oryx Press, 1987.

12. American National Standard Guidelines for Thesaurus Structure, Construction and Use. New York: American National Standards Institute, 1980.

13. Thesaurus of Psychological Index Terms. 4th ed. Washington, DC: American Psychological Association, 1985.

14. Macrothesaurus for Information Processing in the Field of Economic and Social Development. 3rd ed., prepared by Jean Viet. New York: United Nations, Department of International Economic and Social Affairs, 1985.

15. Weinberg, Bella H . [Review of] Macrothesaurus for Information Processing in the Field of Economic and Social Development. Journal of the American Society for Information Science 39, No. 1, p. 23 - 24, Jan. 1988.

16. Weinberg, Bella H.; Cunningham, Julie A. The Relationship Between Term Specificity in MeSH and Online Postings in MEDLINE. Bulletin of the Medical Library Association 73, No. 4, p. 365 - 372, Oct. 1985.

17. Medical Subject Headings. Annotated Alphabetic List, 1988. Bethesda, MD: National Library of Medicine, 1987.

18. Medical Subject Headings. Tree Structures, 1988. Bethesda, MD: National Library of Medicine, 1987.

19. Announcing EMBASE Plus. Profile: the Excerpta Medica Newsletter 5, No. 4, p. 1-7.

20. Smith-Yoshimura, Karen; Tucker, Alan. RLIN East Asian Character Code and the RLIN CJK Thesaurus. Stanford, CA: Research Libraries Group, May 1985.

21. LCSH in Microfiche: The New Look. Cataloging Service Bulletin. No. 37, p. 54 -58, Summer 1987.

22. Searching DIALOG: The Complete Guide. Palo Alto, CA: Dialog Information Services, August 1987, p. 7-5.

23. Kesselman, Martin; Perry, Irene. What Online Searchers Should Know About Indexing and What Indexers Should Know About Online Searching. Proceedings of the Fifth National Online Meeting, p. 141-148, April 1984.

24. The BRS Aid Page for TERM, April 1983.

25. Knapp, Sara D. Creating BRS/TERM, a Vocabulary Database for Searchers. Database 7, No. 4, p. 70-75, December 1984.

26. BRS TERM Database Guide, p. 11, [1984?].

27. Online Services Reference Manual. Bethesda, MD: National Library of Medicine, 1986.

28. Permuted Medical Subject Headings - 1988. Bethesda, MD: U.S. National Library of Medicine, 1987.

29. Anderson, James D. Indexing Systems: Extensions of the Mind's Organizing Power. In: Information and Behavior, vol.1, ed. Brent D. Ruben, New Brunswick: Transaction Books, 1985, p. 287-323.

JUSTIFYING YOUR INFORMATION CENTER'S BUDGET

Daniel U. Wilde and Nan R. Cooper, NERAC, Inc.

Keywords: Technical Information Center, Technology Transfer, Benefits, Productivity, Innovation

Abstract: When market conditions force corporate belt-tightening measures, often the first budget item to go is that sustaining the information center. Yet, logically, when confronted with business difficulties - be they financial, operational, marketing, managerial or technical - a company should secure all the help it can muster. The technical information center should be the last resource targeted for cutback, because it provides a steady source of technological intelligence fueling innovation and productivity. Regrettably, information managers themselves may unwittingly contribute to this demise. Most feel it is unprofessional to "fight" for their center: they perceive the need for information is so intuitively obvious it requires no formal argument to justify continued funding. The truth is that information's contribution to the company is difficult to quantify, and even before times become tight, information managers should champion their technical information center as an indispensible asset. A superior defense relies on actual measures of the center's performance. One very successful evaluation method involves the identification and reporting of specific examples in which technology supplied by the information center encouraged new products, enhanced efficiency, reduced costs or led to some other such tangible benefit to the company. A formal presentation of case findings serves to illustrate to upper management the vitalizing power of the information center, thus affirming the need for continued funding.

1. INTRODUCTION

   The merit of infusing technical information gathered from sources external to the organization cannot be overstated. A reliable channel of both historical and contemporary information is nothing short of a professional umbilical cord providing sustenance to the R&D process.

   Innovators know, both intuitively and experientially, that fresh intelligence from multiple sources and perspectives is vital to creativity. It can unveil background data in new or unfamiliar areas, confer currency and a more cosmopolitan perspective, and fuel creativity. It also permits the scientist or engineer to investigate markets, market needs and trends; to monitor patents and gather competitive intelligence; and to avoid duplicating existing, tested technologies. Outside information reduces chances of pursuing ultimately unprofitable or unworkable R&D ventures. It also is a wellspring of fresh ideas and a stimulant to creativity and productivity.

Despite these undeniable benefits, corporate management may not fully appreciate the critical relationship between exposure and innovation. Or they may simply underestimate the effect in relation to cost. This orientation is not wholly unexpected. It frequently stems from limited contact with the day-to-day activities occurring in the "trenches", the breeding ground for innovative thinking.

Other problems are the difficulty of measuring how effectively outside information stimulates performance, and a tendency by administrators to evaluate cost without consideration for qualitative results such as cost avoidance.

This problem is a perceptual discrepancy founded in poor communication. How is the gap bridged? Corporate skepticism is overcome through presentation of tangible evidence that beneficial applications ensued from information provided by the corporate information center: that is, bottom-line proof in the form of case studies. This method "commodicizes" the information exchange process so that a cost/benefit analysis may be made.

2.   DOCUMENTATION OF BENEFITS: A DISCUSSION

A clear link must be drawn between the information conveyed and the end-user's exploitation of it for some beneficial result, be it technical currency, cost savings, creative thought, enhanced productivity or market intelligence. The most valid, consistently reliable and expedient evidence is obtained by directly contacting the information consumer - the scientist or technician - and soliciting his/her evaluation.

A followup methodology must be designed which effectively captures the desired feedback and allows for critical analysis. Some important considerations are timing, degree of disruption to the information user and quality of feedback. Obviously, the ideal method is timed such that the user has fully digested and employed the information but still accurately recalls the source, nature and value of the information to the R&D effort. Likewise, the method should intrude minimally on the user's productivity by its brevity, and it should elicit the most thorough and candid response possible.

Common methods for obtaining feedback include use of either open-ended qualititative or structured quantitative questionnaires, and person-to-person verbal interviews. Possibly, a combination of the two is optimal for detail and accuracy. The end result of this intelligence-gathering process should be a collection of individual case studies which permit inferences to be drawn as to the cumulative use and adjudged valuation of the outside information source. In companies that rely upon several information sources, this evaluation process allows management to compare the alternatives, to determine which is perceived by users as most useful, and perhaps to reallocate financial resources for greater productivity.

The results of a user followup program should be presented to the decision-making management as substantiation of the use and effectiveness of the information service.

3. NERAC'S EXPERIENCE

The success of this strategy in compiling a convincing argument to management is borne out through NERAC's experience, which is shared below. First, however, it is appropriate to offer some background about NERAC. In 1958, Congress passed the National Aeronautics and Space Act mandating NASA to "Provide for the widest practicable and appropriate dissemination of information concerning its activities and the results thereof." To accomplish this task, NASA designed the Technology Utilization Program. A network of centers was founded nationwide to aid and promote technology transfer by helping businesses, academic institutions, state and local governments gain access to relevant technical information.

The New England Research Application Center was established at the University of Connecticut in 1966 under co-sponsorship of NASA. In July of 1985, both co-sponsors concluded their experiment was a success. At that time, an independent, not-for-profit corporation was founded to continue the technology transfer task. The company is NERAC, Inc., and today it is the largest technology transfer center in the United States.

NERAC has learned that a user followup program accomplishes several important objectives for the information source itself. Within the framework of the NASA technology transfer program, it is requisite for sponsorship. Given its awesome task, NASA needed a means to substantiate the performance of its channels in effecting technology transfer. Each Technology Utilization (TU) network member must "identify and document the benefits that are being derived by private industry, the nation and NASA and the TU program."

The information center itself stands to gain significant knowledge from user contact. It affords a pulse on market satisfaction, enabling the information center to attack weak areas and concentrate on program augmentations to meet the demands of a dynamic marketplace. In turn, by responding to user concerns, the information source is better able to meet client needs and to earn client loyalty.

The organization subscribing to the information service can benefit from this same feedback. It enables the company to concentrate its resources for greater performance and to identify departments that are under-utilizing the information source, offers management a prime view of the types and progress of work occurring in R&D departments, and indicates the relative value of information sources utilized.

4. USER FEEDBACK MECHANISMS

A key consideration for NERAC, in designing a useful user feedback mechanism, was how to define "benefits." While this may vary between - even within - companies, benefits resulting from technology transfer may include labor/time savings; financial savings from new procedures and processes or from cost avoidance; identification of alternate materials, suppliers or distribution networks; new or improved products and processes; increased productivity; market intelligence and identification of new markets; and contact with knowledgeable experts in new or specialized areas.

Over time, NERAC's models for assessing technology transfer have undergone considerable evolution as the Company itself has grown. Early models relied upon leads generated from such sources as feedback reply cards returned by users, recommendations by in-house technical staff who worked with clients, and mandatory reports prepared by the collaborating Small Business Administration staff. Given a potential lead, the benefit reporter would then phone the user and attempt to document the case, including such details as the technology conveyed, application, expected benefits to society from this new product/process, and assessed value of information conveyed. Though somewhat haphazard in approach, this methodology unveiled cases of significant technology transfer.

Experience, and NERAC's growth in clients and usage, compelled the Company to design a more controlled, focused strategy capable of rendering qualified responses. The new strategy seeks to encroach minimally on the participant's time, thus respecting the corporate environment; to elicit strong, qualified leads from users who are willing and able to disclose information; and to attain substantive details of the beneficial application.

While several lead sources are still employed today, two mechanisms are found to deliver superior clues. First is the NERAC marketing force. Sales representatives have a special relationship with clients. Their frequent contact with participants, plus knowledge of internal corporate structures and personalities, make them a valuable resource. Another superior source of leads is a document followup form which accompanies each NASA document order fulfilled through the Company's document service. This form captures excellent detail from users about the technology transferred and how it was beneficially applied. In brief, NERAC's benefit identification and reporting mechanism transpires something like this:

The salesman learns of potential leads through personal contact with users, followup reply cards and document followup forms, or unsolicited testimonials from participants. He verifies the lead's legitimacy, evaluates the climate for disclosure, and obtains details of the transfer. This information is shared with the benefits reporter, who uses this intelligence, along with that supplied by the attending NERAC technologist, to prepare a draft report. If the company permits, the reporter interviews the user directly to verify and ascertain details. Then a final report is prepared and submitted to the user and his/her superiors for approval.

This strategy has proved most effective and efficient, and it has produced substantive profiles of beneficially applied technology. It is appropriate to note here that presentation of the report to upper management within the client corporation accomplishes two important objectives. First, it lets the company censor any potentially damaging revelations from the report. Second, it provides them a bird's-eye view of specific benefits to the company from subscribing to the information service. A few examples illustrate NERAC's success with this strategy.

5. BENEFIT EXAMPLES

5.1 Bio-Polymers, Inc.

Bio-Polymers, Inc. of Farmington, CT, was founded exclusively to manufacture and market a synthetic version of a natural superglue produced by ocean mussels. Mussels secrete the glue-like substance from their single foot, and it forms a powerful bond with the nearest solid surface, enabling the mussel to secure itself within the harsh ocean environment. The "glue" is nonbiodegradable and non-toxic, making it ideal for many adhesive applications. An enormous number of mussels are needed to produce just one kilogram of the substance, however, so synthesis was imperative.

Dr. J. Herbert Waite, biochemist and Assistant Professor of Orthopaedics at the University of Connecticut Health Center, isolated and identified the key protein in the natural glue, leading to development of the synthetic adhesive of parallel properties. NERAC's role was in helping the company gain critical research monies and in identifying near- and long-term applications. Besides saving the company an estimated $4,000 and many days of research time, NERAC unveiled such potential medical applications as: adhering broken bones, coating sutures for infection prevention following surgery, use in general tissue culturing in research laboratories, and closing corneal puncture wounds and preventing astigmatism after ophthalmological surgery.

5.2 Alcide Corp.

Several years ago, a young company called Alcide Corporation, located in Norwalk, CT, developed a new sterilant disinfectant compound. This nontoxic, biocompatible demand-release oxidizing agent effectively despatches bacteria, fungus and virus. Its effectiveness over a range of dilutions and pH values, and its various forms (gel, liquid, cream and powder), make it useful in many diverse applications.

The company initially was unsure of possible markets. They credit NERAC with opening their horizons to a diversity of potential applications and business markets, and with providing them critical research information. Today, scientists at the National Cancer Institute have endorsed the company's products for disinfecting equipment and health-care workers in contact with AIDS patients' blood and tissue samples. Ongoing research may open the door to use of Alcide by blood banks to cleanse stores of potentially contaminated blood; one formulation is being clinically tested in Europe for treatment of primary human genital herpes; the FDA has approved sale of Alcide for cleaning and sterilizing hemodialyzers used in kidney dialysis; formulations are now used to maintain germ-free conditions in animal breeding quarters; and one version is now being distributed as a sterilant/disinfectant to the professional dental market.

5.3 Touch Scientific

Touch Scientific, a new entrepreneurial research firm based in Raleigh, NC, develops diagnostic products for the eye-care market. Many of the company's products are diagnostic machines to be used by ophthalmologists and optometrists in analyzing key biochemical characteristics of a patient's eyes and that person's tolerance for extended-wear contact lenses. Others, in the initial stages of R&D, involve simple, reliable, inexpensive procedures that will permit users to extract tear liquid and chemically treat it to determine the level of glucose present or to test for the presence of glaucoma. The company's objective is to significantly reduce the number of cases of blindness caused each year by these two diseases, both domestically and in underdeveloped countries.

Touch has sought assistance from NERAC on many occasions to learn the state of the art in biochemical analyses and interactions, to identify existing patents, investigate methods not previously considered, and to enhance productivity. The company credits NERAC with providing valuable scientific data and redirecting the R&D focus on certain products.

6. CONCLUSION

A systematic, well-conceived process which surveys users of the information service for their feedback and candid evaluation of the service is an invaluable mechanism. It enables employees to express their satisfaction or dissatisfaction with the information center used, and to discuss cases of successful technology transfer. Carefully prepared, the resulting reports form a composite picture that is useful in convincing upper management of the particular utility and effectiveness of the service.

From management's view, this process brings them closer to the real heart of the R&D departments, affording them better a vantage point on work in progress. It also gives them a valid premise by which to assess the utility of the information center.

Finally, the information center also benefits from user followup and reporting procedures, in that valuable feedback is captured. Problems, or perceived problems, in the quality of service may be immediately resolved. Technological trends may unveil themselves, enabling the information service to enhance its resources in such areas. And client loyalty to a responsive, effective service is engendered.

IN SEARCH OF GNP AND 30 MILLION OTHER SERIES: DRI'S NEW DIMENSION IN ON-LINE SEARCHING

Roger M. Winsby and Samuel Solomon, Data Resources/McGraw-Hill

Abstract: There is a growing demand for information specialists to search numeric data bases for their organizations. However, numeric data bases are not structured in ways that are familiar to most searchers. The kinds of on-line classification schemes that aid information specialists in searching full-text and partial-text data bases are simply not available. Aids for searching numeric data bases are still very primitive, consisting primarily of hard-copy documentation organized by name of concept. The authors have undertaken a major project to build an on-line classification scheme for the DRI economic and financial numeric data bases, drawing upon the knowledge base in the textual field but also developing new tools particular to the context of numeric data. They are also researching the kinds of user interface attributes that will appeal most to information specialists.

INTRODUCTION

The purpose of this paper is to share with you what DRI is doing in the area of improving on-line exploration of numeric data bases. Searching quickly and effectively for specific concepts in numeric data bases is a subject close to our hearts at DRI because we maintain more than 30 million data series in over 125 data bases, covering the vast spectrum of economic and financial information for the United States and much of the world.

Having the ability to conduct powerful searches both within and across data bases is important for DRI both externally and internally. Externally, offering easy search and retrieval is important because these 125-plus data bases are directly available to the public. Use of DRI data bases by worldwide business, financial, and government clients comprises a significant and growing share of our business. Internally, we are faced with a tremendous training effort for both our client support staff and our economists who use the data bases in support of DRI's ongoing forecasting and analysis work.

It is our goal to meet the internal challenge and further encourage external demand by providing increasingly sophisticated, powerful, and easy-to-use ways of searching for numeric information. Making our data easily available is not a new goal, of course. Ease of access has always been central to our business. However, the U.S. and world markets for information have been changing rapidly, and the industry, including DRI, must be investing in ways to respond to these changes in user requirements and delivery modes.

THE WAY IT WAS

In the 1970's and first part of the 1980's, the approaches to making known the contents of numeric data bases centered on three areas: maintaining a large field staff to work with clients on identifying the appropriate numeric concepts for their analysis; producing printed documentation for each data base with the information generally organized alphabetically by series retrieval code or mnemonic; and offering a range of on-line tools for searching the series descriptors of an individual data base or a small, related set of data bases. These solutions worked well for a long time, because there were fewer and smaller data bases then, and many clients were able to devote substantial amounts of research assistant time to learn the mnemonics and to work with the field staff.

However, by the mid-1980's, cutbacks in corporate staff, the corresponding reduction in field staff by numeric data vendors, and expansions in the breadth and depth of numeric data demanded by clients advanced the challenge significantly. Most data base vendors now offer clients an 800 # hotline to call in order to provide a more focused level of support. DRI and a few others have also developed catalogs of the available data bases with cross-references by subject as searching tools. Beyond that, there have been no other major advances in systems for identifying numeric data.

ORGANIZATION OF NUMERIC DATA

The lack of advances is not due to lack of interest. There are challenges to be met, as a few concrete examples should convey. Most numeric data bases are organized around one of three basic paradigms: data source, geography, or industry. DRI has several data bases that are the product of a single governmental agency or corporation, such as the International Monetary Fund's Direction of Trade data base or the Standard & Poors Compustat II data base. Then there are data bases organized around a country or set of countries where DRI experts have assembled the important economic and financial indicators from several sources, such as the DRI Canadian Primary Source data base or the DRI Current Economic Indicators data base covering the U.S., Europe, Japan and selected developing countries. Examples of the third type of data base, those organized around industries, include products covering steel, chemicals, agriculture and energy, which again, draw upon multiple sources for their information.

Thus, the challenge of finding the right numeric information is a two-dimensional problem. First, a user must identify which data bases have the appropriate information. Second, a user must find the specific series and then its mnemonic. In the case of a user wanting worldwide information about steel, he/she would have to search not only the steel industry data base, but also the country-organized data bases for government measures of price indices, production and employment and the source data bases for trade and financial statistics.

TEXT VS. NUMERIC

These issues must certainly sound familiar to on-line searchers of textual data bases. Along the dimension of finding the right file to search, text-based vendors have been investigating a variety of methods for years. The recent introduction of multiple-file searches adds the first significant expansion of capabilities for these users. Our research certainly supports the notion that much of the growth in information demand will come from users who will not spend the time to become expert on the relative merits of the various data bases available.

For within-file searches, textual data bases clearly have the upper hand over numeric. For example, users of a given text product may have the benefit of keyword searching with full Boolean capabilities on the entire record or just specified fields. They may have the benefit of menu-driven (and/or keyword searchable) hierarchical subject thesauri. In fact, they may have the benefit of both full text AND menu-driven subject searching during the same search session.

In contrast, users of a given numeric product may have the benefit of referring to a foot high stack of paper that lists series alphabetically within a one level subject scheme, with 3 to 18 character alphanumeric mnemonics that must be typed into the system in order to retrieve any data. TYPED CAREFULLY.

That may be overstating the present situation, but not by much. What is going on here? Why does text have it so much better than numeric? Is there an intrinsic difference of some kind? Is there some insight which will help in the creation of more robust search capabilities for numeric data bases? It is an interesting area of question. It will put us directly aboard the train of thought many of us at DRI have been riding lately.

The conclusion we have arrived at is, basically, that to be searched as effectively as we would like, numeric data bases have got to acquire more of the characteristics of textual data bases. And the main characteristic we are thinking of acquiring is ... more text. Textual data bases provide information in the form of words. Numeric data bases provide information in the form of numbers. That is the intrinsic difference. In textual data bases, text is retrieved, and text is searched on. In keyword search, in fact, the same text items are both searched on and retrieved. It's very efficient: The record describes itself; a single word sells itself and its neighbors. In numeric data bases, however, numbers are retrieved but they cannot be searched on by themselves. Numbers are abstract entities. By themselves, they have no significance, no meaning. To be meaningful, numbers need definitions. Whatever things they measure must be known.

THE DRI DECISION

It is no great intellectual leap, then, to realize that the best way to retrieve numbers is to search on their definitions, and that these definitions need to be in text form. Furthermore, to avoid the issue of which file to search, the searching system must cut across the DRI data bases.

What DRI is going to do is make the labelling of its individual time series more useful. We are going to upgrade and make consistent our data definitions, and we are going to construct and store these definitions in ways that, with the addition of a new interface, will vastly improve the search capabilities of our users.

Having made that commitment (not a small one, considering the amount of data that DRI has on hand), we came directly to the first problem ... and then an appreciation of the opportunity it offered. The problem was the state of our present definitions. The impression should not be had that the numbers in DRI or any one else's numeric data bases are not defined. Fortunately, definitions do exist, supplied either from outside sources, or from DRI editing of outside sources. In the data bases where DRI has organized the information, there is a general consistency of terminology within each data base. Unfortunately, when you combine the language differences across data bases including those where the definitions come directly from the sources, there are a sizeable number of problems to confront. Initial forays into the dictionary of terms across many of our data bases show that there are large numbers of close but different references to similar concepts such as "employment," "employed," "employees," "labor force," and "personnel."

The opportunity, of course, is that, given this situation, we can build our definitions very much as we want them without significantly meddling with the numeric data bases, themselves, or inconveniencing clients accustomed to the present finding aids.

Having decided to take action, and having discovered that we would have a comparatively free rein in doing what we wanted, we began to address the major questions: What (at what level) should we define? Where should we put the definitions? How should we structure the definitions? And the big question: What attributes of the data should be defined? For the remainder of this paper, we would like to share our thinking on those questions, then briefly touch on subject and other thesauri and, last but not least, the user interface.

AT WHAT LEVEL TO DEFINE

The general decision to create definitions leads to the specific question: Definitions of what? What entities? Do you create and store a full definition for every datapoint, for groups of related time series (i.e., a table), or somewhere in between? The decision has implications for storage requirements, development effort, and degree of user-friendliness. The point of the last is that, since the definitions will find data, the data found should be a manageable amount.

The decision we have made is to define single time series in almost all of the economic and financial data bases. This follows what we feel to be our present pattern of client usage. By defining at this level -- looking briefly at time series -- a customer may acquire the whole series with practically a single keystroke, a single datapoint by specifying only its date, and a "table" by requesting two or more time series (probably closely related in definition and therefore "adjacent" at the interface).

Complication. There are a few data bases, the DRI Securities data base and several of the trade data bases, where the data are defined along three dimensions: company, concept, and time for the securities data; and reporting country/partner country, concept, and time for the trade data. Representing each concept in a two-dimensional way would dramatically expand the size of this data base. We are working on ways to link search capabilities tailored to these data bases into the basic system.

WHERE TO PUT THE DEFINITIONS

The "where" is meant literally. The two extremes were rejected immediately: on paper, because that was one of the problems we were trying to solve; in the same files as the numbers, because it would be unwieldy and restrictive.

The decision has been made to create a separate definitions file, a unified data base of consistently formatted records, one for each series or individual data item we have decided to define. This will provide a unified and consistent structure to overlay many separate and inconsistently formatted numeric data bases. Benefits we anticipate, in addition to the obvious advantages in the area of searchability, include portability. The definitions data base need not reside in the same location as the data. Also, there should be advantages in the areas of development, updating, and quality control: we will be dealing with a set of like elements.

HOW TO STRUCTURE THE DEFINITIONS

At issue here is the fact that the structure of the records being created will define search functionalities. Structure will also affect the appearance and contents of the data definitions or "citations" appearing at the interface, which will guide users in refining their searches and selecting data for retrieval.

Each record, clearly, must be composed of a consistently defined set of fields, one for each data attribute we care to define. The contents of each field will be consistently formatted or worded across the file. (e.g., the word "employment" will always be used, if that is a "subject attribute" of the data, not, variously, "employees, employee number, and employed"). The storage of individual attributes in consistent form in consistent fields opens up rich possibilities for search capabilities -- not only for free text on one or more fields, but also for menu-driven searching supported by geographic and hierarchical subject thesauri, SIC and other standard classifications, data frequency, etc. And also, as stated above, this approach allows us to tailor consistent citations.

WHAT ATTRIBUTES TO DEFINE

The issue is simple: How much information about each series or data element should be rounded up and placed in the record? The decision, however, has implications for development effort, storage requirements, and interface design.

We have decided to tell all we know. The benefits of providing the richest search capabilities and fullest citations possible outweighed the higher development effort and other costs. At present, we plan to store in separate fields and make available the following types of information, as appropriate for the series or other element being covered. This list is not necessarily complete:

- current mnemonic
- long name (series title)
- units of measure
- data source (agency)
- source publication
- anomalies in statistical methodology
- data frequency (as stored)
- start date
- end date
- DRI data base of storage
- subject or concept term(s), to be selected from the subject thesaurus under construction
- geographic location
- specific industry (SIC, SITC)

433

- specific commodity
- issuer (for financial instruments)
- ticker symbol
- exchange
- bond or equity type
- maturity date
- coupon rate

Most if not all of the above will be searchable free text. The attributes which are conventional statistical classifications, such as subject/concept, geographic area, industry, and commodity will also be searchable through single or multi level menu-driven routines.

SUBJECT AND OTHER THESAURI

The topic of subjects or concepts -- the things the data are about -- deserves a brief separate mention. Many searches of text data bases begin at a very general level of terminology (such as finance) and then proceed down a logical tree to more and more specific terms (such as U.S. Treasury 3-month bills). A feature of many such systems is the ability to browse through the subject terms of the system in search of relevant categories.

As discussed above, the current DRI series descriptions are an amalgam of source agency descriptions from many countries and DRI-edited descriptions. To facilitate the searching across data bases, there must be some standardization of terminology within the searching facility. DRI is building a relatively large subject thesaurus as well as thesauri for some of the other classification categories. The subject thesaurus will relate terminology across countries, agencies and companies through use of synonyms and related terms. The thesaurus will also have a hierarchical term structure to guide users through a search in unfamiliar terminology. For example, the subject term "inflation" is rarely used in our series descriptions: instead the more technical terms "price deflators" and "price indices" are used. We need to provide an environment which preserves the technical specificity that is crucial to numeric data definition, and which offers a more informal language structure at the front-end.

THE INTERFACE

We will end this discussion of DRI plans and goals at that point where DRI customers will first encounter the results -- at the user interface. DRI plans to provide access in the ways described above to truly immense numbers of records, literally millions: data covering the entire spectrum of economic, business, financial, and even demographic interests.

This will be accomplished through a single user interface. To provide easy access to such large amounts of disparate information, search capability must be not only robust, but also exceptionally flexible. Accordingly, it is quite a challenge to devise an interface which will place the full range of functionalities at the user's fingertips, but also be natural and intuitive to use. Intuitive and easy use is a constant goal. At the interface, for many users, "flexibility" can translate too easily into "complexity." This is especially true for first time users, and we hope this product will attract many of those.

We do not plan to compromise either functionality or ease of use at the interface. The process of defining requirements, discovering problems, and finding solutions continues. We have explored several on-line and CD-ROM based interfaces for textual searching programs and are encouraged by the sophistication and responsiveness of the technology we have found. We are confident we will succeed.

SEARCHERS BY THE THOUSANDS: THE DEVELOPMENT OF A PROGRAM AND SOME RESULTS OF THE EXPERIENCE

Lucy Anne Wozny, Drexel University

Abstract: Over the last four years, 6,000 college students at a mid-sized, private university have been trained to do database searching in a mandatory Freshman Research Paper course. Initially, a training program dealt with the instructors' and students' inexperience with equipment and database searching. As the program matured, instructors reluctantly made necessary adjustments in the course to accommodate searching. Training took the forms of large group and classroom instruction, and an individualized computer simulation of the searching process. A recent study of the search process found that students learned the mechanics of searching very well, but had trouble formulating search strategy. They relied heavily on their own university's library, followed by area university and public libraries for information when looking for materials from the online searches. Sixty percent of the students reported finding materials from the searches in a library, but only 5% of the references in research papers' bibliographies were attributable to the online searches.

1. INTRODUCTION

Over the last four years, 6,000 college students at a Drexel University have been trained to do database searching in "Reading and Research," a mandatory freshman research paper course. This activity was inspired by Drexel's Microcomputer Program, which began requiring students to have access to an Apple Macintosh microcomputer in 1982. When the Microcomputer Program was announced, two professors from the Humanities and Communications Department conducted a pilot program incorporating online searching into four sections of "Reading and Research" (Ref. 1). The professors spent about two hours of class time and 1/2 hour per student outside of class, teaching search strategy and the mechanics of database searching. The pilot was a success, so the head of the department, seizing a opportunity to show that the Humanities Department could use microcomputers for something more than word processng, decided to make it mandatory for the course in the coming terms. That year, and every year thereafter, 1500 freshman performed database searching as a part of "Reading and Research."

This paper will describe the scope of the instructional portion of the project, the search experience, and the subsequent student use of materials from their online searches. It will also describe the current status of the project.

2. INSTRUCTION METHODS AND CONTENT

2.1 Initial Instructor Training

Drexel in 1988 is a different university than Drexel in 1983. The Microcomputer Program has had a profound effect on the faculty and students of the university. Using a Macintosh for everyday tasks is taken for granted now; however, it was quite different in December 1982 when the University was preparing over 40 full-time and adjunct faculty to teach database searching to 1500 students in the Winter quarter. The training program at that time dealt with the instructors' and students' inexperience with both equipment and database searching.

The two instructors from the pilot study and a member of the Office of Computer Services' Micro User Support Group trained the faculty in a series of three one-hour workshops modeled on the introductory training workshop of BRS, the chosen vendor. In three hours, the trainers defined a database and the information in it, explained search terms and Boolean operators, performed sample searches, offered teaching strategies and materials, and gave each instructor the opportunity to perform his or her own search. If they desired, instructors could set up appointments to do extra searching.

From the beginning, it was clear that there would be a great deal of variability among the instructors in terms of their understanding and enthusiasm for online searching. Some saw it as a technique to further their research interests while others wondered about the minimum effort it would take to implement the searching portion of the course. One concern that was voiced was the disparity in the content of the databases with regard to potential student topics; BRS was known to be more oriented to science and engineering while the research topics were geared to the humanities. Some professors were also leary of the microcomputers, since most would have only a month's more experience on them than the first students to receive Macintoshes. Finally, instructors wondered how much time they would have to devote to database searching in a course already tightly scheduled.

2.2 Student Instruction

In order to support the project and respond to instructors' concerns about database searching, the Office of Computing Services and the pilot instructors created a BRS simulator, offered large group and classroom instruction, and provided student consultants for the actual online sessions.

One of the pilot instructors applied for and received a grant administered by the University to develop a computerized searching simulator with the help for Drexel's Software Development Group. The application simulated the mechanics of searching using BRS' command language and interpreted the logic of search statements entered by the user. In addition, it contained a small database of bibliographic citations with one-line abstracts on the topic of 19th century U. S. immigration. This database was created from a search of Sociological Abstracts and was an attempt by the developer to show that BRS treated social science topics adequately. Students who didn't want to search the sample database could still use the simulator to practice syntax and Boolean structures. The software, packaged with a manual containing a tutorial, thesaurus for the database, and a hints and tips section, was sold at the University book store.

Instructional support also took the forms of lecture hall and classroom presentations by the training coordinator in the Office of Computing Services. In a 45 minute session, she presented the contents of a database, database selection, Boolean logic, command syntax, truncation, and the mechanics of searching using a microcomputer. She suggested databases with which students are most successful based on previous term paper topics. She did not include any discussion of controlled vocabulary; because of severe time constraints, her discussion taught students how to perform free text searches. The overwhelming amount of material presented in this session was supplemented by the search simulator and a second instructor-guided class session to review the process.

During the first term, instructors' concerns about learning and using the Macintosh were moot, since the Macintoshes, though announced, did not begin shipping until well into the term. This gave the instructors eight to ten weeks to practice their microcomputer skills. Once the Macs were on campus, the students' knowledge of the Macintosh and their lack of knowledge of online searching were evident during the initial training session. Students rarely asked questions about the mechanics of searching, presumably because they were still assimilating the information and didn't know the questions to ask. However, knowing the operation of the Macintosh, they had difficulty grasping the concepts of telecommunications on a microcomputer. For instance, the BRS print command only displays items on the screen and does not automatically send them to a printer. Quitting from a database does not automatically quit the software program as well. Saving a search on the Macintosh does not affect the telecommunications link. It was difficult to explain the dual functions, local and online, operating simultaneously through a single computer.

As a final way to support the project, the Office of Computing Services provided student consultants, well-versed in telecommunications and knowledgeable about BRS, for the actual searching experience. The consultants would help log the student searchers on to BRS, interpret system-generated errors and messages, and, depending on the instructor, offer advice on search strategy.

3. <u>SEARCHING</u> <u>A</u> <u>TOPIC,</u> <u>SEARCHING</u> <u>FOR</u> <u>MATERIALS</u>

The online searching experience consisted of two 1/2 hour sessions: an instructor-guided search and an optional independent search. The instructors found that they could direct a maximum of eight students simultaneously, and so would schedule their classes over one or two class periods to accommodate all the searchers.

The experience was evaluated in the summer of 1986 when 36 search transcripts, 23 bibliographies from the resulting research papers, and 25 questionnaires administered to the students were analyzed. The search

Type of Trouble	# of Students n=25	% of Students
With Database Searching	11	44%
Database choice	5	20
Keywords	3	12
No documents	6	24
Too many documents	4	16
Didn't know commands	1	4
With Equipment or Software	5	20
With Library Search	6	24

TABLE 1: PERCEIVED TROUBLE

transcripts were used to characterize the searchers. The bibliographies were compared to the transcripts to discover if students were actually using materials retrieved online in their papers. The questionnaires provided information about student perceptions of the search process.

3.1 Students Had Trouble With Search Strategy

The different methods of instruction emphasized the mechanics of database searching, and students learned them well. Command language errors were few, with most errors generated from the complicated print command syntax. However, students had trouble with search strategy. One-third of the students retrieved ten or fewer full bibliographic citations, as a result of making their searches too specific. Sometimes, they would retrieve a reasonable number of citations only to combine the search set with another term.

Student reports of trouble confirm the findings in the transcripts. Table 1 shows that 11 students (44%) reported trouble with database searching, as opposed to equipment, software, or library research. Specifically, they didn't know how to choose a database or keywords for their topics, or how to expand or limit their searches. Only one student, though, reported not knowing the commands.

3.2 Students Had Trouble Finding Materials

Table 2 shows where students looked for online materials. Forty percent either did not look for online materials or could not find anything when they did. Those who did locate online materials looked further than the University library. For the most part, these students used the near-by University of Pennsylvania library and the Free Library of Philadelphia.

This can possibly be explained by Drexel University's library holdings. The library focuses on science and engineering, rather than on the students' social science and humanities topics. In addition, Drexel's library held 51% of the 289 unique journal titles retrieved online. Students who wanted to locate a title from the half not held by Drexel would necessarily have to visit other libraries.

3.3 Students Did Not Use Online Materials in the Bibliographies

Presumably, if a database search is successful, the researcher will include the most relevant materials in the paper's bibliography. For these students, this did not happen: only five students included any references from the search in the bibliographies of their papers. References attributable to online searching in the bibliographies accounted for 5% of the total. This result is similar to reports in two other studies on

Where Student Found Online Materials	# of Students n=25	% of Students
Did not look for online materials	2	8%
Did not find online materials	8	32
Used only University library	3	12
Used other libraries only	4	16
Used both University and other libraries	8	32

TABLE 2: LIBRARY USAGE TO LOCATE ONLINE MATERIALS

introducing online searching with high school students, but raises serious questions about the effectiveness of online searching in the student research process (Refs. 2 and 3).

4. RECENT CHANGES AND CONCLUSIONS

The continuing concerns of the instructors of "Reading and Research" have changed the original scope of the online searching program at Drexel. Beginning in Fall 1986, online searching was no longer mandatory in the course. Some instructors felt it simply consumed too much class time that would be better spent on other concepts. In addition, the pilot instructors, the department head (a strong advocate of the program from the beginning), and the training coordinator in the Office of Computing Services left those posts. The following fall, the department decided to change vendors from BRS to Dialog; instructors were never fully satisfied with the range of databases offered via BRS.

In fact, the results of the Summer 1986 study might offer some explanation for the general malaise of the faculty. Online searching, as students experienced it in "Reading and Research," was often a frustrating experience. The difficulties associated with developing a good search strategy from the limited classroom and independent learning, and then locating the resulting materials is simply too great to ignore. The fact that the students did not include online materials in their bibliographies, and that this finding replicates that in other studies, is a strong indication that the role of online searching by students and the methods used to teach it needs further study.

REFERENCES

1. For a complete description and philosophy of the pilot program, see Kollmeier, Harold H. and Kathleen Henderson Staudt. "Composition Students Online: Database Searching in the Undergraduate Research Course." Computers and the Humanities 21, pp. 147-155, 1987.

2. Wozny, Lucy Anne. "Online Bibliographic Searching and Student Use of Information: an Innovative Teaching Approach." School Library Media Quarterly 11, no. 1, pp. 35-44, Fall 1982.

3. Mancall, Jacqueline C. and Dreama Deskins. High School Students, Libraries, and the Search Process; an Analysis of Student Materials and Facilities Usage Patterns in Delaware Following Introduction of Online Bibliographic Database Searching. Wilmington Institute. November 12, 1984.

NATIONAL AGRICULTURAL TEXT DIGITIZING PROJECT: SYSTEM STARTUP AND OPERATION

Judith A. Zidar, National Agricultural Library

Keywords: OCR Scanning, Text Digitization, Information Dissemination, Full-Text Retrieval, Preservation.

Abstract: The startup and early operational procedures of the National Agricultural Text Digitizing Project are described. This includes system planning and acquisition, selection of publications, document structure design, scanning procedures, conversion of bit-mapped images to ASCII text, quality control, and pre-mastering of data onto 9-track tape.

1. INTRODUCTION

Much of the U. S. and world literature of agriculture remains difficult to access because of the cost of in-depth indexing and/or abstracting by humans. Much of that same literature is subject to eventual disappearance because of the disintegration of the acidic paper on which it appears. The National Agricultural Text Digitizing Project (NATDP) is a cooperative effort by the National Agricultural Library (NAL) and forty-two landgrant university libraries to test a new method of capturing this literature in digital format for publication on CD-ROM laser discs. The discs will contain both the page images and the full text of selected publications, providing local, in-depth retrieval of the information and a convenient medium for storage and dissemination.

The system to be tested utilizes a laser scanner which captures a page (both text and graphics) as a digitized, bit-mapped page image for storage in a microcomputer. The page image is then processed by a "recognition server" which converts the text portions to ASCII code. The ASCII is processed by computer software, which creates an index. The resulting page images, ASCII text, and index are stored on CD-ROM for dissemination and retrieval on microcomputer workstations.

This paper will focus on how we have gone about implementing the first phase of NATDP, from system planning and acquisition to pre-mastering of the data for the first CD-ROM. The first disc contains approximately 6,000 pages of aquaculture material, both the page images and the full text. It is one of four discs that will be produced on different topics and using different retrieval software, as part of our pilot study of this technology. For an in-depth overview of the design, concept, and purpose of NATDP, please refer to Andre, 1988 (Ref. 1).

2. SYSTEM PLANNING AND ACQUISITION

Since scanning and optical character recognition (OCR) technology is rapidly changing and developing, we did not attempt to purchase a system directly. Instead, we chose to go through a systems integrator with experience in the field. We chose Science Applications International Corp. (SAIC), who was working on a system at the Smithsonian Institution which was functionally similar to what we wanted.

2.1 System Specification

In our specifications to SAIC, we stated what we wanted the system to do rather than how it should be configured. SAIC chose or designed the hardware and software, installed the system, prepared an operating manual, and provided training for the NATDP staff. NATDP provided space for the equipment (12- by 15-foot area), electrical hookup (two 20-amp lines), and data structure specifications (see below). In addition to the scanning workstation (see Appendix I for a list of components), SAIC set up a second workstation, which has been networked to the scanning station, to be used for editing the scanned documents and testing retrieval.

Our agreement with SAIC included a six-week acceptance test period during which 3000 pages of material selected by NAL would be scanned, converted to ASCII, indexed, stored on an archival medium (a 5 1/4" WORM disc), and written to 9-track tape in preparation for mastering onto CD-ROM discs. The system had to pass this performance test before we would certify that we had received the system specified in the contract.

2.2 Selection of Publications

We decided that the first CD-ROM would contain aquaculture material because of the wide-spread interest in this growing field of agriculture, and because of the support expressed by the aquaculture community for the project. NAL's Aquaculture Specialist selected the publications to be put on the disc, many from the shelves of NAL and others donated by universities and aquaculture organizations. The publications were numbered by the Specialist, based on their perceived usefulness as reference materials. The publication considered most useful was assigned the number "1", the next most useful was assigned the number "2", and so on in sequence. Then the Specialist prepared a list of the publications and their numbers. This list has been invaluable for keeping track of the 102 books, journals, bulletins, etc., while they were processed by different branches at NAL (i.e., Cataloging, Indexing, and NATDP).

2.3 Data Structure

After scanning and conversion accuracy, data structure is the single most important component of this (or any!) full-text retrieval system. Our data structure committee consisted of two database managers and two reference librarians. Working within the constraints of the chosen retrieval package (FastFind Plus), a structure was adopted which provided both full-text and bibliographic level retrieval. It was decided that indexing terms should be assigned to each document by an experienced NAL indexer to provide a further level of access.

All publications on the disc are in one large file. Each publication is divided into "documents" consisting of a chapter in the publication or some other logical dividing point. In addition to its individual chapters,

each publication may have a title page, preface, table of contents, etc., which are all included into a single document called the "host item record". All documents from a single publication are linked together, so that a user can easily go from one to another by use of a function key and without doing a separate search. In addition, the ASCII version of a document is linked to the image version, so that users can easily access pictures. All words, except for stop words such as _and_ or _the_, are searchable as part of the
full-text level retrieval.

For each document, a "relational header" is keyed in when it is scanned. This consists of certain fields that are especially important for searching, including title of publication (host item title), title of document, author, publication date, publisher, and other bibliographic information. The indexing terms assigned to the document are also included, as descriptors. The relational header is linked to its associated document. It is the only place where information from the document can be tagged for specific access.

One last component of the database is the MARC records. An OCLC/MARC cataloging record is created for each publication by an NAL cataloger and given to NATDP staff in machine-readable form on a floppy disk. When all 6,000 pages have been scanned, each MARC record will be loaded into the database and linked to its associated publication and to all the documents (chapters) in that publication. These records are searchable as part of the full-text level retrieval.

3. **IMPLEMENTATION**

The acceptance test period gave the NATDP staff a chance to learn about the scanning system, discover and work out bugs in the software, and develop an organized approach to production. SAIC performed the scanning and some of the data entry, and NATDP staff assisted with data entry and performed editing tasks.

3.1 **Log**

The first step we took was to develop a log. In addition to tracking documents through production, we wanted to record the amount of time that was required for each step, the system down time, and the impact of publication format (bound vs. loose copy; single vs. multiple columns; page size; normal vs. landscape page layout) on the quantity and quality of scanning and conversion. Our log book contains the following columns:

Date Scanned	Doc. No.	No. of Images	Description of Publication	Image Edit	Date Converted	Text Edit	Date Indexed

All date columns include space for recording the time (in minutes). The "Doc. No." is a number assigned to each document by the scanning system. The "Description of Publication" contains the publication number (assigned by the Aquaculture Specialist), the title, and a brief physical description (e.g., "bound, multi-col"). In the two "Edit" columns, we record date and time (in minutes.) If there is system down time, this is recorded in the log on a separate line. After a period of three or four months, we expect to have some solid information about system performance and staffing requirements.

3.2 Scanning

Before scanning a document, the operator must key in the information for the relational header. Some of this information appears on a worksheet prepared by the NAL indexer who assigns the descriptors. But many items, such as the publisher and authors, must be looked up in the publication.

Scanning is carried out on a Ricoh scanner at 300 dpi and is fairly straightforward, since it is much like making copies on a photocopier. However, documents vary widely in quality and format, and these variations may require adjustments in the settings for brightness, size, columnation, and orientation. All operational functions are menu-driven, and these adjustments are easy to make, but the operator must have a keen eye and a penchant for detail. As each page is scanned, its digital image appears on the high resolution monitor, where it is reviewed for quality and alignment. If the image includes text, the operator "marks" it electronically for later conversion to ASCII. At any time until the document has been converted to ASCII, the operator can re-scan, delete, or insert page images.

3.3 Conversion to ASCII

Conversion is performed by a Palantir compound document processor (recognition server). The Palantir works from the digital page image stored in the computer. It goes through the image, determines what is text, and then creates machine-readable ASCII text from the image. The page image itself is left intact. Converting a page image to ASCII takes anywhere from 1 1/2 to 4 minutes, depending on the quality and format of the text image. Pages which include some pictures take longer than those with text alone.
Multi-column pages take longer than single-column. Adding filter or spelling software slows the process even more. Since the scanning workstation cannot be used while the recognition server is converting, we decided to run this task at night, in batch mode. We have experienced some problems with this, however. If the Palantir does not "like" a document, the conversion process stops. The following morning, the operator must restart the batch job, tying up the system for a few hours. As we work with the system and gradually debug it, we expect such batch interruptions to occur less and less frequently. We also hope to upgrade to the faster Palantir 9000, which will greatly reduce conversion times.

3.4 Editing Text and Images

Editing (quality control) is done in two stages. First, the page image portion of the database is reviewed, along with the relational headers. Any necessary corrections are made to the header of a document, and then the images for that document are briefly reviewed.

The second stage of editing is done after the document has been converted to ASCII. Using WordPerfect, the reviewer goes through the text, correcting any obvious errors. When the review is finished, the document is marked as completed. Once so marked, the document, both text and images, is written to a "history" file on the hard disk, where it remains until it is archived to a WORM optical disc for permanent storage, using the WORM drive configured with our system.

We have not yet performed a statistical analysis, but it appears that good quality publications have about a 5-10% error rate in the ASCII text.

Poor quality runs up to a 30% error rate. As part of the pilot study, we will be evaluating the trade-offs between editing the text (a time-consuming task) and letting it stand as produced by the Palantir. The question is: How does this affect retrieval?

3.5 Creation of Full-Text Index

The indexing task will be performed by the FastFind Plus indexing module and is entirely software driven. It can be performed on completed documents as we go along or on all documents at once when scanning for the first disc is completed (a point we have not reached at this writing). As the indexing is performed, the links described in Section 2.2 will be created. This entire task should take no more than several hours.

3.6 Pre-Master to WORM and 9-Track Tape

Once the indexing is done, the entire database, including page images, ASCII text, index, and linkages, will be written to a WORM disc. The WORM will be used to test retrieval capabilities using the FastFind Plus retrieval software. This will be a preliminary in-house review, simulating the final product on CD-ROM. Note that the retrieval WORM and the archival WORM are two separate discs.

Once we are satisfied with the retrieval of data from the WORM, the entire database will be written to 9-track tape using the 9-track tape drive included in our system configuration. A partial tape dump will be done to determine the accuracy of the data transfer, and the tape will be ready to send to a CD-ROM mastering facility, such as Sony or 3M.

4. CONCLUSION

Because we are just beginning this pilot study, there are really no useful conclusions that can be drawn concerning the technology. We plan to gather data concerning system performance, staffing requirements, and the value of disseminating information in this way; this data will be shared with both the technological and agricultural communities as soon as it is available. It is safe to say that this method of information storage is very promising, since it addresses our concerns about space limitations, data access, preservation, and distribution.

5. REFERENCES

1. Andre, Pamela Q. J., National Agricultural Text Digitizing Project. Library Hi Tech, 1988 (In Press).

APPENDIX I

System Profile

Type: Digital Information Management System

Functions: Scanning and text recognition system which provides image capture, verification display, recognition and storage capabilities for a variety of page and image materials.

Hardware: <u>Microcomputer</u>

PC AT 286 Microcomputer Compatible
Internal 230mb RLL Harddisk
Ethernet Interface Board

<u>Mass Storage Device</u>

Alloy PC-9Track
Ricoh Writable Optical Disk Subsystem 800mb

<u>Palantir Compound Document Processor</u>

<u>High Resolution Display Subsystem</u>

Monitor Controller
Decompression Processor
High Resolution Monitor

<u>Scanner Subsystem</u>

Compression Processor
Ricoh High Speed Scanner

<u>Laser Printer Subsystem</u>

Ricoh Laser Printer
Laser Printer Controller

<u>System Software</u>

Operating System (PC DOS 3.1)
Full Text Search Software

Titles of Papers Presented at the Meeting for which Text does not Appear in the Proceedings

Development of Electronic Services to Provide User Access to Published Information Sources
    M.J. Allen
    Galxo Group Research Limited

Paving the Way for AI in an International Trade Database
    Michael DuBrow
    CED Intellibanc Corp.

Library Patron Acceptance of CD-ROM
    Paul E. Elsener
    Harborfields Public Library

AIDS School Health Education Databases—Online to the School
    Christine Fralish
    Center for Disease Control

Developing CD-ROM Products and Applications for Business and Financial Markets
    Steve Goldspiel
    Disclosure, Inc.

Hypertext Retrieval for CD-ROM
    Tim Oren
    Apple Computer

International Information from the NEXIS Service
    David A. Robson
    Mead Data Central

User Interface and Graphics on CD-ROM
    Elizabeth Ross
    KnowledgeSet Corporation

The Japan Telecommunication Market
    Rob Seitz
    Rob Seitz Communications

Online Searching: A Tool for Collection Development
    Leny Struminger
    Rutgers University

INDEX

The index is based on terms in the titles, added keywords supplied by the author, author last names, and first word of the author's affiliation. All are sorted together in a single index which was edited to provide consistency. All entries point to the first page of the associated paper. Page numbers are in sequential order.

ABI/Inform 141, 247.
ABI/Inform Ondisc 141.
Academic environment 275, 353, 437.
Academic libraries 37, 233, 365.
Academic rates 353.
ACCESS 389.
Access 199, 449.
Adventures 49.
Agricultural 443.
AI see Artificial intelligence.
AIDS 449.
Allen, M.J. 449.
American Chemical Sociaty 91.
Americans 37.
Apple Computer 99, 449.
Apple Macintosh 99.
Applications 449.
APS 191.
Area 149.
Aries Systems Corporation 99.
Artificial 169.
Artificial inputs 281.
Artificial intelligence 1, 107, 169, 449.
Assessment 27.
Associative retrieval 1.
Audino, Nancy 5.
Automated 107.
Automated patent system 191.
Automated translation 315.
Availability 115.
Badger, Edward W. 337.
Badger, Robert C. 7.
Bechtel, Hanns 9.
Bedord, Jean Newman 17.
Behavior 205.
Beilstein 7.
Beilstein Institute, West Germany 7.
Bell, Steven J. 21.
Benefits 421.
Bibliographic Access and Control System (BACS) 259.
Bibliography formatting software 383.
Blake, Virgil L. P. 27.

Borbely, Jack 5.
Bowling Green State University 275.
Brown University 131.
BRS 235, 411.
Budget 421.
Burr, Robert L. 37.
Business 5, 337, 449.
Business information 337.
Business practices 17.
Butkovich, Nancy J. 43.
Butler, Matilda 49.
C language 169.
California State Library 217.
Carlos, Gina D'Ascenzo 53.
Cartoons 81.
CAS 353.
CAS Online 63, 353.
CAS Registry 7.
Case study 185.
Cavanagh, Joseph M.A. 59.
CD-ROM 37, 49, 79, 99, 141, 161, 199, 311, 359, 449.
CED Intellibanc Corp. 449.
Center 421.
Centers for Disease Control 449.
Central Michigan University 287.
Challenge 79.
Charts 81.
Chemical 7.
Chemical Abstracts 9, 353.
Chemical Abstracts Service 191, 337.
Chemical Abstracts Service/STN International 371.
Chemical structures 7.
Chris Olson and Associates 293.
Clustering 301.
Clustering retrieval 301.
Code of practice 397.
Collection 449.
College students 71.
Columbia University 281.
Command 169.
Common command language 169.

Communications software 21, 315.
Compact Disc see CD-ROM.
Competitive analysis 337.
Competitive intelligence 377.
Computers 27, 67.
Computer security 27.
Computer-Assisted Instruction see Training, Education.
Computers see Apple Computer, Macintosh, PC.
Continental Insurance 67.
Control 275.
Cooper, Nan R. 421.
Core concept 333.
Core concept database 333.
Corporate see also Business, 5.
Corporate and Industry Research Reports 79.
Costs 233.
Cunningham, Julie A. 411.
Dalessandro, Glen Key 67.
DARC/Questel 7.
Data Resources, Inc. 429.
Database 1, 7, 9, 91, 107, 115, 247, 281, 287, 293, 315, 333, 337, 449.
Database applications 281.
Database development 333.
Database publishing 99.
Database searching 149.
Database selection 107.
Database--Online 449.
Databases see Database.
DataTimes 307, 213.
Decision-making 169.
Defense Technical Information Center 169.
Des Chene, Dorice 63.
Design 411.
Designing 235.
Development 265, 437, 449.
DGIS 169.
DIALOG Information Services, Inc. 7, 17, 123, 411.
Digitized information 281.
Digitizing 443.
Dillon, Martin 327.
Dimension 429.
Disclosure, Inc. 449.
Disk 141.
Display 191, 227.
DOD 169.
DoD Gateway Information System 169.
Dow, Victoria E. 71.
Downloading 67, 123.

Drexel University 437.
DRI see Data Resources Inc.
DuBrow, Michael 449.
E mail 389.
Economic databases 429.
Education 449.
Educational promotion strategies 293.
Effect 371.
Electronic 265, 449.
Electronic Branch Library 37.
Electronic Database see Database.
Elsener, Paul E. 449
End users 21, 71, 91, 199, 275, 281, 353, 403.
End-user instruction 63.
End-user profiles 353.
End-user searching 37, 199, 259.
End-user training 353.
English Language Databases 115.
Environment 21, 149, 353.
ERIC 411.
Evaluation 107, 233, 383, 403.
Evaluation criteria 161.
Executives 377.
Experience 437.
Expert systems 1, 43.
Extended learning support 37.
F-TAS 327.
Fact 213.
Factors 287.
Ferragamo, Ralph 79.
Fiction 213.
Financial 449.
Financial databases 429.
Florida State University 205.
Format 383.
Fralish, Christine 449
Freeware 67.
Front end 371, 377.
Full text 81, 91, 213, 239, 327, 443.
Full-text Access System 327.
Full-text retrieval 327, 443.
GaIN 259.
Gateway 107, 169, 397.
Georgia 259.
Georgia Interactive Network for Medical Information (GaIN) 259.
Glaxo Group Research Limited 449.
GNP 429.
Goldspiel, Steve 449.
Gonzaga University 37.
Gordon, Martha J. 327.
Government 217.

Graphic displays 307, 311.
Graphics 7, 311, 449.
Guide 383.
H. R. 145 Telecommunications Security 27.
Hackleman, Karen 293.
Harbofields Public Library 449
Hard 213.
Hardy, Nancy F. 81.
Hazardous 67.
Health 449, 67.
Health information systems 259.
Hearty, John A. 91.
Herner and Company 221.
High-Tech 161.
Highlights 1.
Highways 59.
Holmes, Lyndon S. 99.
Hu, Chengren 107.
Human factors 327.
Human-computer interaction 327.
Hurdles 17.
Hypermedia 59, 131, 235.
Hypertext 1, 59, 235, 449.
Hypertextbook 235.
I.S. Grupe, Inc. 359.
Ikushima, Keiko 115.
Image 221.
Image databases 221.
Image display 227.
Image processing 221.
Image processing issues 221.
Image processing systems 221.
Image processing trends 221.
Image reproduction 227.
Image retrieval 191, 227, 307.
Image storage 307.
Images 191.
Implementation 17, 43.
In-house 5.
Indexing 81.
Indexing policy 9.
Industry information 123.
Inform 141, 247.
Information centers 149.
Information Dimensions, Inc. 239.
Information dissemination 443.
Information markets 99.
Information policy 27.
Information retrieval 131, 337.
Information retrieval costs 233.
Innovation 421.
INPADOC 315.
Instructional Programs 37.

Insurance 185.
Integrated systems 91.
Integration of information 131.
Intelligence 169, 281.
Interactive 259, 311.
InterBrowse 131.
Interface 107, 311, 449.
Interface design 327.
International 17, 449.
International Patent Documentation Center 315.
Investment 337.
Jacobs, Leslie R. 123.
J. A. Micropublishing 79.
Japan 449.
Japanese Databases 115, 315.
Japanese literature 115.
Japanese periodicals 115.
Jochum, Clemens 7.
Johns Hopkins University 161, 333.
Justifying 421.
Kahn, Paul 131.
Kanji alphabet 315.
Karp, Nancy S. 141.
Kibirige, Harry M. 149.
Knowledge 53.
Knowledge Access International, Inc. 49.
Knowledge base 333.
Knowledge Set Corporation 449.
Kosmin, Linda Joyce 161.
Kriebel, Gail 71.
Kristofco, Robert E. 293.
Kuhn, Allan D. 169.
Kuntz, Lynda S. 185.
Kurtenbach, Gary M. 191.
Language 17, 169.
LANs 149.
Learning 205.
Learning styles 205.
Lee, Donna 199.
Lehigh University 71.
Lesch, Sigrid 7.
LEXX 53.
Libraries 37, 149, 161, 311, 449.
Library instruction 311.
Library needs 161.
Local 149.
Local area networks 149.
Logan, Elisabeth L. 205.
Long, Arlene F. 213.
Low, Kathleen 217.
Loyola University, New Orleans 365.
Lunin, Lois F. 221.

Lynch, Clifford A. 227.
Macintosh 99.
Management 213.
Maps 81.
Markee, Katherine M. 233.
Market 99, 499.
Market realities 161.
Marketing 79, 91, 217, 265, 377.
Marketing intelligence 337.
Marketing research 293.
Marketing strategies 91.
McClelland, Bruce 235.
McDonald, Michael A. 239.
McDonald, Tim 247.
McInnis, Kimberly A. 259.
McLane, John F. 265.
Mead Data Central 81, 449.
Media 161.
Mediated searching 199.
Medical 53, 235, 259.
Medical ARchival System 53.
Medical information 359.
Medical library 259.
Medical literature 293.
Medical literature databases 293.
MEDLINE 199, 293.
Meeting 79.
Mental peripheral 281.
Mercer University 259.
MeSH 411.
Metal alloys 9.
Metallgesellschaft AG 9.
Metallurgical 9.
Microcomputer 17.
Miko, Chris J. 275.
Miller, Tim 281.
Million 429.
Mini-Databases 247.
Model 275.
Modes 205.
Molkick 7.
Monitor 233.
Monitor online costs 233.
Moore, Ann S. 43.
Moore, Gary 333.
Mortland, Bruce 327.
Mystery 365.
National Agricultural Library 443.
National Library of Medicine 411
Native Americans 37.
Natural intelligence 281.
Natural language processing 53.
NERAC, Inc. 421.

Networks 149, 259.
Neuro 333.
News services 389.
Newspaper 213, 389.
NEXIS 81, 213, 449.
NFAIS 397.
NLM see National Library of Medicine.
Non-profit organization search service 233.
Novice searchers 205.
Numeric databases 429.
O'Dell, Judith E. 287.
OCLC 327.
OCR scanning 443.
Off-campus 37.
Office automation 149.
Olson, Christine A. 293.
Online 1, 5, 21, 37, 107, 115, 149, 185, 205, 217, 233, 235, 287, 315, 353, 411, 429, 449.
Online displays 411.
Online information retrieval 149, 281.
Online search costs 233.
Online search instruction 63.
Online search services 217.
Online searching 205, 337, 353, 403, 63.
Online systems 107.
Online thesauri 411.
Online training 293.
Operation 5, 443.
Opportunities 99.
Optical 191, 311.
Optical Media 161.
Optical storage 191.
Oren, Tim 449.
Outline 131.
Overview 221.
Pao, Miranda Lee 301.
Paschal, Allen W. 307.
Patent 191.
Patent images 191.
PATOLIS database 315.
Patron 449.
Paving 449.
PC 131, 315.
Performance 403.
Performance measures 403.
Periodicals 115.
Peripheral 281.
Personal computer see PC.
Perspectives 5.
Peters, Charles 311.
Photographs 81.
Physician 293.

Physician end user 293.
Pictures 81, 307.
Pilch, Wolfgang 315.
Pirate 67.
Planning 49.
Potomac Consultants 185.
Prasse, Michael J. 327.
Preservation 443.
Price 49.
Pricing 79.
Primary information 91.
Private 49.
Problems 49.
Processing 221.
Production 49.
Productivity 421.
Products 49, 449.
Program 7, 301, 437.
Project 443.
PROLOG 169.
Promoting Online 91.
Promotion 49, 217, 293.
Prospects 49.
Prototype 49, 169, 301.
Psych 333.
Public 49.
Public domain 67.
Published 449.
Pugh, W. Jean 333.
Purdue University Library 233.
Quality 275.
Quality control 275.
Quality filtering 333.
Queens College, CUNY 149, 27.
Query 7.
Reality 371.
Reference assistance 43.
Remote access 353.
Removing 365.
Repka, Anthony 327.
Reproduction 227.
Resolution 27.
Resource sharing 149.
Responsibilities 397.
Results 437.
Retrieval 5, 149, 191, 213, 239, 449.
Retrieval strategy 9.
Rich, Carol L. 337.
Rights 397.
Risk reduction 265.
Rob Seitz Communications 449.
Robson, David A. 449.
Role 199.

Ross, Elizabeth 449.
Ross, Johanna C. 353.
Rutgers University 449.
Sales 79.
Schipma, Peter 359.
School 449, see also Academic environment, Education.
Science 115.
Scientific and technical 115, 337.
Scientific information 337.
Search 233, 315, 365, 403, 429.
Search preparation 411.
Searchers 205, 437.
Searches 9.
Searching 7, 21, 123, 429, 449.
Security 27.
Seitz, Rob 449.
Selection 107, 287.
Series 429.
Services 37, 217, 265, 449.
Set-Up 21.
Shareware 67.
Shoval, Peretz 53.
SIC see Standard Industrial Classification.
Smith, Cynthia G. 91.
Snow, Maxine Leeds 365.
Software 17, 21, 371.
Software design 301.
Software development 301.
Software Jungle 383.
Solomon, Samuel H. 429.
Sources 449.
Springer-Verlag 7.
St. John's University 411.
Stack 141.
Staggenborg, Lisa M. 371.
Stanat, Ruth E. 377.
Standard Industrial Classification Codes 123.
Standards 17.
Startup 443.
State libraries 217.
State University of New York at Stony Brook 59.
State University of New York, Albany 403.
Statistics 81.
Stigleman, Sue E. 383.
Stillman, Stanley 389.
STN 7.
Storage 191.
Strategic Intelligence Systems, Inc. 377.
Strategic planning 337.
Structure 7.

Struminger, Leny 449.
Student instruction 63.
Student preferences 63.
Substructure searching 7.
System 5, 17, 107, 169, 443.
Tables 81.
Taylor, Kathryn L. 43.
Technical information center 421.
Technology 1, 37, 115, 221, 311.
Technology transfer 421.
Telecommunications 17, 185, 449.
Tenopir, Carol 115.
Texas A & M University 43.
Text 443, 449, 5.
Text digitization 443.
Textual Information Management Systems 239.
Theory 371.
Thesaurus 53, 411.
Thesaurus structure 411.
Thousands 437.
TIMS see Textual Information Management Systems.
Tool 449.
Towers, Perrin, Forster and Crosby 5.
Trade 449.
Trainer 71.
Training 71, 353, 365.
Training methods 71.
Training the trainer 71.
Trialware 67.
U.S. Patent and Trademark Office 191.
Ultimate 21.
UMI/Data Courier 247.
Undergraduates 43.
Universal 7.
University of Arizona 311.
University of California, Berkeley 227.
University of California, Davis 353.
University of Cincinnati 63.
University of Hawaii 115.
University of Illinois 1, 107.
University of Maryland 293.
University of Michigan 141, 301.
University of North Carolina at Chapel Hill 383.
University of Pennsylvania 21.
University of Pittsburgh 53.
University of Vermont 199.
Unruh, Betty 397.
User 293, 311, 365, 397, 449.
User costs 233.
User interfaces 311, 327.

USPTO 191.
Vendor 5.
Videodiscs 161.
Vries, John K. 53.
VU/TEXT 213.
VU/TEXT Information Services, Inc. 213.
Walker, Geraldene 403.
Weinberg, Bella Hass 411.
West Virginia 293.
West Virginia University 293.
Wilde, Daniel U. 421.
Williams, Martha E. 1.
Wilson & McLane, Inc. 265.
Wilsondisc 71.
Winsby, Roger M. 429.
Wozny, Lucy Anne 437.
Zidar, Judith A. 443.